ST. THOMAS AQUINAS

1274-1974

COMMEMORATIVE STUDIES

PRINTED BY UNIVERSA — WETTEREN — BELGIUM

ST. THOMAS AQUINAS

1274-1974

COMMEMORATIVE STUDIES

Foreword
by
Etienne Gilson

PONTIFICAL INSTITUTE OF MEDIAEVAL STUDIES
TORONTO, CANADA
1974

ACKNOWLEDGMENTS

These volumes have been published with the help of a grant from the Canada Council.

Thanks are also due to the University of St. Michael's College, Toronto, for its generous support through its Varsity Fund.

CONTENTS

VOLUME ONE

IV ST. THOMAS AND HIS PREDECESSORS

VOLUME TWO

VII ST. THOMAS IN THE 20TH CENTURY

V

ST. THOMAS AND HIS CONTEMPORARIES

WILLIAM OF AUVERGNE, JOHN OF LA ROCHELLE AND ST. THOMAS AQUINAS ON THE OLD LAW

Beryl Smalley

I

INTRODUCTION

"Then I saw the patriarchs and prophets exulting in wondrous joy at having reached that country which once they greeted from afar, at witnessing the fulfilment of what they had foreseen in the spirit, and at having passed from weary waiting to eternal glory."

THESE words are spoken by *Desiderium vitae aeternae*, describing the joys of heaven in a dialogue *De custodia interioris hominis* ascribed to St. Anselm of Canterbury.[1] *Desiderium* expresses the medieval Catholic view of the Old Testament in pictorial form. Moses, both patriarch and prophet, gave a divinely revealed law to God's chosen people as a preparation for the New Law of the Gospel, which would come in the fullness of time. Then the ceremonial and judicial precepts of the Mosaic Law would be superseded, though the moral precepts would remain as having timeless value. So much was common doctrine throughout the middle ages. Readers will expect me to add that the ceremonial and judicial precepts of the Old Law were held to "prefigure" the New Law in their allegorical sense, being interpreted of Christ and the sacraments of the Church, and to signify moral teaching in their tropological sense.[2] So indeed I should have said before reading the *De legibus* of William of Auvergne. Since reading it, I prefer to say that belief in the allegorical and tropological interpretation of the Old Law was general, but not quite universal. Even supposing that it *was* universal, however, the common doctrine raised many questions on the nature and effects of the Mosaic precepts, which admitted of diverse answers. My aim in this paper is to study St. Thomas's place in the chain of question and answer: "...ici comme souvent, il synthétise une

---

1 *Memorials of Saint Anselm*, ed. R. W. Southern and F. S. Schmitt (Auctores Britannici Medii Aevi i, London 1969) 358. The tract originated in St. Anselm's circle; see ibid. 354-5.
2 See H. de Lubac, *Exégèse médiévale. Les quatre sens de l'Ecriture* (Paris 1959-1964).

large tradition, qu'il perfectionne en la dotant d'une forte structure intellectuelle", as Dom Gribomont wrote of his theology on the bond between the two Testaments.[3] The evolution of this wide tradition and its
complexity need more detailed analysis than they have received
hitherto.

The Law, as transmitted in the Old Testament, posed problems as
difficult, though different, for those who read it "all of a piece" as it
does for modern scholars who see it as "composite". Its divergent
traditions, its traces of magic and primitive rites, and the miscellaneous
grouping of many precepts were baffling. How could one reconcile a
God-given code, strange and anomalous as it was, with that beauty,
reason and harmony which belonged to the divine plan for the universe
and for man's place within it? Lack of the tools of modern research
closed one approach to the problem; but others were tried. A striking
change of approach came about in the twelfth and thirteenth century
schools.

The patristic tradition as known to medieval scholars stemmed from
the Latin translation of Origen. He approached the Old Law as an
apologist for the faith against both pagan philosophers and Jews and as
a preacher to Christians. To the Jews, who continued to observe their
Law, he exposed and derided the irrationality and seeming futility of
many precepts: he sought and found biblical texts where precepts contradicted one another; other texts commanded practices which were
"absurd" and even impossible to act upon; they made sense only if interpreted as figures of the Christian revelation to come. To pagan
philosophers he argued that the Old Testament should be read in its
spiritual sense. He urged upon Jews and pagan philosophers alike that
irrational, absurd and impossible precepts had the function of pointing
us to the need for a spiritual interpretation. Some precepts had no
literal sense at all; most of them demanded a spiritual interpretation of
"the letter". Origen admitted the historical reality of much of his text,
but history as such did not interest him.[4] As a preacher he couched his
teaching to the faithful in his spiritual interpretation of the Old
Testament. These homilies won for themselves a unique place in
medieval spirituality.[5] St. Gregory the Great's exegesis reinforced the

---

3 "Le lien des deux Testaments, selon la théologie de Saint Thomas", *Ephemerides
Theologicae Lovanienses* xxii (1946) 71.

4 R. M. Grant, *The Letter and the Spirit* (London 1957) 95-6; M. Simon, *Verus Israel. Etude
sur les relations entre chrétiens et juifs dans l'empire romain (135-425)*, 2nd ed. (Paris 1964) 87-
121, 189-203, gives a general background.

5 See among numerous studies on the subject J. Leclercq, *Receuil d'études sur S. Bernard et ses
écrits* (Storia e letteratura xcii, Rome 1962) passim.

stress on spiritual interpretation. Both Origen and St. Gregory contributed largely to the compilation of the *Glossa ordinaria* on the Pentateuch.[6] St. Jerome's Hebrew scholarship and St. Augustine's more
practical discussion of difficulties arising from the literal sense of the
Law also influenced the glossators, but could do little to alter a settled
mode of thought.[7] A monastic commentary on *Leviticus* by Ralph of St.
Germer of Flaix, written towards the middle of the twelfth century,
achieved the distinction, rare for a monastic book, of becoming a standard school text:[8] it was priced in the Paris stationers' list of 1275-1286.
Ralph on *Leviticus* came too late to be quoted in the *Gloss*, but excerpts from it were often copied into the margins of manuscripts of the
Gloss and it served as a standard supplement to the *Gloss* in lectures on
Leviticus until the late thirteenth century. Ralph's commentary on the
central book of the Law passed on the patristic spiritualist interpretation in its most extreme form. Paradoxically, he shows what a
literally minded exegete could make of it. The schoolmen therefore had
to come to terms with him, accepting, rejecting or modifying what they
found in the *originalia*, in the *Gloss* excerpts and in their standard
medieval commentary.

Ralph set out to dissuade his brethren at St. Germer from overrrating
Jewish arguments in favour of the permanence of the whole Mosaic
Law. The Jewish case for it was known to them, and perplexed the
more simple minded. He counter-attacked along three lines. God himself witnessed through his prophet Ezechiel "quod dederat eis praecepta
non bona" (*Ezech.* xx, 25).[9] Other texts from the prophets denounced
sacrifices as inefficacious or insufficient. This proved that the
ceremonial precepts given by Moses were not good in themselves, but
were merely "the image of righteousness" or "foreshadowings". Moses

---

6   R. Wasselynck, "L'influence de l'exégèse de S. Grégoire le Grand sur les commentaires
bibliques médiévaux", RTAM xxxii (1965) 157-204. Gilbert the Universal compiled the *Gloss* on
the Pentateuch, in concert with the circle of Anselm of Laon, at some time between c. 1110 and
1128; see B. Smalley, *The study of the Bible in the Middle Ages*, 2nd ed. (Oxford 1952) 60-62; "Les
commentaires bibliques de l'époque romane: glose ordinaire et gloses périmées", *Cahiers de
civilisation médiévale* iv (1961) 15-22; R. Wasselynck, op. cit. 186-92.

7   A gloss in the standard *Gloss* on *Lev.* xix, 27-28, a ban on shaving the beard and making incisions in the skin, offers a rational explanation; these things were forbidden as pagan practices:
"Sicut barbari faciunt....nec in honore demonum cicinnos nutrire et vovere, sicut student pagani
puerorum capita demonibus offerre, quod maxime videtur hic prohibere." It represents a garbled
version of Raban Maur's commentary on the text (PL 108, 457-458). But this type of explanation is
rare enough in the *Gloss* to stand out as remarkable.

8   B. Smalley, "Ralph of Flaix on Leviticus", RTAM xxxv (1968) 35-82; I shall refer to it as
"Ralph". I also draw on material to be published in a paper in RTAM on "The influence of Ralph
of Flaix".

9   This text has been variously interpreted throughout the history of exegesis; see for instance
J. Lindblom, *Prophecy in Ancient Israel* (Oxford 1965) 184.

and the wise men of the Old Testament understood them in this manner. The divine revelation to Moses included a prophetic vision of Christ's coming and even of Christian values, such as the pre-eminence of virginity. The rank and file of the Jewish people, on the other hand, took the precepts in their literal sense, since they could not understand the inner meaning. Moses veiled his face, so that they failed to perceive the brightness of his countenance (*Exod.* xxxiv, 33-35). In the same way he concealed the prophetic secrets of the Law under dark sayings. Ralph goes on to make his third point: many precepts, besides being inconsistent with others or childish, would not "stand according to the letter"; that is, they could not have been observed; they had no literal meaning and were put there in order to prove to the wise that their true meaning must be sought in the spiritual sense only. Ralph examined each precept in the course of his commentary to test whether it could "stand according to the letter". For instance, an example to the contrary, which struck him as the most telling of all, was provision for leprosy in clothes and houses (*Lev.* xiii, 47, xiv. 36). "How can clothes and houses be leprous?" he asked. [10] It must be added that Ralph did his best to establish the literal sense where he thought he could do so, and he appreciated literal *moralia*. Precepts enjoining kindness to travellers and strangers called forth warm admiration. He credited observance of the Law with positive value, in that it taught obedience to the one true God. But the gist of his commentary is to present the Law as a cryptogram.

His readers had to cope with another tradition, deriving from St. Jerome and from contemporary Jewish rabbis. Master Andrew of St. Victor, stimulated by the example of his master Hugh, wrote commentaries on the literal sense of Old Testament books, beginning with the Pentateuch (before about 1147). He learned some biblical Hebrew and consulted rabbis on their exegesis. His Jewish teachers drew mainly on rabbinic tradition and on the standard works of Rabbi Solomon of Troyes (d. 1105) in what they told him. [11] There is no evidence to suggest that Andrew doubted the validity of the interpretation according to the four senses. He probably thought of himself as "laying

---

10 Quoted in "Ralph" 64: "Cum in plerisque locis, immo pene ubique satis appareat, legem spiritualiter intelligendam esse, dum ea sepius loquitur que nisi ad mysteria relata fuerint insipida prorsus et fatua sentiunt; nescio tamen si alicubi apertius quam in hoc lepre tractatu, ubi vestis leprosa et sicut sequentia continent domus leprosa introducitur". See "Ralph" 52-67 for anti-Jewish polemic.

11 See my *Study of the Bible in the Middle Ages*, op. cit. 83-185 and "L'exégèse biblique du 12ᵉ siècle", *Entretiens sur la renaissance du 12ᵉ siècle*, ed. M. de Gandillac and E. Jeaneau (Paris 1969) 273-293. My pupil Mrs. G. A. C. Hadfield (née Ten Kate) is preparing a doctoral thesis on Andrew's exegesis, with special reference to his knowledge of Hebrew and to his Jewish sources.

the literal foundation" for the spiritual interpretation, which he left to others. He was accused of "judaising" in his exegesis of the prophet Isaias, but never of a "judaising" approach to the Old Law. What distinguished him from Ralph was that he took for granted the historical fact of *legalia*. All precepts had a literal meaning for Andrew, even when it escaped him. He had never seen leprosy in clothes and houses; if the texts referred to stains, then who should judge which were leprous and which were not?[12] He did not dismiss these precepts as verbal puzzles. His factual approach to the Old Law had more importance than his discussion of its details. His treatment of them was skimpy compared with his much fuller comments on Old Testament history and prophecy. Like Ralph, he wrote after the compilation of the *Gloss*, but he supplied "masters of the sacred page" with a guide to the literal sense of those books which he expounded, until Nicholas of Lyre replaced him in the fourteenth century.

Discovery of an anonymous commentary on *Leviticus*, probably written in the 1120s or '30s in a North French school, shows that St. Victor was not the only centre of biblical scholarship. The anonymous commentator must have been a contemporary of Hugh of St. Victor, but he worked independently. He, too, learned Hebrew and drew upon rabbinic sources. He, too, accepted all precepts as literally true.[13] His commentary deserves mention here, even though it remained almost unknown, because it helps to account for Andrew's success in the schools. The Anonymous proves that the literal sense of the Law was evoking a new curiosity.

Masters of the sacred page preferred the Victorine approach to Ralph's. They came round to it slowly. Hugh had stressed that the literal foundation must be properly laid; Andrew obeyed him. At first, however, masters would quote Andrew on the literal sense along with Ralph and earlier sources, without noting the contrast of method. That is hardly surprising, seeing that Andrew never discussed method; he merely set an example by studying the literal sense. We can see how Ralph's influence persisted in a marginal note to the *Histories* of Peter Comestor on the precepts concerning leprosy: "It is clear that not all which is said of the diverse kinds of leprosy can be taken according to

---

12   Quoted in "Ralph" 66: "Lepram in vestibus vel domibus vel huiusmodi, de quibus lex agit, in nostris partibus vel nostris temporibus non vidimus, nisi forte lepram dicit maculas quasdam, quas in huiusmodi frequenter inveniri constat. Sed que macula sit leprosa, que autem non, qui diiudicare nosset non facile inveniri posset".

13   B. Smalley, "An anonymous commentary on the literal sense of Leviticus of the early twelfth century", RTAM xxxvi (1969) 78-99.

the letter".[14] Peter the Canter, in his lecture-commentary on *Leviticus*
(c. 1170-1196), quoted much from Ralph and did not criticise his
position at all. His blind acceptance of Ralph's method had an un-
toward effect, since Hugh of St. Cher borrowed from the Chanter in his
postill on *Leviticus* (1230-1235). His borrowings included many
quotations from Ralph; Hugh also quoted from Ralph directly. The
Dominican master's postills on Scripture became a standard school text.
Hence he popularised certain passages where Ralph had queried the
literal sense or else rejected it outright. Nevertheless, rethinking on the
validity of the literal sense was already in process: Hugh's incautious
use of the Chanter did not deflect the current trend. Stephen Langton,
teaching at Paris c. 1180-1206, took pains to discriminate between the
senses. Annotators of the *Gloss* and the *Histories* of the late twelfth and
early thirteenth centuries show an increasing anxiety to distinguish the
senses from one another, deciding which glosses expound the literal
sense and which the spiritual. Finally William of Milton or Middleton
O.F.M. achieved clarity in his lectures on *Leviticus* about 1248.[15] He
handles Ralph in a masterful way, quoting him independently of his
sources on both the literal and the spiritual senses, distinguishing between them, and avoiding all those passages where Ralph had rejected
"the letter".

The masters had worked out a method for the practical purpose of
lecturing on the books of the Law. They treated it as an historical fact
instead of trying to decode a cypher. But a satisfactory theory of the
relations between the senses had to wait for St. Thomas. The trouble
was that lecturing on Scripture, as practiced in the schools, gave
masters little opportunity to discuss the Law as a whole. The master
began with an introductory lecture on his book or group of books
setting out the facts on authorship, date and intention, in so far as these
were known to him. Then he expounded his text phrase by phrase. The
procedure did not lend itself to discussion of general problems. Further,
he aimed at making his text *praedicabilis*. He was instructing his pupils
on their religious and moral duties as future prelates and preachers and
was training them to preach in their turn: lectures provided raw
material for sermons. Exegesis according to the four senses offered a
commodious hold-all for the combination of biblical scholarship and

14   PL 198, 1206. It is not known whether the glosses printed in the Migne edition of the
Histories were written by the Comestor himself or by a pupil or reader.
15   P. Glorieux, *Répertoire des maîtres en théologie de Paris au XIIIᵉ siècle* (Paris 1933/4) no.
304; A. B. Emden, *A Bibliographical Register of the University of Cambridge* (Cambridge 1963)
407. It is not certain that the Paris and Cambridge friars of the same name were identical, though
it seems probable from the dates. The lectures on *Leviticus* must have been given in Paris, judging
from the diffusion of manuscript copies.

homiletics. The proportion varied from one master to another; the ingredients remained the same. The Bible supplied every need. A writer of the late twelfth century, "B", a priest or canon of Troyes, lists a series of metaphors in praise of Scripture. Most of them are conventional enough, but one is striking. "B" compares "the letter" of Scripture to "a harlot, open to any sense whatsoever". He specifies:

> Sicut enim meretrix multis, immo quam plurimis, sese exponit, ita in littera multiplex est sensus: est enim sensus historialis, allegoricus, tropologicus. [16]

He expresses crudely but truthfully the aptitude of the biblical text to convey any Catholic teaching which the lecturer found suitable to his audience. To give one example: the creatures allowed or forbidden as food in the Law were traditionally interpreted tropologically as virtues and vices. The theme could be developed and spiced with satire on contemporary manners at the lecturer's pleasure.

The allegorical interpretation linked the two Testaments together. William of Auxerre explains the meaning of *rota in medio rotae* in Ezechiel's vision when writing his *Summa aurea* (1222-1225). Tradition taught that it signified the two Testaments: how do they form "a wheel within a wheel"? William gives a traditional answer: "The masters say that the New Testament is in the Old according to prefiguration, and the Old in the New according to exposition". [17] It is easy to see why the rules of their faculty obliged masters of the sacred page to lecture on a book of the Old and a book of the New Testament concurrently. The theme of promise and fulfilment gave unity to their piecemeal exposition of texts.

The *Summa aurea* makes a convenient bridge between lectures on Scripture and theological *quaestiones*, sentences, sentence-commentaries and treatises. This type of discussion encouraged deeper

---

16 Quoted by E. Jeauneau, "'Nani gigantum humeris insidentes'. Essai d'interprétation de Bernard de Chartres", *Vivarium* v (1967) 94-95. The writer tells me that the comparison "litterameretrix" occurs in the *Quaestiones naturales* of Adelard of Bath, ed. M. Müller, *Beitr. zur Gesch. der Philos. etc.* xxxi (2) 1934, 12: "Omnis quippe littera meretrix est, nunc ad hos, nunc ad illos affectus exposita."

Adelard was referring to philosophic texts, not to Scripture. The context of his remark is: "...prius ratio inquirenda sit, ea inventa auctoritas, si adiacet, demum subdenda."

It is not clear whether "B. of Troyes" took his comparison directly from Adelard and applied it to Scripture or whether it was current when he wrote.

17 Ed. Paris, 1500, foll. 243vb-244ra. William of Auxerre is discussing the contrast between the burdens imposed by the Old and the New Law respectively. It is objected by some that Ezechiel's vision would imply that they were of equal weight. William has to answer the objection. I use the *Summa aurea* for illustration because it was widely read. On William of Auxerre see C. Ottaviano, *Guglielmo d'Auxerre (Biblioteca di Filosofia e scienza* xii, Rome 1950).

thought on problems arising from *legalia*. [18] First of all, did writers in a theological context regard all precepts of the Old Law as literally true? The answer is that we do find traces of the same confusion as appears in lectures on Scripture, but they are early and few. Peter of Capua in his *Summa* (c. 1201-1202) raises the question: Did the Old Law include precepts impossible to observe? He gives an opinion ascribed to "quidam" without committing himself: all precepts were imposed upon all Jews, not as binding each Jew to observe them all *ad litteram*, but as binding each to observe *ad litteram* such as he could, and to observe all "mystically", at least. [19] "Mystically" may refer to a spirit of obedience here; it is used rather ambiguously. Roland of Cremona, the first Dominican master to teach at Paris, takes Ralph's interpretation uncritically into his *Summa* (1228-1230):

> Likewise there was something in the Law which could not be understood according to the letter in any way, such as: *You shall eat the oldest of the old store: and new coming on, you shall cast away the old* (*Lev.* xxvi, 10). That precept would force the Jews to resort to the spiritual understanding.... [20]

It seems strange that an innocent promise of abundance should have struck commentators as meaningless according to the letter, until we turn to the ingenious objection made by Ralph on the words *Vetustissima veterum comedetis*: why eat the *oldest* before the *old*?

> Let the Jew, who accepts the fleshly sense only of abundance, tell the reason why the *old* should be cast out and the *oldest* eaten, when they should rather have cast out the *oldest* and eaten the *old*. [21]

Ralph had interpreted the *stores* as the sacraments of the Old and New Laws respectively. [22] Hugh of St. Cher telescoped the passage into:

---

18   See especially A. M. Landgraf, *Dogmengeschichte der Frühscholastik* iii, 1 (Regensburg 1954) 19-108.
19   Quoted ibid. 34: "Quidam etiam dicunt, quod cuilibet erant omnia precepta, non ut ad litteram omnia observaret, sed quedam ad litteram, que posset, et omnia saltem mistice".
20   Quoted ibid. 59: "Similiter aliquid erat in lege, quod nullo modo poterat intelligi ad litteram, ut istud: vetustissima veterum comedetis et novis supervenientibus vetera abicietis. Istud cogebat iudeos recurrere ad spiritualem intelligentiam". I use the Douai version as the most faithful translation of the medieval Latin Vulgate.
21   *The New English Bible. The Old Testament* (Oxford/Cambridge 1970) 167. "Your old harvest shall last you in store until you have to clear out the old to make room for the new."
22   Ed. Marburg/Cologne, 1536, lib. XIX, cap. viii, pp. 295-296: "Que igitur sunt vetera, quae praedicuntur proiicienda? Nos vetera intelligimus legis sacramenta....Haec igitur vetera, novis supervenientibus proiiciuntur, quia dum novi testamenti suscipimus instituta, legis caeremonias servare contemnimus.....vetustissima veterum comedimus, quia iam non iustitiae figuris sub tempore datis oneramur, sed ipsius iustitiae, que apud Deum aeterna est, pane reficimur. Aliaque dicat iudeus, qui carnalem tantum in his amplectitur abundantiam, quae sit ratio ut vetera proiiciantur et vetustissima comedantur, cum quod vetustissimum est magis proiici, vetera vero comedi deberent. Quod si haec non solum in scripturis, verumtamen in nostris affectibus velimus advertere, vetus est cupiditas, quae veterem facit hominem...."

> Obiectio contra iudaeos: nam et si vetera proiiciuntur, multo fortius vetustissima. Mystice vero non est obiectio. [23]

Roland would sometimes deny that his text had a literal or historical sense in his commentary on Job;[24] he carries over the ambiguity of terms into his *Summa*.

However, such passages are exceptional. Masters generally assumed that the precepts could be taken as literally true. The framework for their discussions was a saying, sometimes ascribed to St. Augustine:

> The Law was given as a sign to the perfect, as a burden and scourge to the froward, as tutor to the simple and sucklings. [25]

The first phrase safeguarded the mystical sense of the Old Law, as understood by the élite, the second its penal character, and all three enabled theologians to interpret it as "burdensome" rather than nonsensical or absurd. William of Auxerre takes it in this way. He answers objections raised by texts from the prophets declaring that sacrifices were unpleasing to God. Such texts had figured in Ralph's arguments against the Jews. William gives three reasons for God's displeasure: the sacrifices were offered in the wrong spirit, without right intention; they were offered at the wrong time, after truth had dispersed shade (i.e. the prophets were foretelling the New Law); God did not prescribe sacrifices *voluntate absoluta, sed quasi coacta*. He imposed them as preventive of evil, not as good in themselves, to restrain the Jews from idolatry, just as he permitted divorce, since otherwise they would have

---

23 *Post. in Bib.* (Paris 1530-1545) i, fol. 120rb: "Obiectio contra iudeos: Nam et si vetera proiiciuntur, multo fortius vetustissima. Mystice vero non est obiectio. Nam vetustissima sunt unitas essentie trinitatis personarum, que comedere debet omnis homo et masticare dentibus fidei".

24 Quoted by A. Dondaine, "Un commentaire scripturaire de Roland de Crémone 'Le livre de Iob'", *Archivum Fratrum Praedicatorum* xi (1941) 124: "Sensus ystorialis hic nequaquam invenitur. Non enim piscatores, ut opinor, sagenas implent pelle ceti, neque gurgustium piscium capite illius." The text is *Iob*, xl, 26.

Roland's commentary followed his *Summa*, to which he refers in it; ibid. 118-123. Hence he may have used Hugh of St. Cher's postill, compiled soon after 1230.

25 William of Auxerre, *Summa aurea*, ed. cit. fol. 243va: Solutio: "ut dicit beatus Augustinus, lex fuit data perfectis in signum, duris et superbis in onus et flagellum, rudibus et mamotrectis in pedagogum"; ibid., fol. 101ra: "Lex data est rudibus in pedagogum, duris in flagellum, perfectis in signum."

See *Gal.* iv, 24: *Itaque lex paedagogus noster fuit in Christo*, also *Mat.* xxiii, 4; *Luc.* xi, 46. The saying occurs in various forms, as in Peter the Chanter's *Summa*, ed. J.-A. Dugauquier, *Analecta mediaevalia Namurcensia* iv (1954) 13: "Queritur de sacramentis legalibus que data sunt in signum perfectorum et iugum superborum et pedagogum infirmorum." It is found earlier in *Sententie divine pagine, Sententie Anselmi, Ysagoge in theologiam*; see the references given by Dugauquier, ibid; also Hugh of St. Victor, ed. O. Lottin, "Questions inédites de Hugues de Saint-Victor", RTAM xxvi (1959) 202, no. 27: "Multis de causis data est lex... Quibusdam de se presumentibus data est in onus... Quibusdam, scilicet perfectis, ut Moysi et Aaron et aliis iustis, data est in signum...."

None of the editors has identified the saying as a quotation.

killed their unwanted wives. William goes on to consider the objection that certain precepts were absurd. He tackles it apropos of a classic puzzle: why did the priest who sacrificed the red heifer have to cleanse himself afterwards? Rabbinic tradition, though William may not have known it, also regarded the precept (*Num*. xix, 1-10) as obscure: King Solomon understood the causes of all the sacrifices except that of the red heifer. [26] William classifies the impurity incurred by the priest as "burdensome"; he compares it to the ban on eating pork. Neither precept had any other literal cause or reason: the true cause must be sought in allegory or morality. Pork was forbidden in order to signify that we should not imitate a dirty, greedy animal. The sacrifice of the red heifer signified the Eucharist: the celebrant must beware of sullying his conscience after performing the holy rites. William at least allowed historical reality to precepts for which he could find no literal cause or reason beyond the fact that they were intended to be burdensome. [27]

Some theologians made an effort to clarify the link between St. Augustine's first and third phrases: the Law was given as a sign to the perfect and as a tutor to the simple. They asked themselves what it was like for the simple people, who had to perform burdensome, and to them incomprehensible duties. Simon of Tournai in his *Summa* (towards 1165) compared them to the simple laymen of his own day, who would recite the Lord's prayer with devotion, but without understanding; they knew only that it profited them to salvation. [28] Roland of Cremona probed further. The very fact that some precepts of the Law put a strain on belief would lead simple Jews to enquire from spiritual men or prophets what the true meaning was. Roland instances the sending of the scapegoat into the wilderness, carrying the sins of Israel written on a scroll tied to its head, and the apparent nonsense in

---

26 Quoted by Maimonides, *Guide of the Perplexed* iii, 26, translated by S. Pines with introduction and notes by L. Strauss (Chicago 1963) 507-8. The source is given by the editors.

27 *Summa aurea*, op. cit. fol. 243va: "Erant igitur multa in lege que ad litteram non habebant aliquam causam sue institutionis nisi onus et flagellum; secundum vero allegoriam et moralitatem causam aliquam habebant, sicut quod iudei non comederent carnes porcinas ad litteram non habebat aliquam causam nisi onus, sed secundum moralitatem patet ratio; non enim debemus imitari gulosos et immundos. Similiter immunditia illa, quam contrahebat sacerdos ex immolatione vitule rufe, tantum instituta fuit in onus secundum litteram, sed secundum moralitatem sacerdos ille qui immolabat vitulam rufam significabat sacerdotem nostrum qui confixit eucharistiam, qui postquam celebravit timere debet ne indigne contrectaverit. Unde immundum se debet reputare usque ad vesperem, id est usque ad contritionem que est finis et consumptio peccati".

28 Quoted by Landgraf, op. cit. 32: "Litteralis doctrina non erat superflua rudibus, licet non caperent spiritualem intelligentiam, quia venerabantur litteram continentem spiritualem intelligentiam.....Quo modo nunc aliquis simplex profert dominicam orationem non intelligens eam, et devotione prolationis et veneratione littere citra eius intellectum, quod orat, imperat et salvatur...."

the promise on the oldest and the old stores.[29] The Dominican friar, belonging to a later generation than Simon of Tournai, thought more highly of the intelligence to be found among the "simple". Both men were feeling their way towards a question which would be raised still later: why did the spiritual leaders and prophets of the Old Testament keep simple Jews in the dark, instead of enlightening them on the mystical significance of the legal precepts? Why did they fail to imitate Christian preachers, who expounded the spiritual senses of Scripture from their pulpits?

These were fringe problems, raised *en passant*. Theologians naturally took more interest in the effects of observance on the Old Testament Jews. What merit did observance of *legalia* confer? How far was it meritorious and justificatory? They had to harmonise many conflicting texts from the Bible and the Fathers.[30] A more positive evaluation of observance came slowly to the fore. It had been generally accepted that faith in God's promises as a ground for obedience conferred merit: the righteous men of the Old Testament were justified, even though they had to wait for deliverance until Christ came to save them.[31] Theologians reached agreement on the effects of circumcision at an early stage: circumcision had the same effect as baptism in that it freed from original sin.[32] The parallel between baptism and circumcision was so current as to find expression in poetry:

> Circumcisa caro lavit sub lege reatus,
> illud agens quod agit fons sub cruce sanctificatus,

wrote Hildebert of Lavardin (d. 1133).[33] The efficacy of other sacraments and ceremonies of the Old Law offered more difficulty and provoked much discussion. Eventually it came to be held that they did not confer grace, as did Christian sacraments; nor was observance meritorious in itself; but faith and charity sufficed to make observance meritorious and justificatory. The simple did not need to have explicit faith in the inner meaning of *legalia*; general belief in the Law's divine

---

29 Quoted ibid. 58-59: "Non enim poterat aliquis homo, qui sensum haberet, credere, quod ideo, quod hircus portabat cedulam, in qua erant scripta peccata iudeorum, in desertum, quod ideo eis erant dimissa peccata. Et ideo cogebantur credere in aliquem venturum, qui dimitteret peccata, vel ad minus cogebantur querere a viris spiritualibus vel a prophetis, quid hoc esset, et ipsi eis exposuisse misterium et ita fidem acquisivissent, et ita iustificati fuissent.... Similiter aliquid erat in lege, quod nullo modo poterat intelligi ad litteram....Istud cogebat iudeos recurrere ad spiritualem intelligentiam, et ita quodam modo iustificabat eos...."

30 Landgraf, op. cit. 59-60.

31 Ibid.

32 Ibid. 61-108.

33 *Carmina minora* no. 39 II, ed. A. B. Scott (Teubner 1969) 29. There is no evidence for the date of no. 39.

character and charity they did need. William of Auxerre and others reached a clearer formulation by distinguishing between *opus operans* and *opus operatum*. William answers the question "whether *legalia* justified" as follows:

> The *opus operans* is the action itself, that is the sacrifice of a bull or a lamb, which justified when it was done in charity. The *opus operatum* is the actual flesh of the bull or lamb which was sacrificed, which certainly did not justify. In the New Law, on the other hand. both *opus operans* and *opus operatum* justify, because the flesh of Christ (the *opus operatum*) is justificatory. Thus, when it is asked whether the sacraments of the Old Law justified, we grant that they did as *opus operans*, as the foregoing reasons have proved; but they did not justify as *opus operatum*.[34]

The outcome of discussion had been to raise *legalia* to a higher level than the Lombard had allowed them in his *Sentences*. By the early 1220s a more indulgent view was being taken of observance, if not of the literal content of *legalia*.

Perhaps the Catharist heretics in Italy and the *terra Albigensium* prompted the change of attitude. Cathars rejected the Old Testament as devilish: it emanated from the god of this bad visible world, in their view. Hence they forced defenders of the Catholic Church to stress the divine origin and beneficient character of *legalia*. Preaching missions and debates with heretics before and during the Albigensian crusades brought a spate of tracts against the heretics.[35] The crisis must have made an impression on teachers in the northern schools: some joined in polemic. Although its effect is elusive, we can suppose that the crisis stimulated thought in two ways: the Cathars made an arbitrary use of the spiritual interpretation, dismissing the literal sense altogether in favour of a spiritual sense, where it suited them, They therefore brought out the need for careful definition of the relationship between the senses in Catholic exegesis.[36] By attacking the Old Law as wholly evil, they led

---

34   *Summa aurea*, op. cit. fol. 243va. On the origin of the distinction between *opus operans* and *opus operatum* see Landgraf, op. cit. 54-60.

35   See Christiane Thouzellier, *Catharisme et Valdéisme en Languedoc à la fin du XIIᵉ et au début du XIIIᵉ siècle*, 2nd ed. (Paris/Louvain 1969).

36   Durand of Huesca, a Valdesian who returned to Catholicism and wrote against the heretics, gives examples of how the Cathars interpreted Gospel texts according to the spiritual sense only; he replies to them that the mystical sense does not destroy, but derives from the literal or historical sense; ed. Christiane Thouzellier, *Une Somme anti-cathare. Le liber contra Manichaeos de Durand de Huesca* (Spicilegium sacrum Lovaniense. Etudes et documents xxxii, 1964) 94, 149, 150, 159, 207. But Durand uses the mystical sense in a confused and ambiguous way himself on *Job* xxviii, 6: *Locus sapphiri lapides eius* etc.: "Sed nos sensum eorum exuflando, quia istorice non potest apte intelligi, ad sensum misticum recurramus....Et sic intelligenda est predicta sentencia beatissimi Iob, ab hereticis depravata" (258). His mystical interpretation is that the earth signifies the Synagogue, the source of Scripture, and the holy Jews of the Old Testament. What he has done is to reject the "literal sense" because it contains a metaphor, and pass straight to the allegorical

Catholic theologians to think more deeply about its literal sense as a guide to God's chosen people. The dualist heresies may explain in part why Maimonides' *Guide of the Perplexed* found eager readers, when it reached the schools in its Latin translation.

Maimonides or Rabbi Moses (1135-1204) finished his *Guide* soon after 1190.[37] Its contents interest us here only in so far as it deals with the Law. Maimonides, as a Jewish philosopher and practicing Jew, had much the same aim as his predecessor Philo Judaeus (d. soon after 40 A. D.). He wanted to harmonise the Law with a philosophic account of the deity and the cosmos, without compromising its sacred and binding character for Jews. Philo solved his problem by presenting the Law as an allegory, though he regarded its literal sense as true and binding on his people. The content of philosophy had changed since then. Maimonides had to take another road. He read Plato's *Republic* and noted its philosopher kings, also Aristotle's *Politics* with its insistence on the common good as a criterion for good government. The Jews for whom he wrote were perplexed by the untidiness and irrationality of their Law. Maimonides guided them not by allegorising, but by rationalising. He defended the political and religious value of the Law as it stood. He presented Moses in the dual role of a prophet and of a philosopher ruler, transmitting wise laws for the constitution and running of the Jewish state. The Law as a whole united the tribes of Israel and joined them together as a community, whose cult brought social and religious cohesion. Maimonides dwelt on the justice and mercy of many precepts and on the ethical values inculcated by commands such as those concerning good treatment of neighbours and pity to birds and beasts. Such precepts had "clear utility". His main argument on those precepts whose utility was not so clear amounted to a wide application of the principle that sacrifices and ceremonies aimed at weaning the Jews from idolatry. Moses taught his people to avoid the superstitions and pagan rites of the Egyptians and other gentiles, with whom they had contacts, by prescribing a cult which bore no resemblance to any other. This dictated the choice of animals to be offered as sacrifices and the mode of slaughter, for example. Maimonides "traces an impressive, but quite unhistorical picture of paganism in biblical times" in order to contrast Mosaic to pagan worship. The Jews, emerging from slavery in

---

sense. Mlle Thouzellier dates his *Liber* 1222-1223, *Catharisme*, op. cit. 299. Although, as she shows, Durand had had a good education and was well-read, he was out of touch with the northern schools, where the confusion between the metaphorical and the mystical senses of Scripture was being cleared up at the time.

37 On Maimonides' life and writings see G. Vajda, "La pensée religieuse de Maïmonide", *Cahiers de civilisation médiévale* ix (1966) 29-49, where a full bibliography is given.

Egypt and tainted by gentile customs, needed settled rules and prescribed ritual; without such precepts, they would have lapsed into idol
worship like their neighbours. Blood sacrifices, prohibitions and
purifications all led them to honour God and to feel a holy awe in his
presence. Maimonides does not explain why a code adapted to the state
of Jewish society at a particular point in its history should retain its
value after paganism had disappeared.[38] This failure on his part could
only increase his appeal to Christian readers, since they could fill the
gap in his argument. They saw *legalia* as a passing phase in the history
of salvation.

His explanation had the further advantage that the general covered
the particular. He presented the ceremonial precepts as "God's gracious
ruse" to draw men to himself;[39] hence not every detail need have a
cause assigned to it. Worship called for rules and regulations. Numbers
and kinds of offerings had to be specified; but specification was not
always significant in detail. The whole Law commanded nothing absurd; its seemingly petty orders could be subsumed in its general plan,
to provide for the common good of Israel.

The perplexing reproaches made by the prophets against sacrifices,
and Ezechiel's saying that the precepts were not good (xx, 25) fell into
place quite easily. Maimonides could explain the text of Jeremias:
*When I brought your forefathers out of Egypt, I gave them no com-
mands about whole-offering and sacrifice* (vii, 22), a dictum, he says,
"which has been regarded as difficult by everyone whose words I have
seen or heard."[40] The first intention of the Law was worship of the one
true God. The sacrifices, prescribed at a later stage, were only means to
an end. The prophets blamed the Jews for neglecting the first intention;
God reproaches his people through his prophets:

> You, however, came and abolished this end, while holding fast to what
> has been done for its sake. For you have doubted my existence...And still
> you continue to repair to the temple of the Lord, offering sacrifices,
> which are things that have not been intended in the first intention.[41]

The *Guide* offered reasons to an age in love with reason. It had another
point of contact with scholastic exegesis: its author shared the
philosophers' low opinion of the capacities of the common people. The
Law gave to the vulgar all they needed to know in the perfect city.[42]

38   Ibid. 46.
39   *Guide* iii, 32 and 45, ed. cit. 526, 580.
40   Ibid. iii, 26, 27, 508-510.
41   Ibid. iii, 32, 530-531.
42   Vajda, op. cit. 48.

Moses and the élite understood the philosophy behind the words. Scripture included all science and metaphysics. Significantly, Maimonides writes that to forbid formal worship and sacrifices would have been equivalent to forbidding formal prayers in favour of pure meditation in his own day.[43] His belief in a hierarchy of wisdom corresponded to the Christian teaching that the élite of the Old Testament already belonged to the New, in that they perceived the prefiguration of the Gospel in *legalia*. Hence the *Guide* accorded with Christian tradition in presenting the Law as wholesome for all, sufficient for the people, and a mine of deeper wisdom for the élite.

There is still no study of the text of the Latin translation.[44] The *Guide* was written in Arabic, but was soon translated into Hebrew and thence into Latin. Michael Scot has been credited with the Latin version on plausible evidence. He would have made it in Italy after leaving Toledo "by 1220 at the latest".[45] It used to be thought that William of Auvergne was the first schoolman to quote from the Latin version about 1230. We now know that Alexander of Hales O.F.M. anticipated him. Alexander quotes Maimonides' classification of the Old Testament precepts under fourteen heads in his *Glossa* on the *Sentences*, given as lectures at Paris while he was still a secular, probably 1223-1227.[46] He ascribes the quotation, copied in full, to "quidam expositor, licet non sanctus". As it comes towards the end of his *Glossa*, we can deduce that the Latin *Guide* had reached Paris not long before 1227, and that it made a quick entry into the schools. Alexander of Hales and William of Auvergne were followed by John of La Rochelle in his contribution to the *Summa* which goes under the name of Alexander, by Vincent of Beauvais O.P., the encyclopaedist, and by St Thomas.[47] The *Guide*

43 *Guide* iii, 32, 526. The two central places in Scripture for philosophic and mystical teaching were the account of creation and Ezechiel's vision of the chariot.

44 F. van Steenberghen has noted this as one desideratum among many, *La philosophie au XIIIe siècle* (Louvain/Paris 1966) 339. For a list and analysis of some Latin MSS and the early editions, see W. Kluxen, "Literargeschichtliches zum lateinischen Moses Maimonides", RTAM xxi (1954) 23-35.

45 L. Thorndike, *Michael Scot* (London 1965) 28-29. Michael was at Bologna by 1220. It is not known when he entered the service of the emperor Frederich II, perhaps in 1220, perhaps not until 1224; ibid. 32-33.

46 *Glossa in quatuor libros sententiarum Petri Lombardi* ii (Quaracchi 1954) 471 (*Bibl. Franc. schol. med. aevi* xiv). The quotation is from the *Guide* iii, 36. It occurs in the earliest recension of the *Glossa*, designated by the editors as 'A'; a later recension, 'E', of the 1230s, adds 'Moyses' after "licet non sanctus". On the dates of the various books of the *Glossa*, see xii, 110*-116*, xiii, 21*; xv, 18* of *Bibl.Franc.* etc.

47 The best account of the Latin translation and its influence on the schoolmen is still J. Guttmann's "Der Einflüss etc." in *Moses Ben Maimon*, ed. W. Bacher, M. Brann and M. Simonsen (Leipzig 1908) 135-230. Guttmann could not have known of the recent research on Michael Scot nor of the quotation of the *Guide* in Alexander's *Glossa*, which was not discovered until 1946.

reached Oxford in time to be quoted by Richard Fishacre O.P. in his commentary on the *Sentences* about 1243; he quotes Rabbi Moses at least three times on the literal reasons for *caeremonialia*.[48] It is an impressive picture: the *Guide*, probably translated into Latin by Michael Scot in Italy soon after 1220, was used by a secular teacher at Paris soon before 1227, then by another secular, William of Auvergne, and then by Franciscans and Dominicans alike. A book catches on if it broaches problems which concern its readers and if its answers forestall or put more clearly what readers had in mind beforehand. The *Guide* had just this relevance in the early thirteenth century.

Still, much depended on the first Christian writer who sponsored the *Guide* in a big way. William of Auvergne was the first to unlock and display its teaching. Any suspicion of unorthodoxy on his part would have compromised it. On the other hand, a timid use would have blurred its significance. William was a theologian of high repute and unimpeachable orthodoxy. He grasped its meaning and drew out the implications boldly. We shall see how he fitted it into the framework of his doctrine. His commitment to it was so personal and so daring as to pose problems to his successors. We shall not understand St. Thomas's approach to the Old Law unless we begin by looking at its presentation in William's *De fide et legibus*. Since his ideas and his temperament coloured his use of the *Guide,* we must start by making a general study of William.

---

48   MS Oxford, Oriel College 43, foll. 333ra, 336rb, 338va on *Sent.* IV, i, 4,5,7. Fishacre quotes the opinions that uncleanness was instituted in the Law in order to induce feelings of reverence and fear, that all ceremonies were intended to strengthen faith in God and to prevent idolatry, and that regulations on circumcision had reasonable causes. On Fishacre see A. B. Emden, *A Bibliographical Register of the University of Oxford to A. D. 1500* ii (Oxford 1958) 685, and especially D. A. Callus, "The Introduction of Aristotelian Learning to Oxford", *Proceedings of the British Academy* xxix (1944) 259.

II

WILLIAM OF AUVERGNE

William came from Aurillac in the Auvergne.[1] He studied at Paris and then taught as a doctor of theology from sometime before 1222 to 1228; he was a canon of Notre-Dame by 1223. A disputed election to the bishopric of Paris brought him to Rome in 1228 to forward an appeal lodged by his chapter. Gregory IX quashed the election as uncanonical and provided and consecrated William to the bishopric, which he held until his death in 1249. His career as scholar and bishop corresponds to the ideal picture painted by masters of the Sacred Page in their sermons and lectures: the scholar must prepare himself for pastoral care by his study of Scripture; as master he will lecture, dispute and preach; finally, when raised to prelacy, he will practice what he has learnt and taught to his pupils. William strongly resembles Robert Grosseteste, his contemporary, bishop of Lincoln 1235-1253, another living model of a scholar bishop, as the scholars saw him.[2] Both William and Robert threw themselves heart and soul into the duties of pastoral care, striving to reform abuses, making visitations, preaching and promoting study, giving spiritual guidance and befriending the mendicant friars as precious helpers in their task. Both were strict disciplinarians. Both had to negotiate difficult business with their respective governments and with the papal Curia, though William showed more diplomacy and less intransigeance than his English colleague. Their output as scholars also has features in common. Both had an exceptionally wide range of interests. Neither of them used the normal scholastic mode of presentation, partly because they lacked the necessary feeling for system and order, and partly for the more positive reason that it would have cramped their style. They preferred to preach and teach and discuss theological problems in the same treatise, instead of using separate compartments. Further, they shared a rare gift of originality. The resemblance ends at this point, since each was original in his own way.

We have no comprehensive study of William, but detailed work on early scholasticism has built him up as an innovator: "He was one of the great thirteenth-century thinkers and has received less than his due only

---

1   See the notice and bibliography by P. Viard in *Dictionnaire de la spiritualité* vi (1967) 1182-92.

2   M. Gibbs and J. Lang, *Bishops and Reform 1215-1272* (Oxford 1934); *Robert Grosseteste Scholar and Bishop*, ed. D. A. Callus (Oxford 1953, reprinted 1969); S. Gieben, "Bibliographia universa Roberti Grosseteste ab an. 1473 ad an. 1969", *Collectanea Franciscana* xxxix (1969) 362-418.

because even greater men followed him".[3] His early lectures on *Proverbs*, *Ecclesiastes* and the *Canticle* show him as one of the first to bring the *Libri naturales* to bear on exegesis and to argue against current doubts on the immortality of the soul. His praise of the new religious Orders shows his receptivity.[4] His lectures on the *Canticle* struck Dr. Riedlinger as a marked contrast to the average school treatment of this book. William dwelt on the corruption of the Church, the bride of Christ, in more personal, violent language than any other exegete of the time permitted himself. His satire bit so deep that Hugh of Saint-Cher, basing his postill on William's, felt obliged to muzzle him. Hence William on the *Canticle* circulated through a Dominican medium with the mordancy softened.[5] We shall see how a Franciscan applied the same process to *De legibus*. William's *De bono et malo*, another early work (1223-1228), has been edited recently. It brings out his interest in human nature and his fondness for Cicero's *De officiis*.[6] His *Magisterium divinale*, a collection of tracts put together to form a *Summa*, serves the historian as a quarry for discovery of new or budding ideas. William's extensive early use of Arabic philosophers and scientists has been noted.[7] He was a precursor of St. Thomas in seeking rational proof for God's existence, rejecting St. Anselm's ontological argument.[8] He was a precursor, too, in his teaching on the unity of the soul; he was original on the problem of synderesis; he was one of the first Paris masters to attach liberty to the will[9] and to arrive at the concept of *Limbus puerorum*.[10]

Nowhere does he strike a line of his own more forcibly than in *De legibus*, which concerns us here. It formed part V (together with its twin, *De fide*) of the *Magisterium divinale*. A reference in *De legibus* to his *De sacramentis*, written about 1228, and another in his *De universo*, 1231-1236, date *De legibus* between these years. It therefore belongs to the beginning of his episcopate, probably about 1230.[11]

---

3   R. Weberberger, "*Limbus puerorum*. Zur Entstehung eines theologischen Begriffes", RTAM xxxv (1968) 128.

4   B. Smalley, "Some Thirteenth-Century Commentaries on the Sapiential Books", *Dominican Studies* ii (1949) 326-337; for MS Arsenal 64 read 84.

5   *Die Makellosigkeit der Kirche in den lateinischen Hohenliedkommentaren des Mittelalters* (BGPTM xxxviii, 3, 1958) 241-256.

6   J. R. O'Donnell, "Tractatus Magistri Guillelmi Alvernensis *De bono et malo*", *Mediaeval Studies* viii (1946) 245-299.

7   R. de Vaux, *Notes et textes sur l'Avicennisme latin aux confins des XIIᵉ-XIIIᵉ siècles* (Paris 1934) 17-22, 37-38.

8   A. Masnovo, *Da Guglielmo d'Auvergne a S. Tommaso*, 2nd ed. (Milan 1945-1946) i, 41.

9   O. Lottin, *Psychologie et morale aux XIIᵉ et XIIIᵉ siècles* (Louvain 1942-1960) i, 463; ii, 134-137, 340.

10   R. Weberberger, op. cit. 128-133.

11   J. Kramp, "Des Wilhelm von Auvergne *Magisterium divinale*", *Gregorianum* i (1920) 538-

William distinguishes himself from contemporaries by his grasp of a situation. He listened to men who did not raise their objections in formal academic debate. Hence he uncovers areas of doubt which might have gone unrecorded. To take a striking example: he attacks those who hold that the adherent of any faith, law or sect may be saved, provided that he believes sincerely that it comes from God. His deeds are pleasing to God, they say, provided that he does them for God's sake. William gives their reasons. An exclusive view of religion would mean that the multitude of the damned and the tiny proportion of the saved would reflect on God's mercy. Further, Christians presume in claiming salvation for themselves alone; and as only good Christians will be saved it follows that hell will be overcrowded: God could not be so pitiless as that. The background to such doubts was probably disputations with Jews and conversions to Judaism on the one hand.[12] The Church reacted by tightening regulations against the Jews and by burning the Talmud at Paris; William took a leading part in this. On the other hand, Islam was victorious in the Holy Land and the Reconquest of Spain disclosed hordes of Muslims, who resisted conversion. It was natural that Christians should wonder whether their religion counted as the only true one.[13] But William exposes an elusive frame of mind when he selects it for frontal attack. He does not say who the doubters were, only that they were numerous. He answers them by pointing out first that the doubter should have recourse to prayer: God will surely enlighten one who seeks the truth earnestly. Secondly, he compares the natural and supernatural orders: nature produces many vile in contrast to very few precious things; hence we need not be surprised that few go to heaven. Thirdly, he argues from God's love of justice.[14] St. Thomas's *Contra gentiles* shows up as a more sophisticated

---

584; ii (1921) 42-78. I have used a photographic reproduction of the Paris/Orleans, 1674 edition of William's *Opera*. My references will be to pages of vol. i. I have slightly altered punctuation and spelling. Collation of this edition with an early manuscript for selected passages is reassuring; variants are few and do not materially alter the sense where they occur; see appendix, below, p. 69.

12 For some recent work on disputations between Jews and Christians and on judaising Christians, see B. Z. Wacholder, "Cases of Proselytizing in the Tosafist Responsa", *Jewish Quarterly Review* N.S. li (1960-1961) 288-315; S. Stein, *Jewish-Christian Disputations in Thirteenth-Century Narbonne. An Inaugural Lecture delivered at University College London* (London 1969).

13 Doubt found collective expression in the parable of the three rings. Three sons each inherit a ring given him by his father. The rings look alike, but one is genuine and the others counterfeit. They stand for the three faiths, Christian, Jewish and Muslim. God, the Father in heaven, alone knows which is the true one. For variants of the story and its significance see M. Penna, *La parabola dei tre anelli e la toleranza nel medio evo* (Turin 1953).

14 *De Legibus* xxi, p. 60. Lottin, op. cit., ii, 409-411, points out that William of Auxerre also taught that prayer would be efficacious for the solution of doubts. There is a great contrast, however, between the types of doubt envisaged: William of Auxerre thought in terms of casuistry

argument on the same theme. It aimed at providing a reasoned defence of the Christian faith for use against Jews and Muslims and against Christians led astray by Greco-Arabic philosophy.[15] William's arguments are unconvincing in comparison, just as the objections that he answers are less intellectual. But William at least gives the simpler doubters a right to be heard. His willingness to confront objections will help to explain his attitude to exegesis.

His use of the *Guide* is already well known. It has been asked why he never quoted the author by name, whereas he did not scruple to name Avicenna. The reason is surely that Avicenna died in 1037 and Maimonides in 1204; hence he came within the conventional span during which later writers would not quote him by name; near contemporaries were called *quidam* or *aliqui*.[16] In the same way, Alexander of Hales had quoted him as *quidam expositor, sed non sanctus*, to distinguish him from Christian scholars, as we have seen. William advertised instead of concealing his debt to Maimonides. Alexander quoted from the *Guide* once only; he did not mention the author's rationalisation of precepts which had no obvious reason, such as the ban on wearing clothes woven of wool and flax together (*Deut.* xxii, 11). Such precepts were figurative, though Alexander accepted that they had a literal meaning (if not a reason) for the Old Testament Jews.[17] William, on the contrary, took over the leading idea of Maimonides: *legalia* aimed at weaning the Jews from idolatry; hence they forbad all practices which recalled pagan rites. William echoed the *Guide* on other reasons: the offering of unblemished beasts in sacrifice taught the honour due to God; the burning of offerings and the sending out of the scapegoat signified repentance, in that sins were symbolically destroyed or cast out, in order to teach the sinner to set his sins behind him.[18] He mentions the marvellous cures reported in the *Guide* in discussing the precepts on leprosy.[19] The influence goes deeper than mere quotation.

and scruples of conscience; William of Auvergne was concerned with the more fundamental question of rival religions.

15 M.-D. Chenu, *Introduction à l'étude de Saint Thomas d'Aquin* (Paris 1950) 247-254.

16 The reasons previously suggested (see Masnovo, op. cit. i, 118-124) are that William would not quote Maimonides by name because he was a Jew, and alternatively that the *Guide* was presented as a compilation, rather than as an original work. Neither reason convinces me.

17 *Glossa*, op. cit. 460-461: "Nam alia sunt praecepta mystica, alia non. Mystica autem, alia sunt caerimonialia, alia sacramentalia...Caerimonalia sunt quorum non est evidens ratio, quale est hoc: *Non indues contextum ex lino et lana*. Haec autem et illa dicuntur figurativa. Sed figurativa sunt rei faciendae, aut rei futurae....Quae autem sunt figurativa rei faciendae manserunt in thurificio et aqua benedicta." Ibid. 543: "Erit ergo duplex adimpletio (Veteris Legis), scilicet cum sacramenta Novae Legis succedunt aliis, et cum succedunt litteralibus intellectibus caeremonialium intellectus spirituales."

18 *Guide* III, 46, 584, 589, 591; *De legibus* viii, 38, 40.

19 Ibid. xi, 43.

William made the *Guide* his own. He will elaborate on the arguments, finding further evidence for those pagan practices and superstitions, which according to Maimonides the Law combatted by prescribing their opposites.[20] Even more interesting, he criticises Maimonides openly or by implication, in the belief that he, as a Christian bishop, could give better reasons for the literal causes of precepts than a Jewish philosopher could do.

William is both a personal and digressive writer. Professor Gilson points to the influence of Avicenna on his dialogue with his reader, addressed as *tibi*, and in his constant use of phrases like *revertamur ad id in quo eramus*;[21] the former at least could have derived from Maimonides as well. It will clarify his thesis, therefore, if we begin with his conclusion and then work backward through his proofs. He claims to have made the following points:[22] 1) seemingly absurd precepts had just and reasonable causes and hence must be understood in their literal sense; they were imposed on a simple people, needing to be weaned from idolatry; the time demanded them; 2) many similar bans obtain "among us" even today; certain practices are forbidden as superstitious and recalling Judaism or "Saracenism". All the more reason why the Old Law should have warded off contamination.

Why did William feel a compulsion to defend the literal reasons for *legalia*? The *Guide* stimulated him to go one better in doing so; but other influences worked on him. They appear in his account of the nature and purpose of law in general at the beginning of *De legibus*: nothing but the best was worthy of the divine lawgiver. Hence the Old Law had to fit into his concept of what law ought to be.

He begins with a few remarks on the law of nature, stressing its intrinsic character: laws imposed from without are not laws at all, properly speaking; moral values reside in the soul, radiating from divine wisdom.[23] St. Isidore's list of the attributes of good human law supplies the framework for William's. Isidore wrote:

> Erit autem lex honesta, iusta, possibilis, secundum naturam, secundum

---

20 Ibid. xiii, 44.

21 "Avicenne en Occident au moyen âge", AHDLMA xxxvi (1969) 91-93.

22 *De legibus* xv, 46: "Licet autem ex his clarum tibi sit, et merito, quod iuxta litteram intelligenda sunt ea quae absurda videntur esse in lege, et quia causas habent iustas et rationabiles suae praeceptionis et suae prohibitionis, et quod tempus illud et populi ruditas et ineruditio idolatriaeque proximitas et vicinitas praecepta et prohibitiones huiusmodi requirebant, ostendimus etiam tibi quod magna pars eorum etiam apud nos extant, sicut prohibitiones observationum superstitiosarum, quas proxime enumeravimus, et quia etiam tales praeceptiones et prohibitiones fiunt apud nos propter speciem Judaismi et Saracenismi aliarumque superstitionum suspiciones. Et propter hoc merito ex similibus causis similes praeceptiones et prohibitiones primitivo illo populo, et idolatriae innutrito et circumquaque obsesso, multo fortius faciendae fuerunt."

23 O. Lottin, *Le droit naturel chez Saint Thomas d'Aquin et ses prédécesseurs* (Bruges 1931) 40, n. 1.

consuetudinem patriae, loco temporique conveniens, necessaria, utilis, manifesta quoque...[24]

William renders this in his own words, quoting a current dictum in addition:

Dicamus igitur quia lex verissima ratione nihil aliud est quam honestas legibilis, id est descripta religionis praeceptis, iuxta quod dictum videtur: lex est scriptum assistens honestis, prohibens contrarium...[25] Lex est honestas integra seu completa, legibilis et descripta litteris et ad observantiam imperata.[26]

The definition of good law sets the tone for William's treatment of *legalia*. The outward observance imposed on the Jews must have echoed the precepts of the law of nature and have measured up to the standards set by Isidore for good human laws. Taking the Ciceronian *honestum* as a starting point, he presents the Law of Moses as an *alphabetum honestatis*. True, it formed part, not the whole, of the perfect, eternal Law of the Gospel. Its function was to prepare an uneducated people to receive the Gospel, by teaching them their *alphabetum honestatis*, according to their limited understanding, "quia naturalis honestatis regulas continet et mandata." William justifies his description of the Old Law, which he will then prove in detail:

The whole Law contains nothing which lacks a rational cause for commanding, forbidding or narrating. There is nothing absurd or irrational in it, and this appears clearly in many items which have obvious worth and usefulness.[27]

His defence aims at showing that the Old Law reached Isidorian standards. It was worthy or decorous (*honesta*); it accorded with nature; it was suited to its time and place; it was necessary and useful, just and possible; it was manifest, having been published and set down in writing. William realised only too well that his predecessors had found

---

24   *Etym.* II, x; V, xxi, ed. W. Lindsay (Oxford 1911). This passage from St. Isidore forms the subject of an article of the *Summa* (Ia2ae, q. 95, a. 3). It was so well known previously that we find it in a gloss added to a copy of the *Gloss* on the Psalter, soon after the mid twelfth century, MS Paris, B.N. lat. 105: *Beatus vir.* Ab honesto incipit. *In cathedra pestilentie non sedit.* Ab utili. *Erit tanquam lignum.* A possibili.
See B. Smalley, "Les commentaires bibliques de l'époque romane", *Cahiers de civilisation médiévale* iv (1961) 19-20.
25   This dictum, "lex...contrarium", was current in the thirteenth century, with slight variations. St. Albert ascribed it to Cicero, but it is not in his works; see O. Lottin, *Psychologie et morale*, op. cit. ii, 16-17.
26   *De legibus* i, 18. I cannot find the actual verbal source of William's definition of law; it may be his own.
27   Ibid. ii, 29. See also xvi, 47: "Et quoniam iam defendimus et declaravimus litteralem intelligentiam legis, in his quibus absurda penitus et nullatenus possibilia videbatur..."

many precepts quite the opposite; they had been regarded as unworthy, unfitting, useless or impossible to observe.

He first defends the multiplicity of laws: why did the *alphabetum honestatis* have to include so many precepts? Maimonides explained it on the grounds that the Jews had to be warned against many diverse kinds of idolatry. William adds two other reasons: children cannot understand generalisations; they need instruction in detail, just as bread must be broken before they can chew it;[28] secondly, God provided what would occupy their minds; the Law offered ample matter for study.[29] Scarcity of books and fewness of precepts would have turned the Jews towards profane learning and would have led them astray. This danger appeared later in their history, especially when they were overrun by the Saracens. Then they studied pagan philosophy, which led them to apostatise, since many precepts began to look absurd and futile.[30] William had Maimonides' apologetic purpose in mind at this point in his argument. The *Guide* was written for perplexed Jews, who doubted in consequence of their philosophic studies.

We pass from content to enforcement. Maimonides justified the harsh penalties imposed by the Law in the interests of good order: "To the wicked the existence of a judge who renders tyranny impossible is harmful and grievous."[31] William heartily agrees. He discourses at length on the need for *disciplina*. Men still have to be forced as well as taught to act rightly. He sums up as follows:

> This is the surest and firmest ground (of the judicial penalties), that discipline must be applied, and not teaching only.[32]

He goes on to argue against those soft-brained persons who illogically disapprove of the death penalty, while accepting the need for lesser deterrents.[33] The Church, as he noted, still had to legislate against the survival of pagan practices in the form of superstition and magic: "We shall refute those errors concerning idols which have existed, and still do," he says in his preface.[34] Many Old Testament laws against idolatry had kept their relevance. Maimonides could have given even more

---

28 *De legibus* i, 24. A common analogy for God's condescension to human understanding; see R. W. Southern and F. S. Schmitt, *Memorials of St. Anselm*, op. cit. 274: apples have to be cut up for children on account of their soft teeth and small mouths.

29 This idea derives from Augustine's *De vera religione* xvii, PL 34, 136.

30 *De legibus* i, 24.

31 *Guide* II, 39, 380-1; III, 35, 536.

32 *De legibus* i, 27.

33 Ibid. William's experience as a bishop on the need for *disciplina* corresponded to St. Augustine's, though William does not quote him; see Peter Brown, *Augustine of Hippo* (London 1967) 236-241.

34 *De legibus*, 2.

weight to the argument in their favour. William's sharpest criticism of
the *Guide* turns on the interpretation of *Deut.* xxii, 6: the wayfarer who
finds a nest with a sitting bird in it may take the young, but must let her
go, that he may prosper and have a long life. Maimonides grouped this
text among precepts which inculcated pity: if God requires mercy
towards birds and beasts, then how much more to men?[35] William
dismisses the explanation as laughable and childish. Had pity been the
object of the precept, then it would have been less cruel to take the hen
bird and leave the young; the blessing attached to the precept,
moreover, seems too great for so trivial an action. He explains it instead
as directed against magicians, who used birds and their eggs or chicks
for fertility rites and auguries: "Many fools still think it lucky to find
certain objects and keep them as pledges of good fortune: old women
cannot be weaned of the idea." Similarly, Christians still make incisions
in the skin and carry figures, drawn or engraved, just as the Jews were
forbidden to do (*Lev.* xix, 28); this is yet another detestable relic of
idolatry. The Church today would sternly correct persons who observed
Jewish or Saracen customs, even if these were harmless in themselves,
such as refraining from servile work on Saturdays.[36] William draws on
his experience as bishop and director of conscience here: he tells us in
De virtutibus that he used to be consulted on temptations by demons.[37]

He also brings his personal scientific interests to bear on the
diagnosis of leprosy by the priests of the Law. Earlier commentators
had stumbled over the references to "leprosy in walls" (*Lev.* xiv, 36).
Ralph of Flaix regarded it as the clearest proof of the absurdity of the
Law *ad litteram*; others had followed him or had done their best to
"save" its literal meaning.[38] William had no difficulty with the text. He
had himself been questioned about a stone in a certain abbey, which
was said to be "cancerous" because it was rotting away; and he had observed dry rot in wood.[39]

We see a gentler side of him when he christianises Old Testament
worship. The sacrifices were not prescribed with the sole intention of
weaning the Jews from idolatry, "as certain persons have held". *Quidam*
refers to Maimonides, who wrote:

> The first intention of the Law consists only in your apprehending Me
> and not worshipping someone other than Me....Those laws concerning

---

35   *Guide* III, 48, 600.
36   *De legibus*, xiv, 45-46.
37   Ibid. xi, ed. cit. 131.
38   See above, p. 13, n. 8.
39   *De legibus*, xi, 42-43.

sacrifices and repairing to the Temple were given only for the sake of this fundamental principle.[40]

William was hardly fair to his author, reading *"first* intention" as "one and only";[41] he could pick up hints on other purposes in the ritual precepts. However, he puts forward seven other reasons in addition to prevention of idolatry. The sacrifices were instituted to honour God and to teach the Jews to observe the rites which he alone had prescribed for them. The slaughter of animals signified God's justice and mercy; the Jews learnt the lesson that God in his justice could have visited them with death for their sins, instead of sparing them in his mercy. The act of sacrifice impressed on their minds what they read in their books. William invented a pious thought (*cogitatio*) which would have been used by those making sacrifice:

> Mors nobis imminebat quemadmodum istis animalibus, cui utique de iustitia tua tradere nos poteras, sed per misericordiam tuam vel liberati sumus vel liberari nos petimus, O Deus.

A cross-reference sends us to a later passage, where he invents prayers for use at sin offerings:

> He who slaughtered or burned the animals would state in deed, and also in word, as we believe: "The sins for which I offer these animals perish and vanish, just as they do".[42]

William wrote a treatise on Christian prayer, *De rhetorica divina*, the most popular of his books. It includes a choice of prayers for use by the faithful.[43] He could easily surmise what devotions would have suited the Israelites. The sacrifices were a memorial to divine goodness. The offerers gave part of them to God and kept part for themselves, to signify that they owed all to God's blessing. The sacrifices sanctified those who offered, cleansing them from the stains of their sins, by God's virtue and mercy. Here William commits himself to the much-discussed view that *legalia* sanctified.[44] They also brought men into closer relationship to God. The offering of gifts and sharing at the holy table made them seem in some way to be table-mates with him, just as the family table

---

40   *Guide* III, 32, 530; see also ibid. 527 and III, 29, 517-518 and III, 46, 582.

41   I checked the Latin translation of the *Guide* from MS Oxford, Bodl. 437, to see whether the translation had led William astray, but it has "prima intentio legis est", and "prima intentio...", foll. 91, 92, 93v, 94.

42   *De legibus*, ii, 29; xxiv, 72.

43   P. Viard, *Dict. de spiritualité* op. cit. 1190. He lists a "prayer to Moses" among them, which would be interesting, but it must be a mistake; I cannot find any prayer to Moses in *De rhetorica divina*.

44   He explains later that this was not *propria virtute*, in contrast to Christian sacraments. See below, p. 42.

brings men into closer relationship with their human parents. God indicated his presence from time to time by sending fire from heaven to consume his share of the sacrifices, as though in his stead. Sacrifices unified God's people, drawing many individuals together to make up one household and family. Sharing bodily food is the distinctive mark of the latter. Similarly sharing of spiritual food and drink makes one spiritual family and household. William defines "spiritual food and drink" as that which is hallowed, and where spiritual rather than bodily nourishment is sought. This definition enabled him to classify the Old Testament sacrificial meals as "spiritual". Finally, the sacrifices had a social-religious function in bringing men to worship together;[45] here again he draws on his experience:

> Food and drink cause men to assemble in the same place on the same occasion as nothing else does. That is why the Church has founded infirmaries, where physical refreshment is prepared; otherwise few or none would assemble there. Hence God in his great wisdom and mercy willed that food and drink should be shared in his house and at his altar, in order that the community of his people should be brought there and should be bound to them more closely. He willed that sacrifices should be sacred to him, in order that the people should partake of them as God's gifts and not as their own property, and as sacred, not common. The people would therefore acknowledge him as father of the family, who gave them life and food, and would refrain from evil, when they saw themselves admitted to communion or participation in holy things.[46]

William postulated that all his seven reasons for the sacrificial precepts would have been explained to the Jews in sermons. It could not have been otherwise. The wise and holy fathers of old would not have offered sacrifice without praises, blessings and discourses; they would not have left their people in total ignorance of divine matters. Who will believe that God's worship has ever lacked prayer and praise, seeing that these things are foremost and most pleasing to him in our services? The argument was hypothetical, as William knew. Evidence for prayers at sacrifice in the Old Testament is conspicuous by its absence. William got round it by suggesting that evidence had been lost, just as Maimonides had pointed to lost evidence on the nature of pagan

45   The *Guide* gave William a lead by implication on the subject of pilgrimage, III, 46, p. 592. The reason for the utility of pilgrimage is well known. For such a gathering results in a renewal of the Law, this being a consequence of people being affected by it and of the fraternity that comes about among them because of it. See also III, 39, 551 on the social function of the second tithe, which was to be spent on food in Jerusalem, and hence brought men together.

46   *De legibus*, ii, 29-30. The same point is made later: people would not frequent confraternity meetings unless cooked meals were provided; xxviii, 97.

practices.[47] "If these prayers and praises had come down to us", writes William, "they would have taught us clearly the causes and uses of this kind of rite".[48] A further reason for the sacrifices was to provide for the needs of the priests and leave them free to attend to divine service and to teach their people.[49]

William made a real effort to think himself back into Old Testament times. He tried to recreate the value and ethos of the Old Law, as administered by his predecessors, the levites, He could sympathise with them in their struggle to educate their flock. The Old Law, according to him, had a positive content, as well as a negative purpose against idolatry. Earlier Christian commentators had dwelt lovingly on the Tabernacle and its physical appearance. It took William to set up a pulpit beside the Jewish shrine. His historical method was anachronistic, in that he made the past look much like the present, as was usual in the middle ages. The interesting point is that he brought it to bear on the educative value of *legalia*, taken *ad litteram*.

Having expounded his own view, he turns to earlier exegesis. Commentators had interpreted the precepts all too often in a spiritual sense only. They had seen *legalia* as a veil or foreshadowing of the New Law and had neglected their literal value for the ancient Jews. William names no one, but he may well have directed his reproaches against Ralph of Flaix, since the latter's commentary on *Leviticus* was standard. The whole tradition, deriving from Origen and exemplified by Ralph comes in for criticism. Certain precepts had been classified as "absurd according to the letter". William turns the objection upside down. Absurd indeed they would have been, if they had lacked a literal meaning. The law-giver and his law would have been "barbarous", had they been incomprehensible. What could be sillier than to suppose that a wise prophet and lawgiver would have ordered his people to observe what they could not comprehend? It would have amounted to deception and mockery on his part. How could a leader and teacher fulfil his office unless he explained the law he gave? If he failed to do so, he would lead his people astray. To propound commandments which had no literal meaning, without announcing the fact, would have led the recipients to suppose a literal sense, where none was, or else left them, an ignorant people, to work out the secret, hidden meaning for themselves. Would a wise, loyal man refuse to speak openly to the people whom he had undertaken to teach? That would have involved him in

47 *Guide*, III, 29, 521.
48 *De legibus*, ii, 30.
49 Ibid.

fraud and dissimulation. William quotes a tag from rhetoric: "Sermo interpres animi est".[50] A lawgiver who refused to speak plainly would have concealed his mind instead of revealing it. Moses had followers, too. Would all later doctors of the law have left the people in ignorance of its hidden meaning? The prophets at least would have mentioned it, since God sent them to correct errors. According to the traditional view, the precepts and bans of the Old Law were addressed to the "new people", the Christians. They alone could understand the hidden meaning, which was reserved for them and not for the ancient Jews. William counters this objection. He begins by quoting St. Paul: *Now we know that what things soever the Law speaketh, it speaketh to them that are within the law (Rom.* iii, 19). He goes on to argue that the Law had no need to carry an inner, spiritual meaning for the benefit "of us, who were not yet there". There was no need for the Law to speak to us in figures after the Church had been established, for then the Gospel truth reached us, bare and plain. He thought it most unlikely that the whole Jewish people, dedicated for so long to the study of their Law, would not have discerned the error of taking it in its literal sense only, if there had been another. William ends by anticipating a query which might be raised. It occurred to him that he was claiming to understand the moral value and rational character of *legalia* better than "the modern Jews" did themselves: they ignored the literal reasons for their laws. Was he not making the literal sense as difficult to grasp as the spiritual? He answers that the learned men among the ancient Jews would have understood well enough. The uneducated could have been brought to understand quite easily, given the prevalence of idolatry around them, which supplied the most obvious reason. That their former knowledge has perished is due to the passage of time, to their afflictions and dispersal and to their neglect of study. The reasons for their negligence in studying their Law are avarice, to which the Jews are prone, and love of gentile philosophy.

To sum up: William has anticipated St. Thomas in accounting the whole intention of the sacred writer as included in the literal sense. Further, he was the first commentator, to my knowledge, to break away from a narrow verbal concept of "the letter". Medieval exegetes had been dogged by it. Even scholars who took the literal interpretation seriously had still thought in terms of the *superficies litterae*. When commenting on the literal sense of *legalia* they restricted themselves to the exact form of the rites prescribed and took small pains to bring out their meaning for the ancient Jews. True, William had the advantage of writing in the framework of a treatise, instead of lecturing on his text,

50   Ibid. xv, 46, from Cicero, *De Legibus* i, 10: "Interpresque mentis oratio..."

clause by clause, as was done in the schools; but he also benefited from his careful reading of the *Guide*. Now he must leave the *Guide* and pass to the spiritual sense of *legalia*. So far, he has never denied that the Law has a spiritual sense for Christians. He has merely insisted that it had a literal sense for the Jews, who could understand it and profit from its lessons. *De legibus* presents it as an *alphabetum honestatis* and not as a veil or cryptogram.

What will he make of the spiritual meaning? The answer is rather elusive: perhaps it was intended to be. Conventional passages alternate with eccentric ones. William first states the proposition that Law of necessity has not only a literal, but a manifold spiritual meaning "from God", deducible from the literal, which enlightens the mind and edifies the soul. He proves it from the Law and the prophets themselves.[51] Many texts show us that the Law had an inner meaning. David the psalmist, to quote only one illustration, prayed that his eyes might be opened to consider the wondrous things of the Law (*Ps.* cxviii, 18). He had wit enough to understand the literal meaning of the Law (which William has already described as comprehensible even to simple men); therefore, he must have prayed for understanding of its higher meaning. The proof texts are buttressed by an argument from analogy. A human master teaches the pupils in his school according to their individual needs; some are dull and others clever. How much more does God, the supreme teacher, adapt his lessons to his pupils' various grades of intelligence? The Scriptures offer infinite variety, like a table groaning with good fare, where each guest will find nourishment suited to his appetite. William then launches into praise of Scripture of a traditional kind.[52] It sounds like part of a *principium*, the lecture in praise of Scripture given by a doctor at his inception. William may have used his own or borrowed from someone else.[53] So far, so good. Disconcertingly, however, he does not specify the content of the inner meaning which David prayed to have revealed to him. Did it refer to an understanding of the Old Testament prophecies of Christ? William may have presupposed that such was the case; but how odd that he fails to mention it!

51 Ibid., xvi, 47: "Patefaciemus post haec quia non solum litteralem intelligentiam habet lex. sed etiam spiritualem multiplicem a Deo, ut omnino intellectus illuminativus et aedificativus animarum, qui ex ea elici potest in ea necessario sit; et primum ostendemus hoc ex ipsius legis et prophetarum testimoniis."
William has already mentioned the existence of an élite among the Jews, though without elaborating on it; see cap. i, 23: "Quemadmodum nec omnes Hebraei temporis illius ad vetus testamentum pertinebant, ut dicit Augustinus: immo erant in populo illo qui ad novum pertinent" (*sic*).
52 Ibid., 47-8. Scripture is likened to a mine, having veins of precious metals and jewels, to a garden of delights, to a wine cellar and to a medicine chest.
53 None of the many sermons listed by J. B. Schneyer, *Wegweiser zu lateinischen Predigtreihen des Mittelalters* (Munich 1965) looks like a *principium* or inaugural lecture, but William must have given one.

There is still a chance for him to bring it in, since he passes to the spiritual senses of Scripture, after proving their existence. And here comes the novelty. [54] The spiritual interpretation, he tells us, proves a stumbling block to many; it strikes them as "imposition" rather than "exposition". He will try to satisfy them. His apology for the spiritual senses against their critics falls into four parts. Nobody can take offence at two modes of interpretation. Prophetic signs, expressed by means of deeds or speech were intended to be understood figuratively; he gives examples of what today we should call symbolic gestures or metaphors. On his own showing, these should really have been covered by the literal interpretation, since they belonged to teaching designed for instruction of Old Testament Jews. The third mode of interpretation is inoffensive also: we find a spiritual sense by drawing out the consequences of the literal. Thus bans on bodily idol worship had a moral significance: the command not to worship golden idols signified that plain gold must not be worshipped either, and forbad the sin of avarice. Paris masters of the sacred page classified William's third mode of interpretation as *moralitas secundum litteram*; they distinguished it from moralisation of texts, since it represented a deduction from the literal sense; it was not a "morality" in the strict sense of the term. [55] Logically, William should have included it in his account of the literal interpretation, since he argued that the precepts conveyed moral teaching according to their literal sense and reasons.

The fourth mode of interpretation gives offence to many. William sees the force of their objections and goes at least half way to meet them. This fourth mode is by comparison. There is no harm in it, if only exegetes would stick to comparisons instead of using signification. But they make things signify what they were never meant to, which is abusive. God did not teach in that way, when he spoke through his prophets. He used comparisons. William illustrates comparison in carefully chosen words:

> *As a woman that despiseth her lover, so hath the house of Israel despised me (Ierem.* iii, 20). God did not say that the woman's contempt signified the children of Israel's contempt nor that her lover signified himself.... Rather he expressed a mode or obvious likeness between the woman's contempt of her lover and the conduct of the children of Israel.

The prophet should serve as a model to exegetes. William continues:

> If exegetes and doctors would only speak in this way in their allegories and tropologies and anagogical interpretations, they would do justice to

---

54 See appendix, pp. 69-71 for the full text, which I summarise here in translation, giving references to the quotations in it.
55 B. Smalley, *The Study of the Bible in the Middle Ages*, op. cit. 234.

Scripture and would not insult the intelligence of their readers and hearers.

Instead, they make one thing signify another as a figure or prophecy, when it was neither said nor done in order to signify any other thing, which gravely offends their hearers. William gives a sample of this kind of distortion. He chooses the story of David's adultery with Bethsabee and the slaying of her husband Uria (II *Reg.* xi-xii). David acted as an adulterer, traitor and murderer. Yet he is said to signify Christ, while the good Uria is said to signify the devil. David's adultery with Bethsabee is said to signify Christ's pure, stainless union with the Church of the gentiles. This sort of teaching angers many. It destroys or at least weakens their faith in holy exposition of Scripture. William has picked on a current allegorical interpretation, deriving from St. Gregory's *Moralia*, as he must have known.

The objectors see two flaws in the use of signification. First, David's action was not intended to signify something else. Secondly, they think it most unlikely that the action was recorded in order to signify something else either. William (more or less identifying himself with them) explains how the David story may be used as a comparison: *just as* David loved Bethsabee and procured the death of her husband, *so* Christ loved the Synagogue and freed her from those who had held her in subjection, in order to honour her in spiritual marriage and make her his queen in heaven. If exegetes would make and explain such comparisons in a fitting way, they would run no risk of offending their hearers and would be listened to gratefully. Use of comparisons is a natural mode of teaching, found in Scripture, too. Commentators raise further scandal by their unskilled, fanciful inventions, which do violence to their text; they neglect St. Jerome's warning against excessive use of tropology. Instead of keeping to the point, they go off at a tangent, as when they interpret the branches and baskets in the dreams told to Joseph (*Gen.* xli) as signifying something different from what Joseph said they meant.

William closes this surprising chapter with a second conventional passage in praise of Scripture; but a trenchant summary of his views comes immediately after:

> We have explained that the Law has all the meaning proper to wholesome teaching, which can be deduced from it, in addition to its literal sense; but this is not whatever can be imposed abusively and violently upon it, repugnant to the letter. Such twisting of the Scriptures is not exposition, but rather abusive imposition. God in his goodness intended that all the meaning proper to wholesome teaching, which can be deduced from it *fittingly*, should be understood in Holy Scripture.

He has thrown overboard the current technique of lecturing on Scripture according to the four senses. Those *distinctiones*, which listed the properties of things for use in the spiritual exposition, rank by implication as idle fancies. Comparisons are admissable, significations are not:

> Verbum ergo significandi est quod in parte ista graviter offendit auditores atque lectores.[56]

Finally, William explains why *legalia* have been banned by the Church as superfluous under the new dispensation. Now, if ever, was the time for him to describe them as *umbra futurorum*. He does not. He explains instead that the sacrifices had no power to cleanse of themselves: they pleased God only because they demonstrated devotion and obedience and had useful purposes, such as maintaining the priesthood. The Church has found better ways of providing for divine worship and maintaining her priests.[57] Hence *legalia* no longer serve the needs of the new spiritual people, which has spiritual knowledge in the Gospel. William passes to two questions. First, why were *legalia* imposed on the righteous, as well as on the weak and ignorant, seeing that the righteous did not need symbolic actions to teach them to avoid sin and idolatry? Secondly, why did God withhold the true means of sanctification from his chosen people? The answer to the first question is that the righteous observed the ceremonial precepts in order to avoid scandal and schism. The second question receives the familiar answer that the people as a whole would not have understood them.[58] William now makes a new point: the prophets marked a further stage in education. They invited the people to spiritual worship and inner holiness, blaming mere outward observance.[59] The teaching of the prophets succeeded to that of the Law and came closer to perfection. Then at last, came the perfect excellence of the Gospels.[60] *De legibus* closes with an account of the

---

56 See appendix, below p. 70.

57 *De legibus*, xxviii, p. 97: "Manifestum est quod postquam ista offeruntur, necesse habent illa cessare tanquam superflua quantum ad emundationem et sanctificationem, quare quamcito ista imposita et exposita sunt, cessare oportet illa, et ideo spirituali populo interdicta sunt merito, evangelio coruscante. Spirituali enim populo, hoc est spiritualia cognoscenti, nec necessaria sunt ad eruditionem neque ad emundationem vel sanctificationem neque ad eas quas diximus, scilicet ad conservationem et retinentiam in Dei honorificantia et cultu, neque ad alimoniam sacerdotum, cum alias et melius et honestius provideatur sacerdotibus spiritualibus. Quare manifestum est nullo modo ea esse necessaria. Deo autem accepta vel placita impossibile est esse, nisi propter utilitatem populi sui. Ergo manifestum est quia, facto spirituali populo, nec Deo placita sunt...."

58 Ibid., 98.

59 He quotes *Ierem.* iv, 3; vi, 10; ix, 26. The crucial text *Ezech.* xx, 25: *Dedi eis praecepta non bona* is not mentioned, however.

60 *De legibus*, xxviii, 99: "Unde postmodum per prophetas paulatim ad spiritualem cultum et interiorem sanctificationem invitati sunt, sicut apparet Hierem. 4, ubi dicitur... Iam igitur manifestum est, quia nec veritas nec virtus nec salubritas huiusmodi sacrificiorum causa fuit ut imponeretur populo Hebraeorum, sed sicut generaliter verum est quia pro rudibus et novitiis perfecta

seven sacraments of the Church, which have superseded the legal sacrifices. William's last opportunity to present the latter as figurative of the former has passed.[61] It follows that he could not allow the righteous of the Old Testament any presage of Christian sacraments.

The omission must have been intentional. We can see the influence of Maimonides in William's view of the superior type of wisdom possessed by the Old Testament élite. Like Maimonides, he restricts it to a higher concept of holiness and understanding of true religion or philosophy. It contrasted with external religion, though the latter had its uses, as wise men realised. This view in its turn sends us back to the beginning of De legibus, where William presents law in general as depending on the dictates of mind and heart. But this wisdom, it seems, excluded an understanding of legalia as umbra futurorum.

Full of curiosity, I turned next to William's lectures on Scripture, to his aids to preaching and to his sermons, to discover whether he put his theories into practice. Did he avoid allegories and tropologies, substituting comparison for signification? His lectures belong to an early stage of his career as a teacher. Here he used allegories and tropologies, as did everyone else.[62] He had not yet begun to criticise them. A study of his many unprinted sermons would have taken too long; but one has been edited, a university sermon, preached 1230-1231,[63] and therefore roughly contemporary with De legibus. Here he avoids allegories and tropologies altogether. His colleagues, Philip the Chancellor and others, preaching in the same year, use them freely.[64] William produced two aids to preachers, both undated. One has been edited by de Poorter. It does not mention the four senses. William dwells on the usefulness of fitting comparisons:

ab initio non traduntur vel imponuntur... Et doctrinae legis successit doctrina prophetarum tanquam perfectioni vicinior; tandem autem advenit evangelicae perfectionis excellentia, ultra quam non est quo se extendat in vita ista perfectio sanctitatis, et ideo praenominata rudimenta et initialia in adventu eius penitus cessaverunt et interdicta sunt toto orbe..."

61 Ibid. Several pages are devoted to the sacraments of the Christian Church to conclude De legibus, but nowhere here are they described as having been prefigured or foreshadowed by legalia.

62 See B. Smalley, "Some Thirteenth-Century Commentaries etc" op. cit. 330. I looked again at the copy of William on Proverbs in MS Oxford, Bodl. 292. Here is a specimen of his exegesis: "Dominus sapientia fundavit terram (iii, 19): Ad litteram planum est...Mistice autem terram ecclesie fundavit Christus...Stabilivit celos prudentia. Celos vero enim contemplativos stabilivit...Pes tuus non impinget (23)... Pes autem iste caritas intelligitur..." (foll. 371vb, 372rb).

63 Edited by M. M. Davy, Les sermons universitaires Parisiens de 1230-1231 (Etudes de philosophie médiévale xv, 1931) 149-53. William takes as his theme Numquid ordinem caeli nosti (Iob xxxviii, 33). He distinguishes the literal from the spiritual order of the heavens, but he includes in the literal interpretation of the text: "hujus caeli litteralis ordinem non videntur nosse. Ordo caeli litteralis possunt vocari stellae et hujusmodi... Secundus ordo caeli spiritualis et sublimis est, ubi sedet auctor universitatis, deinde seraphim..." (150).

64 Ibid. 161, 193, 244-5, 365.

> Convenienter rerum similitudo multum valet ad loquendum, sicut videri potest quando aliter rei natura sive proprietas explicatur.

Thus the Holy Spirit may be likened to fire or Christ to the sun, provided that the preacher explains the likeness. He stresses the need for logical order of ideas and he admits the use of *distinctiones, divisiones, interpretationes et definitiones*. The *distinctio*, which he cites as an example, lists only the literal senses of the word: "est pax peccatoris, praedicatoris etc".[65] The unprinted *De faciebus mundi* again recommends comparisons, drawn "from the book of nature and of art", with many examples.[66] Again it does not mention the four senses. So William satisfied me that he was consistent. He avoided allegories and tropologies, as soon as he had begun to reflect on their arbitrary character and had heard them attacked in the schools. Then he resorted to comparisons as a better mode of teaching.

One difficulty remained. William praised the Cistercian abbot, Joachim of Fiore, as having displayed *donum intellectus* in his commentary on the Apocalypse and in his *Liber concordie novi et veteris testamenti*. This passage, which has been discussed by students of Joachism, occurs in William's *De virtutibus*,[67] following next but one to *De legibus* in his *Magisterium divinale*. Joachim's type of spiritual exposition should not have pleased William on the evidence of *De legibus*. However, the praise of Joachim must be taken in its context. William is explaining how the "gift of understanding" differs from the spirit of prophecy and from faith. The prophet sees by divine illumination. The gift of understanding, on the other hand, enables us to discover the inner meaning of hidden things and signs:[68]

> Huic dono loquentur caerimoniae legis omnes et figurae,[69] similiter parabolae, aenigmata et visiones prophetarum, ut dicit Iob, quia intelligentia est opus in visione.[70]

In other words, prophets have the vision; those gifted with understanding expound their utterances. Men have the gift of understanding in varying degrees; it calls for effort and exercise. It may

---

65   A. de Poorter, "Un manuel de prédication médiéval", *Revue néo-scolastique* xxv (1923) 198, 203.

66   MS Oxford, Bodl. Digby 30, fol. 50-50v. On this treatise see H. Caplan, "Mediaeval *Artes Praedicandi*. A Hand-List", *Cornell Studies in Philology* xxiv (1934) 30; "A Supplementary Hand-List", ibid. xxv (1936) 20, 23.

67   M. Reeves, *The Influence of Prophecy in the Later Middle Ages* (Oxford 1969) 41-42.

68   *De virtutibus* xi, 152-3.

69   *Iob* xx, 3: *Spiritus intelligentiae meae respondebit mihi*.

70   *Dan.* x, 1.

attain to such clarity and sharpness as to resemble the spirit of prophecy. He cites Joachim as an example:

> Debes etiam scire quia istud donum, scilicet donum intellectus, tantae claritatis est et acuminis in quibusdam, ut valde assimiletur spiritui prophetiae, qualem crediderunt nonnulli fuisse in Abbate Joachim et ipsemet de seipso dixisse dicitur, quia non erat ei datus spiritus prophetiae, sed spiritus intelligentiae. Si quis autem inspexerit libros eius, quos scripsit super Apocalypsim et super concordiam duorum testamentorum, mirabitur donum intellectus in eo.

He goes straight on to explain that the gift of understanding differs from faith in that its object is deep, hidden matters, which are veiled in mystery or suggested by means of signification, whereas faith concerns basic principles. *Donum intellectus* carries neither the certainty of vision nor the certainty of truth which is arrived at by demonstration; exegetes of the Law and the Prophets do not use proofs, but "declarative narrations" only. The point of the definition comes at the end. William stresses that everything which is understood by *donum intellectus* can be acquired by teaching (*doctrina*). Every prophecy and mystery of which the gift confers understanding can be explained by teaching and set down clearly in writing by its possessor. Each virtue described in *De virtutibus* has its corresponding vice. The vice opposing *donum intellectus* is brutish idleness, which leads to neglect of study and reading.

De virtutibus raises the same problem as *De legibus*, in that William refers to exposition of the inner meaning of the Law and other mysteries without specifying its content. What manner of understanding them did *donum intellectus* confer? He does not tell us. His main aim in describing it comes out clearly, nonetheless. He was pleading for diligent application to study and teaching of the mysteries of Scripture. Joachim served as an example of a man who disclaimed the gift of prophecy (so it was said), but who applied himself to study and who published his studies for the benefit of others. Whether William accepted Joachim's findings, or whether he reserved judgment, cannot be decided from what he wrote. Joachim's exegesis, daring as it was, had no place for the mechanical allegories and moralities that William disliked. He wanted to keep abreast of current trends, as we know from his defence of the new Orders. Joachim's authentic writings were being discussed; the scandal which would break out on *spuria*, circulated by his disciples, had yet to come. William may therefore have been noting new ideas, perhaps without examining them.[71]

---

71 He certainly did not entertain any idea that a third and more spiritual age was still to come, since the gospel had brought full spiritual perfection within men's reach.

I have defended his consistency in applying his theories. Their internal coherence cannot be defended. William's account of the spiritual interpretation and its relationship to the literal is incomplete and muddled. As I understand it, he saw the spiritual interpretation as an extension of the literal; it was not to be "imposed" at the whim of the exegete. The story of David's adultery was not enacted or even recorded as an allegory: why impose allegory upon it? The thesis raised basic problems, which he did not formulate, on the relationship between the Old and New Testaments. The Old Law educated and prepared the chosen people to receive the New. He was sure of that. But was it a prefiguration, perceived by the wise, in addition to serving as an *alphabetum honestatis*? Had the Old Testament élite an implicit or explicit faith in the doctrines of the Trinity, the Incarnation and the Redemption? *De legibus* gives no answer. It raises questions instead; and these are crucial. We hear that many persons canvassed the exclusive truth of Christianity. Even more surprisingly, we hear that many persons took offence at the exposition according to the four senses. We cannot identify the former; the latter must have been students in the faculty of theology at Paris, since William writes that they read and heard expositions of Scripture. William deplores the first type of doubting, but shares the second. The vogue for allegorical interpretation of sacred texts has gone in waves. Each crest has been followed by reaction and "debunking". Yet it has always survived criticism.[72] We depend on *De legibus* for the surprising information that one period of reaction against allegory occurred at Paris in the second quarter of the thirteenth century.

William wrote under its impact. He threw out suggestions which would have altered the technique of medieval exegesis, had they been followed. They were not followed; allegory survived. William's theory suffered from a fatal combination of flaws. It was both original and inchoate, too original to appeal and too inchoate to be adopted. We shall see that it failed to win acceptance in the schools.

---

72   J. Pépin, *Mythe et allégorie. Les origines grecques et les contestations judéo-chrétiennes* (Paris 1958).

III

John of la Rochelle

De legibus was quoted, though not swallowed whole. Much of it is woven into the texture of the *Tractatus de praeceptis et legibus* which forms part of the *Summa* ascribed to Alexander of Hales O.F.M. Modern research has established that John of la Rochelle O.F.M. compiled the *Tractatus*. It is older than the *Summa*. John collaborated with Alexander in preparing some parts of the latter, 1236-1245, but his teaching on natural law differs from Alexander's, as we have it in Alexander's *Sentences*, to such an extent that we must credit John with authorship of the *Tractatus*; it represented an original contribution to the *Summa*.[1] John was master of theology at Paris in 1238 and died in February, 1245. The exact date of his *Tractatus* is not known, but he must have been writing it during William's lifetime, while William was bishop of Paris, 1228-1249.[2] This would explain why he always quoted or referred to *De legibus* anonymously.

John quotes it verbally and sometimes slavishly. He copies out the passage on leprosy, where William wrote that he himself had seen dry rot in wood.[3] But slavish transcription of what appealed to him in *De legibus* went together with a critical and selective treatment of William's doctrine on the Old Law. This is important for two reasons: it shows how a contemporary reacted to the novelties in *De legibus*; it decided the form in which *De legibus* was passed on to the many readers of "Alexander's" *Summa*. Direct knowledge of William's treatise must have been rarer than knowledge of it *via* John's *Tractatus* as contained in the famous *Summa* of the Franciscan school.

John's reaction to *De legibus* can be put quite simply. He held to the traditional doctrine that *legalia* had not only a literal, but also a spiritual sense as signs, foreshadowings or figures of the New Law. William never said so: John keeps recurring to it in no uncertain terms. He classifies the precepts of the Old Law according to their three pur-

---

1 O. Lottin, op. cit. i, 128, 135; ii, 19, 52; W. H. Steinmüller, "Die Naturrechtslehre des Joannes von Rupella und des Alexander von Hales", *Franziskanische Studien* xli (1959) 310-422.
2 I shall quote the *Tractatus* from the edition in *Summa theologiae Alexandri Halensis*, part iii, vol. IV (Quaracchi 1948), using the editors' numbers and page references. They give exact references to both quotations from and allusions to the *De legibus*.
3 No. 518, p. 774. John copies "sicut vidimus".

poses: *moralia* clarified the law of nature; *iudicialia* repressed evil desires and served as a scourge for the wicked; *caeremonialia* signified the law of grace:

> ...figurae erant futurorum. et quantum ad hoc erat (lex) iustis in signum. [4]

William had described "signification" as a stumbling block. [5] John defends it explicitly. The ceremonial precepts were given

> ad manifestationem et testimonium futurae gratiae. [6]
> Sed lex Moysi, quantum ad figuralia, facit cognitionem
> credendorum et ad ipsam pertinet. [7]
> ...lex Moysi includit legem naturalem per explicationem in moralibus, legem vero gratiae per figurationem in caeremonialibus. [8]
> Lex quantum ad figuralia erat ducens in Christum. [9]

The figurative nature of the Old Law raises the question: did the ancient Jews who offered sacrifice according to its precepts understand their significance as prefigurations of the coming Redemption? The command of the psalmist, *sing ye wisely* (xlvi, 8), argues that they should have, since wisdom involves understanding. John answers that doctors and priests were bound to understand the true significance of their sacrifices explicitly. Simple men, on the other hand, were bound to realise only that they were pleasing to God, which carried with it an implicit understanding of their value as signs. He draws a parallel: scholars and prelates are bound to understand the articles of the faith explicitly, but simple men only implicitly. [10] It has already been stated that these figures were a sign of future grace *quoad perfectos*. [11] John adopts the traditional doctrine that *caeremonialia* carried signs of future grace for the Old Testament élite, who could understand their spiritual meaning, whereas the rank and file could not. Again he departs from *De legibus*. William never identified the inner meaning of the Old Law, as studied by the wise among the Jews, with prophecies or figures of Christ. He had asked why signs should have been written into the Old Law for the benefit of Christians, who were still unborn. John answers his query without raising it explicitly: The *figuralia* of the Old

4   No. 259, p. 367-8.
5   "Verbum ergo significandi est quod in parte ista graviter offendit auditores atque lectores". See below, p. 70.
6   No. 259, p. 369.
7   No. 260, p. 370.
8   Ibid.
9   No. 262, p. 373.
10   No. 531, p. 807.
11   No. 267, p. 392.

Law still remain for us to read as past signs of the future, even after their fulfilment and abrogation. [12]

John's very arrangement of chapters shows how wedded to tradition he was. Before considering the literal sense of *caeremonialia*, he establishes that they had a spiritual sense in two chapters on *De intellectu praeceptorum caeremonialium*. This was to reverse the order of their treatment in *De legibus*. John begins by asking: "Utrum in caeremonialibus universaliter sit intelligentia litteralis", as some (William) have held. [13] He puts forward William's arguments in favour of the proposition: the legislator would have failed in his duty had he veiled his meaning instead of teaching his people plainly, and so on. His reply is that the alleged inconveniences are just the opposite: it is fitting that divine wisdom and divine law should be conveyed darkly. John's reasons betray some confusion, since he adduces both parables and metaphors to prove his point; these should have been included in the literal sense, strictly speaking. He adds that the spiritual sense was put there for the benefit of an élite. His conclusion is to deny the proposition, with the proviso that although it is not true *universaliter*, *most* of the precepts did have a literal sense and reason as well as a spiritual; *a few* of them, however, had a spiritual reason only. [14] Then he argues that they *all* had a spiritual meaning in a section headed "Qualiter in praeceptis caeremonialibus sit intelligentia spiritualis". [15]

Here he adapts William's account of the spiritual sense ingeniously to fit his thesis. First, he records objections to the spiritual interpretation. According to St. Augustine in *De doctrina christiana* all teaching is conveyed either by things or by signs. Some (William) ascribe a literal sense to all the ceremonial precepts. In that case, teaching is conveyed by things; these things cannot also be signs; consequently they convey no spiritual meaning. Secondly, it is abusive to deduce signs from things which were not intended to signify, and hence to seek a spiritual meaning in them (William again). Thirdly, the prophets taught by comparisons and not by significations; therefore it is unfitting to seek a spiritual interpretation where none was intended (William again).

---

12 No. 269, p. 398: "... immo adhuc habent eam (auctoritatem signandi) ut possit adhuc homo legere in ipsis; sed quod prius significabant ut futurum, modo significant ut praeteritum, et sic remanet significantia non mutata".

13 No. 516, p. 759.

14 Ibid., p. 760: "Ex iis igitur manifeste relinquitur non esse necesse in praeceptis caeremonialibus Legis universaliter esse sensum sive intelligentiam litteralem. Propterea breviter dicendum est, quod clarius erit in sequentibus, quod in aliquibus et pluribus praeceptorum caeremonialium praeter spiritualem intelligentiam sensus fuit et ratio litteralis, in aliquibus vero et paucis tantum ratio spiritualis, propter rationes praedictas quod infra manifestabitur".

15 No. 517, p. 760.

Fourthly, one thing designates another more fittingly and surely univocally than equivocally: a thing should have one meaning only. The
spiritual interpretation must be fitting. Therefore each word or deed
recorded in Scripture should have one spiritual meaning only. All the
holy expositors who find multiple meanings err in doing so. It is fitting,
too, that good should signify good, and bad, bad. John adduces William's objection to the allegorical interpretation of David's adultery
with Bethsabee as referring to Christ and the Church. He names St.
Gregory (as William had not done), so as to leave no doubt as to the
authentic source of the allegory. This last objection also derives from
William. All in all, John has made a fair and logical survey of William's
arguments against "abusive" allegories and moralities.

He answers them by making William argue against himself. The first
objection is disposed of by a distinction: the ceremonies were "things",
and as such they were ordered to the worship of the Creator; they were
also "signs", and as such they prefigured the Saviour's grace. He then
quotes William's defence of what William regarded as legitimate
spiritual interpretation, that is, the elucidation of metaphor or symbol,
deduction *per consequentiam* and teaching by the method of comparison. William's conventional praise of Scripture is quoted, with his
statement that all wholesome teaching may be drawn from it. John adds
a gloss of his own:

> Most fittingly are many meanings signified by one, in order that the
> Law's intention may correspond to God's goodness.

The gloss falsifies William's thought. John's sleight of hand is
remarkable. He has answered William's objections to the traditional
spiritual interpretation by manipulating William's own words and adding to them. The spearhead of William's attack has been blunted.

A more straightforward use of *De legibus* appears in the next chapter,
De ratione caeremonialium praeceptorum.[16] Having given priority to
the spiritual sense of the ceremonies, and denied a literal reason for
them *en bloc*, John felt free to approve the notion that many or most
had a rational cause *ad litteram*. He supplemented *De legibus* by a
direct study of the *Guide*, which is sometimes quoted by name independently of *De legibus*.[17] John copies at length from William's
defence of the precepts as rational and from his rebuttal of charges that
some of them were irrational, futile or absurd in the literal sense.

---

16   No. 518, p. 763. The full extent of John's use of *De legibus* is shown by the Quaracchi
editors in their admirable footnotes.

17   This also appears in the footnotes; John refers to Rabbi Moses, no. 263, p. 377 and to "Expositor legis Iudaeorum", no. 518, p. 763; there are other examples.

William's rather jumbled presentation of his defence is even improved upon. John classifies its heads in a more logical order. There were four reasons for the precepts in their literal sense. Some were necessary for the institution of religion, as were circumcision and the Passover, some to warn against error, some to promote worship of the Creator, and some for a compound of the last two reasons. John says apropos the third reason that three things are required to attract the rational mind to divine worship: decorum, dignity and cheerfulness (*decorum, honestum, iucundum*). These things appear in the precepts. Here we have an echo of William's account of Old Testament rites. John made further use of *De legibus* in a detailed study of the sacrifices,[18] "Utrum sacrificia legalia fuerint vera sacrificia". Oddly enough, he did not single out any precept as having no literal reason but only a spiritual, although he had refused to allow them a literal reason *universaliter*. His reservation protected him against the charge of too close adherence to *De legibus*, but did not need to be applied in particular, it seems. He dots the "i"s and crosses the "t"s in a later section headed "De differentiis sacrificiorum in Lege",[19] where he sets out the spiritual (allegorical and moral) interpretation of the sacrifices, in addition to the literal reason that they were instituted for the honour of God.

Hence the gist of William's rationalisation of *legalia* passed into school tradition via the *Tractatus*. John took just as much from *De legibus* as would fit into his conservative framework, and no more. But his quotations are full and verbal enough to convey some of the original warmth and power. William's defence of the literal reasons for the precepts became acceptable when once it had been isolated from its dangerous context. He was alive, and a highly respected prelate, when John wrote his *Tractatus*. John processed *De legibus* discreetly so as to avoid open criticism. One would like to know what William thought of the alterations.

18 No. 525, p. 797.
19 No. 537, p. 814.

IV

St. Thomas Aquinas

St. Thomas needed his clear mind when he turned to the literal and spiritual senses of Scripture: he had to fight a war on two fronts. On one front, he had to engage in a mopping up operation. Masters of the sacred page had widened the literal sense of Scripture so as to include verbal simile, metaphor, parable and symbolic action or gesture. Words and actions recorded in Scripture had to be explained according to their first intention; their spiritual interpretation was an addition, not a substitute. But the masters had worked their way to this method without accounting for it by any systematic reasoning, as far as we know. Consequently their terminology remained confused. Neither William of Auvergne nor John of la Rochelle achieved consistency in his handling of biblical metaphor and symbolism. Maimonides either raised or brought to a head a further problem on the literal interpretation of the Old Law. Had all its precepts, excluding *moralia*, some literal reason, as well as a literal sense (as a code actually given to the Jews)? Or were some precepts to be taken as irrational in their literal sense, apart from their divine purpose to prefigure the New Law? The question had wide implications, since it made scholars think about the legislator's aims in their historical context. On this front St. Thomas put forward a theoretical justification for the wider meaning now currently accorded to the literal sense, and distinguished it from the spiritual senses more clearly than had been done before.

On his second front, the traditional three spiritual senses had come under fire from William of Auvergne, voicing the objections of unnamed masters or students. St. Thomas was conservative enough to defend the spiritual senses. It would be interesting to know whether he read William's *De legibus*; if so, he met the attack in its full force. He certainly read and used John's *Tractatus*, where he could find a bowdlerised version of *De legibus* and perhaps guess at the original. Lottin, whose opinion must be respected, thought it probable that St. Thomas read *De legibus* directly and not only *via* the *Tractatus*.[1] I have

---

1   O. Lottin, *Psychologie et morale*, op. cit. iii, 592, 709. On St. Thomas's use of John's *Tractatus* see also G. Lafont, *Structures et méthodes dans la Somme théologique de Saint Thomas d'Aquin* (Paris 1961) 213.

found no textual proof that he did. More important, is the evidence of his *quaestiones disputatae*, given during his first regency at Paris, 1256-1259.[2] The regent master would announce the subject for disputation beforehand; then he presided over the exercise and "determined" at its close. Naturally he would choose a subject connected with some live issue, which would stir up interest and controversy.[3] Among the questions chosen by St. Thomas are: Whether Holy Scripture has senses other than the literal hidden in its words? How many spiritual senses are there? Are they to be found in writings other than Scripture? The choice of these three questions indicates that William's attack on allegories, tropologies and anagogies still had echoes in the schools. Some of St. Thomas's colleagues and pupils in the theological faculty must have doubted the validity of the fourfold interpretation, at least as currently practised, or wanted to be assured that it rested on a valid theory. He posted the problem for disputation in order to satisfy doubters.

The first question was crucial. Once the existence of a spiritual sense "Hidden in the Letter" had been established, it would be plain sailing to make the traditional threefold division of the spiritual into allegorical, moral or tropological and anagogical. The first two objections come from *De legibus*, retailed in John's *Tractatus*:

> Quia dictionibus semel sumptis non est utendum aequivoce vel multipliciter. Sed pluralitas sensuum facit multiplicem locutionem. Ergo in eadem locutione sacrae Scripturae non possunt plures sensus latere. Praeterea, sacra Scriptura ordinata est ad intellectum...Sed multiplicitas sensuum obnubilat intellectum. Ergo non debet in sacra Scriptura multi sensus esse.[4]

In substance it is objected that the purpose of Scripture is to instruct us clearly on one thing at a time. The third objection must have occurred to many masters of the sacred page in the course of their lectures: if there are several senses in Scripture, it will give rise to error, since interpretation will be arbitrary; the exegete will have no check on his arguments. The fourth follows on: the literal sense alone has authority in argument; therefore we cannot posit a spiritual sense as well. The fifth and last objection brings us back to William and John:

> Praeterea, quicumque sensus ex verbis alicuius trahitur quem auctor non intendit, non est sensus proprius; quia auctor per unam scripturam non

---

2 M. D. Chenu, *Introduction à l'étude de Saint Thomas d'Aquin* (Paris 1950) 241-242.
3 Ibid., 242-245; P. Glorieux, "L'enseignement au moyen àge. Techniques et méthodes en usage à la Faculté de Théologie de Paris au XIIIᵉ siècle", *AHDLMA* xxxv (1969) 123-128.
4 *Quodl.* VII, q. vi, a. 1, ed. R. Spiazzi, i (Rome/Turin 1928) 145.

potest intelligere nisi unum, quia non contingit plura simul intelligere, secundum Philosophum. Ergo non possunt esse plures sensus proprii sacrae Scripturae.

This gives the gist of William's argument which he illustrated by the story of David's adultery: we should keep to the sense intended by the sacred writer, instead of making him mean something else and turning his factual record into an allegory of Christ and the Church.

St. Thomas's solution of these problems is too well known to need more than a bare summary here.[5] He focussed attention on the twofold authorship of Scripture, human and divine, and hence on the diverse methods employed first by the human authors and then by the Holy Spirit who inspired them. The human authors would sometimes convey their teaching by means of metaphor, symbolism, analogy and parable. We find the same genres in pagan literature, especially in poetry. The literal sense includes all that the writer meant to express, a rule which applies to both sacred and profane literature. Prophecy and moral instruction, for instance, may be expressed in Scripture through figures of speech or action. We must include both the author's teaching and his way of putting it over to his audience in our reading of the literal sense. This definition of the literal sense as "all that the writer intended" cleared up a persistent muddle in terminology. The spiritual sense, in contrast to the literal, depended exclusively on the intention of God, the first cause and author of Scripture. God, as cause and author of all history, could give a significance to the events recorded and to the things described by the human authors of Scripture, which they, inspired though they were, could not possibly grasp, but which later revelation made plain. The Holy Spirit could express the divine meaning in figures over and above those employed by his human instruments:

> Sicut enim homo potest adhibere ad significandum aliquas voces vel aliquas similitudines fictas, ita Deus adhibet ad significationem aliquorum ipsum cursum rerum suae providentiae subiectarum.[6]

Hence the spiritual interpretation in its threefold division is "founded on the literal"; St. Thomas gave new content to the stock phrase. According to him, interpretation in the spiritual sense meant beginning from where the literal interpretation ended and only after it had been exhausted. His distinction between the senses made firmer ground for the rule (already partly accepted) that argument must proceed from

---

5 *Quodl.* VII, q. vi, p. 145-148. St. Thomas returns to the senses of Scripture in the *Summa* 1a, q. 1, a. 8-10. His treatment of it here is both more comprehensive and more succinct than in the *Quodlibet*. I have taken both the *Quodlibet* and this part of the *Summa* into account in summarising his solutions.

6 *Quodl.* VII, q. vi, a. 3, p. 148.

the literal sense only. God saw to it that everything needed for salvation should be found somewhere in Scripture according to the letter. The distinction between literal and spiritual senses enabled St. Thomas to mark off the Bible from other literature. In the Bible the actual course of the history recorded had a spiritual significance unknown to its actors and writers. That could not apply to any other kind of writing, but only to Scripture, of which the Holy Spirit was author and man merely the instrument.[7]

The solution neatly disposed of William's objections to the allegorisation of King David's misdeeds: they were not committed, nor probably were they recorded, in order to signify Christ's marriage to his Church; so William argued.[8] According to Thomist theory there could be no question of intention to signify either on the part of King David or of the historian. The Holy Spirit intended that the misdeeds and their record should have an allegorical significance, which was unrecognisable at the time. All carping at allegories, moralities and anagogies would cease when this touchstone was applied to them. Their justification in Thomist theory would make it otiose to resort to comparisons instead of significations, as William had urged upon exegetes. The spiritual interpretation could be used without doing violence to the sacred writers' intentions. It must have relieved the scrupulous: allegories, moralities and anagogies had divine authority, whereas comparisons represented mere human inventiveness.

Thomist doctrine on the four senses has been much discussed. Personally I see it differently after reading William's *De legibus*. Before that surprising experience I put too much emphasis on St. Thomas's care for a better definition and better understanding of the literal sense.[9] Now I would classify this as a mopping up operation, designed to remedy confusion and to justify deeper study of the literal sense. His more powerful guns, as I picture it in the light of *De legibus*, were trained in defence of the traditional fourfold interpretation against William's attack. Further study of the section *De veteri lege* in his *Summa* has confirmed my change of mind. St. Thomas was more middle-of-the-road than he seemed to me on first acquaintance with his teaching.

In any case, his doctrine on the senses is incomplete and leaves a gap to be filled in. He allows for Old Testament prophecies of Christ within the context of the literal sense. He justifies the allegorical interpretation, according to which historical events signify Christ and his

---

7 Ibid.
8 See above, p. 41, and appendix, below, p. 70.
9 See my *Study of the Bible*, op. cit. 300-306.

members as shadows of truth; then he explains that when Christ is referred to (directly) by means of a simile or metaphor, this does not go beyond the literal sense; the image of *the stone cut out of a mountain without hands* in Daniel's interpretation of King Nabuchodonosor's dream (*Dan.* ii, 34) is given as an example of a prophecy of Christ according to the literal sense.[10] The problem how to distinguish passages which had a Christological meaning in the literal sense, as intended by the lawgiver or prophet, from those which were allegories, had already presented itself to exegetes. They were left to fumble. By what rules should the exegete judge whether a text which had been traditionally interpreted as a prophecy of Christ belonged to the literal sense or the allegorical? What limits should he set to the prophet's foresight? St. Thomas gave no guidance here. Did he offer guidance in the application of his own principles to exegesis? His literal exposition of the book of Job is a brilliant example: he treated the content as a discussion of the ways of divine Providence.[11] But the choice of this book suited his genius as a philosopher theologian perfectly. The precepts and institutions of the Old Law demanded a different approach. *De veteri lege* shows him applying the principles set forth in *De veritate* and at the beginning of the *Summa*.

A study of *De veteri lege* must begin with its sources. It fits into the framework of the whole section *De legibus*, a treatise on divine, eternal, natural and human law. St. Thomas had a strong feeling for the rational character of law in general. He has been claimed as a true jurist, in spite of his lack of legal training: "Saint Thomas se situe admirablement dans la ligne spirituelle des grands romanistes médiévaux."[12] We know that he read and pondered the *Guide*: he quoted Rabbi Moses independently and directly.[13] The going gets harder when we confront *De veteri lege* with its main secondary source, John's *Tractatus*.[14] The Dominican doctor took up the problems of the Old Law where the Franciscan had left off. He rearranged and rethought the *Tractatus*, though he neither copied it verbally nor mentioned it by name. No one as yet has collated the two. All I can undertake to do in this paper is to

---

10   *Quodl.* VII, q. VI, a. 2, op. cit. p. 147.

11   *Expositio super Iob ad litteram, Opera* xxvi, ed. Leon., 1965.

12   J. M. Aubert, *Le droit romain dans l'œuvre de Saint Thomas* (Paris 1955) 76, 79, 139.

13   See the thorough survey by J. Guttman, *Das Verhältniss des Thomas von Aquino zum Judentum und zur jüdischen Literatur* (Göttingen 1891) 33-92; on his criticism of Maimonides see H. Liebeschütz, "Eine Polemik des Thomas von Aquino gegen Maimonides", *Monatschrift für Geschichte und Wissenschaft des Judenthums* lxxx (1936) 93-96.

14   I have used the edition and translation with occasional minor changes in the new publication of the *Summa* on the Old Law by the English Dominicans, xxix (London 1969) by D. Bourke and A. Littledale. Unfortunately the editors confine themselves to cross-references and to authors quoted by name in the *Summa*. They ignore the relationship between the *Summa* on the Old Law and John's *Tractatus*. Otherwise the volume is very useful.

offer an impressionistic sketch of the order of questions and articles in the *Tractatus* and the *Summa* respectively. The samples that I have chosen relate to the nature and content of the Old Law and to the ceremonies in particular. Sections on *moralia* and *iudicialia* will be omitted. The comparisons will show that St. Thomas posed much the same questions as John. Differences between the two scholars occur mainly in the ordering of their material. St. Thomas sometimes altered the sequence of articles given by the *Tractatus* inside one question; sometimes he made more drastic changes.

Tractatus I	*Summa* 1a 2ae
Q.I: De latione Legis mosaicae	Q. 98
259 a.1) De utilitate lationis Legis	a.1) Utrum lex vetus fuerit bona
260 a.2) An lex Moysi sit necessaria ad salutem	(included in a.1)
261 a.3) De tempore lationis Legis	a.6) Utrum lex vetus convenienter data fuerit tempore Moysi
262 a.4) Quibus debuit dari Lex	a.4) Utrum lex vetus dari debuit populo Judaeorum
263 a.5) De Legis latore. An lex Moysi sit lata a bono et a solo Deo	a.2) Utrum lex vetus fuerit a Deo
264 a.6) Utrum lex Moysi sit lata a Deo per ministerium angelorum	a.3) Utrum lex vetus data fuerit per angelos

The *Summa* follows a more logical order than the *Tractatus*. St. Thomas proceeds from the top downward. The Old Law was good; it was given by God as necessary to salvation by the ministry of angels to the Jews at a fitting time. His a.5 explains why the Old Law, given to the Jewish people, as stated in a.4, was not binding upon all. St. Thomas's a.5 corresponds to a much later article in the *Tractatus*, where John considers a miscellany of questions, under the heading *De personis* (no. 530).

Q.II of the *Tractatus* deals with points which St. Thomas had condensed into q. 98, a.1, *Utrum lex vetus fuerit bona*. A glance will show how he abridged his source; one article sufficed for all the following:

Tractatus (265-268)

a.1) De continentia Legis quantum ad genera contentorum; a.2) De continentia Legis quantum ad qualitatem contentorum; (i) Utrum omne quod continetur in Lege sit sanctum (ii) bonum (iii) iustum.

Tractatus	*Summa*
269 Q.III: De impletione legis Moysi per Christum	Q.106: De lege evangelica etc
271 Q.IV: De onere observantiae legis mosaicae	Q.107, a.4) Utrum lex nova sit gravior quam vetus
274 Q.V: De iustificatione per Legem[15]	Q.100, a.12; Q. 103, a.2.

St. Thomas preferred to tackle problems arising from comparison between the Old and New Laws after, not before, he had finished discussing the content of the Old Law. Again, his arrangement looks tidier than John's. The question whether observance of the legal precepts in Old Testament times justified the observers made a bridge between the two and fitted into discussion of the legal precepts. Hence it came earlier in the *Summa* than in the *Tractatus*.

Tractatus II, sect. iii: De caeremonialibus	*Summa*
516 Q.I, cap. i: Utrum in caeremonialibus universaliter sit intellectus litteralis	Q.102, a.2) Utrum habeant causam litteralem, vel solum figuralem
517 cap.ii: Qualiter in praeceptis caeremonialibus sit intellectus spiritualis	(included in a.2)
518 Q.II: De ratione caeremonialium praeceptorum. An habeant causam observantiae litteralem, an solum mysticam et figuralem	a.1) Utrum praecepta caeremonialia habeant causam (also included in a.2)
A. in generali	(also included in a.2)
B. in speciali	
1) in circumcisione	a.5) De causis sacrorum
2) in Phase	
3) in victu	a.6) De causis observantiarum
4) in vestitu	(included in a.6)
5) circa actum indifferentem	
6) circa immunditiarum cavendarum	
7) purificationis immunditiarum	
8) sacrificiorum, in genere, in speciali	a.3) De causis sacrificiorum
9) altaris	a.4) De causis sacramentorum
10) tabernaculi	(included in a.4)
11) circa ordinationem ministrorum	
12) circa ornatum sacerdotum seu ministrorum	
13) solemnitatum	

15   The numbers 270, 272-3 of the *Tractatus* deal with subordinate points. I have omitted them in order to make the scheme of my comparison clearer.

St. Thomas has succeeded in reducing thirteen articles to six by dividing ceremonies into categories: sacrifices, sacraments, sacred things and observances. He considers most of the points raised by John within the scope of fewer articles.

Tractatus	Summa
Q. III	
519 De numerositate caeremonialium	Q.101, a.3) Utrum debuerint esse multa caeremonialium praecepta
520 De differentia caeremonialium in genere	a.4) Utrum caeremonia veteris legis convenienter dividantur in sacrificia, sacra, sacramenta et observantias

Again, it was tidier to clear up the problem of why there were so many ceremonial precepts before descending to particular items and to group them under separate headings. St. Thomas therefore inverted John's order. As we have seen, he divided them into categories; and he saved himself from redundancy in considering their causes: John's thirteen articles are more than halved in the *Summa*.

My comparison will have shown that St. Thomas had the *Tractatus* on his desk or at least in his mind, when he compiled *De veteri lege*. The sketch will have given some idea of how he set its questions in his own order. He makes one major change of structure in that he treated the ceremonial precepts before instead of after the judicial.[16] A comparison of the internal matter of separate articles, where the questions coincide, gives the same impression: St. Thomas borrowed arguments *pro* and *contra* from John, sometimes conflating them. Thus in q. 101, a. 2, on whether the ceremonial precepts are figurative, he abridges six objections, taken by John (no. 516, p. 759) from William of Auvergne, into one:

> It is the duty of every teacher to make himself easily understood, as Augustine says. This seems necessary most of all in propounding a law, since its commands are conveyed to the people. Hence a law ought to be clear, as Isidore says. If then the ceremonial precepts were given as figurative of something, it would seem that Moses, in failing to explain what they figured, did not transmit them in a proper manner.

But he adds other objections of his own. His replies and conclusions often agree with John's in substance.

---

16 St. Thomas probably did so out of respect for the biblical text: *Haec sunt praecepta et caeremoniae atque iudicia (Deut.* vi, 1). He quotes it in q. 99, a. 4. A further difference between his treatment of *iudicia* and John's is that St. Thomas limits himself here to the judicial precepts of the Old Law, whereas John spreads his net wider; he discusses contemporary judicial problems.

There is no time for a more detailed collation here. St. Thomas restructured his source into a clearer, more logical pattern. He sorted out the pieces and fitted them together as it pleased him. What did he make of its doctrine? The short answer is that he rethought it in terms of his theory of causality.

This appears in his very first questions on the Old Law in general, "whether it is good", (q. 98, a. 1). St. Thomas replies to objections by defending the Old Law on the grounds that it conformed to reason by restraining the appetite and by forbidding all sins which are contrary to reason. Then he considers "the ordering of things to a given end". Human law is directed towards the temporal peace of the State, divine law towards bringing man to the attainment of his goal of eternal happiness. Hence the latter has to do more than regulate external actions: "it is required to make man totally equipped to share in eternal happiness, something which can be achieved only by the grace of the Holy Spirit". It follows from consideration of ends that the Old Law is good, but imperfect in comparison with the New Law; the conferring of grace was reserved to Christ. The crucial text: *I gave them statutes which were not good (Ezech.* xx, 25) has taken its place as the first authority *contra.* St. Thomas refers it to the ceremonial precepts, as had normally been done. Ralph of Flaix, representing the older tradition, had used it to discredit the educative value of *caeremonialia,* whereas William of Auvergne, following Maimonides, had taken *not good* as referring to the disposition of those who performed ceremonies unworthily. John of la Rochelle did not consider the Ezechiel text. St. Thomas steers a middle course. The ceremonial precepts were said by the prophet to be *not good* because they showed up man's need for cleansing (being instituted as sin-offerings etc.), but they did not (in contrast to the sacraments of the New Law) confer the grace by which men could be cleansed of their sins. Thus he relates the Ezechiel text to the nature and purpose of the Old Law; it was good, but imperfect.

He begins his discussion of the ceremonial precepts *secundum se* (q. 101, a.1) by framing a question of his own: "Does the reason of the ceremonial precepts reside in the fact that they concern the worship of God?" This question gives him scope to explain his principle. The ceremonial precepts, even those which at first sight do not seem to belong to divine worship, are particular applications of the moral precepts which order man to God, just as the judicial precepts are applications of those which order man to his neighbour. "Whatever is preparatory to a particular end comes under the science dealing with that end". The ceremonial precepts are rules of salvation, which order man to God. "Accordingly those which concern the worship of God are called ceremonial". St. Thomas has stated his own formula just before he begins to draw on John's *De legibus*, which cannot have been accidental. The theme of "ends" will recur even when he is borrowing. Thus he answers the question (a. 2), whether the ceremonial precepts had a literal cause or only a figurative, by relating them to their purpose: "The reason for whatever is done in view of an end must be looked for in that end. Now the end of the ceremonial precepts was twofold; they were ordained for the worship of God at that time, and for prefiguring Christ". Their purpose was *ordinatio mentis in Deum*, as he states repeatedly (q. 101, a. 2-4, q. 102, a. 1-5). He also fits *ordinatio* into his doctrine on the body-soul relationship (q. 101, a. 2): "Worship is twofold: internal and external. For since man is made up of soul and body, both must be used for the worship of God, the soul by interior worship, the body by exterior....As the body is ordered to God by the soul, so exterior worship is ordered to interior".

We may now turn to his teaching on the significance of *caeremonialia*. St. Thomas subscribed to and underlined John's argument that they had both a figurative and a literal cause. Like John he begins by establishing that they had a figurative cause: divine teaching had to be adapted to a crude people; divine mysteries must be expressed in figures (q. 101, a. 1). Like John he argues that they had a literal cause as well (q. 102, a. 2). His arguments have a more cutting edge than his predecessor's. The objections are (1) circumcision and the sacrifice of the paschal lamb were signs only: how much more so the other ceremonies? (2) the effect is proportionate to the cause. All the ceremonial precepts are figurative. Therefore they have a figurative cause only; (3) many precepts, such as the number of animals prescribed for sacrifice, are indifferent in themselves; therefore they cannot have any literal cause. He replies by arguing for a literal cause on the ground that ceremonies provided for divine worship "at that time". They warded off idolatry, recalled God's goodness and disposed the mind to his worship. St. Thomas draws a parallel between legal precepts and prophetic words. The prophet spoke words which applied to his own time and which also figured what was to come. Similarly, circumcision and the passover signified God's covenant with Israel and her delivery from Egypt according to their literal sense, but they also prefigured the sacraments of the New Law. The other ceremonies likewise were instituted not only as figures of the future, but also to regulate divine worship there and then. The answer to objection (2) is that it would be conclusive only if the ceremonial precepts were given *solely* to prefigure the future. The answer to the objection on indifferent precepts (3) disposes of the whole difficulty once and for all, though particular cases come

up for discussion later. St. Thomas refers back to his treatment of
particulars in human laws (q. 96, a. 1 and 6). Human laws should be ordered to the common good of the body politic in principle. Their particulars vary according to the will of their framers. In the same way
"many particulars in the ceremonies of the Old Law have no literal
cause, but only a figurative, though *taken in the abstract, they have also
literal causes*". His parallel between human and divine laws enabled St.
Thomas to steer a middle course. He avoided making a categorical
statement that some precepts had no literal cause, as John had done; he
avoided making the equally categorical statement that *all* precepts had
a literal cause, as William had done. Divine and human laws alike, in
Thomist theory, were directed to an end in principle, which covered
particular applications.

The literal reasons for *caeremonialia* interested him. He studied their
particulars, supplementing John by direct recourse to the *Guide*. He did
not always agree with John. The Franciscan had argued, copying
William, that the precept against boiling a kid in the milk of its dam
(*Exod.* xxiii, 19) was directed against idolatry, and gave no other reason
for it. The same applied to John's explanation for the precept not to
take the hen with her young from a nest (*Deut.* xxii, 6). Here again, he
followed William, who had scouted Maimonides' suggestion that such
precepts inculcated pity. St. Thomas preferred to hold that they did in-
culcate pity, as well as warning against idolatry and superstition. He expands on the argument:

> As to the affection arising from sentiment, it is operative also with
> regard to animals; for since pity is roused by the sufferings of others, and
> animals can feel pain, man can feel pity for them. And if he is often
> moved in this way, he is more likely to have compassion for his fellow-
> men... Therefore the Lord, in order to stir to compassion the Jewish
> people, naturally inclined to cruelty, wished to exercise them in pity even
> to animals, by forbidding certain practices savouring of cruelty to them
> (q. 102, a. 6).

His thoughtful interest in literal reasons for particular precepts did
not prevent him from tipping the balance in favour of John's defence of
their figurative reasons. *Caeremonialia* as figures have a privileged
place in the Thomist scheme. This comes out in the contrast made between ceremonial and judicial precepts (q. 104, a. 4). The judicial
precepts were figurative in a different way from the ceremonial (q. 104,
a. 2): "It seems to be characteristic of the ceremonial precepts that they
were instituted as figures of something." They regulate divine worship;
things pertaining to God must be conveyed in figures, as being beyond
our reason, whereas what concerns our neighbour is not beyond our

reason. St. Thomas explains that a precept may be figurative in two ways: "First, primarily and in itself, in that it was enacted primarily to be a figure of something. The ceremonial precepts were figurative in this way; for they were instituted in order to be figurative of something connected with the worship of God *and the mystery of Christ*". Here, then, he classifies under the heading "figurative" the purpose of the ceremonies, both as regulating divine worship at that time and as prefiguring Christ. He sees their primary meaning as figurative in both senses. The judicial precepts, on the contrary, were figurative only in the way that the whole history of God's chosen people was figurative: the judicial precepts of this people, like their deeds and wars, are interpreted allegorically and morally as well as literally. Those of gentile peoples differ from the Jewish in that they are not interpreted allegorically and morally; they have a literal meaning only. St. Thomas is applying his doctrine on the senses of Scripture: God, as the first author of sacred history, has given it a mystical content peculiar to Revelation. But *caeremonialia* have a special place within it. Their special character is brought out again on the question: "Do the judicial precepts bind in perpetuity?" (a. 3). St. Thomas answers that neither the ceremonial nor the judicial precepts bind in perpetuity: both have been voided by the New Law. But they were voided in different ways. The ceremonies "became not only dead, but deadly to those who should keep them after Christ had come, and particularly after the promulgation of the Gospel. The judicial precepts, on the other hand, are dead, since they have no binding force, but not deadly". The reason given is that "the ceremonial precepts were figurative primarily and in themselves, being instituted principally as figuring the mysteries of Christ yet to come. Consequently their observance would militate against the truth of faith, in which we profess that these mysteries are now fulfilled". A legislator today might re-enact Old Testament *iudicialia* without committing mortal sin, provided that he did not order them to be observed "as binding through enactment in the Old Law". "The judicial precepts were not instituted as figuring, but as ordering the state of that people, which was directed to Christ".

St. Thomas has made a clear statement: the ceremonial precepts were instituted *principally as figuring the mysteries of Christ yet to come*. Hence they fall into a different class; St. Thomas has set them apart from the rest of Old Testament history, including *iudicialia*. Their literal meaning for the Jews slips into the background, as soon as he contrasts them with the judicial precepts. He repeats the traditional allegories and moralities concerning ceremonies in what strikes a modern reader (and his modern editors) as tedious detail. Much of it is

borrowed from John, but the borrowing stems from St. Thomas's determination to apply his principle at whatever cost in tedium. A principle
was at stake indeed. Since the primary significance of ceremonies included their figurative meaning, that is, allegories and moralities, then
the latter must be set forth at length. It seems that William of Auvergne's neglect or rejection of the figurative sense of the ceremonies
had spurred on St. Thomas to emphasise it, whether he knew of
William's attack at first hand or indirectly. He defended the figurative
sense of the ceremonies at unusual length; such prolixity is too rare in
the *Summa* to be accidental. The theme recurs in other sections too:
Christ's passion was a true sacrifice, prefigured by the blood offerings of
the Old Testament, though truth surpassed its figure (3a, q. 48, a. 3).

Modern experts on Thomism put forward divergent views on the
structure and organisation of the *Summa*, seen as reflecting its author's
mind. Some would interpret the sequence as outlining the process of
withdrawal and return to God; others see it as Christ-centred;[17] others
find the key in the author's concept of *Heilsgeschichte*.[18] All agree on
one point: St. Thomas was constrained by his reasoning to interpret the
Old Testament ceremonies and sacraments as prefigurations of the
New; the structure and doctrine of the *Summa* demanded that he
should.

St. Thomas's re-shaping and re-thinking of John's *De legibus* thus
tied it into his *ensemble*. He produced a more convincing justification
of the figurative meaning of *caeremonialia* than had been offered
previously. It was more telling in two ways: St. Thomas gave a general
theory on the relations between the senses as a background; he understood and allowed for the new enthusiasm for discovering a literal
reason in the precepts. He both satisfied critics and upheld the
traditional view of ceremonies as figurative. A moderate position,
clearly argued, will often win acceptance. So it did here: we hear
nothing further of William's attack on "significations".

Finally we must ask the question: how much, in St. Thomas's view,
did Moses and other wise men of the Old Testament perceive of the
figurative meaning of ceremonies? The distinction between élite and
common herd belonged to tradition and could be taken for granted.
Ralph of Flaix ascribed understanding of the figurative meaning to
Moses and the élite, but denied it to the people, from whom, indeed,

---

17 G. Lafont, *Structures et méthodes dans la Somme théologique de Saint Thomas d'Aquin*
(Paris 1961), gives a summary of earlier views and his own.

18 M. Seckler, *Le salut et l'histoire. La pensée de saint Thomas d'Aquin sur la théologie de
l'histoire*, transl. from the German (Paris 1967).

their teachers took pains to hide it behind the veil of the literal meaning. William of Auvergne challenged this traditional view on the grounds that all precepts of the Old Law had a literal reason, which teachers were bound to explain to the people. He admitted that wise men could gain a deeper understanding by dint of study than could be conveyed to the people, but its content he never specified. William avoided stating that the deeper meaning acquired by study included understanding of the prefigurative value of *caeremonialia*. John of la Rochelle re-stated the traditional view in a modified form. His distinction between explicit and implicit belief enabled him to put it more precisely and to allow the Jewish people a better understanding of their rites: "modern" scholars and prelates are bound to understand and believe in the articles of the *credo* explicitly, but simple men only implicitly. Just so, ancient doctors and priests were bound to understand the true figurative meaning of their sacrifices explicitly, whereas the people were bound to implicit belief only. The people had only to believe that their sacrifices would please God for reasons which passed their understanding.

St. Thomas agreed with John and he explored the subject further. He decided in *De veritate* that the ancients knew the whole faith, *quasi in universali implicite credentes*.[19] But the elders and leaders of the people were bound to believe some truths of the faith explicitly. They were bound to explicit belief in the Trinity, even before the Fall. After the Fall, they were bound also to explicit belief in redemption to come.[20] Explicit belief in a future redemption carried implicit faith in the incarnation and passion with it (2a 2ae, q. 1, a. 1). All those who resisted the devil before Christ's passion were able to do so through faith in his passion, although it had not yet come to pass (3a, q. 49, a. 2). The faith of the ancients was the same as ours, apart from the difference in period. They believed, explicitly in some matters, implicitly in others, truths which would come about in the future, whereas we believe truths which have been manifested to us in the past. The ancient fathers, as teachers of this faith, received from God such knowledge as they needed to convey to their people at the time, whether openly or in figures. Full knowledge would come with Christ. Understanding was given by stages, as God adapted his teaching to men in the various periods of their history: boys have to learn the lesser things first, and a crowd must be brought to understanding of things unheard of previously by degrees.[21]

---

19 *De Veritate*, q. 14, a. 12; ed. R. Spiazzi i (Rome/Turin, 1948) p. 304.
20 Ibid. a. 11, p. 302-3.
21 *Summa contra gentiles* 4, 23; ed. Leon. (Rome 1934) 517.

St. Thomas accepted the traditional three stages: before the Law, under the Law, the time of grace.

Did revelation by stages mean that implicit belief in the figurative value of ceremonies became more explicit as time went on? We might expect the answer to be "yes", since St. Thomas says that those who lived closer in time to Christ had more explicit knowledge, giving St. John the Baptist and the apostles as examples (2a 2ae, q. 2, a. 1-2). But the answer is really "no". The negative comes out clearly in his questions on prophecy (2a 2ae, q. 174, a. 1-2). Moses was the greatest of the Old Testament prophets *simpliciter*. The quality of prophecy did not improve within each of the three stages of salvation (before the Law, under the Law, time of grace). On the contrary, the first revelation within each of the three stages excelled those following in its own stage. Hence the revelation granted to Moses excelled those granted to later prophets under the Law, just as the Gospel excelled anything which followed it in the time of grace. The Baptist and the apostles, therefore, shared in the first and best revelation of the third period. St. Thomas refused to admit a progressive revelation within each of the stages of the history of man's salvation. His refusal formed the crux of his case against the Joachites. He rejected their hope of a new gospel of the Holy Spirit. [22] It is more important here that he differed from William of Auvergne also. William had stated his belief in a progressive revelation "under the Law". The prophets of Israel, according to William, called their people to a more interior worship than the legal precepts enjoined. He presented the Law as wholesome and rational, but argued that it could be supplemented and improved upon, though not voided, before it ceded to the New Law of Christ. [23]

In the Thomist view of revelation the best comes first in each successive stage. That is why the figurative value of ceremonies and sacrifices claims a central place in his synthesis. They give coherence to his picture of the history of salvation. The ceremonial and sacrificial precepts conveyed implicit faith to the whole Jewish people, who practised them for the honour of God (1a 2ae, q. 101, a. 2). They all observed rites which signified the future expiation of sin by Christ. They shared in this expiation "by professing faith in the Redeemer in figurative sacrifices" (ibid. q. 102, a. 5). But the Jewish people were divided into two groups. The priests had more explicit knowledge than the rest, just as they played a more direct part in divine worship:

> Hence the high priest alone, once a year, entered into the inner tabernacle, the Holy of Holies, signifying that the final perfection of man is his

22 See M. Reeves, op. cit. 67-69, 161.
23 See above, p. 42.

entrance into that world. Into the outer tabernacle, the Holy Place, the priests entered daily, but not the people, who only had access to the court, because the people could conceive what was corporeal, but the inner meaning could only be seen by the wise through reflection (q. 102, a. 4, ad 4).

To the state of the Old Law the people and the priests were related in different ways. The people looked on at the bodily sacrifices offered in the court. The priests, however, were intent on the meaning of the sacrifices, since they had more explicit faith in the mysteries of Christ, and so they entered into the outer tabernacle, for some things were veiled from the people concerning the mystery of Christ, while they were known to the priests, though even to them they were not fully revealed, as subsequently in the New Testament (ibid.).

St. Thomas, like John of la Rochelle, transposed the distinction between priests and people, clergy and laity, as he knew it, back into the Old Testament. The priests of the Old Law shared with Moses and the élite a more explicit understanding of the ceremonial mysteries than was vouchsafed to the people. As he explained in *De veritate, minores* in Christian times were bound to have explicit faith in the creed in general and in the Church's teaching; explicit faith in each article of the creed could not be demanded of *minores* as it was of *maiores*.[24] The same sort of difference obtained under the Old Law.

To sum up the results of this long enquiry: St. Thomas on the Old Law stands out from his background as an intelligent conservative. He thought out the traditional doctrine and put his learning at its disposal. It corresponded to his most cherished convictions on the divine scheme of salvation. The patriarchs and prophets still "greet their country from afar". St. Thomas yielded to none of his predecessors in the foresight which he accorded to the Old Testament élite. Priests and elders understood the figurative meaning of ceremonies and sacrifices explicitly, though they could not foresee the Gospel story in detail. The whole Jewish people was bound to believe implicitly what their elders believed explicitly. *Caeremonialia* had a central place in revelation. Their significance broke through the limits which St. Thomas himself had set to the definition of the literal sense of Scripture. The spiritual sense of Scripture, as he taught elsewhere, eluded the sacred writers' understanding, having been put there by God: The New Testament alone revealed the spiritual senses to Christians. But Moses and the élite had a partial understanding of the mystical sense of ceremonies. "Partial" is perhaps too weak an adjective for the explicit faith and clear pre-view which enabled them to pierce the veil of their legal code, as St. Thomas imagined things.

24 *De Verit.* p. 303-4. See also *Summa* 2a 2ae, q. 2, a. 6.

Dom Gribomont has made the pertinent comment that St. Thomas in speaking of implicit (I would add "partially explicit") knowledge, always stresses knowledge of reality implied in the object, as clearly known. Today, as Dom Gribomont says, we think more of the consciousness of the knowing subject. We feel more curiosity about the sacred writers' psychology. [25] The insight applies to medieval scholarship in all fields. The medieval clerk read both profane and sacred books for the sake of their content, as sources of wisdom. His authors interested him less than their teaching; he did not envisage them clearly as persons. So we need not wonder that St. Thomas focussed his attention on the content, literal and mystical, of the Mosaic Law, without enquiring what Moses had in mind. Paradoxically, this neglect of the question has the result of making the Thomist treatment of the Old Law look less dated and anachronistic today than William of Auvergne's. St. Thomas avoided rash speculation on its historical setting. William floundered in a quagmire because he ventured on to the terrain of biblical and ancient history. The schoolmen as a class had little use for history as such and were ill equipped to deal with it. St. Thomas dammed up William's line of enquiry and turned speculation into more profitable channels. He clarified and fortified tradition, partly in reaction to William's attack on allegories and moralities. John had bowdlerised *De legibus*; St. Thomas supplied a powerful counter argument, sustained throughout his *Summa* wherever he touched on ceremonies. *De legibus* therefore had a negative rather than a positive effect: it provoked refutation. St. Thomas's genius took its toll, as genius will, in making men forget his predecessors.

And yet was it all gain that he put William's opinions on the shelf, to moulder there permanently? William's answer to the question "What do we know about Moses?" would amuse a modern biblical scholar. [26] But the questions he asked matter more than his naïve answers. What did Old Testament history convey to readers or hearers when it was first recorded? What was the lawgiver's purpose? What did the Law mean when it was first received? Few of the questions raised in the schools have kept such relevance today. William was no match for the Angelic Doctor in the middle ages. For that very reason he seems closer to us when he discusses the Old Law. St. Thomas had the better mind; William showed more curiosity and imagination.

25 Op. cit. (above, p. 12, n. 3), 80. The difference between medieval and modern approaches to authors makes it hard to adapt Thomist doctrine on the interpretation of Scripture to problems of modern exegesis and theories on inspiration and revelation; see the account of various attempts to do so by J. T. Burtchaell, *Catholic Theories of Biblical Inspiration since 1810* (Cambridge 1969) 131 and passim.

26 See. G. Widengren, "What do we know about Moses?", *Proclamation and Presence. Old Testament Essays in Honour of Gwynne Henton Davies*, ed. J. I. Durham and J. R. Porter (London 1970) 21-47.

APPENDIX

William's account of the spiritual senses in *De legibus* is so novel that it seemed advisable to check the edition from an early manuscript. The editors do not state what manuscripts they used. I chose MS Paris, Bibl. nat. lat. 15755 as the earliest available; it belonged to the Sorbonne. Mlle Marthe Dulong kindly described it and collated it with the edition for me. She puts it probably in the mid-thirteenth century. It is written in black ink in a rather tremulous hand, "more like a hand used for documents than a real book hand". The chapters are marked by red and blue initials. There are no chapter headings or numbers and no marginalia, at least on these pages. The manuscript has some variations from the edition, which do not alter the sense in any material way. Some of the manuscript readings are inferior to the edition; others suggest slight improvements. I transcribe the text of the edition (pp. 48-49), noting the MS variants in brackets (fol. 49vb).

Quarta significatio est per similitudinem rerum, quae non ad hoc factae sunt ut significent; et haec est quae multos offendit, et propter hoc quia abusivum eis videtur res ad (in) signa trahere, quae non ad significandum factae sunt, quale est id (illud) Hieremiae 8 (xiii):[1] Nunquid sicut facit figulus iste non potero vobis (*add.* facere) domus Israel, ait Dominus. Dissipatio enim vasis quae prius fiebat, et formatio vasis alterius (*add.* non ad hoc)[2] factae sunt ut significarent; et cum eis ad significandum usus est Deus (Dominus), neque offenderetur quis audiens huiusmodi expositiones seu interpretationes, si diceretur ei hoc modo: Quemadmodum dicit (ibi dixit) Dominus: Nunquid non sic facere vobis potero? ubi de significatione nihil locutus est, sed de similitudine tantum. Quemadmodum et Hieremiae tertio, non dixit quicquam de significatione, sed similitudinem et modum tantum expressit dicens: Quomodo si mulier contemnat amatorem suum, sic contempsit me domus Israel (*add.* etc).[3] Non dixit, quia contemptus huius mulieris significaret contemptum filiorum Israel, nec dixit quod amator huius significaret ipsum, neque dixit quod dissipatio aut reformatio vasis prophetia esset vel parabola eius quod ipse operatus (operaturus) esset in populo Israel (*add.* hoc modo), vel quod figulus esset figura ipsius, sed expressit modum seu similitudinem notam inter opus figuli et opus suum, et inter factum mulieris contemnentis amatorem suum et factum populi Israel, quo modo si loquerentur sacri expositores et doctores in allegoriis et tropologiis suis (*add.* et) etiam anagogicis

---

1   xviii, 6.
2   The MS reading is better here: the breaking of one vase and the making of another were not meant to signify, but to resemble what God could do to Israel.
3   iii, 20.

interpretationibus, et scripturae satisfacerent et audientium sive legentium intellectus non offenderent. Sed quia dicetur (dicunt): "Tale quid significat tale quid, et est figura seu prophetia aut parabola talis rei", cum alterum propter alterum significandum nec factum nec dictum videatur, offendunt graviter audientes. Quemadmodum se habet in facto David et Uriae, quod legitur in 11 (*add.* secundi) et 12 Regum, ubi dicitur quod David, qui utique proditor erat in facto illo, et adulter atque homicida, significat Christum, Urias autem, vir sanctus et fidelis, diabolum (Dyabolus). Et iterum (*add* de) adulterina illa copula Davidis de (David et) Bersabee, proditione et homicidio execrabili⁺ significat sanctissimum matrimonium et immaculatissimam copulam Christi et Ecclesiae de gentibus, quae (*om.*) auribus multorum multam indignationem ingerunt, fidemque sacrarum expositionum aut penitus in eis abrogant aut multum laedunt. Primum, quia istud non est factum ad significandum, nec verisimile est multis quod propter hoc sit scriptum. Si autem ita dicerent: "Quo modo rex David Bersabee adamavit et pro (MS pre) amore ipsius mortem viri procuravit, quo modo illam regali connubio honoravit et regali solio exaltavit, sic rex coelorum Christus Dominus synagogam adamavit et, procurata morte magistratus seu principatus eius, cui velut marito suberat, eam connubio suo spirituali honoravit et coelestis regni solio sublimavit", si, inquam, de modo tantum aut similitudine mentionem facerent, et ipsam similitudinem decenter et diligenter prosequentes exponerent, absque offensione ulla audientium hoc fieret. Eodem modo de Ecclesia de (et) gentibus, quod procurata morte diaboli, morte (*om.*) scilicet spirituali, cui velut marito suberat, unde et vocabat ipsum Bahalim, quod interpretatur vir meus,⁵ quod sic et sic ei fecit, non solum pacifice, sed gratanter (graviter) etiam audiretur. Verbum ergo significandi est quod in parte ista graviter offendit auditores atque lectores, quamquam verum sit quod omnium duorum similium, quorum alterum est intellectui nostro propinquius, nobisque notius, signum naturale est id (*om.*)⁶ minus noti atque ab intellectu nostro remotioris. Signum, inquam, est naturale illius et velut liber in quo legitur; unde et quasi natura docente altero ad alterum declarandum utimur. Hoc ergo modo sacri doctores et expositores sane et absque offendiculo ullo dicere possunt quia (quod) factum illud de Bersabee factum significavit ecclesiae de gentibus; significavit (*add.* inquam) propria similitudine, tanquam naturali designatione. Licet autem Spiritui sancto et scriptoribus eius notioribus similibus (similitudinibus)⁷ uti ad minus nota significanda et declaranda. Secundo, propter rerum dissimilitudinem et nimiam (nimiamque distantiam), ubi magis violenta est significatio (significationis impositio)⁸ in ipsis quam rerum significatarum expositio. Et in hoc errant imperiti multi, qui nesciunt qualiter tractandum sit verbum veritatis, sed ingenium suum, ut ait Hieronymus, facere nolunt ec-

---

4 Both MS and edition seem to omit several words: "dicunt quod" would make sense.
5 Jerome gives "vir eius" as the meaning of *Bala* (*Ios.* xix, 3), *Liber de interp. nom Hebr.*, PL 23, 802, but it does not relate to the context. William's allusion is obscure. Perhaps another passage has dropped out of the text.
6 A better reading.
7 A better reading.
8 A better reading.

clesiae sacrificium (sacramentum),[9] et propter hoc dixit super Abacuc: Tropologia libera est et tantum legibus circumscripta, ut pietatem sequatur in intelligentiae sermonisque contextu (intelligentia sermonisque contextum), nec in rebus multum inter se contrariis violenta sit copulandis.[10] Tertium, est ignorantia explicandi prosequendique similitudines, ex quo defectu accidit et illud quod diximus, ut non credatur expositionibus, maxime ubi ex similitudine potissimum significant. Cessante namque in his rerum similitudine, cessat et significatio apud audientes. Quartum, est ignorantia eius videlicet quod solum in negotio significat, sicut accidit in somniis quae exposuit Ioseph in 40 et 41 Genesis. Tres enim propagines et tria canistra panum propter numerum tantum significaverunt tres dies, de quibus agitur, et solus ternarius quantum ad dies (om.) illos significat. Erraret enim intolerabiliter qui canistra vel propagines in significationem dierum detorquere vellet. Propter hoc dictum est (add. quod) sacra scriptura est velut cithara, in qua non omnia sonant (sanant).[11]

9 Wrong reading.
10 On Abac. i, 6-11, PL 26, 1281-2: "Historia stricta est et evagandi non habet facultatem. Tropologia libera, et his tantum legibus circumscripta, ut pietatem sequatur intelligentiae sermonisque contextum, nec in rebus multum inter se contrariis violenta sit copulandis."
11 Wrong reading. See Augustine, *Contra Faustum*, PL 42, 463.

THE *QUINQUE VIAE*
AND SOME PARISIAN PROFESSORS OF PHILOSOPHY

William Dunphy

H ISTORICAL studies on the influence of Thomas Aquinas have
focused naturally enough on his fellow theologians. A recent work
entitled *The Early Thomistic School* names five Oxford and nine
Parisian professors as strongly influenced by Aquinas, all of whom were
theologians.[1] There have been fewer studies of Aquinas's influence on
his contemporaries in the Faculty of Arts,[2] though we know in what
high esteem he was held by the Parisian Masters of Arts thanks to the
remarkable letter sent by them to the General Chapter of the Dominican Order immediately after Aquinas's untimely death in Italy.[3] We
have no reason to believe that a comparable letter was sent from his
own Faculty of Theology. Further, given the troubled relations between
the Faculties of Arts and Theology at Paris during the 1260's and
1270's, it is certainly extraordinary that all the Masters of Arts should
have looked upon a theologian as a co-worker in their task of shedding
light on the mysteries of nature and in interpreting the writings of the
great philosophers.

Indeed, the growing suspicion by theologians concerning the
Christian orthodoxy of these Masters of Arts matched a growing
resentment on the part of some philosophers at what they considered to
be unwarranted interference in their affairs by theologians. The Lenten
Collationes of St. Bonaventure bear witness to the former,[4] while

---

* The research for this article was supported by a grant from the Canada Council.

1 F. J. Roensch, *The Early Thomistic School* (Dubuque 1964). One of them, however, is Peter
of Auvergne, who had a notable career in the Faculty of Arts before becoming a theologian.

2 See, for example, O. Lottin, "Saint Thomas d'Aquin à la faculté des arts de Paris aux ap-
proches de 1277," *Recherches de théologie ancienne et médiévale* 16 (1949) 292-313: R. A.
Gauthier, "Trois commentaires 'averroistes' sur l'Ethique à Nicomaque," *Archives d'histoire doctrinale et littéraire du moyen âge* 16 (1947-48) 187-336.

3 The text of the letter can be found in A. Birkenmajer, *Beiträge zur Geschichte der Philosophie des Mittelalters*, XX, 5 (1922) 2-4. See also his "Neues zu dem Brief der Pariser Artistenfakultät über den Tod des hl. Thomas von Aquin," *Xenia Thomistica* 3 (Rome 1925) 57-72.

4 See especially the *Collationes in Hexaemeron* delivered at Paris in 1273 in *Opera Omnia* V
(Quaracchi 1891) and in another version edited by F. Delorme (Quaracchi 1934).

Boetius of Dacia's *De aeternitate mundi* is a passionate statement of the latter.[5]

The *Cartulary* of the University of Paris documents these disturbing developments within the Faculty of Arts and the severe reactions to them by the Bishop of Paris, Stephen Tempier. First, the Bishop condemned thirteen carefully selected philosophical propositions in 1270 and, seven years later, he followed this intervention with the wholesale condemnation of two hundred and nineteen theses. This latter condemnation provides indirect testimony to Aquinas's influence within the Faculty of Arts. The Bishop denounced those "studying in Arts at Paris" who had overstepped the limits of their own Faculty by proposing the condemned propositions for discussion. Since a number of them were drawn from the writings of Thomas Aquinas, Dom O. Lottin has suggested that one of the targets intended by the Bishop was Aquinas and this, precisely because of his influence on the Faculty of Arts.[6] A more thorough study of Aquinas's presence to these professors of philosophy in the period between the condemnations of 1270 and 1277 could assist our understanding of this important moment of tension in the history of western thought.

I propose in this article to examine in some detail the different ways in which two Parisian philosophical commentaries on Aristotle's *Physics* and *Metaphysics* utilized certain theological texts of Thomas Aquinas on the question of God's existence. Both commentaries are in the style of "Questions" and both were composed during the crucial years between 1270 and 1277.

One is a set of questions on Book Eight of the *Physics* found in manuscript Munich Clm. 9559, fol. 40rl-vl, edited in 1941 by Philippe Delhaye and ascribed by him to Siger of Brabant.[7] Since a number of scholars have questioned that attribution,[8] (successfully, I think), this work will be designated simply as the Munich *Questions on Book Eight of the Physics*. The other set of questions on Book Twelve of the

---

5 See the edition by G. Sajó (Berlin 1964).

6 *Chartularium Universitatis Parisiensis*, ed. H. Denifle and E. Chatelain (Paris 1889) I, 449-560. For the text of the decree of 1270, see 486-87; for that of 1277, see 543-58. See also O. Lottin, art. cit. 312.

7 *Siger de Brabant, Questions sur la Physique d'Aristote*, ed. P. Delhaye (Louvain 1941). Although these questions are published as one work with the *Questions on Physics I-IV* that immediately precede them in the manuscript, they were copied by different scribes and were apparently joined together by the compiler of the manuscript.

8 See, for example, A. Maier, "Les Commentaires sur la Physique d'Aristote attribués à Siger de Brabant," *Revue philosophique de Louvain* 47 (1949) 334-350; A. Zimmerman, *Die Quaestionen des Siger von Brabant zur Physik des Aristoteles* (Cologne 1956); G. Sajó, "Boèce de Dacie et les Commentaires anonymes inédits de Munich sur la Physique et sur la Génération attribués à Siger de Brabant," *Archives d'histoire doctrinale et littéraire du moyen âge* 25 (1959) 21-58.

Metaphysics are from Peter of Auvergne's *Quaestiones in Metaphysicam* and are edited for the first time below.

A simple inspection of the titles of a few questions from these two works reveals their significance for a study of the influence of St. Thomas on the Parisian Faculty of Arts. The Munich *Questions on Book Eight of the Physics* ask:

> Utrum primum principium esse sit manifestum in entibus.
> Utrum primum principium esse in entibus possit demonstrari.
> Utrum sit ponere Primum in entibus.

Peter of Auvergne's *Commentary on Book Twelve of the Metaphysics* asks:

> Utrum ex se sit manifestum aliquas substantias separatas esse.
> Utrum substantias separatas esse possunt demonstrari.
> Utrum necesse sit ponere substantias aliquas separatas.
> Utrum sit ponere primum principium.

Historians of mediaeval thought are generally agreed that the triadic sequence of questions concerning 1) the need to demonstrate God's existence, 2) the possibility of such a demonstration, and 3) examples of such a demonstration, seems to have originated with Thomas Aquinas.[9] His *Summa contra Gentiles* (*SCG*) 1, 10-13 and his *Summa theologiae* (*ST*) 1, 2, 1-3 use the successful fulfillment of the third step as the indispensable foundation for all that follows in those works.[10]

In his earlier work, the *SCG*, directed to those intellectuals who do not accept the testimony of either the Old or New Testaments, St. Thomas proposes "to set forth the arguments by which both philosophers and Catholic teachers have proved that God exists."[11] It is interesting that in this chapter the philosophers' arguments come first, in great detail, with many specific references to the text of Aristotle. It is only in the thirty-fifth and final paragraph that he proposes an argument formulated by a Catholic teacher, John Damascene, but with the observation that this argument is also hinted at (*etiam innuit*) by Averroes.

---

9 A possible foreshadowing of this logical sequence of questions can be found in Avicenna's discussion of the subject matter of metaphysics, where he rejects the position that God is that subject because no science proves the existence of its subject and God's existence is proven in metaphysics. Here is the key text in that discussion: "Igitur aut (Deum esse) est manifestum per se aut desperatum per se quod non possit manifestari ulla speculatione. Non est autem manifestum per se, nec est desperatum posse manifestari quia signa habemus de eo." *Meta.* 1, 1 (Venice 1508) fol. 70r2.

10 "Inter ea vero quae de Deo secundum seipsum consideranda sunt, praemittendum est, quasi totius operis necessarium fundamentum, consideratio qua demonstratur Deum esse. Quo non habito, omnis consideratio de rebus divinis necessario tollitur." *SCG* I, 9.

11 Ibid. 1, 13, 1; tr. A. Pegis (New York 1955) 85.

In the *ST*, however, directed to an audience of beginners in the study of Catholic truth, where St. Thomas had promised to set forth "briefly and clearly" the things that pertain to sacred doctrine, he introduces examples of proofs of God's existence with the flat statement that "the existence of God can be proved in five ways."[12] There is only one specific reference to a philosopher, Aristotle, and this occurs in the fourth way, which most historians ascribe rather to the Platonic tradition.

In what ways then would professors in the Parisian Faculty of Arts find use for Aquinas's theological treatment of the question of God's existence? A Christian professor, charged with guiding his students through a reading of Aristotle's *Physics*, might naturally associate a demonstration of the existence of a first unmoved mover in Book Eight with a proof for the existence of God. Even more so, a Christian commentator on Book Twelve of Aristotle's *Metaphysics* could scarcely dissociate in his own mind a proof of God's existence from a demonstration of the existence of an eternal immaterial substance, wholly in act, especially since in this book Aristotle expressly calls such a being God.[13]

In fact, similar associations had already been made, albeit in different ways, by Avicenna and Averroes. Indeed, their handling of the question of demonstrating God's existence was so different that no professor in the Arts Faculty could avoid taking sides in the controversy as to whether such a proof belongs to the science of physics or metaphysics.

Avicenna, with his recognition of a *causa agens* (the *creator mundi*) that is not merely a source of motion but a source of being (*principium essendi*), insisted that it is in the science of metaphysics that we demonstrate the existence of "the Most High God."[14] Averroes, on the contrary, denied the philosophical need for any creative causality and insisted that it is impossible to prove the existence of an immaterial being except by way of motion.[15] Thus the existence of God or the prime mover is properly and exclusively proved in the science of physics. The task of the metaphysician is to demonstrate that the prime mover, whose existence had already been proven in physics, is the principle of sensible substance in the orders of formal and final causality.[16] He

---

12 St. Thomas, *ST* 1, 2, 3.
13 Aristotle, *Meta.* XII, 7, 1072b 30.
14 Avicenna, *Meta.* VI, 1, fol. 91r2, and 1, 1, fol. 70rl-2.
15 Averroes, *In XII Meta.* c. 5 (Venice 1574) fol. 293 C.
16 Ibid. c. 6, fol. 294 K-L; see also *In II Meta.* c. 6, fol. 31 E.

sharply criticized Avicenna's proof of God's existence, saying that it is false, weak, and in no way demonstrative, for even the more certain of its statements do not pass beyond the merely probable. [17]

How then did mediaeval Christians handle this controversy? The thirteenth century interpreters of Aristotle whose main concerns were theological did not hesitate. Obviously, they could not prefer an Averroistic Aristotle whose first principle was not a creator, i. e., where the notion of efficient causality was restricted to that of a *causa movens*. On this point at least, the Avicennian view of efficient causality would carry the day, so that in attempting to formulate proofs of the existence of God these theologians would feel free to view them as properly metaphysical rather than as restricted to a proof from motion in physics.

Albert the Great, for one, while agreeing with Averroes that in physics we primarily study material and moving causes and in metaphysics formal and final causes, nevertheless insisted that demonstrations of God's existence were proper to metaphysics. Even proving the first cause by way of motion is not a physical proof, for we do not arrive at just a first cause of motion *qua* motion, but rather at the first cause of that motion which serves as the instrumental cause of the outpouring of all being from the First. [18]

Thomas Aquinas also, in this instance, preferred Avicenna to Averroes. By including the case of the emanation of a particular being from a particular agent within the emanation of the whole of being from the universal cause who is God, Aquinas regularly uses as interchangeable the terms *causa efficiens, causa movens* and *causa agens*. Thus he can call God both the prime unmoved mover of the *Physics* and the first, wholly actual, eternal substance of the *Metaphysics*. [19]

But what about those mediaeval Christians whose professional interests required them to explain the writings of Aristotle and other philosophers to students in a university Faculty of Arts? Certainly at

17 Averroes, *In I Phy.*, c. 83, fol. 47 F-H; *In VII Phy.*, c. 3, fol. 340 E-F.

18 "Et si accipiatur per motum prima causa, hoc non est, ut sciatur, inquantum est movens talem motum, sed potius inquantum ipse ambit virtute sua mobile et motum quod est instrumentum fluxus totius entis ab ipso, et hoc modo non considerat ipsum physicus." Albert, *In XI Meta.* tr. 1, c. 3; ed. B. Geyer, *Opera Omnia* XVI (1960-64) 462, 53-463, 10. For a complete understanding of Albert's own views, however, one must bear in mind his numerous protestations that in his Aristotelian commentaries he is primarily concerned with merely presenting the peripatetic position.

19 "Et sic terminat Philosophus considerationem communem de rebus naturalibus in Primo Principio totius naturae qui est super omnia Deus benedictus in saecula saeculorum. Amen." St. Thomas, *In VIII Phy.* lect. 23. "Et hoc est quod concludit, quod est unus princeps totius universi, scilicet primum movens, et primum intelligibile et primum bonum, quod supra dixit Deum, qui est benedictus in saecula saeculorum. Amen." *In XII Meta.* lect. 12.

Paris in the second half of the thirteenth century the detailed commentaries of Averroes on Aristotle would prove more immediately
useful to them in resolving textual difficulties than the more personal
philosophizing of Avicenna, whose works were not intended as a textual
commentary on Aristotle. As Aristotle merited the title "the Philosopher," so Averroes truly merited the title "the Commentator."
But believing, as good Christians, in a universe produced *ex nihilo* by a
creating God, how far could they follow Averroes's insistence that since
no creating cause was needed in philosophy, the existence of a God
conceived as the first unmoved mover could and must be demonstrated
only by way of motion, and that only in physics? Clearly, some accommodation was in order.

Two of the better known of these Parisian professors, Siger of
Brabant and Boetius of Dacia, usually identified by historians as "Latin
Averroists,"[20] used neo-platonic doctrines found in Proclus and the
Liber de Causis to make this accommodation. Boethius, while ruling
out any proof for the existence of a creating God in the science of
physics, apparently locates such a demonstration in metaphysics. In-
deed, as authorities for a metaphysical notion of creation, he cites the
Liber de Causis and *Averroes*![21]

Siger of Brabant appears to be more concerned on this point not to
undermine the interpretative authority of Averroes. In the classic *locus*
at which to raise the Avicennian-Averroistic dispute, namely in
discussing the question whether the subject matter of metaphysics is
being *qua* being or God, Siger rejects the contention of Averroes that it
is God. However, he softens this rejection by noting Averroes's insistence, against Avicenna, that the metaphysician must accept from the
natural philosopher God's existence as already proved. What ought I to
hold, Siger asks? Well, he argues, it is not necessary that it belong to
one and the same science to posit both the conclusion of a demonstration and the middle term whereby it is demonstrated. Now the middle term whereby God is proved in metaphysics is drawn from nature,
as Aristotle does in Book Twelve of the *Metaphysics*: "quasi hoc sup-
ponens *ex physicis*." Therefore, on this point, Averroes is right.[22]

Against this background, let us now see how the author of the
Munich *Questions on Book Eight of the Physics* and Peter of Auvergne

20 See, for example, E. Gilson, *History of Christian Philosophy in the Middle Ages* (New York 1955) 389-402.

21 Boetius of Dacia, *De aeternitate mundi*; ed. G. Sajó (Berlin 1964). For the exclusion of creation from the consideration of the natural philosopher, see p. 45. For the metaphysician's proper concerns in treating creation, see pp. 50 and 54. Note his citation there not only of the *Liber de Causis*, but also of Averroes.

22 Siger of Brabant, *Quaestiones in Metaphysicam* 1, 1; ed. C. Graiff (Louvain 1948) 4.

selectively use the theological texts of Aquinas in dealing with the question of God's existence.

Before addressing himself to the actual text of the *Physics* and the question of the eternity of motion, the author of the Munich commentary inserts a block of five questions that one might expect to find in a commentary on the *Metaphysics*. He introduces the first two questions as follows: "Since the metaphysician accepts the existence of the first principle from the natural philosopher, first of all we ask: Whether the existence of a first principle in beings is self-evident; second, Whether this existence can be demonstrated."[23] The third question asks: Whether it belongs to the metaphysician to demonstrate the existence of a first principle. In his generally Avicennian answer to this question the author contends that the existence of God is not accepted as proven in any science other than *this one*, since all sciences other than *this one* deal with some determinate being that is less than *ens commune*. Hence, if God's existence is to be proven in any science, it ought to be done in *this one*.[24] On this basis it is clear that *this science* is metaphysics, and the author appears to conclude against his initial assumption, namely that "the metaphysician accepts the existence of the first principle from the natural philosopher."

The fourth question, which sets forth three proofs for the existence of God in close textual affinity with Aquinas's *ST* 1, 2, 3, explicitly names Avicenna as the author of the *tertia via*. The fifth of these introductory questions extends the metaphysical problematic by asking whether beings other than the first could be *ex se necesse esse*.[25] From these introductory questions one might infer that the author was interested in placing before his students a solution to the philosophical enigma of God's existence other than Averroes's prior to turning to the text of the *Physics* with its proof, based on the eternity of motion, of a first unmoved mover.

As we have seen, the first of the Munich questions asked: Whether it is manifest or self-evident that there be a first principle among beings. The first argument for an affirmative answer closely parallels the second affirmative argument in the *ST* to the question: Whether the proposition "God exists" be self-evident. Those propositions are said to be self-evident that are known simply by knowing the meaning of the terms. Thus, by knowing the meaning of the name "God," we also know that God exists. Unlike Aquinas, the Munich question does not

---

23 Ed. Delhaye, 188.
24 Ibid. 192-3.
25 Ibid. 193-6.

reflect the famous Anselmian argument in the *Proslogion*.[26] In fact, as might be expected, both Peter of Auvergne and the author of the Munich text regularly eliminate any purely theological traces from the texts of Aquinas when they transfer them to the context of discussions in the Faculty of Arts.[27] We shall not specifically note each one of these eliminations.

The second argument for the affirmative parallels the third affirmative argument in Aquinas's *ST*, namely that the existence of some truth is self-evident, for he who denies that there is truth must affirm at least that the denial is true. From this we can infer the existence of that which is most true or Truth, which is then identified with the first principle or God.[28]

A single argument *contra* appears in slightly different form in these works and is drawn from Aristotle: No one can think the opposite of that which is self-evident; but some have denied the existence of a first principle. The reader is left to draw the conclusion that it is not self-evident that there be a first principle.[29]

Both the Munich question and the *ST* begin their solutions of the question with a twofold distinction between the ways in which something can be self-evident, namely *quoad nos* and *non quoad nos*. Both develop the argument, though in slightly different ways, to the conclusion that the proposition "God exists" is indeed a self-evident proposition in itself, but not *quoad nos*. The *ST* explicitly refers to a Boethian text from *De Hebdomadibus*, while the Munich text simply uses Boethian phrases from that text.[30] It then easily disposes of the two arguments for the affirmative by using the above distinction.[31]

The parallel text from Peter of Auvergne asks a slightly different question. Instead of inquiring about God, Peter asks: Whether it be self-evident that some separate substances exist. One reason for this would be that the Aristotelian text on which he is commenting sought to prove the existence of a class of substances separate from matter. Peter an-

---

26   Ibid. 188; *ST* 1, 2, 1, obj. 2.

27   For example, neither author follows Aquinas who, in the *ST*, cites passages from Exodus, The Psalms, John, Paul, Damascene and Augustine.

28   Ibid.

29   Ibid. 189.

30   Ibid. The Munich text also uses the Boethian distinction between those *per se notae* propositions whose terms are known commonly by all men, and those whose terms are known by wise men only (*cujus terminorum rationes sunt notae ipsius sapientibus*). It does not, however, go as far as the *Impossibilia* of Siger of Brabant which argues that "*Deum esse est verum, etiam necessarium, et sapientibus per se notum.*" See P. Mandonnet, *Siger de Brabant et l'averroïsme latin*, (Louvain 1911) II, 74-5.

31   Ibid.

nounces his intention to deal with separate substances before treating of God's existence.[32]

Peter's first argument for an affirmative answer to the question is basically the same as that found in the Munich text, but it is more closely related to the *SCG* than to the *ST*. It is interesting that Peter here uses a phrase which betrays a certain difficulty he felt in maintaining his resolve to treat universally of separate substances before God. His argument is based on the principle that "no proposition is more true or manifest than one in which the same item is predicated of itself." Now this is the case with the proposition "Separate substances exist," because nothing is predicable of separate substances other than their very substance. But here Peter hastens to add the revealing reservation: "at least in the case of the first substance."[33]

Peter's second argument does not correspond to that of the Munich text, but rather to an argument found in both the *ST* and the *SCG*. Here again his language is closer to that of the *SCG* than to that of the *ST*. It states that things naturally known are self-evidently known, and that separate substances are in that category because knowledge of them is naturally desired by man as his supreme perfection and happiness.[34]

Before solving the question, Peter attempts a general explanation, clearly inspired by the *SCG*,[35] why some people would think it idle to question whether the existence of separate substances be self-evident. According to him, their conviction arises from a custom which acquires the force of nature with us. From an early age we have been accustomed to hearing from others that separate substances exist, and so it seems self-evident to us that some separate substances exist as though that knowledge were natural to us.[36]

Peter solves the question by making the philosophical distinction between those things more knowable in themselves but less knowable to us, and those things less knowable in themselves but more knowable to us. Then he argues that while separate substances are supremely in act, nevertheless they are at the furthest remove from sensible things whence our knowledge takes its origin. Hence they are not clearly knowable to us. After all, as Aristotle said, our intellects are, with

---

32 Peter of Auvergne, *Quaestiones in Metaphysicam* XII, 6a. See below, II, p. 95.

33 Ibid.

34 Ibid.

35 Ibid., p. 96. Cf. St. Thomas, "Praedicta autem opinio provenit partim quidem ex consuetudine qua ex principio assueti sunt nomen Dei audire et invocare. Consuetudo autem, et praecipue quae est a puero vim naturae obtinet: ex quo contingit ut ea quibus a pueritia animus imbuitur, ita firmiter teneat ac si essent naturaliter et per se nota." *SCG* 1, 11, 1.

36 Ibid. Note that once again Peter shifts from the discussion of separate substances in general to *ipse Deus*.

respect to the most knowable things in nature, as the eye of the bat is to the light of the sun.[37]

Comparable textual affinities are to be found in the next question where the issue is the possibility of demonstrating the existence of God (*ST, SCG*), the first principle (Munich text), or separate substances (Peter's text). The Munich question's two arguments for the negative side are identical in substance with the second and third arguments of the *ST*; Peter's two arguments are more closely related to two of those in the *SCG*, but with one interesting difference. The *SCG* relates an argument based on the words of certain philosophers who show that, in God, what answers the question *quid est* is identical to what answers the question *an est*. Now, since we cannot know through reason the *quid est* of God, then neither can we by reason demonstrate the existence of God.[38]

The argument in Peter's work starts, as does the Munich text and the *ST*, with the declaration that what-a-thing-is (*quod quid est*) is a principle of demonstration. But, unlike the other two texts, the minor premise of which is that we cannot know the *quid est* of God, Peter's argument states that the *quod quid est* of separate substances is identical with their *esse*. Then, instead of affirming with the *SCG*'s argument that we cannot know the *quid est* of God, Peter's argument states that since there is nothing about separate substances that does not belong to their *quod quid est*, we cannot demonstrate their existence because it is not possible to demonstrate the same thing from itself.[39]

All the passages we are comparing use the Aristotelian distinction between demonstration through the cause (*propter quid*) and demonstration through the effect (*quia*) to maintain respectively that the existence of God or a first principle or separate substances can indeed be demonstrated, but only through effects. The ways in which they make use of this distinction, however, differ sufficiently for us to observe the selectivity of the two philosophical commentaries in their use of Thomistic texts.

Since the *SCG* merely states that "the art of demonstration teaches us to conclude to causes from effects,"[40] Peter turns here to the text of the *ST*. This text is more concise than are the two commentaries in setting forth the two kinds of demonstration. Both the author of the Munich text and Peter expand those descriptions providing a close verbal link with a distinction they had made in their preceding questions, namely

---

37 Ibid. p. 96.
38 St. Thomas, *SCG* 1, 12, 3.
39 Peter of Auvergne, below, pp. 96-7.
40 St. Thomas, *SCG* 1, 12, 6.

between those things which are more or less knowable *secundum naturam et quoad nos*. Peter, for example, describes *propter quid* demonstration as proceeding from those things which are more known according to their nature to those things which are more unknown according to their nature, whereas the *quia* type proceeds *ex ignotioribus secundum naturam, notioribus tamen nobis, ad notiora secundum naturam, ignotiora quoad nos.*[41]

A similar expansion of the more compact text of the *ST* occurs where Aquinas said simply that from any effect the existence of its proper cause can be demonstrated. The Munich text expands the notion of effect to include both proximate and remote effects, those proportioned to the cause and those not so proportioned. Further, where Aquinas simply concluded that the existence of God is demonstrated through effects known to us, the Munich text asserts that "since all things other than the First have their being (*esse*) from that First itself as from their cause, and (since) a cause is not able to produce any effect, except according to its being, the existence of the first principle can be demonstrated from the existence of its effects."[42]

The text of Peter's response presents further proof that he is thinking about God while talking about separate substances. He moves from talk about demonstrating the existence of the *substantia prima*, through a mention of the *causa prima* discussed by the *Liber de Causis*, to concluding that we can demonstrate (*quia*) the existence of separate substances by using as middle term the nominal definition of separate substances as this is drawn from their sensible effects.[43]

Here the Munich text interjects the question as to where one properly demonstrates the existence of God, i.e., in physics, as Averroes claimed, or in metaphysics, as Avicenna held. A look at the Munich author's resolution of this problem, together with a report of Peter's position, will enable us to judge the extent to which these authors introduce non-Thomistic elements into their handling of the *quinque viae*.

The Munich author contrasts the position of Averroes to that of Avicenna in terms of the effects claimed to be the most appropriate for the demonstration of the existence of the first principle. If one chooses the nature of motion itself, then Averroes is correct in insisting that the demonstration is proper to physics. If, however, one chooses the nature of being, the possible and the necessary, then Avicenna is right. But if we recognize that in *quia*, unlike *propter quid*, demonstrations there can

---

41 Peter of Auvergne, below, p. 97.
42 Ed. Delhaye, 190.
43 Peter of Auvergne, below, p. 97.

be as many different demonstrations of the cause as there are different kinds of its effects, then we need not regard the positions of Averroes and Avicenna as mutually exclusive. Thus, the Munich author concludes, both the natural philosopher and the metaphysician prove the existence of the first principle, but they do so in different ways. The natural philosopher begins with an effect, namely motion, that is more known to us through sensible evidence. The metaphysician starts from an effect, namely being or the possible and the necessary, that is more known to us through intellectual evidence. [44]

Although the author does not state his preference for the Avicennian or metaphysical proof, one can infer this from the implied superiority of intellectual over sensible evidence and from his remark that the effects with which the metaphysician begins are effects *per se* of the first principle and belong to the first principle as such (*ut sic*). [45]

Peter of Auvergne's treatment of this question is found within his answer to the question raised at the beginning of his commentary as to what constitutes the subject matter of metaphysics. [46] There, after noting Averroes's charge that Avicenna erred (*peccavit*) in this matter, Peter insists rather that it was Averroes who had erred. He begins by repeating the general principle laid down in the Munich text, namely that since the *esse* of an effect can come only from its cause, we can demonstrate the existence of that cause from an effect more known to us. However, Peter adds a consideration which enables him to include an Averroistic proof from motion, while at the same time subordinating it to the more essential and truer (*essentialius et verius*) metaphysical proof: "When a conclusion can be demonstrated through several middle terms, it is demonstrated more truly through that middle term which is more proportioned, similar and akin to that conclusion." Now, Peter continues, the nature of the possible, as used by the metaphysician, is closer to the conclusion "God exists" than the effect, motion, used by the natural philosopher. This is so because the proximate effect of the First is not motion but rather the "being" of something mobile. Thus, Peter concludes, although the existence of God can be demonstrated in both physics and metaphysics, it is done more essentially in metaphysics. [47] We will return to this hierarchical ordering principle of the proofs when we compare Peter's position with that of Thomas Aquinas.

44   Ed. Delhaye, 191-2.

45   Ibid., 192.

46   Peter of Auvergne, *Q. in Meta.* 1, 1. This text has been edited by A. Monahan, *Nine Mediaeval Thinkers* (Toronto 1955) 152-55.

47   Ibid. "Quare etsi in utraque scientia, scilicet naturali et divina, probetur Deum esse, essentialius tamen in scientia divina." 154.

Since Peter intends to treat the question of proofs for the existence of separate substances before the proofs for the existence of the first principle, we can see how one professor adapts the *quinque viae* of Aquinas to two different problems. The arguments denying the existence of separate substances stress the self-sufficiency of an eternally moving world of generable and corruptible beings; such a world has no need of any separate substances. In fact, as Averroes argues against the Platonists, there could be no efficient causal relationship between such substances and our world.[48]

After an appeal to the evident intention of Aristotle's proofs in Book Twelve of the *Metaphysics* and Book Eight of the *Physics*, Peter's argument *in oppositum* begins with a statement of Aristotle that in every genus there is something first and greatest which is the principle and measure of everything else in that genus. The argument affirms that this is the case in the genus of beings. It concludes that this "first," precisely as indivisible and non-accidental, must be a substance, and a separate or immaterial one at that.[49]

Peter begins his answer to the question by stating that Aristotle seems to have produced two arguments in this matter. The first, in Book Eight of the *Physics*, is based on the eternity of motion, while the second, in Book Two of the *Metaphysics*, is based on the order that obtains among efficient causes.[50]

The first demonstration, starting from the familiar axiom "Everything that is moved must be moved by another" and the manifest fact that we see something being moved, concludes to the existence of a something wholly immobile. Mindful of the question asked here, Peter concludes that this wholly immobile substance cannot in any way be material, and therefore we must posit the existence of separate substances.[51]

The second of the Aristotelian demonstrations, which Peter had identified as based on the order of efficient causes, is clearly located within the realm of Aristotelian moving causes. It is interesting that, in this question, Peter consistently couples the following terms: *in causis agentibus vel moventibus; agens sive movens; causa agens et movens prima.* We might also notice that Peter avoids any development of his conclusion that there is some immobile and immaterial substance, to Aristotle's next step, namely that there is a plurality of such substances.[52]

48 *Q. in Meta.* XII, 6c, below, p. 98.
49 Ibid. We will see in the following question how this argument, reminiscent of the *quarta via* of the *ST*, is seemingly downgraded by both Peter and the Munich text.
50 Ibid.
51 Ibid.
52 Ibid. p. 99.

Peter next offers a further demonstration for which he gives credit to Avicenna. Starting from the complete division of being into the possible and the necessary, and assuming that there exists some determinate being, he concludes to the necessity of positing some first being which is necessary of itself. Since this being is first, it must be simple and therefore prior to all composition, and thus immaterial. Once again Peter's conclusion is in the singular. [53]

Noteworthy among Peter's replies to the three arguments that deny the necessity of positing separate substances is his widening the scope of the discussion of an eternal world from the plane of "moving cause" to that of "agent causality." He agrees with the first argument's statement that "everything that is generated is generated by something similar to itself in name and in species," but he restricts this to the immediate cause of generation. Peter denies that such a causal explanation of our world can be sufficient. To be sufficient, it must include a cause of being as being, which cause is both first and being itself through its own substance, such that no other beings have existence except in so far as this first cause bestows being on them and also conserves them in being. [54]

Returning to our texts, let us consider their treatment of the question: Whether God (first principle) exists. With minor differences, there is a strict correspondence between the two arguments presented by the Munich text, Peter, and the *ST* to show that God (first principle) does not exist. [55] The first of these two arguments is based on the contrary to fact conclusion that evil would not exist if we posit the existence of God understood to be someone infinitely good. The reason for this is that, if one of two contraries were infinite, it would destroy the other. [56]

The second argument is based upon the assertion that since nature, for natural effects, and intellect or will, for rational effects, are sufficient causes to explain the totality of phenomena (*omnium apparentium*), there is no necessity to posit any further cause such as God (first principle). [57]

There is, however, a marked difference in their respective treatments of the arguments *contra*. The *ST* simply cites the text from Exodus: *Ego sum qui sum*, the author of the Munich text uses an argument similar to the *quarta via* of the *ST*, whereas Peter presents arguments paralleling both the fourth and fifth ways.

---

53   Ibid.
54   Ibid.
55   Since the *SCG* is not in the form of a *quaestio*, there can be no comparisons with it until we come to the actual examples of demonstrations.
56   Ed. Delhaye, 193; Peter of Auvergne, below, p. 101; St. Thomas, *ST* 1, 2, 3, obj. 1.
57   Ed. Delhaye, 193; Peter of Auvergne, below, p. 100; St. Thomas, *ST* 1, 2, 3, obj. 2.

The Munich text's presentation of the *quarta via* as merely one of its arguments *contra* would seem to imply a judgment that this kind of demonstration is not of sufficient quality to be included in the Master's own determination or solution of the question. Perhaps to him it had too strong a Platonic flavor, although it is here that Aquinas chose to make his only explicit reference to Aristotle in the *quinque viae*. Perhaps also, for our commentator, Aristotle's denial that "being" is a genus in the strict sense of the term, would preclude the use here of the Aristotelian principle cited in the *ST*, namely that *quod dicitur maxime tale in aliquo genere, est causa omnium quae sunt illius generis.*

At any event, the author of the Munich text avoids using the term "genus" and simply says that where there is a more and a less, there must be posited a greatest (*maxime tale*); now this is the case among beings, for there are greater and lesser beings, all of which are called "beings" by reference to a First Being; therefore there is a First Being whose nature it is to exist (*ens enim primum dicimus illud cujus ratione existere*).[58]

Peter of Auvergne also seems to demote the *quarta via* by making it the first example of his arguments *in oppositum*. He may have felt that this was fitting in a commentary on Aristotle, since even the *SCG* introduces this proof by saying only that it may "be gathered from the words of Aristotle" and that it requires a still further inference to reach the conclusion that there exists something that is supremely being whom we call God.[59]

Peter points to the Second and Fourth Books of Aristotle's *Metaphysics* for the principle that *in quocumque genere est ponere magis et minus tale, et simpliciter tale*. Now in the genus of beings there are some that are more and less perfect, so that we must posit in beings something that is most perfect, in the sense of absolutely, and in the prime instance, perfect. This is the first principle.[60]

The reluctance of these two commentators to include this argument among those contained in their personal resolutions of this question may reflect their greater professional sensitivity and fidelity to the text of the historical Aristotle than was the case with the less historical and freer theological perspectives of Aquinas's *ST* and *SCG*.

Peter's second argument *in oppositum* parallels the *quinta via*, which Aquinas says is based on the governance found among things, although

---

58 Ed. Delhaye, 193.
59 St. Thomas, *SCG* 1, 13, 34.
60 Peter of Auvergne, below, p. 101.

Peter does not mention the role of a directing intelligence for such governance. The argument's major premise is that among several things ordered with respect to one another, something one must be posited as first among them. For, as Proclus proved, every order both begins from, and terminates in, something one. Now there is an order among beings, as Aristotle proves further on; therefore there exists some one first being ordering them, whom we understand to be the first principle. [61]

Once again, there seems to be a downgrading of this proof as seen from its location within the structure of Peter's text. Perhaps one of his criteria for inclusion within his personal solution of the question was whether an argument had actually been used by some philosopher to prove the existence of a first principle or God. Even St. Thomas, in his *SCG*, intended its version of the *quinta via* to be an example of an argument whereby Catholic teachers proved that God exists, and indeed explicitly credits the Christian theologian, John Damascene, with it. [62]

We turn now to the treatment of the *prima via* by our three authors. All give basically the same argument from motion, and all see the need to link the conclusion, namely that some unmoved mover exists, to the further statement that this indeed is what we call "God" or "the first principle." [63]

The *secunda via* of each text, however, provides more striking comparisons. The Munich text and the *ST* announce that it is based upon the nature of efficient causality. Peter, however, says that it is based on the necessity of arriving at a First within an order of causes, and while he also concentrates on the order of efficient causality, he mentions the possibility of proving the existence of a first principle from the orders of formal and final causes. [64]

Further, while all our texts speak of an order of efficient causes, they use quite different terminology, a diversity that seems to reflect different preoccupations or concerns. As we noted above, Averroes and Avicenna held different views on the nature of efficient causality. Averroes was faithful to Aristotle in restricting this kind of causality to that which originates a change through motion. Avicenna was faithful to his own vision of reality by subordinating moving causality to a higher way of causing something to be, namely by creation. As Etienne Gilson has justifiably pointed out, if we assume that the *prima via* of St. Thomas concludes to the first efficient cause of motion, then the

---

61   Ibid.
62   St. Thomas, *SCG* 1, 13, 35.
63   Ed. Delhaye, 193-4; Peter of Auvergne, below, pp. 101-2. St. Thomas, *ST* 1, 2, 3.
64   Peter of Auvergne, below, p. 102.

secunda via becomes superfluous.[65] Why then did St. Thomas use the *secunda via*, and, in the *SCG*, even attribute it to Aristotle? And, a more important consideration for Thomas's contemporaries, if Averroes could endorse the *prima via* yet reject the *secunda via*, and if Avicenna reversed this position, how could Aquinas simply use them both?

Gilson's answer to this question concerns at its deepest level the fundamental attitude of Thomas Aquinas as a theologian toward philosophers and the progress of philosophy in search of truth:

> In effect, if one could demonstrate the existence of a First Unmoved Mover by the way of Averroes, and that of a First Efficient Cause by the way of Avicenna, the two ways are good because they both conclude to the existence of a First Being whom we name God. It matters little that their authors do not agree since, in the thought of Thomas himself, the moving cause is only one variety of efficient cause, namely the efficient cause of movement.[66]

Professors in the Faculty of Arts, however, charged with leading their students through the works of the great philosphers, could hardly adopt such a supra-philosophical perspective. Here, the author of the Munich text seems to fall into a trap. After announcing that his second demonstration is based *ex natura efficientis*, and that it is found in Book Two of Aristotle's *Metaphysics*, he asserts that an efficient cause does not move except in virtue of a First, with the result that if we posit no first mover (*primum movens*), there will be no other movers. Now since there are other movers, it is necessary to posit a First. This is the trap. Faithful as Averroes had been to the text of Aristotle, the author of the Munich text has given, not a second demonstration, but rather another variation of the *prima via*. He seeks to avoid this by adding a final sentence: "Since therefore it is evident that there exists some subsequent being (*aliquod posterius ens*), clearly there will be some first being (*aliquod ens primum*)."[67] The case of Peter of Auvergne is quite different. He had several times earlier in his work[68] made good use of the distinction between efficient causes *unde principium motus* and *unde principium esse*, and had identified the proof from motion as

65   E. Gilson, "Trois leçons sur le problème de l'existence de Dieu," *Divinitas* 5 (1961) 30-2.

66   Ibid., 60-1. See also 64-6 and especially note 7, 66.

67   Ed. Delhaye, 194. If the author of the Munich *Questions on Book Eight of the Physics* were also the author of the *Questions on Physics I-IV* published as one work by P. Delhaye, he could have used here the twofold efficient cause *unde principium motus* and *unde principium esse* developed in Book II, 12 (p. 100) together with the account given there to explain why Aristotle always defined efficient causality in terms of the *unde principium motus*.

68   Peter of Auvergne, *Q. in Meta.* III, 3 and III, 4. See my "Two Texts of Peter of Auvergne on a Twofold Efficient Cause," *Mediaeval Studies* 26 (1964) 287-301.

proper to the science of physics. An effect of God less remote from Him
than motion, namely the *esse* of changing things, could be used for a
different demonstration that would be proper to the science of
metaphysics.[69] Thus, when Peter begins his *secunda via*, he uses a different terminology in order to emphasize its distinction from the *prima
via*. He speaks of a *causa activa*, and takes as his starting point
something newly made (*quod hoc factum est de novo*) to arrive at a
faciens non factum who is first in the order of *causis agentibus*, and not
acted upon either *per se* or *per accidens*. Peter then adds that all understand this to be the first principle.[70]

The *tertia via* also reveals the close dependence of the Munich text
on the *ST*, together with a corresponding independence of Peter's text
vis à vis the *ST*. The *SCG* is, of course, not involved in the comparative
study of the *tertia via* for the simple reason that it is not found there.
Both commentaries explicitly attribute this proof to Avicenna and
follow the *ST* for its starting point, namely that we find in reality some
beings that are possible in that they are able to be and not to be. Peter
alone gives the example that Aquinas used in the *ST*: we experience
beings undergoing generation and corruption.[71]

But now there is a curious shift. St. Thomas, for his own reasons and
no doubt within the theological designs of his work, follows Moses
Maimonides in constructing from some remarks of Aristotle a demonstration that if all beings were corruptible, i.e., containing the
possibility not to be, then in an eternal world all such possibilities
would at some time come about, and thus at some time nothing at all
would exist. Both Maimonides and Aquinas conclude from this that
there must exist some being whose existence is not merely possible but
necessary. Both theologians further conclude from this that there exists
a necessary being whose necessity is uncaused, and indeed is the cause
of whatever necessity other beings have. This necessary being all call
"God" and, as a devout Jew, Maimonides adds, "may His name be
sublime."[72]

The author of the Munich text, though attributing this proof to
Avicenna, follows Aquinas in the Maimonidean blend of Avicenna and
Aristotle. He concludes to the existence of some being whose existence
is necessary, and further concludes to the existence of some being whose
necessity to exist is of itself, namely the first principle.[73]

---

69   *Q. in Meta.* I, 1; ed. Monahan, 154.
70   Ibid. XII, 6d. See below, p. 102.
71   Ed. Delhaye, 194; Peter of Auvergne, below, ibid.
72   St. Thomas, *ST* 1, 2, 3; See Moses Maimonides, *The Guide of the Perplexed*, II, 1, tr. S.
Pinès (Chicago 1963) 247-9.
73   Ed. Delhaye, 194.

Peter of Auvergne, however, after announcing the Avicennian pater-
nity of this proof, sticks more or less closely to the text of Avicenna.
Since nothing which is of itself indeterminate with respect to being or
not being can determine itself to be, every possible being that actually
exists is determined by another. That other has the necessary determination of its existence either from itself or from another. Since we
cannot push on indefinitely in these causal determinations of the
possibilities to exist, we must come to some being whose existence is
necessary of itself, which, Peter adds, we call the First Being. [74]

Here Peter adds some remarks which, had they counterparts in the
texts of Thomas Aquinas, might have simplified the attempts of count-
less historians to synthesize the *quinque viae*. [75] "Although," Peter says,
"the preceding demonstrations are different in words, nevertheless they
are essentially the same except for the fact that one is more universal,
the others less universal." Following this principle of communality or
universality, the *tertia via* is judged to be more common, followed by
the *secunda via* and last of all, the way from motion. [76]

We have already seen the philosophical reasons for this rating. In a
quia type of demonstrating the existence of a cause, there can be different demonstrations depending on the choice of effect as their starting
points. And depending on how much affinity, proportionality and near-
ness the effect has to the cause, the truer and more essential the demonstration of that cause will be. But what does Peter mean by saying that
one demonstration is "more common" or "universal" than another?

It would seem that, viewing God as a universal cause, i.e., as one
whose causal power extends to every being as to its effect, the most immediate effect of God's creative causality, namely being, would be the
most universal or common effect. The remainder of the effects of this
divine causality could then be ranked according to the number of intermediate or secondary causes required to produce it. Thus some effects could be considered as more remote and thus less universal or
common. This seems to reflect a neo-platonic influence such as the doctrine of the *Liber de Causis*, which holds that the first, in the sense of
the most immediate, effect of the Creator is *esse*, which is thus more
common, say, than the effects "life" or "rationality." Further, the view
that the demonstration based on the division of being into the possible
and the necessary is more common, i.e., as closer to the causality of the
First, than the demonstration based on the notion of the agent and its

---

74 Peter of Auvergne, below, pp. 102-3. Cf. Avicenna, *Meta.* I, 7, fol. 73r1-2.
75 See Gilson's remarks on these attempts in his "Trois leçons...," op. cit. 39-46.
76 Peter of Auvergne, below, p. 103.

effect (*ex ratione agentis et acti*) seems clearly to be of Avicennian parentage.

Continuing his theme of the basic similarity of the three proofs, Peter next says that they all rest on two principles: 1) that it is impossible for the same thing in the same respect to be at once in act and potency; 2) that their starting points are evident to the senses.[77]

The second of these two common principles is of interest for the subsequent history of how mediaeval theologians evaluated philosophical proofs for the existence of God. Given Peter of Auvergne's hierarchical ordering of the three proofs, with Avicenna's in first place because it is "more common" than the other two, historians might consider Peter to be a possible forerunner of the position taken by the theologian, Henry of Ghent, because Henry also expresses a preference for Avicenna over Aristotle. The reason for this preference, Henry tells us, is that Avicenna's proof proceeds *ex via propositionum universalium intelligibilium, non ex via testificationis sensibilium.*[78]

Peter's second principle, however, places him squarely in the empirical tradition of Aristotle and St. Thomas. Common to all three ways to prove the existence of God, Peter affirms, is the foundational principle that they are based on the sensible evidence that something in fact exists, namely as being moved, as causing something efficiently, and as possible.

What conclusions emerge from this brief study? First of all, given the selective use our authors made of the Thomistic texts, it would be quite rash to speak of an "early Thomistic school" within the Parisian Faculty of Arts. The author of the Munich *Questions on Book Eight of the Physics* does not manifest much awareness of the *SCG*; he follows more closely the order and treatment of the *ST* on the question of God's existence. He does adapt this treatment to the Faculty of Arts by eliminating its obvious theological elements. One notable failure, however, is the lack of any clear distinction between his first and second proofs. What made sense within the freer theological perspectives of Aquinas requires an explicit translation within its new context in a philosophical commentary.

Peter of Auvergne reveals a more magistral touch in his approach to Aquinas for help on the Aristotelian text. His selective use of both the *SCG* and the *ST* in dealing with this question of God's existence shows a greater familiarity with Aquinas's work than does the Munich text. It

---

77 Ibid.
78 Henry of Ghent, *Summa Quaestionum Ordinariarum Theologiae...* A. 22, q. 5 (Paris 1520) fol. 134v D. See the three-part article by A. C. Pegis, "Toward a New Way to God: Henry of Ghent," *Mediaeval Studies* 30 (1968) 226-247; 31 (1969) 93-116; 33 (1971) 158-179.

reveals also his appreciation that the purpose and method of the *SCG* makes it more adaptable to an audience in the Faculty of Arts. Peter's excursions beyond the letter and meaning of the Thomistic texts should be evaluated in their own right in terms of the independence and depth of his personal philosophy rather than, as in the past, in terms of his fidelity or infidelity to a supposed discipleship to Aquinas.

Finally, much work remains to identify the author of the Munich text, formerly ascribed to Siger of Brabant, and to evaluate in its own right the thought of Peter of Auvergne. One thing, however, is clear. We find here two Masters in the Faculty of Arts who do not hesitate to use the writings of a Master in the Faculty of Theology to further their work of interpreting the writings of the philosophers. And they do this at a time of great friction between their respective Faculties, just after one of Bishop Tempier's ecclesiastical condemnations of selected philosophical propositions and on the eve of another, more massive, condemnation. Thus, the choice of Aquinas by these two commentators as the theologian to help them handle the controverted question of how a philosopher deals with the question of God's existence is a factual confirmation of the sentiments so movingly expressed in the letter from the Masters in the Faculty of Arts on the occasion of the death of Thomas Aquinas.

TEXT

While there are eleven manuscripts known to contain Peter of Auvergne's *Quaestiones in Metaphysicam*,[1] I have chosen to edit the following four questions from Book XII as they are found in a single manuscript, Vienna lat. 2330, fol. 95rl-96rl.[2] There are a number of reasons for this choice. First of all, the first three of these four questions are not found in any of the other manuscripts. However, a marginal note in the Vienna text explains that they are taken *ex reportatione antiqua*.[3] Secondly, the manuscript which I have used as a basic text in editing other questions from this work, namely Paris, BN lat. 16158, fol. 163rl-258v2, breaks off abruptly just before the *solutio* of our fourth question. Further, the Vienna text does not contain any significant variations from the six manuscripts containing this latter question, with the exception of three brief passages which I call attention to in my apparatus. Finally, the Vienna text appears to be the oldest one we have. There is both internal evidence for a *terminus a quo* of 1274[4] and external evidence for a conjectured *terminus ad quem* of 1277.[5]

---

1   Until recently, we knew of only seven of them, which are listed and briefly described in my "Two Texts of Peter of Auvergne on a Twofold Efficient Cause," *Mediaeval Studies* 26 (1964) 288-9. C. J. Ermatinger first called my attention to two more manuscripts containing this work of Peter. The first, Vatican, Pal. lat. 1059, fol. 1rl-9v2, contains Peter's commentary on Books I-II, while the second, Vat. lat. 2173, fol. 78rl-209vl, has a collection of questions on Books I-IX and XII culled from the works of three or four authors, including Peter, whose questions comprise four of the six questions of Book VIII, all but one in Book IX, and all of those in Book XII. A. Zimmerman, in his *Ontologie oder Metaphysik?* (Cologne 1965) 211, first pointed to Peter as the author of the *Commentary on the Metaphysics* I-IX found in ms Oxford Merton College 292, fol. 240rl-323v2, hitherto tentatively ascribed to Simon of Faversham, and to a truncated version of Peter's work in ms Cambridge Peterhouse 152, fol. 117rl-127rl, which breaks off at question 23 (not 17) of Book I. While these recent discoveries add little to the purpose of this article, they do provide much information of assistance in investigating the complex relationships that obtain at least among the three versions of Peter's work that have come down to us.

2   See the extensive inventory of this manuscript by the Dominican scholars, A. Dondaine and L. J. Bataillon, "Le manuscrit Vindob. lat. 2330 et Siger de Brabant," *Archivum Fratrum Praedicatorum* 36 (1966) 153-261.

3   Fol. 95rl.

4   There is a textual reference in XII, 6d to Simplicius's *Commentary on the De Caelo* which, while translated by William of Moerbeke as early as June, 1271 and apparently promised to the Parisian Faculty of Arts by Thomas Aquinas, had not been received by them at the time they wrote their remarkable letter to the Dominican General Chapter at Lyons in May, 1274.

5   The external evidence involves the alteration of attributions of four works from Siger of Brabant to Peter of Auvergne in an index to the manuscript, plus two cryptograms in the upper margins of two of the works identifying them as actually belonging to Siger. See the cautious conjectures by Dondaine and Bataillon, op. cit., 154-60 and 176. They describe them as "particulièrement fragile," but they do indicate that the alterations could be linked to the period following the Parisian condemnation of 1277.

PETRI DE ALVERNIA

Quaestiones in Metaphysicam
Liber XII, Quaestio 6a

Utrum substantias separatas esse sit manifestum ex se.

Sed quoniam tres erant substantiae, etc. [1]

Quaeritur circa partem istam in qua Philosophus incipit determinare de primis principiis substantiarum quae sunt substantiae sempiternae* et a materia separatae. Probat autem Philosophus quod necesse est esse aliquam substantiam sempiternam, immobilem, semper agentem et actu existentem, iterum immaterialem omnino. Et quia talis substantia ponitur esse principium primum, ideo quaeritur circa illud, utrum sit ponere principium primum.

Sed ante hoc quaeratur universaliter de substantiis separatis, utrum scilicet ex se sit manifestum aliquas substantias separatas esse.

[1] Quod sic videtur: Nulla propositio verior et manifestior est illa in qua idem de se praedicatur. Sed ista est hujusmodi, "Substantiae separatae sunt," quia omne quod praedicatur de substantiis separatis nihil est aliud quam substantia ipsarum, saltem de prima substantia. Quare manifestum est ex se aliquas esse substantias separatas.

[2] Item, quae naturaliter sunt nota, ex se nota sunt et manifesta. Substantiae autem separatae notae sunt naturaliter. Quod enim secundum naturas suas notae sint, patet secundo hujus;[2] vocat enim Aristoteles eas manifestas in natura. Quod etiam nobis naturaliter notae sint, patet, quia cognitio earum naturaliter appetitur a nobis, cum felicitas et summa perfectio humana consistat in cognitione principiorum separatorum; et unumquodque naturaliter appetit suam perfectionem. Patet ergo quod universaliter cognitio substantiarum separatarum naturaliter appetitur a nobis. Et cum nullus appetitus sit frustra, oportet quod ipsae sint naturaliter nobis notae.

Oppositum arguitur: Illud non est ex se manifestum in cujus cognitione contingit errare, sicut voluit Aristoteles quarto hujus.[3] Haec enim est ratio prin-

---

* Following the other MSS. The Vienna MS. reads *separatae*.

1 Aristotle, *Meta.* XII, 6, 1071 b3.
2 Aristotle, *Meta.* II, 1, 993 b11.
3 *Meta.* IV, 3, 1005 b11-14.

cipii per se noti, quod circa ipsum non contingat errare. Multi enim philosophorum circa principia erraverunt. Posuit enim Empedocles universaliter principia prima agentia esse litem et amicitiam; alii autem posuerunt alia.

Ad hoc est intelligendum dictum aliquorum, quod consideratio substantiarum separatarum, cum sint separatae, frivola est, quia viso quid est quod significatur per nomen, statim manifestum est ipsas esse. Et istud dictum habent ex consuetudine quae quasi quaedam natura est. Quia enim ex principio aetatis nostrae consuemus audire ab aliis quod sunt aliquae substantiae separatae, et ipse Deus, ideo istud quasi nobis naturaliter est notum; et ideo credimus ex se manifestum esse quod sint aliquae substantiae separatae.[4]

Notandum tamen est quod aliqua notiora sunt secundum naturam suam, ut simplicia magis et quae magis habent rationem actus. Alia autem sunt notiora nobis, ignotiora autem secundum naturam suam, ut composita quae sunt propinquiora sensibilibus; et cognitio nostra ex sensibilibus ortum habet.

Dicendum ergo est ad quaestionem quod substantiae separatae secundum naturam suam manifestissimae sunt, ut quod maxime rationem actus habent; nobis autem immanifestae, ut quod sunt a sensibilibus remotae. Et hoc dicit Aristoteles secundo hujus,[5] quod intellectus noster se habet ad manifestissima in natura sicut oculus vespertilionis ad lucem solis.

Ad primam rationem dicitur quod haec propositio, "Substantiae separatae sunt," manifestissima est secundum naturam suam, nobis autem non. Vel dicendum quod propositio illa in qua idem de se praedicatur manifestissima est cum rationes terminorum nobis manifestae sunt; hujus autem propositionis rationes terminorum nobis manifestissimae non sunt. Non enim nobis manifestissimae sunt substantiae separatae, nec omne quod de ipsis praedicatur.

Ad aliud dicitur quod illa quae naturaliter nota sunt, ex se sunt manifesta secundum naturam suam, nobis autem non sunt manifesta, (fol. 95r2) ut dictum est. Et quod arguitur, quod nobis sunt etiam manifestae substantiae separatae, dicendum quod cognitio ipsarum naturaliter appetitur a nobis. Et cum appetitus sive desiderium non sit respectu habenti sed magis respectu habendi, concludi potest quod non habemus cognitionem substantiarum separatarum secundum quod in natura sua sunt cognoscibiles.

Quaestio 6b

Utrum possit demonstrari substantias separatas esse.

Consequenter, quaeritur utrum substantias separatas esse possunt demonstrari.

[1] Videtur quod non: quod quid est enim principium est demonstrationis; nunc autem in substantiis separatis idem est quod quid est et etiam ipsum esse. Non enim est aliquid in eis quod non pertineat ad quod quid est ipsarum.

---

4 Cf. St. Thomas, *SCG* I, 10, 1 and I, 11, 1.
5 *Meta.* II, 1, 993 b9-11.

Cum ergo non contingat idem ex seipso demonstrari, non contingit demonstrari esse ipsas substantias separatas.

[2] Item, principium cujuscumque demonstrationis est definitio. Substantiarum autem separatarum non est definitio; sicut enim patet ex septimo hujus,[1] substantiae simplicis non est definitio. Quare, etc.

In oppositum est opinio omnium philosophorum. Probat enim Aristoteles hic, et etiam octavo *Physicorum*,[2] quod necesse est esse aliquas substantias separatas.

Ad hoc est dicendum quod dupliciter est demonstratio, sicut patet ex primo *Posteriorum*,[3] scilicet 'quia' et 'propter quid'. Demonstrare autem propter quid est demonstrare effectum per causam, et illa est demonstratio potissima. Alia est demonstratio quae est quia, quae demonstrat causam per effectum. Prima autem demonstratio procedit ex notioribus secundum naturam ad ignotiora secundum naturam. Secunda autem procedit ex ignotioribus secundum naturam, notioribus tamen nobis, ad notiora secundum naturam, ignotiora quoad nos.

Dicendum ergo quod substantia prima non potest demonstrari esse demonstratione 'propter quid' quia ejus non est altera causa. Potest tamen demonstrari ex effectibus ejus qui nobis manifesti sunt. Possumus enim ex istis aliquo modo demonstrare causam primam esse, quamvis causa prima sit super omnem narrationem, sicut scribitur *Libro de Causis*;[4] et hoc quantum est ex natura sua et ex se. Potest tamen in narratione nostra cadere secundum analogiam ad alias causas primas. Medium autem quo possunt substantiae separatae demonstrari est definitio significans quid est quod dicitur per nomen. Nomen autem ipsarum sumptum est ex eis quae sunt principia cognoscendi ipsarum. Haec autem sunt sensibilia ab ipsis causata.

Ad primam rationem dicendum quod ad demonstrandum non accipitur pro principio quod quid est quod est tota substantia ipsius, quia ipsum praesupponit esse. Quaestio enim 'quid est' praesupponit quaestionem 'si est', ut patet ex secundo *Posteriorum*.[5] Sed ad demonstrandum esse de aliquo debet accipi pro medio definitio significans quid est quod dicitur per nomen.

Ad secundam rationem dicendum quod, etsi substantiae separatae non possint habere definitionem significantem quid est ipsius rei, quia solum talis definitio est substantiae compositae ut patet ex septimo hujus,[6] substantiae tamen separatae potest esse definitio quae significat quid est quod dicitur per nomen. Haec autem definitio medium est ad demonstrandum aliquid de ipsis.

---

1 *Meta.* VII, 15, 1040 a9.
2 Cf. *Phy.* VIII, 6.
3 Aristotle, *Anal. Post.* I, 13, 78 a22.
4 *Liber de Causis*, prop. VI.
5 Aristotle, *Anal. Post.* II, 1, 89 b34.
6 Cf. *Meta.* VII, 15.

Quaestio 6c

Utrum necesse sit ponere substantias separatas.

Consequenter, quaeritur utrum necesse sit ponere substantias aliquas separatas.

[1] Quod non videtur, quia si sic, aut hoc esset propter generationem entium aut propter conservationem. Non propter generationem, quia omne quod generatur, generatur ex sibi simili nomine et specie, et ex materia quae manet in re generati. Substantiae autem separatae non conveniunt cum substantiis inferioribus generabilibus et corruptibilibus nomine et specie, nec etiam sunt materia ipsorum. Quare non est necesse ipsas ponere propter generationem ipsorum entium nec etiam propter conservationem ipsorum in esse, quia sicut res esse consequitur ex principiis suis intrinsecis ita ex eisdem potest conservari in esse; eadem enim sunt principia dantia esse et conservantia in esse. Quare, etc.

[2] Item, non necesse habemus ponere substantias separatas nisi propter transmutationem istorum inferiorum generabilium contingentiarum. Nunc autem ipsae non possunt esse principia transmutationis substantiarum materialium, quia immateriale non transmutat materiale, sicut Commentator vult septimo hujus[1] contra Platonem.

[3] Item, non ponit Aristoteles substantias separatas immobiles et aeternas nisi ut sint principia motus aeterni. Sed propter hoc non est eas necesse ponere. Virtus enim in magnitudine aeternaliter alterat ista inferiora. Quare propter motum non est necesse ponere substantias immateriales aeternas.

Oppositum patet ex intentione Aristotelis in libro isto et octavo *Physicorum*.[2]

Item, in unoquoque genere est aliquod primum et maximum* quod est principium et mensura omnium eorum quae sunt in genere illo, ut visum est decimo hujus.[3] Et sic est in genere entium. Et hoc est indivisibile, ut patet in eodem decimo.[4] Istud autem primum non potest esse aliquod corpus nec aliquod materiale quoniam tunc esset divisibile. Quare, etc. Item, nec potest esse aliquod accidens, quoniam accidens non est principium esse ipsius substantiae. Est ergo substantia immobilis et immaterialis.

Ad hoc dicendum quod necesse est ponere aliquas substantias separatas. Et ad hoc videtur Aristoteles adducere duas rationes, quarum prima est ex aeternitate motus, ut in octavo *Physicorum*,[5] alia ex ordine causarum efficientium ad invicem, secundo hujus.[6]

Prima autem demonstrationum est haec. Omne quod movetur, necesse est ab alio moveri, sicut probatum est septimo *Physicorum*.[7] Nunc autem videmus

---

* MS. reads *minimum*.
1 Averroes, *In VII Meta.* c. 28 (Venice 1574) fol. 178 C.
2 Cf. *Phy.* VIII, 6.
3 *Meta.* X, 1, 1052 b18-20.
4 Ibid. 1052 a30-1.
5 Cf. *Phy.* VIII, 1.
6 *Meta.* II, 2, 994 al-19.
7 *Phy.* VII, 1, 241 b24-242 a15.

aliqua manifeste moveri. Ergo ab alio moventur. Et istud aliud aut movetur aut est immobile. Si movetur, ulterius ab alio movebitur et eadem erit quaestio de illo alio sicut prius. Et ita vel procedetur in infinitum in mobilibus et motis, quod probatum est esse impossibile in septimo *Physicorum*[8] et secundo hujus,[9] aut erit tandem devenire ad aliquid immobile penitus. Istud autem non potest esse aliqua substantia materialis quoniam omnis talis mobilis est, cum materia sit principium passivum transmutationis. Necesse ergo habemus ponere substantias separatas praeter motum ipsum.

Alia demonstratio Aristotelis est quia in essentialiter ordinatis, primum movens est causa omnium moventium posteriorum, ut si A moveat B, et B moveat C, tunc A movet B per se et movet C per ipsum B. Aut ergo in mobilibus et motis erit devenire ad movens primum aut in ipsis procedetur in infinitum. Si procedatur in infinitum, cum in infinitis non sit primum, et in essentialiter ordinatis (fol. 95vl) si non est primum, nec est aliquod posteriorum quia primum causa est omnibus posterioribus, ut dictum est; et ita si in causis agentibus vel moventibus sit processus in infinitum, sequitur quod penitus non sit agens sive movens, quod est omnino impossibile. Necesse est ergo ponere aliquam substantiam quae sit causa agens et movens prima ómnium aliorum entium. Illa autem non potest esse substantia mobilis et materialis. Quare ex ordine causarum agentium necesse habemus ponere aliquam substantiam immobilem et immaterialem.

Avicenna etiam in *Metaphysica* sua[10] aliam demonstrationem adducit, quae sumitur ex parte necessitatis ipsius esse. Omne enim quod est aut ex se necesse est esse aut ex se possibile esse. Necesse enim et possibile totum ens universaliter evacuant et dividunt. Sumatur ergo aliquod ens determinatum. Quaero aut illud necesse est esse ex se aut possibile est esse. Si primo modo, tunc ex seipso determinatur ad esse, et tunc erit ens primum. Et si sic, tunc de necessitate erit substantia simplex et immaterialis, quia quacumque substantia materiali et composita est aliquid prius, saltem componentia ipsa. Quare, etc.

Si autem illud ens ex se tantum possibile sit esse, tunc ex se non determinatur ad esse, sed ex alio. Et tunc eadem fiet quaestio de illo alio sicut de isto. Et ita vel procedetur in infinitum, quod est impossibile, vel tandem devenietur ad aliquod ens primum quod ex se est necessarium; et tale erit substantia immobilis et immaterialis, ut prius ostensum est.

Ad primam rationem dicendum quod substantiae separatae necessariae sunt, et propter productionem entium in esse et propter conservationem* eorum in esse. Non enim producitur aliquod causatum in esse nisi ex causa sufficiente. Non est autem causa sufficiens in istis transmutabilibus antequam reducantur ad transmutans intransmutabile, ut probatum est octavo *Physicorum.*[11] Et ideo quamvis omne quod generatur ex sibi simili nomine et specie generetur quantum ad generans immediatum, istud tamen non potest

---

* MS. reads *productionem*.

8 Ibid.

9 *Meta.* II, 2, 994 a11-19.

10 Avicenna, *Meta.* I, 7 (Venice 1508) fol. 73rl-vl.

11 Cf. Aristotle, *Phy.* VIII, 1.

esse causa sufficiens antequam reducatur in causam primam quae quidem est ipsum esse per substantiam suam. Et ideo causa est entis secundum quod ens. Et ita alia ab ipso non sunt entia nisi inquantum largitur eis esse; sic et ea conservat in esse.

Ad secundam dicitur quod dupliciter est transmutatio: quaedam quae est aeterna quae solum est motus localis, et hujusmodi tantum circularis, ut probatur octavo *Physicorum*;[12] quaedam autem sunt transmutationes quae non possunt esse aeternae aequaliter, ut generatio et corruptio et hujusmodi. Cum ergo dicit Commentator[13] quod immateriale non transmutat materiale, dicendum quod verum est immediate nisi mediate corpore intransmutabili secundum substantiam suam, transmutabili tamen secundum ubi. Haec autem transmutatio aeterna est; et ita substantiae separatae non possunt immediate transmutare aliquid transmutabile transmutatione non aeterna. Transmutare tamen possunt aliquid transmutabile transmutatione aeterna.

Ad aliud dicitur quod motus aeternus non sit nisi a virtute infinita. Omnis autem virtus in magnitudine existens, finita est. Et haec probata sunt octavo *Physicorum*,[14] ex quibus in fine concludit Aristoteles[15] quod movens primum non est virtus in magnitudine. Et quod arguitur de sole et aliis corporibus superioribus, quod aeternaliter alterant ista inferiora, dicendum quod hoc non est nisi in virtute moventis primi, quod est virtutis infinitae; quod etiam necesse est ex se modo agendi. Omnia autem alia necessaria ex se sunt modo recipiendi, sicut dicit Commentator supra octavum *Physicorum*.[16]

Quaestio 6d

Utrum sit ponere primum principium in entibus.

Consequenter quaeritur, descendendo specialiter ad primam substantiam quae omnium primum principium, quamvis de hoc dictum sit, utrum scilicet sit ponere primum principium.

[1] Videtur quod non: Primum principium non ponitur esse nisi ex ipso possint reddi causae omnium eorum quae fiunt hic. Si ergo aliquo modo possint reddi causae omnium apparentium et eorum quae fiunt aliter quam ponendo primum principium, non erit tunc necesse ponere ipsum. Nunc autem hoc bene contingit; eorum enim quae fiunt a natura, natura est sufficiens principium et causa. Naturaliter enim homo ab homine generatur et equus ab equo, nec oportet illud reducere in principium aliud. Eorum etiam quae fiunt ab intellectu, intellectus est causa seu voluntas. Quare cum omnia quae fiunt per se, fiant hoc modo vel illo, manifestum autem est quod non necesse est ponere aliud principium ab istis. Quare, etc.

---

12 Cf. ibid. 7-9.
13 Averroes, *In VII Meta.* c. 28, fol. 178 C.
14 Aristotle, *Phy.* VIII, 10, 267 b19-26.
15 Ibid.
16 Averroes, *In VIII Phy.* c. 83, fol. 432 C-D.

[2] Item, per primum principium intelligimus aliquid optimum. Probat enim Philosophus consequenter[1] ipsum esse optimum. Sed impossibile est aliquid optimum esse in natura quia optimum est quod est bonum infinitum; si autem unum contrariorum infinitum esset, corrumperet alterum, ut dicitur tertio *Physicorum*.[2] Quare cum tali bono infinito contrarietur malum, si poneretur esse tale bonum in entibus, tunc malum penitus non esset. Excludere autem malum ab entibus omnino est inconveniens. Quare inconveniens est ponere aliquid quod sit optimum in natura. Principium autem primum est tale quod est optimum. Quare, etc.

Oppositum arguitur: In quocumque genere est ponere magis et minus tale et simpliciter tale, ut dicitur secundo et quarto hujus.[3] Sed in genere entium sunt quaedam magis et minus perfecta. Quare est ponere in entibus aliquid perfectissimum quod simpliciter et primo est tale. Hoc autem est principium primum. Quare, etc.

Item, in quibuscumque est ponere aliqua plura habentia ordinem ad se invicem, in eis est ponere aliquod unum primum. Omnis enim ordinatio ab uno incipit et secundum unitatem terminatur sibi coelementarem, ut probat Proclus.[4] Sed ordo est in entibus. Omnia enim ordinata sunt, ut consequenter probabit Philosophus.[5] Ergo est unum primum ordinans ea. Illud autem non intelligimus esse nisi primum principium. Quare, etc.

Primum principium esse in entibus manifeste declaratur ex motu. Secundum enim Aristotelem in *Physicis*,[6] omne quod movetur, ab alio movetur; quia movens secundum quod movens in actu est, motum autem secundum quod hujusmodi est in potentia. Si ergo impossibile est unum et idem esse in actu et in potentia primo, impossibile erat unum et idem primo habere rationem moventis et moti et respectu ejusdem. Manifestum est autem aliquid moveri in entibus, puta solem; quare ab alio movetur. Aut ergo illud aliud est movens immobile omnino, aut est movens mobile. Si est movens omnino immobile per se et per accidens, tunc illud est simpliciter primum, et ita erit ponere primum simpliciter. Si autem est mobile, tunc ab alio movetur vel per se vel per accidens, (fol. 95v2) et tunc fiet quaestio de illo alio. Aut enim est mobile movens aut movens immobile penitus; si secundo modo, tunc est primum simpliciter, si primo modo tunc fiet quaestio eadem.[7] Quare vel procedetur in infinitum vel erit devenire ad movens penitus immobile. Procedere autem in infinitum in moventibus et motis est impossibile, quia in quibus non est primum, nec aliquod posteriorum, et loquor in essentialiter ordinatis. Si ergo

---

1 Aristotle, *Meta.* XII, 7, 1072 b14-29.

2 Aristotle, *Phy.* III, 5, 204 b24-29.

3 Cf. *Meta.* II, 1, 993 b19-30; *Meta.* IV, 2.

4 Proclus, *Elementatio Theologica*, prop. XXI; ed. C. Vansteenkiste *Tijdschrift Voor Philosophie* 13 (1951) 273.

5 Aristotle, *Meta.* XII, 10, 1075 a16-19.

6 *Phy.* VIII, 1, 241 b24.

7 This sentence differs markedly from the text of the other manuscripts containing this question. There are two other instances in this question (see n. 9 and n. 12) where the Vienna text goes its own way, usually in the direction of a more concise treatment. In these three places, the other manuscripts contain many variant readings among themselves as well as many scribal errors.

in moventibus et motis procedatur in infinitum, cum in infinitis non sit
primum, quare non erit primum movens aliquod, et per consequens nullum;
auferetur ergo motus in entibus. Cum ergo videamus entia movere et moveri,
manifestum est quod non procedetur in infinitum in moventibus et motis. Erit
ergo devenire ad aliquod primum movens immobile per se et per accidens.
Hoc autem dicimus esse primum principium. Quare ipsum necesse est ponere
in entibus.

Hoc etiam probatur ratione magis universali, quae potest haberi ex dictis
Philosophi secundo hujus,[8] ubi probat statum in causis. Nam impossibile est
quod aliquid sit causa activa sui ipsius; tunc enim respectu ejusdem primo
esset in actu et in potentia. Omne ergo quod est actum, ab alio primo est actum. Sed manifestum est quod aliquid primo est actum, puta quod hoc factum
est de novo; quare ipsum est actum ab alio. Et tunc de illo quaeram: aut est
[f]actum faciens* aut non est factum faciens eam. †Si est faciens non factum,
tunc ipsum de necessitate primum est, et habetur propositum. Si autem est
faciens factum, tunc factum est ab alio priori, et de illo fiet eadem quaestio.
Et sic vel procedetur in infinitum vel standum erit in aliquo quod est faciens
non factum, per se vel per accidens. Procedere autem in infinitum in causis
agentibus est impossibile propter[9] eamdem rationem quae prius dicta est, quia
tunc non esset agens aliquod, quod est impossibile. Erit ergo dare aliquod
agens quod non sit actum, nec per se nec per accidens,[9] sed est agens omnia
alia et ipsum non est actum ab alio. Hoc autem omnes intelligunt primum
principium; quare necesse est esse tale in entibus.

Sicut autem primum principium probatur esse ex causis agentibus, ita etiam
posset probari ex statu in causis finalibus et formalibus. Forma enim prima
omnium et terminus ultimus est primum principium, quod secundum se ipsum
bonum est, et omnia alia boni rationem et appetibilis habent ex ipso.

Avicenna[10] autem aliam rationem adducit ad probandum primum principium, quae sumitur ex ratione possibilis et necessarii. Et est propria huic
scientiae quidquid dicat Commentator[11] contra ipsum. Necessarium enim et
possibile consequuntur totum ens secundum quod ens. Arguit autem sic: In entibus est aliquid possibile, quod etiam transmutatio ostendit, puta generatio et
corruptio in ipsis entibus. Generatio enim et corruptio, et universaliter omnis
transmutatio, inest alicui secundum hoc quod in potentia est, quia motus est
actus entis in potentia. Quare in entibus est aliquid quod possibile est esse.
Quod autem tantum possibile est esse, ex se non determinat se ad esse, quia
nihil quod de se indeterminatum est ad esse et non esse, ex se determinatur ad
esse. Quare determinatur a quodam alio. Et illud vel est necessarium ex se vel
ex alio. Si sit necessarium ex se, tunc ipsum est primum; hoc enim dicimus
primum quod ex se necesse est esse. Si autem determinetur ad esse, vel sit
necessarium ex alio, tunc respectu illius est possibile, et tunc fiet quaestio de

---

*   faciens: i.m.
†   est factum faciens eam: i.m.
8   Aristotle, *Meta.* II, 2.
9   See above, n. 7.
10   Avicenna, *Meta.* 1, 7, fol. 73rl-vl.
11   Averroes, *In I Phy.* c. 83, fol. 47 F-H; *In VII Phy.* c. 3, fol. 340 E-F.

illo respectu cujus dicitur esse possibile. Et sic vel procedetur in infinitum vel
devenietur ad aliquid quod sit necessarium ex se. Illud autem dicimus esse
primum principium. Quare, etc.

Rationes autem praetactae, etsi diversificentur in verbis, eaedem tamen
sunt secundum se, nisi quod una est communior, altera autem minus communis. Ratio enim quae sumitur ex possibili et necessario communior est,
deinde vero illa quae sumitur ex ratione agentis et acti. Minus autem communis est illa quae sumitur ex ratione moventis et moti.

Et omnes istae rationes fundantur super hoc, quod impossibile est idem
respectu ejusdem esse primo actu et potentia; super hoc etiam quod
manifestum est ad sensum quod aliquid est possibile in entibus, et quod
aliquid agit et movetur.

Ad rationem autem, cum arguitur "principium primum non ponitur nisi ut
ex ipso possint reddi causae eorum quae fiunt," dico quod verum est. Et cum
dicitur quod hoc contingit facere etsi primum non sit, dico quod falsum est. Et
ad probationem, cum dicitur "eorum quae fiunt natura, natura est principium
et causa," dico quod natura non est tota causa. Est enim natura principium ac-
tivum in virtute alterius activi primi, quia opus naturae est opus intelligentiae.
Non est igitur natura prima causa eorum quae natura fiunt.

Nec est etiam intellectus sufficiens causa eorum quae fiunt ex proposito,
cum ex se non habeat quod sic operetur, sed in virtute prioris. Unde est quasi
causa media inter ea quae fiunt ab eo et inter causam priorem dantem sibi
primum esse et virtutem qua operatur. Sicut igitur nulla causa intermedia est
sufficiens causa effectus, sic intellectus non est sufficiens causa eorum quae
fiunt ab eo.

Ad aliud, cum dicitur si[12] sit ponere primum tunc et optimum, dico quod
verum est. Et cum dicitur non est tale ponere,[12] dico quod immo. Et cum
dicitur "si unum contrariorum esset infinitum corrumpere[t] alterum, et sic
auferetur totaliter malum in entibus," dico quod si unum contrarium esset infinitum existens in natura corrumperet suum contrarium si ipsum ageret ex
necessitate naturae suae, ut ignis agit in aquam et calidum in frigidum. Si
tamen agat secundum rationem cognitionis et per intellectum, non oportet
quod agat ad corruptionem sui contrarii. Sed sic aget secundum quod accepit
agendum esse circa ipsum. Primum autem principium agit per intellectum et
cognitionem; ideo non agit excludendo malum nisi secundum praecon-
ceptionem et ordinem suae scientiae. Quia igitur est conceptum non ex-
stirpandum esse omnino malum si universum debeat manere, quia multa sunt
bona quae sine malo non eveniunt, ut generatio hujus vel illius est quoddam
bonum et tamen generatio hujus est corruptio alterius. Et hoc idem dicit Simplicius, auctoritate Platonis, fine secundi *Caeli et Mundi*.[13] Ideo contingit

---

12 See above, n. 7.

13 Cf. Simplicius, *In Aristotelis de Caelo Commentaria* I, 12. The latin edition, Venice 1544,
was not available to me. However, the latin text of the passage cited by Peter of Auvergne is contained in the greek edition of Simplicius, ed. I. L. Heiberg (Berlin 1894) 364. The editor explains
the presence of this latin text in the following note: "finem libri primi, quem omisit editio Venata
e cod. Collegii Balliolensis Oxon. 99 sumpsi."

quod primum agens, quamvis fuerit optimum, non tamen agit corrumpendo totaliter malum.

Vel potest dici (fol. 96rl) aliter ad rationem, quod videlicet bonum et malum non sunt contraria sed sunt privativa; malum enim est privatio boni. Et ideo falsum accepit ratio illa.

Alio autem modo potest dici sicut aliqualiter tactum est: cum dicitur "si est aliqualiter optimum in entibus tunc corrumpet malum," dico quod verum est sicut possibile est ipsum corrumpi. Non enim agens agit nisi quod est possibile agi, nec corrumpit nisi quod possibile est corrumpi. Nunc autem, manente ordine universi, impossibile est malum universaliter corrumpi; oportet enim generationem et corruptionem existere in entibus. Non autem existerent si auferetur ratio mali.

Item, in motu primo aliqualiter reperitur ratio mali. Acquisitio enim unius ubi est corruptio alterius. Corruptio autem malum est. Non ergo est possibile malum universaliter excludi ab entibus.

CERTITUDE OF REASON AND FAITH
IN ST. BONAVENTURE AND ST. THOMAS

John Francis Quinn C.S.B.

AS a doctor and master of theology, Thomas Aquinas taught without interruption from 1256 to 1274, the year of his death. During those years, he produced an extraordinary number of writings in which he treated many problems several times, including the certitude of reason and faith. Although St. Bonaventure also died in 1274, his teaching as a doctor and master of theology lasted only from 1254 to 1257, the year of his election as Minister General of the Franciscan Order. Because the period of his teaching was short, Bonaventure did not produce as many writings as Aquinas, nor did he have the opportunities that Aquinas had to handle repeatedly the critical problems of their day. As Minister General of his Order, however, Bonaventure managed to write some mystical treatises and, from 1267 to 1273, to review some crucial problems, particularly the problem of certitude, in theological conferences at the University of Paris when it was seriously disturbed by the teaching of some unorthodox Christians, notably Siger of Brabant and Boethius of Dacia. In view of the historical circumstances differentiating the teaching careers of Bonaventure and Aquinas, we are obliged to approach the certitude of reason and faith in Aquinas on the basis of those texts in Bonaventure that can be used to compare the doctrine of the one with the other. Hence beginning with the doctrine of Bonaventure, we shall compare with it the doctrine of Aquinas inasmuch as his texts deal with the same aspects of the problem in question.

According to Bonaventure, there are four different kinds of certitude. The first kind comes from demonstration and is so compelling that a man, though unwilling, must assent to the truth of the demonstration. When certitude of this sort predominates, faith is made void. The second kind depends on authority and generates faith, as Augustine says: "What we believe we owe to authority."[1] Since the doctrine of

---

[1] *De utilitate credendi*, 11. 5 in Migne, *Patrologia latina* (PL), v. 42, c. 83 (42.83): this collection will be noted as the parentheses indicate.

Scripture is intended to generate faith, therefore, because an end imposes a necessity on the means, Scripture has a certitude of authority. This is why the teaching of Scripture is transmitted by way of narration rather than by means of reason, or demonstration, for faith arises from free assent. Although the certitude of authority has little weight in the human sciences, because men often lie, it has great force in Scripture which comes from the Holy Spirit, who can never lie. The third kind of certitude, perfecting and consummating faith, is due to an interior illumination pertaining to the gift of grace. The fourth kind, following faith, is the certitude of persuasion resulting from the use of suitable and efficacious reasons to bring about an understanding of the objects of belief. Bonaventure is referring here to the certitude of knowledge in the doctors of theology, whose writings contain reasons and arguments both strengthening and nourishing Christian faith while terminating in an understanding of its truth.[2]

The certitude of demonstration has to do with the human sciences, which are formed by the natural power of reason. Thus, our first topic is the certitude of natural reason in general, of human science in particular, and so we are dealing specifically with the certitude of natural knowledge. Both the certitude of authority in Scripture and the certitude of illumination in faith belong to the order of divine revelation, which is given by the power of the Holy Spirit. Since the Christian accepts divine revelation by an infused virtue of faith, our second topic consists in the certitude of infused knowledge obtained through faith and sustained by the doctrine of Scripture. The certitude of persuasion pertaining to theology depends primarily on the articles or principles of faith, presupposing the authority of Scripture, and secondarily on the principles of reason. Consequently, our third topic, completing the first and second, will be the certitude of theological knowledge.[3]

---

2 *Commentarius in Evangelium sancti Ioannis*, Prooem., n. 10, q. 2, Resp., ad 1-2 (6.243). The numbers in parentheses show the volume and page of Bonaventure's work in *Opera omnia* (Quaracchi 1882-1902), 10 vv. Where two enumerations are shown, the second (*ed. min.*) refers to *Opera theologica selecta* (Quaracchi 1934-64), 5 vv. His *Commentaria in quatuor libros Sententiarum* will be noted by the number of the book, the title, and the numbers of the distinction, part, article, question etc., for instance: 1 *Sent.*, 27.2.2.2, ad 3 (1.661; *ed. min.*, 1.526); similar abbreviations will be used for his other writings, and for those of Aquinas. The works of the latter will be noted with the volume and page numbers (in parentheses) of *Opera omnia*, editio Leonina (Romae 1882-). Works not in that critical edition will be noted (with the name of the edition) and identified as they appear, first with full title, then as shown in a shorter form. An exception is made for the following work: *Scriptum super libros Sententiarum* (Parisiis 1929), vv. 1-2, cura P. Mandonnet (1933, 1947), vv. 3-4, edidit F. Moos; references to this work will be similar to those for the *Commentaria* of Bonaventure.

3 For Bonaventure, as we shall see, theology is subalternated to Scripture and shares at once in the certitude of both reason and faith.

CERTITUDE OF NATURAL KNOWLEDGE

To know any thing with certitude, Bonaventure teaches, the human intellect must see it in the light of its eternal reason in God. This does not mean that His eternal reason is the whole and sole ground of certitude in human knowledge, for otherwise natural knowledge would not differ from infused knowledge nor any knowledge in the present life from the knowledge possessed in beatitude. The men of the Old Academy erred, therefore, in saying that a thing is known with certitude only in the archetypal or intelligible world. Their opinion gave rise to the greater error of the New Academy, which held that nothing at all could be known with certitude, since the human mind could not see the intelligible world. It is not sufficient, on the other hand, to say that the intellect needs only the influence of God's eternal light, so that, in knowing with certitude, it need not arrive at His eternal reason. This is not sufficient for Bonaventure on two accounts. First, because it is contrary to the very clear teaching of Augustine, who demonstrates that the human mind, to know with certitude, must be regulated not by a habitus of the mind itself, but by the immutable and eternal rules above it in the eternal truth. Secondly, because the influence of God is either general with respect to all creatures or special with respect to grace. If the certitude of human knowledge is excluded from His general influence, then it is included in His special influence; but this cannot be true on the ground that all human knowledge would be infused and none would be natural or acquired. Consequently, to have knowledge with certitude, the human intellect of necessity must be moved into act and be regulated in its action by the eternal reason of God, which is attained only in part, or according as it can be reached by the intellect with its own principles.[4]

Explaining the conditions required for certitude, Bonaventure maintains that it necessitates both a nobility of knowledge and a dignity of the knower. The nobility of knowledge entails an immutability on the side of the object and an infallibility on the side of the knower. Because every creature is brought into being from non-being, the truth of a creature taken in itself is not immutable absolutely, and the light of a created intellect according to its own power is not entirely infallible. As

---

4 *Quaestiones disputatae de scientia Christi* (DSC), q. 4, Resp. "... statum vitae." (5.23). See also *fa.* 1-8 (5.17-18), where Bonaventure cites the texts of Augustine to show that the human mind sees truth in the immutable truth, which is God, and judges things in their eternal reasons that cannot be judged by the mind, to which they are superior and, as the immutable rules of truth, in whose light even an immoral man sees what is right and just.

a consequence, the human intellect cannot know the truth of creatures with the certitude of science if it knows them in its own light alone and only as they have being either in themselves or in a created mind. To obtain the certitude of science, the intellect must know the truth of creatures according to the being that they have in the eternal design or reason of God. It is necessary for the intellect, therefore, to have recourse to His wholly immutable and stable truth, so that this truth confer immutability on the object of science, and to His entirely infallible light in order that it give infallibility to the knower. The second condition for certitude, the dignity of the knower, is said by Bonaventure to consist in the image of God which is found in the superior part of the rational spirit. This is the part of the rational soul by which a man attains the eternal reasons of God and through them defines with certitude whatever he judges and defines in both the speculative and the practical order. To attain His eternal reasons in that manner, a man needs the cooperation of God. Now, as the principle of being and creation, God cooperates in a general way with the natural work of every creature inasmuch as it is a vestige of His essence. As the source of grace and reparation, God cooperates in a special way with the meritorious work of any rational creature which is reformed as a likeness of the Trinity. God cooperates in a particular way, however, as both the moving principle and an object of knowledge, with the intellectual work of every rational creature according to its natural capacity as an image of the Creator. Consequently, for Bonaventure, the certitude of science is due to every man as an image of God who, moving the human intellect into act and cooperating with its action, makes known to each man His eternal reasons of things. Those reasons are not known clearly and distinctly by any man in this life; nor are they known according to their plenitude of truth. They are known only to the extent that the divine truth is known by the natural power of the human intellect, namely, by means of its own principles of knowledge, which are similitudes of the things that it abstracts from phantasms. When the intellect arrives at the eternal reasons of God, it reaches Him so to say as the manifestation of light to every created mind and as the ground of knowing every true thing.[5]

Although Augustine teaches that the human mind knows corporeal things through the senses and spiritual things through itself, or in its own intellectual light, Bonaventure insists that this does not exclude the

---

5   DSC, q. 4, Resp. "Quod autem ..." (5.23-24); see also *fm.* 34 (5.20-21). Bonaventure's conditions for certitude are influenced to a great degree by Augustine and to some degree by Aristotle: *fa.* 17-33 (5.19-20).

cooperation of God with the human mind. The light and principles of created truth are so included in the light and principles of the uncreated truth that the human mind knows creatures not only in its created light of truth, but also in the uncreated light of God, and so it knows created things in His eternal truth.[6] Aristotle has shown, nevertheless, that the power of the intellect and the principles acquired by it through sensation and experience are sufficient for perfect knowledge, and thus there is no apparent need to know things in the light of their eternal reasons. In Bonaventure's judgment, Aristotle shows only the necessity for the concourse of the light and the principles of created truth in order that the intellect acquire knowledge; nevertheless, this does not exclude the light and principles of the eternal truth by whose influence and cooperation the intellect knows the truth of creatures.[7] Hence, handling the problem of natural certitude in an original manner, Bonaventure reconciles the doctrines of Aristotle and Augustine. Though he accepts the teaching of Augustine that the human soul is in contact with the eternal laws of God, even so, Bonaventure holds as indubitably true the teaching of Aristotle that human science comes to be in the intellect by way of the senses, memory and experience.[8]

Combining Aristotelean and Augustinian doctrines, then, Bonaventure synthesizes them in a twofold solution to the problem of natural certitude. On the one side, he maintains that the created light and principles of truth, though they are both necessary for human knowledge, are insufficient to cause certitude without the extrinsic help of the uncreated light and eternal reasons of God. On the other side, he affirms that the intellect is moved both by the eternal truth of its objects and by the created truth of its own principles, so that it sees the eternal reasons of God as they are reflected in its created principles. The intellect attains the certitude of science, therefore, by correlating its abstract similitudes of things with their eternal reasons through the mediation of its first principles.[9]

---

6 DSC, q. 4, sc 3-4 (5.21), ad 3-4 (5.24). See Augustine, *De Trinitate*, 9.3.3 (PL 42.962-63), 12.15.24 (PL 42.1101).

7 DSC, q. 4, sc 7-9 (5.21), ad 7-9 (5.25). See Aristotle, *De anima*, 3.5-6 (430a10-430b21) ; *Analytica posteriora*, 2.19 (100a4-8).

8 *Sermo IV, Christus unus omnium magister (Sermo IV)*, nn. 17-18 (5.571-72; *ed. min.*, 5.303-04). In this sermon, Bonaventure attributes to Christ as the Word of God the teaching of any truth known by reason, thus appropriating to Him the truth that philosophy can discover about God's action on the intellect. Accepting the truth of philosophy as such, Bonaventure goes beyond it through faith to show that Christ teaches all truth infallibly, so that He is the one illumining the mind with certitude to know the necessity of its objects. See also: *In Ioannis*, 1.4.12 (6.249); *Collationes in Hexaëmeron*, 12.5 (5.385).

9 DSC, q. 4, sc 14-16 (5.22), ad 14-16 (5.25).

The texts of Augustine used by Bonaventure in solving the problem of natural certitude are interpreted somewhat differently by Aquinas. His approach to the problem is one of understanding the way that we see the immutable truth of God, or His eternal reasons, according to which we judge the truth of created things. Augustine himself, Aquinas notes, acknowledges that truth is in the human soul, which he proved to be immortal from the eternity of truth. Now truth is in the soul, according to Aquinas, as God is present by His essence in all things, so that they are true inasmuch as, by their own natures, they are similitudes of God. Wherefore, His truth through its similitude is in all things, including the human soul. Because the soul knows truth, however, the divine truth is also in the soul by a special likeness inasmuch as there exists in the soul, when it knows the truth of other things, a sort of similitude of the divine truth. From the one divine truth, moreover, many truths come to be in the minds of men. Although many men differ with regard to the truth of some things, all men concur in the truth of the first principles, both speculative and practical, for they form in every human mind a kind of image, so to speak, of the divine truth. When any mind knows something with certitude, therefore, it sees the object in those principles according to which it judges all things. Thus, by analyzing the object into the first principles, the human mind is said to see the thing in the divine truth, or in its eternal reasons, according to which the mind is said to judge all things. Aquinas confirms his solution to the problem with the words of Augustine, who says that the truths of the sciences are seen in the divine truth as visible things are seen in the manifestation of light by the sun. It stands to reason, Aquinas comments, that corporeal things are not seen in the body of the sun, but in its manifestation of light; so also the truths of the sciences are not seen in the divine truth itself, but in the manifestation of its light.[10]

In the view of Aquinas, differing evidently from Bonaventure, the certitude of natural knowledge does not necessitate a seeing of the eternal reasons beyond their reflexions in the human mind through its first principles. Because those principles are impressed on the mind by the exemplar causality of the first truth, which they resemble as its similitudes, the intellect knows the truth of its objects in their eternal reasons, or the immutable truth of God, simply by judging them according to its first and self-evident principles.[11] This position is not the

---

10 *Liber de Veritate Catholicae Fidei contra errores Infidelium seu "Summa contra Gentiles"* (SCG), textus Leoninus diligenter recognitus, cura et studio C. Pera (Romae 1961), vv. 2-3; see 3.47 "Difficultatem autem ..." (v. 3, pp. 61-63; nn. 2241-45: the texts of Augustine are well documented here); cf. *Summa theologiae* (ST), prima pars (1a), 8.3 (4.86-87).

11 *Quaestiones disputatae de veritate* (DV), 1.4, arg. 5 (22.13), ad 5 (22.14-15); 10.6, arg. 6 (22.310), ad 6 (22.313-14); 10.11, arg. 12 (22.335), ad 12 (22.338).

one taken by Bonaventure, who holds that the intellect must see the eternal reason of its object, though God himself is not seen, since His eternal law is attained of necessity in conjunction with the first principles, which are its effects. Aquinas insists that the eternal law can be known only in its effect and not in itself: just as the sun is seen only in its irradiation and not in its substance, so the eternal law is seen by a man only according to its irradiation or effect in his mind, and thus all human knowledge of truth is a sort of participation in the eternal or immutable truth. [12]

How then does Aquinas account for the influence and cooperation of God in regard to the natural work of the intellect? He maintains, with Bonaventure, that all human knowledge is caused by the influence of God on the intellect. His influence is such for Aquinas, however, that human knowledge is acquired by the intellect through its self-evident principles of truth. Now the whole certitude of science comes from the certitude of principles, for the conclusions of science are known with certitude when they are understood in accordance with its first principles. When a man knows something with certitude, therefore, he has that certitude from God because the certitude of first principles is made known to him in the natural light of reason that God gives to him and through which God teaches him the truth. As a consequence, the man is said to understand and to judge all things in the light of the first truth according as the natural light of reason is, as it were, an impression on his mind of the uncreated truth. God influences the work of the intellect in acquiring certitude, then, through the similitudes of His light and truth in the natural light and self-evident principles given by Him to human reason. Since it is as a similitude of the first truth that a created thing is knowable to the intellect, Aquinas can say that God is known implicitly in every thing that the intellect knows, and so he comes close to Bonaventure's view that the light and principles of the uncreated truth are included in the light and principles of created truth. [13] Aquinas is also close to Bonaventure in some respects regarding God's cooperation with the work of the intellect. In the judgment of Aquinas, God cooperates with the intellect not only by moving it into act and giving it the similitudes necessary for knowledge, but also by conserving continually in being both the power of the intellect to understand and the similitudes of the things that it understands. As the first cause of intelligence, God moves the intellect into act by giving it the light of in-

12   ST, 1a2ae, 93.2, Resp. (7.163).
13   DV, 11.1, Resp. "Processus autem ..." (22.351-52); ad 13, 17 (22.353-54); 22.2, ad 1. See also: ST, 1a, 88.3, ad 1 (5.368); SCG, 1.11 "Ad quintam..." (Pera, 1.15; n. 71).

telligence, or its power of understanding; so, as a second cause of intelligence, the intellect depends on the cooperation of God in order that it understand. Moreover, all created beings pre-exist in God as the first cause of their being, so that, in the order of intelligence, they exist first in God according to their eternal reasons and, secondly, in the created minds actually understanding them by the similitudes derived from those reasons. Thus, by impressing the similitudes of things on the intellect, God causes and cooperates with its natural act of understanding. Though the intellect cannot operate without the cooperation of God, nevertheless, its natural power of intelligence and the cognitive similitudes of its objects are, under the action of God, a sufficient cause of its knowledge. The perception of truth by the intellect, therefore, is attributed chiefly to God not only as the cause and the conserving principle of its being and light of intelligence, but also as the principal agent directing it to see the truth of its objects.[14]

Approaching the position of Bonaventure to some degree, Aquinas ascribes the certitude of natural knowledge to God on the part of the object, which He presents to the intellect, and on the part of the knower to whom He gives the natural light of intelligence. The certitude of every truth in the human intellect, consequently, is derived from God as the first truth, for the truth of human knowledge has its certitude from the power of the divine truth, just as the conclusions of science have their certitude from the power of the first principles.[15] Both the intellectual light of the mind and its first naturally known principles have the power to manifest truth from their assimilation to the divine truth, which confers an infallibility on the one and an immutability on the other. This assimilation consists in the image of divine truth that God, as exemplar cause, stamps on the human mind, thus giving it the ability to know truth according to the first truth, but without seeing the divine truth in itself.[16] Although Aquinas differs from Bonaventure on the effect produced by God in the human mind, even so, they concur in regarding God as the primary source of the infallibility of the mind and the immutability of its truth, the two conditions required for the certitude of human knowledge. The one notable difference between Aquinas and Bonaventure has to do with the reason why God must

14   ST, la, 105.3, Resp., ad 1-3 (5.473); *Expositio super librum Boethii de Trinitate (Expos. de Trin.)*, recensuit Bruno Decker (Leiden 1955), 1.1, ad 2, 6, 8 (pp. 61-62).

15   *Compendium theologiae*, 1.129 "Deus autem ..." in *Opuscula theologica*, cura et studio R. A. Verardo (Taurini 1954), p. 62, n. 258.

16   *Quaestio quodlibetalis (Quodl.)*, 10.4.1 (10.7), Resp. in *Quaestiones quodlibetales*, editio nona, cura et studio R. Spiazzi (Taurini 1956), p. 203. See also DV, 10.8, Resp. "Si vero ..." (22.322).

cooperate with the natural work of human intelligence. In this regard, Bonaventure stands alone, inasmuch as the reason that he assigns is the necessity for God to cooperate with the human mind because of the natural condition of the rational spirit, which is created as an image of God. It is in this context that Bonaventure describes the certitude of natural knowledge as an effect of an illumination from God, and so we must now consider his doctrinē from that point of view.[17]

NATURAL ILLUMINATION OF REASON

All human knowledge, according to Bonaventure, begins with the senses. They perceive their objects by way of the species received from them in the bodily organs and causing the sense powers, both exterior and interior, to apprehend the different kinds of bodies and their common properties. In apprehending those things, the exterior senses judge them, as sight distinguishes a white from a black body, and the interior sense judges by its power of estimation whether a thing is salutary or harmful. To judge why a thing has such qualities belongs to the power of reason, which knows the thing in abstraction from every condition of place, time and motion. Since a sense power is confined by nature to a definite object, as hearing is bound by sound, the certitude of sensation depends only on God's general cooperation with creatures. Because the intellect is open to an understanding of all things, it must be fixed in certitude by the cooperation of the light and the reason of eternal truth, for they alone are free from the imperfections of fallibility and mutability. Consequently, turning to the fount of all certitude, the intellect judges corporeal things according to their unchangeable, timeless and endless reasons in God, thus attaining a higher degree of certitude than the senses. The cause of all things, God is the infallible rule and the light by which the intellect judges anything with certitude, and so it must apprehend corporeal things according to their eternal reasons, or their infallible, immutable and indubitable laws in God. Imprinted indelibly on the memory, those laws can neither be violated nor, as Augustine says, be called into account by a judgment of the intellect. It

---

17 With regard to the immutability of truth, Aquinas concurs with Bonaventure in ascribing an absolute immutability to the divine truth alone, because only the divine being (*esse*) is immutable absolutely. For Aquinas, the being of all creatures, and consequently their truth, is mutable on the ground that they would return to nothing unless God conserved them; an additional mutability is found in the truth of contingent things because of the variable condition of their being. Since the truth in the intellect depends on the true condition of its object, the truth of the intellect is immutable provided there is no change in the being of its objects, which are true according as they are related to the divine truth. See the following: 1 *Sent.*, 19.5.3 (1.494-98); DV, 1.6 (22.22-25); ST, 1a, 16.8 (4.216).

is impossible for the intellect to judge anything with certitude, therefore, apart from the necessary, unlimited and eternal reason of God whose exemplar form is the rule directing the production, conservation and distinction of all created things.[18]

Now, as an image of God, the rational creature is directed from its memory toward eternity, from its intelligence toward the immutable truth, and from its will toward the highest goodness. Reflecting God's eternal laws, the perpetual principles and axioms of the sciences are included among the things retained continually by the memory. Those rules of the human sciences recall to the mind the invariable truths made known to it in the immutable light of God. Relying on the memory, the intellect seeks to understand the terms, propositions and inferences of demonstration. The meaning of terms is grasped by the intellect when it comprehends each one by a definition, and this necessitates an analysis of its particular meaning until the term is understood according to its principal meaning. The definition of a particular substance, for instance, is known in full only when it is known as a being through itself (*ens per se*), which cannot be known without the help of God, the absolute and eternal being in whom are the perfect reasons of all created beings. The intellect truly comprehends the meaning of propositions when it knows with the certitude of science that they are true, which is to know that it cannot be deceived in comprehending their meaning. Having an infallible certitude, therefore, the intellect knows that the truth it comprehends cannot be otherwise, and so it knows that this truth is immutable. Since the human mind is mutable, it can see such a truth shining immutably only through the radiance of the altogether immutable light of God. The significance of an inference in a demonstration is rightly perceived by the intellect when it sees that the conclusion follows necessarily from the premises with regard not only to necessary and contingent terms, but also to existing and non-existing things. The necessity of those inferences is not due either to the existence of the thing in itself or to its existence in the human mind, but to the exemplarity of truth in God, who arranges all things in such a way that, reflecting His eternal design, they are adapted and related to one another. It is thus evident to Bonaventure, following Augustine, that the intellect of every man reasoning truly is illumined by the eternal truth through which alone his intellect can grasp any true thing with certitude. Taking counsel with the intellect, the will inquires about the varying degrees of goodness in creatures un-

---

18   *Itinerarium mentis in Deum (Itiner.)*, 2.3-6, 9-10 (5.300-02; *ed. min.*, 5.188-90, 191-92); DSC, q. 4, ad 11 (5.25). See in Augustine: *De libero arbitrio*, 2.12.34 (PL 32.1259) ; *De vera religione*, 31.58 (PL 34.148).

til it reaches the supreme good, which is attained of necessity from its impression on the memory. The action of counsel ends in a judgment made with certitude according to the divine law as it is seen through the memory and which the mind knows to be both right and beyond its power to judge. As a result of counsel, the will has a desire chiefly for the very best good, or the beatifying good and ultimate end for whose sake every other good is desired, unless a man is deceived and errs by mistaking for the truth an image and likeness of the supreme good. The acts of the memory, the intelligence and the will lead the mind in the order of faith to a consideration of the Trinity with the help of the philosophical sciences, which inform and perfect the human mind as an image of God. But the philosophical sciences have in the order of reason certain and infallible rules descending into the mind, so to speak, as manifestations and rays of truth from the eternal law of God. The brilliance of divine truth so illumines a man's mind that, unless it is blind, he can be drawn toward a contemplation of God.[19]

For Bonaventure, then, the certitude of intellectual knowledge, including both science and wisdom, is caused by an illumination from God. Without His illumination, no man can know any truth with certitude, as Augustine shows. When the Apostle Paul says that we live, are moved and have our being in God (*Acts*, 17.28), he speaks of our intellectual life in the interpretation of Augustine, who sees the Apostle saying that God is the cause of being, the source of intelligence, and the order of living. Commenting on Augustine's interpretation, Bonaventure teaches that God, as the cause of being, is present in the human soul as its productive principle; as the order of living, God dwells in the soul through the gift of grace regulating its actions according to the rule of the Christian life. As the source of intelligence, however, God is the intellectual sun, so to speak, illumining every human mind and conferring certitude on its acts of understanding by raising them above the mutable conditions of the creature.[20]

19 *Itiner.*, cap. 3 (3.303-06; *ed. min.*, 5.193-99); see Augustine, *De vera relig.*, 39.72 (PL 34.154). Note Bonaventure's closing passage: "Huius autem lucis irradiatio et consideratio sapientes suspendit in admirationem et econtra insipientes, qui non credunt, ut intelligant, ducit in perturbationem ..." This does not mean that only the Christian can have wisdom with certitude, even though other texts seem to support such a view, for instance: DSC, q. 4, ad 2 (5.24); *Sermo IV*, n. 15 (5.571; *ed. min.*, 5.302). Bonaventure speaks of natural wisdom in a number of texts, such as: 3 *Sent.*, 35.un.1, Resp. (3.774; *ed. min.*, 3.778-79); 35.dub.1 (3.787; *ed. min.*, 3.793-94). He has some texts on both natural and Christian wisdom, including their certitude, for example: DSC, q. 5, Resp. (5.29-30); 3 *Sent.*, 35.dub.4 (3.788; *ed. min.*, 3.795). Finally, he describes the certitude of natural wisdom as depending, in the same way as human science, on the eternal reasons or the infallible and indubitable norms by which the wise man makes his judgments: *Coll. in Hexaëm.*, 2.9-10 (5.337-38).

20 *Collationes de septem donis Spiritus sancti*, 8.15 (5.496-97). See in Augustine: *De Trin.*, 14.15.21 (PL 42.1052), 14.12.16 (PL 42.1048); *De civitate Dei*, 8.4 (PL 41.228).

The doctrine of Aquinas, no less than Bonaventure's, on the natural illumination of reason is a part of his doctrine on its natural certitude. Now, as Aquinas knows, Augustine says that the human mind cannot judge the truth of corporeal things, because they are mutable and similar in a way to what is false. Augustine also says that the mind, though mutable, sees the immutable rules of truth and judges things according to a light above the mind. Since every human judgment is made according to the agent intellect, it seems that this intellect is God, who illumines the mind.[21] Regarding the problem, Aquinas holds that the human mind judges truth in one way by its own power, which is the agent intellect, and in another way by drawing conclusions from principles, which Augustine indicates, for nothing mutable or seemingly false can be an infallible rule of truth. To understand Augustine properly, Aquinas observes, it is necessary to see the historical reasons for his words. The ancient philosophers, not rising above the senses, said that we could not have certitude of truth because of the instability of being in things and the inability of any man to settle different opinions about them. Augustine referred to those two reasons in saying that the mind cannot know the truth of corporeal things. Moreover, seeking to stabilize the certitude of science, Plato posited immobile species separated from sensible things and, in man, a mind or an intellect illumined by a sort of superior and intellectual sun. Consequently, he put science in the mind as it participated in the truth of the separate species of things. Augustine, following Plato as far as Catholic faith allowed, did not posit the species of things as self-subsistent, but put their eternal reasons in the divine mind, so that the human mind as it is illumined by the divine light judges truth through them, and they are seen only by their impression on the mind. Proceeding differently, Aristotle showed that there was something stable in sensible things and that the judgment of a sense power, though it could be deceived accidentally, was true concerning their proper qualities. He also showed that man had an intellective power which judges truth, not through some intelligible principles existing beyond the mind, but through the light of the agent intellect. It is not going much beyond Aristotle to say, Aquinas remarks, that this light and the truths that it makes known participate in the light and truth of God. Hence, the immutable rules seen by the mind are the first principles made known by the light of the agent intellect as a participation in the

---

21 *Quaestio disputata de spiritualibus creaturis*, a. 10, arg. 8-9 in *Quaestiones disputatae*, editio nona (Taurini 1953), v. 2, p. 406. See in Augustine: *De diversis quaestionibus*, q. 9 (PL 40.13-14); *De Trin.*, 14.15.21 (PL 42.1052).

divine light, and so God illumines the mind by giving it the natural light of its agent intellect.[22]

Thus, combining Aristotelean and Augustinian doctrines to his own advantage, Aquinas takes a different stand than Bonaventure on the natural illumination of reason. In the position of Aquinas, this illumination falls under the providence of God, who bestows on the human mind an intellectual light sufficient of itself for knowing the truth of corporeal things, provided always that He moves the intellect into act and cooperates with its action. As Aristotle suggests, the agent and possible intellects are sufficient when conjoined in operation to cause a perception of truth, for the power of the agent intellect has a proper efficacy to manifest the natural truth of first principles and the conclusions deduced from them. When Augustine says that God is the intellectual sun illuminating the mind interiorly, he is to be understood to speak about the natural light of the soul, because this light is the illumination by which God enlightens it to know the things pertaining to natural knowledge. In short, for Aquinas, the intellect has no need to receive from God an additional light or illumination to know what it can know sufficiently by its natural power of reason.[23]

In Bonaventure's position, the agent intellect, with the possible intellect, has the power to form a knowledge of corporeal things. Because the operation of reason depends, however, both on the certitude or necessity of corporeal things and on the work of the senses, the human intellect cannot know those things by its own power without the aid of God, whose knowledge of such things does not depend on them. Needing the help of the divine light, therefore, the created light of the intellect is not sufficient of itself to operate, even after God produces it. In conserving the intellect, God conforms its light to His eternal light and causes the created light to act by adding to it the influence of His supreme light.[24] As understood by Bonaventure, then, the natural illumination of reason does not necessitate from God an additional light in the intellect, but requires in addition to His conservation the influence of His light to move into act the created light of the intellect which He conforms to His uncreated light. It is in this way that Bonaventure attributes to God an illumination conferring on the intellect the infallible certitude and the immutable truth with which it

22 *De spirit. creat.*, a. 10, ad 8-9 (Taurini 2.409-10); see also: *arg.* 1 (2.405), ad 1 (2.408). Cf. ST, 1a, 87.1, Resp. (5.355-56).

23 *Expos. de Trin.*, 1.1, sc 1-4, Resp. (Decker pp. 58-61); ST, 1a2ae, 109.1 (7.289-90). See Augustine, *Soliloquia*, 1.6 (PL 32.875); and Aristotle, *De Anima*, 3.5 (430a10-15).

24 *Commentarius in librum Ecclesiastes*, 7.1, q. 3, Resp. (6.54-55); 2 *Sent.*, 17.1.1, ad 6 (2.412; *ed. min.*, 2.242).

knows indubitably the necessity of the things that it sees in the light of their eternal reasons. His position on the problem combines in a different way than that of Aquinas the doctrines of Aristotle and Augustine. When Bonaventure holds that the object of human knowledge is necessary in itself and certain to the knower, he follows Aristotle's teaching on this knowledge as certain whenever a man knows that he knows the cause of a thing, and that the thing cannot be otherwise than it is. When Bonaventure maintains that immutability belongs solely to the eternal truth of God, he follows Augustine's teaching on the necessity of the mind to see the truth of creatures in their eternal reasons, which are the immutable rules or laws guaranteeing the certitude of human knowledge. For his own part, Bonaventure adds that the knower must have an infallibility of truth, as otherwise he could be deceived and would not understand the truth of his objects with certitude. Finally, showing a predominantly Augustinian influence, he affirms that, because the light of every created intellect can be obscured, no created intellect is sufficient of itself to comprehend any truth with certitude apart from the uncreated light of God.[25]

Certitude and Illumination of Infused Knowledge

Because the teaching of Scripture is intended to generate faith, which has a proper certitude from a divine illumination, Bonaventure assigns to the doctrine of Scripture the certitude of authority. Explaining this certitude, he says that particular deeds cannot be proved by human reason, but must be believed, and so Scripture teaches by narrating truth rather than by relying on the certitude of reason. Thus, precluding doubt about the doctrine of Scripture, God provides in place of the certitude of reason the certitude of His authority, which can neither deceive nor be deceived. Hence, resting on the infallible authority of the Holy Spirit, Scripture presents the truth in a perfectly authentic

---

25 *Sermo IV*, nn. 6-10 (5.568-70; *ed. min.*, 5.297-300). Bonaventure identifies the intellect's natural power of judgment, as Augustine speaks of it, with the agent and possible intellects: "Lumen innatum est lumen naturalis iudicatorii sive rationis ... id est non solum intellectum possibilem, sed etiam intellectum agentem." — *Coll. de donis*, 4.2 (5.474); see Augustine, *De lib. arbit.*, 3.20.56 (PL 32.1298). The Augustinian expression *naturale iudicatorium* is also used by Aquinas: ST, 1a2ae, 71.6, ad 4 (7.9). He holds, with Bonaventure, the Aristotelean principle that a man knows a thing with certitude by science whenever he knows that it is impossible for it to be otherwise than it is: SCG, 3.39 "Praeterea ... ultima felicitas." (Pera 3.45; n. 2171); see Aristotle, *Anal. poster.*, 1.2 (72b1-4).

manner, not through human investigation, but through divine revelation. [26] Now the believer accepts divine revelation by an act of faith, which looks in a general way to the teaching of Scripture and in a special way to the articles of the Christian creed. When assenting to the creed, the Christian assents to God as the supreme truth, whom he believes most of all while placing himself in the service of Christ. As a consequence, he believes not only things subject to reason, but also other things either above reason or contrary to sense experience, thus assenting to truths that are not apparent or evident to natural reason. To make such an assent, he must have those truths manifested to his mind by an illumination of faith elevating his reason above its nature. To assent to them without doubt, he must also have the testimony of authority supporting Scripture and strengthening his mind in its belief. Both the illumination of faith and the authority of Scripture come from the Father through His Word, Jesus Christ, and through the Holy Spirit, the teacher of truth, who gives the Christian his power to believe divine revelation. According to Bonaventure, therefore, the authority of God upholds Christian faith, which assents to His authority, and this authority resides chiefly in Scripture. Because the whole of Scripture is the work of the Holy Spirit and is ordered to generating Christian faith, the teaching of Scripture and the true faith of the Christian are in perfect harmony. [27]

The object of faith is so true and certain, in Bonaventure's judgment, that it cannot contain anything false or doubtful. The assent of the mind to the truth of faith is made according to an illumination manifesting the foreknowledge of God. Since nothing false can fall under His foreknowledge, no falsehood can fall under faith. The divine foreknowledge, not depending on creatures, is most certain of things that will necessarily come to be and of things that may or may not come to be, so that God cannot be deceived about either necessary or contingent things. The virtue of faith, guided by God's foreknowledge, has such a certitude of both illumination and belief that the believer can neither be deceived nor be in error by his faith concerning future and even contingent things, though they cannot of themselves come to be. In Bonaventure's view, a thing foreknown by God can possibly not come to be through itself and absolutely, because it is impossible that it come to be with His foreseeing of its opposite. God would be deceived if, foreseeing the latter, the former came to be. Likewise, depending on the divine foresight, the virtue of faith is not deceived in assenting to a

26 *Breviloquium*, Prol., n. 5 "Quoniam igitur..." (5.207; *ed. min.*, 5.13).
27 *Brevil.*, 5.7 "... non ficta." (5.260-61; *ed. min.*, 5.114-15).

contingent thing that cannot of itself come to be, because it would not be an object of faith if, at the same time, it could not come to be. Consequently, nothing false can fall under faith, since falsehood in an object of belief cannot stand at the same time with truth in the believer, or in his faith. [28] Bonaventure does not restrict infallible certitude regarding future and contingent events to the virtue of faith. He considers it possible for a man by his natural reason to be infallibly certain about some events of that sort. There are things having a determinate and unfailing (*infallibilis*) cause, such as events determined by the movements of celestial bodies, whose actions cannot be impeded. These things can be known with certitude by the man who knows them in their cause, as he knows, for instance, the time of an eclipse. Terrestrial things have a determinate cause in the ordinary course of nature, but their cause is fallible because of the numerous impediments that can prevent it from producing its proper effects. A field of corn will yield a bountiful harvest, for example, if the soil is rich and the weather is favourable. The true course of such contingent events can be foreseen with some degree of certitude by the man who knows the nature both of terrestrial things and of the causes influencing their actions. Things brought about by the human will have, in one way, an indeterminate cause in the inclination of the will to opposite courses of action and, in another way, a fallible cause owing to the many obstacles that can discourage a man from acting, though he is willing to act. It is the future and contingent events depending on the human will that a man can know with certitude only by divine revelation. [29]

For Bonaventure, then, the assent of faith has an infallible certitude from an illumination manifesting the divine foreknowledge. His understanding of the divine foreknowledge is given in connexion with God's knowledge of predestination. His foreknowledge is harmonious because it is true, for God knows a present event just as it is, and He knows a future event occurring, just as it will. His foreknowledge is also certain because it is independent of the event, which God foresees clearly and indubitably according to His eternal light, so that, knowing with supreme certitude, He is equally certain of all things. Consequently, the divine foreknowledge is infallible because it is the whole power (*totum posse*) comprehending the thing that God foreknows, and so He cannot in any way be deceived or forestalled by His foreknowledge. Although the predestination of a man depends on his freedom of choice, nevertheless, with the certitude of infallibility and

---

28 3 *Sent.*, 24.1.1, Resp. (3.509; *ed. min.*, 3.500).
29 2 *Sent.*, 7.2.1.3, Resp. (2.194; *ed. min.*, 2.188-89).

the impossibility of being deceived, God so foresees this contingent event that it will come to be as He foresees it. The divine foreknowledge of predestination also has an immutable certitude, since God does not dispose and order things so variably that He now chooses one man and, changing His choice, then another. In short, His foreknowledge of predestination has the certitude of both infallibility and immutability.[30]

Aquinas speaks of the teaching of Scripture in a way similar to Bonaventure, though Aquinas does not say explicitly that Scripture has the certitude of authority. In his consideration, Scripture teaches eternal things by its truth and in words having an authority originating from God. This authority is to be believed infallibly because God is truth, and because of the plenitude of His knowledge and the power of His words. Imposing a necessity to believe, Scripture teaches truth by way of precept, or of instruction, directing the intellect through faith and forming the will through love, thus moving the believer to act according to his faith. The truth of Scripture, having a uniformity of doctrine in all its parts, is both immutable and eternal, so that, disposing us for the life of grace, it guides us to the life of glory. Consequently, originating from God and promising eternal life, the doctrine of Scripture is the divine wisdom transcending all human reason.[31] As seen by Aquinas, Christian faith is fostered by the divine revelation made to the prophets and the apostles. This revelation is set down in Scripture written by human authors as instruments of the Holy Spirit, who has spoken through the prophets and the apostles. Because the Holy Spirit is the principal author of Scripture, it can contain nothing false, and neither can Christian faith, which is taught by Scripture.[32]

All the elements of the certitude of authority assigned to Scripture by Bonaventure are present in Aquinas, even though he does not use the term *certitude* in his consideration of Scripture. Its authority, coming from God, provokes a necessary and infallible belief in an immutable truth made known without falsehood, or deception, through a divine revelation given to us by the Holy Spirit, who is the principal author of Scripture. Showing its harmony with Christian faith, Aquinas indicates

---

30 1 *Sent.*, 40.2.1, ad 1-3 (1.707-08; *ed. min.*, 1.561-62); 40.2.2, Resp., ad 5 (1.712-13; *ed. min.*, 1.565-66).

31 *De commendatione et partitione sacrae Scripturae*, prima pars (*Opusc. theol.*, pp. 435-36); *De commendatione sacrae Scripturae*, prima pars (*Opusc. theol.*, pp. 441-42). Aquinas says also that Scripture teaches truth by way of narration: 1 *Sent.*, Prol., a. 5, Sol. (1.17-18). Bonaventure holds that the doctrine of Scripture is uniform throughout all its parts: *Brevil.*, Prol., nn. 1-4 (5.202-06; *ed. min.*, 5.5-12).

32 ST, 1a, 1.8, ad 2 (4.22): 1.2, ad 2 (4.9); SCG, 4.17 "Ex sacris ... divinae naturae." (Pera, 3.279-80; nn. 3536-38); *Quaestiones disputatae de potentia Dei*, 4.1, Resp. "... eius sensus." (Taurini 2.104-05); *Quodl.*, 7.6.1 (7.14), ad 5 (Spiazzi, p. 146); 7.6.3 (7.16), Resp. (p. 148); ST, 1a, 1.10, Resp. "Quia vero..." (4.25).

that the principles of faith are taken from the teaching of Scripture and drawn up in the apostolic creed, which summarizes and proposes for belief the truth diffused in Scripture.[33]

The act of the human intellect is good, according to Aquinas, because it has to do with what is true. For this reason, science is an intellectual virtue, since it is such that, by its means, the intellect is infallibly true. To be a virtue, then, faith must adhere to the sort of testimony in which truth is found infallibly. Now, just as created being (*esse*) is void and wanting in itself apart from its conservation by the uncreated being (*ens*), so also is every created truth apart from its rectification by the uncreated truth. Hence, the testimony of a man or an angel can be accepted infallibly only inasmuch as the creature manifests the testimony of God. The virtue of faith, therefore, moves the intellect to adhere to the truth of God, who is the first truth.[34] Thus, for Aquinas, the virtue of faith depends on the infallible truth of God. His testimony is manifested in the divine revelation received by the men whose minds God illumined to see things beyond the natural light of reason. This divine illumination made their minds so certain of His revelation that those men could propose it with certitude for belief by other men.[35]

Accounting for the act of belief, Aquinas compares it with the natural acts of the intellect, which is related in diverse ways to both sides of a contradiction. Regarding self-evident propositions, or first principles, the intellect adheres totally to the one side whose truth, appearing infallibly, is perceived at once or immediately. When the intellect, knowing the definition of terms, adheres wholly to one of the two sides by the power of first principles, it does not perceive the truth of that side immediately, but by way of a middle term, as a man of science knows the conclusions of a demonstration. If the intellect cannot be fixed in truth either immediately or by a middle term, then, under the influence of the will, provided there is sufficient motivation, the intellect can be made to assent firmly to one of the two sides of a contradiction. Such is the act of Christian faith by which the intellect, moved by the promise of eternal life, assents to the truth of revelation under the influence of the will. The reason inclining the will to move the intellect, however, is the first truth itself, which is infallible, and so the will gives an infallibility of truth to the intellect by causing its assent to the articles of faith.[36] This assent is made by the intellect to

33   ST, 2a2ae, 1.5, ad 2 (8.17); 1.9, ad 1 (8.23). See also 3 *Sent.*, 25.1.1, Sol. 3, ad 1 (3.786-87).
34   DV, 14.8, Resp. (22.459-60); cf. ST, 2a2ae, 1.2 (8.7-8).
35   SCG, 3.154 "Deinde ... sine istis." (Pera 3.229; nn. 3257-58).
36   DV, 14.1, Resp. (22.436-38); 3 *Sent.*, 23.2.4, Sol. 1, ad 2 (3.737). Cf. ST, 2a2ae, 2.1 (8.26-27); 3 *Sent.*, 23.2.3, Sol. 1 (3.731-32).

the revelation that God gave to the men through whom He has spoken. The assent of faith, then, is caused in the believer by the authority of God, who makes the articles of faith known to him by an infused light of faith. The object of faith is beyond natural reason, not because there is no act of reason in believing, but because the ground of faith is such that it cannot provide the evidence for the believer to see what he believes.[37] A man ought to believe the truths of faith, therefore, not because of human reason, but for the sake of divine authority. Assenting to what is unseen, the intellect of the believer is convinced by that authority through a command of the will in obedience to God.[38]

In the judgment of Aquinas, taking a different view from that of Bonaventure, the certitude of faith is found immediately in its principles, which are known self-evidently by the illumination of Christian faith. Just as the habitus of first natural principles gives the intellect an immediate understanding of their truth with complete certitude, so the habitus of faith gives the intellect an immediate and most certain perception of the principles or truths revealed by God. The intellect adheres firmly to those truths under the choice of the will, which is moved by divine authority to command the intellect's assent. Certitude of truth is found also in the intellect from its assent through science to conclusions drawn with the evidence of its objects from indemonstrable principles. It is proper to science that a man have certitude with regard to what he knows through science, for he is certain that he has the science. Likewise, because certitude belongs to the perfection of the intellect, it is proper to faith that the Christian have certitude regarding the things that he believes, since he is certain that he has the virtue of faith.[39] Acting from his faith, the Christian believes in God not only by accepting what He reveals, but also by assenting to it in the light of faith infused by God into his mind. According to Aquinas, the virtue of faith is more sufficient to move the intellect than any demonstration, because men are frequently deceived in thinking that to be a demonstration which is not, though a true demonstration never produces a false conclusion. Moreover, the light of faith is more sufficient for bringing about an assent than the natural light by which the intellect adheres to first principles, for the latter light is often impeded by bodily infirmities. Now the light of faith is, as it were, a sort of seal of the first

---

37 DV, 14.2, ad 9 (22.443-44); cf. 1 *Sent.*, Prol., a. 3, Sol. 2, ad (1.14).

38 ST, 2a2ae, 2.10, Resp. (8.38-39); 4.1, Resp. "Habitudo autem ...", ad 5 (8.44); 5.2, Resp. (8.56).

39 *Commentarium in Epistolam ad Hebraeos,* 11.1, lect. 1 "Consequenter cum dicit ...", *Opera omnia* (Vivès 1876), v. 21, pp. 687-88; ST, 1a2ae, 112.5. ad 2 (7.327).

truth in the human mind, and so this light cannot be deceived, just as God cannot be deceived, nor can He lie. Consequently, depending on the infallible truth of God, Christian faith cannot contain anything false.[40] Thus, presenting to the mind always and only what is true, the act of faith so perfects the intellect that it tends infallibly toward the supreme good, which is the first truth. Again, resulting from a command of the will, the act of faith is so formed through charity that the believer is directed infallibly to the ultimate end for whose sake the will adheres to the first truth. Since Christian faith is a virtue, therefore, Aquinas insists that it cannot contain any falsehood, because the act of belief relies on the infallibility of the divine truth.[41]

There are undoubtedly many points of similarity between Bonaventure and Aquinas on the certitude of Christian faith. Both theologians teach that the act of faith, while it looks to the articles of the creed, involves an assent with certitude made principally to God as the supreme or first truth and secondarily to the things that He has revealed as they are written in Scripture. The two theologians also teach in common, but with some differences, that the indubitable assent of faith is caused by the authority of God who, perfecting reason beyond its nature by a divine illumination, convinces the intellect to accept what He has revealed, though it is not evident to natural reason. In this regard, Aquinas explains the rôle of divine authority in the certitude of faith by a comparison with the certitude of the natural acts of the intellect. As a result, applying his understanding of natural certitude to the certitude of faith, he attributes an immediate infallibility to the articles of faith because their truth is perceived at once in the light of faith. By that means and without weakening the dependence of faith on the divine authority, he gives to the light of faith a power similar to and even more efficacious than the one belonging to the natural light of reason. Bonaventure refers to the divine authority without relating the certitude of faith to the natural certitude of reason. Rather, submitting the intellect as illumined by faith to the supreme truth, and subjecting the will as rectified by charity to the supreme good, he speaks of the divine authority taking the place of reason and persuading the heart of the Christian to believe.[42] Although Bonaventure does not handle this question in the same way as Aquinas, nonetheless, they concur in saying

---

40 *Expos. de Trin.*, 3.2, ad 4 "Unde et ..." (Decker pp. 114-15); 3 *Sent.*, 24.1, Sol. 3 (3.765). See also ST, 2a2ae, 1.3 (8.13-14).

41 ST, 2a2ae, 4.5, Resp., ad 2 (8.48-49).

42 See 3 *Sent.*, 23.1.1, Resp., ad 3 (3.471-72; *ed. min.*, 3.461-63); 23.2.2, ad 2 (3.491-92; *ed. min.*, 3.481-82).

that the assent of faith is made by the intellect at a command of the will.[43]

The two theologians differ greatly in the way of establishing the infallibility of Christian faith, even though they treat it in the same context: no falsehood can fall under faith. Bonaventure finds faith to be infallible by its dependence on the divine foreknowledge, which so safeguards the mind of the Christian that he can never be deceived or be in error because of his faith. Aquinas ascertains the infallibility of faith simply by its dependence on the first truth, which is infallible and cannot deceive the human mind, because God is beyond deception and cannot lie. For his part, then, Aquinas establishes the infallibility of faith without referring to the divine foreknowledge, even in regard to future and contingent things. He holds in the same way as Bonaventure, however, that some of those things are known with certitude by natural reason, while others can be known with certitude only as they fall under God's foreknowledge, which cannot be deceived, and so they are known solely by divine revelation. Thus, revealing future events, God supports our faith in the prophets by His foreknowledge through which He upholds Scripture, the source of instruction for our Christian faith.[44]

It is in the context of the revelation of contingent things that Bonaventure compares the certitude of faith with human science. The latter must be conformed to its object because it depends on the object as this exists, not only in itself, but also in its inferior causes and reasons. Christian faith has to be conformed to its object solely as it exists in its uncreated cause, for the knowledge obtained by faith and revelation depends, not on the thing revealed and believed, but on the infused light illumining the mind in order that it know the truths of faith and revelation. Because this light gives certain knowledge of contingent things, Christian faith, which is conformed to and relies on that

43 "Et quoniam intellectus non habilitatur ad assentiendum ipsi Veritati primae secundum suum iudicium, sed secundum voluntatis imperium ..." — 3 Sent., 23.1.2, in Resp. (3.476; ed. min., 3.466). Bonaventure also teaches, with Aquinas, that the Christian is certain that he has the virtue of faith: 3 Sent., 23.dub.4, Resp. (3.503-05; ed. min., 3.494-96).

44 ST, 3a, 46.2, arg. 4 (11.437), ad 4 (ibid.); cf. 3 Sent., 24.1, Sol. 3, ad 1 (3.765). On the certitude of natural and revealed knowledge concerning future and contingent things see: 1 Sent., 38.5, Sol. (1.909-12); 2 Sent., 7.2.2, Sol., ad 5 (2.189-91): cf. Quaestiones disputatae de malo, 16.7, Resp. (Taurini 2.683-84); ST, 1a, 86.4, Resp. (5.353). For the infallibility of the divine foreknowledge see: SCG, 1.67 "... non sint." (Pera 2.78; nn. 556-59); 3.154 "Possunt tamen ... et sanatis." (3.230; nn. 3265-66): cf. ST, 1a, 14.13, Resp. (4.186); Comp. theol., 1.140 (Opusc. theol. p. 27). Aquinas, like Bonaventure, speaks of a cause as certain when it never fails to produce its effect: "... tractum est nomen certitudinis ad ordinem causae ad effectum ut dicatur ordo causae ad effectum esse certus quando causa infallibiliter effectum producit." — DV, 6.3, in Resp. (22.185); see also: 2 Sent., 4.1.2, Sol. (2.135-36); ST, 1a, 22.4, ad 1 (4.269).

light, cannot be falsified nor can it waver for the sake of the contingency of a thing believed.[45]

According to Bonaventure, furthermore, when faith and science deal with the same objects, faith is always more certain absolutely than science. No philosopher has ever known by natural reason, for instance, the truth 'God is a creator' with so great a certitude as the Christian knows it by faith. With respect to other objects, science has the greater certitude of speculation, which is in the intellect, but faith has the greater certitude of adhesion, which is in the will. Since the speculation of the intellect looks merely to truth, science can give a man certitude so strong regarding some things, such as first principles, that he can in no way doubt or deny them, nor ever in his heart contradict them. Because the adhesion of the will flows from love, faith moves the believer to cling to what he believes more than science moves a man to cling to what he understands. This is evident to Bonaventure from the martyrs, who suffered torture and death rather than deny their faith, which no man would do for a speculative conclusion of science unless, as faith dictates, he ought not to lie.[46]

The position of Aquinas on this question is also similar in some respects and dissimilar in others to the one taken by Bonaventure. As seen by Aquinas, intellectual certitude is the greater according as its cause is the stronger. Certitude of human knowledge is attained by the natural light that causes the intellect both to assent and to adhere to a thing, because its truth is evident and certain. The certitude of infused faith comes from the first truth, which causes the intellect to assent and, consequently, to adhere firmly to the things it believes, though their truth is not evident, at a command of the will. Since the first truth is a stronger cause than the natural light of the intellect, the certitude of faith, regarding strength of adhesion, is greater than the certitude of human knowledge, but the latter has the greater evidence for the things to which assent is given.[47] Thus, having the more certain cause, the virtue of faith is more certain than any form of human knowledge, including science and wisdom. From the point of view of the intellect, however, the virtues of human knowledge are more certain than the virtue of faith, which looks to things above the intellect. Nonetheless, because a thing is judged absolutely according to its cause, faith is the more certain absolutely, since it rests on the certitude of divine truth.[48]

---

45   3 *Sent.*, 24.1.1, ad 1-2 (3.509-10; *ed. min.*, 3.500-01).

46   The adhesion of a true Christian to his faith is so great, in Bonaventure's judgment, that he would prefer to lose the whole of philosophy, if he had it, rather than ignore even one article of the creed: 3 *Sent.*, 23.1.4, Resp. (3.481-82; *ed. min.*, 3.471-72).

47   3 *Sent.*, 23.2.2, Sol. 3 (3.728-29); DV, 14.1, ad 7 (22.438).

48   ST, 2a2ae, 4.8, Resp., ad 3 (8.52-53).

CERTITUDE OF THEOLOGICAL KNOWLEDGE

Laying a foundation for theological knowledge, Bonaventure denies in one respect but grants in another the possibility of an increase in the certitude of faith. No increase is possible in relation to the divine truth, which is most certain and beyond deception, so that, assenting to it, the Christian cannot go any further in certitude. Some increase is possible, however, in relation to the believer. Following Hugh of St. Victor on this point, Bonaventure teaches that faith can grow in the Christian both by a wider knowledge of its principles and, having a clearer illumination, by a deeper knowledge of them. The certitude of faith can grow or increase, then, because of a better knowledge of its truth and, as a consequence, because of a greater devotion toward God. Faith is more certain when, reaching the level of science, it empowers the intellect to know the object of belief more plainly and, strengthening the will stead-fastly, moves the Christian to a more devout acquiescence in the truth that he believes. Indeed, for Bonaventure, faith grows fundamentally in certitude according to the devotion with which the Christian adheres to the truth revealed by God. In this respect, as Hugh of St. Victor says, there are three different kinds of believers. Some Christians, choosing to believe from piety alone, do not comprehend by their reason whether or not they should believe. Other Christians approve by their reason what they already accept on faith. A number of Christians not only ap-prove their faith by reason, but also experience what they believe, and so, understanding it with a purity of belief, they apprehend the certitude of faith.[49]

The approbation of faith by reason gives rise to theological knowledge, which brings faith up to the level of science. Since an end imposes necessity on the means, as Aristotle points out, Bonaventure assigns to the science of theology an argumentative procedure for the general purpose of promoting Christian faith. This method is useful in particular regarding three sorts of men kept in view by a theologian. The method has weight, as Augustine teaches, in defending faith against its adversaries. By the use of probable arguments, according to Bonaventure himself, the method of argumentation has force to strengthen Christians weak in their belief, just as God strengthens them in charity by providing temporal benefits. As Richard of St. Victor

---

49   3 *Sent.*, 25.2.3, Resp. (3.550-51; *ed. min.*, 3.542-44); see Hugh of St. Victor, *De sacramentis*, 1.10.4 (PL 176.332).

shows, this method brings to light hidden though necessary reasons for the things of faith, thus giving delight to perfect Christians in understanding what they believe, as Bernard of Clairvaux says: "We understand nothing more willingly than what we already grasp by faith."[50]

The use of argumentation is proper to theology, in Bonaventure's view, even though the science is rooted in Scripture, which proceeds by way of narration. Theology is related to Scripture as a subalternate to a principal science, for the two sciences consider revealed truth according to different principles. The science of Scripture, resting on divine authority, considers the object of belief as such; adding reason to faith, the science of theology deals with the object of belief as it can be understood. Consequently, theology has a proper mode of procedure, just as it has a proper mode of certitude: whenever the certitude of reason is lacking to theology, this inferior science has recourse to the certitude of authority upholding Scripture and exceeding every certitude of reason.[51] Thus, as seen by Bonaventure, the object of belief belongs to the virtue of faith as that object is grounded in the first truth, to which the Christian assents for its own sake alone. The same object pertains both to Scripture, inasmuch as this science adds to it the principle of divine authority, and to theology, which unites reason to divine authority and the first truth to produce arguments proving the truth of Christian faith.[52] This is not to say that the theologian proves the things of faith by natural reason. On the contrary, assenting from faith to the things narrated in Scripture, the theologian proves them by adding reason to divine authority, so that the whole strength of his arguments rests on the prior assent of faith. Bonaventure illustrates the fact with the truth of the resurrexion, which is proved by the authority of Scripture and the words recorded there from the Apostles. Their words are known to be true because the Apostles were illumined by the Holy Spirit, who gave them their certitude of faith and our guarantee of that certitude is rooted in the faith received by us from God. It is correct to say, therefore, that faith uses reason to prove the truth of the resurrexion, but not to say that faith in the resurrexion is proved by reason.[53] Hence, the certitude of theological knowledge is not due to reason as it is used, for instance, by a philosopher to acquire his science. It is due rather to reason both as elevated by faith to assent to the first truth and as per-

---

50 1 *Sent.*, Prooem., q. 2, Resp. (1.10-11; *ed. min.*, 1.9-10); cf. sc 2-b (ibid.). See the following: Aristotle, *Physica*, 2.9 (199b34-200a14); Augustine, *De Trin.*, 1.2.4 (PL 42.822); Richard of St. Victor, *De Trinitate*, 1.4 (PL 196.892); Bernard of Clairvaux, *De consideratione*, 5.3.6 (PL 182.1691).
51 1 *Sent.*, Prooem., q. 2, arg. 4 (1.10; *ed. min.*, 1.8-9), ad 4 (1.11; *ed. min.*, 1.10.)
52 1 *Sent.*, Prooem., q. 1, ad 5-6 (1.8; *ed. min.*, 1.8).
53 3 *Sent.*, 23.dub.5 (3.505; *ed. min.*, 3.496-97).

fected by the gifts of science and understanding, which enable the theologian to comprehend what he believes. As long as he assents from faith to the first truth and not to any reason for its own sake, the theologian retains the merit of belief and, moved by charity, desires to have reasons for its truth. Consequently, finding reason a source of solace for Christian faith, he relies principally on the authority of God as the first truth and only secondarily on the reasons used to prove the things accepted on that authority by the assent of faith.[54]

Although Aquinas concurs with Bonaventure in maintaining that faith does not change essentially, or increase substantially, Aquinas does not consider directly the possibility of growth in the certitude of faith. Both theologians hold many things in common on the necessity of Christians to believe explicitly several truths, such as the Incarnation, that were believed implicitly before the time of Christ. They also hold commonly that simple Christians are bound to believe the articles of the creed explicitly only in a general way, though their implicit belief in any particular article must preclude in its regard all dissent from the teaching of the Church. An explicit or distinct belief in each article is required of those Christians, such as prelates, pastors and theologians, who have a duty to teach and to explain the articles of faith to the people, who can advance in knowledge of their faith.[55]

Aquinas subscribes with Bonaventure, then, to the view that the theologian, as a doctor of faith, ought to know with the perfection of science the things that he believes. In the particular view of Aquinas, faith cannot be more or less with respect to its object, which is essential to the virtue and always stays the same. The act of faith, however, following the condition of the believer, can grow in efficacy either because of the intellect or because of the will. With respect to the intellect, faith can grow both by thinking, or knowledge, and by assenting: virtues in the intellect need time and experience to grow, so that faith increases in time according to a greater knowledge of the articles; assent gives constancy to the act of faith, for assent entails the firmness and certitude of belief. Faith grows by devotion with respect to the will, which gives the certitude of belief to the intellect and forms faith by charity. Because the will always has dominion over its acts, an increase of faith according to both constancy and devotion results in some believers from a promptness given to the will by grace, which is infused more plentifully now than before Christ.[56] Thus, in the view of Aquinas,

54 1 *Sent.*, Prooem., q. 2, ad 5-6 (1.11; *ed. min.*, 1.10).
55 See Bonaventure: 3 *Sent.*, 25.1.2.-2.2 (3.539-49; *ed. min.*, 3.530-42). See Aquinas: 3 *Sent.*, 25.2.2, qa. 2-4 (3.801-03, 805-09); 4 *Sent.*, 6.2.2, qa. 1, Resp. (4.251); DV, 14.11, Resp., ad 3, 6 (22.470-72); ST, 2a2ae, 1.7 (8.19-20), 2.7-8 (8.33-35): cf. 3a, 71.1 (12.121).
56 3 *Sent.*, 25.2.2, Sol. 1 (3.803-04); see also: ad 1, 5 (3.804-05).

faith cannot be more or less in different men with regard to its object, which is the one and simple first truth, though men can differ more and less with regard to an understanding of the articles. The act of faith can cause a greater participation in its truth by a believer, so that his faith can increase on the part of his intellect, because of a greater firmness and certitude of belief, and on the part of his will, which moves him to believe with either a greater confidence or a greater devotion, and so more promptly. In short, by subjecting himself more certainly and devoutly to the first truth, which he prefers to all others, one Christian can have a greater faith than another.[57]

Approaching the problem only indirectly, Aquinas does not differ essentially from Bonaventure on the increase of faith and its certitude. He differs profoundly from Bonaventure, however, on the certitude of the understanding of faith that constitutes theological knowledge. As seen by Aquinas, the science of theology, directing man to his ultimate end, takes its reasons immediately from the inspiration of the divine light and not from creatures. Hence, ordering the end of all natural knowledge to its own end, theology commands and uses all the other sciences. In doing so, theology has its certitude from the divine light giving the science its power to know not only the things revealed by God, but also the things of nature falling under human reason.[58] The certitude of theological knowledge, therefore, is due to the efficacy of the divine light. Because of that efficacy, theological knowledge perfects man both in action and in contemplation, but chiefly in contemplation, for the end of theology is contemplation of God in beatitude. As a science, moreover, theological knowledge has to do with necessary things and has a proper certitude from its own principles, namely, the articles of faith as they are known infallibly by the superior science or knowledge of God to which the science of theology is subalternated. Theological knowledge, consequently, is most properly wisdom and he who has it is most certain of what he knows, since a man of faith assents more firmly to what he believes than even to the first principles of reason. Led by faith, reason has a fuller grasp of the objects of belief while advancing toward an understanding of them, for the end of our faith is that we arrive at an understanding of what we believe.[59]

57 ST, 2a2ae, 5.4, Resp., ad 2 (8.59).

58 1 *Sent.*, Prol., aa. 1-2 (1.6-10). Cf. ST, 1a, 1.1 (4.6-7), 1.3 (4.11-12); *Expos. de Trin.*, 3.1 (Decker pp. 107-15).

59 1 *Sent.*, Prol., a. 3, qa. 1-3 (1.11-14); *Expos. de Trin.*, 2.2, ad 5, 7 (Decker pp. 89-90). Cf. ST, 1a, 1.2 (4.8-9); 1.4 (4.14).

The obvious difference between Aquinas and Bonaventure on the certitude of theological knowledge, thus far, is rooted in their individual conceptions of theology as a subalternate science. In Bonaventure's conception, theology is subalternated to Scripture which, in its turn, is subject to the first truth as it is known through faith. As a consequence, assenting first and foremost from faith to God as He is revealed in Scripture, the theologian knows the object of faith with certitude by a theological knowledge resulting from the addition of reason to the authority of Scripture on the ground of the first truth. For Bonaventure, then, certitude of theological knowledge is due primarily to the illumination of faith and the divine authority upholding Scripture; this certitude is due secondarily to the reasons taken from creatures and added to both faith and the divine authority with the assistance of the gifts of science and understanding. In the conception of Aquinas, theology is subalternated to the divine science, or the knowledge of God, so that theological knowledge is formed by reasons taken immediately from the divine light as the one source of both reason and revelation. Consequently, for Aquinas, certitude of theological knowledge is due immediately to the divine light and proximately to the articles or principles of faith as they are known infallibly by God in His science. Following this conception, Aquinas differs also from Bonaventure on the mode of procedure by which theology has certain knowledge of the things of faith. As described by Bonaventure, theology proceeds properly in an argumentative way, though respecting and basing its arguments on the narrative mode of the superior science of Scripture.[60] Aquinas makes room in theology not only for the argumentative method, particularly in regard to defending the faith and to understanding its truth, but also for the narrative mode of Scripture as a means of confirming the faith and imparting moral instruction. Thus, coming close in a way to Bonaventure's position, Aquinas puts in Scripture the roots of theology through its proper mode of procedure. He holds that the theologian, in defending and proving the truths of faith, such as the reality of our resurrexion, must proceed from the superior science of Scripture, or from the principles of divine revelation. In that manner, Aquinas rests the arguments of theology on authority, though he refers to the authority of the authors of Scripture, who received the divine revelation, rather than to the authority of God. Theology uses human reason, therefore, not to prove Christian faith, but to serve it by manifesting truth in accordance with the demands of theological reasoning. Accordingly, arguing principally from faith, theology relies

60 See *Brevil.*, Prol., nn. 5-6 (5.206-08; *ed. min.*, 5.12-16).

necessarily only on the divine revelation made to the authors of Scripture. When a theologian uses reason to serve faith in such a theological way, his arguments neither destroy Christian faith nor take away the merit of his belief.[61]

In saying that theological knowledge perfects man in action and in contemplation, but chiefly in contemplation, Aquinas elevates theology above the philosophical sciences, thus considering it to be nobler than they as both speculative and practial. In the speculative order, theology is nobler because of its certitude and of its matter, or subject. The certitude of theology comes from the light of divine science, which cannot be deceived; the certitude of the other sciences comes from the natural light of reason, which can err. The subject of theology has to do principally with things transcending human reason, whereas the philosophical sciences deal only with things subject to reason. In the practical order, theology directs man to his eternal beatitude, or the ultimate end to which all the ends of the other practical sciences are ordered, and so theology is nobler than those sciences.[62] It is according to this line of thought that Aquinas looks upon theology as most properly wisdom and upon the wise theologian as most certain of the truth that he understands. By comparison with natural wisdom, speculative or practical, theology is wisdom absolutely because it considers God, who is the highest cause of the universe, not only as He is knowable from creatures, but also as He alone knows himself and communicates this knowledge to others through revelation. Consequently, as wisdom, theology orders the philosophical sciences and judges their principles in accordance with divine wisdom, which orders all human knowledge and from which, by revelation and not natural reason, theology receives its own principles.[63]

The position taken by Aquinas on theology both as wisdom and as chiefly speculative marks the deepest difference between him and Bonaventure on the certitude of theological knowledge. This difference does not entail a fundamental departure of Aquinas from Bonaventure regarding the superiority or nobility of theology with respect to philosophy. Bonaventure sees theology alone as the perfect science, since it starts from God as the first principle and ends at God as the ultimate and eternal reward. Theology alone is also perfect wisdom, because it begins where philosophy ends, namely, from the supreme

61   1 *Sent.*, Prol., a. 5 (1.16-19); ST, 1a, 1.8-10 (4.21-26): cf. 1.5, ad 2 (4.16). See also: *Expos. de Trin.*, 2.1, ad 5 (Decker, p. 84); 2.2, ad 4-6 (pp. 88-89); 2.3 (pp. 90-97).
62   ST, 1a, 1.5, Resp. (4.16); cf. *Expos. de Trin.*, 2.2, Resp. (Decker, pp. 86-87).
63   ST, 1a, 1.6, Resp., ad 1-2 (4.17-18); cf. 1 *Sent.*, Prol., a. 3, Sol. 1 (1.12). See also: *Expos. de Trin.*, 2.2, ad 1 (Decker pp. 87-88).

cause as the principle of all caused things, and because it returns to God as the reward of all merit and the end of every desire.[64] In Bonaventure's view, then, philosophy is concerned solely with the being of things in nature and in natural knowledge. Founded on faith and the revelation of Scripture, theology is concerned with the being of things in grace, in glory and in the eternal wisdom of God. Hence, making a substrate of philosophy and taking only what is necessary from natural things, theology constructs a mirror, as it were, reflecting divine things and erects a ladder, so to speak, with its feet on the earth and its peak in heaven thus moving between heaven and earth through Christ, who is both God and man. In every respect, therefore, theology is nobler than philosophy, which theology uses to serve the needs of Christian faith.[65]

The very deep difference between the two theologians flows from the necessity posited by Bonaventure, but not by Aquinas, for the operation of certain gifts of the Holy Spirit to have the knowledge obtained with certitude in theology by subordinating reason to faith. This necessity governs Bonaventure's position that theology is chiefly practical and not speculative. In his judgment, the end of the whole of Scripture is to make men good; this is also the end of theology as the knowledge of Christian faith, which is rooted in Scripture and without which it is impossible to please God or to live rightly (*Heb.*, 11. 6). To achieve that end, the theologian needs the gift of understanding to perfect his speculative thinking and the gift of science to perfect his practical thinking. Moreover, to unite his speculative and practical thought, he needs the higher perfection of the gift of wisdom. Since the latter gift consists at once in knowledge and love, the whole of theology, though it leads to contemplation, is concerned principally with making men good.[66]

Relying on the gift of understanding, the theologian goes beyond the simple assent of faith to reach a comprehension of its truth with the help of human reason. By his theological use of reason, he contemplates the Creator as God is known through faith and, within the order of faith, as He is understood both from His own properties and from the properties of His creatures, especially the rational creature, which is an image of God. This contemplation is not purely speculative, but is intended to move the Christian to believe God more devoutly and to love

---

64 *Brevil.*, 1.1 (5.210; *ed. min.*, 5.19).

65 *Brevil.*, Prol., n. 3 (5.204-05; *ed. min.*, 5.9-10); cf. n. 1 (5.202-03; *ed. min.*, 5.5-7). For the way that Bonaventure subordinates all the philosophical sciences to the science and wisdom of theology see: *De reductione artium ad theologiam* (5.320-25; *ed. min.*, 5.218-28).

66 1 *Sent.*, Prooem., q. 3 (1.12-13; *ed. min.*, 1.10-11).

Him more ardently.[67] The gift of science gives to every Christian an inclination from faith to know moral truth and inclines his will toward the good of moral action. This gift, taken properly, directs the Christian to act according to the prior demands of the rule of faith, so that, as the law of nature dictates, he returns good for good and, following both the law of grace and the example of Christ, returns good for evil. Taken widely, however, the gift provides the Christian with a knowledge of his faith as the principal foundation of moral actions and, thereafter, with a knowledge of Christ as the model of the true way of life. Thus, inclined by the will under the influence of this gift, the theologian develops the practical science of Scripture from the principles or articles of faith with the aid of the moral science of natural reason. The latter science, inclining the will toward action, is acquired by the virtue of prudence from the principles of natural law, which orders men toward rectitude and probity of life. The theological knowledge obtained through the gift of science, therefore, is intended principally to direct the Christian by his faith and the divine law both to act and to live in a holy manner after the pattern of Christ. To have such a theological knowledge of the Christian life, the theologian must first have an understanding of the revelation of Scripture.[68]

Bonaventure speaks of two sorts of theological wisdom. The first sort is a knowledge of God according to piety and, as Augustine says, is attained in the Christian religion by worshipping God through faith, hope and charity. The second sort is an experiential knowledge of God attained by the gift of the Holy Spirit. The act of the gift of wisdom is begun in knowledge and consummated in love; acting chiefly from the will, the gift involves a tasting or savour of the divine sweetness, thus giving the Christian an experiential knowledge of the divine goodness.[69] The wisdom of Christian piety is the one to which Bonaventure refers, as we have seen, in connexion with an increase in the certitude of faith by a more devout acquiescence in the truth of faith. To possess this wisdom, then, the Christian must live a holy life founded firmly on faith, though he is not required to understand its truth as this is comprehended on the level of science. The gift of wisdom is the one contributing fundamentally to the growth of faith in certitude, a growth stemming from a fervent adherence by the Christian in piety, holiness and love to the truth of faith. The gift of wisdom, moreover, includes

---

67   3 *Sent.*, 35.un.3, Resp. (3.778; *ed. min.*, 3.783).
68   3 *Sent.*, 35.un.2, Resp., ad 3-4 (3.776-77; *ed. min.*, 3.781-82). See also: 3 *Sent.*, 25.1.1, Resp. "... Symbolo continentur." (3.535; *ed. min.*, 3.526); ad 2 (3.537; *ed. min.*, 3.528).
69   3 *Sent.*, 35.un.1, Resp. "Tertio modo ..." (3.774; *ed. min.*, 3.778-79); see Augustine, *De Trin.*, 14.1.1 (PL 42.1035-37).

and completes the increase in the certitude of faith that the theologian
has by his understanding of the object of belief. Perfecting the virtue of
faith, the gift of understanding directs the theologian principally to consider spiritual creatures and solely according to their eternal reasons,
which are the way to an understanding of the truth of faith. It is by the
eternal reasons of God, therefore, as they are reflected in spiritual
creatures, that the theologian is guided toward the supreme truth as he
assents to it from faith. As a result, he is able to contemplate the
Creator through the reflexions of His eternal reasons in spiritual
creatures. Take, for instance, the truth of the Trinity. The theologian
believes this truth, but he knows, through the gift of understanding,
from the ternary condition of a spiritual creature as an image of the
Creator why the Trinity ought to be in God: just as a word is generated
by a created mind and as a love, binding the two, proceeds from both
the mind and its word, so also the Word and Son of God is generated by
the Father and, binding the one to the other, the Holy Spirit proceeds
from both the Father and the Son. In that way, increasing the certitude
of faith in the speculative order, the clearer illumination of the gift of
understanding removes some of the obscurity surrounding the object of
belief. In a similar way, perfecting the infused virtue of prudence, the
gift of science increases the certitude of faith in the practical order.
This gift directs the theologian to treat of both spiritual and corporeal
creatures; taking account of the natural law, he treats them according to
their temporal reasons while thinking about moral action on the principal ground of the truth of faith. The gift of wisdom, acting initially in
the order of knowledge, completes the theologian's speculative and
practical knowledge of truth by directing that knowledge to the good of
the Christian life. This gift guides the theologian toward a contemplation of God from His eternal reasons according as they are the
way to an experiential knowledge of His goodness. By drawing the
theologian's contemplation of the Creator toward a consummation in
love, the gift of wisdom binds his intellect to his will and, acting chiefly
from love, perfects his theological knowledge by the virtue of charity,
which disposes him to taste the goodness and sweetness of God. Thus,
completing the increase in the theological certitude of faith, the gift of
wisdom perfects in charity the knowledge obtained by the theologian
both of creatures and of their Creator through the gifts of science and
understanding. The experiential knowledge of God attained by the gift
of wisdom gives a far greater delectation, Bonaventure says, than the
intellectual delight flowing from the contemplation of God by the gift of
understanding. Because the gift of wisdom unites knowledge and love,
the way of knowing God by experiencing His goodness is the best of all

and is much more excellent, noble and delightful than the way of knowing Him by the method of argumentation. [70]

Aquinas limits the action of the gifts of the Holy Spirit to the personal perfection of the Christian. The gift of understanding perfects his perception of the truths of faith and the gift of science perfects his judgment of them; in that way, both gifts assist the Christian to assent with perfect certitude to God as the first truth. [71] The gift of wisdom also contributes to the certitude of faith, particularly by assisting the Christian to judge things rightly according to the divine truth, or their uncreated cause, and so this gift differs from the gift of science, which helps the Christian to judge things with certitude according to their created causes. [72] A Christian whose faith is perfected by the gifts of science and wisdom can use his knowledge to perfect other men by manifesting to them the truths of faith and of moral action. This ability is not due to the gifts, however, but to a special grace given to some Christians by the Holy Spirit according to the disposition of His will (1 *Cor.*, 12. 8). [73] For Aquinas, therefore, the action of the gifts of the Holy Spirit does not pertain to the certitude of theological knowledge. The act of judgment, bringing about certitude, belongs to theology according as it is attained by study or inquiry, even though its principles are received through revelation. [74]

CONCLUSION

Bonaventure and Aquinas attribute the certitude of natural reason to God as the primary source of truth and the principal agent of intelligence. They consider the human intellect to be a second cause in the formation of knowledge and in judging things with certitude. This judgment is made in the natural light of reason and according to the truth of first principles, but in such a way that the infallibility of the one comes from the eternal light of God, who alone is entirely infallible, while the immutability of the other comes from His supreme truth, which is alone absolutely immutable. The action of God in causing the certitude of human knowledge is seen by the two theologians to consist in an illumination of the intellect. Although they concur in placing this

---

70   3 *Sent.*, 35.un.3, ad 1-6 (3.778-79; *ed. min.*, 3.783-85); 35.un.1, ad 5 (3.775; *ed. min.*, 3.779-80). The eternal reasons known by faith have to do with things coming to be according to the hidden disposition of God's will and not according to the necessity of nature: DSC, q. 4, ad 21 (5.26).
71   ST, 2a2ae, 8.1-6 (8.66-72); 9.1-3 (8.74-76); cf. 3 *Sent.*, 35.2.2-3 (3.1196-1205).
72   ST, 2a2ae, 45.1-5 (8.339-43); cf. 3 *Sent.*, 35.2.1 (3.1191-96).
73   ST, 2a2ae, 9.1, ad 2 (8.74); 45.5, Resp. (8.343).
74   ST, 1a, 1.6, ad 3 (4.18).

illumination within God's conservation of the intellect, their particular views do not coincide on His action both as influencing and as cooperating with the natural work of the intellect. For Bonaventure, the created light and principles of the intellect are not sufficient of themselves to move it, so that God must add to them, even after their production, the influence of His uncreated light and principles of truth. In cooperating with the intellect, which pertains to the soul as an image of God, He regulates its operations according to its natural capacity to grasp truth. The combined influence and cooperation of God is such that the intellect judges things not only by its own light and principles, but also in His infallible light and eternal reasons. Consequently, the infallible certitude and immutability of truth are not due immediately to the human intellect. For Aquinas, the influence of God on the intellect involves simply the production of its natural light and self-evident principles. God moves the intellect into act by giving it a light of intelligence and by impressing on it similitudes derived from His eternal reasons. Cooperating with the acts of the intellect, He directs it according to its own light and principles, so that they are sufficient of themselves for the intellect to judge things without going beyond the created similitudes of His eternal truth. As a result, an infallible certitude and immutability of truth are due immediately to the light and principles of the intellect. Though Bonaventure and Aquinas, following Aristotle and Augustine in distinctive ways, differ regarding the effect of God's action on the intellect, they hold in common, speaking absolutely, that the light of His immutable truth is the infallible rule of certitude in human knowledge.

Christian faith, to both Bonaventure and Aquinas, is more certain absolutely than human knowledge, which has the greater certitude in relation to what is evident to reason. The two theologians ground Christian faith in Scripture, which teaches truth by the authority of God, who cannot deceive or be deceived. Upheld by His infallible authority, Scripture contains a divine revelation made known by the power of the Holy Spirit. The Christian, as seen by Aquinas and Bonaventure, assents to this revelation by a divine illumination so perfecting his intellect that it adheres with an infallible certitude to God as the first truth. In adhering to God, the intellect responds to a command of the will in accordance with His authority, which causes in the intellect, for Bonaventure, an indubitable assent to truth and, for Aquinas, an infallibility of truth. Bonaventure safeguards the indubitability of faith by a dependence on the divine foreknowledge, which is infallible because it is the whole power comprehending what God foresees. In that way, the infallible certitude of faith rests immediately on the divine authority rather than on the divine illumination conforming the intellect to the light of God. Aquinas protects the infallibility of faith by a simple reliance on the infallibility of divine truth, so that the illumination of faith, in full dependence on the divine authority, gives rise immediately to an infallible certitude from the principles of faith. In the final analysis, however, the two theologians guarantee the infallible certitude of faith by the impossibility of the intellect ever being deceived by God, who can never lie.

Neither Bonaventure nor Aquinas allows the possibility of an increase in the certitude of faith with respect to its principal object, which is the divine and simple truth, the one that is most certain and beyond deceit. Both theologians admit, though in slightly different ways, that the ordinary Christian can grow in his belief not only by obtaining an understanding of his faith, but also and especially by a more steadfast and more devout assent to its truth, thus increasing the certitude of his belief. Bonaventure and Aquinas also acknowledge that the theologian, having the task of teaching Christian faith, ought to obtain an understanding of its truth at the level of science, and so to attain the perfection of theological certitude. Although Bonaventure and Aquinas concur in many respects on the various elements entering into the constitution of theology, particularly regarding its mode of procedure and its superiority over philosophy, they diverge considerably on the certitude of theology as a subalternate science and, as a consequence, very profoundly on the manner in which theological knowledge arrives at its proper certitude. Aquinas sees theology as subalternated directly to the knowledge or science of God. As a result, the certitude of theological knowledge is due immediately to the divine light, as the one source of truth whether natural or revealed, and proximately to the principles of faith as they are known in the divine science. While theology has recourse to human reason for the manifestation of truth, the certitude of theology has no necessary dependence on the reasons taken from creatures; the science uses those reasons only as an extrinsic means to serve the needs of faith. Since theology reaches an understanding of God not only as He is known by revelation, but also from creatures according to their divine truth, theology is most properly wisdom and, as such, most certain to the Christian possessing it. Because theology directs the Christian, even in his actions, to the ultimate contemplation of God in beatitude, theological knowledge is chiefly speculative as both science and wisdom. Bonaventure sees theology as subalternated to the science of Scripture through which it depends on the first truth as this is known by faith. Consequently, theology attains its certitude by adding reason to the authority of Scripture on the ground of the first truth, so that the certitude of theological knowledge results primarily from the illumination of faith and secondarily from human reason as it is perfected in faith by the gifts of the Holy Spirit. Thus, relying in a necessary but not a subordinate way on human reason, the certitude of theological knowledge is established in the speculative order by the gift of understanding, which directs the theologian from Christian faith to a contemplation of God by way of His spiritual creatures; it is established in the practical order by the gift of science, which inclines the theologian on the foundation of Scripture, though taking due account of the natural law, to consider both spiritual and corporeal creatures while thinking about the good of moral action according to the law of grace and the example of Christ. By uniting the speculative and practical knowledge of theology, the gift of wisdom completes the theological certitude of faith and, binding knowledge to love, directs the theologian toward the good of the Christian life. Predominantly practical, then, theology has complete perfection when its contemplation is consummated in charity, thus giving rise to an experiential knowledge of the goodness of God. Aquinas limits the action of the gifts of the Holy Spirit to the personal perfection of the Christian with regard to the perception and judgment of the truths of faith. The judgment giving certitude to theological knowledge is not due to the gifts of the Holy Spirit, but to the industry and study of the theologian, even though he receives the principles of theology from divine revelation. Their deep-rooted differences regarding theological knowledge notwithstanding, Aquinas and Bonaventure are united fundamentally in grounding the certitude of theology principally in the revelation made in Scripture on the authority of God and accepted by the Christian through the illumination of faith.

Since St. Thomas and St. Bonaventure have each been honoured for many centuries as a Doctor of the Church, it is well to ask in 1974, the seventh centenary of their death: what can they contribute to our understanding of the certitude of the doctrine and faith of the Church? This is no idle question inasmuch as, representing the Christian tradition in the thirteenth century, they contributed in no small measure to the reform of the Church undertaken at the Council of Lyons in 1274. To answer the question, it would be necessary to analyze their positions not only on the faith of the Church and the source of its authority, but also on the sort of authority given by Christ to His Church to secure its faith and to teach the truth.[75]

75 St. Thomas and St. Bonaventure, regarding the magisterium of the Church, do not speak directly about a papal infallibility; rather, appealing to Scripture, they refer to the pope's plenitude

From our short study of their doctrines on certitude, both of natural and of revealed knowledge, it is clear that St. Bonaventure and St. Thomas can show us the way to maintain inviolably the truth of divine revelation while, at the same time and with the help of human reason, developing particular forms of theological knowledge that do not separate Christians from one another.

of power or authority to teach the truth and to decide the things that pertain to faith. For the relevant texts in St. Thomas see: ST, 2a2ae, 1.10 (8.22-23); 5.3 (8.57-58); 11.2, ad 3 (8.99): cf. *De pot. Dei*, 10.4, ad 13 (Taurini 2.268-69). See in St. Bonaventure: 1 *Sent.*, 11.un.1, Resp. "Similiter ..." (1.212; *ed. min.*, 1.172); *Quaestiones disputatae de perfectione evangelica*, 2.2, ad 19 (5.147): Replicatio "Qui autem ..." (5.155); *Brevil.*, 6.12 "Postremo ..." (5.278; *ed. min.*, n. 5, 5.150); *Quare Fratres Minores praedicent ...*", nn. 2-3 (8.375); *Apologia pauperum*, 1.1 (8.235): cf. *Commentarius in Evangelium sancti Lucae*, 9.20.34 (7.727), 24.44.56-58 (7.601).

JOHN PECHAM AND THE BACKGROUND
OF AQUINAS'S *DE AETERNITATE MUNDI*

Ignatius Brady O.F.M.

NOTWITHSTANDING Saint Thomas's customary calm and quiet
mode of procedure, he was sometimes driven by his own inner zeal
to the point of exasperation when faced by the faults and defects of his
contemporaries. He shows his impatience or surprise when their
arguments are slipshod and inconsistent, and reveals his indignation
when Christians propose arguments that militate against their faith and
their duties as Christian teachers.[1] How this trait reveals itself in attacks on such masters as William of Saint-Amour or Gerard of Abbeville, or against contemporary Radical Aristotelians, is too well-known
to need proof here.

The same characteristic of the Angelic Doctor is equally apparent in
his short work *De aeternitate mundi*, against a hitherto unknown adversary — to the point that he bluntly addresses to him or them a
paraphrase of the words of Job to his would-be counsellors: *Ergo illi qui
tam subtiliter eam* [*repugnantiam*] *percipiunt, soli sunt homines, et cum
eis oritur sapientia?*[2] Nonetheless, to understand Thomas's indignation,
his use of this verse, and indeed the whole import of this work, requires,
we may truthfully say, more investigation into the background of the
argument than has hitherto been undertaken.

I. Contra Murmurantes?

It is rather apparent, first of all, that the title of the work is simply
De aeternitate mundi; and that in consequence we should abandon the
later appendage: *contra murmurantes,* and not build up history (or a
story) on a foundation not laid by Saint Thomas. At least, it is the conclusion of Martin Grabmann that in the oldest catalogs of Saint

---

1   I have but paraphrased here the words of A. Dondaine, O.P., in his *Praefatio* to *S. Thomae
de Aquino Expositio super Iob ad litteram, Opera omnia* 26 (Romae 1965) 17.

2   Cf. *Iob* 12, 2: *Ergo vos estis soli homines, et vobiscum morietur sapientia?*; and St. Thomas at
this verse (ed. cit., 179b).

Thomas's works and in all the manuscripts of the *De aeternitate* save Siena *U.IV.9* (late fourteenth century), the words *contra murmurantes* are not to be found.[3] By contrast, the same criteria lead to the conclusion that Thomas did add the qualification *contra Averroistas* to the title of the *De unitate intellectus.*[4] It is not too much to conjecture that some one later thought it apropos to add a like designation to the *De aeternitate mundi,* at least in the catalogs of Thomas's writings.

Yet such an addition is at variance with the very contents of the work and carries with it an interpretation which has little or no justification in history. Certainly a close examination of Aquinas's thought and the course of his whole argument shows that while he is attacking a specific person or persons, he is not directing his words to some one who has berated his position. Hence the work is not to be regarded as "against the complainers": that is, it is not a reply to those contemporary theologians who felt his position on the subject was heretical; nor again, a rebuke addressed to some group (apparently headed by Saint Bonaventure) which clung to the doctrine of a temporal creation. Rather, as we shall attempt to show below, it represents what Fr. Dondaine calls Saint Thomas's impatience and surprise, and even his indignation, at the lack of clear thinking (and the use of his *Summa theologiae* against himself) on the part of one young Franciscan master, John Pecham.

Even in such a historical context we might find some justification for the subtitle *contra murmurantes,* if we were to interpret it less in the specific sense of a murmur or complaint (as used frequently in the Vulgate), and more in the generic meaning of an indistinguishable or unintelligible sound. It could then be predicated of one who speaks so low that his arguments are not loud and clear: not a grumbler, but a mumbler! Such an interpretation is possible, though it strains the range of probability.

II. THE POSITION OF SAINT THOMAS

At this juncture we should examine again the text of Saint Thomas, to discover what *his* complaint is. For the moment we must limit ourselves to his own words, leaving the full story to reveal itself after the examination of extraneous texts in the endeavour to discover the object of Aquinas's indignation.[5]

---

3   M. Grabmann, *Die Werke des hl. Thomas von Aquin,* 3. Ausg., BGPTMA 22, Heft 1-2 (Münster 1949) 341, and description of codices, 155-238.
4   Ibid., 44-118 (ancient catalogs), 138-218 (mss.).
5   We use the text and divisions of J. Perrier, *S. Thomae Aquinatis Opuscula omnia necnon opera minora* I (Paris 1949) 52-61.

We take it for granted, begins Saint Thomas, that according to Catholic belief the world did not exist from eternity, but had a beginning. Yet we may raise the question, as in fact it has already been raised, whether the world could have always existed. If this were to mean that the world or anything else could have existence independently of God because not made by Him, not only faith but philosophy also would reject such a view. On the other hand, if the question means that something (the world as a whole, for example) always has been and nonetheless has been caused by God, we have here a genuine question. If such is not possible, it will be either because God could not make a creature that always has been, or because such a creature is intrinsically impossible, even if God had the power to make it. Since all agree that by reason of His infinite power God could bring into being an eternal creature (n. 1), the question is reduced to the second alternative: whether it is possible that something come to be which has always existed (n. 2).

Only two reasons can be offered against this possibility: either that it would do away with passive potency, or present two mutually exclusive concepts (*intellectus*). The first argument is not very valid: if it is question of a spiritual being, an eternal angel for example, such a being does not and never did possess passive potency, since it is immaterial; and if it is question of an eternal material being, one cannot affirm without heresy that its passive potency has always existed. Hence according to the faith we must concede that something caused by God has not always existed. Yet from this it does not follow that God cannot bring it about that there come into being something that is *semper ens.*

The second reason offered, that the two concepts of a "created something" (*aliquid creatum a Deo*) and "eternal existence" (*semper fuerit*) are mutually opposed and exclusive, deserves more attention (nn. 2-7). If they are incompatible, then it would be false to say that such could be done by God. If there is no repugnance, it would not only not be false, but even possible; otherwise we would do injustice to God's omnipotence.

This is indeed the very heart of the question: whether "to be wholly and substantially created by God" and "to have a duration without beginning" are mutually exclusive. This would be true either if an agent cause, God in this case, had to precede its effect in duration; or if not-being of necessity preceded being in duration (since what is caused by God is said to be made from nothing); or if both alternatives together excluded such a possibility.

There is ample proof that God, had He so willed it, need not exist before His creature: He is a cause that produces His effect immediately (*subito*), not through a series of steps (*per motum*); therefore the beginning and end of His action are not only simultaneous, but one and the same.[6] This perhaps is not easy to grasp, especially if one's imagination influences his thinking. Men are so used to considering causality *per motum* (with a corresponding time-gap), that they find it hard to accept the concept of an agent which does not precede its effect in time or in duration of some kind. Again, God causes through His will, without discursive deliberation; which again implies there is no need that the will precede the effect in duration (n. 4). Other arguments can be offered that lead to the same conclusion (n. 5).

On the other hand, if there is anything abhorrent to the intellect in stating that something which is made never was not, it would arise from the necessity that its non-being must precede its being, since creation of its very essence means that something is made from nothing. Yet, as Saint Anselm makes clear,[7] the proper understanding of *nihil* reveals that it is pure non-being, in no way a something (*aliquid*); and that in consequence there is no real relationship between what is made and *nihil*, as though the creature had first to be "nothing" and then be "something" (n. 6). Even if we suppose that such an order or relationship exist, and interpret it as meaning that the creature is made from nothing, that is after nothing, it does not follow that "after" must be taken in the order of time or duration. For such order or relation a priority of nature, not of duration, will suffice, namely that "nothing" be prior by nature to "being." The being the creature has is from another; left to itself, taken only in itself, in its nature, it is nothing. This does not signify that it is therefore at once nothing and being, since there is no question of a time-difference. Hence if some creature always has been, this does not imply that at some time it was a nothing; but that its nature is such that left to itself it would be a nothing (n. 7).

Thus far Saint Thomas has argued from reason (even if our paraphrase is all too halting) that there is nothing repellent to our mind in the proposition that something was made by God and yet never was not. He now turns to the great minds of the past as living proof of his position. If there were any such repugnance, it is remarkable that Augustine (a prime authority, we may surmise, for Thomas's opponent or opponents) did not see it (n. 8). This would be the most effective way of overthrowing the thesis of an eternal world; and yet while Augustine offers many arguments against such a teaching in books XI and XII of

---

6   See also the presentation of this proof in the *Summa theologiae* I, 46, 2, ad 1 (ed. Ottawa 297b 10-20).

7   *Monologion*, c. 8 (PL 158, 156 C; ed. F. Schmitt I, 23).

The City of God, he passes over completely such an approach. Indeed, he hints in the tenth book that there is no such repugnance, and again in book XI, chapter 4.[8] It is equally astounding that the noblest of the physicists (or the philosophers, according to a variant reading), who while they claimed the world to be eternal said at the same time that it was made by God, did not find therein any contradiction or repugnance (n. 9). *Ergo illi qui tam subtiliter eam percipiunt, soli sunt homines; et cum eis oritur sapientia?*

Finally, since *they* cite certain authorities in their favour, it remains for us to show that in reality such arguments are a weak foundation for their position. If two which they offer, from John Damascene and from Hugh of Saint-Victor, both plainly say that no thing can be co-eternal with the First Principle, such statements and others like them should be interpreted in accordance with Boethius's distinction between a continuous or progressive eternity, interminable, without beginning or end, and the *tota simul et perfecta possessio* which is proper to the true eternity of the divine being (n. 10).

If we make this distinction, then what some offer against an eternal creation does not follow, namely that thereby a creature would be equal to God in duration. No creature, certainly, can share the unchangeableness of God who is without beginning or end and without any succession, in the full and simultaneous possession of interminable life. This Augustine makes clear in his *De civitate Dei* XII, 15, where he shows that since even in the immortality of the angels there is a certain past and present, they cannot be co-eternal with God. So too in *De Genesi ad litteram* VIII, he writes: "Since the nature of the Trinity is entirely unchangeable, it is thus so eternal that nothing can be co-eternal with It." Almost the same thing is found in book XI of the *Confessions*. But we have no grounds to conclude therefrom that in no manner whatever can any thing be co-eternal with God, since successive and changing eternity is not excluded (n. 11).

Lastly, *they* adduce reasons which the philosophers touched on and solved. Among such the most difficult is that based on an infinity of souls: if the world always has been, then at the present moment the number of souls must be actually infinite. Yet this argument does not touch the heart of the matter, since God could have made the world without men and souls; or He could have created men when He did, even if the physical universe as a whole were eternal. Besides, we have yet to demonstrate that God cannot cause an actually infinite number of

8   Thomas had cited the same authorities earlier, but in reverse order, in *Summa theologiae* I, 46, 2, ad 1 (ed. cit., 297b 1-10).

beings. We pass over their other arguments either because we have already answered them elsewhere[9] or because some of them are so weak that their very weakness suggests that the opposite position is probable (n. 12).

III. *Quidam Dicunt*: Who are They?

The *De aeternitate mundi*, as even our slight synopsis makes manifest, is a historical document directed against a definite historical opponent — not necessarily some one who directly attacked Saint Thomas, but quite apparently some contemporary who, engaged in a dispute on the eternity of the world, had taken an approach or viewpoint different from that held by the Angelic Doctor from the days when he was a bachelor of the *Sentences*: that though by faith one must reject the position favoured by the philosophers of an eternal world, one cannot at the same time offer a genuine demonstration against such a thesis or for the Christian doctrine of creation.

Whoever this opponent might have been, his disputation took place around or shortly before the syllabus of 10 December 1270, whereby Stephen Tempier condemned thirteen articles currently taught or asserted at Paris.[10] One proof of this is the acknowledged fact that the treatise of Aquinas is part of a collection of writings of current interest which Master Godfrey of Fontaines collected during the years 1270-1272.[11] Even apart from this extraneous proof, the text itself shows it must date from the same period; more specifically, from the second regency of Saint Thomas at Paris, from about January 1269 to April/May 1272.

Since the tract plainly enough is directed against a specific person and a specific disputation, it seems in order to institute some slight search among the masters at Paris who either shortly before or precisely during the second regency of Saint Thomas undertook to discuss the question, in hope that we can identify the object of his wrath.

Let us start with one well-known adversary, Gerard of Abbeville,

---

9 Saint Thomas had already considered the question of an eternal world in his *Scriptum super II Sent.*, d. 1, q. 1, a. 5 (before or about 1256); in *Contra Gentiles* II, cc. 32-38 (about 1261-1264); *De potentia* III, a. 17 (Rome after 1265?); and *Summa theologiae* I, 46, 1-2 (Italy c. 1265-1267). Dates are based on I. T. Eschmann's *A Catalogue of St. Thomas's Works*, appendix to E. Gilson, *The Christian Philosophy of St. Thomas Aquinas* (New York 1956) 385, 387, 391.

10 Cf. H. Denifle-E. Chatelain, *Chartularium Universitatis Parisiensis*, n. 43; tom. I (Paris 1889) 486-487.

11 Cf. P. Glorieux, "Un recueil scolaire de Godefroid de Fontaines (Paris, Nat. Lat. 16297)," *Recherches de théologie ancienne et médiévale* 3 (1931) 37-53.

whose Quodlibet XIV[12] not only contains a short question (X): *Utrum sit ponere mundum eternum* (and questions on at least three other topics touched on in the condemnation of 1270), but begins with a lengthy dispute *de statu diversarum personarum in ecclesia*, which gives the work its place in history, since this opening question is a frontal attack on the twentieth chapter of Aquinas's *De perfectione vitae spiritualis,* to which Thomas replied by adding the last six chapters of his treatise.[13] The Quodlibet is correspondingly dated as of Advent 1269.

There is nothing, however, in the tenth question[14] which shows any relationship to the *De aeternitate mundi.* It opens with two reasons from Aristotle[15] that time and motion neither begin nor end; and then argues against an eternal world on the basis of paschal reckonings, which would have no meaning if the course of the sun and moon were eternal; or again, with the briefest of references to Augustine, *De civitate Dei* XII, c. 4, from the incompatibility of changing time and unchanging eternity; and finally from an interpretation of Scripture according to which all movement of the heavens will cease when the number of the elect is complete. The answer to the argument from Aristotle provides a more philosophic approach, with the conclusion: *Salve tamen pace Augustini, Jeronymi et Bede et aliorum expositorum non probavit Aristoteles motus et temporis eternitatem sed coevitatem...*

Though Thomas refuted Gerard on other matters, he does not show any interest in this rather prosaic approach to our question.

Of the secular masters of the period Gerard alone seems to have left any literary remains. Perforce then our next step is to turn to the Franciscan masters between 1265 and 1270: Friar William de Baliona (Baglione, Vaglon, etc.), regent 1266-1267; Walter of Brugge, 1267-1268; Eustace of Arras, 1268 until probably the end of 1269; John Pecham, January 1270-1272 (?).[16] Of these, only de Baglione and Pecham have questions on the eternity of the world. At least, according to our present knowledge neither Walter nor Eustace seems to have

---

12   Edited by Ph. Grand, "Le Quodlibet XIV de Gérard d'Abbeville. La vie de Gérard d'Abbeville", *Archives d'histoire doctr. et litt. du moyen âge* 31 (1964) 222-269.

13   Cf. P. Glorieux, "Pour qu'on lise le *De perfectione* de saint Thomas d'Aquin," *Vie spirituelle* 23 (1930), suppl. 97-126; id., "Les polémiques *Contra Geraldinos.* Les pièces du dossier," *Rech. de théol. anc. et méd.* 6 (1934) 8-9; and his "*Contra Geraldinos.* L'enchaînement des polémiques," ibid. 7 (1935) 129-155.

14   Ed. cit., 265-268.

15   *Physic.* VIII, c. 1, text 11 and t. 10 (251b 20, and 251b 12); not identified by the editor.

16   Cf. I. Brady, "Questions at Paris c. 1260-1270," *Archivum Franciscanum Historicum* 61 (1968) 447-461; 62 (1969) 681-689. Pecham perhaps left Paris in the spring of 1272, as did Saint Thomas, and went to teach at Oxford.

touched on any of the tendencies or errors then current in the faculty of Arts, perhaps because they judged such problems to have been sufficiently treated by their immediate predecessor.

William of Baglione merits our attention for his concern with problems which were very much to the forefront at Paris in the decade before the condemnation of 1270.[17] In his series of questions *De symbolo* (a name we have elsewhere given them, since they follow the order of the Creed), two are devoted to the problem of an eternal world. The first: *Utrum mundus habuerit sue duracionis inicium vel sit ponere mundum esse ab eterno,* exists in two forms: in the codex Florence, Bibl. Naz. *Conv. soppr. B. 6. 912,* ff. 13d-16d (= F), we possess, it would seem, the script of the original dispute; in the ms. Vatican, *Pal. lat. 612,* ff. 154a-154d (= V), a revised version in a somewhat shorter and more polished form. Since in the Response (in both versions) the author declares: *Credo absque dubio hoc, scilicet quod mundus non est ab eterno per efficacissimas raciones esse demonstrabile* (F 15b; V 154c), he proceeds to ask in a second question: *Quaeritur utrum mundum non esse eternum sit demonstrabile, ita quod per raciones necessarias possit istud probari,* and to claim in answer: *Cum creaturam esse coeternam Deo fides et racio condemnet, sicut dicit B. Augustinus, XII De civitate, c. 15, et eternitas mundi necessario inferat istam coeternitatem, absque dubio mundum non esse nec posse esse eternum certissimis et efficacissimis racionibus potest ostendi.*[18]

Such a position, we need not be reminded, is directly opposed to that taken by Thomas in the *De aeternitate*; and well it may be, since the Questions of Master William are an attack on Aquinas's answer to the same question in his Script on the Sentences.[19] In at least four, if not five, of William's arguments in the F version (of which only one is retained in V) and in several phrases in the latter part of the Response in F (which here differs from V), Thomas's arguments and objections are cited and answered.[20]

---

17 Cf. I. Brady, "Background to the Condemnation of 1270: Master William of Baglione O.F.M.," *Franciscan Studies* 30 (1970) 5-48.

18 Cf. I. Brady, "The Questions of Master William of Baglione, O.F.M., *De Aeternitate mundi*," *Antonianum* 47 (1972) 362-371, 576-616.

19 Cf. *Scriptum super II Sent.,* d. 1, q. 1, a. 5 (ed. Parma 1856) VI, 390b-395b.

20 Thus, in the Sed contra, arg. 10 (or k), which becomes arg. 12 (or m) in V: "Forte dices [id est Thomas, ad 6 in contrarium]: ad hoc responderent philosophi: primo ille Algazel, quod anime separate non habent dependenciam. Averroes diceret quod omnes anime sunt una anima. Sed ista absurda sunt, et ex hiis mendicare responsiones non videtur nisi fugam querere; et verbo suo convinci dicendo quod non potest demonstrari mundum non esse ab eterno quia ista racio de infinitate animarum valet [ad] demonstracionem saltem huic qui nescivit aliter respondere vel ad minus non ostendit se scire. Nec decet theologum ut recurrat ad errores philosophorum" [F 14d; V 154b]. — Later in F, part of the response would be unintelligible without reference to Thomas:

Nonetheless, the Questions of this almost unknown Friar Minor are not the object of Thomas's *De aeternitate mundi*. A priori, the time-gap between the regency of William and the second regency of Saint Thomas does away with the sense of immediacy and urgency that pervades the opuscule of Aquinas. But a stronger argument is to be found in the questions themselves: while they claim that an eternal world is intrinsically impossible, and make ample use to this effect of Augustine, especially of the *De civitate Dei*, adducing likewise the argument from infinity of souls, they lack the two authorities, of Damascene and Hugh of Saint-Victor, which Thomas says (n. 10) are used by his opponent. Besides, the Questions of John Pecham fit that opponent like a glove.

*
* *

In a well-known though often misinterpreted remark[21] Roger Marston testifies that at an inception at Paris under Gerard of Abbeville, Brother Thomas of Aquino and Brother John of Pecham were present with some twenty-four other doctors. The ceremony and concurrent disputations, if one may judge from the chronology of Gerard, Thomas and Pecham, took place in the first months of 1269 (Parisian style), that is 1270.[22] Pecham himself must have incepted shortly before, in late 1269, since he replaced as regent Eustace of Arras, who left Paris on 15 March 1270, in the company of Saint Louis and his crusaders.[23]

Given the agitation that troubled the University at this time and which led to the syllabus of 10 December 1270, it is not at all surprising that Pecham should enter the fray. Besides his questions on the creation and/or eternity of the world edited below, he disputed at least two others related to the errors condemned by Tempier: one on the reality of hell-fire (art. 8), another on the unicity of the intellect (art. 1). In Quodlibet IV, the eighth question reads: *Quaeritur per oppositionem de malicia, utrum anima racionalis damnata paciatur ab igne materiali*

"Unde exemplum de puero nutrito in loco solitario quod ipsi ponunt nihil facit ad propositum" (f. 15b); cf. Saint Thomas, Respond. (392b-393a).

21 See his *Quaest. disp. de emanatione aeterna*, q. 6, in *Fr. Rogeri Marston, O.F.M., Quaestiones disputatae* (Quaracchi 1932) 116f. See the study of the late D. A. Callus, O.P., who shows that no condemnation of Saint Thomas is here implied: "The Problem of the Unity of Form and Richard Knapwell, O.P.," *Mélanges offerts à Etienne Gilson* (Toronto-Paris 1959) 152f.

22 Cf. I. Brady, *Prolegomena* to *Fr. Rogeri Marston, O.F.M. Quodlibeta quatuor* (Quaracchi 1968) 10*; the chronology therein presented needs some slight emendation, since I am now convinced (see the following note) that Pecham did not begin his regency with the Michaelmas term of 1269, but the Hilary term (to use Oxford expressions for Paris) of 1270.

23 Cf. I. Brady, "Questions at Paris...," *Arch. Franc. Hist.* 62 (1969) 687 f.

imaginarie tantum an vere.[24] This is followed[25] by the fourth question *De anima: Quaeritur per oppositum utrum unus est intellectus in omnibus hominibus.*[26] This latter group of questions is, it seems to me, posterior to the questions on the eternity of the world; and more probably the same can be said (on the basis at least of more maturity of treatment) of Quodlibet IV. A partial proof may be found in the opening question *De anima,* which is much more explicit than the Response of Question I (below), on Augustine's rejection of the soul as made from the substance of God[27]; a more substantial proof can be deduced from the fourth question (on the unity of the intellect), wherein argument 30 discourses at length on a proof drawn from an infinity of souls,[28] thus developing what Question II (below), argument i, touches on in passing.

Since the problem of chronology is relatively unimportant at the moment, let us return to the questions on the eternity of the world, to see if they indeed provoked Thomas's reaction in the *De aeternitate mundi.*

There seems little in the first question that might have caused such a reaction. It is true, Thomas would have recognized the *Summa theologiae* I, 25, 4, and several articles of q. 45, as source-material for certain arguments. At the same time, he clearly saw that Pecham remained close to Bonaventure's opening questions on Book II, dist. 1, of the *Sentences,* even to the extent that the Response is hardly more than a paraphrase and expansion of the Seraphic Doctor's position. There is no attempt to demonstrate creation philosophically, but to investigate the problem intellectually and theologically. The only parallel to the *De aeternitate mundi* appears to lie in the citation from Hugh of Saint-Victor,[29] which Thomas states (n. 10) is used by his opponent. Yet Pecham seeks thereby to illustrate the power of God and not the question of an eternal world.

The case is quite other, however, in respect to the second question.

---

24 In cod. Flor. Bibl. Laurenz. Plut. XVII sin. 8, f. 75c-d; cf. V. Doucet, "Notulae bibliographicae de quibusdam operibus Fr. Ioannis Pecham O.F.M.," *Antonianum* 8 (1933) 317. The major part at least of the Response is reproduced by Roger Marston, Quodl. IV, q. 21 (ed. cit. 410-412).

25 The title *Quodlibet IV* is given by way of convenience (as the last discovered, by Fr. Doucet), and has nothing to do with chronology. That it precedes the *Quaestiones de anima* is shown by Doucet, art. cit., 322f.

26 Edited by H. Spettmann, *Johannis Pechami Quaestiones tractantes de anima,* BGPTMA 19, Heft 5-6 (Münster 1918) 38-59.

27 *Qq. de anima,* q. 1, resp.; ed. cit., 5-6.

28 *Qq. de anima,* q. 4, arg. 30, and resp.; ed. cit., 44f, 58f.

29 See below, Quaestio I, resp., at note 31.

Thomas could not help noting that the *Summa* I, 46, 1: *Utrum universitas creaturarum semper fuit,* furnished material for this question, and that not always to the purpose intended by him. More than once, indeed, his answers to arguments are themselves rebutted.[30] In the Response creation in time is said to be an article of faith, in agreement with Thomas (I, 46, 2); which merits to be investigated by reason helped by faith. Then against the warning of Saint Thomas (ibid.), not to attempt to demonstrate this truth by adducing so-called necessary reasons, which leave the faith open to ridicule, Pecham proceeds to offer five reasons, none of which Thomas would qualify as necessary. Small wonder, if this question is the object of his attack, that the *De aeternitate* opens by emphasizing anew the distinction between faith and reason in respect to the problem at hand.

Yet we can hardly say that the opuscule of Saint Thomas goes on to attack point for point the demonstrations of Pecham. Such a facile proof of identity would be almost too much to expect. Nonetheless, since these five arguments labour under the deficiences Thomas had previously warned against in the *Summa* I, 46, 1-2, and now repeats in the *De aeternitate,* nn. 4-7, especially the failure to see that there is no repugnance between the concept of something created and that of always existing, we have something of a case, at least in respect to the first two proofs of the Franciscan. To this we must add Thomas's rejection of an authority from Damascene (n. 10) as of value in the debate: precisely that authority cited by Pecham in the third proof. Our thesis stumbles a little in respect to his fourth argument. Hugh of Saint-Victor is cited indeed; but what Thomas quotes from him (n. 10) and interprets away is the authority used by Pecham in the first question. Yet it is likely that Thomas is relying on his memory, without the text of Pecham before him, and recalls the use somewhere of the words of Hugh. Both authorities, as we have seen earlier, are offset by the distinction made by Boethius of a successive eternity and the unchanging eternity of God; which distinction leads Thomas to reject (n. 11) as a non-sequitur the objection that a creature would equal God in duration, because God's duration is total, whereas that of the creature is a constant succession. To affirm this Thomas cites at length the words of Augustine in *De civitate* XII, 15. Yet this same authority in shorter form[31] is used by Pecham in the fifth proof, and is followed by the general conclusion: *Dico igitur quod mundus nullo modo capax fuit*

---

30 See arg. 6; and in the *Contra*, arg. k, 1, and o.
31 Perhaps the lacuna of four lines at this point in F (see Quaest. II, note 145) has some significance.

aeternae et interminabilis durationis. The same position is taken by Pecham in answer to the second argument, on the basis of Augustine's words *Super Genesim* VIII, also quoted by Thomas in number 11.

Finally, our opponents, remarks Thomas (n. 12), adduce reasons touched on and solved by the philosophers, including the difficult one based on an infinity of souls. The latter argument appears in almost every scholastic who disputed the question; in Pecham it is used as argument i of the second question.

The cumulative effect of the rather consistent parallels between the Question(s) of Pecham and the *De aeternitate mundi* leads, it seems to me, to only one conclusion: that the opuscule of Aquinas was indeed provoked by the disputation of the Franciscan. Our thesis lacks only one more element: to put it into a historical setting.

IV. PARIS, EARLY 1270

Relations between Pecham and Thomas at Paris are known to have been not overly cordial, even though the Minor later spoke reverently of "Brother Thomas de Aquino of holy memory"[32] and claimed that on one occasion he alone stood by him in a dispute over the unity of form.[33] On the other hand, Bartholomew of Capua was to testify at the Naples inquiry prior to Thomas's canonization that on the occasion of a dispute Iohannes de Pizano answered Thomas in bombastic and pompous language.[34] This may mean that Pecham as a baccalaureus formatus was respondent at some disputation; or, since masters did not attend ordinary disputed questions of other masters, that he participated in the inception of a student of Saint Thomas (or even of another student, when both were present); or that this disagreement happened in connection with Pecham's own inception.

---

32   In his letter (1 January 1285) to the cardinals of the Curia; ed. C. T. Martin, *Registrum Epistolarum J. Peckham, Archiepiscopi Cantuariensis* III (London 1885) 871.

33   Letter to the Bishop of Lincoln (1 June 1285); ed. cit., III, 899. We pass over Pecham's later reactions as Archbishop to nascent Thomism at Oxford. The matter has been amply discussed by D. A. Callus, art. cit., 126-136, and by Theod. Crowley, O.F.M., "John Peckham, O.F.M., Archbishop of Canterbury, versus the New Aristotelianism," *Bulletin of the John Rylands Library* 33 (1951) 242-255.

34   Cf. *Acta Sanctorum Martii* I (Antverpiae 1668) 712a; and *Fontes vitae s. Thomae Aquinatis* IV (Var 1934) 374. The Dominican chronicler Nicholas Trivet (early fourteenth century) also says of Pecham: "erat...gestus afflatusque pompatici, mentis tamen benignae, et animi admodum liberalis," *Annales sex regum Angliae (1126-1307)*, ed. T. Hog (London 1845) 299. It is far and beyond the data of Bartholomew's account to create a story of a "famous debate" when "Aquinas presided at the disputation of the question of the death of Christ, which involved the doctrine of unicity" (cf. F. J. Roensch, *Early Thomistic School*, Dubuque 1964, 10; and 22, note 35, where Marston's words are twisted once more).

This last alternative seems much more probable in view of an incident related by William of Tocco in his Life of Saint Thomas: as an example of Aquinas's humility he cites the Saint's reaction at the inception of a certain religious.[35] Tocco's details of the acts involved in an inception are faulty; yet the essentials no doubt are trustworthy. At the vesperiae, he says, this unnamed religious upheld an opinion contrary to the truth which the Doctor had previously determined in his schools. Thomas said nothing, lest he harm the reputation of the new master. But on the way back to the friary, when his students upbraided him for such gentleness, he promised to do what he could on the morrow to repair the injury done them and himself. When next morning the faculty and students were gathered in the hall of the Bishop for the aulica, the second part of the ceremony, the same questions and their determinations were repeated. This time Thomas quietly rebuked the new master: "This opinion of yours cannot be held because it is against such and such a Council." A dispute followed between them, until Thomas forced him to confess his error and beg for instruction.

Was this religious John Pecham? Dominic Prümmer, O.P., the editor of Tocco, is of this opinion.[36] On the other hand, the noted Dominican scholar, C. M. J. Vansteenkiste grants the scene was Paris, but considers the chronology uncertain, since it could have taken place during Thomas's first regency (1256-1259), and makes no reference to Pecham.[37] Yet it is not improbable that the religious was a Franciscan, since Orders other than the Preachers and the Minors did not present candidates before 1269 or later. If the incident took place during the first regency, the Minor would have been Eudes de Rosny or Godfrey of Vierzon, of whom we know almost nothing. In the second regency, Pecham would have been the only Franciscan candidate, together with perhaps Dom Albert (of the College of Cluny) and Gilles du Val (of the Fratres Vallis Scholarum).[38] But if we link together the account of Tocco, who may not have known the name of the religious or may (more likely) have left him anonymous out of respect for a prelate (the Life formed part of the first dossier presented to John XXII), and that of Bartholomew, which is later, Pecham appears to be the master in question.

At the same time, from our knowledge of the acts of inception[39] we

---

35 *Historia b. Thomae de Aquino*, c. 5, n. 27, in the *Acta Ss. Martii*, I, 668D-F; c. 26, in ed. D. Prümmer, *Fontes* II, 99.

36 "Iste Religiosus videtur esse Johannes Peckham"; *Fontes* II, 99, note 1.

37 In his article "Tommaso d'Aquino," in *Bibliotheca Sanctorum* 12 (Roma 1969) col. 556.

38 Cf. P. Glorieux, *Répertoire des maîtres en théologie de Paris au XIIIᵉ siècle*, II (Paris 1934) 269, 278.

39 Cf. P. Glorieux, "L'enseignement au moyen âge. Techniques et méthodes en usage à la

must change some of the details provided by Tocco, who had not been a student at Paris. The candidate (*aulandus*) circulated beforehand four questions on some common topic, two for the vesperiae, two for the aulica.[40] Of these, he was to dispute the second in the first ceremony with two of the oldest masters; and the third in the aulica. The other two were disputed respectively by the bachelors as they awaited the masters for the vesperiae, and by the masters at the end of the aulica. Finally, at the first available opportunity the new master was to hold the *resumptio* in the presence of all the masters and students, at which he repeated the second and third questions, filling in lacunae and presenting in full his determination of each question, which, we may suppose, he had meanwhile put into writing.

Hence, I would suggest, fully conscious of all the probabilities involved, that the two Questions of Pecham on the eternity of the world are his resumption of the dispute at the earlier ceremonies; and that perhaps the two older Masters at the vesperiae may have been Thomas and Gerard of Abbeville. That the texts represent the *resumptio* is somewhat suggested by the frequent use of *respondebatur*, an echo of the actual disputation; and again by Pecham's fairly accurate use of the words of the *Summa theologiae*. Thomas may courteously have spared Pecham on the more formal occasion of the vesperiae and aulica, and then have reacted publicly at the *resumptio*, though one would be hard-pressed to identify any Council he might have cited. He certainly reacted thereafter in his *De aeternitate mundi*.[41]

Faculté de Théologie de Paris, au XIIIᵉ siècle," *Archives d'hist. doctr. et litt. du moyen âge* 35 (1969) 141-148.

40   Two (or more likely, three) clear examples have survived: for Nicholas of Pressoir, 1273; cf. V. Doucet, in *Arch. Franc. Hist.* 26 (1933) 214, where another (anonymous) set of four questions follows; and for Durandus of Saint-Pourçain, 1302; see J. Koch, *Durandus de S. Porciano*, BGPTMA 26, Halbbd. I (Münster 1927) 161-168.

41   This article quite unintentionally is an answer to that of Thomas Bukowski, "An Early Dating for Aquinas, *De aeternitate mundi*," *Gregorianum* 51 (1970) 277-304, which came to my notice only after I had sent my contribution to the Editors (1970). If some remarks are in place, one might say that Prof. Bukowski has not made full use of the *De aeternitate* itself, since he fails to locate arguments and authorities advanced by the scholastic Thomas is opposing: it cannot be Bonaventure. Again, if the treatise is supposedly early (1259 or before), and was then given to the public, it is surprising that William of Baglione knows nothing of it, despite his attack (1266-1267) on Thomas's position. I think I have established beyond reasonable doubt that Aquinas is *not* "almost certainly arguing against St. Bonaventure," as the author claims (p. 280) with too many others.

JOHN PECHAM

*QUAESTIONES DE AETERNITATE MUNDI**

* The first Question of Pecham is taken from the only known manuscript, Florence Biblioteca Nazionale, *Conv. soppr. J.1.3*, ff. 59c-61a |=F|. The second Question is based on the same codex, ff. 61c-63a, and on a second, Florence Bibl. Medicea Laurenziana, *Santa Croce PL. XVII sin. 8*, ff. 97a-99c |=L|. I have not found any other manuscript.

F is well-known as devoted wholly to the works of John Pecham, and has been described more than once. Cf. F. Tocco, in *Fratris Johannis Pecham Tractatus tres de paupertate* (British Soc. of Franc. Studies II, Aberdeen 1910) 99-108; H. Spettmann, *Johannis Pechami Quaestiones tractantes de anima* (Beiträge zur Gesch. der Phil. u. Theol. des Mittel. 19, Heft 5-6; Münster 1918), xxii-xxvii. For our Questions the text is very defective, with many lacunae (some of several lines in length), poor readings (as is evident from the text of some authorities cited), few corrections (errors are often marked with a cross in the margin, and sometimes by a cross over a word, but are not corrected; a later reader apparently had no other copy from which to correct the text). At the end, as also in codex L, the second question stops after the response to the eleventh objection.

L contains several works of Pecham; yet the present (second) Question is somehow included in a series of Questions that otherwise are to be attributed, at least in part, to Bartholomew of Bologna. See V. Doucet, "Notulae bibliographicae de quibusdam operibus Fr. Ioannis Pecham O.F.M.," *Antonianum* 8 (1933) 309-328; and M. Mückshoff, *Die Quaestiones disputatae De fide des Bartholomäus von Bologna O.F.M.* (Beiträge 24, Heft 4; Münster 1940), xxxiii-xxxv, and xliv. The text is, as a whole, of greater accuracy than that of F, and thus serves to correct the latter in many difficult passages.

It is quite evident, however, that there is no immediate or direct relationship between the two manuscripts. Both are almost assuredly of Parisian provenance; but F seems more likely to be the work of a student close to Pecham's term as magister regens, whereas L is later, at least after the regency of Bartholomew (c. 1275-1277).

We should likewise note that Pecham's question in his commentary on the Sentences I, dist. 44, q. 3: *Quaeritur si potuit creare mundum antiquiorem* (cod. Florent., Bibl. Naz. *Conv. soppr. G.4.854*, f. 121c) is of no help either doctrinally or textually. — I am grateful to Dr. G. Etzkorn for making the original transcription from codex F of the two Questions published here; the text has since been critically compared to the manuscript itself.

I

Quaeritur utrum aliquid factum sit vel fieri potuit de nihilo ordinaliter.[1]

Et ostenditur quod non:

1. Quia teste Hieronymo:[2] "Cum Deus omnia possit, non potest tamen corruptam facere virginem." Sed maior est convenientia entis ad ens quam non-entis ad ens. Si igitur non potest Deus de corrupta facere virginem ordinaliter, multo magis nec de non-ente ens. — Respondebatur quod corruptio transit in praeteritum et non potest esse idem praeteritum et non praeteritum: ideo de corrupta non potest facere virginem.

2. Contra: eodem modo non-esse creaturae transit in praeteritum; ergo eadem ratione ei non potest succedere esse.

3. Item, maior est convenientia Creatoris cum creatura quam non-entis cum creatura, cum inter Creatorem et creaturam sit analogia entis. Sed Deus non potest facere de Creatore creaturam, cum Creator sit immutabilis et creatura mutabilis. Ergo multo magis non potest facere de nihilo esse quod nullo modo convenit cum eo.

4. Item, si potest facere de non-ente ens, ergo cum infinita sit distantia non-entis ad ens, infinita distantia potest pertransiri.[3] Quod est falsum, quia secundum Philosophum:[4] "Infinitum non potest pertransiri nec a finito nec ab infinito."

5. Item, si potest super hanc distantiam quae est infinita, eadem ratione poterit super quamcumque aliam. Ergo potest inter distantiam quae est inter Creatorem et creaturam, cum una distantia infinita sit maior alia.

6. Item, omnis actio est per contactum vel corporalem ut in corporalibus, vel virtualem ut in spiritualibus. Si igitur Deus producit creatum [per] contactum virtutis suae: aut creatum prius est quam tangatur (dico 'prius' naturaliter), aut prius tangitur quam sit. Si primo modo: sed prius non causatur a posteriori; ergo creatura non creatur a contactu divinae virtutis. Si autem prius tangitur quam sit, contra: omne verbum includit in suo intellectu esse et addit super ipsum, secundum grammaticos. Unde sequitur: tangit, ergo est tangens; et tangitur, ergo est tactum. Si igitur prius est simplex quam compositum, et posterius est quod est ex additione ad alterum, prius est esse quam tangi, et ita ut supra: ipsum esse non creatur a contactu divinae virtutis.

7. Item, si creatura incepit esse, accipiamus instans quo incepit esse, et sit A. Item, si creatura prius habuit non-esse, accipiamus aliquod instans in quo non fuit, et sit B. Ergo inter A et B, cum se habeant secundum prius et prius, fuit tempus. Si dicas quod illud 'prius' fuit nunc aeternitatis,

---

1 de nihilo *apparently deleted*; in the list of questions provided in F [f. 19c], the title reads: *Utrum aliquid sit factum de nichilo ordinabiliter.*

2 *Epist. 22 (ad Eustochium)*, n. 5 (PL 22, 397; CSEL 54, 150). Cf. St. Thomas, *Summa theologiae* I, 25, 4, sed contra (ed. Ottawa 175a 43-45).

3 Cf. St. Thomas, *Summa theol.* I, 45, 2, arg. 4 (284b 53-285a 2).

4 Aristotle, *Post. Anal.* I, 3 (72b 10-11); and more directly, *Metaph.* X (XI), 10 (1066a 35-1066b 1).

8.   Contra: ergo inceptio temporis fuit post aeternitatem vel nunc aeternitatis. Sed hoc est falsum, quia nunc aeternitatis omnia complectitur tempora; ergo etc.

9.   Item, Deus secundum immensitatem essentiae comparatur ad mundi magnitudinem; secundum comparationem suae aeternitatis vel durationis comparatur ad mundi durationem. Sed, quamvis sit infinitas [= infinitus] magnitudine et mundus finitus, non tamen est extra mundum; ergo quamvis sit |in|finitus[5] aeternitate, non tamen fuit ante mundum.

10.   Item, si non-esse praecedit esse: aut prioritate naturae, et hoc non, quia nihil non dicit naturam, ergo nec ordinem naturae; aut prioritate temporis, et hoc non, quia tempus prius non fuit; aut aeternitatis, et hoc non, quia aeternitas Dei est ipse Deus. Sed ipsum nihil non est in Deo, ergo nec in aeternitate Dei.

11.   Item, nobilior est affirmatio quam negatio, et habitus quam privatio, et |59d| esse quam non-esse. Sed esse naturae non mensuratur aeternitate, ergo multo magis nec non-esse.

12.   Item, simplicius est nunc aeternitatis quam nunc temporis infinitum. Ergo, si propter simplicitatem instantis temporalis non praecessit in eo esse nec non-esse creaturae, ergo multo magis in nunc aeternitatis non possunt stare simul esse et non-esse. Sed si non-esse creaturae fuit in aeternitate, et postea suum esse est in aeternitate, opposita sunt in ipsa aeternitate. Ergo hoc est impossibile, quod hic ponatur aliquod fundamentum, scilicet esse ex nihilo.

13.   Item, si aliquid factum est ex nihilo, simul fuit ens et non-ens. Probatio: quod tantum natura praecedit alterum potest simul esse cum illo, sicut natura |sonus| praecedit cantum,[6] et tamen simul tempore generatur. Sed si creatura habuit aliquando non-esse, suum non-esse solum natura praecessit suum esse; ergo etc. Probatio assumptae: quia certum est quod non fuit prius tempore, nec prius aeternitate, quia tunc sequitur quod tempus esset post aeternitatem; quod falsum est, quia simul est cum ipsa.

14.   Item, si creatura est et non fuit, si affirmatio et negatio de eodem, ergo idem suppositum est subtractum esse; et quod prius subtractum fuit puro[7] non-esse; et ita esse et purum non-esse aliquid habent commune, quod est falsum. Respondebatur quod idem est commune secundum rationem.

15.   Contra: secundum rem vere et proprie quod est non fuit, et quod non fuit est; idem ergo est commune; ergo etc.

16.   Item, omne quod fit, possibile erat fieri antequam fieret.[8] Si ergo aliquid est creatum de nihilo, prius potuit creari. Sed potentia non est sine possibili. Ergo quod creatur fuit aliquid antequam crearetur. Respondebatur quod non fuit nisi in potentia Creatoris.

17.   Contra: "In aeternis non differt esse et posse,"[9] quia omnipotentia suo actui semper coniunctum est; ergo nullam habet actum ex temporis novitate.

---

5   A cross is found in the margin, indicating either an error or an omission.

6   [sonus] *lacuna in text*; supplied from St. Augustine, *Sonus cantum (praecedit origine)* in *Confession.* XII, c. 29, n. 40 (PL 32, 842; CSEL 33, 340).

7   puro *corr. marg. for* po *in text.*

8   Cf. St. Thomas, *Summa theol.* I, 45, 2, arg. 3 (284b 42-52).

9   Aristotle, *Physic.* III, text 32, c. 4 (203b 29).

18.   Item, quia dicebatur quod posse creari non dicit potentiam nisi rationis, contra: posse creare et posse creari sunt diversorum subiectorum, quia posse creare est agentis primi, posse creari est ipsius creabilis. Ergo differunt essentialiter istae duae potentiae. Ergo, sicut vere differunt Creator et creatum, sic vere creare et posse creari.

19.   Item, hoc probatur quia differunt, quia potentiae differunt sicut causae. Sed posse creare terminatur ad creationem actionem, posse creari ad creationem passionem. Ergo sicut creatio actio et creatio passio differunt essentialiter, sic istae potentiae. Ergo, si aliquid est creatum, praecessit potentia vera; quod repugnat creationi; ergo etc.

20.   Item, creatio est actio. Actio autem requirit non quid agat, sed in quid agat. Ergo praesupponit materiam.

21.   Item, Deus est causa creaturae in triplici genere causae: efficientis, formalis et finalis. Ad agendum non indiget alio efficiente, quia ipse est virtus infinita et est ipse sua virtus, nec agit alio[10] a se. Item, nec indiget alio exemplari a se diverso ad producendum, quia ipse [est] essentialiter exemplar. Nec eget alio fine, quia ipse est finis ultimus. Sed si exemplar differret ab esse essentialiter, indigeret alio exemplari a se diverso ad producendum. Similiter de virtute et fine. Ergo cum materia, quae est quarta causa, ab eo sit penitus diversa, non potest agere nisi praesupposita materia.

22.   Item, si educitur de non-esse in esse: aut quando est, aut quando non est. Si educitur quando est: sed quod est non eget eductione,[11] et quod non eget, non educitur. Ergo non creatur quando est.

23.   Item, si creatura accipit esse vel si fit de non-creante creans, hoc est per mutationem ipsius creantis. Probatio: quia non est per mutationem creaturae, quia Deus creat antequam creatura creetur; creatio enim eius [= est] actio aeterna. — Respondetur quod creatio connotat effectum. — Contra: nihil connotat nisi quod dicitur de creante; connotat ergo [60a] actionem et non passionem. Actio autem non est sine termino actionis. Ergo prius est creatura quam actio. — Item, duplex est creatio: creatio actio et creatio passio. Sed creatio passio est accidens creati. Sed nullum accidens est prius suo subiecto. Ergo impossibile est creationem passionem praecedere creatum. Sed creatum non posset esse nisi praecederet illud ordine naturae creatio passio, cum sit via ad esse. Via autem praecedit terminum; ergo etc.

24.   Item, potentia creabilis remotior est ab actu quam potentia numeri, quia potentia creabilis nihil dicit in actu aut potentia reali. Potentia autem numeralis dicit aliquid in actu in quo fundatur realis potentia. Sed potentia numeri ad infinitas species non potest educi in actu; ergo multo magis nec potentia creabilis.

25.   Item, materia nullo modo potest esse a Primo. Hoc probatur, quia omne agens agit secundum quod est in actu.

26.   Item, agens a proposito educit sibi simile in specie. Sed materia est ens penitus[12] in potentia. Deus autem est ens plene in actu. Ergo non habet aliquam convenientiam materia cum Deo; ergo ab ipso esse non potest.

---

10   alio] alio id est per aliud *add. marg.* F².
11   eductione] vel eductore *add. marg.* F².
12   penitus] est ens *repeated*; I have placed the words after *autem*, where they evidently belong.

27.   Item, in creaturis sunt multi defectus. Aut igitur sunt in creaturis unde ex nihilo, aut ratione materiae. Si primo modo, tunc omnes creaturae aeque plenae sunt defectibus; quod falsum est. Si ratione materiae, ergo materia non est a Deo ex nihilo; vel si ipsa est ex nihilo, adhuc omnia erunt aeque plena defectibus[13] quaecumque ipsam participant.

28.   Item, si aliquid creatur, aut materia [est] aut forma aut compositum. Si est compositum, contra: actio indivisibilis non terminatur ad divisibile. Sed creatio est actio indivisibilis; ergo non terminatur ad compositum. Quod est indivisibilis patet, quia est summae simplicitatis et in [ens] indivisibiliter terminatur, quia nihil est medium inter ens et non-ens. Item, nec materia creatur, quia actio nobilissima non terminatur ad summum ignobile. Materia autem est summe ignobilis. Item, nec materia [= forma] creatur, nec [= quia] forma praesupponit materiam; ergo etc.

CONTRA:

a.   Avicenna, VI *Meta.*[14]: "Philosophi non intelligunt per agentem principium mutationis [= motionis] tantum, sicut intelligunt naturales, sed principium essendi et creatorem [= datorem] eius, sicut est creator mundi."

b.   Item, causa quanto prior, tanto prius [= plus] influit.[15] Ergo prima influit super totum.

c.   Item, materia est secundum quam unumquodque potest esse et non esse, secundum Philosophum.[16] Ergo materia multum communicat cum non-esse. Si ergo forma est productibilis, quae dat esse, multo magis materia est productibilis, a qua est non-esse. Sed materia non producitur de materia, quia sic esset ire in infinitum; ergo producitur de nihilo.

d.   Item, agens quod agit secundum aliquid sui, per virtutem suam scilicet, potest reproducere secundum partem, ut fit per generationem in qua transit commune subiectum a specie in speciem. Ergo agens quod agit secundum se totum, cuius [= cui?] subest sua actio, producit rem secundum suam totam essentiam, scilicet secundum materiam et formam.[17]

e.   Item, duplex est actio Dei, intrinseca et extrinseca. Ergo, sicut intrinseca productio ostendit infinitatem Dei, sic et extrinseca debet[18] manifestare infinitam potentiam Dei. Sed hoc non est nisi....

RESPONSIO:

I.   Creatio est articulus fidei et nunquam ad plenum alicui infideli illuxit.[19] Hinc et quod quidam posuerunt mundum omnino a Deo non fuisse

---

13   A cross in margin would indicate the text is incomplete.
14   VI Meta.] dicenti *ms.* Cf. Avicenna, *Metaph.* VI, c. 1 (ed. Venice 1508, 91b).
15   Cf. St. Bonaventure, *In II Sent.*, d. 1, p. 1, a. 1, q. 1, fund. 1; *Opera omnia* II (ed. Quaracchi 1885), 14b; whence we have interpreted *prius* as *plus*. The argument depends on the *Liber de causis* prop. 1; ed. A. Pattin (Louvain s.a.), 46.
16   Aristotle, *Metaph.* VI (VII), c. 1 (1042a 25-28).
17   Cf. St. Bonaventure, loc. cit., 14b-15a.
18   debet] decet (docet?) F. The final word (*nisi*) is followed by a lacuna of some three lines.
19   Cf. St. Bonaventure, *In II Sent.*, d. 1, p. 1, a. 1, q. 1, resp. (II, 16b); and St. Thomas, *Summa theol.* I, 46, 2, resp. (297a11 ff.). — What follows from Augustine is rather a paraphrase of *De*

productum, sicut recitat Augustinus, *De civitate* XI, cap. 4, dicens contra eos:
"Mobilitas et immobilitas partium mundanarum ad idem tendentium clamat
totum mundum habere idem principium." Alii peius [60b] errantes, quia non
potuerunt intelligere aliquid fieri ex nihilo, mundum istum factum esse de Dei
substantia posuerunt. Quod etiam per eandem viam improbatur. In pluribus
enim locis probat Augustinus[20] animam non fuisse factam de Dei substantia
ideo quod mutabilis est. Et ideo alii, ut Platonici, |posuerunt|[21] mundum esse
productum |ex materia| praeexistenti aeterna et increata. Unde Ambrosius,
in *Hexaëmeron*[22]: "Plato tria posuit increata et sine initio: Deum et exemplar
et materiam. Deum vero non tanquam creatorem materiae, sed tanquam ar-
tificem." Propter quod Philosophus dicit[23]: "Plato solus generat mundum."

Sed istud primo improbatur, quia unumquodque quanto durabilius est tanto
melius est. Si igitur materia omnibus aliis durabilior est, omnibus aliis melior
est. — Item, quantitas rei cognoscitur per virtutis mensuram et materialis [?].
Ergo, si materia habet mensuram infinitam, habet et virtutem infinitam, quod
est impossibile. — Item, Richardus probat, *De Trinitate* V,[24] quod eo ipso
quod persona Patris non est ad aliam, omnis alia persona et natura est ab ipsa.
Et probat sic: quoniam si habet esse a se, non habet esse [secundum] participationem essendi; et si non secundum participationem, ergo secundum
plenitudinem. Sed ubi est plenitudo essentiae et potentiae, ibi est omnino
posse, quia suum posse est omne posse. Ergo ex ipsa est omne posse et omne
esse. — Item, negare non potest quin esse a se sit nobilissima conditio et
proprietas principii. Ergo si materia est a se, convenit in nobilissima
proprietate cum primo principio.

Item, si materia est increata: aut simplex est aut composita. Si simplex est,
penitus ergo de ipsa nunquam fiet compositum, nisi pars compositi fiat de
nihilo. Si autem sit composita, omnis compositio est a componente simplici.
Ergo necesse est aliam esse causam materiae, et ita non est a se. — Item, esse
a se dicit proprietatem dignitatis et actum nobilem essendi, ut dictum est.[25]

---

civitate Dei XI, c. 4, n. 2: "Exceptis enim propheticis vocibus, mundus ipse ordinatissima sua
mutabilitate et mobilitate et visibilium omnium pulcherrima specie quodammodo tacitus et factum
se esse, et nonnisi a Deo...fieri se potuisse proclamat" (PL 41, 319; CSEL 40-1, 515; CCL 48, 324).

20   Cf. *De Genesi ad litt.*, VII, c. 2, n. 3, and c. 3, n. 5 (PL 42, 356, 357; CSEL 28-1, 202, 203);
and especially *Contra adversarium legis et prophetarum* I, c. 14, nn. 21-22 (PL 42, 614f); and Peter
Lombard, *Sent.* II, d. 17, c. 1, n. 5 (Quaracchi 1970) I, 410f.

21   The text is marked by a cross in the margin; I have essayed to repair it.

22   Book I, c. 1 (PL 14 [1845], 123A; CSEL 32, 3); cf. P. Lombard, *Sent.* II, d. 1, c. 1, n. 2 (ed.
cit. 330), where Strabus is quoted to the same effect.

23   Cf. *Physic.* VIII, c. 1 (251b 17-18). More exactly, as used by other scholastics, the authority
should perhaps read: *Solus Plato genuit tempus*; cf. Gerard of Abbeville, *Quodl. XIV.* q. 10; ed. Ph.
Grand, "Le Quodlibet XIV de Gérard d'Abbeville: La vie de Gérard d'Abbeville," *Archives d'hist.
doctr. et litt. du moyen âge* 31 (1964) 267.

24   Ch. 4 (PL 196, 951 D; ed. J. Ribaillier ₉[Paris 1958] 199). Cf. John Pecham, *In I Sent.*, d. 27,
q. 1, a. 1: "Igitur primitas Patris innascibilitate significatur; et quia eo ipso quo innascibilis est, a
nullo est, sequitur ut omne aliud et omnis alia res quaecumque sit ab ipso, sicut docet Richardus
De trin. 5 c. 4...Ergo innascibilitas Patrem distinguit aliquo modo, immo ut supra habetur ex
Richardo, rationem dicit communicandi"; cod. Florent., Bibl. Naz. *Conv. soppr. G. 4. 854*, f. 80d;
cited by M. Schmaus, *Der Liber propugnatorius des Thomas Anglicus und die Lehrunterschiede
zwischen Thomas von Aquin und Duns Scotus*, BGPTMA 29 (Münster 1930) 586, note 57.

25   Cf. some seven lines above.

Ergo convenit rei digniori. Sed dignior est forma quam materia. Ergo si non convenit formae, nec convenit materiae. — Item, quod est alterius causa amittendi esse, ipsum esse non habet ex se. Sed contrariorum contrariae sunt causae. Sed materia est in quolibet quod potest non esse; ergo etc.

De rerum vero principio primo non habet Aristoteles manifestam sententiam, quamvis dicat quod non est virtus nisi a Deo.[26]

II. Hi igitur errores omnes professione fidei excluduntur, dicente Scriptura quia *In principio creavit Deus caelum et terram*.[27] Hanc veritatem fidei nullus sapientum mundi intellexit ad plenum, quia aut eam negaverunt aut erronee posuerunt, sicut Avicenna, qui sic eam attribuit Creatori quod etiam eam attribuit creaturae.[28] Et idcirco omnibus his erroribus praeexclusis, sciendum est omnia in primo instanti temporis fuisse producta de nihilo.

Ad cuius intelligentiam sequestranda est imaginatio philosophorum naturalium qui quaerunt commune subiectum, et ad intellectualem indaginem, ut est possibile, ascendendum. Quod igitur omnia sint ex nihilo creata, patet tam considerando conditiones ipsius Creatoris quam etiam ipsius creaturae.

Primo, dico, attendamus quantitatem potentiae |a parte producentis|,[29] quoniam quanto potentia est virtuosior, tanto paucioribus indiget adminiculis et dispositioni ad productionem sui effectus.[30] Ergo potentia quae [in]finite excedit omnem alteram potentiam circa aliquid producendum, infinite minus requirit quam alia potentia. Sed infinite minus quocumque ente non est nisi pure non-ens. Ergo inifinita potentia eo quo infinita potest producere quemcumque effectum de pure non-ente. Unde Hugo I *De sacramentis*, parte 1, cap. 1[31]: "Omnipotentiae virtus ineffabilis, sicut non poterat aliud praeter se habere coaeternum quo in faciendo iuvaretur, ita sibi cum voluit suberat ut quod voluit et quando et quantum |60c| voluit de nihilo crearetur."

Secundo, hoc idem patet considerando modum producendi res in esse. Agit enim per intellectum suum, per Verbum suum, quod est ipsa eius operativa potentia, nec differunt in eo cognitio et operativa potentia, sicut in omni creatura differunt. Sicut igitur eadem facilitate intellectus divinus apprehendit entia et non-entia, sic necesse est ut virtus eius eadem facilitate producere possit aliquid sicut de ente, ita de non-ente. Unde Augustinus, *Confessionum* XI[32]: "Verbo tibi coaeterno et sempiterno dicis omnia quae dicis, et sic quidquid dicis ut fiat non aliter quam illo facis."

Item, idem patet tertio considerando perfectionem divini exemplaris, quia perfectiones divinae sunt exemplaria creaturarum exprimendo se in creatura. Sicut igitur omne vivens est a Deo sub ratione vitae, immo vita eius est exem-

---

26   Cf. *Ethic. Nic.* I, c. 9 (1099b 10), and II, c. 1 (1103a 25).

27   Gen. 1, 1.

28   *Metaph.* IX, c. 4 (f. 104d-105a); cf. St. Thomas, *Summa theologiae* I, 45, 5, resp. (288a 35ff).

29   The manuscript has a lacuna of some ten letters; since the argument follows St. Bonaventure, we have supplied the omission from *In I Sent.*, d. 1, p. 1, a. 1, q. 1, fund. 2 (II, 14b).

30   Cf. Aristotle, *De caelo* II, t. 62, c. 12 (292b 4ss); the argument is taken from St. Bonaventure, loc. cit.

31   PL 176, 187 B; quoted by St. Thomas, *De aet. mundi*, n. 10.

32   Chapt. 7 (PL 32, 813; CSEL 33, 287).

plar omnis vitae, ita esse in eo est exemplar omnis esse. — Item, quia esse divinum est omnipotentius[33] in exprimendo quam vivere divinum, immo quodammodo perfectius in causando in quantum generalius se diffundit, quod tamen ut in Deo est nullum dicit gradum, unde Dionysius, V *De divinis nominibus*[34]: "Nihil est exsistens cuius non sit substantia et aevum ipsum esse. Convenientius igitur cunctis aliis principalius." Ergo non habet minus de vi expressiva quam aliae perfectiones divinae, "sicut exsistens Deus laudatur ex digniore donorum aliorum eius." Igitur, cum Deus sit esse purum et per-fectum, necesse est ut illud suum esse sit expressivum cuiuslibet alterius esse, ut sicut unum [= una] vita dat vivere non-viventi, sic unum ens dat esse sim-pliciter non-enti. Unde in eodem capitulo[35]: "Ante alias ipsius participationes esse propositum est, et est[36] ipsum secundum se esse senius eo quod est per se vitam esse," etc.

Et haec est sententia Avicennae in loco auctoritatis allegatae.[37] Item, dicit alibi, eodem libro, quod "creatio est dignior omnibus modis dandi esse."

1. Ad obiectum primum dicendum quod Deus potest quidquid in se est possibile et suae perfectioni non repugnat. Tunc autem illud in quo con-tradictio implicatur cadit a ratione, sicut ubi est contradictionis implicatio; verbi gratia in omni impossibili per accidens. Tanta enim est impossibilitas ut pransus fieret ieiunus, sicut ut corruptus fieret incorruptus. Quia igitur corrup-tio transit in praeteritum, non potest non fuisse facta, et ita corruptam fieri virginem implicat contradictionem.[38]

2. Ad secundum dicendum quod non est simile, quia esse creaturae non ex-cludit non fuisse, sicut esse virginem excludit esse corruptam.

3. Ad tertium dicendum quod abusiva est comparatio cum dicitur quod 'maior est' etc., quia in comparando creaturam Deo sunt deo extrema; in com-parando creaturam nihilo, non est nisi unum extremum, quorum unum caret omni possibilitate pro utroque extremo mutationis. Non sic creatura, quia in nihilo non est possibilitas, sed tantum esse creaturae est possibile.

4. Ad quartum dicendum quod revera non est ibi distantia, quia non est nisi unum extremum; et ideo proprie non pertransitur, quia extrema non con-currunt vel sequuntur se circa idem supremum.

5. Ad quintum dicendum, sicut patet, quod ibi non est distantia. Item, ex-tremum distantiae inter Creatorem et creaturam caret omni possibilitate initiali et finali.

6. Ad sextum dicendum quod hoc est in hac productione singulare, quia contactus est causa huius quod tangitur in tactu suo. Unde, quia ipse tactus dat esse, prius natura est tactus quam sit res ipsa quae tangitur. — Ad obiectum autem quod dicit quod tangi est esse tactum et esse tactum addit supra esse, ergo posterius est eo, respondeo quod illud addit super alterum secundum rem vel sicut tactum ab ipso vel [sicut] cursu rerum naturali posterius est eo quia

33   est omnipotentius] enim est impotentius F.
34   Num. 5 (PG 3, 820 B; *Dionysiaca* I, ed. Chevalier [Solesmii 1937], 338).
35   Num. 5 (PG 3, 820A; *Dionysiaca* I, 337).
36   est] quoniam *add.* F. Then below, for *senius*, the codex reads *se minus* (with cross over it).
37   Cf. note 28 above; then, *Metaph.* VI, c. 2 (f. 92a).
38   Cf. St. Thomas, *Summa theologiae* I, 25, 4, resp. (175a 48-175b 18); and *Quodl.* V. q. 2, a. 1.

addit super eum secundum rem. Sed in proposito addit secundum modum loquendi, quia quod additur non causatur a principiis subiecti nec ordine, nec sequitur ipsum, sed naturaliter praecedit sicut creari.

7. Ad septimum breviter respondeo quod omnes negativae concedendae sunt in talibus et nulla affirmativa. Haec enim vera est [60d]: creatura non fuit nisi in instanti [A]. Haec autem falsa: prius fuit suum non-esse, quia per hoc ponitur mensura distincta a tempore secundum prius et posterius; et propter hoc non est dandum aliquod instans prius per modum aeternitatis, sicut nec extra mundum datus est locus, videlicet ubi est. Tamen divina maiestas transcendit mundi capacitatem. Sicut qui de [= quidem?] aeternitatis [sempiternitas?],[39] sic est prius quod est simul cum tempore et semper. Unde inter nunc temporis primum et aeternitatem quae semper fuit, nihil cadit medium. — Concedo ergo quod mundus incepit et non fuit prius. Et nego istam: suum non-esse fuit prius quam suum [esse], quia hoc ponit mensuram distinctam a tempore secundum prius et posterius. Unde concedi potest ista: mundus semper fuit. Unde Augustinus, *De civitate* XII, cap. 15[40]: "Angeli, si semper fuerunt, creati sunt; ac per hoc nec si semper fuerunt ideo Creatori coaeterni sunt. Ille enim semper fuit aeternitate incommutabili, isti autem facti sunt; sed ideo semper fuisse dicuntur, quia omni tempore fuere."

9. Ad nonum dicendum quod sicut [Deus] non est extra mundum, ut 'extra' dicat dimensionem positionis, cum non sit extra mundum per immensitatem virtutis quia continet mundum et mundo non collimitatur, ita fuit ante mundum, non quidem secundum extensionem sed secundum simplicem aeternitatem. Unde etiam [= dicit?] Augustinus, *De civitate* XII, cap. 15[41]: "Si Deus fuit semper dominus, semper habuit creaturam suo dominatui servientem, de nihilo factam nec sibi coaeternam; erat quippe ante illam quamvis nullo tempore sine illa; non eam spatio praecurrens, sed manente perpetuitate praecedens." Haec Augustinus. Igitur praecessit sine dimensionis extensione sicut transcendit mundum cui non collimitatur sine distensione. — Item, Augustinus, *De civitate* XI, cap. 5: "Si dicunt inanes esse cogitationes quibus [infinita] imaginantur loca, cum nullus sit locus praeter mundum, respondetur eis isto modo inaniter cogitare homines praeterita tempora vacationis Dei, cum tempus nullum sit ante mundum."

10. Ad decimum dico quod non-esse non praecessit esse. Concedo enim negativas nihil ponentes, et nego omnes affirmativas ponentes durationem extensionis vel ordinatae secundum prioritatem respectu instantis temporis.

11. Ad undecimum dico quod verum concludit, quia non-esse omni mensura caret.

12. Ad duodecimum respondeo: Haec est falsa: 'non-esse mundi fuit in nunc aeternitatis,' quia puro non-esse nulla est mensura. Esse autem creaturae est in tempore. — Quod si adhuc velles omnino dicere quod non-esse fuisset in nunc aeternitatis, non est [idem] simplicitati instantis, quia simplicitas in-

39 A conjectural reading to fill in a lacuna of 8 letters.
40 Num. 2 (or in modern edd., c. 16); the original text is somewhat varied (PL 41, 364; CSEL 40-1, 593; CCL 48, 372).
41 Num 3, or c. 16 (PL 41, 365; CSEL 40-1, 594; CCL 48, 372). — This is followed by a reference to Book XI, c. 5 (PL 41, 321; CSEL 40-1, 518; CCL 18, 326).

stantis est simplicitatis paucitatis vel arctationis, et ideo plura complecti non potest. Simplicitas autem nunc aeternitatis non est paucitatis sed multiplicitatis immensae, unde omnia tempora complectitur. — Quidam aliter dicunt quod non sequitur, quia non-esse mensuratur immediate ab aeternitate, esse autem mediate. Sed illic nihil est quia nobilius esset non-esse quam esse, quia immediatius aeternitati.

13. Ad decimum tertium dico quod quomodocumque dicatur 'prius', ista est falsa: 'prius fuit non-esse mundi quam esse mundi.' Haec autem vera: 'non prius fuit esse mundi,' quia, ut prius tactum est, dicendo 'prius fuit non-esse mundi' copulatur mensura habens prius et posterius respectu temporis ex necessario, quia omnis mensura habens prius respectu temporis aliquid habet se posterius, quia hic est sermo de prioritate extensionis.

14-15. Ad decimum quartum dicendum quod affirmatio et negatio est de eodem, non ut ente sed ut apprehenso ab intellectu. Res enim ut apprehenditur ab intellectu, apprehenditur absque suo esse vel suo non-esse. Non enim est suum esse. Aliquid ergo est commune utrique, non secundum rem, sed quantum ad intellectum; vel si secundum rationem, non tamen ut entem sed ut intellectu apprehensibilem. — Et sic patet ad decimum quintum.

16. Ad decimum sextum dicendum quod cum dicit 'omne quod fit, possibile erat fieri,' distinguo: quia si sit secundum cursum naturalem possibile est fieri secundum cursum naturalem; si vero sit supra cursum naturalem, possibile erat potentia supernaturali, potentia scilicet Creatoris, quae quantum ad intrinseca semper est actui coniuncta, quantum ad extrinseca minime.

17. Ad decimum septimum iam patet, quia de actu interiori verum est, de actu exteriori falsum est.

18. Ad decimum octavum dicendum quod possibile circa aliquid dicitur proprie secundum potentiam quae est in ipso. Large tamen dicitur aliquid possibile alicui quia aliquis potest super ipsum. Cum ergo dicit quod posse creari est alterius potentiae [61a] contra posse creare, si posse creari proprie dicatur quod sit posse subiecti creabilis, verum est, sed tunc posse creari nihil est. Si autem posse creari dicatur secundum rationem, quia Creator potest super creabile, tunc idem est posse creari et creare. Quod autem dicitur quod posse creari non dicitur de Creatore, verum est quantum ad modum loquendi; secundum rem tamen diceretur de ipso.

19. Ad decimum nonum dicendum quod potentiae differunt sicut termini quando secundum veritatem sunt diversae potentiae. Sed in proposito una est Dei potentia naturae mancipata a qua possunt esse diversi effectus.

20. Ad vigesimum dicendum quod creare non est agere, sed facere. Unde Augustinus, *De Trinitate* V, cap. 11[42]: "Quod autem ad faciendum attinet, de solo Deo verissime dicitur." Facere igitur non [requirit] in quid agat. — Aliter tamen loquitur Philosophus[43] de agere et facere, vocans actilia quorum finis est in ipsa operatione, sicut [in] actu cytharizandi et opere virtutis de quibus nihil relinquitur post factum. Factilia sunt quae post operationem manent, ut

42 More correctly, c. 8, n. 9 (PL 42, 917; CCL 50, 216).
43 Cf. *Ethic. Nic.* VI, c. 4 (1140a 1-24); then below, for the distinction between prudence and art, *Ethic. Nic.* VI, c. 4, and c. 7 (1140a 9-10; 1141b 22).

aedificia et consimilia. Unde dicit Philosophus quod prudentia est habitus vera ratione activus; ars vero habitus vera ratione factivus. — Item, de his aliter loquitur Augustinus, *Contra adversarium legis,* cap. 15,[44] dicens: "Facere est quod omnino non erat; creare autem, ex eo quod iam erat ordinando aliquid constituere; ideoque dictus est Deus creans mala."

21. Ad vigesimum primum dicendum quod aliud est de causa materiali, quae omnino est imperfectionis et in Deum nullo modo cadere non [sic!] potest, aliud de aliis causis.

22. Ad vigesimum secundum dicendum quod eductum educebatur quando erat, quia simul educebatur et eductum est. Et cum dicitur: 'quod erat non indiget Creatore,' verum est de eo quod est post acceptionem esse; sed de eo quod accipit esse simul et creationem,[45] non est verum.

23. Ad vigesimum tertium dicendum est quod creatio actio non dicit actionem Dei intrinsecam tantum, sed coniunctionem eius cum effectu exteriori quem connotat communicatio[46] quae simul est cum creato. — Ad obiectum quod actio non est sine termino actionis, dicendum quod verum est. Tamen aliter est in actione divina quae est tota causa acti, aliter in aliis.

24. Ad vigesimum quartum dicendum quod non est simile de potentia creabilis et de potentia numeri, non ratione subiecti potentiae nec ratione termini, quia potentia creabilis est in creante, iuxta illud Augustini, *Ad Volusianum*[47]: "In rebus mutabilibus tota ratio [facti] est potentia facientis." Item, nec ratione termini, quia creabile ordinatur ad actum purum, potentia autem numeri ad actum mixtum cum potentia, quia unus numerus via est ad alium.

25. Ad vigesimum quintum dicendum...[48]

II

Utrum mundus potuit fieri ab aeterno.[1]

Quaeritur, hoc supposito, si[2] mundus potuit ab aeterno creari.
Et ostenditur quod sic:

1. Quia dicit Dionysius, *De divinis nominibus*[3]: "Bonum est sui diffusivum." Et Augustinus, *Contra adversarium legis*[4]: "Istorum producendorum causa sola bonitas Dei fuit." Ergo, sicut simul sunt lux et diffusio lucis, sic bonum et dif-

---

44 Book I, c. 23, n. 48 (PL 42, 633); cf. St. Thomas, *Summa theol.* I, 45, 1, arg. 1 (283b 29-32). Cf. Isaiah 45.7.
45 Highly conjectural; *cũ* in F.
46 communicatio (conject.)] concreatio F (with cross above it).
47 *Epist. 137,* c. 2, n. 8 (PL 33, 519; CSEL 44, 107).
48 Lacuna at this point of some twelve lines.
1 Title taken from the list of questions, F., f. 19c.
2 hoc supposito si] utrum L.
3 Cf. *De divinis nominibus,* c. 4, n. 1 (PG 3, 693; *Dionysiaca* I, 146); the axiom is more derived than direct (*ut ex verbis Dionysii accipitur,* remarks St. Thomas, *Summa theologiae* I, 5, 4, arg. 2; 30a 2). On its use in Scholasticism before St. Thomas, cf. J. G. Bougerol, "Saint Bonaventure et le Pseudo-Denys l'Aréopagite," *Etudes franciscaines* 19 (1969), suppl. annuel, 81-104.
4 Book I, c. 7, n. 10 (PL 42, 609).

fusio bonitatis. Sed bonum fuit ab aeterno, ergo et diffusio eius quae est creatio.

2. Item, Augustinus, *De Trinitate* VI, cap. 1[5]: "Est coaeternus Patri Filius, sicut splendor qui gignitur ab igne atque diffunditur coaevus[6] est illi, et esset aeternus, si ignis[7] esset aeternus." [F 61b] Si igitur ignis a se habet effectum diversum sibi coaevum, ergo et Deus potest. — Respondebatur[8] quod creatura non potest capere aeternitatem.— [3.] Contra: Augustinus, *Ad Volusianum*[9]: "In rebus artificialibus[10] [L 97b] tota ratio facti est potentia facientis." Sed creatio est operatio summe mirabilis; ergo totaliter dependet a potentia Dei. Ergo nulla impotentia repugnat a parte recipientis.

4. Item, quando creatura non est, nihil potest recipere quantum est a parte sui, nec esse nec aeternum esse, quia a pari est impossibilitas ad utrumque. Ergo qua ratione potest recipere unum, et reliquum.

5. Item, plus potest Deus de nihilo quam creatura de aliquo. Sed si ignis fuisset ab aeterno, genuisset splendorem suum ab aeterno, ut dicit Augustinus.[11] Ergo Deus potuit ab aeterno producere mundum[12] de nihilo.

6. Item,[13] posita causa sufficienti, ponitur effectus. Sed Deus est causa mundi solus et sufficiens. Sed haec causa fuit aeterna; ergo et creatum. — Respondebatur[14] ad hoc argumentum quod non sequitur de causa[15] voluntarie agente, quia eius effectus est secundum modum voluntatis suae. — [7.] Contra: ergo si voluisset ab aeterno mundum produxisse, potuisset. — Respondetur quod verum est quantum est ex parte sui. — [8.] Contra: Deus quantum est ex parte sui nihil potest nisi quod posse esse est possible,[16] cum 'posse' dicat respectum ad obiectum potentiae. Ergo, si Deus potuit ab aeterno mundum producere quantum est ex se, mundus potuit ab aeterno produci.

9. Item, aeque potens Deus est producere finitum sicut infinitum. Sed produxit ab aeterno infinitum, scilicet Filium suum. Ergo et potuit[17] ab aeterno producere finitum.

10. Item, mundus non incepit esse; ergo fuit ab aeterno. Probatio primae: si incepit esse, aut in tempore, aut in instanti. Non in tempore, quia inter ens et non-ens non est medium. Ergo incepit in instanti. Sed hoc est impossibile; ergo non incepit. Quod sit impossibile,[18] probatur: quia eadem est ratio de mundi inceptione et eius desitione. Mundus autem si desineret, non desineret in instanti.

---

5   PL 42, 923; CCL 50, 228; cf. P. Lombard, *Sent.* I, d. 9, c. 2, n. 3 (ed. cit., 103-104).
6   coaevus] coeternus L.
7   ignis...Si *om.* (homoioteleuton) L.
8   Respondebatur F, respondetur L.
9   *Epist. 137,* c. 2, n. 8 (PL 33, 519; CSEL 44, 107).
10   artificialibus F, mirabilibus L, talibus *Aug.*
11   Above, in arg. 2.
12   mundum *trp. after* potuit L.
13   Cf. St. Thomas, *Summa theol.* I, 46, 1, arg. 9 (294a 11-20).
14   Respondebatur F, respondetur L. — Cf. St. Thomas, ibid., ad 9 (295b 47-296a 5).
15   de causa *om.* L.
16   est possible L, posuit F (with a cross in margin).
17   potuit F, est possibile L.
18   ergo...impossibile *om.* (*hom.*) L.

11. Hoc probatur sic: quia si mundus verteretur in nihilum, mundus in sua annihilatione non esset, et annihilatio mundi esset terminus sui[19] esse. Sed mensura annihilationis esset cum annihilatione, sicut mensura omnis motus est cum motu et mutationis cum mutatione. Ergo si annihilatio est in instanti, instans est cum annihilatione. Sed annihilatio est[20] post esse mundi; ergo et instans quod est eius mensura. Ergo, si mundus annihilatur in instanti, instans est[21] post esse mundi. Sed hoc est impossibile, cum pars non sit sine toto, nec accidens sine subiecto; ergo etc. — Respondebatur[22] quod annihilatio est in nunc aeternitatis. — Contra: Quidquid est in nunc aeternitatis est aeternum. Sed annihilatio illa, hoc[23] casu posito, non esset aeterna; ergo etc.

12. Item, si mundus non potest esse aeternus, hoc non nisi quia habet esse post non-esse. Quod[24] est falsum; ergo primum. Quod non habeat esse post non-esse probatur: quia nec post secundum[25] naturam, cum non-esse non dicat materiam.[26] — Item, quia prius tantum natura simul est tempore cum posteriori, sicut materia cum forma. Nec prius tempore, quia non prius erat tempus[27]; nec prius aeternitate, quia non-esse mundi non fuit in aeternitate. Sic enim non-esse vel nihil esse esset in perfectissimo esse [L 97c] et negatio in affirmatione purissima; ergo etc.

13. Item, praeteritum et futurum sunt aequalia in suppositis. Quidquid enim est praeteritum, fuit futurum; et quidquid est futurum erit praeteritum. Ergo, qua ratione est unum infinitum, et reliquum est vel esse poterit infinitum.

14. Item, Boethius, *De consolatione* V[28]: "Neque Deus conditis[29] rebus antiquior videri debet. Ergo Deus non est antiquior mundo; ergo si Deus aeternus, et mundus.

15. Item, in habentibus materiam quod est ab agente per artem est secundum modum agentis, quantum patitur conditio materiae. Ergo quod est ab alio[30] sine materia, est totaliter secundum modum agentis. Sed mundus sensibilis exprimitur a mundo architypo sine praeiacente materia; ergo est[31] secundum modum agentis omnino. Ergo, si mundus architypus vel exemplaris est aeternus, et mundus [F 61c] iste sensibilis erit aeternus.

16. Item, Deus[32] est agens naturale et voluntarium. Si igitur produxit de novo[33] mundum: aut in quantum agens naturale vel per principium quod est natura, aut per principium quod est voluntas. Si primo modo: sed natura agit

---

19 sui *om*. F.
20 est *om*. F.
21 est F, autem L.
22 Respondebatur L, respondetur F.
23 hoc *om*. L.
24 Quod F, sed hoc L.
25 secundum *om*. F.
26 materiam F, naturam L.
27 tempus F, tempore L.
28 Prosa 6 (PL 63, 859 B; CCL 94, 101).
29 conditis] conditor L.
30 alio F, aliquo L.
31 est *om*. F.
32 Deus *om*. F.
33 de novo L. deus F.

uniformiter et determinate unum. Ergo aut ab aeterno produxit, aut nunquam produxit. Si autem produxit in quantum agens voluntarium: sed non est impotentior natura quam voluntas. Ergo ab aeterno potuit producere sicut si[34] ex natura produxisset.

17. Item, quod non repugnet conditio[ni] creaturae produci ab aeterno, probatur: quoniam dicendo mundum creatum fuisse ab aeterno, duo dico: et mundum semper fuisse, et semper ab alio esse habuisse. Sed[35] in hoc si aliquid repugnat rationi creaturae, quaero: aut quia potentia esse ab alio aeternaliter, et hoc non,[36] quia Filius est ab aeterno; aut quia potentia[37] ab aeterno diversitate substantiae, et hoc non, quia si caelum fuisset ab aeterno motus fuisset aeternus, qui tamen essentialiter differt a caelo[38]; aut quia in hoc aequipararetur Deo,[39] et hoc non, quia aeternitas eius esset aeternitati Dei incomparabilis, cum haberet partem post partem; et sicut modo esset duratio mundi successiva cum simplici aeternitate Dei, sic potuisset, ut videtur, si ab aeterno fuisset.

18. Item, si Deus produxit mundum ex tempore proposito aeterno, ergo[40] mutatus est implendo propositum. Probatio consequentiae[41]: quia quod voluit ab aeterno producere, productum actu voluit. Causa autem aut[42] fuit a parte mundi; et hoc non videtur, quia mundus cum produceretur nullam habuit[43] causam suae productionis; aut fuit a parte Dei, et ita Deus implendo ex tempore quod ab aeterno disposuit, mutatus est.

19. Item, res habent comparationem ad causam materialem et efficientem. Sed materiatum potest esse coaevum[44] materiae sicut cantus sono; ergo et efficienti. Probatio: nihil fit[45] de materia nisi cum mutatione materiae. Sed quod fit a Deo, fit sine mutatione Dei vel etiam sine mutatione proprie dicta eius quod est sic, quia creatio non est mutatio proprie dicta.[46] Ergo magis potest aliquid creatum[47] coaeternum esse creanti quam materiae de qua est.

20. Item, Deus dat creaturae aliquid mediantibus principiis suis, aliquid sine concursu alicuius principii, sicut in creatione. [L 97d] Sed dat creaturae perpetuitatem sui esse quia convenit suis principiis a parte post. Ergo potest eidem dare aeternitatem a parte ante quam dat mediantibus principiis.

21. Item, productio creaturae ex tempore causam habet solum Dei voluntatem. Sed quod[48] ex sola causa tali pendet, ipsa sola mutari potest. Ergo si Deus vellet, aliter esse posset vel fuisse potuisset.

34   si *om.* F.‖ produxisset L, potuisset F.
35   Sed *om.* F.
36   non] est *add.* F.
37   potentia L, est F.
38   celum eternum implicat opposita *marg. note* F².
39   Deo *om.* F.
40   ergo *om.* L.
41   consequentiae L, consequentis F.
42   Causa autem aut F, tamen causa L.
43   habuit F, haberet L.
44   coaevum] corporeum F (marked by cross).
45   fit F, est L.
46   mutatio proprie dicta L, proprie mutatio F.
47   creatum *om.* F ‖ coaeternum esse *trp.* L.
48   quod *om.* F.

22. Item, si mundus productus est in instanti, hoc non potest esse quia instans est copulatio[49] duorum temporum, et ita ante tempus esset tempus.

23. Item, inter processionem aeternam, quae est in identitate substantiae, et temporalem, quae est in diversitate essentiae, medium est: vel processio in identitate naturae ex tempore, vel processio in diversitate naturae ab aeterno. Primum est impossibile; ergo secundum est necessarium.[50]

24. Item, aut Deus ab aeterno potuit mundum producere, et voluit; aut potuit, sed noluit; aut voluit, sed non potuit. Si primum est verum, ergo produxit. Si secundum est verum,[51] ergo invidus fuit, sicut de generatione Filii arguit Augustinus.[52] Si tertium est verum, impotens fuit. Sed haec duo ultima sunt impossibilia; ergo primum est necessarium.

25. Item, potuit fuisse mundus mille annis antequam[53] fuit, per mille annos et iterum per mille, et sic in infinitum. Ergo potuit ab aeterno.

26. Item, *De ecclesiasticis dogmatibus* X[54]: "In principio creavit Deus omnia, ut non esset otiosa Dei bonitas." Ergo si non creavit ab aeterno, fuit otiosus ab aeterno.

27. Item, Deus est causa rerum in triplici genere causae. Sed ad perfectionem exemplaris pertinet ut sit aeternum. Ergo ad perfectionem efficientis similiter.

28. Item, si mundus incepit in aliquo [F 61d] instanti, verbi gratia in A, ante A mundus non erat. Ante autem A, quando mundus non erat, dicatur B. Sed inter A et B, cum non sint simul, cadit[55] medium, et tempus per consequens. Ergo ante mundum[56] fuit tempus.

29. Item, si fit aliqua prima mutatio, sit A. Ergo cum A incepit, prius fuit verum dicere A non esse actu sed potentia. Sed quidquid exit de potentia in actum, exit per mutationem. Ergo ante primam mutationem[57] fuit mutatio.

30. Item, Augustinus videtur docere quod non sit impossibile mundum fuisse ab aeterno. Unde dicit, *De civitate* XI, cap. 4[58]: "Qui a Deo mundum factum fatentur, non eum temporis volunt habere sed suae creationis initium, ut modo quodam vix intelligibili semper sit factus." Haec Augustinus. Sed mundus iste est vix intelligibilis; ergo non impossibilis. Nullum enim Deo impossibile est intelligibile, cui *non* est[59] *impossibile omne verbum*, dicitur Lucae primo.

31. Item, Deus non creavit mundum nisi quia bonum est mundum esse. Sed

---

49 copulatio L, copula F.

50 necessarium] quia semper alterum concomitatur (?) *marg. note* F[2].

51 est verum *om.* F.

52 "Deum quem genuit, quoniam meliorem se generare non potuit (nihil enim Deo melius), generare debuit aequalem. Si enim voluit, et non potuit, infirmus est; si potuit, et non voluit, invidus est. Ex quo conficitur aequalem genuisse Filium"; *De divers. Quaest. 83*, q. 50 (PL 40, 31s); cf. P. Lombard, *Sent.* I, d. 44, c. 1, n. 2 (ed. cit., 304).

53 mundus...antequam F, mundura (?) priusquam L.

54 Gennadius, *De eccl. dogm.* (PL 58, 983 C-D); the text is abbreviated.

55 cadit] tempore *add.* L ‖ tempus] tempore L.

56 mundum F, medium L.

57 mutationem] non *add.* F.

58 PL 41, 319; CSEL 40-1, 515; CCL 48, 324; quoted in part by St. Thomas, *Summa theol.* I, 46, 2, ad 1 (297b 1-4). — Below, Luke 1, 37.

59 est F, sit L. ‖ impossibile] apud deum *add.* L.

melius est esse ab aeterno quam non ab aeterno, cum esse ab aeterno conveniat Deo; ergo etc.[60]

CONTRA:

a. Gen. 1, 1: *In principio creavit Deus caelum et terram.*[61] Et loquitur Moyses de principio temporis quod continuatur per dies inferius enumeratos in canone.[62]

b. Item contra:[63] Avicenna. VI *Metaphysicae*[64]: "Postquam res |L 98a| ex seipsa[65] habet non-esse, sequitur tunc ut eius esse sit post non-esse et fiat postquam non fuerat."

c. Item, mensura est per quod[66] cognoscitur quantitas. Ergo quae est actio duarum invicem quantitatum, eadem erit proportio invicem mensurarum suarum. Deus habet quantitatem virtutis, mundus habet quantitatem molis.[67] Sed non est aliqua quantitas creaturae quae posset commensurari[68] quantitati vel magnitudini divinae. Deus enim ita est in hoc mundo quod posset esse in mundo alio[69]; si etiam esset maior in infinitum, nec etiam[70] posset facere mundum sibi conproportionalem. Ergo nec duratio mundi potest ex aliqua parte aequari aeternitati.[71] Sed aequaretur si esset factus ab aeterno. Ergo impossibile est Deum creasse mundum ab aeterno.

d. Item, si mundus creatus est non in tempore, quia inter esse et non-esse purum non est medium, ergo creatus est in instanti; quaero: aut instanti initiali temporis aut mediali[72] aut finali, cum non sit aliud cogitare. Tertium est manifeste falsum; similiter et secundum, quia tunc tempus fuisset ante mundum. Ergo creatus est in instanti temporis[73] initiali. — Quod etiam patet per aliam viam. Cum enim creatio dedit mundo esse, ergo instans creationis fuit terminus essendi ipsi mundo a parte ante. Sed nihil huiusmodi[74] est vel esse potest aeternum; ergo etc.

e. Item, si mundus duraverit per tempus infinitum et duraturus est similiter per tempus infinitum, tantumdem ergo[75] durabit quantum duraverit et non plus. Ergo[76] sicut non impediente infinitate praeteriti temporis[77] totum tempus

---

60   Lacuna of two lines in F.

61   et terram] etc. L. ‖ Et loquitur Moyses L, loquitur F.

62   Again a lacuna of two lines in F.

63   contra *om.*. L.

64   Chapt. 1 (f. 91c).

65   seipsa] se L.

66   quod F, quam L.

67   Cf. Augustine, *De Trin.* VI, 7 (PL 42, 929; CCL 50, 237); in P. Lombard, *Sent.* I, d. 8, c. 4, n. 3 (ed. cit., 99).

68   posset commensurari F, possit mensurari L.

69   alio *om.* F.

70   etiam *om.* F.

71   aeternitati] trinitati F.

72   initiali...mediali *trp.* both FL.

73   temporis *om.* F.

74   huiusmodi F, tale L.

75   tantumdem ergo L, ergo tantum F. ‖ et non plus *om.* L.

76   Ergo] est ut videtur corruptum exemplar *marg. note* F[2].

77   praeteriti temporis *om.* F. ‖ praeteriit sic L, preteritum F.

praeteriit sic ut nihil eius sit futurum, similiter non obstante infinitate temporis futuri aliquando sic erit praeteritum ut nihil eius sit futurum. Sed[78] illud cum aliquando nihil erit futurum, penitus desinet. Ergo tempus est infinitum futurum et tamen aliquando deficiet omnino, quod est impossibile.

f. Item, creatio et versio opponuntur, quia creatio incipit a non-esse sicut versio terminatur in non-esse.[79] Item, versio respicit futurum sicut creatio[80] praeteritum. Ergo sicut impossibile est mundum verti in nihilum et tamen durare in infinitum a parte post, ita impossibile est mundum eductum fuisse de nihilo et[81] tamen durasse per tempus infinitum a parte ante.

g. Item, si mundus duraverit per tempus infinitum et durabit[82] similiter, accipiatur ergo instans [F 62a] mediae diei, quod sit A; dicaturque totum tempus praeteritum A-praeteritum, et omne tempus futurum[83] A-futurum. Similiter sumatur aliud instans mediae diei, quod sit B; dicaturque totum tempus[84] praeteritum B-praeteritum, et totum futurum B-futurum. Item[85] hiis positis supponatur quod duorum aequalium quidquid est maius uno et reliquo, et quocumque unum est maius, et reliquum. Item supponatur quod quidquid sustinet alterum cum alio superaddito sit maius ipso vel totum ad[86] ipsum. Item, quod duo infinita ab eodem[87] indivisibili procedentia[88] sint aequalia. Ex hoc sic: A-praeteritum et A-futurum [L 98b] sunt aequalia, cum unum per impossibile alteri suppositum nec[89] excedat ipsum nec excedatur ab eo. Similiter B-praeteritum et B-futurum sunt aequalia. Sed B-praeteritum est maius quam A-praeteritum, et totum ad ipsum. Ergo est maius quam A-futurum. Sed B-praeteritum et B-futurum sunt aequalia. Ergo B-futurum est maius quam A-futurum; sed A-futurum est totum ad B-futurum. Ergo pars est maior suo toto, posito quod tempus fuerit[90] sine initio.

h. Item, omne esse est aliquod bonum, et duratio maior est[91] melior minore. Ergo infinite maior, infinite melius alio. Ergo impossibile est aliquod creatum infinito tempore durasse.

i. Item, mundus duravit duratione infinita; sed mundus est propter hominem; ergo infiniti homines praecesserunt. Cum[92] ergo animae rationales sint immortales, sunt actu infinitae. Forte hoc non habebit pro inconvenienti qui volet contrarium sustinere. Sed contra: Infinita esse actu est omni philosophiae contrarium.[93] — Aliter docet alius haereticus animas interire

---

78 Sed *corr. to* Si F[2]. ‖ cum L, tamen F.
79 The whole sentence is omitted in L.
80 creatio] respicit *add.* L.
81 et] tempus *add.* L.
82 duraverit...durabit F, durabit...duravit L. ‖ similiter *om.* L.
83 A-praeteritum...futurum *om.* (*hom.*) L.
84 tempus *om.* F.
85 Item] ex *add.* F. ‖ supponatur F, supponitur L.
86 ad *om.* L.
87 eodem *om.* L.
88 procedentia] precedentia F.
89 nec F, non L. ‖ excedatur ab eo F, ab ipso excedatur L.
90 fuerit L, fuit F.
91 est *om.* F.
92 cum *trp. after* rationales F.
93 Lacuna of three lines in F. — The whole argument is dependent on St. Bonaventure, *In II Sent.*, d. 1, p. 1, a. 1, q. 2, fund. 5 (II, 21b); and to a lesser extent on St. Thomas, *Summa theol.* I,

cum corpore, quod est contra omnes nobiles philosophos; vel dicit omnium hominum esse animam unam, quod est contra rectissimam philosophiam, quae formam propriam dicit esse propriae materiae et unum esse motorem[94] unius mobilis; vel dicit quod animae successive revolvuntur in corpora diversa, et hoc est a Philosopho improbatum et inter pythagoricas fabulas reputatum. [95]

k. Item, Richardus, I *De Trinitate*, cap. 8,[96] dicit quod id quod est a seipso necessario est aeternum. Ergo per oppositum, quod non est a seipso est ex tempore; et loquor[97] de eo quod est ab alio essentialiter diverso. Haec consequentia sic probatur: quod est a seipso, eo ipso habet esse et esse posse; et quidquid aliud est ab ipso, ab ipso[98] participat esse et posse. Sed nullum participans ab altero aequatur in aliqua conditione illi quod participat. Ergo quod[99] participat recepit esse participatum ab eo quod est aeternum, [sed] non recipit ab aeterno. — Ad hoc respondetur[100] quod si mundus semper fuisset, non tamen Deo parificaretur, quia esse divinum est esse totum simul. — Contra: aequaretur suo modo, quia tantum durasset quantum[101] aeternitas Dei.

l. Item, omne pertransitum et acceptum est finitum. Ergo si omnes revolutiones caeli pertransitae sunt, sunt[102] finitae. — Ad hoc respondetur[103] quod transitus intelligitur a termino in terminum. Quaecumque autem praeterita dies signetur, finiti[104] sunt dies ab illa ad istam, et non oportet quod omnes sunt infiniti. — Contra: caelum pertransit revolutionem diurnam istam et aliam. Ergo si infinitae revolutiones praecesserunt, finitum transiit infinita, quod est contra rationem infiniti, [F 62b] cuius ratio est quod eius quantitatem accipientibus, semper est accipere aliquid extra.

m. Item, omne praeteritum fuit futurum. Totum tempus praeteritum est praeteritum.[105] Ergo totum tempus[106] fuit aliquando futurum. Sed quando totum fuit futurum, fuit in principio sui esse et durationis. Ergo omne tempus habuit initium suae durationis.

n. Item, omne quod factum est, aliquando fuit in fieri. Sed mundus factus est. Ergo aliquando fuit in fieri, hoc est in aliquo instanti. Sed nullum instans

---

46, 2, arg. 8 and ad 8 (296b 33-39; 298a 44-298b 17). Later in his so-called *Quodlibet Romanum* (that is, disputed at the Roman Curia), Pecham was to argue in Question V: "Item, si mundus fuisset ab aeterno, essent infinita actu, scilicet infinitae animae rationales, nisi ponantur animae interire cum corpore vel revolvi in corpora diversa: quorum quodlibet est impossibile theologiae et philosophiae [more likely: theologice et philosophice]"; ed. F. M. Delorme, *Ioannis de Pecham Quodlibet Romanum* (Romae 1938), 17, 1-4.

94   motorem L, mortem F (with cross in margin).
95   *De anima* I, t. 53, c. 3 (407b 20-26).
96   PL 196, 894 D; ed. J. Ribaillier, 93.
97   loquor L, loquitur F.
98   ab ipso *om.* L.
99   quod F, si L. ‖ participat] deficit *add.* L. ‖ recepit...recipit *om.* L.
100   This is taken literally from St. Thomas, *Summa theologiae* I, 46, 2, ad 5 (298a 3-7).
101   quantum L, sicut F.
102   sunt *om.* F.
103   From the *Summa theol.* I, 46, 2, ad 6 (298a 9-13).
104   finiti F (and Thomas), finitae L. So also below.
105   est praeteritum *om.* L.
106   tempus *om.* L.

[L 98c] distat ab instanti[107] infinite; ergo mundi creatio praecessit finite hoc instans.

o. Item, in causis efficientibus non est abire in infinitum. Ergo si pater est causa filii, non praecesserunt patres infiniti.[108] — Respondetur quod in causis per se ordinatis ad effectum aliquem non est abire in infinitum, sicut quod lapis moveretur a baculo et baculus a manu, et hoc in infinitum. Sed in efficientibus per accidens ordinatis non est impossibile; verbi gratia, accidit huic homini generare in quantum est genitus ab alio, quia generat in quantum homo, non in quantum genitus ab alio. — Contra: infinitas in causis accidentaliter ordinatis non potest esse nisi ab infinita virtute Creatoris. Cum igitur inter effectum istum signatum et Deum, qui est infinitus, simpliciter sint infiniti gradus causarum possibiles, non est ratio quare non possit esse[109] infinitas in causis ordinatis essentialiter sicut in ordinatis accidentaliter. — Item, ratio II *Metaphysicae*[110] videtur esse contra hoc. Et est talis: In agentibus ordinatis primum est causa medii et medium est causa ultimi, sive sit unum sive plura media. Remota autem causa, removetur illud cuius est causa. Remoto ergo primo, medium non potest esse causa. Sed si procedatur in[111] causis efficientibus in infinitum, nulla causarum erit prima; ergo nulla erit secunda. Istud videtur sequi tam in causis essentialiter quam accidentaliter ordinatis.

p. Item, Philosophus, in fine...[112]

RESPONSIO:

Creatio mundi ex tempore quamvis sit articulus fidei,[113] tamen ratione, ut videtur, potest investigari. Nec hoc est in praeiudicium fidei, dum non propter rationem fidei assentitur, sed merito fidei ad eius intelligentiam pervenitur. Unde qui sine fide de creatione locuti sunt, omnes erraverunt vel diminute,[114] non eam attribuendo Deo, vel superflue, attribuendo eam alii a Deo.

Mundum[115] igitur fuisse ex tempore et non ab aeterno creatum patet considerando primo in ipso veram praeteritionem fieri[116]; secundo participationem essendi; tertio modum suae originis; quarto mensuram suae productionis; quinto totum decursum temporis.

Prima ratio.[117] Primo dico, considerando praeteritionem ipsius fieri

---

107 instanti *om.* F.

108 The argument is based on arg. 7 of the *Summa theol.* I, 46, 2 (296b 26-32). The response is rather literally from ad 7 (298a 16-43), with a mangled use of St. Thomas's own words.

109 esse *om.* L.

110 A-minor, t. 6, c. 2 (994a 11-18). Cf. St. Thomas, loc. cit., arg. 7.

111 in L, a F.

112 Lacuna of five lines in F; whole line omitted in L, which proceeds immediately to the Response.

113 Cf. St. Thomas, loc. cit., sed contra, and resp.

114 diminute L, dimitti (*corr. in* dimitte) sunt (= non?) F, *with* loquti sup. *add. marg.* F². ‖ non eam *trp.* L. ‖ superflue *om.* F. ‖ attribuendo] etiam *add.* F.

115 Mundum F, Quemadmodum L.

116 fieri F, fiendi L.

117 Prima ratio *marg.* L, *om.* F (so also below).

mundi, quoniam suum fieri vere transiit in praeteritum. Omne autem praeteritum aliquando fuit praesens et non praeteritum. Nullum autem tale fuit ab aeterno. Ideo dicit Augustinus, *Super Genesim contra Manichaeum*[118]: "Non coaevum Deo mundum dicimus, quia non eius aeternitatis est mundus, cuius aeternitatis est Deus. Mundum quippe Deus fecit, et cum ipsa creatura quam Deus[119] fecit tempora esse coeperunt." Ergo si fecit, fieri transiit in praeteritum quod est temporis initium.

Secunda ratio. Item secundo, considerando participationem essendi. Eo[120] enim quo participat esse, non habet esse plenum, sed contractum et limitatum et quantum ad essentiam et quantum ad modum.[121] Igitur sicut participat esse finitum, sic et modum essendi finitum.[122] Sed habere esse sine limitatione[123] dicit modum [L 98d] essendi infinitum. Ergo non [F 62c] convenit[124] habenti esse participatum. Quod dicat talem modum essendi multipliciter[125] patet: quia excedit omne esse ex tempore in infinitum. Item,[126] quia secundum hoc, tantum est suum esse vel tam diuturnum extensive sicut esse divinum intensive, et tam longa volubilitas temporis quanta simplicitas aeternitatis; quod est impossibile, sicut invenire mundum tantum quantitate molis sicut Deus est quantitate virtutis. Unde Augustinus, *De civitate* XI, cap. 5[127]: "Si infinita spatia temporis ante mundum cogitant, in quibus non videtur eis Deus ab opere cessare potuisse, similiter cogitent extra mundum infinita spatia locorum," quia idem est iudicium de ante et de extra mundum. — Quod si dicas non esse simile, quia ponere magnitudinem infinitam est ponere infinitum actu; ponere autem[128] tempus infinitum non est ponere aliquid[129] actu infinitum, quia partes temporis non sunt simul; contra: tempus est aliquod ens; ergo tempus infinitum, ens vel essentia infinita creatae durationis aequans aeternitatem Dei; et si non in simplicitate, tamen in durationis immensitate a parte ante.

Item, quod modus sit infinitus, probatio: quia infinitas a parte prima[130] est possibilis quia semper est actu finitum quod acceptum est et infinitum in potentia tantum. Sed in infinitate a parte ante est econtra infinitum in actu et in potentia. In actu inquam,[131] quia tantum habet in actu quantum habet acceptum; et in potentia, ut de futuro dictum est. Haec sententia colligitur ex

118 Book I, c. 2, n. 4 (PL 34, 175).
119 Deus *om.* F.
120 From *Eo enim* to *immensitate a parte ante* (i. e., the end of the paragraph), the text is incorporated by Roger Marston into his *Quodl.* I, q. 1, nn. 9-10; ed. G. F. Etzkorn — I. C. Brady (Quaracchi 1968) 8-9.
121 modum] essendi *add.* Marston.
122 Igitur...finitum *om.* F.
123 limitatione F, initio vel principio L. (this sentence is omitted by Marston).
124 convenit *om.* F.
125 multipliciter *om.* L.
126 Item *om.* L.
127 PL 41, 320; CSEL 40-1, 517; CCL 48, 325.
128 ponere autem] sed ponere L.
129 aliquid *om.* L.
130 prima L, ante primo F. (*post* would seem to be called for).
131 inquam L, nunquam F.

Augustino, *Super Genesim contra Manichaeum*, dicente[132]: "Cum ipsa creatura quam fecit Deus tempora esse coeperunt; et ideo dicuntur aeterna tempora. Non tamen sic sunt aeterna tempora quomodo aeternus est Deus, quia Deus est ante tempora, qui fabricator est temporum, sicut omnia quae fecit Deus bona sunt valde, sed non sic bona sunt quomodo bonus est Deus qui illa fecit." Ergo ex hiis verbis patet quod sicut bonitas est penitus infinite minor bonitate, ita duratio duratione.

Tertia ratio. Item, tertio hoc patet ex modo suae originis, quia est ex nihilo, et ita aliquando non fuit. — Respondetur[133] quod intelligendum est negative: mundus factus est de nihilo, hoc est de non-aliquo, ita quod non-esse non[134] praecessit esse secundum durationem, sed esse mundi nihil praecessit. — Sed istud improbatur per rationem praetactam,[135] quoniam sicut versio in non-esse non potest stare cum infinitate a parte post, ita nec eductio de non-esse cum infinitate a parte ante. Item, accipere esse non de aliquo dicit maiorem novitatem quam accipere esse de aliquo, quia quod accipit esse ab aliquo non totaliter producitur, sed secundum aliquid[136] prius fuit. Sed si mundus factus fuisset de aliquo, habuisset esse novum et ex tempore, ut probat Philosophus.[137] Ergo multo magis si habuit esse non de aliquo, habuit esse novum necessario. Damascenus, cap. 8[138]: "Creatio ex Dei voluntate opus exsistens, [L 99a] non coaeterna est cum Deo, quia non aptum natum est quod ex non-ente ad esse deducitur coaeternum esse ei, qui sine principio est et semper est." Et haec est etiam ratio Anselmi, *Monologion*, 24 cap.[139]

(IV.) Item, hoc patet ex mensura suae productionis, quae est nunc aevi vel nunc temporis. Nunc autem creationis est terminus sui esse a parte ante. Quod autem habet terminum initialem, non habet essendi infinitatem. Ergo si mundus productus est in tempore, productus est in temporis[140] initio. De instanti productionis dicit Hugo, parte prima, cap. 5[141]: "Credimus unum et idem prorsus momentum temporis fuisse, ut in tempore creata sit rerum visibilium corporaliumque materia, [et invisibilium in angelica natura essentia]." [F 62d]

---

132 Book I, c. 2, n. 4 (PL 34, 175).
133 Respondetur] Si respondetur L; cf. St. Thomas, *Summa theol.* I, 46, 2, ad 2 (297b 25-33).
134 non L, rerum F.
135 See arg. f, above; and a parallel text in Pecham's *Quodl. Romanum*, q. V: "Respondeo. Hic implicantur duae difficultates. Una est: An mundus potuit esse vel creari ab aeterno. Et certum est quod non. Probatur sic: quia habuit esse post non-esse, id est creatus est de non-aliquo. Sicut igitur impossibile est mundum durare in infinitum a parte post et tamen verti in nihilum, ita impossibile est quod fuerit ab aeterno ex parte ante et tamen fuerit eductus de nihilo"; ed. cit., 16, 16-22.
136 aliquid F, quid L.
137 *Physic.* VIII, t. 2 and 10, c. 1 (250b 24: 251b 17).
138 *De fide orthodoxa* I, c. 8 (PG 94, 814 A-B); versio Burgundionis, c. 8, n. 4 (ed. E. M. Buytaert, St. Bonaventure, N. Y. 1955, 32). Quoted by R. Marston, *Quodl.* I, q. 1, n. 2 (ed. cit., 4); and in part by St. Thomas, *De aeternitate mundi*, n. 10.
139 Thus St. Anselm writes: "Nam vel hoc solo veram aeternitatem soli illi inesse substantiae, quae sola non facta sed factrix esse inventa est, aperte percipitur; quoniam vera aeternitas principii finisque meta carere intelligitur; quod nulli rerum creatarum convenire, eo ipso quod de nihilo factae sunt, convincitur"; PL 158, 178 A.
140 temporis *om.* F.
141 PL 176, 189 D; at the end of the citation there is a lacuna in F (only) of somewhat over two lines, which we have endeavoured to supply from Hugo's text.

(V.) Item, hoc patet considerando decursum temporis, quoniam[142] revolutio una tardior est quam alia, quia plures praecedunt unam quam aliam, sicut dies crastina[143] tardior est quam hodierna. Igitur revolutio omnis quam infinitae praecedunt vel praecesserunt, est infinitae tarditatis. Sed quod est tale, nunquam eveniet. Ergo si mundus infinito tempore duravit, hodierna vel crastina revolutio nunquam eveniet. Ideo dicit Augustinus, *De civitate* XII, cap. 15[144]: "Tempus quoniam mutabilitate transcurrit, aeternitati immutabili non potest esse coaeternum. Et ita motus quibus tempora peraguntur Creatori coaeterni esse non possunt."[145]

Dico igitur quod mundus nullo modo capax fuit aeternae vel interminabilis durationis. Qui autem posuerunt mundum Deo coaeternum ex falso fundamento ad hoc moti sunt: vel quia sine mundo Deum credebant esse[146] otiosum; vel quia imaginati sunt temporis spatium praecessisse mundum; vel quia non credebant Deum aliquid facere novum nisi voluntate affectum et per consequens mutatum. Unde Augustinus, XI *De civitate*, cap. 4,[147] loquens de ponentibus mundum aeternum dicit: "Dicunt quidem aliquid unde sibi Deum videntur velut a fortuita temeritate defendere, ne subito illi credatur venisse in mentem quod nunquam ante venisset, facere mundum, et accidisse illi voluntatem novam, cum in nullo omnino sit mutabilis." Quae falsa fundamenta Augustinus refellit, ut patebit respondendo ad argumenta.

1. Ad primum de diffusione boni et lucis, dicendum quod duplex est diffusio illius boni vel lucis: quaedam est diffusio boni[148] interior per aeternas emanationes, quaedam exterior per rerum temporalium[149] productionem. Interior de necessitate est aeterna propter uniformitatem et perfectissimam actualitatem divinae naturae. Secunda autem, quae est temporalium et temporalis,[150] de necessitate est secundum quod congruit creaturae. Unde sicut universum est finitum nec capax infinitatis in magnitudine, ita nec tempus capax erat infinitatis actualis ex aliqua parte, et ideo ipsum, cum sit pars universi, certo termino et mensura est perventum. Aliter finitum esset susceptivum modi infiniti, ut dictum est. Et quod |L 99b| dicit Augustinus[151] quod sola bonitas Dei fuit causa istorum, dico quod verum est, sed non causa defectuum, sicut novitas et vertibilitas et parvitas quae sequuntur creaturam in quantum ex nihilo. Novitas, quia ab alio facta est; vertibilitas, quia ex[152] nihilo facta est; parvitas, quia participative facta est.

2. Ad secundum dicendum quod aeternitas soli Deo convenit, nec potest[153]

---

142   Marston uses *revolutio...tale nunquam eveniet* in *Quodl.*I, q. 1, n. 4; ed. cit., 4.
143   dies crastina] postcrastina L.
144   Num. 2, or chapter 16 in newer editions (PL 41, 364s; CSEL 40-1, 594, 1-9; CCL 48, 372, 83-92). Augustine's words are cited at greater length by St. Thomas, *De aeternitate mundi*, n. 11.
145   Lacuna of four lines in F only.
146   esse *om.* F.
147   Num. 2 (PL 41, 319; CSEL 40-1, 515; CCL 48, 324).
148   est diffusio boni *om.* F.
149   temporalium F, naturalium L.
150   temporalium et temporalis] temporalium et temporis F, naturalium et temporalis L.
151   See above, in the first arg. of the present question.
152   ex F, de L.
153   potest] fecit F.

alii convenire, sicut dicit Augustinus, *Super Genesim* VIII[154]: "Incommutabilis est natura Trinitatis, et ob hoc ita aeterna ut aliquid ei coaeternum esse non possit." Quod etiam plures non possunt esse aeternitates[155] probat Anselmus, *De incarnatione Verbi*, cap. 14.[156] — Tamen aliquando aeternum dicitur largius: sicut super[157] Gen. 3, 22: *Ne sumat de ligno vitae et comedat et vivat in aeternum*, id est per magnum spatium temporis, sic ubi[158] Apostolus dicit, II ad Timoth. I, 9: *Quae data est nobis ante tempora saecularia*, ibi littera Augustini habet *ante tempora aeterna*. Quod exponit, *Super Genesim contra Manichaeum* I, dicens[159]: "Mundum fecit Deus et cum ipsa creatura quam fecit Deus tempora esse coeperunt; et ideo dicuntur aeterna tempora." Ergo sensus est: si ignis fuisset aeternus,[160] hoc est quantumcumque amplius fuisset quam fuit, vel si fuisset in principio ipso[161] temporis in specie distinctus. Quodsi dicatur aeternum Deo coaevum, implicatio est oppositorum, quia ponit accidens infinitum in subiecto finito, et sequitur ut splendor esset aeternus, sicut posito impossibili sequitur quod impossibili implicatur. Et sic dicendum de vestigio [F 63a] pedis in pulvere rationibus consimilibus.

3. Ad tertium dicendum quod 'tota ratio facti est potentia facientis'. Sed tamen defectibilitas sequitur creaturam in quantum ex nihilo est, cuius causa Deus non est. — Item, cum dico posse rei creabilis, licet nihil dicam positive nisi potentiam Creatoris, dico tamen cum hoc privationem prohibitionis[162] sui esse. Quaedam enim prohibent suum esse, ut omnia in quorum intellectu negatio clauditur. Licet igitur creabile non dicat potentiam aliam a potentia Creatoris, tamen excludit impedimentum, quia termini non repugnant.

4. Ad quartum dicendum quod non est impossibilitas[163] a pari ad utrumque, quia in eo quod est 'creaturam esse aeternam' opposita clauduntur, non autem in eo quod est 'creaturam creari'.

5. Ad quintum dicendum quod plus potest Deus de nihilo in eo quod posse est posse, sed hoc posse non est posse.

6-7. Ad sextum dicendum quod illud argumentum procedit ex falsa imaginatione, quasi Deus spatio mundum praecessit. Amplius, dico quod Deus nihil potest velle nisi secundum leges sapientiae. Ideo non potest velle aliquid infinitum inesse subiecto finito.[164] — Et sic patet ad septimum.[165]

---

154   *De Genesi ad litteram* VIII, c. 23, n. 44 (PL 34, 389; CSEL 28-1, 262).
155   aeternitates] trinitates F.
156   PL 178, 282 B.
157   super *om.* F.
158   ubi] hic F.
159   Chapt. 2, n. 3 (PL 34, 175).
160   See the words of Augustine in the second argument.
161   in principio ipso F, a principio L.
162   prohibitionis] probationis F.
163   impossibilitas] argumentum L.
164   In the margin of F at this point there is one note deleted and partly covered by another (at third hand?), which is quite illegible; it seems to refer to the lack of a response to the seventh argument.
165   septimum] sextum L.

8. Ad octavum[166] dico quod verum est ex parte sui pro tanto quod non procedit ex impotentia quod non producit; sed tamen non congruit omnino potentiae suae.

9. Ad aliud dicendum quod aequipotens est producere finitum sicut infinitum, sed non simul finitum et infinitum.[167]

11. Ad undecimum dicendum[168] quod non est simile de creatione quae terminatur ad esse, et ideo potest habere mensuram; et de versione quae |L 99c| terminatur ad non-esse, et, quia est defectio, ideo nulla sibi respondet mensura; sed ipsum esse habet ultimum instans sui esse cui nihil succedit nisi non-esse.

166 octavum] vii L.
167 A marginal note in F: Hic autem (?) deest decimi solutio.
168 undecimum dicendum F, aliud L.

UN ADVERSAIRE DE SAINT THOMAS:
PETRUS IOHANNIS OLIVI

Marie-Thérèse d'Alverny

1. L'INTERPRÉTATION DE *NOLITE POSSIDERE*

L E 6 août 1325, Dame Prous Boneta, de Montpellier, arrêtée comme suspecte d'hérésie, fit une longue confession devant le tribunal d'inquisition de Carcassonne.[1] La béguine proclamait les révélations dont elle aurait été favorisée, comparait le pape régnant, Jean XXII, à Caïphe, à Hérode, à "Lucibel," à Simon le Magicien et même à l'Antéchrist, car il avait persécuté les béguins fidèles à la pauvreté évangélique, et détruit l'écriture du saint frère "Petrus Ioannis." Elle adjurait Prêcheurs et Mineurs de revenir à la pureté de leur règle primitive, et de ne plus s'occuper d'inquisition. Les réminiscences bibliques fournissant à l'imagination de Dame Prous des similitudes frappantes, elle mit ainsi en cause le frère Thomas d'Aquin, que le mauvais pape venait de mettre sur les autels: De même qu'Adam engendra d'Eve Abel et Caïn, de même, le Seigneur Dieu eut deux fils de cette Eglise moderne, qui peut être appelée Eve par similitude, à savoir Abel et Cain. Le fils de l'Eglise qui ressemble à Abel fut le frère Pierre Jean, et l'autre, Cain, fut ce frère Thomas d'Aquin, de l'ordre des Prêcheurs, qui a été récemment canonisé; de même que Cain a tué son frère Abel corporellement, de même, ce frère Thomas a tué son frère, à savoir le dit frère Pierre Jean, spirituellement, c'est à dire quant à ses écrits.[2]

Cette vue dramatique et un peu sommaire du conflit idéal entre deux théologiens dont Dame Prous n'avait pas lu les ouvrages savants[3] devait être un écho des opinions exprimées par les Franciscains Spirituels avec

---

1 Cf. W. H. May, "The Confession of Prous Boneta, Heretic and Heresiarch," *Essays in Medieval Life and Thought presented in honor of A. P. Evans* (New York 1955), pp. 3-30. Edition du texte, pp. 7-30, d'après le vol. 27 de la collection Doat à la Bibliothèque Nationale, f. 51-79v. La confession est datée du 6 août 1325. Cette confession est analysée par R. Manselli, *Spirituali e Beghini in Provenza* (Roma 1959), pp. 239 sqq. (Instituto storico italiano per il Medio Evo. Studi storici, 31-34).

2 Ed. cit., p. 24.

3 Des écrits du Spirituel, traduits en langue d'oc, circulaient parmi les Béguins; c'étaient surtout des opuscules pieux, dont certains sont encore conservés; cf. D. Zorzi, *Testi inediti francescani in lingua provenzale*, Miscellanea del Centro di Studi Medievali, ser. I (Milan 1956), pp.

lesquels la béguine avait l'occasion de s'entretenir. La canonisation de saint Thomas,[4] survenue au moment où l'agitation était vive dans le Midi de la France parmi les dévôts qui vénéraient la mémoire du "saint frère Pierre Jean," mort à Narbonne le 14 mars 1298, et où la controverse au sujet de la pauvreté évangélique[5] suscitait la rédaction de nombreux traités ou consultations, pouvait paraître une marque de la politique de Jean XXII, favorisant les Prêcheurs et condamnant les Spirituels, en particulier le culte et les écrits apocalyptiques du plus célèbre d'entre eux.

De fait, si saint Thomas d'Aquin avait eu le dessus dans une lutte imaginaire, c'était bien dans une vision intemporelle, car il avait dû ignorer totalement l'existence d'un jeune franciscain qui faisait des études à Paris au cours de sa vie terrestre. Par contre, "Abel" avait porté à son illustre prédécesseur un certain nombre de pointes, qui risquaient de se retourner contre lui.

Les sentiments de Pierre Jean Olieu,[6] dit communément Olivi par les historiens contemporains, à l'égard du grand maître en théologie qu'il avait peut-être aperçu de loin dans sa jeunesse, ne sont pas aveuglément hostiles, bien que son attitude soit le plus souvent critique et ses propos peu amènes. Dans le dernier quart du XIIIᵉ siècle, époque de l'activité

249-268; édition du texte latin de quatre opuscules par R. Manselli, op. cit., pp. 274 sqq. Il y avait aussi, d'après Bernard Gui, des traités sur la pauvreté, la mendicité, les dispenses, traduits en langue vulgaire: "ex aliquibus tractatibus quos ipse fecisse Beguini dicunt et credunt, unum videlicet de paupertate et alium de mendicitate et quemdam alium de dispensationibus et quibusdam etiam aliis....que omnïa habent in vulgari transposita." *Practica inquisitionis*, ed. G. Mollat, 1 (1926), p. 110. Il s'agit probablement, d'après cette description, d'extraits des questions sur la perfection évangélique. Des extraits du commentaire sur l'Apocalypse ont dû également circuler, mais il n'est pas probable que des ouvrages d'exégèse et de théologie théorique aient été traduits.

4 Le P. Pierre Mandonnet a publié à l'occasion de l'anniversaire de la canonisation une étude historique: "La canonisation de saint Thomas," *Mélanges thomistes* (Paris 1923), pp. 1-48 (Bibliothèque thomiste 3). Il relève dans un récit des faits relatifs à la canonisation fait par un témoin la relation d'un sermon prononcé par le pape: "Et mirabiles commendationes proposuit tam de predicatorum ordine quam de sancto. Inter cetera dixit quod iste sanctus in ordine sancto predicatorum gessit vitam apostolicam, cum ordo nichil habet in proprio et in speciali, licet habeat in communi, addens: et hanc vitam apostolicam reputamus."

5 Il y a une grande quantité de publications sur les Spirituels et la controverse sur la pauvreté évangélique. Nous renvoyons à la bibliographie récente publiée par S. Gieben, "Bibliographia Oliviana" (1885-1967), *Collectanea franciscana* 38 (1968), 167-195, en particulier les nn. 117-154.

6 A. Thomas, "Le vrai nom du frère mineur Petrus Iohannis Olivi," *Annales du Midi*, 1913, 68 sqq., a ainsi interprété le surnom latin du Spirituel, avec des attendus philologiques et historiques qui paraissent valables. Nous nous permettons de suivre l'avis d'un savant amateur d'étymologies pour parler de notre compatriote occitan. Sur la vie et les œuvres d'Olieu, cf. la "Bibliographia Oliviana" que nous venons de citer en ce qui concerne les éditions et études. Le P. D. Pacetti a donné une liste des œuvres connues d'Olieu, en grande partie encore inédites, complétant celle qui a été dressée par Fr. Ehrle dans son étude fondamentale: "Petrus Iohannis Olivi, sein Leben und seine Schriften," *Archiv für Literatur und Kirchengeschichte des Mittelalters* 3 (1887), 402-452. Cette liste est comprise dans l'introduction de l'édition: Petrus Ioannis Olivi, *Quaestiones quatuor de Domina*, 1954, pp. 15*-29*. Il faut compléter cette liste pour les commentaires bibliques par le *Repertorium biblicum* de Fr. Stegmüller, nn. 6679-6725.

littéraire de Pierre Jean, Thomas d'Aquin n'est pas encore une autorité, même parmi ses confrères; la plupart des maîtres séculiers de l'Université de Paris ont des positions différentes des siennes. Quant aux Franciscains, leur attitude est défiante; l'un d'entre eux, Guillaume de la Mare, a rédigé une mise en garde contre une série de thèses thomistes qui paraissent contestables ou périlleuses.[7] Au chapitre général de Strasbourg, tenu à la Pentecôte de l'an 1282,[8] une décision marquait cette réserve de manière officielle; il n'était permis aux Lecteurs de l'Ordre d'utiliser la *Somme théologique* qu'accompagnée du *Correctoire* de frère Guillaume de la Mare:

Minister generalis imponit ministris provincialibus quod non permittant multiplicari Summam fratris Thome nisi apud Lectores rationabiliter intelligentes, et hoc nonnisi cum declarationibus fratris Guillelmi de Mara, non in marginibus positis, sed in quaternis, et huiusmodi declarationes non scribantur per aliquem secularem.

Ce texte, bien connu, permet de constater que la valeur de la *Somme théologique* était suffisamment admise pour que sa lecture fût autorisée avec restrictions; la première d'interprétation délicate, car tous les Lecteurs devaient, il faut le supposer, être considérés comme "rationabiliter intelligentes."

Olieu n'ignorait pas le *Correctoire* et il s'y réfère à plusieurs reprises dans un écrit polémique rédigé sans doute à une date un peu antérieure à celle du Chapitre: *Impugnatio XXXVIII articulorum* (fratris Ar.).[9] Il discute en termes fort vifs un certain nombre de thèses doctrinales, sur lesquelles il est en désaccord avec son confrère, et son texte est à la fois une riposte et une attaque. Il accuse son adversaire, qui est certainement un Lecteur, étant donné les références à son enseignement,

---

7 Une bibliographie récente au sujet des Correctoires et des études qui les concernent a été donnée par le P. V. Heynck, "Zur Datierung des 'Correctorium fratris Thomae' Wilhelms de la Mare; ein unbeachtetes Zeugnis des Petrus Iohannis Olivi," *Franziskanische Studien* 49 (1967), 1-2.

8 Cf. G. Fussenegger, "Definitiones Capituli generalis Argentinae celebrati 1282," *Arch. fr. hist.* 26 (1933), 139.

9 L'*Impugnatio* fait partie d'une série d'écrits polémiques d'Olieu contenus dans un volume imprimé à Venise, L. Soardi, sans date. Ce recueil a été analysé par Fr. Ehrle, op. cit., pp. 467-469; il est fort rare et Ehrle, ibid. pp. 466-467 raconte qu'il l'a vainement cherché à Paris. Il s'y trouve cependant à la Bibliothèque Mazarine, sous la cote: Incunable 1315, avec un ex-libris du XVIe s. "Est S. Justine de Padua." L'*Impugnatio XXXVII articulorum adversus opiniones doctorum quorundam quorum ipse supprimere voluit* se trouve f. 42-52v. Le personnage visé est un certain frère *Ar.* qui aurait fait une liste d'erreurs d'Olieu. Ehrle avait suggéré que ce frère *Ar.* pourrait être Arnaud de Roquefeuil, provincial de Provence en 1285, op. cit. pp. 477-479; J. Koch, "Die Verurteilung Olivis auf dem Konzil von Vienne und ihre Vorgeschichte," *Scholastik* 5 (1930), 499 propose le nom de frère Arnaud Galhard, qui eut également maille à partir avec notre Spirituel. C'est de cet écrit qu'il est question dans l'article cité du P. V. Heynck, qui suit J. Koch, et tend à dater ce texte polémique de 1280-1281.

de "suivre Thomas" ainsi qu'Aristote, qui est lui même dans l'erreur![10]

L'intransigeant franciscain n'avait du reste pas besoin d'encouragements de la part des supérieurs de l'Ordre pour formuler des réserves au sujet d'une doctrine qui différait trop souvent de celle de "nos maîtres," c'est à dire surtout de saint Bonaventure.

Dans son ouvrage sur les doctrines philosophiques d'Olivi, d'après les Questions sur les *Sentences* éditées par B. Jansen,[11] le P. E. Bettoni[12] a exposé divers points de divergence ou d'opposition entre les thèses défendues par le franciscain et celles de Thomas d'Aquin (divergences déjà en partie notées par l'éditeur). Il remarque que, conformément à l'usage lorsque les "moderni" sont en cause, Olieu ne nomme pas frère Thomas. Mais l'importance de ce "moderne," est tacitement reconnue, même en cas de dissentiment, car il est placé parmi les "quidam magni."[13] S'il arrive que Thomas se trouve, selon lui, d'accord avec saint Augustin et Bonaventure, il consent plus volontiers encore à le ranger parmi les auteurs de poids, et même, fait surprenant, à s'abriter derrière lui en face de ses censeurs. Le cas est assez remarquable pour être noté.

Dans sa Question XI sur le second livre des *Sentences*: An conseruatio rerum in esse sit aliud quam earum creatio,"[14] Olieu, après avoir énuméré les arguments *contra*, déclare: "Alii autem non mediocribus placet quod conseruatio non differat a creatione seu actione secundum rem, nisi quantum esse vel fieri in sequenti tempore vel nunc differt ab esse vel fieri priori nunc."

Lui-même ajoute un peu plus loin qu'il convient de distinguer les termes: "videtur igitur tenendum quod conseruatio non differat secundum speciem a creatione, sed solum numero, sicut supradictum est, nomen creationis non possit proprie praedicari de conseruatione, pro eo quod non significat absolute et in generali factionem creaturae."

10 Le P. V. Heynck, art. cit., p. 10, a relevé rapidement les pointes d'Olivi contre s. Thomas et plus longuement, pp. 13-16, les citations et références au Correctoire de Guillaume de la Mare, d'après le texte contenu dans l'imprimé et les mss Vat. Borgh. 46 et 54. Cf. aussi au sujet des rapports du Correctoire et des ouvrages d'Olivi, F. M. Delorme, "P. I. Olivi quaestio de voto regulam aliquam profitentis," *Antonianum* 16 (1941), 131 sqq.

11 B. Jansen, Fr. Petrus Iohannis Olivi...*Quaestiones in secundum librum Sententiarum*, I-III (Quaracchi 1922-1926).

12 E. Bettoni, *Le dottrine filosofiche di Pier di Giovanni Olivi* (Milan 1959).

13 Cf. Q. 36 sur les *Sentences*, ed. Jansen, I, p. 629. La question concerne l'angélologie, sur laquelle Olieu conteste la position de saint Thomas: "Quaeritur an (angelus) intelligat et videat omnia per species innatas. — Ad quod quidam magni dixerunt et dicunt quod sic..." Dans son *Impugnatio XXXVII articulorum*, Olieu précise que son adversaire "dicit quod per species innatas quicquid est angelis naturaliter cognoscibile est eis cognitum...quod autem eum ad hoc moverit, nescio, nisi forte quia voluit in hoc sequi Thomam cuius est positio ista (il s'agit probablement de l'article 18 de la *Prima pars*, qui est également relevé par Guillaume de la Mare. Cf. P. Glorieux, *Le Correctorium corruptorii Quare*, Kain, Belgium, 1927, p. 79) sequens in hoc philosophos qui de cognitione intelligentiarum tanquam de cognitione deorum loquuntur." Ed. cit., f. 46.

14 Ed. Jansen, I, pp. 197 sqq.

Olieu ne nomme pas alors ces "non mediocres," à l'avis desquels il se range: "Istis autem ad praesens magis consentiendum mihi videtur, quoniam non solum rationi, sed et dictis sanctorum et philosophorum magis conforme videtur." Cet adversaire des philosophes consent, pour une fois, à leur accorder quelque crédit. Ayant été attaqué sur ce point, (car dans une liste de 19 erreurs qui lui sont imputées l'article 9 se rapporte à la question sur la création que nous venons de citer: "quod Deus continue res creat ita quod earum conseruatio est continua eorum creatio,") le franciscain rectifie l'imputation et précise sa position réelle, en spécifiant qu'il est en bonne compagnie:[15]

De hoc dixi quod faciendo vim in propria significatione nominis, quod conseruatio non debet dici creatio, quia creatio secundum nomen suum proprie significat primam factionem creaturae; dixi tamen quod conseruatio in his quae immediate a Deo conseruantur est quaedam continua factio, non tamen prima factio rerum, et si inspiciatur quaestio fratris Bonauenturae, ubi dicit qualiter aeuum sit successiuum sine innouatione, ubi et dat exemplum radii continue orientis a sole, fortasse videbitis quod hoc idem dicit ibidem, quamuis sub aliis verbis...si tamen pie ac fideliter mihi ostendatur quod in hoc dicto aliquid erroneum contineatur, et quod in hoc Augustinus, Bonauentura et Thomas[16] rem erroneam et periculosam dixerunt, libentissime cedo...

Dans sa seconde réponse aux observations des maîtres parisiens chargés par le Ministre général d'examiner ses écrits, datée de Nîmes en 1285, Olieu donne une explication analogue au sujet de cette imputation: "Ista opinio non est mea, sed fratris Thomae de Aquino

15   Ce texte est contenu dans une lettre apologétique adressée à un certain frère Raymond et à ses très chers compagnons qui doivent être à Paris, d'après le contexte. Elle se trouve dans l'imprimé de Venise, f. 51²v-53² (par suite d'une erreur de foliotation de l'imprimé plusieurs folios portent deux fois le même chiffre). Une autre copie a été découverte par le P. Gratien dans le ms. n. acq. lat. 774 de la Bibliothèque Nationale, et publiée partiellement: "Une lettre inédite de Pierre de Jean Olivi," *Etudes franciscaines* 29 (1913), 414-422.

Le nom du destinataire dans l'imprimé est: fr. R. de Camliaco, qu'il faut probablement lire: Caviliaco; dans le manuscrit il est désigné: frère Raymond *Gaufredi*, qui devint général de l'ordre en 1289. Cette dernière identification a peut-être été trop vite adoptée, car le ton de la lettre paraît un peu familier pour s'adresser à un personnage qui devait être assez important dans l'ordre, même avant son généralat. La date de la lettre est également discutée. Le P. V. Heynck, suivant J. Koch, pense qu'elle est antérieure au chapitre de la Pentecôte 1282, art. cit. p. 12; le P. Pacetti, op. cit. p. 17*, suivant les suggestions de F. Ehrle et du P. Gratien, la situe vers 1286. Notre texte n'est pas cité dans l'éd. Gratien.

16   Olieu se réfère vraisemblablement pour s. Thomas à la *Prima pars*, q. 104, a. 1, car c'est là qu'on trouve une citation de s. Augustin, *De Genesi ad litteram*, IV, 12: "...sicut aer, praesente lumine fit lucidus, sic homo, Deo praesente, illuminatur"; ce que s. Thomas interprète ainsi: "...sic autem se habet omnis creatura ad Deum sicut aer ad solem illuminantem." Cf. aussi *Quaest. de potentia*, q. 5, a. 1: "Utrum res conservantur in esse a Deo." Pour s. Bonaventure, il s'agit d'un passage de son commentaire *In Sent.* II, d. II, p. 1, q. 3, dans lequel il emploie la comparaison du rayon de soleil pour indiquer la continuité de l'action divine. Olieu n'a pas étudié de trop près les textes, car s. Thomas n'est pas d'accord avec s. Bonaventure sur la question de l'*aevum*.

sequentis in hoc sententiam Auicennae, et videtur esse fratris Bonaventurae in quaestione: An aeuum sit successiuum."[17]

En regard de ce cas favorable, pour lequel Olieu a jugé bon de se
réclamer de frère Thomas d'Aquin, il faut bien constater que beaucoup
plus souvent le fougueux méridional se déclare en désaccord avec le
maître dominicain et le traite sans ménagements. Les termes employés
par Guillaume de la Mare dans ses critiques des thèses thomistes sont
fort modérés en comparaison.

Le motif principal de l'irritation d'Olieu est l'attitude de saint
Thomas vis à vis d'Aristote et des philosophes arabes, que celui-ci cite
dans les questions théologiques, en prenant leurs arguments en sérieuse
considération, et en les adoptant lorsqu'ils lui paraissent valables du
point de vue de la raison naturelle. Il arrive à Olieu de citer Aristote, et
parfois Avicenne ou même Averroes, mais il considère avec méfiance,
voire avec animosité ces corps étrangers à la chrétienté.[18] Aussi sévère
que saint Jérôme, comparant les auteurs païens à la captive du
Deutéronome qui ne doit être tolérée qu'après avoir été rasée et
dépouillée de tout ornement superflu, Olieu déclare qu'il convient de
traiter les philosophes païens et arabes comme l'esclave Agar, et non de
les vénérer comme des maîtres.[19] Pour lui, Thomas entre dans la
catégorie des "philosophantes" qui se détournent de la saine doctrine en
suivant Aristote, Platon et leurs disciples musulmans.[20]

Les attaques directes contre saint Thomas se remarquent surtout dans
la série d'écrits polémiques et apologétiques rédigés entre 1281 et 1286
environ, à l'époque ou un certain nombre de thèses tirées de son enseignement avaient été attaquées et dénoncées; les expressions vives
d'Olieu, ses boutades parfois drôles contre les "philosophantes" sont
sans doute provoquées par l'amertume de se voir soupconner d'opinions
suspectes par ses propres confrères. Il faut convenir cependant que son
attitude vis-à-vis des aristotéliciens est consistante à travers toute son
œuvre. Le P. Delorme, dans son introduction à l'édition du petit traité:
De perlegendis philosophorum libris,[21] dans lequel Olieu expose ses

17   Texte contenu dans l'imprimé de Venise, f. 54-54v, 43²-50²v et réédité par D. Laberge, "Fr.
Petri Ioannis Olivi tria scripta sui ipsius apologetica annorum 1283 et 1285," *Arch. fr. hist.* 28
(1935), 130-155, 374-407; cf. 153.
18   Cf. O. Bettini, "Olivi di fronte a Aristotele," *Studi francescani* 55 (1958), 176-197; et surtout
la récente étude de D. Burr, "The Apocalyptic Element in Olivi's Critique of Aristotle," *Church
History* 40 (1971), 15-29.
19   "Responsio fratris Petri Ioannis ad aliqua dicta per quosdam magistros parisienses de suis
quaestionibus excerpta," éd. D. Laberge, art. cit. p. 406.
20   Cf. E. Gilson, "Les *Philosophantes*," *Archives d'histoire doctrinale et littéraire du moyen
âge* 19 (1952), 134-140.
21   F. M. Delorme, "Fr. Petri Ioannis Olivi tractatus 'De perlegendis philosophorum libris',"
Antonianum 16 (1941), 31-44.

vues sur l'utilisation des philosophes, a essayé de présenter la position de l'auteur comme plus modérée qu'il n'apparaît à la simple lecture; il a rappelé les circonstances historiques qui ont pu provoquer la méfiance du franciscain, qui a étudié au Studium de Paris au moment de l'invasion de l'averroïsme. Ces circonstances étaient les mêmes pour la plupart des contemporains, et nous ne pensons pas qu'aucun d'entre eux se soit insurgé avec autant de vigueur contre Aristote et contre les théologiens qui lui attribuent une autorité.

Ce n'est pas à titre de "philosophans" que Thomas d'Aquin a subi une réfutation en règle de deux passages de la *Somme théologique* de la part d'Olieu, mais parce qu'il y traitait de ce qui tenait le plus au coeur du Spirituel; nous devons même dire qu'il s'agissait de la cause à laquelle il avait voué sa vie et le meilleur de son éloquence; la défense de la règle de vie évangélique instituée par saint François, et plus particulièrement de la pauvreté. La valeur prédominante attribuée à la vertu de pauvreté dans l'ordre franciscain s'appuyait sur des textes scripturaires qui avaient sans doute constitué la première règle. Un verset de l'évangile selon saint Matthieu exprimait les recommandations du Christ aux Apôtres en les envoyant prêcher la Bonne Nouvelle: Ne possédez pas, ni or, ni argent, ni monnaie dans vos ceintures, ni sac pour la route, ni deux tuniques, ni chaussures, ni bâton.[22] Ces paroles indiquaient le chemin de la perfection vers laquelle devaient tendre ceux qui voulaient mener une vie conforme à celle des Apôtres et suivre les traces de celui qui avait imité le dénuement du Christ, François d'Assise. L'interprétation stricte de la règle évangélique impliquait la renonciation à toute propriété, tant en propre qu'en commun. La pauvreté volontaire pratiquée par saint François et laissée en exemple aux Frères Mineurs était un idéal difficile à soutenir pour un ordre religieux, mais si, en fait, il était nécessaire de s'accommoder plus ou moins aux circonstances, les Spirituels intransigeants, tels Olieu, réclament sans défaillir l'application stricte des principes, et ne tolèrent pas de voir atténuer, ou interpréter différemment, les principes eux-mêmes.

Aussi, la position prise par saint Thomas dans la *Somme théologique*, en premier lieu au sujet du sens et de la portée des préceptes évangéliques donnés dans ces versets du chapitre X de saint Matthieu; en second lieu, au sujet de la perfection à rechercher dans les différents états de vie des ordres religieux, et du rôle de la pauvreté, a-t-elle indigné le franciscain, qui a vigoureusement pris à partie le grand Docteur.

---

22 Mt. X, 9-10.

Cette diatribe a été trouvée par F. Ehrle, à l'état isolé, dans un recueil de questions et de traités d'Olieu conservé à la bibliothèque du Vatican, le manuscrit Vat. lat. 4986. Il l'a présentée et en a publié des extraits dans sa remarquable étude sur la vie et les oeuvres de Pierre Jean Olivi. [23] Le texte ainsi mis en lumière est en réalité partie intégrante de l'une des œuvres les plus importantes d'Olieu, la *Postilla* ou *Lectura in Matthaeum*. Replacée dans son contexte, l'explication du chapitre X et du verset: *Nolite possidere*, la riposte d'Olieu aux passages incriminés de la *Somme*, qu'il cite du reste presque intégralement, prend un sens plus précis, et l'on apprécie mieux sa portée, puisque saint Thomas est accusé d'erreur dans un commentaire biblique qui correspond à un enseignement, et qui paraît avoir eu une assez large diffusion.

Les commentaires scripturaires du frère Pierre Jean datent probablement de l'époque de son enseignement au Studium de Florence, ou il fut envoyé en 1287 par le ministre général Matthieu d'Aquasparta, et au Studium de Montpellier, où le nomma le général Raymond Gaufredi après 1289. [24] La *Postilla in Matthaeum* peut en tous cas être située par rapport à d'autres oeuvres de l'auteur, car celui-ci a coutume de se référer souvent à ses propres écrits. Il cite ses deux premières questions sur la pauvreté rédigées avant la publication de la bulle *Exiit qui seminat*, promulguée par le pape Nicolas III le 14 août 1279 au sujet de l'interprétation de la règle des frères Mineurs; ces questions: "An status altissimae paupertatis sit simpliciter melior omni statu diuitiarum" et: "An usus pauper includatur in consilio seu voto paupertatis euangelicae, ita quod sit de eius substantia et integritate," dans lesquelles Olieu expose pleinement sa conception de l'idéal et de la pratique de la pauvreté évangélique sont respectivement la huitième et la neuvième de la série des questions *De perfectione evangelica* décrite par Ehrle d'après le manuscrit Vat. lat. 4986 et que l'on trouve, en groupe ou isolément, dans quelques autres manuscrits. [25] D'après la référence d'Olivi, il est possible que la collection des questions n'ait pas été encore ordonnée au moment où il rédigeait la *Postilla*. Une question sur la dispense des voeux par le pape, également décrite par Ehrle, [26] est

23 Op. cit. pp. 519-523.

24 Cf. F. Ehrle, *ALKGM* III, 431, qui tire ces renseignements biographiques d'un écrit d'Hubertin de Casale, disciple d'Olivi, le libelle "Sanctitati apostolicae"; sur lequel cf. F. Ehrle, *ALKGM* II, 389.

25 Cf. sur la série des questions et les manuscrits qui les contiennent la liste donnée par D. Pacetti; il faut ajouter, pour la question sur l'*usus pauper* le ms. Paris Nat. lat. 3699, f. 13-26v, de la fin du XIII° s. ou début XIV° qui contient en marge des annotations qui doivent dater de l'époque du concile de Vienne, car on y relève les points incriminés par la Communauté dans la doctrine d'Olieu. Nous avons nous-même étudié ces questions dans le manuscrit de la Laurentienne, S. Croce, cod. XXXI, sin. 3 et dans des manuscrits du Vatican.

26 "An papa possit in omni voto dispensare et specialiter an in votis evangelicis"; cf. Ehrle, op. cit. pp. 528-530.

aussi citée, au chapitre XIX de saint Matthieu, ainsi que la question sur le voeu d'obéissance, au chapitre X, à la fin de la réfutation de Thomas d'Aquin.[27] Dans le chapitre V de la *Postilla*, Olieu se réfère à l'une de ses questions sur les *Sentences*, sur le péché véniel,[28] et à une "expositiuncula" sur le Pater.[29] D'autre part, la *Postilla in Matthaeum* est antérieure à la *Postilla in Lucam et Marcum*, à la *Postilla in Ioannem*, à la *Postilla super Actus Apostolorum*, à la *Postilla super Isaiam*, à la *Postilla super libros regum*; par contre, il semble, d'après une allusion à la fin du chapitre V que la *Postilla in Epistolas canonicas* ait été rédigée auparavant. Dans son *Expositio regulae fratrum Minorum*, au chapitre 3, Olieu renvoie ses lecteurs à son exposition du chapitre X de saint Matthieu.[30]

La *Lectura in Matthaeum* est l'une des oeuvres les plus intéressantes et les plus élaborées d'Olieu. Tout en commentant la lettre du texte, il traite des questions théologiques qui peuvent se poser à ce propos. Ces digressions sont assez importantes, aussi ne peut-on considérer la réfutation de saint Thomas comme une addition exceptionnelle dans le corps de l'ouvrage. Une liste de questions a été jointe à une partie des manuscrits de la *Postilla*; les premières se rapportent à l'introduction générale sur les Evangiles, qui constitue le prologue, puis dans chaque chapitre sont énumérés les points discutés en particulier. Il nous parait probable que cette liste a été élaborée, sinon par l'auteur, du moins par des disciples qui ont voulu utiliser le commentaire pour l'enseignement.

Alors que les boutades contre saint Thomas contenues dans les écrits apologétiques n'ont pas dû dépasser un petit cercle de l'ordre franciscain, les critiques longuement développées dans la *Postilla* ont été remarquées et ont suscité des réactions, d'après quelques témoignages dont le moins parlant n'est pas l'examen de la tradition manuscrite. Aussi, après avoir exposé le corps du délit, c'est à dire les points essentiels de l'exposé de saint Thomas et de la réplique d'Olieu, donnerons nous quelques précisions à ce sujet.

27 "De voto obedientiae evangelicae"; cf. Ehrle, op. cit. p. 523, qui donne un abrégé d'après le ms. Vat.4986, f.79-81v. Le dernier point envisagé est la valeur relative des trois vœux de religion, et Olieu, sans le nommer, s'oppose à l'opinion de s. Thomas, *Secunda Secundae*, q. 88, a. 6, ce dont on ne se rend pas compte en lisant Ehrle, car il a transcrit l'argument *contra* en l'attribuant à Olieu: "doctores communiter in hoc consentiunt quod votum obedientie sumptum in suo culmine est perfectius quam alia duo." Olieu réfute cette thèse, et pose la thèse contraire, à savoir que le vœu de pauvreté est le plus parfait, et comprend les deux autres.

28 *Quaest. in Sent.* q. 118; éd. Jansen, III, pp. 375 sqq.

29 Ed. F. M. Delorme, "L'explication littérale du Pater selon Pierre Jean Olivi," *Archivio italiano par la storia della pietà*, 1 (1951), 185-194.

30 Cf. Ehrle, op. cit. au sujet de la *Postilla in Ioannem* et de l'*Expositio Regulae*, éditée dans le *Firmamentum trium ordinum* (Venise 1513), f. 106-124v; V. Doucet, "De operibus mss. Fr. Petri Ioannis Olivi in bibliotheca Universitatis Patavinae asservatis," *Arch. fr. hist.* 28 (1935), 162-168, pour les Postilles "super Actus, super Isaiam, super Lib. Regum," trouvées par lui dans les mss. 1510 et 1540 de Padoue.

Le premier passage incriminé se rencontre dans la *Somme théologique* I-II, q. 108, a. 2, réponse à la troisième objection. Saint Thomas, ayant successivement étudié la loi naturelle, puis la Loi de l'ancien Testament, en vient à la Loi nouvelle, qui est celle de l'Evangile, dans les questions 106 et suivantes. Il envisage quatre points au sujet de la Loi nouvelle dans la question 108; les deux premiers concernant les œuvres ou actes extérieurs: La Loi nouvelle doit-elle prescrire ou interdire des actes extérieurs? A-t-elle suffisamment ordonné les actes extérieurs? Sur le premier point, saint Thomas établit que les œuvres extérieures doivent être rapportées à la grâce, soit qu'elles puissent la conférer, comme les sacrements, soit qu'elles puissent être inspirées par la grâce. Parmi les actes humains, certains peuvent être conformes ou contraires à la grâce; il faut alors qu'ils soient l'objet de préceptes ou d'interdictions. Pour les actes qui ne sont pas nécessairement conformes ou contraires à la grâce, les fidèles sont libres d'agir au mieux. Les mêmes principes sont invoqués dans la discussion de l'article 2; la Loi nouvelle ne considère les œuvres extérieures que par rapport à la grâce; elle n'a ordonné ou prescrit aucun acte extérieur, sinon les sacrements et les préceptes de morale qui appartiennent en soi au fondement de la vertu. Il répond à la troisième objection, dans laquelle était allégué le verset: *Nolite possidere*, en expliquant que les préceptes donnés par le Seigneur aux Apôtres ne sont pas des observances rituelles, mais des recommandations morales. On peut considérer, avec saint Augustin (*De consensu evangelistarum*, II, 30) que ce sont, non des préceptes, mais des concessions accordées aux prédicateurs, ceux-ci devant attendre de recevoir ce qui leur est nécessaire de ceux auxquels ils prêchent l'Evangile, ou considérer que ce sont des statuts temporaires qui ont été abolis au temps de la Passion, temps de la liberté parfaite où désormais les Apôtres devraient user de leur libre arbitre pour agir dans les actes qui n'appartiennent pas en soi et nécessairement à la vertu.[31]

Cette opinion mesurée est en opposition complète avec l'exégèse stricte que Pierre Jean Olieu donne du verset de saint Matthieu, indiquant en outre une interdiction qui lui paraît s'imposer. Selon la lettre, le Christ interdit aux Apôtres la possession de trésors, c'est à dire d'or et d'argent, le port de monnaie, de victuailles ou de nourriture, de chaussures, de plusieurs vêtements et de bâtons, en ajoutant que les ouvriers du Seigneur méritent de recevoir le nécessaire, tant de la part

---

31 Il convient de signaler que l'attaque d'Olieu contre ce passage de la *Somme* correspond à un article du *Correctoire* de Guillaume de la Mare: "Quod ista verba: Nihil tuleritis in via, etc. non pertinent ad perfectionem"; cf. P. Glorieux, *Le Correctorium corruptorii Quare*, pp. 383 sqq. Mais alors que le *Correctoire* ne donne qu'un résumé, Olieu cite intégralement le texte de saint Thomas.

des hommes que de la part de Dieu. De plus, enlevant aux Apôtres la possession des biens meubles, il sous-entend que la possession des immeubles est interdite; s'il n'en fait pas mention expresse, c'est parce que déjà, de fait, et selon la vie à laquelle ils s'étaient voués, les Apôtres avaient tout abandonné. Il n'est pas question de transformer les préceptes en concessions ou en recommandations provisoires. Olieu récuse l'interprétation d'Augustin telle que l'entend Thomas, en déclarant que quelques paroles d'un saint isolé n'ont pas de valeur en regard des autorités convergentes de tous les autres saints, des souverains pontifes, et surtout de saint François, le parfait imitateur du Christ. Du reste, d'après saint Augustin lui-même, il semble que ce soient les instructions de recevoir le nécessaire des fidèles auxquels les Apôtres prêchent qui soient une simple concession.

C'est à propos de ce passage de la *Postilla in Matthaeum* que l'évêque carme Gui Terré, dans sa *Concordia evangelistarum*, écrite probablement entre 1328 et 1334, prend la défense de saint Thomas contre les sectateurs de la doctrine erronée de Pierre Jean, qui, au chapitre X de sa *Postilla in Matthaeum* prétend que saint Thomas a erré et écrit une erreur au sujet du précepte du Christ de ne pas porter de monnaie. Comment peut-on oser dire que saint Thomas, qui a exposé les paroles évangéliques de si belle et si catholique manière, conformément à la doctrine des saints docteurs catholiques, ait pu écrire de façon erronée, contrairement à l'évangile? Gui Terré réfute point par point l'argumentation d'Olieu; il paraît certain qu'il avait sous les yeux un exemplaire de la *Postilla*. L'ouvrage était donc bien connu des adversaires des Spirituels. [32]

Olieu reproche en second lieu à saint Thomas la position que celui-ci prend au sujet de l'abdication de la propriété, en traitant des états de vie et particulièrement de l'état des religieux dans la *Secunda Secundae*. [33] Saint Thomas déclare en effet que la pauvreté n'étant qu'un moyen de tendre à la perfection (*instrumentum perfectionis*), doit être considérée quant à la fin d'un ordre religieux; par conséquent, pour apprécier les degrés de renoncement souhaitables, il convient d'examiner de quelle manière ils concourent à réaliser l'idéal de l'ordre qui les pratique. Les ordres hospitaliers et militaires ont besoin de posséder quelques biens. Les religieux contemplatifs ne doivent pas être

---

32 Ed. Cologne 1650, p. 275. Cf. sur cet ouvrage B. M. Xiberta, *De magistro Guidone Terreni* (Rome 1925), p. 174. Gui Terré a fait partie de la commission des huit maîtres désignés par Jean XXII en 1318 pour censurer la *Postilla in Apocalypsim*; cf. Ehrle, op. cit. pp. 451-452; texte édité dans Baluze-Mansi, *Miscellanea* II, pp. 258-270, d'après le ms. Paris Nat. lat. 4190.

33 *Secunda Secundae*, q. 188, a. 7. Les citations d'Olieu ne sont qu'en partie littérales. Il a abrégé, omis, et transposé quelques passages.

gênés dans leurs prières par le souci continuel de se procurer le nécessaire. La mendicité est justifiable pour les religieux voués à la prédication et à l'enseignement, mais, pour ceux-ci, conserver en commun les aumônes reçues et les distribuer à chacun selon ses besoins ne diminue pas la perfection de l'Ordre, à la condition de garder une juste modération. Il ajoute que l'abdication totale de la propriété présente de graves inconvénients; posséder en commun les choses nécessaires à la vie n'est pas un obstacle à la perfection; c'est au contraire le meilleur moyen d'éviter une sollicitude exagérée des choses terrestres; il s'appuie en cela sur l'exemple du Christ et des Apôtres.

Olieu avait déjà répondu à une série d'arguments analogues dans sa première question sur la pauvreté. Dans le commentaire de saint Matthieu il réfute point par point les raisons exposées par Thomas d'Aquin. La fin principale d'un ordre religieux, dit-il, doit être dans le domaine des choses spirituelles, même s'il a une fin secondaire temporelle, comme l'assistance des pauvres ou la lutte contre les infidèles; par conséquent, même si ce motif secondaire semble exiger des possessions, celles-ci demeurent toujours un empêchement pour le but supérieur. Les ordres hospitaliers et militaires seraient plus parfaits s'ils se bornaient à vivre d'aumônes et de leur travail. Quant aux provisions, sauf en cas de nécessité évidente — et encore n'est-il pas souhaitable de les posséder comme biens propres ou communs — il est complètement faux de dire qu'elles évitent un souci exagéré de se procurer des choses matérielles. Olieu en donne cinq motifs, énumérés avec grande verve dans une gradation progressive, le dernier inconvénient encouru par les possesseurs étant le risque de s'engager dans des procès. De plus, conserver habituellement des provisions en commun est directement opposé aux préceptes du Christ, qui a dit de ne pas s'inquiéter du lendemain, et qui, permettant l'usage indispensable des biens terrestres, a interdit aux Apôtres le droit de les posséder; ni l'adversaire ni ses sectateurs ne peuvent donner un seul exemple démontrant qu'il s'est servi d'argent, sauf en cas de nécessité extrême.

Ramener l'*altissima paupertas* au rang d'instrument de perfection est le reproche le plus grave que le Spirituel formule à l'égard d'un dominicain infidèle, selon lui, à l'esprit de saint Dominique, et qui prétend que la pauvreté est le moins élevé des trois vœux de religion. Si la pauvreté n'est pas la perfection ultime, titre qui convient à la charité, elle est la première des vertus recommandées par le Christ, car elle est la première des béatitudes. O merveille, s'exclame notre Provençal, le Christ, en paroles et en actes, exalte la pauvreté sur toutes les vertus, et celui-là la rejette presque au dernier rang! Je sais que ce n'est pas ainsi que se serait comporté saint Dominique, qui a maudit ceux des siens qui accepteraient des possessions![34]

Traiter aussi cavalièrement un grand maître en théologie était impertinent à la fin du XIIIe siècle, mais sans conséquences. Par contre, sous le règne de Jean XXII, et surtout au moment de la canonisation de Thomas d'Aquin, l'existence de ce texte polémique dans lequel étaient énumérées les "erreurs" du pieux et docte Frère Prêcheur pouvait constituer un grief supplémentaire contre Olieu. L'inquisiteur Nicolas Eymerich, écrivant, il est vrai, plus d'un demi-siècle après les évènements, dit que la *Postilla in Matthaeum* a été condamnée par Jean XXII en même temps que la *Postilla in Apocalypsim*.[35] Cette dernière a été examinée par une commission de censeurs désignés par le pape, qui paraît s'être occupé lui-même de près de l'affaire.[36] La condamnation de la Postille en février 1326 est rapportée par Bernard Gui, qui est un témoin contemporain.[37] Mais aucun document ne confirme l'assertion de Nicolas Eymerich, à notre connaissance.

Les dires de Dame Prous Boneta semblent néanmoins indiquer que l'opposition d'Olieu aux doctrines de saint Thomas était notoire dans le milieu des Spirituels, et le fait que la béguine rend ce dernier responsable de la "destruction de l'écriture de frère Pierre Jean" donne à penser que la note d'Eymerich n'est pas dépourvue de tout fondement. Il paraît assez probable qu'il a été question de la *Lectura in Matthaeum* dans les discussions relatives à la *Postilla in Apocalypsim*, sans qu'elle ait été pour autant condamnée de manière expresse.[38] L'auteur anonyme du factum contenu dans le manuscrit lat. 4190 de la Bibliothèque nationale, rédigé probablement en 1325: "Allegationes super articulis tractis per dominum papam de Postilla quam composuit Fr. Petrus Iohannis super Apocalypsim..." cite des passages de la Postille sur s. Matthieu ainsi que des questions sur la pauvreté et du traité *De usu paupere* d'Olieu.[39]

---

34 "Mira res! Christus verbo et facto paupertatem quasi super omnia extollit; iste vero quasi sub omnibus eam deiecit. Scio quod hoc non fecisset beatus Dominicus, qui maledixit omnibus suis quandocumque possessiones reciperent!" Extrait ed. par Ehrle, op. cit., p. 522.

35 *Directorium inquisitionis*, ed. Pena (Venise 1607), p. 328.

36 Cf. E. Pasztor, "Le polemiche sulla 'Lectura super Apocalypsim' di Pietro di Giovanni Olivi fino alla sua condanna," *Bulletino dell'Istituto storico italiano per il Medio Evo*, 70 (1958), 365-424.

37 *Flores chronicarum*, cit. par Ehrle, op. cit., p. 456.

38 Cf. au sujet des passages de la *Lectura in Matthaeum* contenant des considérations eschatologiques qui se rapprochent de celles qui sont développées dans la *Lectura in Apocalypsim*, R. Manselli, *La 'Lectura super Apocalypsim' di Pietro di Giovanni Olivi* (Rome 1955), pp. 155-159.

39 Cf. sur ce texte et sur le procès de la *Postilla in Apocalypsim*, J. Koch, "Der Prozess gegen die Postille Olivis zur Apokalypse," *Recherches de théologie anc. et méd.* 5 (1933), 302-315; E. Pasztor, art. cit., p. 387. Cette dernière analyse le texte de plus près.

L'un des manuscrits subsistants de la *Postilla*, le Vat. lat. 1001, témoigne de la double réprobation suscitée par les écrits du Spirituel, car le texte a été expurgé du passage litigieux du chapitre X, et des chapitres eschatologiques dans lesquels l'auteur développait des théories joachimites.[40]

Il est probable que la diatribe de Pierre Jean ne devait pas déplaire à la plupart des Franciscains, car la *Lectura* a été le plus souvent recopiée intégralement, en omettant ou supprimant le nom de l'auteur.[41] Les théologiens étrangers à l'Ordre qui se sont intéressés à l'ouvrage ont encore eu moins de scrupules. Nous allons voir que l'Université de Paris, grâce à la générosité de l'un des maîtres de la Sorbonne, conservait soigneusement un bel exemplaire, orné, par surcroît, d'une caricature de saint Thomas.

2. La Tradition Manuscrite de la Postilla in Matthaeum

Nous avons examiné nous-même une partie des manuscrits contenant la *Postilla in Matthaeum*; d'autres nous sont connus seulement par des catalogues. Nous croyons utile de donner un aperçu de la tradition du texte en indiquant les témoins assez nombreux qui subsistent encore, et en décrivant en détail celui qui nous paraît le plus intéressant, en raison de sa date et de son premier possesseur.

Paris, Bibl. nat. lat. 15588

Il s'agit du manuscrit latin 15588 de la Bibliothèque nationale, légué à la Sorbonne par maître Pierre de Limoges, mort en 1306. Ce remarquable personnage, qui joignait à un intérêt fondamental pour la

---

40   Cette dernière lacune a été notée par R. Manselli, op. cit., p. 149. Quant à la première, qui était la suppression de l'attaque contre saint Thomas au c. X, elle a empêché Ehrle d'identifier le texte qu'il avait trouvé dans le ms. Vat. lat. 4986, car il s'était servi du Vat. lat. 1001 pour décrire la *Postilla in Matthaeum*. Nous avons jadis identifié l'extrait et constaté la lacune; cf. *Positions de thèses des élèves de l'Ecole des Chartes*, 1928.

41   L'anonymat de la plupart des manuscrits des œuvres de Pierre Jean Olieu a provoqué quelques confusions et attributions inexactes. Certaines ont été publiés sous le nom de saint Bonaventure, comme la *Postilla in Cantica Canticorum* et les *Principia* dans le *Supplementum* de Bonelli. Un destin plus étrange est celui de l'un des commentaires bibliques le plus fortement imprégné de joachimisme, la *Postilla in Genesim*. Elle a été en partie reproduite dans un commentaire de la Genèse imprimé parmi les œuvres de saint Thomas dans les éditions de Rome, 1570, de Parme, et de Paris (Frette-Vives), ainsi que l'a signalé A. Borst, *Der Turmbau von Babel*, II, 2, pp. 819-822. A. Borst remarque que le contraste entre le symbolisme joachimite d'Olivi et le "rationalisme humaniste" de saint Thomas est assez prononcé pour que la confusion paraisse surprenante. Cf. Stegmuller, *Repertorium biblicum*, n. 6684, pour la *Postilla in Genesim* de Pierre Jean Olivi, et n. 8025 pour le pseudo-Thomas d'Aquin; à partir du commentaire de *Gen*. VIII, 1 jusqu'à l'explicit, les deux textes semblent concorder. A. Borst a collationné en partie le ms. Vat. Ottob. lat. 694 avec l'édition. Néanmoins, celle-ci est partiellement expurgée.

théologie théorique et surtout pratique un goût non moins vif pour les sciences, et notamment l'astronomie, a laissé à ses confrères une belle collection de livres. Pierre a annoté de sa main une partie des volumes; certains recueils ont même été transcrits par lui. Soixante-sept manuscrits subsistants du fonds de la Sorbonne ont été recensés par L. Delisle[1]; A. Birkenmajer en a identifié deux autres à la Bibliothèque nationale, d'après les annotations autographes.[2]

Ce pieux savant ne redoutait pas les esprits aventureux, ni les fortes personnalités. Il fut l'un des premiers admirateurs de Raymond Lulle, qu'il dut connaître pendant le séjour que celui-ci fit à Paris à la fin du XIIIᵉ siècle. Il possédait plusieurs de ses œuvres. Il est possible qu'il ait connu Pierre Jean Olieu, puisque celui-ci a fait des études à Paris et y a peut-être enseigné, mais la curiosité d'esprit et les tendances éclectiques de Pierre de Limoges suffisent à justifier l'acquisition d'un bel exemplaire de la *Postilla in Matthaeum* et d'autres commentaires bibliques du Frère Mineur. Peut-être même le manuscrit a-t-il été exécuté pour lui; l'écriture est méridionale, mais la décoration, d'une richesse exceptionnelle pour ce type de texte, nous paraît plutôt parisienne. Pierre de Limoges a lu avec soin l'ouvrage; la foliotation en chiffres arabes semble de sa main. Il a inscrit en marge du texte des lettres de repère, et il a rédigé un bref index alphabétique des matières transcrit au f. 179. On trouve de plus quelques annotations et corrections de sa main, notamment, au f. 38, la restitution d'un passage omis par le scribe.

Il faut admettre ou que Pierre de Limoges a fait copier le texte, par un scribe originaire d'Italie ou du midi de la France, et a revu l'ouvrage sur l'*exemplar*, ou qu'il s'est procuré un autre manuscrit pour le collationner. Ajoutons que la mention: "Cor." se trouve encore à la fin de plusieurs cahiers; le manuscrit a donc été soigneusement revu et corrigé après son exécution. Ceci, ajouté au fait que le volume a été transcrit peu d'années après la rédaction des commentaires bibliques qui le constituent, et probablement encore du vivant de l'auteur, donne une valeur particulière à cet exemplaire.

Nous ne pensons pas que Pierre de Limoges soit responsable du petit dessin marginal que l'on remarque au f. 68v, en regard des mots:

---

1 Cf. L. Delisle, *Le Cabinet des manuscrits de la Bibliothèque Nationale*, II, pp. 167-169, sur Pierre de Limoges et son legs de manuscrits. Il reproduit la notice de l'obituaire de la Sorbonne, à la date du 3 novembre: "Obiit magister Petrus de Lemovicis quondam socius huius domus, canonicus Ebroicensis qui refutavit duos episcopatus et bis prebendam parisiensem, bacalarius in theologia, magnus astronomus, qui legavit domui plus quam VIˣˣ volumina."

2 A. Birkenmajer, "Pierre de Limoges, commentateur de Richard de Fournival," *Isis* 40 (1949), 18-31. Il signale également le ms Vat. Regin. lat. 1261 qui contient des gloses de la main de Pierre de Limoges.

"Diligenter adverte. Advertendum autem diligenter quod Thomas in Summa sua..." Ce dessin représente un religieux, la tête couverte d'une capuche, dans une chaire. Il est auréolé, aussi est-il probable que cette esquisse est l'œuvre d'un lecteur facétieux après la canonisation de Thomas d'Aquin en 1323.

Après ces remarques préliminaires, voici comment se présente le recueil. Il est écrit sur parchemin, mesure 350 x 230 mm. et comprend 181 ff. à 2 col. Petites initiales et signes de paragraphes bl. ou rouges; grandes initiales ornées peintes bl. et r. à filigranes et à antennes; f. 15, 135, 163, au début des commentaires, grande lettre peinte sur fonds d'or avec encadrement peint et orné. Il y a quelques dessins marginaux à la plume, sans doute un peu postérieurs. Le début du manuscrit, contenant les cinq "Principia in sacram scripturam" a une apparence plus simple que le corps du manuscrit, et l'écriture est de plus petit module; cette section comprend un cahier de 10 ff. et un cahier de 4 ff. On n'y trouve pas de rubriques ni de titres courants. Le corps du manuscrit est constitué de cahiers de 12 ff. avec réclames et mention contemp.: "Cor." Il n'y a pas de rubriques, mais des titres courants peints en lettres alternativement bl. et r.

F. 1, dans la marge supérieure, inscription à l'encre très pâle, qui paraît du début du XIVᵉ s.: "Pos. fratris Io. Petri (sic) Et huius pos. ponitur tabula questionum...de Lemouicis bancha ad volumen q."

I. Les cinq "principia" transcrits au début du lat. 15588 ont été imprimés dans le *Supplementum ad Opera s. Bonaventurae* de B. Bonelli, t. II et I, d'après un manuscrit conservé au couvent des Frères Mineurs réformés de Venise; l'ensemble était ainsi désigné "S. Bonaventura de intelligentia sacrae scripturae."[3] Ces textes sont très rares. En dehors de notre ms. de Paris, l'on ne connaît plus que le ms. Vat. lat. 918, du XIVᵉ siècle, provenant de la Chartreuse de Saycz en Styrie.[4] F. Ehrle reproduit la notice du catalogue de 1369 de la bibliothèque d'Avignon, n. 381: "Item, principia generalia super sacra scriptura...per fratrem P. Iohannis"; mais cet exemplaire semble perdu.[5]

1. "Vidi in dextera sedentis super thronum...(Apoc. V, 1). Consideranti michi scripturarum sanctarum pelagus infinitum... — ...ad hanc igitur visionem nos introducat ipse Dei Filius Ihesus Christus...", f. 1-4.
2. "Quatuor animalia singula eorum habebant alas senas...qui est et qui erat et qui venturus est (Apoc. V, 8). Superineffabilis altitudo doctrine euangelice in iiii. euangeliis apprehense a secretario Christi Iohanne... — ...de resurrectionis et ascensionis tropheis et preconiis," f. 4-5.

---

3 Cf. F. Ehrle, op. cit., p. 495; F. Stegmuller, *Repertorium biblicum*, nn. 6679-6683.
4 Cf. A. Pelzer, *Codices vaticani latini*, II, 1, pp. 319-322.
5 Cf. F. Ehrle, op. cit., p. 460.

3. "Cum essem in medio captiuorum...vidi visionem Dei (Ez. I, 1). Conscendere cum Paulo volentibus in tercium celum ad videndas visiones...
    — ...clauis etiam earum est iubilus caritatis; de istis tamen clauibus et de modo ducendi eas amplior exigeretur tractatus. Explicit tractatus Deo gratias," f. 5-9v.
4. "Ingredere in medio rotarum que sunt subtus cherubin...(Ez. X, 2). Scripturarum sanctarum pelagus et abyssus triformiter se ingerit inuestigatoribus suis... — ...diuinum amorem et dulcorem quem nobis administret Christus Ihesus fons veritatis, equitatis et caritatis in s. s. Amen," f. 9v-12.
5. "Vacate et videte quoniam ego sum Deus (Ps. 45, 10). Sicut inter omnia nichil Deo altius et melius... — ...et videbimus gloriam eius gloriam quasi Unigeniti a Patre, plenum gratie et veritatis in s. s.," f. 12-14v.

II. "Postilla super Matheum." Il n'y a pas de rubrique, mais le titre est peint dans les marges supérieures.

Prol. général à l'exposition des évangiles: "Quatuor facies uni et quatuor penne uni...Ezechiel primo (I, 6). Quemadmodum admirabilis est clausura... — ...qui est fons omnis veri luminis et qui cum Patre et Spiritu sancto perhenniter regnat in s.s.," f. 15-16. — Préambule: "Ad maiorem euidentiam dictorum et dicendorum septem sunt querenda et prenotanda... — ...qui est materia totius libri, scilicet Christum," f. 16-18. — Hiis igitur prelibatis accedendum est ad Matheum qui est in ordine primus... — ...ipse est leo resurgens qui solus meruit et potuit soluere VII signacula libri Dei, cui est honor et gloria in s. s. Amen. Finito libro sit laus et gloria Christo. Amen." f. 18-134v.

III. "Epistola ad Romanos," titre peint dans les marges supérieures.

"Ad contemplandam et prelibandam in summa doctrinam epistolarem diuinissimi Pauli menti mee nichil occurere potuit breuius et clarius quam verbum eiusdem II. Cor. iii dicentis: Ubi spiritus Domini, ibi libertas... — ...quidam dicunt quod *le cui* est positum hic superflue more scripture, sicut ibi: cuius participatio eius in idipsum. Et secundum glossam quidam legunt hoc sine *cui*: ei, qui sic potens est, et qui tanta nobis reuelauit sit per Ihesum Christum gloria in s. s. Amen. Explicit tractatus. Deo gratias." f. 135-163.

Ce commentaire de l'épître aux Romains ne se trouve que dans un autre manuscrit, précieux recueil d'œuvres scripturaires d'Olivi, conservé à la Laurentienne de Florence, Conventi soppressi 240. Il se trouvait dans la bibliothèque d'Urbain V en 1369 (n. 656), puis dans celle de Benoît XIII à Peniscola (n. 153).[6]

---

6 Cf. F. Ehrle, op. cit., p. 462; F. Stegmuller, *Rep. bibl.* n. 6716.

IV. "Postilla in Cantica Canticorum."

"In speculo breui et aperto contueri volentibus continenciam Cantici Canticorum... — ...sponsi pietas sic ad plenum abstergat ut cum electis ceteris ducat eum ad vite fontes aquarum, quas qui bibet non sitiet in eternum. Amen. Explicit liber iste Deo gratias. Amen." f. 153-179.[7]

F. 179v suit une table alphabétique dressée sur 4 colonnes: "Abraham... Ypocrisis." A la suite, une note au premier abord mystérieuse: "Questiones huius libri scilicet super Mat. R < equire > post quodlibet Henr < ici? > ." Les ff. 180-181 sont blancs.

F. 181v. "Iste liber est pauperum magistrorum de Sorbona ex legato magistri Petri de Limouicis quondam socii domus huius in quo continentur postille super Matheum et super epistolam ad Romanos et super Cantica." Au dessous: "Precii X librarum. Cathenabitur. 25us inter postillas mixtas." Il nous paraît que la "tabula questionum" mentionnée dans la note que nous avons relevée ci-dessus est sans doute une liste des questions traitées par Olivi dans son commentaire, à partir du prologue général sur les évangiles jusqu'à la fin du texte sacré. La première est: "primo queritur quare Christus per seipsum non scripsit doctrinam euangelicam"; la dernière: "Queritur etiam an Christus apparuerit matri sue." Ces questions se rencontrent dans un certain nombre de manuscrits de la *Postilla*, et justement avec le titre: "Tabula questionum." Or, parmi les livres légués par Pierre de Limoges figurait un recueil contenant les quodlibets d'Henri de Gand, d'après le catalogue de la librairie de Sorbonne au XIVᵉ s., n. 74. "Item, in uno volumine liber in opere spere volubilis...et scripta de quolibet magistri Henrici de Gandauo; item scripta de quolibet magistri G. de Fontibus...Item questiones de quolibet aliorum, de legato magistri Petri de Lemouicis."[8] Malheureusement ce n. 74 de la section: "Summe questionum" semble perdu, ce qui nous empêche de vérifier notre hypothèse.

Florence, Bibl. Laur. Santa Croce Plut. X dextr. 4

Le manuscrit de la Bibliothèque Laurentienne de Florence, provenant du couvent franciscain de Santa Croce: S. Croce Plut. X dextr. 4, paraît aussi dater de la fin du XIIIᵉ siècle.

Parch. 168 ff. à 2 col. Initiales peintes. Le texte est transcrit avec soin.

F. 1-107. "Postilla in Matthaeum," anonyme, A la fin: "Explicit Lec-

---

7 La *Postilla in Cantica* est imprimée dans le *Supplementum Operum s. Bonaventurae*, par B. Bonelli, I, pp. 50-182. Cf. F. Ehrle, pp. 484-486, et pp. 461, 462 pour les notices des catalogues des papes d'Avignon; Stegmüller, *Rep. bibl.*, n. 6693.

8 Cf. L. Delisle, *Cabinet des manuscrits*, III, p. 31.

tura super euangelium beati Matthaei. Amen." F. 107-108: "Tabula euangeliorum beati Matthei per totum annum." F. 108-109: "Tabula euangeliorum Luce." F. 110-167: "< P. I. Olivi > Lectura super Lucam (et Marcum)." Prol. "Quoniam ex dictis super Matthaei euangelium et Ioannis fere maior pars euangelii Marci et Luce est tacta...—...prout Gregorius in homelia festi Ascensionis exponit."— "Lucas autem primo premittit prologum... — ...Dei unius et trini benedicti et benedicendi in s. s. Amen. Explicit Lectura super Luce euangelium. Deo gratias. Amen." — F. 167-168, table des questions. — F. 168v, notes de la main du frère Thedaldus de Casa, bibliothécaire de Santa Croce vers 1380-1410. Elles ont été reproduites par V. Doucet, "De operibus mss. Petri Iohannis Olivi," *Arch. fr. Hist.* 28 (1935), 164. Thedaldus donne la référence de plusieurs ouvrages de "Petri Ioannis" avec leur incipit. Il savait donc que les deux *Lecturae* contenues dans le manuscrit étaient d'Olivi.— F. 1: "Iste liber fuit ad usum fratris Thedaldi de Casa quem viuens assignauit armario Fratrum Minorum de Florentia anno D. 1406." Sur la reliure, inscription fin XIVᵉ ou XVᵉ s.: "Ista Postilla est ad usum fratris Mathei Guidonis." Sur le f. liminaire qui forme couverture est transcrit le début de la *tabula quaestionum* de la *Lectura in Matthaeum*. Ce volume est-il l'exemplaire de la *Postilla* du couvent de Santa Croce prêté sur sa demande expresse à saint Bernardin de Sienne en 1440? Le P. Doucet ne le pense pas, car saint Bernardin spécifie que le manuscrit de la *Postilla* de Pierre Jean dont il connaît l'existence est mis à tort sous le nom de Nicolas de Lyre. Les deux commentaires, ayant le même incipit scripturaire, une confusion s'explique aisément. La lettre de s. Bernardin est publiée par V. Doucet, art. cit., p. 160. Le point important est l'insistance de s. Bernardin, preuve de la haute estime en laquelle il tenait les écrits du frère Pierre Jean.

Cf. A. M. Bandini, *Catalogus cod. latinorum Bibl. Mediceae Laurentianae, t. IV, continens...recensionem mss. cod...qui olim in Florentino S. Crucis coenobio adseruabantur,* col. 406-407. Nous avons étudié ce manuscrit.

Padoue, Antoniana Scaff. XV. N. 336

Le manuscrit conservé à la Bibliothèque Antoniana de Padoue a, lui aussi, un intérêt historique. Il semble avoir été exécuté, avec un certain luxe, pour l'évêque de Padoue, qui l'a donné au couvent des Frères Mineurs avec des réserves qui montrent la valeur qu'il attachait au texte. En connaissait-t-il l'auteur? Le manuscrit est anonyme. Il contient, après la *Postilla*, le commentaire du *Pater*.

Parch. CCXXII ff. à 2 col. Initiales bl. et r. à filigranes et à antennes; F. 1, encadrement peint; titres courants peints bl. et r. Rubriques.

F. 1-212. < Petrus Ioannis Olivi > "Postilla super Matthaeum." Le passage concernant s. Thomas commence au f. 96.

F. 212v-215v: "Expositio super orationem dominicam ab eodem expositore quam supra edita." "Ad intuendum altitudinem orationis dominice que ponitur Mat. VI... — ...et maxime in mysteriis scripturarum sanctarum."

F. 215: "Iste liber fuit scriptus et completus anno D. I. M°-CCC°XLIIII° de mense Nouembris xiii° indictionis."— F. 216-221v. Table de la *Postilla*, — F. 221v-222v. Canons des évangiles tirés de s. Mathieu avec référence à la *Postilla*, — F. 223v: "Anno D. M°CCC°LII° die xxvi° Septembris venerabilis Pater et Dominus Ildebrandinus D. gr. episcopus Paduanus nomine donationis inter nos dedit et donauit hunc librum fratri Iohanni de Mont. ss. tunc sacri conuentus beati Antonii guardiano recipienti, nomine et vice dicti conuentus, hiis conditionibus appositis, videlicet quod usum dicti libri sibi retinuit in vita sua tantum, ita quod quandocumque predictus dominus vellet dictum librum, guardianus et fratres dicti conuentus ipsum concedere teneantur, et quod predictum librum non possunt ipsi fratres vendere, impignorare, alicui obligare vel appropriare, sed semper remaneat in supradicto sacro loco ad comodum et utilitatem fratrum in hibi (sic) comorantium et quod secus factum fuerit ex nunc prout ex tunc ipsos fratres priuat et priuatos esse vult, et mandat, ac ipsum donat et dat capitulo canonicorum Ecclesie Maioris de Padua. Actum in Palatio sepedicti domini in camera sua, presentibus domino Nicolao abbate Sancte Iustine de Padua, (...) priore Cruciferorum et fratre Antonio de Cortarodulo et al. etc."

Le manuscrit est soigneusement corrigé. On y trouve des notes marginales en cursive du xiv° s.

Cf. *I codici manoscritti della Biblioteca Antoniana di Padova descritti...dal P. M. Antonio Maria Iosa* (Padova 1886). Nous l'avons étudié sur place.

Trois manuscrits de la *Postilla in Matthaeum* sont conservés à la Bibliothèque Vaticane:

Vatican. lat. 10900.

Parch. 207 ff. à 2 col. Ecriture méridionale qui nous paraît du début du xiv° siècle; le manuscrit est probablement d'origine italienne. Initiales peintes en bleu-violet et rouge. La première initiale, historiée, représente un franciscain; petites initiales rehaussées de jaune. Le manuscrit est constitué de quinternions; un cahier arraché après le f. 40; il manque la fin du c. 4 et le début du c. 5. — Titre, en partie gratté, capitula et titres courants rubriqués; notes marginales du xv° et du xvi°-xvii° s.

F. 1-210. "Postilla in Matthaeum," précédée d'une rubrique presque entièrement cancellée: "Postilla fratris P < etri Ioannis Ord. Minor. > super Mattheum." — A la fin, "Explicit Postilla optima *super euangelium Matthei* edita ab egregio sacre theologie professore fratre *Petro Ioannis de Biteris* de custodia Narbone et de provincia Prouincie sacri ordinis fratrum Minorum" (les mots soulignés ont été grattés). — F. 201v-207. Table des questions de la *Postilla*: "Et primo queritur quare Christus per seipsum non scripsit doctrinam euangelicam... — ...Queritur etiam an primo apparuerit matri sue." Inscription du XVIIe s.: "Petrus Ioannis in Mattheum manuscript. 1652." Sur la reliure, nom d'un possesseur: "card. Segna."

Cf. *Codices vaticani latini. Codices 10876-11000*, recensuit J. B. Borino (Roma-Vaticano 1955), p. 117. Nous avons étudié le ms.

Vatican. lat. 1001.

Parch. 165 ff. à 2 col. Ecriture méridionale, première moitié du XIVe s. Initiales peintes en rouge et bleu, ou violet. Notes marginales. Cahiers de 12 ff. sauf un quinion ff. 133-142.

F. 1-162v. *Postilla*, avec le prologue habituel.

F. 163-165. Table des questions de la *Postilla*. A la fin: "Explicit tabula questionum que sunt in Postilla super Matheum secundum Petrum Iohannis de ordine Minorum fratrum et est ad ussum (...) eiusdem ordinis. Precii floren..."

F. 165v. "Die XX Decembris MDLXXVII sanctus Dominus noster Gregorius XIII dedit hunc librum Bibliothecae Vaticanae. Ce manuscrit présente des lacunes volontaires et non apparentes, puisque le scribe s'est simplement abstenu de transcrire les passages litigieux: c. X, passage contre s. Thomas, et c. XXIII, XXIV, XXV, eschatologie. Cette dernière lacune est signalée par R. Manselli, *La "Lectura super Apocalipsim" di Pietro di Giovanni Olivi* (Roma 1955), p. 149.

Il nous paraît probable que le manuscrit a été copié vers l'époque du procès contre la *Lectura in Apocalypsim*, et après la canonisation de s. Thomas.

Cf. *Codices vaticani latini, t. II, pars I. Codices 679-1134*, recensuit A. Pelzer (1931), p. 484. Nous avons étudié ce ms.

Vatican. lat. 8670.

Papier; filigranes italiens de la première moitié du XVe s. 204 ff. à 2 col.

F. 1-196v. "Postilla super Matthaeum," sans titre ni nom d'auteur. A la fin: "Benedictus sit dulcissimus Iesus et humilissima mater eius et totus celestis exercitus. Amen."

F. 197-199v. "Expositio super Pater Noster," sans rubrique ni nom d'auteur: "Ad intuendum altitudinem orationis dominice... — ... et maxime in misteriis scripturarum sanctarum."

F. 200-204v. Tabula questionum. "Primo ad euidenciam totius euangelii... — ...V° queritur etiam an primo apparuerit matri sue. Explicit tabula questionum que sunt in postilla super Matheum. Benedictus Deus."

F. 1, inscription d'une main italienne xvie-xviie s. "Postilla Petri Ioannis super Mattheum."

Ce manuscrit, qui ne porte aucune indication de provenance, a très probablement été transcrit dans un couvent franciscain d'Italie au début du xve s. Nous l'avons étudié nous même; M. Duval-Arnould, Scriptor à la Bibliothèque Vaticane et Mlle D. Jacquart ont bien voulu nous donner des indications complémentaires.

Un manuscrit est conservé à Rome dans le collège des Franciscains irlandais:

Rome, Collegio S. Isidoro I/56.

Parch. 160x115 mm., 176 ff. à 2 col. plus deux ff. de garde parch. au début, avec textes en italien, d'une main cursive du xive s.
Grandes initiales bl. et r. avec dessins filigranés; autres initiales bl. à filigranes r. ou rouges à filigr. violets; petites initiales bl. ou r. sans ornements. Cahiers de 10 ff. Réclames encadrées. De petits ff. de parchemin ou languettes ont été insérées, soit pour combler des lacunes, avec renvoi au texte, soit contenant des additions postérieures. Le manuscrit a été écrit par des mains italiennes circa 1300; l'encre est pâle et l'écriture de tout petit module, très soignée.

F. 1-176. "Lectura in Matthaeum." "Incipit expositio evangelii super Math < eum > O. mitairanni (sic?)" (rubr.) Avec le prologue habituel. "Quatuor facies uni... Quemadmodum admirabilis est clausura... Ad maiorem autem evidentiam dictorum et dicendorum septem sunt querenda...Hiis igitur prelibatis, accedendum est ad Matheum... — ...ipse est Leo resurgens qui solus meruit...in secula seculorum. Amen. Amen." — A la suite, f. 176: "Laus, honor, virtus, gloria, divinitas, imperium et benedictio sit crucifixo Domino Ihesu Dei filio qui me suo preciosissimo sanguine dignatus est redimere. Ad cuius laudem honorem et gloriam sint que facta sunt in secula seculorum. Amen."

F. 174-176. Tabula quaestionum, de la même main que ce qui précède: "Iste questiones sunt per ordinem in postilla super Mat. Et primo ad evidenciam tocius evangelii queritur quare Christus per seipsum non scripsit doctrinam evangelicam... — ...Queritur an primo apparuit matri sue. Explicit."

F. 176v. De la même main, début de l'*expositio super Pater Noster*, sans titre; incomplète par lacune matérielle, car le cahier suivant manque.

Le passage concernant s. Thomas au ch. X se trouve f. 72-78; il a été signalé par un lecteur du XIVᵉ-XVᵉ s. avec un index tendu dessiné en marge et des notes; cf. f. 73v "nota 7m errorem contra sanctum Thomam."

Cf. F. M. Delorme, "L'Explication littérale du Pater selon Pierre Jean Olivi," *Arch. ital. per la storia della pietà*, I (1951), p. 181. Nous avons pu nous-même examiner et décrire ce ms., qui paraît l'un des plus anciens.

Trois autres manuscrits, entiers ou fragmentaires, sont conservés dans diverses bibliothèques d'Italie.

Castiglione Fiorentino, Biblioteca del
Collegio Cosimo Serristori ms. 5.

Nous ne connaissons ce manuscrit que d'après la description très sommaire du Catalogue de Mazzatinti, vol. XXVI, p. 221.

Ce manuscrit, papier et parchemin, de petites dimensions: 15 x 22 cm., 271 ff. date probablement du XVᵉ s. Le titre indiqué au début a peut-être été ajouté: "Postilla optima super euangeliis Mathei aedita a fratre Petro Iohanne de Biterris."

Assise, Bibl. Comunale 361.

Papier, 79 ff. à 2 col. Plusieurs mains du XIVᵉ s.

Ce manuscrit ne contient pas le prologue général sur les Evangiles; il est mutilé de la fin et s'arrête au début du c. VII. "In nomine Domini. Amen. Hec est postilla super Matheum edita a venerabile doctore M. Petro Iohannis sacre theologie magistro" (rubr.). "Ad maiorem autem euidentiam dictorum et dicendorum V. sunt querenda et prenotanda... — ...(c. VII). Nolite iudicare...unde et Augustinus in libro de predestinatione sanctorum dicit: cum res vera...dicentibus."

Le manuscrit est décrit très sommairement dans le Catalogue de Mazzatinti, vol IV, p. 8. Nous l'avons examiné nous même.

Florence, Bibl. Naz. Conventi Soppressi
G. I. 671, f. 132-132v.

Ce manuscrit ne contient que le début de la *Postilla in Mattheum* transcrit à la suite de la *Postilla super Genesim* d'Olivi.

Parch. 166 ff. à 2 col.

Ce manuscrit a été étudié et décrit par le P. V. Doucet: "De operibus mss. Fr. Petri Ioannis Olivi..." *Arch. fr. hist.* 28 (1935), 51 et 414.

Les ff. 6-24v contiennent la "Lectura" de Pierre Olivi "super 4um librum Sententiarum"; les ff. 27-132 la "Postilla super Genesim Pe. Io." Titre rubriqué. A la suite, f. 132-132v, sans titre: "Quatuor facies uni. Quemadmodum admirabilis... — ...videlicet pastorum seu prelatorum, martyrum, doctorum." Le reste du texte a disparu de ce ms.

Deux manuscrits proviennent du Midi de la France, et l'un d'entre eux s'y trouve encore.

Toulouse, Bibl. mun. 48.

Parch. 264 ff. à 2 col. (Foliotation médiévale jusqu'au f. 110). Ecriture méridionale du début du XIVe s. Initiales bl. et r.

Le texte est complet. A la fin, f. 264v: "Explicit lectura super euangelium beati Mathei. Amen. Finito libro sit laus et gloria Christo in perpetuum. Amen. Dexteram scribentis benedicat Filius Dei omnipotentis. Amen. Benedictus sit Ihesus dulcissimus et sanctissima Maria mater eius regina celi et terre. Amen." Il y a des notes marginales de plusieurs mains, les unes admiratives, les autres réprobatives. En regard du c. 1: "Nota quod hec est generalis distinctio siue quadriformis diuisio tocius radiosissimi libri huius." En regard du passage contre s. Thomas, au début de l'énumeration des "erreurs," f. 111: "reprobatio positionis et opinionis Thome" d'une main contemporaine. Mais un peu plus loin, en marge du passage: "auctoritates...quarum aliquas supra in sermone Domini demonstraui," on trouve cette remarque, d'une main plus récente: "caue hanc positionem quia condemnata est." Le manuscrit provient des Dominicains de Toulouse; il est probable qu'il a été copié plutôt par des Franciscains.

Cf. *Catalogue général des manuscrits des bibliothèques publiques de France.* Série in-4., VII, p. 23. Nous avons étudié ce manuscrit.

Escorial Q. III. 2.

Parch. 117 ff. à 2 col. Ecriture méridionale du XIVe s. Initiales bl. et r.

Le texte est complet. Le nom de l'auteur a été ajouté d'une autre main dans la marge supérieure du f. 1: "Hec Postilla est super euangelium Mathei euangeliste per venerabilem Petrum Iohannis compilata." — A la fin: "Hic liber est Michaelis Rubei canonici et sacriste Sancte Marie Maioris civitatis Cesarauguste quem emit Tho < lose > pretio quinque francorum anno < M > CCCC octauo."

Cf. G. Antolin, *Catalogo de los codices latinos de la...bibl. del Escorial*, III, pp. 408-409.

Deux manuscrits sont conservés en Angleterre.

Cambridge, Corpus Christi Coll. 321 (K. 13).

Parch. 3+281 ff. à 2 col.

Transcrit vers le milieu du XIVe s. par un scribe probablement anglais. Initiales peintes bl. avec filigr. r.

F. 1-210. "Lectura in Matthaeum." Texte complet avec prol. A la fin: "explicit lectura super evangelium b. Mathei."

F. 210v-214v. Tabula quaestionum.: "Et primo ad evidentiam tocius evangelii queritur quare Christus per seipsum non scripsit doctrinam evangelicam... — ...quinto etiam an primo apparuerit matri sue."

F. 215-218. Expositio super Pater noster, sans titre: "Ad intuendam altitudinem oracionis dominice... — ...in ultima etiam scilicet in *libera nos a malo* omnes sunt, quia nunquam perfecte a malo liberabimur...in re saltem et in fine Et huius Lucas (sic)."

F. Iv, titre inscrit au XVe.: "Postill. super Mt." et mot gratté: "R...ye." Un f. contenant un fragment de texte anglo-saxon a été inséré après le f. 139.

Cf. M. R. James, *A Descriptive Catalogue of the Manuscripts in the Library of Corpus Christi College, Cambridge*, II, pp. 137-138; N. Ker, *Catalogue of Manuscripts containing Anglo-Saxon*, 1957, p. 106; le ms. a été donné au Collège par l'archevêque Parker en 1575.

Oxford, New Coll. 49.

Parch. 158 ff. à 2 col. Ecriture de la seconde moitié du XIVe s.

Ce manuscrit de grandes dimensions, a des initiales peintes en bl. et r. La première page a un encadrement peint et historié avec les symboles des évangélistes.

Il contient le texte complet de la *Postilla in Matthaeum*, avec le nom de l'auteur à la fin: "Explicit opus Petri Iohannis super euangelium Mathei." Une main plus récente a ajouté une mise en garde: "Erat quidam Petrus Ioannis hereticus unus ex complicibus Ioachimi abbatis heresiarche; cum ergo non constat cuius Petri Ioannis hoc opus sit, non alienum putaui ab officio meo imprudentem lectorem admonere."

Cf. H. O. Coxe, *Catalogus codicum manuscriptorum qui in collegiis aulisque Oxoniensibus adseruantur*, I, p. 14.

Trois manuscrits se trouvent actuellement dans des régions plus lointaines.

Klosterneuburg, Bibl. du Monastère 769.

Parch. 120 ff. à 2 col. XIVe s.

F. 1, note d'une main de la fin du XIVe s. "Lectura magistri Alexandri doctoris Parisius de Hallis de ordine fratrum minorum."

F. 1v-120. Texte de la *Postilla in Matthaeum*, qui semble complet. A la suite, table des évangiles selon l'année liturgique; à la fin: "Explicit postilla super euangelia Matthei. Qui scripsit scribat, semper cum Domino viuat."

La description de ce manuscrit est contenue dans les carnets de voyage du P. Fedele da Fanna, volume 5, p. 92. Elle est conservée au Collège Saint-Bonaventure qui vient de se transporter de Quaracchi près Florence à Grotta Ferrata, et nous a été généreusement communiquée par le P. I. Brady. Celui-ci ajoute que cette description a dû être rédigée au printemps 1876, le P. Fedele ayant séjourné à Vienne et visité les bibliothèques d'Autriche à cette époque, avec deux compagnons, Giovanni Maraspini et Hyacinthe Deimel.

Budapest, Bibl. Univ. 49.

Parch. 259 ff. à 2 col. Ecriture de la deuxième moitié du XIV⁰ s., de type parisien, d'après le catalogue. Initiales peintes bl. ou r. Deux grandes initiales peintes et ornées avec encadrement peint au début des deux œuvres contenues dans le ms., f. 1 et 152.

F. 1-15v. "Postilla in Matthaeum," sans titre ni nom d'auteur.

F. 152-259v. (Vitalis de Furno, Commentarium in Apocalipsim).

Cf. *Codices latini Medii Aevi Bibl. Universitatis Budapestinensis quos recensuit Ladislaus Mazey. Accedunt tabulae...quas posteriores collegit et notis auxit Agnes Bolgar* (Budapest 1961), pp. 75-76.

Wroclaw (Breslau), Bibl. de l'Université I F 61m.

Parch. 152 ff. à 2 col. Seconde moitié du XIV⁰ s.

Initiales rubr. Le texte, anonyme, débute avec le prologue, f. 1 et se termine, incomplet, f. 152, avec le commentaire de Mt. xxvii, 55: "erant ibi mulieres." Au dessous, le rubricateur a inscrit: "non est plus in exemplar." La provenance est inconnue, mais il subiste deux cotes anciennes: "B. 22" et au dessous: "85".

Cf. H. A. Krüss, *Die Handschriften der Staats- und Univers. bibl. Breslau* I (Berlin 1938), p. 66. Dr. Sophie Wlodek a bien voulu nous indiquer que le nom de l'auteur ne figurait pas dans le ms.

Deux manuscrits contiennent des extraits du chapitre X de la "Postilla in Matthaeum."

Vat. Lat. 4986.

Le premier, dont nous avons déjà parlé, le manuscrit Vat. lat. 4986, du premier quart du XIV⁰ siècle, est un recueil de questions théologiques et de traités sur la pauvreté évangélique de Pierre Jean Olieu. C'est une compilation assez mal ordonnée, mais précieuse en raison du grand

nombre de textes importants qu'elle renferme. Elle a été décrite par F.
Ehrle, qui l'a utilisée dans son étude sur la vie et les œuvres d'Olivi. Ce
volume a fait partie dès le xive siècle de la bibliothèque des papes
d'Avignon et a été noté dans les inventaires de 1369 et de 1411. L'extrait concernant saint Thomas est transcrit, sans titre, à la suite de la
question 10 des *Quaestiones de perfectione evangelica*, sur la mendicité,
f. 75-78. Le compilateur a copié également les attaques d'Olivi contre
d'autres détracteurs de la pauvreté évangélique, qui suivent la réfutation
de saint Thomas dans la Postille.

Cf. Fr. Ehrle, "Olivis Leben und Schriften," *ALKGM* III (1887), 473,
461 et 463, 497 sqq. pour les passages des écrits d'Olieu décrits d'après
ce manuscrit, et pp. 519-522 pour les extraits de l'attaque contre saint
Thomas. Le P. V. Doucet a complété en partie la description dans son
article, "De operibus mss. fr. Petri Ioannis Olivi in bibliotheca Universitatis Patavinae asservatis," *Arch fr. hist.* 28 (1935), 413-414.

Vat. Ottob. lat. 522.

Un autre extrait du chapitre X, comportant le commentaire du *Nolite
possidere*, est contenu dans le manuscrit Vat. Ottobon. lat. 522, f. 88-
97v. Ce manuscrit, sur parchemin, comprend deux parties distinctes, la
seconde, plus tardive, f. 142-321 étant le *Liber exemplorum fratrum
Minorum*. La première partie, de la première moitié du xive s., présente
des textes divers, dont trois fragments ou extraits relatifs à la règle franciscaine: F. 76-87, une "expositio regulae," anonyme, qui est celle
d'Angelo Clareno, avec de nombreuses lacunes.

F. 87v, extraits de l'exposition de la règle de saint Bonaventure. C'est
à la suite de ce fragment que se trouve l'extrait de la *Postilla*, qui est en
réalité une paraphrase du texte d'Olieu. Les expressions vives et spon-
tanées de notre auteur ont été atténuées, et les allusions à ses autres
ouvrages ont disparu. Le texte est, naturellement, anonyme: "Nolite
possidere aurum neque argentum, Mt. 6 (sic). Postquam informauit
predicatores euangelicos in abdicatione temporalis prosperitatis..." Le
texte suit le commentaire au delà des passages polémiques contre saint
Thomas, puis contre d'autres objections; il continue, après la reprise de
l'explication de la lettre: "Nunc ad litteram redeamus..." f. 97-97v. Il
s'arrête brusquement, au milieu d'une page, sur les mots: "Et ibant
< Apostoli > velut principales magistri omnis perfectionis a Christo
corporaliter separati..."

Cf. sur ce ms. L. Oliger, "Fr. Bonagratia de Bergamo et eius tractatus
de Christi et apostolorum paupertate," *Ach. fr. hist.* 22 (1929), 317-319.

L'on peut tirer avec prudence quelques conclusions de cet examen de
la tradition manuscrite de la *Lectura in Matthaeum* de Pierre Jean
Olieu.

En premier lieu, malgré la suspicion qui s'attachait aux écrits d'un auteur réprouvé et condamné par les autorités de son ordre, il faut constater que les témoins de l'ouvrage sont relativement nombreux, et peut-être quelques uns se cachent-ils encore dans des fonds incomplètement catalogués.

Il est vrai que l'ordre donné par le ministre général Jean de Murrovalle de brûler les livres du Spirituel est surtout adressé aux ministres des provinces de Provence et d'Aragon,[9] et que les couvents d'Italie n'ont sans doute pas tenu compte de ces instructions. Le nom de "Petrus Ioannis" a été gratté ou omis, dans une bonne partie des exemplaires, mais les frères ont continué à recopier l'ouvrage, le trouvant bon et utile. La présence de la table des questions et de la table des péricopes semble en effet indiquer que la *Lectura* a été, au moins quelque temps, utilisée pour l'enseignement et la prédication. C'est en Italie, d'après notre recension, que l'œuvre d'Olieu semble avoir été le plus longtemps appréciée. Elle a même eu des admirateurs vénérables, tels saint Jean de Capistran[10] et saint Bernardin de Sienne.[11]

En second lieu, bien que la majorité des manuscrits paraisse de provenance franciscaine, le texte a intéressé d'autres théologiens, tels Pierre de Limoges, l'évêque de Padoue qui a confié avec méfiance son beau volume au monastère du *Santo*, et le chanoine de Saragosse, qui a acheté le livre à Toulouse en 1408. Enfin, nous constatons que l'aire de diffusion est étendue, puisque l'on retrouve des exemplaires jusqu'en Autriche, en Hongrie et en Pologne. C'est bien peu en comparaison de la masse des manuscrits de saint Thomas, mais notre franciscain occitan a tout de même réussi à survivre.

Addendum. Pierre de Limoges a acquis, et probablement fait exécuter pour lui une copie de la *Lectura in Genesim* de Pierre Jean Olieu; c'est aujourd'hui le manuscrit Lat. 15559 de la Bibliothèque Nationale. Comme dans le manuscrit Lat. 15588, il a mis une foliotation en chiffres arabes, et a rédigé une table des matières après avoir inscrit des lettres de repère dans les marges; il a également indiqué par des traits en marge les passages qui lui paraissaient intéressants, et parmi ceux-ci, des digressions d'inspiration joachimite. — Nous devons, d'autre part, citer une étude récente sur l'écriture de Pierre de Limoges: M. Mabille, "Pierre de Limoges copiste de manuscrits," *Scriptorium* 24 (1970), pp. 45-47 et pl. 10.

9 Cf. F. Ehrle, op. cit., pp. 444-445, et textes publiés dans son article: "Zur Vorgeschichte des Concils von Vienne," *ALKGM* III, pp. 15, 16, 157.

10 Sur les mss. de Pierre Jean conservés au couvent de Capistran, cf. L. Oliger, "Descriptio codicis Capistranensis continens aliqua opuscula Fr. Petri Johannis Olivi" (Capistr, xxvi), *Arch fr. hist.* 1 (1908), 617-622; A. Chiappini, *Reliquie letterarie Capistranesi* (Aquila 1927).

11 Cf. D. Pacetti, *De s. Bernardini Senensis vita et operibus; ratio criticae editionis* (Quaracchi-Florence 1947), pp. 74-80.

TEXT

PETRUS IOHANNIS OLIVI. *LECTURA IN MATTHAEUM*
EXTRAITS DU COMMENTAIRE DE MT. X, 9-10.[1]

Nolite possidere. Hic quatuor inhibet: primo scilicet possessionem thesaurorum; secundo, deportationem nummorum; tertio, deportationem victualium seu ciborum; quarto, deportationem calciamentorum et plurium indumentorum et baculorum. Quinto, quia possent dicere: de quo viuemus? aut: qualiter nobis dabitur victus? subdit quod tanquam operarii agri Dominici digni sunt sustentari tam ab hominibus quam a Deo. Pro primo ergo dicit: *Nolite possidere aurum et argentum.* Et nota quod auferendo possessionem mobilium subponit interdictam esse possessionem immobilium, quia irrationalis esset abdicatio mobilium, retenta possessione immobilium; de hac autem hic expresse mentionem non fecit, quia iam de facto et ex professione votiua omnia reliquerant. Facit autem specialius mentionem de auro et argento, tum quia sunt illecebrosiora et cupiditatem fortius intendentia, tum quia facilius poterant[2] ab eis recipi et occulte conseruari quam alia, tum quia facilius possent credere quod pro suis necessitatibus liceret eis saltem aliquantulum thesaurum congregare...

Neque pecuniam, id est nummos, *in zonis vestris,* id est in bursis ad zonam pendentibus; ex hac autem additione patet quod per primum intellexit et inhibuit[3] congregationem auri domi seruari et pro tempore longiori; hic vero agit de deportatione que fit pro continuis expensis...*Non peram in via* pera est cassidile in quo pastores portant panem suum...Si per peram intelligitur portatio ciborum, ut quid in Marc. (VI, 8) et Luc. (IX, 3) additur: *neque panem?* Dicendum quod pera posset portari a principio vacua sub spe acquirendi cibos qui postmodum per viam portentur.

Neque duas tunicas, id est: nec duo indumenta...*Neque calciamenta...Neque virgam.* Contra,[4] Marc. 6° (8) dicitur: *Nisi virgam tantum.* Dicendum quod portare virgam in auxilium sue defensionis seu defensiue percussionis fuit eis

---

1 Nous avons établi le texte de ces extraits d'après le ms. lat. 15588 de la Bibl. nationale de Paris, probablement contemporain de l'auteur, en le corrigeant, en particulier les fréquentes omissions par homoioteleuton, à l'aide du ms. 48 de la Bibl. mun. de Toulouse. N'ayant l'intention que d'offrir un texte lisible, nous n'avons pas tenu compte des variantes des mss. de Florence, Laurent. Plut. 10 dextr. 4, Vat. lat. 8670 et 10900 de la Bibl. Vaticane, ni du ms. Vat. lat. 4986, contenant le passage utilisé et partiellement édité par Fr. Ehrle, que nous avions collationnés.
    Ms. Paris lat. 15588, f. 68-71v = P.
    Ms. Toulouse 48 = T.
2 poterant/potest aut P.
3 intellexit et inhibuit T/intellexerat P.
4 contra *om.* P.

prohibitum; portare vero eam in sustentaculum proprie inbecillitatis fuit eis concessum. Potest etiam dici quod virgam defensionis prohibuit, sed virgam correctionis concessit, de qua Apostolus I. Cor. 4° (21) dicit: *in virga veniam ad vos, aut in caritate?* etc. Potest etiam dici quod ad litteram extra casum necessitatis interdixit eis virgam seu baculum quo communiter utuntur peregrini et viatores, quia tamen hoc non ita interdixit eis[5] quin aliquo modo liceret; ideo Marc. hoc excepit ut innueret quod, licet de communi forma euangelice regule fuerit eis inhibitum, sicut referunt Matt. et Luc., et ex condescensione tamen[6] fuit eis concessum, quia hoc non tantum continet perfectionem sicut reliqua.

Aduertendum[7] autem hic diligenter quod Thomas, in Summa sua, questione: "An lex noua sufficienter se habeat circa actus exteriores precipiendos vel prohibendos,"[8] dicit "quod licet ista precepta non dederit Dominus Apostolis tanquam cerimoniales obseruantias, sed tanquam moralia instituta, possunt intelligi dupliciter; uno modo secundum Augustinum,[9] ut non sint precepta, sed concessiones; concessit enim eis ut possent pergere ad predicationis officium sine pera et baculo, et aliis huiusmodi, tanquam habentes potestatem accipiendi necessaria vite ab illis quibus predicabant; unde subdit: *dignus est enim operarius cibo suo.*[10] Non autem peccat sed[11] supererogat qui sua portat ex quibus viuat in predicationis officio, non accipiens sumptus a quibus predicat, sicut Paulus fecit.[12] Alio modo possunt intelligi secundum expositionem aliorum sanctorum ut sint quedam statuta temporalia Apostolis data illo tempore quo ante Christi passionem mittebantur ad predicandum in Iudea. Indigebant enim discipuli, quasi adhuc paruuli accipere a Christo aliqua[13] specialia instituta, sicut et quilibet subditi a suis prelatis, et precipue quia erant paulatim exercitandi, ut temporalium sollicitudinem abdicarent, per quod reddebantur idonei ad predicandum per uniuersum orbem. Nec est mirum, si durante adhuc statu veteris Legis, et ipsis nondum perfectam libertatem Spiritus consecutis, quosdam determinatos modos viuendi instituit, que quidem statuta, imminente passione, remoueret,[14] tanquam discipulis iam pro ea sufficienter exercitatis; unde Luc. XXII° (35) dixit: *quando misi vos sine sacculo,* etc. et post: *sed qui nunc habet sacculum tollat, similiter et peram.*[15] Iam enim imminebat tempus perfecte libertatis, ut totaliter suo demitterentur arbitrio in hiis que secundum se non pertinent ad necessitatem virtutis." Hec prefatus doctor.

---

5   seu baculum...interdixit eis *om*. P.
6   tamenT/n P.
7   Le ms. P porte ici: Diligenter adverte, avant: aduertendum...Le copiste a dû inclure dans le texte une note marginale de son modèle. C'est ici que commence l'extrait contenu dans le ms. Vat. lat. 4986.
8   *Prima Secundae*, q. 108, a. 2, ad 3. La citation est presque littérale.
9   *De consensu Euangelist.* II, 30.
10   *Mt.* X, 10.
11   si superer. P.
12   *I Cor.* IX, 4 sqq.
13   aliq. alia *add*. T.
14   remoueret P/remouit T.
15   *Lc.* XXII, 36.

Et aduertendum etiam illud quod in altera parte Summe sue[16] dicit, questione: "An habere aliquid in communi diminuat de perfectione religionis."[17] Licet enim ibi dicat quod "habere superhabundantes diuicias in communi, siue in rebus mobilibus, siue immobilibus, est impedimentum perfectionis, licet totaliter non excludat eam," plura tamen subdit valde cauenda. Subdit enim quod "habere de exterioribus rebus in communi, siue mobilibus, siue[18] immobilibus quantum[19] sufficit ad simplicem victum non impedit perfectionem religionis, si consideretur paupertas in comparatione ad communem finem religionum, qui est vacare diuinis obsequiis; per[20] comparationem vero ad speciales fines, tanto erit unaqueque religio perfectior quanto habet paupertatem magis proportionatam suo fini." Ex quo infert quod "religio que ordinatur ad militandum et[21] ad hospitalitatem sectandam vel ad alias corporales actiones actiue (vite) esset imperfecta si omnibus diuitiis communibus[22] careret." Deinde subdit quod "religiones que ad contemplationem ordinantur tanto perfectiores sunt quanto earum paupertas minorem sollicitudinem temporalium eis ingerit." Deinde subdit: "Manifestum est autem quod minimam sollicitudinem ingerit conseruare res usui hominum[23] necessarias tempore congruo procuratas. Et ideo tribus gradibus religionum, triplex ratio[24] paupertatis competit; nam illis religionibus que ordinantur ad corporales actiones actiue vite, competit habere habundantiam diuitiarum communium; illis autem[25] que sunt ordinate ad contemplandum magis competit habere possessiones moderatas, nisi ubi oportet tales[26] per se vel per alios hospitalitatem tenere; illis autem que ordinantur ad contemplata aliis tradendum, competit vitam habere valde[27] expeditam ab exterioribus sollicitudinibus, quod quidem fit dum modica que sunt necessaria vite congruo tempore procurata conseruantur." Deinde ostendit quod "Christus, institutor paupertatis hoc suo exemplo docuit, quia habebat loculos...ex quo patet quod conseruare pecuniam aut quascumque alias res communes ad sustentationem religiosorum congregationis eiusdem vel quorumcumque aliorum pauperum est conforme perfectioni quam Christus docuit suo exemplo" ...Deinde subdit quod "paupertas non est perfectio, sed perfectionis instrumentum et minimum inter tria principalia instrumenta perfectionis" ...Subdit etiam quod "non oportet quod religio tanto sit perfectior quanto maiorem habet paupertatem, sed quanto eius paupertas est magis proportionata communi fini et speciali..."

Ut autem pateat que in hiis precipue sunt cauenda, reduco illa ad septem. Primum est quod verba Christi: *Nolite possidere*, etc., non sunt precepta, sed

---

16   Summe sue T. (et cet. cod.)/sic P.
17   *Secunda Secundae*, q. 188, a. 7.
18   s. etiam *add*. T.
19   Quantum *om*. P.
20   per *om*. P.
21   et P/vel T.
22   communibus T/communiter P.
23   hominum P/hominis T.
24   ratio P/gradus T.
25   illis autem T/aut illis P.
26   tal. vel *add*. T.
27   valde P/maxime T.

concessiones. Secundum est quod: qui portat sua in predicando supererogat. Tercium est, quod secundum alios sanctos ab Augustino predicta a Christo fuerunt quedam statuta temporalia secundum se non spectantia ad perfectionem seu ad necessitatem perfecte virtutis, et ideo euacuata sunt tempore passionis a Christo dicente: *et nunc qui habet sacculum tollat, similiter et peram*. Quartum est quod religio ordinata ad militiam vel hospitalitatem vel ad quamcumque actiuam est imperfecta nisi habeat in communi habundantiam diuitiarum, et quod religionem ordinatam ad contemplandum decet et competit habere possessiones moderatas, et si ultra hoc vacat hospitalitati, debet habere habundantes. Quintum est quod habere in communi mobilia et immobilia quantum expedit necessario victui religionis tam pro se quam pro aliis pauperibus in nullo impedit perfectionem religionis ordinate ad contemplandum et ad predicandum vel docendum, et quod conseruare res usui necessarias congruo tempore procuratas minimam sollicitudinem temporalium ingerit et facit habere vitam ab exterioribus sollicitudinibus maxime expeditam, et quod non differt seruare pecuniam aut seruare res alias necessarias, et quod est eadem ratio uti hiis que pertinent ad necessaria vite aut quod communiter conseruentur. Sextum est quod hec probantur Christi exemplo et Apostolorum, quia ipsi ita fecerunt, et quia aliter facere est periculosum, secundum[28] Antonium et Augustinum.[29] Septimum est quod paupertas non est perfectio, sed instrumentum perfectionis, minimum inter vota euangelica; et quod non quanto maior tanto perfectior, sed potius quanto est magis proportionata communi et speciali fini religionis.

Primum igitur est erroneum[30]; primo quia est contra expressa verba Scripture...secundo, quia est contra expressissima[31] et[32] plurima verba[33] sanctorum tam grecorum quam latinorum, quorum adminus XVII auctoritates expressas posui in prima questione de paupertate[34]; et ultra hoc sunt plures auctoritates Basilii in regula sua et sanctorum Patrum in collationibus suis, quarum aliquas supra[35] in Sermone Domini recitaui,[36] et aliquas etiam in hac parte[37]; tertio quia eneruat totam veritatem perfectionis euangelice,[38] sicut ibidem est per

---

28   sec. beatum Ant. *add.* T.

29   Saint Thomas cite, pour s. Antoine, les *Collationes Patrum* II, 2, et pour s. Augustin, le traité *De operibus monachorum* c. 23-24 (2a2ae, q. 188, a. 7, ad 2).

30   En marge de ce passage, le ms. T porte une note: "reprobatio positionis et opinionis Thome."

31   expressiua P.

32   quam *add.* P.

33   verb. multorum s. *add.* T.

34   A la fin de la question: "An status altissime paupertatis sit simpliciter melior omni statu diuitiarum"; cette première question sur la pauvreté évangélique est la huitième question dans la série ordonnée des "Quaestiones de perfectione euangelica"; cf. Ehrle, op. cit., pp. 505-506. Nous avons étudié cette question d'après le ms. Flor. Laurent. Santa Croce XXXI, sin. 3, f. 121-138v. Ehrle en donne quelques extraits d'après le ms. Vat. lat. 4986, f. 23-39v., dans son étude cit., pp. 505-506, mais ne mentionne pas cette série d'autorités.

35   supr. et *add.* P.

36   au chap. 6 de la *Lectura in Mt.*, ms. 15588, f. 57-59.

37   Olivi a cité la règle de saint Basile un peu plus haut, f. 68v du ms. lat. 15588.

38   T porte en marge de ce passage: "Cave hanc positionem, quia condemnata est."

plures vias ostensum.[39] Quod autem pro se Augustinum inducit, miror prudentem virum pauca verba unius sancti velle reducere contra expressissima verba Scripture sacre et omnium aliorum sanctorum, et contra expressa dicta Romanorum pontificum, et contra sententiam, vitam et regulam tanti viri quantus fuit sanctus Franciscus, Christi plagis insignitus, et[40] contra alia verba ipsiusmet Augustini et contra lumen irrefragabilium rationum. Ergo potius debuit vel exponere verba Augustini, vel negare; sicut enim optime dicit frater Bonauentura Apologie sue 7° c°,[41] predicta verba Christi possunt intelligi esse dicta apostolis in persona omnium christianorum qui secundum litteram ad tantam artitudinem non tenentur...possunt etiam secundo intelligi prout dicta sunt Apostolis generaliter in persona omnium doctorum et prelatorum, quibus de iure euangelico competit recipere necessaria a subditis suis; et tunc, si verba Christi predicta referantur solum ad huiusmodi receptionem, dicit Augustinus in libro De concordia Euangelistarum et alibi[42] quod non sunt precepta, sed concessa siue permissa, quod est dicere quod non fuit eis preceptum recipere necessaria ab hiis quibus predicabant, nec etiam fuit eis preceptum[43] quod ut reciperent ab illis non deberent aliunde necessaria accipere, sed solum fuit eis permissum...quamuis autem sub hoc respectu non sunt Apostolis precepta, nichilominus prout perfectionem paupertatis aperte includunt, sunt eis precepta tanquam professoribus altissime paupertatis ad quam non astringuntur hii qui non vouerunt eam. Unde, nec ratio Augustini de Paulo operante manibus[44] aliquo modo vadit contra hoc, sed solum contra primum, sicut patet etiam cecis et surdis...

Secundum etiam, scilicet quod qui in predicando portat sua supererogat, simpliciter loquendo, est falsum et erroneum, quia tunc predicator habens proprium de quo viuit est perfectior paupere euangelico, qui predicando viuit de elemosinis aut stipendiis illorum quibus predicat...Constat autem quod desistere ab opere supererogationis non est sacrilegium neque peccatum, nisi vouisset illud; igitur illud non est simpliciter verum, nisi in facientibus illud instar Pauli, secundum quod tamen supererogat omnis qui stipendium sibi licitum et debitum propter Dei amorem non recipit.

Tercium etiam est erroneum, falsoque ascribitur hoc sanctis, quia non solum hoc non dicunt, immo expressissime contrarium docent, omnium enim auctoritates expresse dicunt eos ista semper obseruasse et obseruare debuisse, et quod ista simpliciter sunt perfectionis et perfecte virtutis et perfectissime exemplaritatis...Ex quibus tamen verbis eius premissis aperte patet quod Christus debuit discipulis suis dare aliquam formam vestitus condecentem statui suo; debuit ergo esse forma mire paupertatis, vilitatis, humilitatis, simplicitatis, austeritatis, nuditatis, et recte[45] talis est forma data eis a

39 vias P/rationes T.
40 et P/est etiam T.
41 *Apologia Pauperum*, c. 7; *S. Bonaventurae Opera omnia* VIII, opusc. XI, p. 279.
42 *Contra Adimantium*, c. 20, 1, cité d'après Bonaventure, loc. cit.
43 recipere...preceptum *om.* P.
44 Cf. *Act.* XVIII, 3.
45 recte T/ratione P.

Christo...nemo sane mentis debet dicere hanc in[46] passione euacuatam esse
tanquam imperfectam, aut tanquam perfectioni virtutis non multam ac-
comodam, et precipue cum non solum innumera verba[47] sanctorum, sed
etiam omnes antique imagines Apostolorum oculata fide nos docent eos sic
per orbem uniuersum semper incessisse.

Quartum etiam quod scilicet religio ordinata ad actiuam, utpote ad militiam
vel ad hospitalitatem est imperfecta nisi habeat habundantes diuicias est noua
et inaudita doctrina. Quis enim usque nunc audiuit in noua Lege sic diuicias
commendari ut dicatur aliqua religio esse imperfecta, non solum si non habeat
diuicias, sed etiam nisi habeat diuicias habundantes? Quero autem an, dato
quod aliqui milites pro cultu Dei sic exponant se religiose militie quod penitus
nichil querant nisi sumptus sibi gratis a Christianis dandos, an isti sint in cultu
et religione Dei imperfectiores quam si sibi ad hoc coaceruent castra et regna
et certe nullus sane mentis dicet quin illud sit maioris virtutis.

Preterea in statu et actu militie religiose principaliter debet intendi
spiritualis salus eorum qui sunt in statu illo et spiritualis cultus Dei. Constat
enim quod si absque omni[48] dominio temporalium, solis stipendiis officio suo
competentibus sunt contenti, et ubi desunt sunt prompti ferre patienter propter Deum, quod tanto sunt elongatiores a superbia et auaricia et luxuria
eneruante militare studium et a seditione dissipante exercitum et totum
militare negocium, essentque promptiores ad obediendum suis ducibus et
fidentiores in Deo et eius auxilio; essetque Deo et suo populo honorificentius
per tales vincere quam per diuiciis affluentes, maiusque exemplum darent[49]
mundo, contempnandi mundum et colendi Deum, et pure bellandi propter Dei
amorem; et huiusmodi exemplum de facto probamus in pluribus, qui, dum[50]
essent pauperiores pro Deo suo optime militarunt, facti autem diciores, super-
biis, opulentiis et luxuriis atque rixis, inuidiis et seditionibus vacant, or-
bemque totum malo exemplo replent et ideo nec Deus curat eis auxiliari.

Preterea, secundum hoc, decrescentibus diuiciis, semper decrescit regularis
eorum perfectio, et cum crescentibus crescit, acsi in ipsis diuiciis formaliter
consistat perfectio religionis illius, quod non solum est erroneum, sed etiam
ridiculosum et tantum quod apud Romanos nundum christianos exercicio tam
morum quam armorum[51] affluentia diuiciarum, que est mater gule et luxurie et
litigiorum domesticorum reputaretur valde nociua, et e contra pauperies
dilecta reputata sit prodesse predictis.   Preterea, esto quod in militia haberet
hoc locum, quis dicet quod religio que cum summa paupertate de solo opere
ac labore proprio vacat hospitalitati non sit perfectior illa que de sola super-
fluitate suarum diuiciarum elargitur pauperibus; et certe dixit Christus quod
paupercula vidua mittens duo minuta in gazophilacium Dei misit plus quam
omnes diuites;[52] cuius ratio secundum Christum est quod ista misit totum victum suum, illi vero de superfluo suo.

46   in Christi pass. *add.* T.
47   verba *om.* P.
48   omni T/.n. P.
49   darent T/daret P.
50   qui dum T/quidem P.
51   quam armorum *om.* P.
52   *Mc.* XII, 42-44; *Lc.* XXI, 2-4.

Rursus, dato quod in hiis qui nesciunt orare nec ferre pauperiem, hoc locum haberet, quis dicet quod religio dedicata contemplationi et non doctrine sit perfectior cum moderata sufficientia possessionum et aliarum rerum quam si instar anachoritarum et monachorum existentium tempore magni Antonii, nichil habentes, viuerent de solo labore? Sed quis ferat quod subditur, scilicet quod si vacat hospitalitati debeat ultra predictum moderamen[53] habere habundantes diuicias? Estne hec doctrina Christi vel Pauli? Dixit hoc unquam aliquis sanctus? Absit!

Sed arguit quod proprius finis predictarum religionum hoc exigit; et nos dicimus quod proprius finis[54] talis religionis potest sumi tripliciter, aut secundum quod est complementum perfectionis sui status, aut secundum quod est[55] remedium infirmitatis eorum, aut secundum quod est solatium carnalitatis eorum.

Primo modo diuitie aut possessiones terrene non iuuant, immo potius obsunt, nisi per magnum contemptum animi virtualiter conculcentur et a mentis affectibus[56] totaliter sequestrentur, quod facere habendo eas est valde difficile, non solum in[57] imperfectis, sed etiam et perfectis. Secundo modo iuuant quidem eo modo quo coniugium est remedium concupiscentie per adulteria et meretricia effluentis;[58] sed iste finis semper presupponit imperfectionem ut sibi annexam. Tertio vero modo semper est culpa et crebro mortale peccatum.

Sciendum etiam quod aliquis[59] dicitur esse specialis finis religionis qui tamen non est semper finis principalis, sed annexus principali. Dilectio enim Dei et proximi et spiritualis salus anime sue ac deinde aliorum est principalis finis religionis; temporalis vero et corporalis impugnatio infidelium et corporalis defensio ac redemptio vel nutritio fidelium non est proprie finis religionis, nisi forte sit finis annexus. In proportionando autem statum suum ad talem finem, non est virtutis perfectio, nisi solum pro quanto illa proportionatio magis vel minus dirigitur ad caritatem et ad perfectionem spiritualem anime sue.

Dato ergo quod habundantia diuiciarum absolute plus prodesset corporalibus commodis fidelium, si tamen ex hoc modo[60] impedimentum maius[61] prestetur spirituali saluti anime sue vel aliorum, non erit[62] perfectio religionis, sed imperfectio.

Quintum autem quantum ad primam sui partem est aperte contrarium doctrine Christi, sicut habunde et diffuse alibi[63] est probatum; et certe secundum

---

53   predictum moderamen T/predictam moderationem P.
54   predictarum...finis *om.* P.
55   est quoddam rem. *add.* T.
56   affectibus T/effectibus P.
57   in *om.* T.
58   effluentis P./affluentis T.
59   aliquis T/aliquid P.
60   modo P/aliquid T.
61   maius P/magis T.
62   erit P/esset hoc T.
63   L'auteur se réfère à ses questions sur la pauvreté qui portent les n° 8 et 9 de la série des "Quaestiones de perfectione euangelica"; cf. Ehrle, op. cit., pp. 505-514, et peut être aussi à son traité "de usu paupere"; cf. Ehrle, pp. 514-517.

hoc debuit dicere Christus: *Vade et vende quod habes, et da pauperibus* vel adiunge ea collegio nostro. Quero etiam quare non fecit apportare ad collegium suum retia Apostolorum, sed potius pro magna laude dicitur quod *relictis retibus secuti sunt eum.*[64] Secundum istam doctrinam nescio ad quid, nisi solum quia parum valebant et ideo collegium Christi paruam ex eis pecuniam habuisset. Quare etiam non dixit eis: *Nolite possidere aurum vel argentum*[65] in proprio, sed in communi collegio prouidete et habete satis, quia hoc non impedit perfectionem, immo potius iuuat? Quantumvero ad secundam partem in qua dicitur quod conseruare res usui necessarias minimam sollicitudinem ingerit, immo et facit habere vitam maxime expeditam a sollicitudinibus, si[66] solum intelligit hoc de conseruatione absque omni iure proprio vel communi, et hoc pro solo tempore in quo est euidens necessitas talia[67] conseruandi, verum dicit, et[68] utinam iste fuerit intellectus! Si vero conseruacionem accipit cum dominio, et necessitatem rerum accipit[69] pro tota vita aut pro magno tempore cuius nondum imminet necessitas, nisi forte apud hominem imperfectum qui non plene se committit dispositioni aut consilio Dei, est falsum et erroneum.

Falsum quidem est; primo, quia talis de pluribus et pro maiori tempore sollicitatur; secundo, quia cum maiori affectu sollicitatur, quia vult eas[70] procurare et conseruare cum pleno dominio in communi, alius non; tertio, quia cum maiori timore amittendi eas conseruat quam alter, quia quanto maiori affectu fertur ad eas tanquam ad res suas et in quibus vult habere dominium et tanquam ad res maioris precii et ad multum tempus utiles et[71] tanto utique plus timet amissionem earum; quarto, quia quanto minus committit se consilio Dei, tanto cum maiori diffidentia Dei eas procurat et conseruat, ac per consequens cum minori cordis quiete ac securitate; quinto, quia in eo quod ipse[72] vult habere ius repetitorium[73] contra quemcumque tollentem, utique non solum maiorem habet affectum ad eas, sed etiam magnam dat ei[74] occasionem distrahendi se contra proximum per causas litigiosas et contenciosas a quibus utique est liber ille qui nullo modo vult ista sibi licere. Verum est autem quod in homine diffidente aut imperfecte confidente de auxilio Dei et molestissime ferente quamcumque penuriam et in omnem euentum volentem habere rerum affluentiam est expedientius, seu minus inexpediens esse in statu inferiori in quo licet thesaurizare, quam esse in statu ita perfecto, iuxta illud Apostoli: *Si se non continent, nubant; melius est enim nubere quam uri.*[75]

---

64   eum *om.* P. *Mt.* IV, 20; *Mc.* I, 18.
65   *Mt.* X, 9.
66   si T/.i. P.
67   talia T/talium P.
68   et quod utin. *add.* P.
69   cum dominio...accipit *om.* P.
70   eas T/eos P.
71   et *om.* T.
72   ipse P/iste T.
73   repetitorium P/petitorium T.
74   ei P/sibi T.
75   *I Cor.* VII, 9.

Erroneum vero est, quia est expresse contra consilia Christi, sicut in precedentibus et etiam alibi[76] est ostensum; nec aduertisse videtur quod radix distractiue sollicitudinis, que scilicet est cupiditas rerum et nimia cura sui et modica fiducia Dei, non ita aufertur per modum quem ponit sicut fit[77] per alterum; non etiam videtur aduertisse quod motus corporis exterior non est formaliter ipsa sollicitudo que distrahit mentem. Unde et sepe videmus quod seruus missus hinc inde ad procuranda debita domini sui modicum anxiatur de habendo vel non habendo; dominus vero domi sedens quam plurimum anxiatur et sollicitatur; licet igitur pauperes euangelici qui[78] non congregant aliquando exteriori motu corporis plus laborent et in hoc[79] plus macerent corpus, non tamen plus sollicitantur quamdiu in sua paupertate et penuria complacentiam habent; immo vadunt et petunt elemosinam sine omni sollicitudine cordis.

Quantum vero ad terciam partem qua dicitur quod non differt seruare pecuniam et res alias necessarias, non est sane dictum, quia non solum sacer textus et omnes sancti, sed etiam multiplicia experimenta clamant quod[80] pecunia super res alias se ingerit amabilem, tractabilem, conseruabilem, multiplicabilem et ad omnem contractum et commutationem[81] valde ductibilem et ad omnia appetibilia gule et luxurie et consimilium procuranda nimium aptam et circa eam facilius[82] interuenit furtum et fraus et thesaurizatio occulta et ypocritalis et ex ea de facili fiunt symonie et lucra inepta. Preterea constat quod usus pecunie non est secundum se ita[83] necessarius victui nostro sicut sunt cibi et vestes.

Quintum etiam quod subditur, scilicet quod eadem est ratio uti hiis que sunt necessaria vite aut quod communiter conseruentur, si[84] de conseruatione que est cum dominio et que est pro usu longi temporis hoc intelligat, falsum est et erroneum. Falsum quidem quia constat quod iurisdictio est longe alterius rationis quam sit solus simplex usus rei; constat etiam quod conseruare res pro futuris temporibus est alterius rationis quam sit solum uti re necessaria de presenti et pro presenti. Erroneum vero est quia est expresse contra consilia Christi qui necessarium quidem usum rerum concedit, immo et precepit, dominium vero rerum et congregationem earum pro futuro tempore cuius necessitas de presenti non iminet, consulit et viris apostolicis interdicit.

Sextum autem sic est erroneum, quod est Christo et apostolis nimis contumeliosum et non est aliud quam scripturam repugnantem violenter intorquere ad suum affectum et ad operculum imperfectionum nostrarum. Expono autem caput meum si ipse cum omnibus sectatoribus suis vel potest

---

76 autre allusion aux Questions sur la pauvreté.
77 fit T/facit P.
78 qui P/quia T.
79 in h. ipso *add.* T.
80 quod P/quia T.
81 commutationem T/communicationem P (mais il s'agit plutôt d'une abréviation mal interprétée par le scribe).
82 facilius P/facillime T.
83 ita *om.* T.
84 si P/scilicet T.

unicum exemplum dare quod unquam Christus vel eius apostoli seruauerint pro[85] se pecuniam, nisi in casu tante necessitatis in quo liceret hoc cuicumque, quantumcumque vouisset abdicationem illius;[86] vel tamen de illismet casibus non legitur multum expresse nec inde potest extrahi, nisi per satis simplicem coniecturam. Quando enim dicitur quod *discipuli iuerant in ciuitatem*,[87] *ut cibos emerent,* certum est quod ibi non dicitur quod ipsi pro hac re pecuniam portarent. Constat autem quod de facultatibus mulierum ministrantium sibi aut de rebus aliquorum credentium, qui ad Christi consilia non erant astricti poterunt emi, aut de elemosinis[88] tunc quesitis vel oblatis. Constat etiam quod hoc fuit in terra Samarie de qua ibidem dicitur quod *non coutuntur Iudei Samaritanis*[89] et ideo presumi poterat quod eis[90] essent inhospitabiles; ista vero et alia satis alibi sunt[91] ostensa, quia pecunia que ponebatur ad pedes apostolorum non dicitur esse posita pro usu vel necessitate eorum, sed potius pro aliis; quia si Petrus habebat pecuniam in communi, falso dixit petenti elemosinam: *argentum et aurum non est michi*[92]; si enim voluit dicere: non habeo in proprio, licet habeam in communi, sermo esset duplicitate et im-misericordia plenus... Preterea, esto quod esset, constat quod tanta persecutio omnium Iudeorum contra eos tunc temporis feruebat quod merito poterat cen-seri esse necessarium uti ea in tali casu quantumcumque usus eius ex voto alias non liceret...

Quia tamen Augustinus dicit quod in loculis Christi ecclesiastice pecunie forma tradita est;[93] sciendum quod in hoc casu et consimilibus aliud est dare formam condescensionis, aliud formam euitande periclitationis, aliud formam cure pastoralis, aliud formam mediocris religionis, aliud formam vitandi erroris. Christus autem usus est, licet raro, loculis, partim condescensiue tam pro infirmis quam pro forma mediocris religionis, partim pietate cure pastoralis, ut ostenderet quod prelatus ecclesiasticas oblationes in usus pauperum potius debet conuertere quam in suos, et ut ostenderet quod sic debet inopias pauperum subleuare et eorum curam habere quod tamen congregationi[94] magnorum thesaurorum non debet etiam pro hac re insistere; usus est etiam partim ad docendum quod in casu periculose seu ineuitabilis necessitatis licitum, immo et debitum est quantumcumque perfectis uti loculis aut aliquo equiualenti...Usus est Christus in condempnationem futurarum heresum dicentium quod nulli christiano, precipue clerico vel prelato, licet habere aurum vel argentum. Docuit etiam per hoc formidandam esse prouisionem et conseruationem temporalium, quia unus ex XII. apostolis ex hoc cecidit in latrocinantem cupiditatem, et in hoc ipso docuit quan-

---

85   pro se/per se P.
86   illius P/ipsius T.
87   *Ioh.* IV, 8.
88   de el. aut t. *add.* P.
89   *Ioh.* IV, 9.
90   eis T/eas P.
91   sunt T/essent P.
92   *Act.* III, 6.
93   *Homel. 62 super Ioh.* (XIII, 29) cité par Bonaventure, *Apologia pauperum*, c. 7, ed. cit., p. 284.
94   congregationi P/congregationem T.

tumcumque[95] fugiendum sit malum cupiditatis ecclesiasticorum bonorum, quia Iudas ex hoc factus est proditor Christi. Docuit etiam in hoc quoscumque prelatos ut dispensationem temporalium etiam necessariorum alteri relinquant, ipsi vero soli orationi et predicationi instent, sicut[96] et apostoli postmodum fecerunt prout habetur Actus 6 (2-4). Docuit etiam ne in hoc nimis curiose timerent de infidelitate dispensantium, anne pro tali timore dispensationem huiusmodi ad se reuocarent cum tollerabilius sit temporalia perdi quam a spiritualibus officiis retrahi.

Septimum autem scilicet quod paupertas non est perfectio, sed instrumentum perfectionis, si intendit dicere quod non est illa finalis perfectio que soli competit caritati, verum dicit; sed tunc ita posset hoc dicere de aliis virtutibus. Si vero intendit quod[97] nullo modo sit virtualis perfectio, contrarium dicit Christo, qui dicit: *Si vis perfectus esse, vade et vende*,[98] etc. et qui primam beatitudinem ponit in paupertate[99]...Quod etiam subditur, scilicet quod paupertas est minimum inter tria vota,[1] falsum est, sicut in questione de hoc specialiter facta alibi est ostensum.[2] Mira res! Christus verbo et facto paupertatem quasi super omnia extollit; iste vero quasi sub omnibus eam deicit. Scio quod hoc non fecisset beatus Dominicus, qui maledixit omnibus suis[3] quandocumque possessiones reciperent.[4]

Quod etiam subdit[5] quod paupertas non quanto maior tanto perfectior, sed quanto[6] est fini suo proportionalior, est mira falsigraphia, quia de omni habente[7] super se finem ulteriorem est universaliter verum quod[8] quanto est fini[9] proportionalius, tanto est melius; sed non ex hoc sequitur quod paupertas, quanto maior, non sit perfectior, nisi probetur quod quanto est maior,[10] non est fini suo proportionalior, sicut nec de castitate hoc sequitur, que utique tanto est maior, quanto[11] est melior. Quod autem paupertas altissima sit proportionalior et utilior perfectioni castitatis et contemplationis omniumque sublimium virtutum, alibi est ita copiose ostensum quod nisi cecus vel maliuolus negare non possunt. Et dato quod nullam aliam rationem haberemus, nisi Christi consilium et exemplum, qui ait se *non habere ubi*

---

95   quantumcumque P/quantum T.
96   sicut *om.* P.
97   quod *om.* P.
98   *Mt.* XIX, 21.
99   Cf. *Mt.* V, 3; *Lc.* VI, 20.
1   vota T/votata P.
2   Référence à la question "de voto obedientie euangelice," que contient, entre autres, le ms. Vat. lat. 4986, f. 79-81v.
3   suis *om.* P.
4   Cité par Olivi d'après s. Bonaventure, *Quaestiones disputatae de perfectione evangelica*, q. II, art. II, ed. *Opera omnia* V, p. 138: "Item, exemplum de sancto Dominico qui in morte sua imprecatus est maledictionem omnibus qui in ordinem suum possessiones conerentur inducere."
5   subdit P/subditur T.
6   quanto T/quantum P.
7   habenti P.
8   quod P/quia T.
9   fini *om.* P.
10   perfectior...maior *om.* P.
11   tanto...quanto P/quanto...tanto T.

caput reclinet,[12] sufficere deberet omni fideli. Fateor tamen quod ubi non habetur maior paupertas in voto, sed solum in obseruantia simplici, sicut quidam abdicationem possessionum non habent in voto, licet de facto ita obseruent, in talibus fortasse verum est quod castitas habita cum voto sollempni maior est tali obseruantia paupertatis,[13] et si hoc dicere prefatus doctor voluit, habeat sibi!

12 *Lc.* IX, 58.
13 paupertatis *om.* P.

BROTHER THOMAS, THE MASTER,
AND THE MASTERS

Edward A. Synan

GREAT men, as experience led the Duke of Wellington to observe, are "much exposed to authors" and Thomas Aquinas has not escaped that exposure. The blameless Brother Thomas, to be sure, had no occasion to anticipate the "Publish and be damned!" which one brush with an author is said to have wrung from the Duke;[1] in compensation, he has been at the mercy of authors for half a millennium longer and in ways the Duke was spared.

One major source of this exposure has been the interest of Thomists in issues to which Aquinas adverted only in passing. To determine his position on such issues, an obvicus strategy is to collect his random remarks and then, if courage does not fail, to follow the precedent Albert set when he noted gaps in the Aristotelian canon. Since Aristotle, or time, had failed to hand down every treatise required for an integral presentation of peripatetic philosophy, Albert promised to supply what might be missing from the tradition.[2] Thus references to 'analogy' are not uncommon in the works of Aquinas, but systematic treatises on analogy are the work of Thomists, not of Thomas.[3]

---

1 "...in his situation as Chancellor of the University of Oxford, he had been much exposed to authors" are the words with which Wellington refused to accept the dedication of a song; see G. W. E. Russell, *Collections* and *Recollections* (London 1898) 23; "Publish and be damned!" is ascribed to Wellington by tradition, but the letter in which he must have written either these or equivalent words is not extant; see E. Longford, *Wellington, The Years of the Sword* (London 1969) 166-169.

2 "Et addemus etiam alicubi partes librorum imperfectorum, et alicubi libros intermissos vel omissos, quos Aristoteles non fecit, et forte si fecit, ad nos non pervenerunt...", St. Albert, *In VIII Physicorum* initio; *B. Alberti Magni... Opera Omnia*, ed. A. Borgnet (Paris 1890-1899) III, 1-2.

3 An impression of the breadth of this production, inaugurated by the classic treatises of Thomas de Vio (Cajetan, 1469-1534) *De Nominum Analogia, De Conceptu Entis*, edd. P. N. Zammit and P. H. Hering (Rome 1952), can be derived from a rapid sampling: H. Chavannes, *L'analogie entre Dieu et le monde selon saint Thomas d'Aquin et selon Karl Barth* (Paris 1969), T. W. Guzie, *The Analogy of Learning; An Essay toward a Thomistic Psychology of Learning* (New York 1960), G. P. Klubertanz, *St. Thomas Aquinas on Analogy; a Textual Analysis and Systematic Synthesis* (Chicago 1960), H. Lyttkens, *The Analogy between God and the World; an Investigation of its Background and Interpretation of its Use by Thomas of Aquino* (Uppsala 1952). E. L. Mascall, *Existence and Analogy; a Sequel to "He Who Is"* (London, New York 1949), R. M.

Platonism in various guises was never far from his thoughts, as an extensive documentation proves, but Aquinas made his subtly discriminating responses to challenges posed by Plato only as the course of argument demanded; their painstaking assembly, organization, and exposition have been the work of a modern author.[4]

I

Like analogy and Platonism, the value of 'authority' and of 'magistral opinion' in theology is a theme on which an essay from the pen of Aquinas would have been welcome, but it is one he did not feel compelled to write. This does not mean that he was insensitive to the virtualities of the university world in which he worked. With all his contemporaries, Aquinas was accustomed to garnish his writings with authoritative texts,[5] to take them as points of departure, to reckon with them in the sword-play of his dialectic, to 'interpret' them with a freedom and ingenuity that would be inexplicable apart from a fundamental respect for those venerable formulations. On occasion, he would reject an authority and give his reasons for so doing. Thomists have often busied themselves with searching out and weighing his explicit comments on the subject. Although another approach is set out in this paper, Peter of Bergamo, Melchior Cano, and M.-D. Chenu must be present at all points, thanks to their classic contributions to our understanding of the Common Doctor's 'procedures of documentation,' both *authentica* and *magistralia*.[6]

Isolated comments on authority and magistral decisions by theologians later than Peter Lombard can be supplemented with evidence of exceptional interest and solidity. A series of questions on which the views of Peter Lombard and those of the Parisian Masters were at odds shows how each commentator on the *Sentences* came to

McInerny, *Studies in Analogy* (The Hague 1968), B. Mondin, *The Principle of Analogy in Protestant and Catholic Theology* (The Hague 1963), B. Montagnes, *La doctrine de l'analogie de l'être d'après saint Thomas d'Aquin* (Louvain, Paris 1963), M. T. L. Penido, *Le rôle de l'analogie en théologie dogmatique* (Paris 1931), G. B. Phelan, *Saint Thomas and Analogy* (Milwaukee 1941), H. G. Pohlmann, *Analogia entis oder Analogia fidei? Die Frage der Analogia bei Karl Barth* (Göttingen 1965).

4 R. J. Henle, *Saint Thomas and Platonism; a Study of the Plato and Platonic Texts in the Writings of Saint Thomas* (The Hague 1956).

5 M.-D. Chenu, "*Authentica* et *magistralia*, deux lieux théologiques aux XII-XIII siècles," *Divus Thomas* (Piacenza) 28 (1925) 257-285 and, by the same author, *Toward Understanding St. Thomas*, tr. A. M. Landry and D. Hughes (Chicago 1964) 126-149; M. Riquet, "Thomas et les *auctoritates* en philosophie," *Archives de philosophie* 3.2 (1925) 117-155.

6 "Procedures of documentation" is the phrase of M.-D. Chenu, *Toward Understanding St. Thomas*, Chapter IV. 126-155.

terms with opposition between the Master and the Masters acting *communiter*. Bonaventure is the first man who is known to have listed explicitly those propositions of the Master that the Parisian theologians had rejected with moral unanimity.[7] At the moment he wrote, these numbered eight, distributed symmetrically, two from each of the *Four Books of Sentences*; the list was destined to lengthen.[8] When Peter of Bergamo drew up his Thomistic indices in the fifteenth century, the positions Aquinas had taken on nine issues, (which coincide only in part with Bonaventure's eight), persuaded him that it was his duty to warn the reader. "The Master of *Sentences* is not endowed with authority, *non est authenticus*; therefore, on many points he is not upheld..."[9]

With this mention of Peter of Bergamo it must be remarked first, that by using the term *authenticus* with respect to Peter Lombard, he has adopted a usage which Chenu would characterize as "a transition in application that was almost abusive."[10] Second, of the nine pericopes adduced by Peter of Bergamo to show that Aquinas did not grant the Master of *Sentences* status as an *auctor*, six are reducible to the first one listed by Bonaventure, that is, the proposition that charity is the Holy Spirit. Two are reducible to Peter Lombard's view that there is a human 'truth,' constituted for babies by what they receive from their parents in conception and for Eve by Adam's rib; these may be related to the fourth opinion in Bonaventure's list. The remaining text invoked by Peter of Bergamo is remarkable in that it correctly reports Aquinas himself writing in the "almost abusive" way: *non est necessarium auctoritatem Magistri Sententiarum sequi in hac parte.* The issue relates to views on grace and nature at stake in the third of Bonaventure's eight controverted questions.

Thomist investigators are understandably fond of noting that Aquinas thought the authoritative Boethius correct in his claim that

7 St. Bonaventure, *In II Sent.* d. 44, dubium 3; *Opera theologica selecta*, editio minor (Quaracchi 1934-1949) II, 1058; see also, ibid., Praelocutio II, 2.

8 F. Stegmüller, *Repertorium Commentariorum in Sententias Petri Lombardi* (Würzburg 1947) I, x; also *Petri Lombardi Libri IV Sententiarum* (Quaracchi 1916) I, lxxvii, n. 1, where the editors have printed a list of twenty-six such questions, dated by Du Plessis d'Argentré at A.D. 1300.

9 *Tabula Aurea... Petri de Bergomo... in Omnia Opera Divi Thomae Aquinatis...* (Rome 1570), a work first printed at Bologna in 1475 and many times since, in part or in whole; the entry cited here is from the *index generalis, s.v.* Magister, where Peter adduced nine passages to support his judgment that, for Aquinas, "Magister Sententiarum non est authenticus:" 1) *Summa theologiae* i, q. 94, a. 4, ad 2; 2) *Summa theologiae* II-II, q. 23, a. 2; 3) *In I Sent.* d. 17, q. 1, a. 1; 4) *In II Sent.* d. 18, q. 1, a. 1; 5) *In II Sent.* d. 30, q. 2, a. 1; 6) *In III Sent.* d. 27, q. 2, a. 4; 7) *In III Sent.* q. 2, a. 4; 8) *Quaestio disputata de virtutibus* q. 1, a. 11; 9) *Quaestio disputata de virtutibus* q. 2, a. 1, ad 12.

10 M.-D. Chenu, *Toward Understanding St. Thomas* 136.

human authority is the most wretched of the resources at the disposal of a philosopher.[11] We shall hardly be unfaithful to his intent if we extend this judgment to all specifically human disciplines, for Aquinas was notably reserved on the scope of human rationality.[12] Aristotle has given mild scandal by dropping his habitual empiric caution to advise his readers that it is sufficient to state the universal attributes of the human species 'once, for all,'[13] whereas Brother Thomas had small confidence in our capacity to know the 'differences' and 'essences' of even the material singulars we are best equipped to know.[14] He would do Aristotle the courtesy of expounding at length upon the Philosopher's *De caelo*, but this consummate exegete of philosophical texts remarked in the course of so doing that philosophy is more than a record of 'what men may have thought,' for the best of authors have achieved — will achieve? — no irreformable conceptual scheme to account for astronomical data. A different and better hypothesis 'to save the appearances' always remains a possibility and nothing less than 'the truth of things,' *qualiter se habeat veritas rerum*, can preside over the work of intelligence as Aquinas understood it.[15]

Although there is massive evidence of his life-long interest in contributing to the work of his philosophical colleagues in the faculty of arts,[16] where the scope of authority is so narrow, Aquinas recognized that, in his own faculty of theology, authority must play a different role.

---

11 *Summa theologiae* I, q. 1, a. 8, ad 2 is the response of Aquinas to an argument based upon the authority of Boethius (*In topica Ciceronis commentaria* IV, PL 64, 1166 and *De differentiis topicis* III, PL 64, 1199); see comment by D. Mosher that the appeal to the authority of Boethius against the value of authority seems to be "some kind of weird variation on the so-called Liar's Paradox." *Crux* 8.1 (1970) 8, n. 4.

12 J. Pieper, *The Silence of St. Thomas*, tr. J. Murray and D. O'Connor (New York 1957) 64-71, 89-91, 94-95.

13 E. Gilson, *Being and Some Philosophers* (Toronto 1949) 50.

14 "... differentiae essentiales sunt nobis ignotae..." *De veritate* q. 4, a. 1, ad 8; *Sancti Thomae Aquinatis... Quaestiones disputatae*, ed. P. Mandonnet (Paris 1925) I, 103; "... principia essentialia rerum sunt nobis ignota..." *Sancti Thomae Aquinatis in Aristotelis librum de anima commentarium* 1, 1, 15; ed. A. M. Pirotta (Turin 1936) 7.

15 "Illorum tamen suppositiones quas adinvenerunt, non est necessarium esse veras: licet enim, talibus suppositionibus factis, apparentia salvarentur, non tamen oportet dicere has suppositiones esse veras; quia forte secundum aliquem alium modum, nondum ab hominibus comprehensum, apparentia circa stellas salvantur." *De coelo et mundo* 2, 12, 17, 2; *Sancti Thomae Aquinatis Opera omnia*, ed. Leonina (Rome 1886) III, 186, 187; "Quidquid autem horum sit, non est nobis multum curandum: quia studium philosophiae non est ad hoc quod sciatur quid homines senserint, sed qualiter se habeat veritas rerum." ibid. 1, 10, 22, 8; III, 91.

16 Of the authentic works listed by I. T. Eschmann, "A Catalogue of St. Thomas's Works," in E. Gilson, *The Christian Philosophy of St. Thomas Aquinas*, tr. L. K. Shook (New York 1956) 379-437, numbers 28-39, 49-52, 54-55, 65-68, 70-71, and 74 are of a nature to interest the faculty of arts; to these ought to be added the works referred to by the Rector and Regent Masters in arts at Paris when they requested both these and the body of Aquinas. See A. Birkenmajer, "Der Brief der Pariser Artistenfakultät über den Tod des hl. Thomas von Aquino," *Beiträge zur Geschichte der Philosophie des Mittelalters* 20.5 (1922) 1-35.

Authority is an essential characteristic, a *proprium*, of sacred doctrine. This in no way entails the conclusion that theologians are in a less dignified posture than are the philosophers who bow only before 'the truth of things'; quite the contrary: *nec derogat dignitati huius doctrinae.*[17] Nothing could be more theological than the tentatives by Job's friends to explain the humanly inexplicable disasters that afflicted him. Indeed, Brother Thomas went so far as to interpret Job's dialogue with the Holy One in terms of a disputed question, of a theological debate in which truth is sought through the stylized moves of thirteenth century dialectic.[18] Neither Job nor his friends wished to diminish the authority of the Lord, yet Job could speak out boldly even to Him, for Job was conscious that he was speaking the truth and that the Holy One cannot fail to sustain created reflections of Himself: Truth is a divine Name. Aquinas was sure that Job was right.[19]

Theologians, however, do their work under a sobering rubric: Truth properly so-called, *quae antonomastice est veritas,* is divine Truth and is strictly incomprehensible by a human intellect. Hilary, the *auctor* Aquinas cited in support of this theological reserve, was right to have said: "Even though I know you will not arrive, still I rejoice that you strive, for the man who seeks infinite goals with piety, even though he sometimes does not attain them, nonetheless will profit always by advancing."[20] If the articles of faith are to sacred doctrine what first principles are to philosophy, then authorities rooted in divine Wisdom are

17 *Summa theologiae* I, q. 1, a. 8, ad 2; see above, note 11.

18 "Postquam ergo auditores reddidit attentos, modum disputationis suae determinat: vult enim disputare quasi cum alio contendens, et hoc est quod subdit *Quis est qui iudicetur mecum,* idest cum quo de veritate disputem?" *Expositio super Iob*, cap. 13, vv. 17-18, ed. Leonina (Rome 1965) XXVI, 87; "Est autem disputatio inter duas personas, scilicet opponentem et respondentem; ingrediens ergo disputationem cum Deo, dat ei optionem utramlibet personam eligendi vel opponentis vel respondentis... Primo autem Deo dat partes opponentis..." ibid. v. 22; "Deinde quasi tacente eo cui partes opponentis dederat, ipse partes obicientis assumit et inquirit de causis suae punitionis..." ibid. v. 24; it must be noted that the editors feel Aquinas has been more discreet than Albert was to be in assimilating the Book of Job to a disputed question, ed. cit. p. 28*.

19 "Sed ulterius considerandum est quod ille qui ad ostendendam Dei iustitiam vel bonitatem mendacio utitur non solum rem agit qua Deus non indiget, sed etiam hoc ipso contra Deum vadit: cum enim Deus veritas sit, omne autem mendacium veritati contrarietur, quicumque mendacio utitur ad Dei magnificentiam ostendendam hoc ipso contra Deum agit." Ibid. vv. 7-9, 85; "Videbatur autem disputatio hominis ad Deum esse indebita propter excellentiam qua Deus hominem excellit; sed considerandum est quod veritas ex diversitate personarum non variatur, unde cum aliquis veritatem loquitur vinci non potest cum quocumque disputet; certus autem erat Iob quod veritatem loquebatur sibi a Deo per donum fidei et sapientiae inspiratam, unde de veritate non diffidens..." Ibid. v. 19, 87.

20 "... etsi non perventurum sciam, gratulabor tamen profecturum. Qui enim pie infinita prosequitur, etsi non contingat aliquando, semper tamen proficiet prodeundo..." Hilary, *De trinitate* 2, 10, PL 10, 58 C-59 A, cited by Aquinas, *Summa contra Gentiles* 1, 8; ed. Leonina manualis (Rome 1934) 7.

the strongest conceivable sources of conviction.[21] The Word of God, first, the Lord Jesus whose decision not to write his teaching can be defended with good reasons,[22] and in the second place, the inspired writings of the Bible, possesses an authority which is absolute.[23] This authority is echoed by the teaching Church; the authority of the greatest Fathers and Doctors stands far below that of her perennial practice. Her traditional recognition, for example, of the right Jewish parents retain to refuse baptism for their children, cannot be shaken by any human protest, no matter how eminent its author may be: 'Not Jerome, not Augustine, not any Doctor whosoever' can enter the lists against her practice.[24] Church authority is expressed especially by the Bishop of Rome[25] and this prestige, participated in varying degrees, is not absent from more modest levels in the teaching Church; if the opinions of the Masters of Theology do not enjoy 'authority' in its most technical sense, they do carry weight.[26]

The scattered remarks by Aquinas persuade us that he can have had no quarrel with Bonaventure's census of the sources available to the student who wishes to 'add reason to faith.'[27]

First, the Word of God, transmitted in the canonical Scriptures; then, in a decrescendo of value, the personal writings, the *originalia*, of the Fathers, the derivative *summae* of the Masters (which are not always free from error) and, last of all, those 'waters of deception,' the gentile philosophers: Plato, Aristotle, Cicero, Plotinus.[28] Despite his reservations, Bonaventure was generous in accounting for deficiencies he ob-

---

21 "... haec doctrina non argumentatur ad sua principia probanda, quae sunt articuli fidei; sed ex eis procedit ad aliquid ostendendum..." *Summa theologiae* I, q. 1, a. 8; ed. Commissio Piana (Ottawa 1948) I, 7b.

22 See *Summa theologiae* III, q. 42, a. 4.

23 "Auctoritatibus autem canonicae Scripturae utitur proprie, ex necessitate argumentando. Auctoritatibus autem aliorum doctorum ecclesiae, quasi arguendo ex propriis, sed probabiliter. Innititur enim fides nostra revelationi Apostolis et Prophetis factae, qui canonicos libros scripserunt..." *Summa theologiae* I, q. 1, a. 8, ad 2; ed. cit. I, 8b.

24 "... maximam habet auctoritatem Ecclesiae consuetudo, quae semper est in omnibus aemulanda. Quia et ipsa doctrina Catholicorum Doctorum ab Ecclesia auctoritatem habet; unde magis standum est auctoritati Ecclesiae quam auctoritati vel Augustini vel Hieronymi vel cuiuscumque Doctoris. Hoc autem Ecclesiae usus nunquam habuit quod Iudaeorum filii invitis parentibus baptizarentur..." *Summa theologiae* II-II, q. 10, a. 12, ad 3; ed. cit. III, 1466b.

25 "Quae quidem auctoritas principaliter residet in Summo Pontifice..." *Summa theologiae* II-II, q. 11, a. 2, ad 3; ed. cit. III, 1469b.

26 M.-D. Chenu, *Toward Understanding St. Thomas* 135-136.

27 "... et sic est credibile, prout tamen credibile transit in rationem intelligibilis, et hoc per additionem rationis; et hoc modo, proprie loquendo, est subiectum in hoc libro." *In I Sent.* Proemii q. 1; ed. cit. I, 7.

28 *Collationes in Hexaemeron* 19, 7-15; *Sancti Bonaventurae Opera omnia* (Quaracchi 1882-1902) V, 421-422; for pagan philosophers, see ibid. 7, 3, ed. cit. V, 365 and *Sermo* IV, 18: ed. cit. V, 572.

served in Aristotle. If the Stagirite has proclaimed the eternity of the world, he might be excused because he spoke precisely as a philosopher of nature and intended to say no more than that the world could not have come to be by nature. [29] Aquinas was equally gentle with Aristotle on the point, but for another reason. Echoing Rabbi Moyses Aegyptius, he reminded his readers that, according to the *Topics*, the eternity of the world belongs among the "dialectical problems on which we do not have reasons,"[30] that is, reasonings of a compelling, demonstrative sort. Bonaventure thought that if Aristotle had missed the awesome realities of punishment and glory in the world to come, this too may have stemmed from his rigor in remaining within the limits of his discipline, this time Ethics; he may have thought that life is eternal despite a silence prompted by the formal focus of his classification of the sciences. Ethics, after all, deals with human living in this world. On the tortuous question as to whether a single and separate Intellect functions for all men, Bonaventure ascribed the affirmative solution, and not without reason, to the Commentator rather than to the Philosopher. [31]

Finally, owing to the fallibility of the Masters, caused in part by their poor understanding of the Fathers: *credunt se intelligere originalia, et non intelligunt,* Bonaventure's advice was to adhere to 'the more common path.'[32]

What stance did Aquinas adopt toward his theological colleagues, that elite corps, the *magistri Parisienses?*

The question resists a summary answer. True enough, the university world, despite occasional verbal lapses, distinguished sharply between the weight given to an *auctor* and the prestige granted to a living university professor. Roger Bacon's celebrated complaint that the practice of citing Alexander of Hales and Albert, the second still living, as *auctores* was a scandalous vagary[33] and Bonaventure's disclaimer that

29 *In Hexaemeron* 7, 1-2; ed. cit. V, 365.

30 "... expresse dicit in I libro *Top.*, quod quaedam sunt problemata dialectica, de quibus rationes non habemus, ut 'utrum mundus sit aeternus'." *Summa theologiae* I, q. 46, a. 1, c.; ed. cit. I, 294b; Moses ben Maimon: "Volo in hoc capitulo ostendere quod Aristoteles non inducit demonstrationem super antiquitate mundi secundum sententiam ipsius... Dicit enim in eo cuius non habemus rationem, vel est difficile ostendere nobis. Scito quod si dixerimus cur ita fuit, defectus est sicut si dixerimus, est mundus antiquus, an non. Haec sunt verba ipsius." *Rabi Mossei Aegyptii, Dux seu Director dubitantium aut perplexorum...* Augustini Iustiniani... recognitus (Paris 1520) 2, 16; fol. 48r-48v; the text of Aristotle is *Topica* 1, 11; 104b 16.

31 "... dicit Commentator quod ipse hoc sensit." *In Hexaemeron* 7, 2; ed. cit. V. 365; the text of Averroes is *In III de anima,* t.c. 5.

32 *In Hexaemeron* 19, 11; ed. cit. V, 422; see also *In II Sent.* Praelocutio, ed. cit. II, 1, for Bonaventure's pledge of allegiance to Alexander above all others.

33 Philosophy, Roger complained, was thought to have come to the Latins and" ... pro auctore allegatur compositor ejus. Nam sicut Aristoteles, Avicenna, Averroes allegantur in scholis, sic et ipse; et adhuc vivit, et habuit in vita sua auctoritatem, quam numquam homo habuit in doctrina."

in writing his imposing *Commentary on the Sentences* he aspired to be
no more than a humble *compilator*, not an *auctor*,[34] are intelligible only
in the presence of that distinction. Still, the whole body of Masters,
above all the Masters of Paris, enjoyed immense prestige when they
spoke with substantial unanimity; the day would come when Melchior
Cano would systematize the sources of theological doctrine and one of
his 'places,' *topoi*, would be the common teaching of the theologians
and canonists of the School.[35] Descartes was far from shy in setting out
the originality and the value of his *Meditations*, but he did not think
support from the Doctors of the Sorbonne nugatory.[36]

Certainly Brother Thomas spoke of them with respect. Did some
propagandist for 'heterodox Aristotelianism,' to borrow the felicitous
phrase of F. Van Steenberghen,[37] teach nonsense in corners to teen-
agers? 'He will find, not only me, the least of them, but many others
who are zealous for truth; through those others either his error will be
brought to a halt or something will be done for his ignorance!'[38] Those
'others' were, of course, the Masters of Paris.

Against this testimonial to teamwork is the well-known report by
Bernardus Lombardi, a few years after the canonization of Saint

---

Fratris Rogeri Bacon Opera quaedam hactenus inedita, ed. J. S. Brewer in: *Rerum Britannicarum
medii aevi scriptores* (London 1859) XV, 30; this remark from the *Opus tertium* bears on the then
living Albert, but there were two such: "Duos enim noto ibi, sed ipse est principalis in re; sed alius
majus nomen habet, qui tamen mortuus est, Ibid., 31 and: "Unus autem illorum duorum est mortuus, alius vivit; qui mortuus est fuit bonus homo... nam quum intravit ordinem Fratrum Minorum
fuit Deo maximus Minor..." *Opus minus*, 325, "Alter qui vivit intravit ordinem Fratrum puerulus...
Et vere laudo eum plus quam omnes de vulgo studentium..." ibid., 327; despite his reservations,
Roger thought Albert better than most Parisian theologians.

34 *In II Sent.* Praelocutio, ed. cit. II, 1.

35 "Septimus est auctoritas Theologorum scholasticorum, quibus adjungamus Juris pontificij
peritos. Nam Iuris hujus doctrina, quasi ex altera parte, scholasticae Theologiae respondet..."
Melchior Cano, *De locis theologicis* 1, 3, *Opera* (Lyon and Paris 1704) 3; like Aquinas, Cano set
limits on the weight to be granted to theological opinion: "Theologorum scholasticorum etiam
multorum testimonium, si alij contra pugnant viri docti, non plus valet ad faciendam fidem quam
vel ratio ipsorum, vel gravior etiam auctoritas comprobavit... Nec enim si quid aut Scoticis aut
Thomisticis pronunciatis contrarium est, error illico est." ibid. VIII, 4; 317.

36 "Atque ideo, qualescunque meae rationes esse possint, quia tamen ad Philosophiam spectant, non spero me illarum ope magnum operae pretium esse facturum, nisi me patrocinio vestro
adjuvetis. Sed cum tanta inhaereat omnium mentibus de vestra Facultate opinio, tantaeque sit
authoritatis SORBONAE nomen, ut non modo in rebus fidei nulli unquam Societati post sacra
Concilia tantum creditum sit quam vestrae, sed etiam in humana Philosophia nullibi major per-
spicacia et soliditas, nec ad ferenda judicia major integritas et sapientia esse existimetur..."
Meditationes de prima philosophia, Epistola, *Œuvres de Descartes* edd. C. Adam and P. Tannery
(Paris 1897-1909) VII, 5.

37 F. Van Steenberghen, *Siger de Brabant d'après ses œuvres inédites* in: *Les philosophes
Belges XII and XIII, Siger dans l'histoire de l'Aristotélisme* (Louvain 1942) II.

38 "... et inveniet non solum me, qui aliorum sum minimus, sed multos alios veritatis zelatores,
per quos ejus errori resistetur, vel ignorantiae consuletur." *Sancti Thomae Aquinatis opuscula omnia*, ed. J. Perrier (Paris 1949), *De unitate intellectus* I, 120.

Thomas, that his view on the distinction between created *esse* and *essentia* was in opposition to that of all the Parisian Masters.[39] He and they were 'zealous for truth', but this had not resulted in unanimity on a fundamental, if metaphysical, issue. The great Masters who had preceded him, of whom Peter Lombard and the Victorines are the most notable, often inspired serious reservations on the part of Aquinas. As for his own contemporaries, he advised students faced with magistral dissent that each one ought to feel free to follow the solution that pleased him best, provided always that the controverted question remained unresolved by the teaching Church.[40] Neither a single Master nor all Masters in concert could generate 'authority' as such; still, it is clear that Aquinas thought their solutions worth weighing. The question remains: How and on what criteria did Brother Thomas nuance the air of *stare decisis* that magistral determinations enjoyed? In the absence of a systematic theoretical treatment by Aquinas on what degree of deference might be due to the Master of the *Sentences*, or to the Masters of Paris when they spoke with one voice, the eight controverted questions listed by Bonaventure make possible an appeal to the practice of Aquinas within limits that match, in their order, the controlled conditions of laboratory experiment.

II

1. In the first of the eight questions the Masters were to reject the view of Peter Lombard that 'The Holy Spirit is the love or charity by which we love God and neighbor,' the 'very same Holy Spirit by which the Father and the Son love each Other and love us.'[41] Had not Saint John asserted unequivocally that 'God is love' (1 Jo 4:16)? Augustine's exposition of that saying proceeds from his profound conviction that nothing is more intimate to the soul than is God: Nothing can be more known to us than is God because nothing is 'more present, more in-

---

39 "In ista questione erunt duo articuli: primus de hoc, quod queritur, an in creaturis differat esse et essencia; secundus, an in Deo sint idem. Quantum ad primum in genere est duplex modus dicendi: Primus est doctoris Sancti Thome, qui ponit, quod in omnibus citra Deum differt esse ab essencia; secundus est omnium aliorum concorditer Parisyensium, qui dicunt oppositum; et isti distinguuntur tripliciter secundum quod ponunt diversas declarationes." Cited by J. Koch, "Durandus de s. Porciano," *Beiträge zur Geschichte der Philosophie des Mittelalters* 26.1 (1927) 330, note 60; see use made of this by E. Gilson, *Being and Some Philosophers* 213, note 28.

40 *Quodlibeta* III, a. 10, c.

41 *Petri Lombardi, Libri IV Sententiarum*, Liber I, d. 17, capp. 1-3, (Quaracchi 1916) I, 106-109; for the commentary by Aquinas *Sancti Thomae Aquinatis, Scriptum super libros Sententiarum Magistri Petri Lombardi Episcopi Parisiensis*, ed. P. Mandonnet and M. F. Moos (Paris 1929-1947) *In I Sent.* d. 17, q. 1, a. 1; I. 391-397.

terior, more certainly grasped.' To be holy is to be emptied of pride and to brim with love; that sanctifying love is God.[42]

Bonaventure noted that Lombard himself had faced 'many opponents' of this authoritatively supported thesis: 'Of old' there had been two opinions on the matter.[43] Aquinas formulated his personal opposition in a *sed contra* which, far from adducing theological authority, invokes three metaphysical arguments.

First, Thomas echoed the Boethian insight[44] that 'whatever is received is received according to the measure of what receives.' The Holy Spirit is 'received' by creatures but as 'participated'; He is received in a finite measure, which is as much as to say that our participation in the divine is finite and, in consequence, creaturely. Second, it is a function of charity as sanctifying love to restore the likeness to God in which our race was created and from which our race has fallen. If Genesis established these facts, a metaphysical conceptual scheme must be ready to assign the ground for this, as for any other, likeness.[45] Every ground of likeness is a determined, finite, and therefore created structuring, that is to say, every ground of likeness must be created form. Third, God is present to those who have been sanctified in a way that transcends His inevitable presence to all and to any of His works. There is a real diversity between the mode in which

---

42 Peter was anxious that his readers recognize the authoritative basis for his opinion, "Ne autem in re tanta aliquid de nostro influere videamur, sacris auctoritatibus quod dictum est corroboremus" loc. cit. I, 106, § 144, chief among them the exegesis of 1 Jo. 4, 16 by Augustine, *De trinitate* VIII, 7-8; PL 42, 957 ff.

43 *In I Sent.* d. 17, pars 1, a. unicus, q. 1; I, 238; the division of learned opinion that Bonaventure noted "ab antiquo" persisted; Albert complained that although "communiter fere omnes meliores concordant," and that "contradicendum est Magistro in ista parte," not all saw it that way: "Hic sunt quaedam absurditates dictae a quibusdam." Duns Scotus was to deal with the issue very briefly in his *Commentarii Oxonienses, Opera omnia* (Paris 1891-1895) X, 39-40, but more at length in his *Reportata Parisiensia*, ed. cit. XXII, 206; his effort to provide Peter Lombard with a pious interpretation involved him in one exchange on devotional experience that was to prompt a harsh comment by Denis the Carthusian: "Introducit demum Scotus... multas difficultates (ut apparet) supervacuas, curiosas, quibus immorari, magis videtur fractio capitis et impedimentum devotionis quam occupatio fructuosa." *In I Sent.* d. 17, q. 1, a. 1; *Doctoris Ecstatici D. Dionysii Cartusiani Opera Omnia* (Tournai 1896-1906) XX, 16 A-B; both Albert, ed. cit. XXV 462, § 3 and 463 ad 3, and Richard of Middleton, *Svper Qvatvor Libros Sententiarvm* (Brixiae 1591) loc. cit.; I, 156, felt that the Master of Sentences had given aid and comfort to the Pelagians, whereas Bonaventure had only the mildest of censures for the Master on this point: "Et in his omnibus verum dixit nec erravit, sed defecit..." ed. cit. I, 238.

44 "Omne enim quod cognoscitur non secundum sui uim sed secundum cognoscentium potius comprehenditur facultatem." *Boethii Philosophiae Consolationis* liber V, prosa 4; edd. H. F. Stewart and E. K. Rand (London and Cambridge, Mass. 1946) 388; "... omne quod scitur non ex sua sed ex conprehendentium natura cognoscitur..." ibid. prosa 6; 398.

45 Is it necessary tor remark that Aquinas was conscious of the enigmas provoked by attempts to account for likeness on any plane? See, for instance, his discussion of Aristotle's rejection of Plato's Ideas, *Metaphysica* I, 9; 990a34 - 991a8, in *Metaphysicam Aristotelis Commentaria*, ed. M.-R. Cathala (Turin 1935) Liber I, lectio 14, 73-76, § 208-216.

God is present to any and to all creatures and the mode in which He is present to His saints. But no diversity within God can be adduced as ground for that diversity; God remains supremely One and free from all inner division: 'With respect to all the real, He possesses Himself in an identical fashion.'[46] Hence, that diversity of the divine Presence to the just, as distinguished from His Presence to all that He has made, must be rooted within creatures, diversely related to Him.[47]

Given these metaphysically based negations, nothing remains but that the just are justified by a finite, created form, an effect of divine Goodness, without which nothing is good,[48] patterned by exemplarity on the Holy Spirit, but effected by the total Trinity. Thanks to this form, which is 'charity,' the justified man is pleasing to God; thanks to the same gift, he can act in meritorious fashion. As God has communicated true being to creatures in His creative act, for He is the efficient Cause of all and has caused the world to be according to exemplarity, so in the order of the New Creation, our being is dependent and participated, but, for all that, autonomous and responsible. The result of creation is no pantheistic extension of the Creator into His creation; each creature exists and acts with an autonomy that is totally contingent and dependent, but also genuinely and incommunicatively its own. In the order of being, the act of existing argues the presence of a corresponding form, and here once more Boethian wisdom is just beneath the Thomistic surface: 'All being is from form.'[49] In the parallel order of grace, meritorious acting discloses the form that is disinterested love or 'charity.'

Against this, as Aquinas read him, Peter Lombard had held that 'charity' is not a habit created within the soul. In his view, created 'charity' could be no more than the act that proceeds from a free choice moved by the Holy Spirit, *ex libero arbitrio moto per Spiritum sanctum*, and it is only Uncreated Love, the Holy Spirit Himself, whom Peter named 'charity' *tout court.*[50]

---

46   Loc. cit. "Sed ista diversitas non potest poni ex parte ipsius Dei, qui eodem modo se habet ad omnia." ed. cit. I, 393.

47   Ibid.; see also *Summa theologiae* I, q. 4, a. 3, especially ad 2 and ad 3, ed. cit. I, 26a-26b; finally, the asymmetrical aspect of our similarity to God is set out in the same place, ad 4; I, 26b, with the support of an authoritative text from the *Divine Names* of Denis.

48   Ibid. I, 394.

49   "Omne namque esse ex forma est." *De Trinitate* II; ed. H. F. Stewart and E. K. Rand (London, Cambridge, Mass. 1946) 8.

50   Aquinas has expressed the Master's opinion more lucidly than he had found it in the *Sentences*: "Magister tamen vult quod charitas non sit aliquis habitus creatus in anima, sed quod sit tantum actus, qui est ex libero arbitrio moto per Spiritum sanctum — quem (that is, the Holy Spirit) "charitatem' dicit" is the line, loc. cit. I, 394; I have adjusted the punctuation of the edition in this citation.

Both Bonaventure and Aquinas rejected an inept comparison made by some theologians between visible light and the Holy Spirit. In itself, those theologians had reasoned, light is but light, whereas, embodied in lightsome material, the same light is a color. Thus, the third Person of the Trinity, in Himself, is styled 'the Holy Spirit' and 'God'; as dwelling within the soul which He moves to loving acts, the same Holy Spirit is styled 'charity.' This uniting of the Holy Spirit with souls was conceived to be the doing of the Trinity of Persons, although 'terminating' with the third Person alone. Aquinas was careful to preclude this bizarre suggestion of what would amount to a kind of incarnation of the Holy Spirit in each of the redeemed on the ground that such an explanation fails to give due weight to the proximate, causal condition of creaturely activity, that is, to created, habitual form.[51] Bonaventure, we may note, argued by exclusion to the same result. If that solution be conceded, then justification is either by nature or by grace; surely not by nature, for redemption is gratuitous; if by grace, then his opponent has been compelled to grant precisely the contrary of what his argument purported to establish, namely, that redeeming charity is a created gift and not the Creator Himself.[52]

When Aquinas came to deal with this issue many years later in the *Summa theologiae* he added the observation that Lombard's exposition tended to diminish rather than to elevate charity. The view proposed by the Master would reduce the human person to the status of a passive object of exterior compulsion in violation of our voluntary structuring as free agents, for such a status is appropriate to merely corporeal beings, bereft of freedom. At best we should be mere instruments for whom 'the voluntary' and 'the meritorious' could have no authentic meaning. Last, the *Summa* discussion is one of the places where Aquinas thought it right to advert to the Platonism with which Augustine had been imbued and to the misleading language this entailed.[53]

2. The second commonly rejected thesis from the *First Book of Sentences* is that the numerical predications used in trinitarian statements

---

51 Loc. cit. I, 394: "ad cujus explanationem..."; Albert, it may be noted, was particularly exercised by the misunderstanding of the nature of light evinced by this analogy ("quoddam valde grossum falsum..." ed. cit. XXV, 464) whereas Bonaventure, like Aquinas, confined himself to a theologically grounded denial: "Sed haec positio non potest stare, quia Spiritus sanctus non est unibilis..." ed. cit. I, 238.

52 Ibid.: "... si esset unibilis, aut per naturam aut per gratiam..."

53 "Hic enim modus loquendi consuetus est apud Platonicos, quorum doctrinis imbutus fuit Augustinus. Quod quidam non advertentes, ex verbis eius sumpserunt occasionem errandi." *Summa theologiae* II-II, q. 23, a. 2, c.; ed. cit. III, 1522b.

have but negative force.[54] Aquinas surveyed speculation on the notion
of unity and found a discrepancy between 'philosophers' and 'masters.'
Avicenna, for instance, identified the 'one' convertible with being with
the 'one' that functions as the principle of number; hence, he could not
deny that predications of the numerical 'one' make a positive addition
to the subjects of which that 'one' is asserted. Avicenna counted as a
philosopher, but there were theologians, that is, masters to follow his
lead. Still, if not all masters opposed the opinion associated with the
Arabian philosopher, not all philosophers had agreed with the position
of Avicenna: Aristotle before him and Averroes after him denied that
the 'one' convertible with being can be identified with the 'one' that
grounds our counting. This, wrote Aquinas, is a rational decision. The
Philosopher and the Commentator held that the numerical 'one' posits
an addition in the order of being, to be precise, in the order of the
'being of measure,' and thus is intelligible in itself and renders intelligible both succeeding numbers and continuous quantities. Aquinas
also reported that some held a middle position: With Avicenna they
demanded only a rational distinction between the 'one' convertible with
being and the 'one' of number, whereas, with Aristotle, they agreed that
the 'one' convertible with being makes no positive addition to the subject of which it is predicated.

As for Aquinas, the 'one' and the 'unity' that belong to quantity can
have no place in divine predication; only the 'one' convertible with

54 *Petri Lombardi, Libri IV Sententiarum,* Liber I, d. 24, cap. unic., ed. cit. I, 153-156;
Aquinas, *In I Sent.* d. 24, q. 1, a. 1, ed. cit. I, 579-585; Peter was persuaded that, should the
authoritative texts be examined carefully, "magis videtur horum verborum usus introductus ratione
removendi atque excludendi a simplicitate deitatis que ibi non sunt, quam ponendi aliqua," loc.
cit. 154. Albert agreed with the Master to a point: "Est enim *numerus* discretae quantitatis... Et ex
illa ratione videtur procedere Magister in *Littera*: quia sine dubio nulla talis discretio separans
unum ab alio est vel potest in divinis..." However, Albert claimed that the Master had failed
to notice another meaning of "number": "Quarto modo dicitur *numerus* ex parte rei numeratae
secundum quid et non simpliciter, scilicet causata pluralitas a distinguente quocumque modo... et
hoc modo solo numerus positive cadit in divinis: et in hac numeri consideratione diminutus est
Magister..." Albert, *In I Sent.* d. 24, A, a. 1; ed. cit. XXV, 606-607. Scotus, like Aquinas, was to
side with the Master. "Ad quaestionem vero secundum ultimam opinionem est dicendum, sicut
Magister dicit, quod numero in divinis magis utimur ad removendum quam ad ponendum
aliquid...," *In I Sent.* d. 24, q. unica; ed. cit. XXII, 281, as did Richard of Middleton, "... unitas in
Deo ponit divinam essentiam, et nihil aliud positiuum dicit..." *In I Sent.* d. 24, a. 1; ed. cit. I, 218;
finally, Durandus drew the fire of Denis the Carthusian, "Durandus quoque circa haec multa
scribit, in quibus praeallegatis contradicit doctoribus in nonnullis, sed inepte: quod prolixitatem
vitans, non prosequor." *In I Sent.* d. 24, q. 2; ed. cit. XX, 178; in fact, Durandus contradicted all
parties: "... Nec potest dicere solum idipsum quod ens et sub eadem ratione, quia esset negatio
dicendo ens unum quod non est verum. Necesse est ergo, quod dicat aliquam rationem circa ens.
Et illa est ratio indivisionis quae est ratio privativa... multitudo quae est de transeuntibus et
reperitur in divinis ut et esse unum quod convertitur cum ente, et de hac dicunt quidam quod eius
formalis ratio est privativa... Istud autem non videtur bene dictum... unius sit privativa oportet
quod ratio multitudinis sit positiva." *In I Sent.* d. 24, q. 1; *D. Dvrandi a sancto Porciano... in Petri
Lombardi Sententias Theologicas Commentariorum Libri IIII* (Venice 1571) I, 71v-72r.

being can be said of the Lord and these terms add no connotation to their denotation. They remain exclusively negative: *nihil addunt...nisi rationem negationis tantum.* [55] Nor was the more mature theologian of the *Summa theologiae* to unsay what he had said in the *Scriptum in Sententias*: 'As far as this is concerned, the Master has expressed the truth in the *Sentences.*' [56] If Aquinas was right, the Masters were wrong *communiter.*

3. The first of the two generally rejected theses from the *Second Book of Sentences* asserted that reward preceded merit in the case of the angels. [57] Genuine merit, in an economy of grace, entails for its theologians the twin perils of Pelagianism and unintelligibility. [58] Aquinas had met the first by his affirmative determination of the question immediately preceding the one here at stake: 'Whether angels needed grace in order that they might be converted to God?' [59] He met the second peril by conceding with candor the incoherence of positing a 'reward' apart from genuine merit, [60] and by distinguishing the order of time from the order of nature. In the prior question, he had made use of the natural parallelism between the 'instant' in which a substantial form

---

55   Loc. cit. 583.

56   *Summa theologiae* I, q. 30, a. 3, c.; ed. cit. I, 201b.

57   *Petri Lombardi, Libri IV Sententiarum*, Liber II, d. 5, cap. 6; ed. cit. I, 328-329; Aquinas, *In II Sent.* d. 5, q. 2, a. 2; ed. cit. II, 152-155; it ought to be noted that Peter introduced a cluster of theological opinions in addition to the one rejected by the Parisian Masters: "Aliis autem videtur, quod beatitudinem, quam receperunt in confirmationem per gratiam tunc appositam, non meruerint, dicentes, tunc non fuisse eis gratiam collatam ad merendum, sed ad beate vivendum; nec tunc eius datum esse bonum, quo mererentur, sed quo feliciter fruerentur. Quod autem tunc in praemium acceperunt, per obsequia nobis exhibita ex Deo obedientia et reverentia, mereri dicunt; et ita praemium praecessit merita..." *loc. cit.* 329. Bonaventure was willing to concede that the view proposed by the Master and his followers was "probabilis," but he thought the opposing one "rationabilior... et melius habet fundamentum." He concluded with a turn of phrase Aquinas would not have used: "Hanc communiter tenent moderní doctores; ideo huic adhaerendum est." *In I Sent.* d. 5, a. 3, q. 2; ed. cit. II, 151.

58   Although Aquinas has not mentioned the Pelagian peril here, he had done so in his presentation of the first of the eight controverted questions, ed. cit. I, 392, 397. See also his *Disputed Question, De caritate*, q. unica, a. 1; *Opera omnia* (Parma 1852-1873) VIII, 581, 583; against this background he wrote in the present question: "...facile intelligi potest ex his quae supra dicta sunt. Sicut enim actus liberi arbitrii est dispositio ad gratiam, ita actus informatus est meritum gloriae. Unde unus et idem conversionis motus est praeparatio ad gratiam secundum quod est ex libero arbitrio, et meritorius gloriae, secundum quod est gratia informatus: et iterum fruitionis actus, secundum quod completur per habitum gloriae." loc. cit. 154.

59   Ed. cit. II, 150-152.

60   In rejecting one proposed solution, an important aspect of Peter Lombard's total position, that grace had been given to the angels, not in order that they might merit, but that they might live well (see above, note 57), Aquinas wrote: "Hoc autem non videtur conveniens, quia beatitudo habet rationem praemii: praemium autem sine merito esse non potest, sicut nec poena sine culpa." loc. cit. 153; Durandus, once more, provides an idiosyncratic view: "Argumentum etiam in oppositum deficit, quia contra iustitiam esset infligere poenam sine demerito, sed gratiae est dare praemium sine merito," *In II Sent.* d. 5, q. 3; ed. cit. I, 143v.

is induced and the non-continuous motion of voluntary decision.[61] In the present question, he has used a comparable philosophical distinction between truly causal and merely chronological sequences. Thus the pious interpretation suggested by Brother Thomas hinges upon a distinction well-grounded in Aristotle[62] and it is one he proposed 'in company with others,' *videtur cum aliis dicendum...*[63]

Thanks to this distinction, Aquinas could conclude that the Master was not wrong, even though the Masters who had rejected Lombard's thesis were right. Had the angels been created 'in grace,' the priority of their merit with respect to their reward would have been beyond doubting; Peter Lombard, however, seemed to have been of the contrary opinion, that is, that the angels had not been created 'in grace.' This had led him to state the thesis that the Masters found disturbing, namely, that the reward of the angels had preceded their merit. Aquinas acknowledged that their misgivings were not empty ones: For him as for them, 'reward' where genuine merit is lacking was as intolerable as 'punishment' without guilt. Still, even had the angels not been created 'in grace,' and if the grace that makes creaturely activity meritorious had been given to them, chronologically speaking, 'with' their reward of glory, it must be said (with the Parisian Masters) that the reward preceded merit for, in the order of nature, this would have been the case. In the chronological order, however, reward would not have preceded their merit (as the Master of the *Sentences* had claimed).

Here, too, the *Summa theologiae* is, if anything, more clearly sensitive to the truth Peter Lombard wished to defend than is the *Scriptum*. The activity of the angels was meritorious in the order of salvation only because it was suffused with grace. That grace stood in an authentically causal relationship to the reward which is beatitude only because it was, in a significant way, prior to that reward: 'They are said to have

---

61 "In eodem enim instanti quod primo est dispositio necessitans in materia, forma substantialis inducitur... Motus autem voluntatis qui disponit ad gratiam est simplex et non continuus; ideo vel primus tantum est sufficiens dispositio ad gratiam, vel ultimus inter plures, qui agit in virtute omnium praecedentium: et ideo cum illo gratia infunditur." loc. cit. 151-152; Durandus would not allow chronological simultaneity and causal priority as a means for easing the difficulty: "... non solum natura, imo tempore meritum praecessit praemium... actus qui includunt oppositionem circa statum operantis non possunt esse simul... mereri est illius qui est in statu acquirentis et tendentis ad terminum. Praemium autem respicit statum non acquirentis sed possidentis, nec tendentis ad terminum, sed iam existentis in termino...", ed. cit. I, 143v.

62 V.g. *Metaphysica* 5, 11; 1018b 9-1019a 14.

63 "Et ideo videtur cum aliis dicendum quod meritum in eis non praecessit praemium tempore, sed natura..." loc. cit. 154; Scotus handled the issue with his accustomed precision: "... aliter dicitur, quod prius natura est meritum quam praemium... Sed an meritum praecedit praemium prioritate durationis? Teneo igitur de bonis, quod prius merentur quam percipiant beatitudinem. Sed de malis angelis dicitur quod non prius duratione peccant quam sint obstinati... fuerunt in termino in primo instanti in quo peccaverunt." *In II Sent.* d. 5, q. unica; ed. cit. XXII, 612.

merited and so, merit preceded reward. And this, I avow, pleases me more,' Peter had written.[64] Aquinas was to echo this in the *Summa* text: 'And, therefore, it is better said that the angel possessed grace before he was rendered blessed — through which grace he merited beatitude.'[65]

4. Next, Aquinas knew that there were those to say, and the Master seems to have shared their opinion, that the 'truth' of the child consists exclusively of what has come to him from his parents. The growth of that parental contribution, therefore, to the quantity that marks the adult, entails no real addition; the food the child eats does not enter into his 'true' being.[66] A cognate view has found expression in our time and it is not without significance that a great novelist has put on the lips of a Cabbalistic mystagogue the jibe that a man is no more than 'a pipe of flesh.'[67] Some mediaeval exegetes, Peter Lombard the most influential among them, thought this a helpful way to understand the saying of Matthew 15:17 — what ends in the drain was never 'truly' man and so will never see resurrection![68]

Brother Thomas arraigned this opinion in his *Scriptum* as 'irrational' for it does justice neither to the man who grows nor to the sustaining food, thanks to which he grows. If Peter Lombard and his followers were right, growth could come to pass only by rarefaction or by the creation of new material; neither alternative is a rational explanation. Nothing remains but to allow that what had been the matter of another corporeal entity has been transmuted by digestion into the body that grows. Much as respect for the coherence of natural sequences had impelled Aquinas to insist that there can be no 'reward' where there has been no genuine merit, so respect for the coherence of biological reality has led him to defend the totality of the human; man is what he eats; what he eats becomes truly man.

How serene the good sense of Aquinas here! Alas, he would not always succeed so well in his efforts to solve scatological dubeities in an eschatological perspective. One contemporary of ours, who rides to the prestige of Aquinas with a loose rein, has mentioned some *topoi* where

---

64   Loc. cit. 329.

65   "Et ideo melius dicendum est quod gratiam habuit angelus antequam esset beatus, per quam beatitudinem meruit," *Summa theologiae* I, q. 62, a. 4, c.; ed. cit. I, 374b.

66   *Petri Lombardi, Libri IV Sententiarum*, Liber II, d. 30, cap. 15; ed. cit. I, 467-468; Aquinas, *In II Sent.* d. 30, q. 2, a. 1; ed. cit. II, 776-787.

67   "... what can we say we really know about man? That he is, when all is said and done, just a passage for liquids and solids, a pipe of flesh..." words ascribed to Balthasar by L. Durrell, *Justine,* Part II, (London 1961) 93.

68   Peter and Brother Thomas cite only Matthew 15:17 in this connection, Brother Bonaventure added Mark 7:18-19 as well as the *Glossa ordinaria* on this pericope.

he holds Aquinas guilty of 'nonsense and superstition' worthy of commendation to 'connoisseurs of the absurd.'[69] Prominent among them is the assertion that the whole man, intestines and all, will rise from the grave, but that 'noble fluids rather than base superfluities will fill them...'[70] Was it not a tactical blunder for Aquinas to have dealt with a syllogism that impugned total resurrection by claiming that full intestines would be too base for the world to come, apart from a certain amelioration, and empty ones impossible in a Nature that abhors a vacuum?

5. In his *Third Book of Sentences* Peter Lombard faced, in company with all Christian theologians, some perplexing questions posed for the philosophy of man by the theology of Incarnation. Peter's way of accounting for the persistent denial by the Church that what the divine Person of the Word assumed in the Incarnation of the Lord is a human person was to claim that a soul is not a person while it is united to some other reality in such a way as to constitute a person with that other reality, a mode of union he designated by the adverb *personaliter*. This entails a conclusion he did not fail to draw: A human soul, separated from the body by death, is a person as is an angel, by nature bereft of body.[71] Since the human soul of Jesus was at no point not united to another Reality, its assumption by the second Person is not the assumption of a person by a Person. Needless to insist, it was not the fact that Jesus is not a human person which was rejected by the theologians who disclaimed Peter's explanation of that fact.

Aquinas noted that many among the 'ancients' had held just a view of man as did Peter Lombard: Gregory of Nyssa (Nemesius), Plato, and Hugh of Saint Victor are the 'ancients' he named, opposed by only one ancient, Aristotle, 'whom all the moderns follow.' The Philosopher's generally accepted conviction that soul is 'united to body as is form to

---

69 D. J. O'Connor, *Aquinas and Natural Law* (London, Melbourne, Toronto 1967) 1, 89; the text is cited from *Summa theologiae*, q. 80, a. 1, ad 2; ed. cit. V, 373*b; as is well known, a fourteenth century editor, whose identity has not been established, continued the *Summa theologiae* of Aquinas beyond III, q. 90, the point at which Thomas had died (see ed. cit. V, v); the material for the argument against total resurrection was borrowed from *In IV Sent.* d. 44, q. 1, a. 2 and the response of Aquinas from *In IV Sent.* d. 44, q. 1, a. 2, quaestiuncula 5, ad 2; the Mandonnet-Moos edition cited hithertofore does not extend this far so the reader is referred to the *Opera omnia* (Parma 1852-1873) VII-II, 1075 ff.

70 "Dicendum quod intestina resurgent in corpore, sicut et alia membra. Et plena erunt, non quidem turpibus superfluitatibus, sed nobilibus humiditatibus." loc. cit.

71 *Petri Lombardi, Libri IV Sententiarum*, Liber III, d. 5, cap. 3; ed. cit. II, 571-573; Aquinas, *In III Sent.* d. 5, q. 3, a. 2; ed. cit.III, 206-207; Peter's opinion is expressed in a line: "... anima non est persona, quando alii rei est unita personaliter, sed quando per se est: absoluta enim a corpore persona est, sicuti Angelus..." loc. cit. 1772.

matter' entails the conclusion that a separated soul is neither an instance of human nature, since a part is not a whole, nor a person, for
the notion of 'part' is opposed by contrariety to that of 'person.' For as
long as a soul is separated from the body it once informed, that soul is
not actually a part of the former composite, but it continues to retain a
structure, thanks to which it is 'born,' adapted by nature, to be such a
part.[72]

Beyond all merely technical philosophical concerns is the dignity and
integrity of the human person. The soul, separated at death from what
it had rendered a human body, cannot be a 'person' in isolation from
that body without demeaning the role of the material in constituting our
reality. If only the name of Aristotle could be invoked against the
ranked 'ancients,' saints included, Brother Thomas and his colleagues
thought reason on the side of the beleaguered Philosopher.

6. The second controverted position from the *Third Book* is closely
related to the preceding one. Lombard argued that Jesus was still truly
a man during the three day period after crucifixion and before resurrection.[73] Hugh of Saint Victor[74] and Peter had reached an identical conclusion by diverse roads. For Hugh, the totality of human personality is
constituted by the soul and thus, the separated soul can be called 'man,'
not only in the case of Jesus, but in the case of Everyman as well. Peter
restricted this state of affairs to Christ alone on the ground that even in
death His human soul and human body remained in some way united
with each other because each remained united with the eternal Word.[75]

Not even this limited claim, Brother Thomas held, can be admitted:
Only when soul informs body is man present. Dead flesh is called

---

72   That of Aquinas is expressed with equal economy: "Unde anima est pars humanae naturae,
et non natura quaedam per se. Et quia ratio partis contrariatur rationi personae... quamvis
separata non sit pars actu, tamen habet naturam ut sit pars." loc. cit. 207, § 111.

73   *Petri Lombardi, Libri IV Sententiarum*, Liber III, d. 22, cap. 1; ed. cit. II, 650-651;
Aquinas, *In III Sent.* d. 22, cap. 1; ed. cit. II, 650-651; Aquinas, *In III Sent.* d. 22, q. 1, a. 1; ed. cit.
III, 662-664.

74   The significance of this is that Peter's departure from Hugh's more simplistic explanation
was both noticed by Aquinas ("... opinio fuit Magistri et etiam Hugonis de Sancto Victore quod
Christus in illo triduo fuerit homo; sed ad hoc movebantur *diversis viis*.") and used by him to con-
trive a pious interpretation, see below, note 76; for the Master claimed that the case of the Incarnate Lord was a special one, not to be accounted for by a theory that would make every human
soul after death a "man": "... Magister non voluit quod alii post mortem essent homines, sed solum
hoc voluit de Christo..."; loc. cit. p. 663, § 12 and § 14.

75   Peter's explanation, far from depending upon an over-arching philosophy of man, invoked
the independence of the mysteries of faith from philosophical restrictions: "... fidei sacramentum a
philosophicis argumentis est liberum... Dicimus ergo, in morte Christi Deum vere fuisse hominem,
et tamen mortuum; et hominem quidem nec mortalem nec immortalem, quia unitus erat animae et
carni seiunctis..." loc. cit. 650.

'flesh' by equivocation only and here, of course, Aquinas is at one with Aristotle: The dead eye is an 'eye' only by equivocation, the dead man a 'man' by equivocation only.[76]

But here Aquinas unexpectedly offered a benign interpretation based precisely upon the Aristotelian pronouncement. Peter had indeed spoken equivocally, but he had intended to do just that. Had not the Master remarked that Christ was termed 'man' between cross and resurrection on grounds other than those that had justified the same predication before His death? Christ was truly named 'man' but not on the same basis as are other men. Aquinas thus departed from the strict letter of Peter's solution, but did not accept to the letter the sweeping condemnation of the Master on this point by the Parisian Masters of Theology.

7. Was the baptism of John such that for some it precluded the necessity of receiving the 'baptism of Jesus' later?[77] Some thought that this had been the case and Aquinas noted that 'it seems this was the opinion of the Master in the text.' The Acts of the Apostles, 19:1-7, speaks of Ephesian believers who had been given the 'baptism of John,' but who had not so much as heard whether there be a Holy Spirit; the Apostles baptized them 'in the name of Jesus,' laid hands upon them, and they received the Holy Spirit. Did this imply, the theologians asked, another set of converts, men baptized by John, but baptized in view of the Lord whose coming he proclaimed and equipped with trinitarian conceptions, for whom baptism by the Apostles had not been necessary? A text from Jerome encouraged Peter Lombard to think that this had been the case: 'Those who were not aware of the Holy Spirit when they received baptism from John were baptized again,' Jerome had written.[78] Ambrose reinforced this impression: 'Some denied that

---

76 Aquinas here has cited Aristotle simply "in IV Metaphysicorum" and the editor has expanded this citation to book *gamma*, chapter 4; by an evident misprint, the Bekker number 1106b, 13, has been substituted for 1006b, 13; but Aquinas seems to have had in mind rather the characterization of man as a "besouled biped" given at *Metaphysica* IV, 4; 1006a 32, see his *In Metaphysicam Aristotelis Commentaria*, Liber IV, lectio 7, ed. M.-R. Cathala (Turin 1935) 206-207, § 613; finally, no reader of Aristotle, and least of all Aquinas, can have failed to remember *De anima* II, 1; 412b 18-25, *De interpretatione* 11; 21a 17-29, especially 23; *Metaphysica* I, 9; 991a 5-8, in all of which equivocal uses of such terms are at stake and the Philosopher cautions us on their use; Aquinas credits the Master with having been fully aware of this and of having legitimately employed a consciously chosen equivocal turn of speech. loc. cit. 664, § 17.

77 *Petri Lombardi, Libri IV Sententiarum*, Liber IV, d. 2, cap. 6; ed. cit. II, 753-754; Aquinas, *In IV Sent.* d. 2, q. 2, a. 4; ed. cit. IV, 100-103.

78 Peter also cited another text from Jerome, ed. cit. 753, note 3, to the same effect; taken to the letter neither pericope supports the inference that, since there were believers baptized by John to whom the Holy Spirit was unknown and who were therefore baptized by the Apostles with a trinitarian formula, there must have been another group whose situation required no more than the laying on of hands.

they knew a Holy Spirit when they said that they had been baptized with the baptism of John — who had baptized, not in his own name, but in that of the approaching Jesus. These, therefore, who had been baptized neither in the name of Christ, nor with faith in the Holy Spirit, could not have received the sacrament of baptism. They, therefore, were baptized in the name of Christ; in the case of these men, baptism was not "repeated" but "newly bestowed," *novatum*.'[79] Peter was moved to complete what seemed to him the implication of the biblical anecdote: 'Those, however, who had not put their hope in the baptism of John and who believed in Father, Son, and Holy Spirit, were not baptized afterwards...'[80]

Thomas Aquinas rejected the opinion of the Master, not on the questionable logic of the exegesis he had adopted, but on two generally applicable principles of sacramental theology. First, the subjective dispositions of hope and faith are irrelevant to the efficacy of sacraments as such; their effectiveness is rooted exclusively in the 'very doing of what is done.'[81] Second, if something pertains to the substance of a sacrament — here the trinitarian formula of baptism and not the trinitarian faith of the baptized — should have been omitted, then the defective 'sacrament' is to be repeated.[82] Of all the eight controverted questions, this one alone has drawn from Aquinas a discussion from which all specifically 'philosophical' considerations are absent.

8. Peter was anxious to defend the claim of Church and priesthood that the Lord has communicated to men the power to forgive sin. Since some theologians has assimilated the power to forgive sin to the power to create in order to deny the first by an *a pari* argument, the Master

---

79   The text cited from Ambrose is notable for the precision that the rite of the Apostles was not a re-baptism but a baptism conferred for the first time.

80   Loc. cit. 754; Scotus is one of those who tried to save the Lombard thesis: "... dico quod Baptisma Joannis potest intelligi uno modo, quod baptizavit tantum in nomine venturi, et sic remanebant obligati ab eo ad suscipiendum Baptisma Christi... Alio modo potest intelligi Joannes baptizasse Baptismo Christi, potuit enim audisse discipulos Christi baptizasse, et formam quam tenerent... Et sic dico quod... non erant iterum baptizandi, et ita potest salvari dictum Magistri..." *In IV Sent.* d. 2, q. 2; ed. cit. XXIII, 573-574; Dionysius the Carthusian stood on firmer exegetical ground: "Verum non reor Joannem baptizasse Baptismo Christi, quia praecursoris habebat officium, et Scriptura apertissime protestatur eum usum baptismo distincto ac differenti a Baptismate Christi. Nec ulla auctoritas videtur hoc edocere, quod Joannes baptizaverit in forma baptismatis quam tradidit Christus..." *In IV Sent.* d. 2, q. 5; ed. cit. XXIV, 95; but the Masters in general, Brother Thomas among them, seem to have avoided the exegetical question and to have used the debate as an occasion for setting out the conditions for a valid baptism.

81   "Sed quia sacramenta novae legis ex ipso opere operato efficaciam habent..." loc. cit. 101, § 128.

82   "Hoc est generale in omnibus sacramentis, quod si omittatur aliquid quod est de substantia sacramenti, oportet illud sacramentum iterari. Unde cum non esset forma debita in baptismo Joannis, oportebat quod iteraretur baptismus. Et hoc habet communior opinio..." loc. cit. 101, § 129.

argued in his *Fourth Book of Sentences* that the Creator can communicate both powers.[83] Peter qualified both communications of power by holding that they can be but ministerial: The creature so acting would not be the 'author' of the new 'creation,' whether in the order of grace or that of nature, but rather the delegate through whom and in whom the Creator would act as, in fact, He does in all our good works.[84]

Aquinas noted that the common opinion of the Masters was against this solution by the Master of the *Sentences*, a point to which he has not habitually adverted. Still, in presenting the debate, Brother Thomas adduced four reasons that might be urged in favor of Peter's position, three more under the rubric *sed contra* against his position, and ended by 'responding' to all seven. For the three against Peter he considered simplistic in their use of the metaphysical notions of non-being, of the First Agent as religiously acknowledged through worship, *latria*, and finally, of act and potency correlations.[85]

Brother Thomas rejected the view that creation bridges an infinite 'distance' between being and 'pure non-being'; for him, pure non-being is only incidentally a term of the creative act, the other term of which is some being. The truth of the matter is rather that 'after non-being' something has come to be; it has come, not from non-being as from some positive antecedent, and so creation can be quantified only on the basis of the resultant being, not on the basis of the 'distance' between nothing and something. All the argument precludes, Aquinas held, is the creation of what is infinite.[86] Put another way, if there is an infinite distance between non-being and being, then the being at stake must be Infinite Being.[87] Still, it is true that 'nothing can be more distant from being than is non-being,' and so it is also true that this enigmatic 'distance' is in one way infinite and in another finite — this last because, if that were not the case, one being could not be less or more removed from God than is any other. Aquinas had remembered and cited Augustine's angel, *prope deum*, and his matter, *prope nihil*.[88]

The argument that *latria*, worship in the supreme degree, belongs to

83 *Petri Lombardi, Libri IV Sententiarum*, Liber IV, d. 5, cap. 3; ed. cit. II, 775-776; Aquinas, *In IV Sent.* d. 5, q. 1, a. 3; ed. cit. IV, 206-211.

84 "Ad quod dici potest... Ita etiam posset Deus per aliquem creare aliqua, non per eum tanquam auctorem, sed ministrum, cum quo et in quo operaretur; sicut in bonis operibus nostris ipse operatur, et nos: nec ipse tantum, nec nos tantum..." loc. cit. 776.

85 Loc. cit. 206, § 39 for the first four arguments; the fifth and sixth are § 40 and § 41 on the same page, the seventh § 42, 207; that Aquinas considered this to be a series is incontrovertible since he responds to them formally "Ad primum, Ad secundum," and so forth, 209-211, § 58 - § 72.

86 Loc. cit. 210-211, § 67, § 68.

87 Loc. cit. 211, § 69.

88 Ibid.; the text of Augustine is *Confessionum* 12, 7.

the Creator exclusively and that therefore the creative power that evokes it cannot be communicated to a creature, he rejected as missing the point. *Latria* is due to the Creator precisely as to the First Agent and what is under discussion is whether a secondary agent might participate in creative power as a secondary agent.[89]

Brother Thomas dismissed the third argument *contra* by arguing that, although it is true that no creature can be 'pure act,' there are creatures, creatures, angels, in whom there 'remains nothing of potency that has not been brought to full realization through act.'[90] Aquinas was with his colleagues in rejecting the position that creativity is communicable to creatures, but his dialectical rigor excluded some of the usual arguments given to support that rejection.

Furthermore, he was willing to extend to Peter Lombard the benefit of benign interpretation here as elsewhere. One might say 'improperly,' that is, imprecisely, that there is 'creation' where something comes to be, not from nothing at all, but from nothing of what comes to be, provided always that it be understood that some Agent, prior to the one who thus acts, has not been excluded. Any production is 'creative' in this less exact sense, because every production is the emergence into being of what had not been and thus from the 'nothing' of what emerges. This was the intent of those philosophers, Avicenna for one, who held for a mediated production of the world.[91] If anyone should wish to 'sustain him on this point,' this is the way Aquinas thought the thing might be done. In any case, the Master had not joined the philosophers who had ascribed a deputed creativity to incorporeal and immaterial substances: Although, in Lombard's perspective, the thing could have been done, he did not think it had occurred.[92]

III

What conclusions impose themselves upon a witness to the way Aquinas has comported himself when obliged to reach his decisions either against the Master of *Sentences* or against the corporate prestige of the Masters of Paris?

The thrust of his conclusions is so varied as to preclude any possibility that he approached his duties with a preliminary bias in favor of either side. In company with his peers, he rejected four out of

---

89   Loc. cit. 211, § 71.
90   Loc. cit. 211, § 72.
91   Loc. cit. 210, § 64, § 65, § 66.
92   "Et sic Magister dicit quod potuit communicari potentia creandi, non est autem alicui communicata." loc. cit. § 66.

eight positions of Peter Lombard (1, 4, 5, 7), a proportion that hardly suggests subservience to the men with whom he was obliged to work. That he agreed unreservedly with Peter on one out of eight impugned solutions (2) will not convince us that his esteem for traditional wisdom went beyond due limits. On the remaining three controverted questions (3, 6, 8), Aquinas held that the Parisian Masters were right to dissent from the Master, but that the Master's solutions were not wholly indefensible. Given the appropriate qualifications and distinctions, pious interpretations did not seem impossible and since Brother Thomas provided them, we must conclude he thought them desirable. The impression is inescapable that the very real respect Aquinas felt for Master and for Masters in no way limited his own freedom of manœuvre. He has matched the virility and discretion of his doctrine on *correptio fraterna* in the presence of moral vagaries with a discriminating independence in matters of intellect.

Second, Brother Thomas found reasons for his personal solutions on seven out of eight questions in philosophical rather than in explicitly theological sources; like the Platonizir.g Fathers of the Church, whose orientation he had diagnosed correctly, he has shown in his theologizing what his philosophical antecedents had been.[93]

His debts to Aristotle are heavy indeed, but he was no more a doctrinaire Aristotelian than he was a conformist to Parisian theological opinion or an armor-bearer for the Master of *Sentences*. An account of causes straight from the *Physics* combined in his perspective with the eminently non-Aristotelian notions of exemplarism and participation in order to justify an exegesis of 'God is love' more urbane than the blunt assertion: 'Charity is the Holy Ghost.' He counted Peter Lombard right on the exclusively negative import of numerical names as yhese are predicated of God and did so with the observation that there was dissent on the issue between 'philosophers' and 'masters.' In fact, he

---

93 "Similiter etiam expositores sacrae Scripturae in hoc (the question at issue was whether the firmament is of the same nature as are the inferior bodies; with Aristotle, Denis the pseudo-Areopagite, and "nunc omnes," Aquinas held that it is not) diversificati sunt, secundum quod diversorum philosophorum sectatores fuerunt, a quibus in philosophicis eruditi sunt. Basilius enim et Augustinus et plures sanctorum sequuntur in philosophicis quae ad fidem non spectant opiniones Platonis:... Dionysius autem fere ubique sequitur Aristotelem ut patet diligenter inspicienti libros ejus..." *In II Sent*. d. 14, q. 1, a. 2; ed. cit. II, 350; this text has been adduced by M.-D. Chenu in his 1925 article, cited above in note 5, 277, note 47, and also in his *Toward Understanding St. Thomas* 143, note 30; in this early mention of Dionysius, the diagnosis of his philosophical antecedents is, of course, incorrect, but a more diligent inspection of his books would permit Aquinas to write later: "Est autem considerandum quod beatus Dionysius in omnibus libris suis obscuro utitur stilo... Accidit etiam difficultas in praedictis libris, ex multis: a) Primo, quidem, quia plerumque utitur stilo et modo loquendi quo utebantur platonici, qui apud modernos est inconsuetus..." *Sancti Thomae Aquinatis In Librum Dionysii De Divinis Nominibus Expositio*, ed. C. Pera (Turin 1950) Prooemium, 1.

showed that the dissent was more complex: Philosophers could be found on both sides. Aristotle and his Commentator held what Peter held; Aquinas supported them against the Parisian Masters, but his reasons owe nothing to 'authority' or to the prestige that attaches to the experts.

The practice of Aquinas, as exhibited in the way he handled these eight questions, is seen to have been as flexible with respect to magistral opinion as his random remarks on the *auctores* and their views might have prepared us to expect. He neither ignored nor despised the achievements of his great predecessors and his eminent colleagues. Thomist assent, however, is compelled neither by the prestige of other Masters nor by the authority of a Church Father. In the Thomist perspective, not even the absolute divine authority is an exception to the rule that truth alone commands the assent of intellect. Divine authority is unconditioned because Truth is a divine Name and, like all biblical names, Truth is an epiphany of What it denotes. Whatever else may be required to make a 'Thomist,' unreserved allegiance to truth as perceived, rather than to an author or to the consensus of experts, cannot be absent.

Was Peter of Bergamo correct in his claim that, for Aquinas, Peter Lombard *non est authenticus*?

Passing over the mild impropriety of using the term *authenticus* with respect to the Master, and we have seen Aquinas indulge in the same impropriety, the contrary seems to have been the case. Peter Lombard embodied in a pre-eminent way human, scientific prestige as Brother Thomas conceived it: A point of departure, endowed with a value that summons a reader to benign interpretation in emergencies, but always in subordination to his best judgement as to where truth might lie. For Brother Thomas granted the Master of *Sentences* a status no worse than the one he assigned to those best of 'authors,' the Fathers of the Church. His views and theirs were sustained, and with extreme ingenuity, except where they were seen to be indefensible. Brother Thomas responded in an identical way to Peter Lombard, to Augustine, to Jerome, to any doctor — or to any doctors, even to the formidable *magistri Parisienses* marching in phalanx, *communiter*.

VI

ST. THOMAS IN HISTORY:
14TH TO 19TH CENTURIES

THE *SUMMA CONFESSORUM*
OF JOHN OF FREIBURG AND THE POPULARIZATION
OF THE MORAL TEACHING OF ST. THOMAS
AND OF SOME OF HIS CONTEMPORARIES

Leonard E. Boyle O.P.

JUST as in the wake of the theological and legal advances of the twelfth century there was a demand for popularization at the beginning of the thirteenth that produced, for example, the *summae* of Robert of Flamborough, Thomas Chobham or Raymund of Peñafort, so in the years that followed the age of Aquinas, Bonaventure and Hostiensis, there was another, and possibly more spectacular, wave of popular treatises that was, for the most part, to endure until about 1500.

Summaries of Bonaventure's commentary on the *Sentences* were numerous by 1300;[1] while as early as 1273, material from the commentary of Aquinas on the *Sentences* was incorporated into a popular *Dialogus de quaestionibus animae et spiritus*[2] by the Dominican, James of Genoa ("Januensis", the author of the influential *Catholicon*, in which there is also much of the moral theology of Aquinas). Later, between 1280 and 1288, the General of the Dominicans, John of Vercelli, commissioned Galienus Ozto to make an abbreviated version of the *Secunda secundae.*[3]

Lesser works of Bonaventure and Aquinas also had their share of popularity, in particular Bonaventure's *Breviloquium* and the *De articulis fidei et de sacramentis* of Aquinas.[4] The most popular work of all, however, was a product of neither Aquinas nor Bonaventure,

---

1 S. Alzeghy, "Abbreviationes Bonaventurae. Handschrifliche Auszüge aus dem Sentenzenkommentar des hl. Bonaventure im Mittelalter," *Gregorianum* 18 (1947) 474-510. See also K. Ruh, *Franziskanisches Schrifttum im deutschen Mittelalter*, (Munich 1965), pp. 192-197, 214-221.

2 M. Grabmann, *Mittelalterliches Geistesleben*, I (Munich 1926), pp. 369-373, and "Die Weiterleben und Weiterwerken des moraltheologischen Schrifttums des hl. Thomas von Aquin im Mittelalter," *Divus Thomas* (Freiburg in d. Schweiz) 25 (1947) 10.

3 Grabmann, art. cit., pp. 5-6.

4 J. Hartzheim, *Concilia Germaniae*, V (Cologne 1763), pp. 401, 414, 423. See also F. W. Oediger, *Ueber die Bildung der Geistlichen im späten Mittelalter* (Leiden-Cologne 1953), p. 123.

although it often circulated under their names: the *Compendium theologicae veritatis* of Hugh of Strasbourg. Written between 1265 and 1270 on a basis of Albert the Great's *Summa de creaturis* and Bonaventure's *Breviloquium*,[5] it had a remarkable influence on popular theology in the 14th and 15th centuries, in England, for example, where it is prominent in William of Pagula's *Speculum praelatorum* (c. 1320), and in the anonymous *Regimen animarum* (1343) and *Speculum christiani* (1360-1370).[6] And if the *De instructione sacerdotum* which Albert of Brescia compiled about 1300 "ex libris et quaestionibus et tractatibus fratris Thomae de Aquino" had no great success,[7] the *Dialogus de administratione sacramentorum* which William of Paris put together between 1300 and 1313 "de scriptis fratris Thomae...ac Petri Tarentoize", proved so useful that it survives in very many manuscripts and in numerous printed editions.[8]

I

Aquinas and Peter of Tarentaise are also at the centre of the subject of the present essay, the *Summa confessorum* of John of Freiburg. Its author was a contemporary of William of Paris, and died a year or so after William. Like William, who also produced several compilations of canon law, he was an indefatigable compiler.

Born at Freiburg-im-Breisgau towards the middle of the 13th century, John was to spend most of his life there as Lector in the Dominican priory. Even when he was unwillingly elected prior of the house about 1290 he was allowed to retain his lectorship by Hermann of Minden, the provincial of Germany, "ne conventus vestrae doctrinae salutaris interim accipiat detrimentum."[9] Until his death in 1314, John continued

---

5   G. Boner, "Ueber den Dominikanertheologen Hugo von Strassburg," *Divus Thomas* (Fr.) 25 (1954) 268-286. In the middle ages the *Compendium* was variously attributed to Albert, Bonaventure, Thomas, Giles of Rome, Peter of Tarentaise, etc. Some of the medieval uncertainty about authorship is reflected in a 15th-century English treatise on the seven deadly sins (Oxford, Bodleian Library, MS. Rawlinson C. 288, f. 5r): 2 "To this answereth a grete clerk (et est sanctus Thomas secundum quosdam, et sanctus Albertus secundum alios) in Compendio theologiae, lib. 3, cap. de avarita."

6   *Speculum praelatorum*: Oxford, Merton College, MS. 217, f. 5r-v; *Regimen animarum*: Oxford, Bodleian Library, MS. Hatton 11, f. 4r; *Speculum christiani*, ed. G. Holmstedt (London 1933), p. 182.

7   M. Grabmann, "Albert von Brescia O.P. (ob. 1314) und sein Werk *De officio sacerdotis*," *Mittelalterliches Geistesleben*, III (Munich 1956), pp. 323-351.

8   A. Teetaert, "Un compendium de théologie pastorale du XIIIe-XIVe siècle," *Revue d'histoire ecclésiastique* 26 (1930) 66-102.

9   H. Finke, *Ungedruckte Dominikanerbriefe des 13. Jahrhunderts* (Paderborn 1891), p. 165.

to combine these offices of "prior per se" and "lector per accidens", as Hermann of Minden nicely put it.[10]

A pupil of Ulrich Engelbrecht, under whom he had studied at Strasbourg before 1272,[11] John the Lector (as he was often known) had accompanied Albert the Great to Mecklenburg in 1269,[12] and may have studied for a time at Paris, perhaps while Aquinas and Peter of Tarentaise were lecturing there.[13] When he entered about 1280 on his function as Lector at Freiburg (which was mainly to hold public lectures which his own brethren and those of the local clergy who so desired would attend),[14] John soon found that Raymund of Peñafort's *Summa de casibus*, the standard work of confessional practice, and other similar compilations, were badly in need of revision.[15] Raymund had written his *Summa* at Barcelona about 1225,[16] and although it had been revised by Raymund himself some ten years later and had been glossed extensively by William of Rennes about 1241,[17] it was, inevitably, very much out of date by 1280. Given his background, it is not surprising to find that when John of Freiburg came to the conclusion after some years of teaching that the *Summa de casibus* would have to be revised, he turned at once to the writings of Ulrich Engelbrecht, Albert the Great, Thomas Aquinas and Peter of Tarentaise, for material which would bring the *Summa* up to date.

As we know from John himself (first prologue to his *Summa confessorum*), the earliest form of his revision of Raymund's *Summa* was a

10 See H. Flamm, "Die Grabstätte des Dominikaners Johannes von Freiburg," in *Zeitschrift der Gesellschaft für Beförderung der Geschichts-, Altertums- und Volkskunde von Freiburg* 31 (1916) 272.

11 A. Fries, "Johannes von Freiburg, Schüler Ulrichs von Strassburg," *Recherches de théologie ancienne et médiévale* 18 (1951) 332-340.

12 H.-C. Scheeben, "Albert der Grosse. Zur Chronologie seines Lebens," *Quellen und Forschungen zur Geschichte des Dominikanerordens in Deutschland* 27 (1931) 53.

13 A. Walz, "Hat Johann von Freiburg in Paris studiert?," *Angelicum* 11 (1934) 245-249.

14 See H.-M. Feret, "Vie intellectuelle et vie scolaire dans l'ordre des Prêcheurs," *Archives d'histoire dominicaine* 1 (1948) 11, 20-24.

15 "Quoniam dubiorum nova quotidie difficultas emergit casuum, doctores moderni tam theologi quam iuristae plures casus et legendo et scribendo determinaverunt qui in antiquioribus compilationibus non habentur,...": John of Freiburg, first prologue to the *Summa confessorum*. — The edition of the *Summa confessorum* (here cited, where convenient, as *SC*) used in the present essay is that of Nuremberg 1517. Since John of Freiburg has arranged his work very carefully, and it is very easy to locate a given reference in any of the editions of the *SC*, it will not be cited here by the page of the Nuremberg edition, but simply by book, *titulus* and *quaestio*, thus: 1.7,1 (Book One, title 7, question 1).

16 S. Kuttner, "Zur Entstehungsgeschichte der *Summa de casibus poenitentiae* des hl. Raymund von Pennafort," *Zeitschrift der Savigny-Stiftung für Rechtsgeschichte*, kan. Abt., 83 (1953) 419-448. The edition of the *Summa de casibus* (cited on occasion as *SdC*) used in this essay is that of Paris 1603, but the work is cited only by book and title, e.g. *SdC* 3.24.

17 A. Walz, "Sanctus Raymundus auctor Summae casuum," in *Acta Congressus iuridici internationalis, Romae 1934*, III (Rome 1936) 25-34.

Registrum: an alphabetical index that combined the matter in the *Summa de casibus* with that in the *Apparatus* of William of Rennes. Then, spreading his net a little, he began to collect *casus* which were not covered by the *Summa* and the *Apparatus*, the result being a *Libellus quaestionum casualium* that followed the order of Raymund's *Summa* but contained much more material. Finally, he embarked on a full-blown *Summa confessorum* of his own, the first *summa*, in fact, to be so called.[18]

The date usually assigned to this *Summa confessorum* by bibliographers and others is 1280 x 1298, the *terminus ante quem* being determined by the fact that John added a supplement to the *Summa* when the *Liber sextus* of Boniface VIII was issued in 1298.[19] This span of years may now be narrowed considerably. For example, John (*SC* 3.13, 12, etc.) quotes Garsias Hispanus on the second Council of Lyons, a commentary written in 1282;[20] he also refers (*SC* 3.35, 5) to the *Summula* of "frater Burchardus", a work that is probably to be dated 1290 x 1295;[21] further, he speaks of a treatise on excommunication by "Hermannus, ordinis praedicatorum, *quondam* provincialis Teutoniae" (*SC* 3.22, 219, etc.), who can only be Hermann of Minden, the provincial who confirmed John as prior about 1290 and who was in office from 1286 to 1290.[22]

If these references take us much nearer to 1298 than to 1280, a further important reference enables the *Summa* to be dated even closer to 1298. In that year Boniface VIII published the *Liber sextus*, and John therefore appended a section correlating his *Summa* with the *Sext*, "ne libri qui de Summa confessorum *iam scripti erant* appositione statutorum domini Bonifatii nuper in suo sexto libro decretalium de novo editorum destruerentur." This, I take it, means that when the *Sext* came to John's attention, a large part of his *Summa* ("libri qui de Summa confessorum iam scripti erant") had already been completed and he was loth to tamper with it, preferring to add "utiles indices in fine ipsius summae sub titulis eiusdem summae." Certainly John was in

---

18   The use of this title in editions of pre-1300 works for confessors is anachronistic, as in F. Broomfield, *Thomae de Chobham Summa confessorum* (Louvain 1968).

19   For example, in H. Finke, "Die Freiburg Dominikaner und der Münsterbau," (Freiburg in Breisgau 1901), pp. 163-171; J. Dietterle, "Die Summa confessorum," *Zeitschrift für Kirchengeschichte* 25 (1904) 257-260; M.-D. Chenu in *Dictionnaire de théologie catholique* VIII.1 (1924), cols. 701-702; A. Teetaert, *La confession aux laïques* (Louvain 1926), pp. 440-444; P. Michaud-Quantin, *Sommes de casuistique et manuels de confession au moyen âge* (Louvain 1962), p. 44 ("vers 1290").

20   London, British Museum, MS. Royal 9 C 1.

21   Dietterle, art. cit., p. 208.

22   P. von Loë, "Statistisches über die Ordensprovinz Teutonia," *Quellen und Forschungen...Dominikanerordens* 1 (1907) 13.

a position fully to analyze the *Sext* before he compiled the index to his
Summa, since he states expressly in his preamble to the index that he is
including there "additiones quas de sexto libro decretalium collectas in
fine summae in speciali tractatu addidi." Given that the *Sext* was
published in March 1298, a date 1297/1298 may therefore be suggested
for the composition of the *Summa confessorum*.

II

In character, the *Summa confessorum* is a mixture of practical
theology and canon law. Like the *Summa copiosa* of the canonist
Hostiensis (d. 1271), upon which John draws extensively, the *Summa* is
in question and answer form, each question being answered "according
to" one or other of several of John's main authorities: Raymund,
William of Rennes' *Apparatus*, Hostiensis, Geoffrey of Trani, William
Durandus the Elder (*Speculum* and *Reportorium*), the *glossa ordinaria*
on the Decretals, Albert, Aquinas, Peter of Tarentaise, Ulrich of
Strasbourg.

Following the plan of Raymund's *Summa de casibus*, John's *Summa*
is divided into four books, each of which reproduces the chapter-
headings in Raymund, from *De symonia* in Book One to *De
donationibus* in Book Four. Like Raymund, John also breaks each
chapter into numbered *quaestiones*, but John's *quaestiones* do not
always coincide with those of Raymund. And where Raymund often
discusses several subjects under a single heading, John gives each new
subject a special *rubricella*, without, however, disturbing the con-
secutive numeration of the *quaestiones*.[23] Thus in *SC* 1.1 (= *Summa
confessorum, libro* 1, *titulo* 1), where there are 92 *quaestiones* in all, the
full *titulus* (from Raymund, *SdC* 1,1), is *De symonia et de iure
patronatus*, but qq. 1-79 are entitled *De symonia*, and qq. 80-92 are
given a *rubricella, De iure patronatus*. Again, where Raymund (*SdC*
3.24) has 70 paragraphs for *De poenitentia et de remissionibus*, John of
Freiburg (*SC* 3.34) has a large number of *rubricellae* embracing some
288 *quaestiones*. On occasion, as in *SC* 3.33, q. 34, John sets up special
but unnumbered *quaestiones* within a single numbered *quaestio*. The
overall impression of the *Summa* as a well-planned and carefully-
executed piece of work is heightened by the author's numerous and very

---

23   John often cites Raymund by paragraph, e.g. *SC* 3.34, 6: "Post haec quaero quot et quae
sunt actiones poenitentiae. Respondeo secundum Raymundum, par. 5."

explicit cross-references, for example, in *SC* 1.4,3, where the reader is
referred from the beginning of the First Book to the middle of the
Third: "vide de hoc infra libro 3, titulo 38, *De transitu clericorum*,
'utrum aliquis'."

Since much of the method and material of the *Summa confessorum*
derives from his earlier compilation, the *Libellus quaestionum
casualium*, John of Freiburg included the preface to the *Libellus* in the
SC, immediately before the preface to the *SC* itself. His purpose, he explains in the first (*Libellus*) preface, was to aid his own Dominican
brethren in the pastoral care:

> Cum igitur quamplurimae quaestiones ad consilia animarum perutiles
> diversorum doctorum per volumina sint dispersae, ego frater Iohannes
> lector de ordine praedicatorum minimus, aliquas ex illis quas magis utiles
> iudicavi in unum decrevi colligere ad meum et aliorum fratrum profec-
> tum, ut si qui forte librorum copiam non habuerint, vel ad tot summas et
> scripta transcurrenda non vacaverint, hic collecta sub compendio multa
> de his inveniant quae requirunt...

To that end he had written his earlier *Registrum* of the *Summa* of
Raymund and of the *Apparatus* of William of Rennes. Now in the
Libellus he has put together *quaestiones casuales* which elaborate upon
Raymund's or are not to be found in Raymund, and which he has taken
from certain canonists and from four theologians of his own Order:

> ...in isto libello quaestiones casuales quae vel non continentur vel minus
> plene continentur in ipsa praedicta summa fratris Raymundi et apparatu
> eius, quas in pluribus doctorum libris et scriptis invenire potui, in unum
> collegi easque sub titulis eiusdem summae et eorumdem librorum et
> titulorum ordine disposui, aliquas insuper rubricellas de specialibus
> materiis quibusdam titulis supponendo. Sunt autem haec collecta maxime
> de libris horum doctorum memorati ordinis, videlicet, fratris Alberti
> quondam Ratisponensis episcopi, fratris Thomae de Aquino, et fratris
> Petri de Tharantasia, postmodum summi pontificis Innocentii quinti,
> magistrorum solemnium in theologia. Item, fratris Ulrici, quondam lec-
> toris Argentinensis eiusdem ordinis, qui quamvis magister in theologia
> non fuerit, tamen magistris inferior non extitit, ut in libro suo quem tam
> de theologia quam de philosophia conscripsit evidenter innotescit, et
> famosorum lectorum de scholis ipsius egressorum numerus protestatur:
> unde et postea provincialatus Theutoniae laudabiliter administrato of-
> ficio, Parisius ad legendum directus, ante lectionis inceptionem ibidem a
> domino est assumptus. Item ponuntur hic aliqua de summa Goffredi et
> plura de summa domini Ebrudunensis quae dicitur Copiosa, qui post-
> modum fuit cardinalis Hostiensis: unde et a quibusdam nominatur summa
> domini Hostiensis. Adduntur quoque hic aliqua de novis statutis sum-
> morum pontificum sive in modernis conciliis editis sive in curia
> publicatis. Sed et hic considerandum est quod cum secunda pars secundae

de summa fratris Thomae praedicti quasi pro maiori parte sit moralis et casualis, plurima de illa sumpta in hoc opusculo posui: et ideo ubicumque solum dicitur "Respondeo secundum Thomam in summa" vel simile, nullo addito, semper intelligendum est de secunda secundae nisi alia pars specialiter exprimatur.

The preface to the *Summa confessorum* itself presumes that one has read the above preface to the *Libellus,* although there is a slight variation on the warning about references to the *Summa* of Aquinas: "quod cum nominatur hic 'in summa Thomae', semper intelligitur de secunda parte secundae nisi alia pars specialiter exprimatur." John is also careful to point out that when he states at the beginning of a reply that he is following a given author, then all of that reply is to be understood as coming from that author:

Nota etiam quod cum cuiuscumque doctoris nomen vel liber ponitur in principio responsionis ad quaestionem, puta cum dicitur "Respondeo secundum Raymundum vel Thomam" aut similia, ab illo accepta est tota solutio quaestionis usque in finem nisi alius doctor interponatur. Cum vero duo vel plures doctores simul ponuntur in principio quaestionis, ut cum dicitur "Respondeo secundum talem et talem," solutio totius quaestionis communis est illis doctoribus, licet aliqua verba ponat unus ad explanationem quae non ponit alius, sed in sententia non discordant.

John explains, too, what precisely he means when he adds (typically, as it happens) at the end of a citation from an author that several other authors (e. g. Thomas and Albert and Peter) support this position:

Verum cum in fine alicuius quaestionis sic dicitur "Concordat" vel "Idem dicit talis et talis", et nullus alius doctor interpositus est, concordia intelligitur totius solutionis vel in sententia et quasi in verbis vel saltem in sententia, nisi solutio plura membra et plures articulos habeat; tunc enim respondet illi versui vel sententiae cui immediate adiungitur, nisi per aliquid additum designetur ad omnia praecedentia vel ad aliqua plura de praedictis esse referendum...

Again, as in the *Libellus*, the audience to which the *Summa* is directed is the "animarum medici". John now hopes that in this present work "multa de his quae requirunt inveniant, et ex diversorum concordia doctorum sciant quid sit probabilius et securius iudicandum."

Now, although John does not claim to be doing anything more than bringing Raymund up to date ("... de summa fratris Raymundi quam quasi totam huic operi includo...": *SC* 3.34,84), his *Summa* is, in fact, a much different work from that of Raymund. For one thing, his range of canonical authorities naturally goes far beyond that of the *Summa de casibus* to include the chief legal writers between 1234 and 1298: Innocent IV, Peter Sampson, Geoffrey of Trani, Garsias Hispanus,

Hostiensis, William Durandus. For another, the tone of the *Summa* is much more theological than that of Raymund. This is largely because of John's adroit use of theological authorities, and in particular of his four Dominican sources. John claims that he is simply filling out Raymund's *summa* with "casus morales", but in fact he presents the reader with quotation after quotation from his "doctores moderni", and thus places some of Raymund's legal solutions in a wider, theological framework.

A good example is Raymund's chapter *De sacramentis iterandis et de consecrationibus ecclesiarum* (*SdC* 3. 24). Raymund is entirely preoccupied with irregularities in this chapter, and only a few lines are allowed to the sacraments as such: "Quoniam quorundam sacramentorum iteratio irregularitates inducit, merito post praedicta impedimenta (sexus, etc.) de hoc aliqua sunt tangenda, pauca sacramentorum generatim praemittendo." As usual, John repeats the opening words of Raymund, "Quoniam...tangenda", but then adds, "et quia de aliquibus sacramentis non ponuntur—puta de baptismo, confirmatione, eucharistia et extrema unctione—quarum notitia non modicae est utilitatis, de his in hoc titulo aliquantulum latius prosequamur, maxime secundum theologos a quibus haec materia perfectius determinatur" (*SC* 3. 24, prologue). As a result, John now devotes 149 elaborate *quaestiones*, with replies mostly from Aquinas, to the four sacraments in question, and a further 14 to a separate *rubricella De consecratione*.

Of course, John never forgets that his primary text is that of Raymund. It was, in its way, sacred in the Dominican Order. For Raymund, who had been a General of the Dominicans for a brief period, was the known compiler of the *Decretales* promulgated by Gregory IX in 1234; besides, his *Summa* was one of the few books to be singled out for mention in the *Ratio studiorum* which a committee composed of Albert, Thomas, Peter of Tarentaise and two others had drawn up for the Order in 1259.[24] This reverence is reflected in the care with which John of Freiburg quotes the *Summa* at length at the beginning of each chapter and keeps to the order of Raymund's paragraphs. Here and there it restrains him when he is tempted to jettison parts of Raymund: "...praetermissa vero hic posui, ne de summa fratris Raymundi...viderer partem notabilem detruncasse" (*SC* 3. 34, 84).

Yet John was quite aware of Raymund's limitations. For example, Raymund has nothing at all on the sacrament of Orders. In fact, under the title *De aetate ordinandorum et de temporibus ordinationum*, he plunges into impediments, without as much as a glance at the nature of

---

24 *Acta capitulorum generalium*, I, ed. B. M. Reichert (Monumenta ordinis praedicatorum historica 3), (Rome 1898), p. 99; see pp. 110,174.

the sacrament: "Repellitur quis ab ordinatione et electione propter defectum aetatis, dist, 77" (*SdC* 3. 22). John, on the other hand, will have none of this too legalistic approach: "De hoc titulo circa ordines, ordinantes et ordinatos magis specialia exequens, primo quaero...quid sit ordo...."; and proceeds in some 54 *quaestiones* to give long quotations from Thomas, Peter of Tarentaise and others, on the meaning of order, character, etc. Again, in the title *De bigamis (SC* 3. 3), John is content to repeat Raymund almost word for word for the first three *quaestiones*, but then breaks away with the question (q. 4): "Sed quare ad perfectionem sacramenti (matrimonii) non requiritur virginitas in viro sicut in muliere?" And his reply possibly has a sting in its tail: "Respondeo secundum Thomam in scripto (4 D. 27, cited earlier by John), quia defectus in ipso sacramento causat irregularitatem....Juristae tamen diversas rationes alias assignaverunt quae stare non possunt...."

By and large, there is scarcely one place where John is satisfied to repeat Raymund without some comment or addition. Sometimes it is simply a question of filling out a casual reference in Raymund, as when in *SC* 3. 34, 6 he adds a *Decretum* reference ("ab Augustino: De pe. dist. 1") where Raymund has a vague, "ut ait Augustinus". At other times, and especially on purely legal matters, there is an unexpected display (for a theologian) of legal learning. Thus, in the title *De negotiis saecularibus, et utrum de illicite acquisitis possit fieri elemosina (SC* 2. 81), John devotes four *quaestiones* (qq. 39-42) to *De iure emphiteosis* where Raymund has only a few desultory sentences.

Of course, John's command of legal sources was not entirely at first-hand. Most of his acquaintance with the finer points of law, and with the major Decretists and Decretalists, was due, as he admits in his prologues, to the *Summa copiosa* of Hostiensis, the *Apparatus* of William of Rennes on Raymund, and the *Summa* of Geoffrey of Trani (not to speak of the *Speculum iudiciale* of William Durandus, which he does not mention there). Thus, in *SC* 3. 33, 245, after what appears to be an uncommon familiarity with some of the Decretists, John admits disarmingly: "Haec omnia in glossa". All the same, John appears to have made a fair attempt to keep abreast of legal scholarship. If it is not unexpected to find him using the *Speculum* (1287) of Durandus, or the *Manuale* of his fellow-Dominican, Burchard of Strasbourg (*SC* 3. 33, 105, 135, etc.) and the *De interdicto* of his former superior, Hermann of Minden (*SC* 3. 33, 219, 226, 251, etc.), it is a little surprising at first glance to note the presence of the commentary (1282) of Garsias Hispanus on the legislation of the Second Council of Lyons (*SC* 3. 13, 12; 3. 34, 221, 227, etc.). But, then, as befitted an assiduous teacher of

practical theology, John had more than a passing interest in the constitutions issued by that Council, for he quotes them often (*SC* 1. 7, 29;
2. 7, 71, 72; 4. 24, 149, etc.).

Since Raymund of Peñafort has many chapters of purely legal content in his *Summa de casibus*, there are, inevitably, some quite long
stretches of almost unrelieved quotations from legal authorities in John
of Freiburg's *Summa confessorum*. Otherwise, John never lets slip an
opportunity of drawing extensively on the "doctores moderni" of
theology. As John states in both his prologues, these theological sources
are generally limited to the writings of Albert, Ulrich of Strasbourg,
Peter of Tarentaise and Thomas Aquinas. Albert and Ulrich, however,
are much less in evidence than Peter and Thomas.

The *Liber de missa* of Albert is quoted extensively on many occasions
(e. g. *SC* 3. 24, 56, 60, 75, 85, 105, 110), but his *Summa de creaturis* is
used sparingly (*SC* 1. 8, 47, 48; 4. 1, 21, etc.), though it is often cited in
support of an opinion of one of the other theologians. One of the more
notable instances of dependence upon it occurs in the *rubricella De
consecratione et velatione virginum (SC* 3. 3, 14-24), where in q. 17
John shows that he is well aware of the relationship between Albert and
Thomas: "Quid de virginibus occultis, si sine scandalo earum consecratio intermitti non potest? Respondeo secundum Albertum in
Summa de quatuor coaequaevis, in tractatu de virtutibus cardinalibus,
di. 58. Et quasi eadem verba sunt Thomae et Alberti, quia Thomas
sumpsit de Alberto, qui doctor eius fuerat in studio Coloniensi."
Although the "Summa de bono" of Ulrich of Strasbourg is cited more
frequently than Albert's *Summa*, it ceases to be prominent after Books
One and Two (e. g. *SC* 1. 1, 2, 3, 4, 6, 12: 2. 5, 64-99), and appears only
fitfully in Book Three (where, as it happens, there is a citation from
Ulrich "in quadam quaestione de quolibet": *SC* 3. 34, 272).

The two theological mainstays of the *Summa confessorum* are, in
fact, Peter of Tarentaise and Thomas Aquinas. The *Quodlibets* of Peter
are quoted only twice,[25] but his commentary on the *Sentences* is almost
as frequently invoked as the *Summa* or the commentary on the *Sentences* of Thomas. Sometimes there are long runs of citations from
Thomas, but just as often there are passages of equal length from Peter,

---

25 "Utrum religiosus teneatur obedire praelato suo praecipienti sibi aliquid contra regulam.
Respondeo secundum Petrum in quadam quaestione de quolibet" (*SC* 3.33, 8). This is Qdl. 1.34 in
P. Glorieux, *La littérature quodlibetique*, II, (Paris 1935), p. 227, and is printed in Glorieux, "Le
Quodlibet de Pierre de Tarentaise," *Recherches de théologie ancienne et médiévale* 9 (1937) 270.
A second reference, "Respondeo secundum Petrum in quaestionibus de quolibet" (*SC* 3.34, 254),
may really be to Peter's *Quaestiones de peccato*, on which see Glorieux, "Questions nouvelles de
Pierre de Tarentaise," ibid., 14 (1947) 98-103.

one after the other. Thus, in *SC* 3. 34, qq. 144-148 (*Pro quibus peccatis requiratur poenitentia?*), all five replies are from Peter; and this block of questions is followed by *De remissione venialium* (qq. 149-158), where Peter is the source called on for qq. 149-152, Thomas for q. 153, Peter again for q. 154, Thomas for qq. 155-156, Peter for 157, and so on. Unless one were to count, and then add up the lines of explicit borrowings from these two authors, it would be difficult to state with any exactitude which one of them is relied upon more than the other in John's *Summa*. But in view of John's own remarks in his prologues, it is not unfair to suggest that Thomas would possibly prove the winner.

Of the works of Thomas quoted in the *Summa confessorum,* the least expected is that known as *De regimine Iudaeorum ad ducissam Brabantiae.* It first occurs in *SC* 1. 4, 9 ("Utrum liceat dominis terrarum aliquam exactionem facere in Iudaeos? Respondeo secundum Thomam in quadam epistola ad ducissam Lotharingiae et Brabantiae..."), and is cited at length on at least 10 occasions — practically all of the letter, in fact (*SC* 1. 4, 9, 10, 11, 12, 13, 14; 2. 5, 34, 36, 40, 41).

John's use of the *Quodlibets* of Thomas is even more striking, for he cites Thomas "in quadam quaestione de quolibet" on at least 33 occasions, and generally in full. Obviously he had searched through the *Quodlibets* and had utilized as much as possible of those with a "pastoral" bearing,[26] e. g., "Utrum clericus praebendatus in duabus ecclesiis, in die quo diversum est officium in utraque ecclesia, debeat utrumque officium dicere...Respondeo secundum Thomam in quadam quaestione de quolibet..." (*SC* 1. 7, 19 = Thomas, *Qdl.* I. 7, 1: all of corpus); "Utrum executor debeat tardare distributionem elemosinarum...Respondeo secundum Thomam..." (*SC* 2. 5, 114 = *Qdl.* VI. 8, 2: all of corpus): "Utrumque aliquis teneatur dimittere studium theologiae, etiam si aptus ad docendum alios, ad hoc quod intendat saluti animarum. Respondeo..." (*SC*. 3. 5. 4 = *Qdl.* I. 7, 2: all of corpus).

Curiously, not all of the *Quodlibets* which John attributes to Thomas prove to be really his. Here and there one's suspicions are aroused by passages which do not have the ring of Thomas, as in *SC* 3. 28, 23: "Utrum periculum sit claustralibus monachis si cura ecclesiarum spectantium ad claustrum negligatur a monachis officialibus? Respondeo secundum Thomam in quadam quaestione de quolibet....Et si esset mihi notum aliquid tale monasterium, non auderem consulere quod aliquis in tali collegio eligeret monachatum." As it happens, this quotation comes

---

26 See L. E. Boyle, "The Quodlibets of St. Thomas and the Pastoral Care," *The Thomist* 38 (1974).

from q. 24 of the first *Quodlibet* (1270) of John Peckham.[27] This is quite interesting, when one remembers that, beginning from 1279, this *Quodlibet* of Peckham occurs in at least 23 MSS of the *Quodlibets* of Thomas, but that only one of these MSS explicitly attributes it to Thomas. This is a late 13th-century MS (Paris, BN, lat. 15351), and it seems reasonable to suppose that the manuscript of the *Quodlibets* of Thomas to which John of Freiburg had access, belonged to that same tradition.[28] At all events, in 11 of the following 33 instances, John of Freiburg turns out to be quoting from Peckham's first *Quodlibet* and not at all from Thomas "in quadam quaestione de quolibet":

		S. confessorum	St. Thomas	Peckham
* 1.	1:	1,66		I.20a
2.		4,4	II.4, 2	
3.		7,19	I.7, 1	
4.		20	V.13, 3	
5.		21	VI.5, 2	
6.		8,62	IV.7, 2	
* 7.		78		I.26
* 8.		79		I.26
9.		9,23	I.9, 2	
10.		10,5	VI.9, 3	
11.		11,23	III.9, 2	
*12.	2:	5,93		I.17
13.		113	VI.8, 1	
14.		114	2	
15.	3:	5,4	I.7, 2	
16.		5	III.4, 1	
*17.		24,23		I.22
*18.		28,23		I.24
19.		32,18	III.4, 2	
*20.		33,6		I.19
*21.		10		I.25
22.		194	IV.8, 3	
23.		34,26	I.5	
24.		48	6, 3	
25.		69	2	
*26.		73		I.23
*27.		74		I.23a
28.		110	III.13, 1	
29.		192	V.7, 2	
30.		236	VI.5, 3	
31.		237	V.11, 3	
32.		249	III.6, 2	
*33.		289		I.18

27 For the quodlibets of Peckham see P. Glorieux, *La littérature quodlibétique* I (1925), pp. 220-222, II (1935), pp. 174-175.

28 See J. Destrez, "Les disputes quodlibétiques de Saint Thomas d'après la tradition manuscrite", *Mélanges Thomistes*, (Paris, 1923), pp. 49-108, at pp. 59-61. The MS. is Paris, Bibliothèque nationale, MS. lat. 15351 (n. 69 in Destrez).

Needless to say, the work of Thomas that is used most of all in the *Summa confessorum* is the *Secunda secundae* of his *Summa*. Other parts of the *Summa*, of course, are cited: the *Prima secundae* occasionally; the *Tertia pars* (with the commentary on 4 *Sentences*) frequently in *SC* 3. 33, qq. 24-167, on Baptism, Confirmation, Eucharist and Extreme Unction. But pride of place is given to the *Secunda secundae*, "cum (as John states in his first prologue) secunda pars secundae de summa fratris Thomae praedicti pro maiori parte sit moralis et casualis..." And in both of his prologues he warns the reader, "quod cum nominatur hic in summa Thomae, semper intelligitur de secunda parte secundae, nisi alia pars specialiter exprimatur."

The *Secunda secundae* is present right from the opening title of the *Summa* (*De symonia*) and it is invoked on every occasion that some moral point is being considered, even in the midst of long legal passages. If it is very notable in sections on the *De lege et consuetudine* (*SC* 2. 5, 203-208), or *De emptione et venditione* (*SC* 2. 8, 7-19), or *De sententia praecepti* (*SC* 3. 33, 5-26, etc.), it is at its most evident in the *rubricella De iudiciis peccatorum* (qq. 196-288) of *SC* 3. 34 (*De poenitentiis et remissionibus*). After some quotations from Raymund, and one from the *Prima secundae*, John introduces a long selection from the *Secunda secundae* with the words, "Post haec descendendo ad spiritualia, de fide primo quaero..." (q. 202). There now follow the essentials of the teaching of Thomas on most of the theological and moral virtues:

S. confessorum	St. Thomas	Subject
q. 202	2.2 2. 6, 7	explicit faith
203	8	"
204	3, 2	confession of faith
205	10, 6	infidelity
206	7	infidels
207	13, 1	blasphemy
208	2	"
209	15, 1	torpor
210	2	despair
211	20, 1	"
212	21, 2	presumption
213	25, 8	charity
214	9	"
215	10	"
216	12	"
217	26, 2	"
218	7	"
219	34, 2	hate
220	35, 1	sloth
221	2	"

222	36, 1	envy
223	2	"
224	3	"
.	.	"
.	.	"
.	.	"
288	168, 2	games

In all of the *Summa confessorum*, however, there is very little to be seen of John of Freiburg himself, apart, that is, from a few asides such as "in hoc tamen casu credo quod..." (*SC* 3. 33, 61), "Ego sine praeiudicio credo" (3. 33, 86), "Fateor dictum fratris Thomae, cum ex ratione procedat, mihi magis placere" (2. 8, 25), "Prima opinio benignior et communior" (3. 30, 12), and from a possibly autobiographical glimpse when he speaks of John de Varzy, a Dominican who taught at Paris in 1266: "Et hanc formam (absolutionis) exposuit magister Iohannes de Verziaco in scholis..." (3. 34, 89).

For all that, it would be a mistake to dismiss the *Summa* as a mere, if gifted, compilation. Rather, it may prove not to be an exaggeration to state that the *Summa confessorum* was the most influential work of pastoral theology in the two hundred years before the Reformation. Certainly it was endowed by its author with a doctrinal character which few manuals before it had possessed — and one which would be imitated but rarely improved upon by the manuals and manualists of the next two centuries.[29]

III

Whatever its originality, the *Summa confessorum* was an immediate success. It attracted followers from professional theologians such as Rainerius of Pisa (*Pantheologia*, c. 1330)[30] and legists such as Albericus de Rosate (*Repertorium iuris*, c. 1338)[31] to humble manuals such as the *Fasciculus morum* (1320 x 1340),[32] the *Cilium oculi* (1330 x 1340),[33] the *Speculum christiani* (1370 x 1400),[34] the *Lucerna conscientiae* (c.

---

29   For a slightly different opinion, see P. Michaud-Quantin, *Les Sommes de casuistique*, p. 50. While allowing that the *SC* has a theological character, he feels that it is so faithful to Raymund that there is no new direction there.

30   *Pantheologia* (Louvain 1570), I, p. 384a; II, p. 896b, etc. The *SC* is not cited as such.

31   See R. Abbondanza in *Dizionario biografico italiano* 4 (Rome 1962), cols. 463-465.

32   Oxford, Bodleian Library, MS. Bodley 332, f. 142vb, etc. The *SC* is not cited by name.

33   Oxford, Balliol College, MS. 86, f. 233rb, etc. Again, there is no explicit reference to the *SC*.

34   Oxford, Bodleian Library, MS. Rawl. C.19, ff. 7v, 8r, etc., but again not by name. This MS. contains a larger, if not an original, version of the *Speculum* as printed by G. Holmstedt (London 1933).

1400),[35] the ethico-medical *Florarium Bartholomaei* (1395 x 1407) of John Mirfield,[36] and the *Speculum iuratorum* (c. 1450) of Thomas Wygenhale.[37] And if we are to believe the *Summa rudium* (c. 1338), Pope John XXII held the *Summa confessorum* in such high esteem that he remarked on one occasion of its author, "Qui istam summam collegit, reputo unam esse de melioribus personis totius ecclesiae."[38] There may be some truth in this report, for, as we know from an inventory of 1327, the *Summa* was indeed among the books in John XXII's study.[39]

Not unexpectedly the Dominicans of the 14th and 15th centuries responded with enthusiasm to the new, up-to-date, pattern of confessional manual set by John of Freiburg. From the earliest days of their Order there had been a sturdy tradition of manuals for confessors, mainly because Honorius III had commissioned them in 1221 to hear confessions and had commended them as confessors to the bishop of Christendom. As a result, the Dominicans had entered the field of theology for the very first time, when manuals of practical theology were hurriedly put together at various points of the expanding Order. At Bologna, a *Summa* by Conrad Höxter was possibly ready by May 1221; in 1222 the Dominicans at St. Jacques combined to produce a handy vademecum for the Paris area; another handbook appeared at Cologne in 1224; and in 1225 a first version of a *Summa de casibus* was composed at Barcelona for the Dominicans of Spain by Raymund of Peñafort.[40] It was in this way that a tradition began which Raymund was to dominate in the thirteenth century, and John of Freiburg from 1300 onwards. Raymund, of course, was a great name all through the middle ages,[41] but it is not unlikely that some of the fame attached to Raymund and the *Summa de casibus* is to a large extent due in the later middle ages to the fact that John of Freiburg's ubiquitous *Summa*, with its superficial likeness to that of Raymund, was sometimes mistaken

35 Oxford, Bodleian Library, MS. Bodley 801, *passim*, but not by name.

36 Cambridge University Library, MS. Dd. xi. 83, f. 82v, etc., but not explicitly. There is a general study of the *Florarium* in P. Hartley and H. R. Aldridge, *Johannes de Mirfield* (Cambridge 1936).

37 Cambridge University Library, MS. Ii. vi. 39, ff. 3v, 4r, etc., but not by name.

38 *Summa rudium*, (Reutlingen 1487), prologue. The 15th-century chronicler Johann Meyer also reports this eulogy, but his source is probably the *Summa rudium*. See H.-C. Scheeben, "Johannes Meyer O.P., *Chronica brevis ordinis praedicatorum*," in *Quellen und Forschungen...Dominikanerordens* 29 (1933) 53.

39 A. Maier, "Annotazioni autografe di Giovanni XXII in codici vaticani," *Ausgehendes Mittelalter* II (Rome 1967), pp. 81-96, at p. 94, n. 28.

40 See P. Mandonnet, *Saint Dominique*, ed. M.-H. Vicaire and R. Ladner (Paris 1938), I, pp. 249-269.

41 A. Walz, "S. Raymundi de Penyafort auctoritas in re paenitentiali," *Angelicum* 12 (1935) 346-396.

(especially by library catalogues) for the *Summa de casibus*, and cited as "Raymundi *Summa confessorum*", through ignorance of its real author.[42]

The readiness with which the Dominicans abbreviated, translated or simply used the *Summa confessorum* leaves little doubt that John had taken over the field from Raymund. The *Summa rudium*, with its eulogy of John, is largely a simplified version of the *Summa* by an anonymous Dominican;[43] another Dominican, William of Cayeux, published an abridgement about 1340;[44] in 1338, Bartholomew of S. Concordia composed at Pisa an influential *Summa de casibus* (often called *Pisanella* or *Magistruccia*) that is basically an alphabetical arrangement of the *Summa confessorum*;[45] about a hundred years later a small Dominican *Tractatus de sacramento altaris* is described by its author as "ex Summa confessorum quasi totaliter extractus."[46]

Dominicans, too, contributed to vernacular versions of the *Summa*. Berthold of Freiburg, John's successor as superior, made a German translation which was to find its way into print at least four times before 1500.[47] In the middle of the 14th century the *Summa* is used, if not directly translated at times, by the *Tugenden Buch*, a work which translates selections from the *Secunda secundae* of Thomas, and with which John of Freiburg himself is credited in some three manuscripts.[48] At the end of the 15th century a French translation was printed of a *Regula mercatorum* which Guy of Evreux had pulled together about 1320 from John of Freiburg's chapters on usury and just price in the *Summa*.[49]

---

42 Thus the *Regimen animarum* (1343): "Compilavi enim hoc opusculum ex quibusdam libris, videlicet, Summa summarum, Raymundi Summa confessorum,...." (Oxford, Bodleian Library, MS. Hatton 11, f. 4r). John of Freiburg himself is partly to blame for any mistake of identity. Shorn of its two prologues, the *SC* could easily have been taken for the *Summa de casibus*. The incipits of both works are largely identical, as are the prologues to each *titulus*.

43 J. F. von Schulte, *Geschichte der Quellen und Literatur des canonischen Rechts*, II (Stuttgart 1877), pp. 528-529; R. Stintzing, *Geschichte der populären Literatur des römisch-kanonischen Rechts in Deutschland* (Leipzig 1867), p. 514; J. Dietterle, "Die Summae....," in *ZKG* 27 (1906) 78-80. Since this article of Dietterle, "Die *Summae confessorum*...von ihren Anfängen an bis zu Silvester Prierias....," is cited often in the following notes, it may be useful to note here that the whole article runs through five volumes of the *Zeitschrift für Kirchengeschichte* (*ZKG*), as follows: 24 (1903) 353-374, 520-548; 25 (1904) 248-272; 26 (1905) 59-81, 350-362; 27 (1906) 70-83, 166-188, 296-310, 431-442; 28 (1907) 401-431.

44 Schulte, II, p. 423; Dietterle, *ZKG* 26 (1905) 59-63.

45 Schulte, II, pp. 428-429; Dietterle *ZKG* 27 (1906) 166-171.

46 Cambridge University Library, MS. Ee. iii. 58, ff. 80r-88r.

47 Dietterle, *ZKG* 26 (1905) 67-77; R. Stanka, *Die Summa des Berthold von Freiburg* (Vienna 1937).

48 K. Berg, *Der tugenden Buch. Untersuchungen zu mittelhochdeutschen Prosatexten nach Werken des Thomas von Aquin* (Munich 1964), pp. 77-78, 97-100, 109-112. The *Summa confessorum* is also present in German works of Nicholas of Dinkelsbühl (ob. 1433), one of the great 15th-century popularizers of scholasticism (ibid., pp. 30-32, 41-52).

49 P. Michaud-Quantin, "Guy d'Evreux, technicien du sermonnaire médiéval," *Archivum Fratrum Praedicatorum* 20 (1950) 216-217.

Finally, if the influence of the *Summa confessorum* is to be seen in the two great Franciscan *Summae* of the end of the 15th century, the *Rosella casuum* of Baptista de Salis[50] and the *Summa angelica* of Angelo Carletti,[51] it is even more present in the last, and perhaps the most ambitious, of the medieval Dominican manuals, the *Summa summarum Sylvestrina* (1516) of Sylvester Mazzolini de Prierio.[52] A man of formidable learning, Sylvester nevertheless draws, as so many others had done for over 200 years, on the *Summa* of John of Freiburg for quotations from the *Quodlibets* and the *Secunda secundae* of Thomas, from the *Summa* of Raymund, from the *Apparatus* of William of Rennes and, need it be said, from the writings of Albert the Great and Peter of Tarentaise. At the end of the *Sylvestrina* there is a long catalogue of the main "summistae" of the preceding centuries. It is surely not inappropriate that the *Summa confessorum* of John of Freiburg should appear there simply and anonymously as "Summa confessorum ordinis praedicatorum".[53] If anything, the impact of the *Summa confessorum* on the manualist tradition at large was as pronounced as that on the Dominican manualists. As early as 1303 it was used (but without acknowledgement) by the Franciscan, John of Erfurt, in the second edition of his *Summa de poenitentia.*[54] About the same time there also appeared the first Franciscan counterpart to the *Summa*, an anonymous *Labia sacerdotis*. While this leans heavily on the pre-1300 manualists, and on Bonaventure, it also cites Thomas, Peter of Tarentaise and Raymund. The *Summa confessorum*, however, is never mentioned. Yet it is clear from the whole layout of the *Labia*, and from its citations from these Dominican sources, that the author had John of Freiburg's work before him.[55]

The most successful attempt to do for Franciscan moralists what John of Freiburg had done for Ulrich, Albert, Peter and Thomas, comes some ten years later with the *Summa Astesana* of Astesanus of Asti.[56]

50 Schulte, II, pp. 448-450; Dietterle, *ZKG* 27 (1906) 431-442.

51 Schulte, II, pp. 452-453; Dietterle, *ZKG* 27 (1906) 296-310; Michaud-Quantin, *Sommes*, pp. 99-101.

52 Schulte, II, pp. 455-456; Dietterle, *ZKG* 28 (1907) 416-431; Michaud-Quantin, *Sommes*, pp. 101-104.

53 *Summa summarum quae Sylvestrina dicitur* (Cologne 1518), ff. xxxvv, clxvr, etc.

54 A first edition of this *Summa* was written c. 1296 (see F. Doelle, "Johann von Erfurt," in *ZKG* 31 (1910) 225-238). A second edition in 1302 (e.g. Oxford, Oriel College, MS. 38) uses the *Summa confessorum*, for example at f. 150r, where, citing Aquinas on the Eucharist through the *SC*, John of Erfurt says, "Ego tamen credo cum Bonaventura...".

55 For example, Oxford, Bodleian Library, MS. Hamilton 34, f. 279r: "Numquid participans excommunicato in casibus non concessis peccat mortaliter? Respondetur. Quidam dicunt sic, ut Ray. et Gau., et istud durum est dicere. Sed Bon., Thomas et Petrus dicunt..." (= *Summa confessorum*, 3.33, 165, without, of course, the reference to Bonaventure).

56 For an account of Astesanus see G. Giorgino, *Sponsalium institutum in fr. Astesani de Ast Summa de casibus* (Caiazzo 1942), pp. 4-17. See also Schulte, II, 425-427; Dietterle, *ZKG* 26 (1905) 35-62; Michaud-Quantin, *Sommes*, pp. 57-60.

Written in 1317, and dedicated to cardinal Giovanni Caetani, it was probably as influential as John's *Summa* over the next two centuries. The preface, which is not unlike that of John of Freiburg,[57] carries a massive list of authorities, mostly Franciscan moralists and theologians such as Bonaventure, William de la Mare, Alexander of Hales and John Scotus ("Famosissimus et subtilissimus"). If there are also the *Quodlibets* of Henry of Ghent, the commentary on the *Sentences* of Richard of Middleton, and the recently-published *Apparatus* of Iohannes Andreae on the *Sext*, the *Astesana,* nevertheless, has a batch of authorities in common with John of Freiburg: Thomas ("famosissimus"), Raymund, William of Rennes, Peter of Tarentaise, Hostiensis, Garsias Hispanus and William Durandus. There is no sign, however, of the *Summa confessorum* among the sources cited, whether in the prologue or the text. This is a little strange. For although the *Astesana* does appear to show some independent knowledge of Raymund, Thomas and Peter of Tarentaise, there are sections where quotations from these authors are undoubtedly through John of Freiburg's work.[58]

The unacknowledged use of John of Freiburg's *Summa* was, in fact, widespread. One of the most striking instances is that of the Berkshire vicar, William of Pagula. In three of his works, and particularly in his very popular *Oculus sacerdotis* (1320-1327), Pagula quietly uses the *Summa confessorum*, without once mentioning it by name, for matter from various canonists and, on many occasions, for quotations from Albert, Thomas, Raymund and Peter of Tarentaise.[59] One small example will suffice to illustrate the point:

Oculus[60]	*Summa* (3. 34, 28)
Tanta potest esse contritio quod tota poena remittitur absque confessione. Nichilominus tamen confessio et poenitentia iniuncta ex-	Utrum contritio possit tollere totum reatum poenae? *Respondeo secundum Petrum:...*
	Tantum potest incendi contritio

57 "...exhortatione ven. patris et domini supra memorati, et etiam plurium fratrum, summam de casibus deo auxiliante compilavi," prologue.

58 Compare, for example, *Summa astesana* (Regensburg 1480), 4.3, 4, with *SC* 3.24, 13. Often, as in *Astesana* 4.3, 4 and 4.3, 5, the author gives a precise reference to Aquinas and Peter of Tarentaise where the *SC* has only a general reference. Anonymous borrowings from John of Freiburg are also to be found in the *Summa de casibus* (c. 1315) of the Franciscan Durandus de Campania: see Dietterle, *ZKG* 27 (1906) 70-78.

59 On the *Oculus* see L. E. Boyle, "The *Oculus sacerdotis*... of William of Pagula," in *Transactions of the Royal Historical Society*, 5th series, 5 (1955) 81-110.

60 Oxford, New College, MS. 292, f. 76r.

pleri debent ńon propter remedium sed propter praeceptum.

Et non solum propter praeceptum tenetur quis confiteri et satisfacere, sed etiam propter incertitudinem, quia non est certus quod
sua contritio fuit sufficiens ad totum reatum tollendum, *secundum
Thomam et Petrum.*

quod tota poena remittitur. Nichilominus tamen confessio et poenitentiae iniunctae expletio requiritur etiam, non propter remedium
sed propter praeceptum.

Concordat his Thomas, et addit
quod non solum propter praeceptum tenetur confiteri et satisfacere
sed etiam propter incertitudinem,
quia, scilicet, non est certus quod
sua contritio fuerit sufficiens ad
totum reatum tollendum.

The same unacknowledged dependence on John of Freiburg is again
to be noted in William of Pagula's *Summa summarum*, a massive and
not unsuccessful compilation of law and theology which was put
together between 1319 and 1322. The same is true of his *Speculum
praelatorum* of much the same period.[61] And when Pagula's *Oculus
sacerdotis* was revised, and in part re-written, some sixty years later by
John de Burgo, chancellor of Cambridge, there is an even greater exploitation of the *Summa confessorum*. But there is a difference. Like
William of Pagula, the *Pupilla oculi* (1384) of de Burgo cites Albert,
Aquinas, Peter, Raymund, etc. through the *Summa confessorum,* but
unlike Pagula, de Burgo explicitly admits that the *Summa* of John of
Freiburg is his source, as when he states in his tract on the Eucharist,
after a series of quotations from Aquinas: "Haec omnia notat Iohannes
in Summa confessorum, lib. 3, tit. xxiiii, c. xxix."[62] Again, his debt to
the *Summa confessorum* is obvious, even though he does not explicitly
acknowledge it, when he says that his exposition of the Peckham
"Syllabus of pastoral instruction" (1281) comes "ex dictis sancti Thomae
in secunda secundae, diversis articulis."[63]

Borrowings from the *Summa confessorum,* whether explicit or implicit, were not at all confined to popular manuals. Thus, John Bacon-

---

61   Thus, at the end of the *Summa summarum* (Oxford, Bodleian Library, MS. Bodley 293, f.
83r): "Quare requiritur maior numerus testium contra episcopos et superiores quam contra alios
simplices homines? Dic quod triplex est ratio...secundum Thomam in Summa" (= *SC* 2.5, 183);
"Quid si testis producatur super re de qua non est omnino certus? Dic secundum Thomam in
Summa...." (= *SC* 2.5, 183), etc. See L. E. Boyle, "The *Summa summarum*...," in *Proceedings of
the Second International Congress of Medieval Canon Law, Boston 1963*, ed. S. Kuttner and J. J.
Ryan, (Vatican City 1965), pp. 415-456, at p. 423.

62   *Pupilla oculi*, 4.10 (Strasbourg 1518), f. xxxiii.

63   Ibid., 10.5 (Strasbourg 1518), f. clxxvr.

thorpe, the English Carmelite theologian, whom one would have expected to have known his Thomas at first-hand, is content in his Postill
on St. Matthew (1336-1337) and *Quaestiones canonicae* on the 4th book
of the *Sentences* (c. 1344) to draw on the *Summa confessorum* for many
passages from Aquinas.[64] What is more interesting, perhaps, is the fact
that although Baconthorpe possessed John of Freiburg's *Summa*, he often quotes Thomas, Peter, etc., not through the *Summa confessorum* but
through William of Pagula's *Summa summarum* which, in turn, was
totally dependent upon the *Summa confessorum*. There are occasions,
indeed, when he prefers to quote Thomas from the *Summa summarum*
rather than from Thomas himself, or, for that matter, from the *Summa
confessorum*, the source of the *Summa summarum*. Thus when he
writes, "In Summa summarum et Summa confessorum habes multos
casus expressos necessitatis excusantes (a ieiunio)....Primo quid de
laborantibus in vineis....Respondetur ibidem (i. e. Summa summarum)
....Sic tenet Thomas in secunda secundae q. 174, art. iv," the wording of
the passage from Thomas is that of the *Summa summarum* and not of
the *Summa confessorum* or Thomas himself. Yet John Baconthorpe
clearly had the *Summa confessorum* of John of Freiburg open before
him at the same time. For where Pagula's treatment of fasting ends simply "secundum Thomam in Summa",[65] Baconthorpe proceeds to give a
more precise reference to Thomas, taking it straight from the *Summa
confessorum*.[66]

While one can understand that a canonist such as William of Pagula
(or, a hundred years later, William Lyndwood in his *Provinciale*)[67]
would have found the *Summa confessorum* convenient for quotations
from the great theologians, it is otherwise in the case of John Baconthorpe or of equally professional theologians such as Antoninus of
Florence (d. 1459) and Robert Holcot (d. 1349). If, for example, the
Confessionale of Antoninus is based mainly on the *Pisanella* of Bartholomew of Pisa, a derivative of the *Summa confessorum*, there are
numerous instances when Antoninus turns (sometimes without
acknowledgement) to the *Summa confessorum* itself for references to
Thomas, Peter of Tarentaise, etc., thus: "Duplex est contritionis dolor
secundum Thomam et Petrum in 4 d. xvii.... Item secundum Petrum
in 4 d. xvii, dolor maior intellectualis debet esse de maiori peccato

64   See B. Smalley, "John Baconthorpe's Postill on St. Matthew," *Medieval and Renaissance
Studies* 4 (1958) 99-110, 119, 143.

65   *Summa summarum*, MS. Bodley 293, f. 149v.

66   Baconthorpe, Commentary on 4 *Sent.* 20.2, 2 (Cremona 1616, II, p. 446). The same passage
is also to be found in the *Postilla in Matthaeum*, Trinity College, Cambridge, MS. 348, f. 120v.

67   *Provinciale* 3.23 (Oxford 1679), pp. 227-235, on Penance, etc. Thus at p. 229, note 1: "In hac
materia dicunt beatus Thomas et Petrus in scriptis, et idem recitat Jo. in Summa confessorum, tit.

habitualiter et non actualiter si considerentur peccata in communi.... Item secundum Thomam in quolibet et Innocentium, contritus debet magis diligere Deum quam seipsum" (= *Summa confessorum* 3. 34, 22-26).[68] Robert Holcot, in his commentary on the fourth book of the *Sentences*, also uses the *Summa confessorum* extensively, but with a certain amount of caution. Citing the *Summa confessorum* for a *Quodlibet* of Aquinas which is, in fact, one of John Peckham's, Holcot voices his suspicions as follows, "Numquid debet baptizari (monstrum) ut unus homo an ut duo? Dicendum est...sicut dicitur in Summa confessorum et imponitur sancto Thomae in quadam quaestione de quolibet. Sed puto quod non est dictum suum. Tamen satis bene dicit...."[69]

Holcot's fellow Dominican and exact contemporary, John Bromyard, probably makes the greatest use of the *Summa confessorum* of all the writers of the 14th and 15th centuries who borrowed from John of Freiburg. Both in Bromyard's *Opus trivium* (c. 1330)[70] and the massive *Summa praedicantium* (1330-1348), there are passages through the *Summa confessorum* "ex responsione sancti Thomae ad ducissam Lotharingiae" (*Summa praedicantium* M. 8, 36; U. 12, 27), from Raymund and the canonists, as well as from Albert, Ulrich of Strasbourg and Peter of Tarentaise. At times Bromyard acknowledges his source, thus "Contrariae vero opinionis sunt sanctus Thomas et Petrus et Ulricus, qui volunt .... Nota s. Thomam ad hoc, prima secundae, q. 64, art. 4. Vide in Summa confessorum, lib. 3, tit. 34, q. 321" (*Summa praedicantium* D. 5, 5). But there are other moments when there is no reference to the *Summa confessorum*, and an unwary reader might be led to conclude that Bromyard had consulted all the numerous sources which he lists, as when he states, "Ad omnia namque haec secundum Hostiensem, Raymundum,...Tancredum, Ulricum, tenentur..." (*Summa praedicantium* R. 6, 2 = *Summa confessorum* 2. 5, 91), or again, "Quibus concordat sanctus Thomas de Aquino in scripto super 4 sent. d. 25.... His etiam concordat idem in Summa q. 100, art. 4. Et Petrus et Albertus in scripto super 4 dist. 25..." (ibid., S. 9, 1 = *Summa confessorum* 1. 1, 1).[71]

---

de penitentiis et remissionibus, rubrica de suffragiis, q. 163...;" p. 232n.: "Sed numquid contritus, non tamen confessus, recipiendo corpus Christi, peccat? Dic secundum Petrum....Et his concordat Albertus d. 16...Notantur haec secundum Jo. in Summa confessorum, lib. 3, c. 24, q. 78."

68 *Confessionale* (Paris 1516), f. 186v.
69 *In quattuor libros Sententiarum* (Lyons 1518), 1.7, casus XVI.
70 *Opus trivium*, R 7 B-C, S 1 C, etc.; London, British Museum, MS. Royal 10 C X, ff. 123v, 125v, etc.
71 *Summa praedicantium* (Venice 1586). On Bromyard see L. E. Boyle, "The Date of the *Summa praedicantium* of John Bromyard," *Speculum* 48 (1973) 533-537.

IV

If the general influence of the *Summa confessorum* of John of Freiburg on canonists, theologians and manualists is impressive, there is, in respect of the works of Aquinas and Peter of Tarentaise, a further point that has not been fully appreciated by scholars. This is the fact that much of the knowledge of the moral teaching of Aquinas and Peter (not to speak of Albert, Ulrich of Strasbourg, Raymund and the others) in the 14th and 15th centuries is due to a great extent to the *Summa confessorum*.[72] So ubiquitous, indeed, was the *Summa* that it is not surprising to find references to Albert or Aquinas or Peter in places as unlikely as the jottings of a confessor's notebook in St. John's College, Cambridge,[73] or the notes scribbled at the end of a Canterbury copy of the *Summa de casibus* of Thomas Chobham,[74] or in the interlinear gloss of the *Manuale confessorum metricum* of a Cologne Dominican towards the end of the 15th century.[75] And if the name of one of John of Freiburg's teachers, John de Varzy, was known to John Gerson in the early 15th century, this is precisely because, as he himself tells us, he possessed a copy of the *Summa confessorum*:

> Petis primo, si apud aliquem doctorem reperiatur forma authentica absolutionis sacramentalis. Respondeo quod sic. Et de hoc videatur Summa confessorum....Tenor quaestionis de qua fit superius mentio in Summa confessorum, lib. 3, tit. 34, q. 91, *secundum quotationem libri mei* sic se habet: ... Respondeo secundum Albertum....Et hanc formam exposuit magister Iohannes de Varziaco....Thomas etiam in ultima parte summae..."[76]

Leaving John de Varzy aside, there is no doubt that Albert, Thomas and Peter of Tarentaise were known in their own right by many scholastics. But where their moral teaching is concerned, and particularly in non-professional circles, the evidence seems to point to the

---

72 Thus, many of the works cited by Grabmann, "Das Weiterleben und Weiterwerken des moraltheologischen Schrifttums des hl. Thomas von Aquin im Mittelalter," in *Divus Thomas* (Fr.) 25 (1947) 3-28, as evidence of the influence of the moral theology of Aquinas in the middle ages, in fact derive much of their knowledge of Aquinas from John of Freiburg, e.g. the *Summa astesana*, the *Summa rudium*, the *Consolatorium* of John Nider (ob. 1438).

73 Cambridge, St. John's College, MS. 355, f. 84r. 15th c.

74 For example, "Utrum satisfactio possit fieri per opera extra caritatem facta? Respondeo secundum Petrum in scriptis d. 15, et Iohannem in Summa, lib. 3, c. de satisfactione...Dicit Thomas...:" Canterbury, Dean and Chapter Library, MS. B.10, f. 23r. 14th century.

75 (Cologne 1498), f. cxxxvii, etc.

76 J. Gerson, *De absolutione sacramentali*, in *Opera omnia*, ed. E. du Pin (Antwerp 1706), II, cols. 406-407.

Summa confessorum and its many derivatives. In the case of Peter and Thomas one has to allow, of course, for the influence of the very popular *Dialogus de administratione sacramentorum* which the Dominican William of Paris compiled between 1300 and 1314 "de scriptis fratris Thomae principaliter...ac Petri Tarentoize."[77] In practice, however, one can rule it out, since, unlike John of Freiburg, William of Paris rarely identifies his quotations.

But even when the *Summa confessorum* is not mentioned by name, it is fairly easy to recognize its presence where there are citations from Albert, Aquinas, Peter of Tarentaise, Ulrich of Strasbourg or Raymund of Peñafort. The juxtaposition of two or more of these names is usually a good indication. The phrase, "ut dicit Thomas in quadam quaestione de quolibet", also provides a strong hint, as in the *Summa summarum* of William of Pagula (1319-1322),[78] the *Manipulus curatorum* of the Spaniard Guido de Monte Rocherii (c. 1330),[79] or the *Speculum curatorum* of the Benedictine Ranulph Higden (c. 1340).[80]

The key, however, is in the formula by which John of Freiburg cites his authorities. He drew attention to it in his second prologue ("Verum cum in fine alicuius quaestionis sic dicitur *Concordat...*"), and he is unfailingly true to it from the very opening chapter of the *Summa*, thus:

> Quaestio prima. Quaero quid sit symonia. Respondeo. Symonia est studiosa voluntas emendi vel vendendi aliquid spirituale vel annexum spirituali. Sic diffinitur communiter a theologis et iuristis. Communiter enim addunt "vel spirituali annexum", ut Thomas in scripto super 4 sent.. dist. xxv, et Petrus de Tarentasia, etiam Albertus, eadem distinctione, et Thomas in Summa q. 100, art. 1....Quare etiam symonia dicitur haeresis? ....Respondeo secundum Thomam in Summa art. i et art. x. Ideo symonia dicitur haeresis quia sicut protestatio fidei exterior quaedam religio est....*Concordat* his Petrus in scripto et Ulricus par. ii....Quare symoniaci dicuntur a Symone...quam Giezite?....Respondeo secundum Ulricum, par. Dicuntur autem, quod completior huius ratio peccati fuit in actu Symonis quam in facto Giezi, nam ille solum vendidit donum Dei....*Concordant* his Thomas et Petrus..."

---

77 A. Teetaert, "Un compendium de théologie pastorale," *Revue d'histoire ecclésiastique* 26 (1930) 66-102.

78 For example (MS. Bodley 293, f. 140v): "An clericus praebendatus in duabus ecclesiis in die quo diversum est officium in ecclesia debeat dicere utrumque officium vel unius ecclesiae officium dicere debet? Dic...*secundum Thomam in quadam quaestione de quolibet*" (= SC 1.7, 19); "An clericus praebendatus in scholis existens tenetur dicere officium mortuorum?... Sciendum...*secundum Thomam in quadam quaestione de quolibet*" (= SC 1.7, 21).

79 *Manipulus curatorum* (Louvain 1552), e. g. at f. 128r : "Sanctus Thomas *quadam quaestione de quolibet* ponit aliquos casus in quibus tenetur existens in peccato mortali statim confiteri" (= SC 3. 34, 69).

80. Cambridge University Library, MS. Mm. i. 20, f. 188v : "Sanctus Thomas *in quadam quaestione de quolibet* dicit quod in foro contentioso creditur homini pro se et contra se et sine probationibus" (= SC 3. 34, 48).

Armed with this key, and remembering in particular John of Freiburg's variations on the "Concordat" theme, it is not too difficult to suggest what must be the source, directly or at a remove, of, for example, a gloss that begins, "Declarantur praefati versus quoad restitutionem secundum beatum Thomam, Albertum et Ulricum, sic...."[81] Above all, it allows us to estimate just how widespread was the direct influence of Thomas or Albert in certain areas of scholasticism, and to cut down to size some of the supposed influence of Peter of Tarentaise and Ulrich of Strasbourg.[82] And if an author claims rather plausibly, as a certain Henricus de Belle of Löwenich does in a fifteenth-century treatise, that he has compiled his work from notes taken "dum studueram in 4 lib. sententiarum", and, further, goes on to urge his readers to study "in libris Thomae et Alberti", this seeming evidence for the availability of certain works of Albert and Thomas to the common clergy of the Rhineland crumbles away when one discovers the said Henricus using phrases such as "et concordant Albertus et Thomas."[83]

As for Raymund and his well-known, if not axiomatic, domination of the penitential theory and practice of the middle ages, much of this was just as vicarious from 1300 onwards as the reputed influence of Albert and Thomas and Peter of Tarentaise on popular (and some nonpopular) theology. Sylvester de Prierio was not far from the truth in 1516 when he gave the label "Summa confessorum *ordinis praedicatorum*" to John of Freiburg's work. For although it never had the blessing of official approval in the Dominican Order that Raymund's *Summa* had had, the *Summa confessorum* was *the* Dominican manual in as much as it had distilled the moral teaching of the greatest of the Dominican theologians, and had placed it at the disposal of a vast audience. From 1300 onwards, Raymund was, in fact, obsolete. It is surely not without some significance that whereas John of Freiburg's *Summa confessorum* was printed twice before 1500[84] and repeatedly in the following century, the *Summa de casibus* of Raymund did not appear in print until 1603.

81 *Manuale confessorum metricum* (Cologne 1498), f. cxxxviiv. For the *Manuale* see Dietterle, *ZKG* 27 (1906) 177-183.

82 J. Daguillon, *Ulrich de Strasbourg, O.P., 'Summa de bono'* (Paris 1930), pp. 3*-5*, and H.-D. Simonin, "Les écrits de Pierre de Tarentaise," in *Beatus Innocentius Papa V* (Rome 1943), pp. 163-335, make no allowance whatever for the *Summa confessorum* when discussing the influence of their respective authors in the later middle ages.

83. Cambridge University Library, MS. Kk. i. 9, ff. 54r-65v, at ff. 54r, 58r. Henricus de Belle was pastor of Löwenich, and his treatise is addressed to his curate, John. Another copy, dated 1470, is in Brussels, Bibliothèque Royale, MS. 2070 (2434-52), ff. 64r-81v.

84. L. Hain, *Repertorium bibliographicum* (Stuttgart-Paris 1826-1838), nn. 7365 (1476) and 7366 (1498). Incunabula of the German translation by Berthold of Freiburg are at nn. 7367-7377.

THE UNITY OF A SCIENCE:
ST. THOMAS AND THE NOMINALISTS

Armand A. Maurer C.S.B.

IT is a commonplace to speak of science as a body or system of knowledge. Contemporary philosophers of conflicting and even contradictory persuasions are alike in using this language. That science is a body of knowledge flows as easily from the pen of a Thomist as from that of a logical positivist, however different their understanding of the words may be. There is general agreement that science is composed of many items, whether they be thought of as propositions, truths, phenomena, or simply data, and that these items are unified in a science so as to constitute a whole. So common is this notion that it has been enshrined in our dictionaries. The *Oxford Dictionary* calls science an "organized body of the knowledge that has been accumulated on a subject,"[1] and *Webster's Dictionary* gives as one meaning of science "any department of systematized knowledge."[2]

It is not difficult to trace the notion of science as a unified body of knowledge to the dawn of modern philosophy. In various guises it is found in the works of Francis Bacon, Descartes, Leibniz, Condillac, Auguste Comte, the French encyclopedists Diderot and d'Alembert, and Kant.[3] It was Kant who gave this notion its classic expression. Science, in his view, is not just any doctrine, but one that forms a system, by which he means "a totality of knowledge arranged according to principles."[4] Kant writes: "... systematic unity is what first raises ordinary knowledge to the rank of science, that is, makes a system out of a mere aggregate of knowledge."[5] Science is no mere aggregate (*coacervatio*) but an organized unity (*articulatio*). Each science is an organic

---

1 *The Concise Oxford Dictionary,* 3rd ed. (Oxford 1934) p. 1065.

2 *Webster's New Collegiate Dictionary* (Toronto 1961) p. 757.

3 See R. McRae, *The Problem of the Unity of the Sciences: Bacon to Kant* (Toronto 1961).

4 "Eine jede Lehre, wenn sie ein *System,* d.i. ein nach Prinzipien geordnetes Ganze der Erkenntnis, sein soll, heisst Wissenschaft..." Kant, *Metaphysische Anfangsgründe der Naturwissenschaft,* Vorrede, *Sämtliche Werke* (Leipzig 1921) IV, p. 547.

5 Kant, *Critique of Pure Reason,* trans. N. K. Smith (London 1950) A 832, B 860.

unity built around an a priori idea, that is to say one that is not derived from experience but is furnished by reason itself. In order to illustrate the organic character of the unity of a science Kant compares a science to an animal body: like a living body it is a self-sufficient whole that grows from within and not by the addition of external parts.[6]

Leibniz was just as certain as Kant that a science is a logically ordered system of truths, though he conceived its unity in a different manner. In his view, an individual science is not a self-sufficient whole with an organic unity but an arbitrary and conventional combination or synthesis of concepts. Strictly speaking, there is but one science — the logical synthesis of all truths. Leibniz granted some value to the ancient division of science into physics, ethics, and logic, but he thought that ultimately the division broke down because each of these sciences could contain the others. Physics, for example, can embrace all the truths of logic and ethics; for physics treats of beings endowed with intelligence and will, and a complete explanation of intelligence requires the whole of logic, and a full account of the will embraces the whole of ethics. Leibniz remarks that the encyclopedists have encountered this difficulty in arranging their dictionaries of science and philosophy. "It is usually found," he says, "that one and the same truth may be put in different places according to the terms it contains, and also according to the mediate terms or causes upon which it depends, and according to the inferences and results it may have."[7] In this connection he praises the nominalists, who (he writes) "believed that there were as many particular sciences as truths, which they composed after the manner of wholes, according as they arranged them."[8]

Who were these nominalists who shattered science into myriad fragments and then arranged them in arbitrary combinations? Unfortunately Leibniz does not name them; but he gives us a clue to their background, and possible identity, when, in a treatise on the contemporary nominalist Mario Nizolius, he gives a brief account of the rise of nominalism in the Middle Ages.

The nominalists, Leibniz writes, were the most profound scholastic sect and the one most in harmony with the spirit of modern philosophy. Almost all the modern reformers of philosophy, he goes on to say, are nominalists, maintaining that individuals alone are real and rejecting the reality of universals, which they consider to be simply names

---

6 *Ibid.* A 833, B 861. For Kant's conception of science, see R. McRae, *ibid.* pp. 123-143.
7 Leibniz, *New Essays concerning Human Understanding,* IV, xxi, 4; trans. A. G. Langley (La Salle 1949) p. 623.
8 Leibniz, *ibid.* See R. McRae, *ibid.* pp. 7-8.

(*nomina*). The sect of the nominalists is said to have begun with Roscelin, and after suffering eclipse for many years it was suddenly revived by William Ockham, a man of the highest genius and of outstanding erudition for his time. In agreement with him were Gregory of Rimini, Gabriel Biel, and the majority of the Augustinian Order. Thus it is that the early writings of Martin Luther reveal an affection for nominalism; and with the passage of time it began to influence all the monks.[9]

Thus Leibniz leads us to medieval nominalism for the origin of the notion of science as a unified body of knowledge. In this paper I should like to suggest that this notion of science indeed began with the nominalist and conceptualist theologians of the late 13th and early 14th centuries, and that its chief theoretician and popularizer was William of Ockham. I am not arguing that the medieval nominalists were Leibnizians or Kantians, but only that in the late Middle Ages there grew up a common notion of science as a collection of truths or propositions unified by principles, and that this notion was passed on by them to early modern philosophers, each of whom interpreted it in his own way. I should also like to suggest that this notion of science was conceived in opposition to St. Thomas' doctrine of science, according to which an individual science is not in essence or primarily a system or body of knowledge but a single and simple *habitus* of the intellect. The story of the development of the notion of science as a body of knowledge is another chapter in the eclipse (and sometimes misunderstanding) of Thomism during the late Middle Ages.

*
* *

St. Thomas inherited from Aristotle the notion of science as a stable disposition or *habitus* ($\xi\zeta\iota\varsigma$) of the intellect. As such it is an intellectual virtue, a perfection of the mind acquired by repeated acts enabling its possessor to demonstrate truths through their causes or principles.[10]

In this view, each of the sciences is a distinct mental facility of demonstration and insight. Ontologically, St. Thomas regards a scientific *habitus* as a simple form or quality: one *habitus* is not composed of many *habitus* (*habitus est qualitas simplex non constituta ex pluribus*

---

9 Leibniz, *Dissertatio de Stilo Philosophico Nizolii*, 28. *Opera Philosophica*, ed. J. E. Erdmann (Berlin 1840) pp. 68-69.

10 Aristotle, *Nicomachean Ethics*, VI, 3, 1139 b 14-35. St. Thomas, *In VI Ethicorum*, lect. 3 (Rome 1969) 47, pp. 340-341.

habitibus).[11] He grants that it involves a multiplicity, in the sense that it extends to many objects. Materially considered, its objects are many, but the scientific *habitus* regards all of them from one formal perspective (*ratio*). In other words, each science has its own formal object, whose unity gives unity to the science.[12] For instance, the unity of the science of theology is based on the unity of its formal object, which is divine revelation. The theologian considers many truths, but all insofar as they have been divinely revealed, or at least insofar as they are related to divine revelation.[13] Similarly, the science of arithmetic treats of all its objects from the formal perspective of number, and geometry considers its many objects from the formal perspective of continuous quantity. Each science has thus a formal unity owing to the formal unity of its object, and in virtue of this unity it is formally distinct from the other sciences. As the habit of an intellect, it also enjoys numerical unity: it is an individual ability or facility of insight and demonstration perfecting the individual intellect of its possessor.

St. Thomas was aware of the serious objection his opponents raised against this conception of the unity of a scientific habit. Following Aristotle, he defines science as the knowledge of conclusions: it is the mental habit that enables us to demonstrate conclusions in the light of their principles.[14] Now there are many conclusions in a whole science such as geometry or arithmetic, and we can have scientific knowledge, both actual and habitual, about any one of them independent of the others. So it would seem that a science is not one single habit but a complex of many.[15]

In replying to this difficulty St. Thomas in no way compromises the unity of a scientific habit. Suppose, he says, that we acquire the knowledge of one conclusion in a science by learning its appropriate demonstration. We then possess the habit of the science, though imperfectly. If we go on to master the knowledge of another conclusion in the science, we do not gain an additional habit; our previous habit simply becomes more perfect by extending to more demonstrations and conclusions, all of which are mutually related and ordered. So there is no need to think that a scientific habit is a complex of many partial

---

11 *Summa Theol.* I-II, 54, 4. On the notion of a habit as a quality disposing one to act well or badly, see *ibid.* I-II, 49, 1.

12 For the distinction of cognitive habits according to their formal objects, see *ibid.* I-II, 54, 2.

13 *Ibid.* I, 1, 3.

14 *In VI Eth.* lect. 3, p. 341, lines 101-116. See Aristotle, *Nic. Ethics* VI, 3, 1139 b 14-35; 6, 1140 b 31-33.

15 *Summa Theol.* I-II, 54, 4, obj. 3.

habits: it is a single quality or form, capable of indefinite increase in perfection by extending to a greater number of objects. [16]

It will be noticed that while St. Thomas is making his main point concerning the unity of a scientific habit, he adds another: that this habit is related to a multitude of mutually related demonstrations and conclusions. From the latter point of view a science appears as having a complex structure. "The conclusions and demonstrations of one science," he writes, "have an order, and one flows from another." [17] Adopting this perspective, a science is seen to have a systematic structure that can be studied for its own sake, for example by the logician. From this point of view St. Thomas analyzes science in his commentary on the *Posterior Analytics*, showing that a science has its own subject and principles, from which it draws its conclusions. [18] In a sense, then, a science is a systematic whole according to St. Thomas. Its demonstrations and conclusions are mutually related and form an ordered whole. But the unity of the system is based on the unity of the single mental habit which is the principle of the whole science. The habit is the principle by which (*principium quo*) the scientist demonstrates all his conclusions and establishes an order among them. Without this one *habitus* there would be no systematic unity in the activities and conclusions of the scientist.

As we shall see, many scholastics of the later Middle Ages lost sight of the unity of the mental habit that essentially constitutes a science. They describe a science simply as an orderly collection of many mental habits or concepts or propositions. In their view, the unity of a science is that of an ordered or systematic whole, and not that of a single mental habit.

Even some Thomists, in their concern to be "modern," interpreted their master in this sense. Cajetan, writing shortly after 1500, refers to certain Thomists who thought St. Thomas vacillated between the opinions that a science is one *habitus* of the intellect and that it is an orderly collection of intelligible species in the mind. [19] They believed that he inclined to the second view. They based this interpretation on statements of St. Thomas describing science as a totality and ordered

---

16 "Dicendum quod ille qui in aliqua scientia acquirit per demonstrationem scientiam conclusionis unius, habet quidem habitum, sed imperfecte. Cum vero acquirit per aliquam demonstrationem scientiam conclusionis alterius, non aggeneratur in eo alius habitus; sed habitus qui prius inerat fit perfectior, utpote ad plura se extendens, eo quod conclusiones et demonstrationes unius scientiae ordinatae sunt, et una derivatur ex alia." *Summa Theol.* I-II, 54, 4, ad 3.

17 *Ibid.*

18 *In I Post. Anal.* lect. 17 (Rome 1882) I, pp. 204-207; lect. 41, p. 305, n. 7.

19 Cajetan, *Comm. in Summa Theol.* I-II, 54, 4 (Rome 1891) VI, p. 345, n. 2-5.

aggregate. For example, in the *Summa contra Gentiles* he speaks of the *habitus* of knowledge in two senses: 1) as an ability (*habilitatio*) of the intellect to receive intelligible species by which it becomes actually understanding, and 2) as "the ordered aggregate of the species themselves existing in the intellect, not in complete actuality but in a way between potency and act."[20] From this and similar texts, these Thomists concluded that a scientific habit is composed of intelligible species and hence that it is an ordered whole or totality.

But as Cajetan rightly remarks, these Thomists (one of whom was Capreolus) misinterpret their master. St. Thomas' constant teaching is that a science is essentially a simple quality or *habitus* of the mind. This *habitus* is produced by repeated acts and by intelligible species, but neither the acts nor the species constitute the *habitus* itself. A text from St. Thomas' *De Veritate* clearly states the relation of intelligible species to a scientific *habitus*: "... an ordering of [intelligible] species produces a *habitus*."[21] Cajetan comments that St. Thomas does not say that the species *are* the *habitus,* but that they *produce* it. He also points out that, according to St. Thomas, we use an orderly group of intelligible species when we think scientifically by means of the *habitus*.[22]

Why, then, does St. Thomas sometimes call an ordered aggregate of intelligible species a scientific habit? The answer would seem to be that he applies the term *habitus* to these species because of their special relation to it. They are the habit in the sense that the habit derives from them and in turn uses them; but properly speaking they do not constitute it. Hence, only in a derived and secondary sense can they be called the habit.

St. Thomas often uses terms in primary and secondary senses in order

---

20 "Omnis autem intellectus in habitu per aliquas species intelligit: nam habitus vel est habilitatio quaedam intellectus ad recipiendum species intelligibiles quibus actu fiat intelligens; vel est ordinata aggregatio ipsarum specierum existentium in intellectu non secundum completum actum, sed medio modo inter potentiam et actum." *Summa contra Gentiles* I, 56, § 6.

St. Thomas holds, contrary to Avicenna, that intelligible species remain in the intellect in a state of incomplete actuality even when they are not actually being employed by the intellect. *Ibid.* II, 74. Hence their orderly arrangement in the intellect constitutes a kind of habitual body of knowledge.

21 *De Veritate* 24, 4, ad 9.

22 Cajetan, *ibid.* p. 347, n. 12. According to Cajetan, the species are the beginnings of the habit and its potential parts. *Ibid.* Likely he has Capreolus in mind as one of the Thomists who misinterpreted St. Thomas on this point. See Capreolus, *Defensiones Theologiae Divi Thomae Aquinatis,* Prol. q. 3, a. 1, concl. 1 (Turin 1900) I, p. 34. Soncinas (d. 1494) also held that a science is not a simple quality but a related grouping of intelligible species: "... tamen magis videtur quod scientia sit aggregatio specierum, vel ut melius dicam quod sit ipsae species aggregatae; et consequenter quod una totalis scientia sit constituta ex multis notitiis partialibus, ita quod per quamlibet demonstrationem acquiratur nova notitia." Soncinas, *Quaestiones Metaphysicales* VI, q. 9 (Venice 1505) fol. 59v.

to express the nuances of his thought. He does not always speak *for-malissime*. His use of the term *habitus* seems to be a case in point. Another instance is his extension of the term to the propositions that are held to be true by means of the habit. In his *Summa Theologiae* he distinguishes between two meanings of the term *habitus*.[23] Essentially and properly it means the habitual inclination or disposition to act in a certain way; but in a secondary and derived sense it means that which is produced or held by the habit. In this latter sense the term can be extended to mean the propositions held to be true by means of the habit. St. Thomas illustrates this distinction by the habit of faith. In the proper sense, faith is the habit by which we believe certain truths; in a derived sense, however, we can speak of "the faith" as that which we hold on faith. In this extended and analogous use of the term it is legitimate to speak of science objectively as a synthesis or system of truths or propositions; but for St. Thomas this is not the primary or proper meaning of the term. Properly, a science is a habit of the intellect, and this habit is radically one and simple.

In later scholasticism the secondary and extended senses of the term "science" gradually came to the fore, supplanting its primary and essential meaning. A science was then conceived as an orderly arrangement of many partial habits of the intellect, or of terms and propositions.

*

*   *

This shift in the meaning of a science was not long in coming. Shortly after the death of St. Thomas a lively debate began whether a science is properly speaking a simple habit of the mind or a synthesis of many habits or acts or propositions. Henry of Ghent was no Thomist, but on this question he held firmly to the Thomistic view of the unity of a scientific habit. In the proper sense, he says, *scientia* has three meanings: 1) the intellectual habit hidden in the intellectual memory, 2) the concept elicited from this habit, 3) the act of understanding by which the concept is conceived.[24] The scientific habit contains within its

23 "Dicendum quod aliquid potest dici esse habitus dupliciter. Uno modo, proprie et essentialiter; et sic lex naturalis non est habitus. Dictum est enim supra quod lex naturalis est aliquid per rationem constitutum, sicut etiam propositio est quoddam opus rationis. Non est autem idem quod quis agit, et quo quis agit; aliquis enim per habitum grammaticae agit orationem congruam. Cum igitur habitus sit quo quis agit, non potest esse quod lex aliqua sit habitus proprie et essentialiter. Alio modo potest dici habitus id quod habitu tenetur, sicut dicitur fides id quod fide tenetur." *Summa Theol.* I-II, 94, 1.

24 "... sunt alii tres modi notitiae quae proprie dicenda est scientia. Unus enim modus notitiae quae est scientia, est habitus intellectualis latens in memoria intellectuali. Alio modo verbum con-

power (*virtualiter*) the whole science, with all its concepts, principles, and conclusions; and it is not really composed of parts, but is a simple form or quality acquired by repeated acts, like the moral virtue of temperance. The habit is not a synthesis (*collatio*) of many propositions — principles and conclusions — but the intellectual facility inclining one to elicit all the acts proper to the science.[25]

For Henry of Ghent, if the word "science" is taken not in a generic but a most specific sense (for example, if it means a specific science like metaphysics), it is not really composed of many items, but it is as simple and incomplex as a moral virtue or the quality of whiteness. Like them, it is a form, simple in itself, but capable of greater or less perfection. The whole reality of the habit is present through the first act that generates it, as the whole reality of whiteness exists as a result of the first act that produces it. At first it exists most imperfectly, but it can increase later to its perfect degree.[26]

A Dominican by the name of Bernard of Auvergne (also called Bernard of Gannat from his birthplace), who lectured at Paris between 1294 and 1297, wrote a long defense of St. Thomas against Henry of Ghent, but ironically he adopted a stand on the unity of a science opposed to his master. On this point Henry was closer to St. Thomas than Bernard. Bernard was not at all pleased with Henry of Ghent's likening the simplicity of a scientific habit to that of a moral virtue. To Henry's conclusion that "science is not a composite," he retorted that if we speak of science as an intellectual habit it is indeed something composite, for it is a suitable arrangement of intelligible species in the intellect (*debita ordinatio specierum intelligibilium*). The habit of science, which enables us to understand promptly and at will, is comprised of many such species, and hence it is really composed of parts.[27] Bernard

---

ceptum ex illo in intelligentia. Et tertio modo ipse actus intelligendi quo concipitur, qui non potest dici verbum nisi ea ratione qua verbo conceptus informatur, ut iam amplius dicetur." Henry of Ghent, *Quodlibet* IV, q. 8 (Paris 1518) fol. 98r.

25 *Ibid.*

26 "Et est dicendum quod quaelibet scientia quae est habitus in specialissimo scientiae consistens, unicus est et simplex in re, carens omni compositione reali ex diversis secundum rem ut partibus existentibus et manentibus in ipso, et hoc aequali simplicitate illi quam habet quilibet habitus affectivus, et universaliter quaelibet forma una recipiens intensionem et remissionem, et hoc secundum modum iam supra tactum. Unde non est minor simplicitas in habitu scientiae Metaphysicae in quocumque gradu habeat eam aliquis quam in habitu temperantiae et quam in albedine. Ita quod per primum actum generativum habitus habetur tota realitas habitus, quemadmodum ex primo actu generativo albedinis habetur tota realitas albedinis, licet in gradu imperfectissimo, a quo habet procedere per intensionis motum ad gradum perfectum." Henry of Ghent, *Quodlibet* IX, q. 4, fol. 355rv.

27 "Ergo habitus scientiae non est habilitas intellectus ad intelligendum sicut sunt habitus qui sunt in viribus appetitivis, sed est ordinatio specierum secundum quam intellectus prompte intelligit cum voluit. Ergo cum ad habitum scientiae requirantur species multae, ex quibus iste

was clearly relying on St. Thomas' statements about science and intelligible species which were quoted above; but, as Cajetan has pointed out, these statements cannot be used to deny the simplicity of a scientific habit. On this question, Bernard, whom B. Hauréau called "one of the most intelligent students of St. Thomas and one of the most zealous defenders of his master,"[28] proves to be less Thomistic than Henry of Ghent.

Few scholastics in the years that followed failed to take up the problem of the unity of a science, generally (because they were theologians) in connection with the science of theology. It would be impossible here to do justice to this debate, which is of considerable importance for the development of the notion of science as a body of knowledge. All that can be done is to touch upon some of its most salient moments.

The Franciscan Peter Auriol, commenting on the *Sentences* between 1316 and 1318, devoted considerable attention to the present problem. He dismisses the opinion of Bernard of Auvergne, that a scientific habit is an orderly collection of intelligible species, and also that of St. Thomas and Henry of Ghent, that a science is a simple and indivisible form or quality of the intellect.[29] After a lengthy discussion of the subject, in which he weighs the opinions of many of his predecessors and contemporaries, he concludes that a science is not one simple individual habit of the mind but a composite of many incomplete and imperfect habits, united to form one whole. What decides the issue for him is the fact that we can acquire the mental facility of demonstrating one conclusion in a science without the facilities of demonstrating others. To him, this proves conclusively that these facilities or habits are really distinct, and that many of them go to make up a total science.[30]

As for the kind of unity these habits have within a science, Auriol denies that they are a mere aggregate (*acervus*), like many stones in a

---

habitus integratur, videtur quod scientia habet talem materiam ex qua fit et per consequens quod sit composita. Bernard of Auvergne, *Contra Dicta Henrici de Gandava quibus Impugnat Thomam, Quodlibet* IX, q. 4, Ms Troyes 662, fol. 123rab. "Praeterea, scientia ut est habitus non est nisi debita ordinatio specierum intelligibilium." *Ibid.* fol. 123ra. On Bernard of Auvergne, see F. J. Roensch, *Early Thomistic School* (Dubuque Iowa, 1964) pp. 104-106.

28 B. Hauréau, *Histoire de la philosophie scolastique* (Paris 1872-1880) II, p. 206.

29 For Auriol's criticism of Bernard of Auvergne, see his *Scriptum super primum Sententiarum,* prooemium, sect. 4, n. 34-39 (St. Bonaventure, New York 1952) I, pp. 260-261. For his criticism of Henry of Ghent, see *ibid.* n. 25-28, pp. 256-258; for his criticism of St. Thomas, see *ibid.* n. 58-62, pp. 270-271. For a more complete account of Auriol's doctrine of the unity of a science, see P. Spade, "The Unity of a Science according to Peter Auriol," *Franciscan Studies* 32 (1972) 203-217.

30 See *ibid.* n. 26-28, pp. 257-258. For Auriol's notion of a scientific habit, see *ibid.* pp. 262-267.

heap. Neither are they linked together like potential parts of a continuous whole, as one whiteness has potentially many parts. Rather, they are parts of one totality, having an inner structure or form. A science has the same kind of unity as a house, which is one because of the unity of its form, or as a geometrical figure, which is one because of the total form resulting from its lines.[31]

Auriol contends that a formal unity of this sort suffices for a scientific habit and is consistent with the way we ordinarily talk about a science. We say that one acquires a science little by little; that one is in error regarding the twentieth conclusion of a science while knowing the first; that there are not as many natural sciences as there are conclusions in the science, and so on. Clearly there is formal unity in a specific science along with a multiplicity of acts and mental habits disposing towards them.[32] As for the ground of this formal unity, Auriol refuses to place it in the formal object of the science. If a science were one because it had one formal object, he contends, this formal object would have the unity of an *infima species*, a subalternate genus, or a most general genus. In the first case, there would be as many sciences as there are *infimae species*; in the second, sciences would be multiplied according to subalternate genera; in the third, there would be only ten sciences corresponding to the ten categories. If being were the formal object of science, there would be only one science, especially if there were only one concept of being. Consequently, the formal unity of a science cannot be based on the unity of its formal object. The unity of a science comes from its unique mode of knowing, of understanding its premises and deducing its conclusions, of abstracting its objects and relating them to the senses, imagination, and the external world. In short, each science has its own logic which distinguishes it from every other science and confers on it its formal unity.[33]

---

31 *Ibid.* n. 54, p. 267. "Haec autem scientia unitatem habet, non simplicitatis et indivisibilitatis omnimodae, sed cuiusdam totalitatis et unius formae. Est autem illa forma connexio omnium partialium habituum, vel secundum longum, vel secundum [latum]; sicut enim dicit Philosophus I Posteriorum, demonstrationes densantur dupliciter, uno modo in post assumendo, ut cum ex una conclusione infertur alia demonstrative; et istarum conclusionum connexio est secundum longum; quae quidem connexio locum habet in passionibus ordinatis, secundum mediationem et immediationem ad primum subiectum. Alio modo densatur secundum latum, ut cum ex eodem medio plures passiones concluduntur de subiecto non ad invicem ordinatae." *Ibid.* n. 56, p. 268.

32 "Quod autem haec unitas sufficiat pro habitu scientiali, patet ex duobus. Primo quidem quia est unitas formalis; sicut enim ratione unionis maioris extremitatis et minoris in medio, syllogismus est unus unitate formali, sic, ratione istius ordinis perfectivi et unionis cognoscitivae, scientia una erit unitate formali. Secundo vero, quia tali posita unitate, salvantur omnia quae de scientia dicuntur..." *Ibid.* n. 57, p. 269.

33 "... unaquaeque scientia habet propriam logicam et proprium modum sciendi... Ex quibus colligitur evidenter quod scientiae habent unitatem specificam ex modo sciendi eiusdem rationis; qui quidem consistit in uniformi acceptione principiorum, et uniformi modo demonstrandi, et

Auriol's commentary on the *Sentences* had been published only a few years when Ockham made his own commentary on Peter Lombard. Ockham acknowledges reading Auriol's work, but for no longer than twenty-four hours.[34] Certainly some of this time was spent on Auriol's Prologue, which contains his lengthy treatment of the unity of a science.

Like Auriol, Ockham refuses all attempts to place the unity of a whole science, such as physics or metaphysics, in one simple habit of the intellect. Each of these sciences, he maintains, is made up of many intellectual habits or propositions arranged in a definite order. If one wishes, he can call a science a single habit or quality, but then he is talking about the facility of demonstrating only one conclusion in a whole science. As the term is generally used, it denotes

> a collection of many items belonging to the knowledge of one or many objects having a definite order. In this sense, science contains both the incomplex knowledge of terms and the knowledge of propositions, both principles and conclusions. It also comprises the refutations of errors and the solutions of sophisms. It also frequently contains necessary divisions and definitions... Science in this meaning of the term is taken as the compilations and treatises of authors and philosophers... This is the meaning of science when the book of [Aristotle's] *Metaphysics* or *Physics* is said to be one science. Science in this sense is not one in number but contains many habits distinct not only in species but frequently also in genus. But they are mutually ordered, and owing to this special order, which other objects of science or knowledge do not have, they can be called, and are called, in common usage, one science.[35]

Ockham appeals to experience to show that science is a stable disposition or habit of the mind. We are aware, he says, that as a result

deducendi conclusiones ex ipsis, et uniformem modum se habendi intellectus penes abstractionem et extensionem ad extra; et quod omnis res, quae exigit ista propria et distincta, habet propriam scientiam." *Ibid.* n. 87, p. 279. See n. 101, p. 282.

34 "... quia tamen pauca vidi de dictis illius doctoris, si enim omnes vices quibus respexi dicta sua simul congregarentur, non complerent spatium unius diei naturalis." Ockham, *In I Sent.* d. 27, q. 3, H (Lyons 1495). See P. Vignaux, "Occam," *Dictionnaire de théologie catholique* XI, 886.

35 "Ad primum istorum dico quod scientia, ad praesens, dupliciter accipitur. Uno modo pro collectione multorum pertinentium ad notitiam unius vel multorum determinatum ordinem habentium. Et scientia isto modo dicta continet tam notitiam incomplexam terminorum quam notitiam complexorum, et hoc principiorum et conclusionum; continet etiam reprobationes errorum et solutiones falsorum argumentorum; continet etiam divisiones necessarias et definitiones, ut frequenter... Et isto modo accipitur scientia pro compilationibus et tractatibus auctorum et philosophorum... Sic etiam accipitur scientia quando dicitur liber *Metaphysicae* vel liber *Physicorum* esse una scientia. Et scientia ista non est una numero, sed continet multos habitus non tantum specie sed etiam frequenter genere distinctos, ordinem tamen aliquem inter se habentes, propter quem ordinem specialem, qualem non habent aliqua alia scibilia vel cognoscibilia, possunt dici et dicuntur, secundum usum loquentium, una scientia." Ockham, *In I Sent.* Prol. q. 1 (St. Bonaventure, New York 1967) I, pp. 8-9. For Ockham's doctrine of the unity of a science, see A. Maurer, "Ockham's Conception of the Unity of Science," *Mediaeval Studies* 20 (1958) 98-112.

of repeatedly knowing some object we are more ready and able to know it than before. Repeated acts of knowing produce in us a new promptness or facility of knowing called *scientia*. The habit may be simply one of apprehending a certain term or proposition; or it may be one of demonstrating a conclusion from principles. In the latter case it is science in the strict sense. It is also a matter of experience that distinct acts of demonstrating conclusions engender in us distinct habits of knowing, or sciences. There are, in other words, as many scientific habits in us as there are distinct acts of demonstrating conclusions.[36]

Both St. Thomas and Henry of Ghent come under Ockham's criticism for making a whole science consist of one indivisible intellectual habit. Their position rests on the presupposition that every scientific habit has one formal object (as St. Thomas claims) or one formal mode of knowing (as Henry of Ghent says).[37] Just as a power of the soul has one formal object (as color, for example, is the formal object of sight), which gives unity to the power and distinguishes it from every other power, so a science has a formal object which gives unity to the science and differentiates it from all others. But Ockham contends that the unity of neither a power nor a habit can be established on the basis of the unity of its formal object; nor can the distinction of powers or habits be based on the distinction of their formal objects. He strikes at the foundation of St. Thomas' doctrine of the unity and distinction of habits and powers by denying the distinction between a material and formal object, for reasons that take us to the heart of his nominalism.

If St. Thomas is correct, Ockham argues, many materially different items share in a common nature (*ratio*). For example, a man and a stone would have in common the nature of being colored. Accordingly, they would fall under the sense of sight, whose formal object is color. Similarly, the objects studied in theology, according to St. Thomas, share in the common *ratio* of being revealed, and so they can be considered by the one science of theology, whose formal object is "the divinely revealable." But in the perspective of Ockham's nominalism, no two items have anything in common. In his view, it is absurd to speak of a number of things presenting to the mind a common intelligible or formal object. Every reality or thing is individual and one in number and it shares nothing in common with anything else. Only terms or concepts are common or universal, in the sense that they are predicable of many things. But *things* themselves are not common or

---

36   Ockham, *Expositio super libros Physicorum*, Prol.; ed. P. Boehner, *Ockham: Philosophical Writings* (Edinburgh, London 1957) 4-7. (Henceforth referred to as *Physics*).
37   Ockham, *In I Sent.* Prol. q. 8, pp. 208-217.

universal. St. Thomas' doctrine of the unity and distinction of sciences based on their formal objects contradicts this basic tenet of Ockham's nominalism. It also compromises the unity of an individual thing as conceived by Ockham. St. Thomas imagines that within one reality there are many distinct *rationes*, which can be the formal objects of distinct powers and habits. But if this were so, Ockham argues, these *rationes* would be distinct realities, and the unity of the original reality would be destroyed. Thus, in Ockham's view the Thomistic distinction between the material and formal objects of sciences breaks down, and along with it the notion that faculties and sciences are distinguished by formal objects. [38]

Ockham's conception of reality as radically individual led to a new interpretation of the object of science. With Aristotle he held that science concerns universals and not individuals as such. [39] But where is the universal to be found? It was generally agreed by his scholastic predecessors that individuals in some way contain natures or essences which are the foundations of our universal concepts and which serve as the objects of science. Ockham was uncompromisingly opposed to this view. It was axiomatic for him that reality is individual and in no way common or universal. He was aware that he was going further than any of his predecessors in adopting an absolute position on this point. He writes:

> All those whom I have seen agree that there is really in the individual a nature that is in some way universal, at least potentially and in-completely; though some say that [this nature] is really distinct [from the individual], some that it is only formally distinct, some that the distinc-tion is in no sense real but only conceptual and a result of the con-sideration of the intellect. [40]

Having proved to his own satisfaction that universality is a property of terms (whether spoken, written or mental), which are found in propositions, he drew the inevitable conclusion: Propositions alone are the objects of science. "Every science," he writes, "whether real or rational, is concerned only with propositions as with objects known, for only propositions are known." [41] In saying this he does not mean that

38 *Ibid.* pp. 208-211. For Ockham's doctrine of universals, see *In I Sent.* d. 2, q. 8 (St. Bonaven-ture, New York 1970) II, pp. 266-292.

39 Ockham, *Physics*, Prol. p. 11. See Aristotle, *Metaph.* XI, 1, 1059 b 26.

40 "In conclusione istius quaestionis omnes quos vidi concordant, dicentes quod natura, quae est aliquo modo universalis, saltem in potentia et incomplete, est realiter in individuo, quamvis aliqui dicant quod distinguitur realiter, aliqui quod tantum formaliter, aliqui quod nullo modo ex natura rei sed secundum rationem tantum vel per considerationem intellectus." Ockham, *In I Sent.* d. 2, q. 7; II, pp. 225-226.

41 "... est sciendum quod scientia quaelibet sive sit realis sive rationalis est tantum de

science in no way concerns reality. The terms of the propositions in some sciences stand for real things; for example those of natural science and metaphysics. Ockham calls these "real sciences" or sciences of reality. The terms of the propositions of logic, on the contrary, stand for concepts in the mind; so logic is called "rational science." The terms of the propositions of grammar stand for written or spoken words. Thus science does treat of individuals, but only in an improper sense, inasmuch as the terms of its propositions stand for them. Properly speaking, science deals with universals, which are terms of propositions.[42]

As for the subject of a science, it is simply the subject term in the proposition which is the object of the science. For example, when we know that every man is capable of learning, the object of this knowledge is the whole proposition: "Every man is capable of learning"; the subject is the term "man."[43]

In a total science whose unity is that of a collection or group there need not be one object or subject. The science derives its unity from the arrangement of its parts and not from the unity of its object or subject. Ockham criticizes Duns Scotus for failing to see this point. According to Scotus, a science has a primary subject which gives unity to the science because it virtually contains all the truths belonging to the science. For example, theology is one science because its primary subject is God, who virtually contains all theological truths.[44]

Ockham opposes the Scotistic explanation of the unity of a science for several reasons. To begin with, he does not think it true that a science has only one subject. He insists that a science has different parts, each of which, being a proposition, has its own subject. So it is meaningless to ask what is the subject of logic, physics, metaphysics, or mathematics. There is no one subject of the entire science; its different parts have different subjects. To ask what is the subject of these sciences is like asking who is the king of the world. There is no one man who is king of the world; one person is king of one part and another of another part. It is the same with the subjects of the various parts of a science. Each part has its own subject.[45] Ockham's comparison of a science to

propositionibus tamquam de illis quae sciuntur, quia solae propositiones sciuntur." Ockham, *In I Sent.* d. 2, q. 4; II, p. 134. See *Physics*, Prol. p. 11.

42   Ockham, *In I Sent. ibid.* pp. 134-138; *Physics*, p. 12.

43   Ockham, *Physics*, p. 9.

44   Duns Scotus, *Ordinatio*, Prol. 3, q. 1-3 (Vatican 1950) I, p. 102, n. 151; *Reportata Paris.*, Prol. 3, q. 2, n. 12 (Paris 1894) 22, p. 51.

45   Ockham, *Physics*, pp. 9-10.

the world is an accurate analogy for both have a unity of order. He writes:

> Hence we have to say that metaphysics is not a piece of knowledge that is numerically one. The same is true of the philosophy of nature, which is a collection of many habits... It is one in the same sense that a city or a nation, or an army, which includes men and horses and other necessary things, or a kingdom, or a university, or the world, is said to be one.[46]

Secondly, Ockham denies — again in opposition to Scotus — that a science has one primary subject. He insists that absolutely speaking there is no primary subject of a whole science. From one point of view one subject may be primary and from another point of view another may be primary. Thus, being is the primary subject of metaphysics in the order of predication, for the metaphysician primarily draws conclusions about being. But in the order of perfection God is the primary subject of metaphysics, for he is the most perfect being known in it. Natural substance is the primary subject of the philosophy of nature as regards priority of predication; but as regards priority of perfection its first subject is man or the heavenly bodies.[47]

Thus the attempt to establish the unity of a science on the unity of a formal object or primary subject fails. Ockham's problem is to find a principle of unity for science, conceived not as a single habit of the mind but as a collection of many items of knowledge: habits of the mind primarily, but secondarily propositions (mental, spoken, and written) which are the objects of these habits. These "partial sciences" do not by their nature belong to the whole science. An item of knowledge may be integrated into a total science, but it does not by nature belong to that science to the exclusion of another science. For example, Ockham says that the truth that God is one, or the habit of demonstrating it, is neither theological nor metaphysical in itself. It does not in itself belong to theology or metaphysics, any more than a man by himself is part of a nation or an army. Just as he can be included in either or both, so a truth can be integrated into one science or many.[48]

---

46 "Ideo dicendum est, quod metaphysica non est una scientia numero, nec similiter philosophia naturalis. Sed philosophia naturalis est collectio multorum habituum, sicut dictum est. Nec est aliter una nisi sicut civitas dicitur una vel populus dicitur unus vel exercitus comprehendens homines et equos et caetera necessaria dicitur unus, vel sicut regnum dicitur unum, vel sicut universitas dicitur una, vel sicut mundus dicitur unus." Ockham, *Physics,* p. 7.

47 *Ibid.* pp. 9-10. See Scotus, *Ordinatio,* Prol. 3, q. 3; pp. 94ff.

48 "Si dicatur quod tunc idem habitus numero esset metaphysicus et theologicus, dico, secundum praedicta, quod accipiendo habitum metaphysicum et theologicum sicut communiter accipitur et quomodo loquimur modo, neuter est unus numero sed continet multos, numero, specie et genere distinctos. Et ideo habitus ille quo cognoscitur ista veritas 'Deus est unus', qui pertinet ad metaphysicam et ad theologiam, nec est habitus metaphysicus nec theologicus, sicut nec est

Ockham is not saying that every truth will fit into every science. He points out that theology considers many subjects and attributes of subjects that are not the concern of metaphysics or any other natural science. Sciences are distinguished by both their subjects and the attributes demonstrated of them. But what determines the exact range of subjects to be treated by any one science? What marks off one body of knowledge from another as a distinct science? What is the "special relation" between the parts of a science that unifies it and makes it one science?

We have seen Peter Auriol place the unity of a science in the form of the science. He conceives a science on the analogy of a house or geometrical figure, whose parts are unified by their supervening form. But this solution of the problem is not acceptable to Ockham, for he does not think the notions of matter and form apply in this case. A science, he says, has no formal cause but only efficient and final causes.[49] Since he believes that theology is a practical science, leading to eternal beatitude, he can appeal to its end as the source of its unity: all truths necessary for salvation are theological and can be integrated into the science of theology.[50] But what is the source of unity of a speculative science like metaphysics? This science, he maintains, has only the unity of an aggregate.[51] At best it has the unity of order, like an army or city. It is made up of many partial sciences (*scientiae partiales*), some of which are still to be discovered. What gives the science its unifying order which distinguishes it from, say, mathematics?

Ockham suggests three possibilities: the order may be found in the predicates of the science, or in its subjects, or in both. In the first case, the science may demonstrate of the same subject many attributes which are logically related as superior and inferior (that is, of greater and less extension). Ockham's example is taken from geometry. This science demonstrates of the subject "figure" the attributes of magnitude, and also its own proper attributes and those of its logical inferiors (for in-

---

metaphysica nec theologia. Unde sicut non est concedendum quod homo est populus vel exercitus, nec domus est civitas vel villa, ita habitus ille nec est metaphysica nec theologia. Si tamen per habitum esse metaphysicum vel theologicum intelligatur istum habitum pertinere ad metaphysicam vel theologiam, sic potest concedi quod idem habitus est metaphysicus et theologicus. Concedo tamen quod idem habitus numero est pars habitus metaphysici et etiam theologici, sicut idem homo est pars populi vel exercitus." Ockham, *In I Sent.* Prol. q. 1, pp. 13-14.

49   "Ideo dicendum est quod, loquendo de virtute sermonis, nulla scientia habet nisi tantum duas causas essentiales, scilicet efficientem et finalem." Ockham, *Physics,* p. 7.

50   Ockham, *In I Sent.* Prol. q. 1; I, p. 7. For the practical nature of theology, see *ibid.* q. 12, pp. 324-370.

51   "Et ita accipiendo unitatem aggregationis pro omni unitate quae non est alicuius unius numero, concedo quod talis scientia (scil. metaphysica) est una unitate aggregationis." Ockham, *ibid.* p. 224.

stance, circle and triangle). Secondly, the order that unifies a science may be found in the subjects of the science, as when general attributes are demonstrated of their primary subjects and also of their logical inferiors. Thus in the science of animals the attributes of animal in general are demonstrated not only of animal but also of the various genera and species of animals. Thirdly, the unifying order of a science may reside in both its subjects and predicates, as, for example, the attributes of animal are predicated of animal, and the attributes of the various species of animal contained under the genus are predicated of these species. Because the terms of a science have a logical relation of this sort, or some similar logical order, it is called one science. Ockham assures us that this is the sense in which Aristotle and the other philosophers and masters understand the unity of a science. [52]

Ockham knew well enough that Aristotle locates the unity of a science in the unity of its generic subject. "A single science is one whose domain is a single genus," writes the Philosopher in his *Posterior Analytics*. [53] This Aristotelian dictum is quoted in one of the objections to Ockham's position. In reply, he does not deny it, but qualifies it in such a way that it no longer applies to a whole science. One science, he says, has one generic subject, but only if the attribute predicated of it is one; otherwise the science will have a unity of order. [54] But Ockham has already said that in a total science, like metaphysics, many attributes are predicated of many subjects. Hence, a whole science can only have a unity of order. [55] Ockham's nominalism prevents him from accepting in its full meaning the Aristotelian doctrine of the unity of a science based on the unity of its generic subject.

Closer to Aristotle in this respect was Gregory of Rimini, a master of theology at Paris and General of the Augustinian Order, who died shortly after Ockham in 1358. We have seen Leibniz list him among the leading nominalists; and indeed according to a tradition going back to about 1500 he was the standard bearer of the nominalists (*Antesignanus nominalistarum*). [56] This does not mean that he was always in agreement

---

52 Ockham, *ibid.* pp. 219-220. See *ibid.* q. 1, p. 14. Natural philosophy is distinguished from the other sciences either by its subjects or predicates; but this does not prevent one and the same truth from belonging to it and to other sciences. Ockham says that he intends to explain how sciences are distinguished by their subjects and predicates in his commentary on the *Metaphysics*, which he does not seem to have written. See *Physics*, p. 15.

53 Aristotle, *Post. Anal.* I, 28, 87 a 38-39.

54 "Ad secundum patet, quod unius generis subiecti est una scientia si passio sit una, vel erit una unitate ordinis." Ockham, *In I Sent.* Prol. q. 8, p. 225.

55 "Ad tertium etiam patet, quod metaphysica, prout dicit totum librum *Metaphysicae*, non est una nisi tali unitate ordinis." Ockham, *ibid.*

56 This title was given to him by Aventinus (1477-1517), according to D. Trapp. See G. Leff, *Gregory of Rimini: Tradition and Innovation in Fourteenth Century Thought* (Manchester 1961) p. 1.

with Ockham, as is clear from his notion of the unity of a science. Like Auriol and Ockham, he denies that its unity consists of a single intellectual habit. If such were the case, he argues, we would know all the principles and conclusions of a science through the one habit. Knowing one conclusion of geometry, we would know all the conclusions of the science, which is contrary to experience.[57]

For this and other reasons Gregory rejects the view that there is one all-embracing habit for one science. What, then, is the source of its identity? Gregory concludes with Aristotle that a science like geometry or medicine has its own generic subject and premises which give unity to the whole science. For example, the subject of geometry is magnitude. Because all the conclusions of the science concern this subject, they form a unity. The conclusions belong to the same science, as do the habits by which they are demonstrated. Gregory specifies that the common genus constituting the subject of a science cannot be one of the widest genera, like "quality" (that is, it is not one of Aristotle's ten categories). Gregory considers this far too universal to unify a science. Neither is the subject of a science a particular species like "man"; this would be too restrictive a subject for one science. At best this could only be the subject of a "partial" or "special" science included within a total science. The subject of a whole science has the unity of a subalternate genus; that is to say, a genus subalternated to one of the widest genera. The example Gregory gives is "magnitude," which is a genus subalternated to the more general genus "quantity." Magnitude is the generic subject of geometry, giving unity to that science. Gregory adds — again following Aristotle — that a science is said to have one subject genus not only if the items known in it are conceived univocally with one common *ratio* or notion, but also if they are conceived analogically, or having a common focus of reference. Gregory makes this qualification in order to include metaphysics among the sciences, for its subject "being" is not a genus.

More is required to unify a science than a common subject according to Gregory of Rimini. If this were sufficient, how would geometry differ from physics, since both concern magnitude? Besides a subject, a science has common premises or principles, and it regards its objects from a formal point of view different from that of the other sciences. For example, both physics and mathematics draw conclusions regarding magnitude, but mathematics has to do with magnitude as such, while

---

57 "Prima [conclusio] est quod non omnium conclusionum talium est habitus unus numero. Secunda est nec unius conclusionis et suorum principiorum est habitus unus numero. Tertia est nec ipsorum principiorum est habitus unus numero." Gregory of Rimini, *Sent.* Prol. q. 3, a. 1 (Venice 1522) fol. 11Q-12A.

physics regards magnitude in the external world. Each of these sciences, accordingly, has not only its generic subject but also its own principles and formal perspective, all of which give the science its identity and distinguish it from the other sciences.[58]

Gregory of Rimini's doctrine of science deserves more detailed attention than can be given here. What has been said makes it clear that his conception of the unity of a science, while in some respects similar to Ockham's, differs significantly from his. In appealing to a common generic subject and a unique formal perspective for each science as the ground of its unity, Gregory parts company with his nominalist contemporary. This is but one indication that what goes by the name of fourteenth century nominalism was really a complex of many doctrines which, though they have common features, were really quite different.

Ockham's theology and philosophy were widely disseminated in the universities of the later Middle Ages, especially through the works of his commentator Gabriel Biel, who died in 1495. Among the many Ockhamist doctrines taught by Biel was that a science is not a single habit of the intellect but a unified collection of habits. The word "science," he says, is as it were a collective name: *quasi nomen collectivum*.[59]

*
*   *

If one wishes to appreciate how widely the unity of a science was discussed by the late scholastics and how diverse their views on this subject were, he has only to read Suarez' popular *Disputationes Metaphysicae,* published in 1597. In his usual thorough manner, Suarez recounts the views of many of his predecessors and contemporaries before giving his own. He cannot agree that a science is a simple and indivisible quality of the mind, as Henry of Ghent, St. Thomas, and many Thomists hold. Neither is it an ordered collection of intelligible species, as Soncinas thought. Suarez is also opposed to the nominalist view that a science is not a habit with an essential unity, but only a collection or coordination of many qualities: the opinion, he says, held by Auriol, Scotus, Gregory of Rimini, Ockham, and Biel. He opts for what he calls a "middle way" between the Thomistic and nominalist opinions, maintaining that a science is a collection or coordination of many qualities, but that these qualities comprise one scientific habit

---

58 *Ibid.* a. 2, fol. 14L-O.
59 G. Biel, *In I Sent.* Prol. q. 1, E (Tübingen 1501).

with an essential unity owing to the unity of the formal object of the science. [60]

Suarez likens the unity of a science to that of a quality of the body, like health or beauty. We speak of health or beauty as though it were one quality, but in fact it is the result of the relation of many bodily qualities. The same is true of a quality of the mind such as a scientific habit. It is the product of the coordination of many simple mental qualities. Every time we learn a new demonstration or principle in a science the mind acquires a real perfection which is not simply an increase in intensity of a previous quality but a new quality of the mind. Each of these simple qualities is a "partial habit" which is integrated into the total habit of the science. Suarez does not favor the nominalist way of speaking, that there are as many sciences as there are simple habits of the mind. Even nominalists like Ockham and Gregory of Rimini, he says, agree that a science such as geometry or theology is *one* science. [61] Suarez wants to keep the usual language when speaking of the sciences, and above all to avoid extreme positions on this subject. Both the Thomists and the nominalists err in this regard: the Thomists because they fail to see that a science is comprised of many mental qualities, the nominalists because they do not realize that these qualities are so closely coordinated that they compose an essential unity. Suarez goes to great lengths to justify his assertion, against the nominalists, that a science has not simply an artificial or accidental unity but constitutes something essentially one. The partial habits that comprise a science, he contends, are linked together by an "effective subordination," because they dispose the mind to demonstrate conclusions one of which is derived from the other. The scientific habits also refer to one total object or essence, such as man, from a knowledge of which many conclusions can be drawn. [62] In the final analysis, then, it is the unity of the formal object of the science, based on the essence of things, that accounts for the unity of the science.

*

*   *

When non-scholastic philosophers took up the question of the unity of a science in the seventeenth and eighteenth centuries they were continuing a discussion that already had a long history, conveniently sum-

---

60 Suarez, *Disputationes Metaphysicae,* 44, sect. 11 (Paris 1877) 26, pp. 697-700, n. 12-19. Suarez here presents the four opinions concerning the unity of a science and adopts the fourth or middle way. On p. 711, n. 55 he asserts that a science is a collection of many simple mental qualities. For the nature of the connection between them, see p. 713, n. 62-63.

61 *Ibid.* p. 713, n. 60.

62 *Ibid.* p. 713, n. 63. The mind, however, also has a role in the unity of a science, so that its unity is not exact or perfect but, in a way, artificial. *Ibid.* p. 715, n. 69.

marized for them in Suarez' *Disputationes Metaphysicae*. Nor were they ignorant of Suarez' work. Descartes had firsthand knowledge of it, and Leibniz boasted that he could read it as easily as most people read novels.[63] To many, the *Disputationes* were, in Schopenhauer's words, "an authentic compendium of the whole scholastic wisdom."[64]

Christian Wolff, professor of mathematics and physics at Halle and Marburg from 1706 to 1754, read Suarez with admiration and praised him as the Jesuit "who among scholastics pondered metaphysical realities with particular penetration."[65] After imbibing scholasticism at the font of Suarez, Wolff could hardly fail to describe a science as a unified whole. Indeed, in his view a science constitutes a system, comparable to an organized animal body.

While treating of natural laws in his *Philosophia Practica Universalis* Wolff says that they constitute a system, by which he means "the close union (*compactio*) by which all of them are interconnected." In general, he defines a system of doctrines as "a close union of mutually connected truths or universal propositions." This is the sense, he adds, in which he often called the first part of his *Theologia Naturalis* a system, even putting in the title of this work that it embraces a whole system, for the truths that it demonstrates about the nature of God are interconnected. In the widest possible sense a system is the close union of interconnected realities. As an example of this use of the word "system" Wolff points out that medical men speak of the nerves, arteries, and veins in the human body as a system when they describe them as diffused throughout the whole body and connected to each other so that they compose as it were one entity. Similarly, there is a system of natural laws if all the laws of nature are interconnected.[66] On this

---

63 *Vita Leibnitii a Seipso,* in Foucher de Careil, *Nouvelles Lettres et Opuscules Inédits de Leibniz* (Paris 1857) p. 382.

64 *Fragmente zur Geschichte der Philosophie* § 6 (Berlin 1847) 6, p. 57.

65 "Sane Franciscus Suarez e Societate Jesu, quem inter Scholasticos res metaphysicas profundius meditatum esse constat..." C. Wolff, *Philosophia Prima sive Ontologia* I, 2, 3 (Hildesheim 1962) p. 138.

66 "Per systema legum naturalium intelligo eam ipsarum compactionem, qua omnes inter se connectuntur. In genere nimirum systema doctrinarum est compactio veritatum seu propositionum universalium inter se connexarum. Immo generalissime systema appellari suevit compactio rerum inter se connexarum. Monuimus enim veritates universales, seu propositiones universales inter se connexas systema doctrinarum constituere... Et in hoc etiam sensu partem primam Theologiae naturalis in parte altera saepius diximus systema et in ipso titulo illius posuimus, quod integrum systema complectatur, quia scilicet veritates de Dei natura notae inter se connectuntur. In sensu generalissimo Medici systema nervorum, arteriarum, venarum vocant, si nervos, arterias, venas eo ordine describunt, quo per totum humanum corpus diffusi diffusaeque inter se connectuntur, ut unum quoddam quasi ens constituant nervi inter se juncti, unum ab eo diversum arteriae, et diversum ab utroque venae. Quamobrem systema legum naturalium habebis, si leges naturae omnes inter se connectantur." C. Wolff, *Philosophia Practica Universalis, Methodo Scientifica Pertractata,* II, c. 1 (Frankfurt, Leipzig, 1789) 2, pp. 65-66, n. 81.

model, too, there can be a system of doctrines, but only if the demonstrative method is used, for only then will all its propositions be mutually connected, one term being contained in the definition of another, and one proposition being the premise from which another is deduced.[67]

Wolff was not the first to use the word "body" (*corpus*) of a doctrinal system. Traditionally, the word was applied to a complete collection of writings on a subject arranged systematically. Thus the Justinian Code of law was called the *Corpus Juris*. The works of Homer were referred to as the *Corpus Homeri*. Cicero and Seneca speak of the book of an author as a *corpus*.[68] In the fourteenth century the bibliophile Richard of Bury reflects this usage when he writes of "the mighty bodies of the sciences."[69] In his *Logic*, Isaac Watts (1725) writes that "The word science is usually applied to the whole body of regular or methodical observations or propositions... concerning any subject of speculation."[70] What appears to be new in Wolff is the analogy between a system of doctrines or laws and a living human body. He sees a science as having a unity on the model of that of a living organism — an appropriate paradigm indeed for a rationalist like Wolff who attempted "to build up a philosophy in which all terms would be unequivocally defined and disposed according to an order as strict as that of mathematical demonstrations."[71]

The analogy of science to a living body was no less appealing to Kant. Wolff appeared to him as the living embodiment of metaphysics. Kant rejected that metaphysics and along with it the Wolffian notion of a scientific system; but he was too strongly influenced by Wolff to deny that science is an organic system of doctrines. As we have seen, Kant makes systematic unity the essential note of scientific knowledge. But for him a scientific system is no mere concatenation and interlinking of

---

67 "Systema doctrinarum condi nequit nisi methodo demonstrativa. Etenim in systemate veritates universales, quae dogmatum seu doctrinarum nomine veniunt, inter se connectuntur. Enimvero veritates inter se connectuntur, si definitum unum ingreditur definitionem alterius, et propositio una demonstrationem alterius tanquam praemissa." *Ibid.* p. 66, n. 82.

Wolff also describes a science in the scholastic manner as a mental *habitus* of demonstrating truths: "Per scientiam hic intelligo habitum asserta demonstrandi, hoc est ex principiis certis et immotis per legitimam consequentiam inferendi." C. Wolff, *Philosophia Rationalis sive Logica*, discursus praelim. c. 2, n. 30 (Verona 1735) p. 9.

68 See references under "corpus" in A. Forcellini, *Totius Latinitatis Lexicon* (Prati 1839) I, p. 778b.

69 "Sed per plurimorum investigationes sollicitas, quasi datis symbolis singillatim, scientiarum ingentia corpora ad immensas, quas cernimus, quantitates successivis augmentationibus succreverunt." Richard of Bury, *Philobiblion* 10 (Oxford 1960) p. 108.

70 Isaac Watts, *Logic* II, 2, n. 9; cited by *The Oxford English Dictionary* (Oxford 1933) 9, p. 221.

71 E. Gilson, T. Langan, *Modern Philosophy: Descartes to Kant* (New York 1963) p. 178.

terms and propositions in the Wolffian manner. "By a system," he writes, "I understand the unity of the manifold modes of knowledge under one idea."[72] Every scientific system for Kant is regulated and constituted by an a priori idea, furnished by reason itself. Empirical knowledge by itself is not scientific unless it is regulated and systematized by a priori principles of reason.

With Kant we come full circle and return to the point where we began this inquiry into the history of the notion of the unity of a science. Standing between Kant and his predecessors is his Copernican Revolution in philosophy, which assumes that instead of our knowledge conforming to objects, objects must conform to our knowledge.[73] Thomas Aquinas lived in an age that believed that through sense experience the mind can gain an insight — however superficial and precarious — into the nature of reality and achieve truth by conforming to it. Being a realist, he was also convinced that the individuals encountered in sense experience are bearers of intelligible characters or natures which, when conceived, are the contents of our general notions. His solution to the problem of the unity of a science depends upon this metaphysical view of reality and human knowledge. For him, each of the speculative sciences has its own generic subject, or formal object, conceived through its unique mode of abstraction. Each science also has its own principles and mode of procedure, which produce in the intellect a *habitus* distinct from that of every other science.[74]

Once the nominalists eliminated intelligible natures or essences from reality a new explanation of the unity of a science had to be found. For Ockham, the object of science is no longer the real world but the propositions we form about it. Corresponding to each demonstrated proposition there is a scientific habit in the intellect. These are "partial sciences" which can be integrated into a "total science," such as physics or metaphysics, by the logical interconnection of the terms of the scientific propositions.

The mediaeval nominalists set the stage for the new notions of the unity of a science in early modern philosophy. Like them, Leibniz locates the unity of a science in the logical synthesis of the truths contained in the science. Not content with this rather loose unity, Kant bases the unity of a science on an a priori idea in the understanding. Between Aquinas and Kant, accordingly, stand the mediaeval nominalists.

72 Kant, *Critique of Pure Reason*, A 832, B 860, trans. N. K. Smith (London 1950) p. 653.
73 *Ibid.* Preface to second edition, B xvi, p. 22.
74 For St. Thomas' doctrine of the subject of science and its modes of abstraction, see *Expositio super Librum Boethii de Trinitate* Q. V-VI (Leiden 1955) pp. 161-218; trans. A. Maurer, *The Division and Methods of the Sciences* (Toronto 1968).

GALILEO AND THE THOMISTS

William A. Wallace O.P.

WHEN Antonio Favaro, the otherwise careful editor of Galileo's *Opere*, came across the name "Caietanus" in Galileo's student notebooks, he assumed that the reference was to Caietanus Thienensis,[1] the Paduan *calculator*; apparently it did not occur to him that the young Galileo would be acquainted with the writings of the Italian Thomist, Thomas de Vio Caietanus.[2] Yet a check of Galileo's citations shows that six of the eight references ascribed by Favaro to Caietanus Thienensis in reality are references to Thomas de Vio Caietanus.[3] Favaro's error here, of course, is more excusable than his failure to identify correctly the more mature Galileo's reliance on the authority of the celebrated Dominican in his letter to the Grand Duchess Christina.[4] There it was a question of the place of the sun in the heavens when Joshua gave his famous command, "Sun, stand thou still," and Thomas de Vio had long been recognized as a competent Scriptural commentator.[5] But De Vio also held distinctive views on matters relating to physical science, as did many of the Thomists of his day, and such views were known and discussed by Galileo in his early writings. Most of these writings, contained in Vol. I of Favaro's National Edition of Galileo's works, show a preoccupation with Aristotle and the problems raised by his philosophy then being discussed in the schools, particularly at Pisa and other Italian universities. Of the 419 pages that go to make up this first volume, in fact, Aristotle is mentioned on 194 pages; the author cited with next greatest frequency is St. Thomas Aquinas, who gets mentioned on 32 pages, followed in order by the Aristotelian commentators Averroës and Simplicius, who are men-

1 Gaetano da Thiene (1387-1465), professor at Padua from 1422 to his death, and author of important commentaries on William Heytesbury and on the *Physics* of Aristotle.

2 Tommaso de Vio, of Gaeta (1469-1534), cardinal, commonly known as Gaetanus or Caietanus from his birthplace; master general of the Dominican Order and principal commentator on the *Summa theologiae* of St. Thomas.

3 See A. Favaro, ed., *Le Opere di Galileo Galilei*, Edizione Nazionale, 20 vols., (Florence 1890-1909), Vol. I, 422; Caietanus Thienensis is cited only on pp. 72 and 172, whereas Thomas de Vio Caietanus is cited on pp. 76, 96, 101, 133, 146, and 153. Favaro ascribed all these references to Thienensis.

4 See Vol. V, p. 347, and index for the entire work, Vol. XX, p. 339.

5 The letter, written in 1615, has been translated into English by Stillman Drake, *Discoveries and Opinions of Galileo* (New York 1957). For the reference to Thomas de Vio and its context, see p. 214; Drake correctly identifies the Italian Dominican.

tioned on 30 and 28 pages respectively.[6] Apart from this recognition of Aquinas as a foremost interpreter of Aristotle, Galileo's early writings reveal also a surprising knowledge of the Thomistic school. On four different pages of the same volume Galileo refers to "the Thomists," and in one of these references he identifies four members of the school. Then, in various individual references, he cites Joannes Capreolus[7] (7 places), Thomas de Vio Caietanus (6 places), Paulus Soncinas[8] (4 places), Ferrariensis[9] (3 places), Hervaeus Natalis[10] (2 places), Dominicus Soto[11] (2 places), and Chrysostomus Javellus[12] (1 place).

This little known acquaintance of the young Galileo with Thomism is worthy of study in its own right, particularly on the part of anyone tracing the impact of the thought of a thirteenth-century scholar like Aquinas on subsequent centuries. From the viewpoint of the history of science, however, there are additional reasons for examining closely Galileo's relationship to the Thomistic school. Although much is known about Galileo, there is a definite *lacuna* in Galilean scholarship in the

---

6 These data are taken from a simple count of Favaro's entries in the "Indice degli autori citati," Vol. I, 421-423. Other authors who are frequently cited include Ptolemy (on 20 pages), Alexander of Aphrodisias (on 19 pages), Plato (on 18 pages), John Philoponus (on 17 pages), Albertus Magnus (on 15 pages), Giles of Rome (on 14 pages), and Archimedes (on 10 pages). Omitted from the index entirely are the Calculator, Richard Swineshead, cited on p. 172, and the Conciliator, Pietro d'Abano, cited on p. 36. It should be noted, moreover, that the citations are distributed selectively throughout the volume; the *Juvenilia*, for example, end on p. 177, and 15 of the Plato citations are given prior to this page and only 3 after, whereas Archimedes makes no appearance before p. 177 and 10 after. Again, in all, 19 writers are cited in both the *Juvenilia* and the unquestionably Galilean works in the volume; 10 writers are cited in the latter but are not mentioned in the former; and 133 writers, including 14 who are mentioned at least half a dozen times each, appear in the *Juvenilia* but nowhere else.

7   John Capreolus, (*c.* 1380-1444), French Dominican and principal expounder and defender of Thomistic doctrine in the century before Cajetan; known especially for his *Defensiones,* cast in the form of a commentary on the *Sentences,* and directed against Duns Scotus and Henry of Ghent, among others.

8   Paul Soncinas (d. 1494), Italian Dominican and admirer of Capreolus, who published a compendium of the latter's work as well as a lengthy Thomistic exposition of the *Metaphysics* of Aristotle.

9   Francesco Silvestri of Ferrara (*c.* 1474-1528), Italian Dominican noted for his commentary on the *Summa contra gentiles* of St. Thomas; among his works is a commentary on the *Physics* of Aristotle.

10   Harvey or Hervé Nedellec (*c.* 1255-1323), master general of the Dominican Order and author of numerous *Quaestiones* and *Quodlibets*; his polemics were frequently directed against Henry of Ghent.

11   Domingo de Soto (1494-1560), Spanish Dominican, theologian and political theorist, but also a commentator on Aristotle's logic and physics; he was regarded by Pierre Duhem as a precursor of Galileo on the basis of his adumbration of the law of falling bodies *c.* 1545. For details, see my articles, "The Enigma of Domingo de Soto: *Uniformiter difformis* and Falling Bodies in Late Medieval Physics," *Isis* 59 (1968), 384-401; "The 'Calculatores' in Early Sixteenth-Century Physics," *The British Journal for the History of Science* 4 (1969), 221-232; and "Mechanics from Bradwardine to Galileo," *Journal of the History of Ideas* 32 (1971), 15-28.

12   Giovanni Crisostomo Javelli (*c.* 1470-*c.* 1538), Italian Dominican, student of Cajetan and colleague of Ferrariensis, who commented on the works of Aristotle and defended a Thomistic interpretation against the Averroists of his day.

area of the *Juvenilia*, which are commonly regarded as notes written down or copied by Galileo during his student days at the University of Pisa, most probably during the year 1584. [13] The notes themselves cover a wide range of topics discussed with a fairly high degree of sophistication, and with a citation of sources that range from classical antiquity through the middle and late scholastic periods to the latter part of the sixteenth century. This mass of material is so refractory to simple analysis that it is not surprising that scholars have contented themselves with rather vague generalities about the early sources of Galileo's ideas. [14] What is needed, as E. A. Moody has already urged, [15] is a detailed study of these early writings, and for this it is necessary to start some place. The present paper is offered as a beginning in this important but hitherto neglected area of scholarship in the hope that it may shed light not only on the development of the Thomistic school but also on its relationships with this celebrated "father of modern science." In structure it will first describe in general Galileo's citations of St. Thomas and the Thomists, then it will narrow the field of discussion to examine in detail Galileo's understanding of the Thomistic positions he cites on the intension and remission of forms and various teachings on the elements, and finally it will conclude with some observations on the possible sources of these sections of Galileo's early writings.

I. Galileo's Citations of St. Thomas and Thomists

Galileo shows little interest in the metaphysical problems that have consistently attracted the attention of Thomistic historians of philosophy, but concentrates instead on the physical problems relating to the heavens and the earth that were to remain a constant concern throughout his life. His citations of St. Thomas in the first volume of the *Opere* are confined to three important references in the treatise *De motu*, with the remaining 29 all occurring in the notes, written in

13 See Favaro's introduction to the *Juvenilia*, I, 12; the argument is based on Galileo's discussion of the origin of the universe, which he attempts to date. In measuring the various epochs he holds that 74 years elapsed from the birth of Christ to the destruction of Jerusalem, and "from thence to the present time 1510 [years]." — *ibid.*, 27.

14 For a general indictment of the lack of specific scholarship in this area, see C. B. Schmitt's essay review, "A Fresh Look at Mechanics in 16th-Century Italy," *Studies in History and Philosophy of Science* 1 (1970), 161-171.

15 Treating of the sources of Galileo's ideas in "Galileo's Precursors," *Galileo Reappraised*, ed. C. L. Golino (Berkeley 1966), 41, Moody writes: "In what form, or through what books, these ideas were conveyed to Galileo, are questions that, if answerable in whole or in part, would cast a good deal of light on the way Galileo's thinking developed. If historians of science had given more time to historical research on this problem, instead of engaging in a priori debates over the validity or invalidity of Duhem's thesis, better insight into the nature of Galileo's scientific achievements might well have been gained."

Galileo's hand, that go to make up the *Juvenilia*. In general these notes treat of two types of problem, the first relating to Aristotle's treatise *De caelo et mundo* and the second to the subject of alteration and the way in which alteration is related to the forms of the elements and their qualities. In the second category there are only eight citations of Aquinas, so that the remaining majority (21 citations) are concerned with the matter of *De caelo et mundo*. Apart from these references in the first volume of the *Opere,* Aquinas is cited seven times in Vol. III, twice each in Vols. IV and V, and once in Vol. XIX, for a grand total of 44 citations, while he is also named, in passing, in at least five other places.[16] Compared to this rather liberal use of Aquinas himself, Galileo's attention to the members of Aquinas's school, "the Thomists," is relatively restricted. Aside from the one citation of Thomas de Vio Cajetan in Vol. V, to which reference has already been made, all of the references to Thomists are to be found in the *Juvenilia* section of Vol. 1. Cumulatively these amount to 29 references, of which 12 pertain to the matter of *De caelo* and 17 to that of alteration and the elements. The content of all of these citations will now be sketched in a general way, outlining first Galileo's rather extensive use of Aquinas's teaching and then his sparser references to the Thomistic school. This survey will provide the background information necessary for the detailed examination, to be undertaken in Section II of this paper, of the specific understanding and evaluation of the Thomistic tradition revealed in the *Juvenilia*.

A. *Citations of St. Thomas*

The *Juvenilia* is a composite treatise that purposes to present, in more or less systematic fashion, the essential content of Aristotle's four books *De caelo* and his two books *De generatione*. The treatise is prefaced by two brief questions where the author[17] inquires first concerning the subject of Aristotle's *De caelo* and second concerning the order, connection, and titling of these books. St. Thomas is mentioned in both questions, first for his view that this subject is the universe according to all its integral parts[18] and secondly for his insisting on the

16 The references in passing occur in Vols. IV, 421; XII, 265; XIV, 260; and XIX, 298 and 319. The remaining citations are located, verified and in most cases explained in detail in what follows.

17 Although the writer of the *Juvenilia* was certainly Galileo, it is not known whether the notes are his own composition or whether they are copied from another source (or sources); hence, reference will be made simply to the "author" throughout the remainder of this section.

18 15.15. In this method of citation, which will be employed throughout, the first number is the page on which the citation occurs and the second is the line number; all such references are to Vol.

title *De caelo et mundo,* along with Albertus Magnus and other "Latins," against the Greek tradition represented by Alexander and Simplicius, who would name the books simply *De caelo* from their "more noble part."[19] Thereupon the work is divided into two tractates, the first concerned with *De mundo* and consisting of four questions and the second concerned with *De caelo* and consisting of six questions.

The tractate *De mundo,* whose title the author seems to understand broadly enough to encompass the world or universe as well as the earth, has two preliminary questions which discuss the origins of the universe first as understood by ancient philosophers and second according to the Catholic faith, but in neither of these is St. Thomas mentioned. In the third question, however, which treats of the unity and perfection of the universe, Aquinas is discussed at some length. He is first invoked in support of the author's contention that the universe is one, based on his argument from the order existing in things created by God.[20] The author's next conclusion is that the unity of the universe cannot be demonstrated by reason, although it is certain from faith that only one universe exists. Here he raises five queries and offers his own interpretation of St. Thomas to resolve the first three of them. One of Aquinas's arguments seems to maintain that earth's natural motion to a center would preclude there being any other earth than this one, but this is to be understood only of what happens according to nature from God's ordinary power.[21] The second query is whether God can add any species to this universe, or make other worlds that have more perfect species that are essentially different from those found here. Both Scotus and Durandus deny this possibility, but Aquinas and practically everyone else hold that God's infinite power would enable Him to make more perfect universes to infinity.[22] The third query is whether God could make creatures more perfect than those He has made in this world, to which the author replies that He could make them accidentally more perfect but not essentially so, and here he adduces Aquinas's example of the number four, whose essence cannot be varied, and argues that other essences are like this also.[23]

I of Favaro's National Edition. To save space, and in view of the general availability of the National Edition, the Latin text will not be given in these notes.

19   21.36.

20   27.31, citing *Summa theologiae,* 1a, q. 46 (given erroneously as q. 43), a. 3.

21   29.13, citing ibid., ad 3, and 29.16-17. Galileo writes "de potentia naturali vel de ordinaria"; St. Thomas speaks only of God's "potentia ordinata" (see 1a, q. 25, a. 5, ad 1), but in his school the expression "potentia ordinaria" became quite common. (Here and henceforth references to the *Summa theologiae* are made by citing only the part, the question, and the article numbers).

22   29.29, citing 1a, q. 25 (given erroneously as q. 21), a. 6.

23   30.7, citing ibid.

The fourth question is whether the world could have existed from eternity, and here the author presents three conclusions: (1) that the world did not exist from eternity since it is of faith that it was created in time; (2) that on God's part there is no repugnance that the world could have existed from eternity; and (3) that there is a repugnance, however, on the part of creatures, whether these be corruptible or incorruptible. [24] These conclusions and their proofs are preceded by four opinions, and Aquinas is mentioned in the discussion of three of them. The first opinion is that of Gregory of Rimini and other nominalists, who maintain that the world could have existed from eternity whether it be made up of successive or permanent entities or corruptible and incorruptible ones. This seems to gain some support from St. Thomas, the author notes, when he proves that the creation of the universe cannot be demonstrated from reason. [25] Also, Aquinas's maintaining that creation does not involve any action going forth from God to creatures[26] is used in a quite complex argument in support of the same conclusion. The second opinion is that of Durandus and "many moderns," which holds that there is no repugnance to eternal existence on the part of incorruptible things, whereas there is of corruptible things, and St. Thomas seems also to support this. [27] The fourth opinion, arguing from other *loci* in St. Thomas, the author identifies as that of Aquinas himself, which is in agreement with the teachings of Scotus, Ockham, the "Parisian doctors," and Pererius. [28] This would maintain that the world could have existed from eternity on the part of incorruptible things, but that there are problems associated with corruptible things; Durandus points out the absurdities that follow from allowing corruptible things an eternal existence, but these can be solved by admitting infinites in

24   The more common Thomistic opinion would agree with the first two conclusions but would disagree with the third, maintaining that there is no repugnance on the part either of the act of production or of the thing produced (whether corruptible or incorruptible) that creatures with a stable nature should have existed from eternity. Apart from St. Thomas, this was held by Capreolus, Cajetan, Ferrariensis, Soncinas, Javelli, Soto, and Banez. St. Bonaventure, on the other hand, held the third conclusion as stated by the author; so did Philoponus, Henry of Ghent and, among the late sixteenth-century authors, Toletus and Vallesius. Giles of Rome, Scotus, and Pererius argued dialectically on both sides of the question and came to no firm conclusion. The author of the *Juvenilia,* surprisingly enough, identifies the opinion of St. Thomas with that of Scotus and Pererius (see fns. 28 and 29, infra).

25   32.10-11, citing *De potentia,* q. 3 (given erroneously as q. 13), [a. 17], and 1a, [q. 46, a. 2]. Identifications in square brackets are not made in the text but are supplied by myself.

26   33.28, citing 1a, q. 41, a. 1, ad 2.

27   34.11, citing 1a, q. 46, a. 2.

28   35.26-29, citing *De potentia,* q. 3, a. 14; *De aeternitate mundi; Contra gentiles,* Bk. 2, c. 38; 1a, q. 46. The reference to "doctores Parisienses" is at 35.29 and it occurs again at 138.5, without further identification. Duhem interprets these citations as showing Galileo's dependence on his "Parisian precursors"; see *Etudes sur Léonard de Vinci.* Troisième série: Les Précurseurs parisiens de Galilée (Paris 1913), 582-583. On Pererius, see fn. 82 below.

act, or infinites that can be actually traversed, or one infinite that is larger than another.[29]

The second tractate *De caelo* begins with two rather technical questions, the first on the unity of the heavens and the second on the order of the celestial spheres, which draw heavily from medieval writers on astronomy but make no mention of Aquinas. In the third question, which inquires whether the heavens are composed of simple bodies, the author argues that the heavens are a body distinct from the four elements and are not composed from these elements. In discussing the opinion of ancient philosophers before Aristotle, who attributed the same nature to the heavens as to the elements, the author documents Aquinas's interpretation of Empedocles's and Plato's teachings on this matter.[30] Again, in reply to various objections that are brought against Aristotle's teaching, the author culls responses from Aristotelian commentators and among these he cites in some detail Alexander, Simplicius, and Aquinas.[31] The fourth question is whether the heavens are corruptible, and here the author's main difficulties stem from whether one is to consider the heavens from their intrinsic principles or in relation to the absolute power of God, who can annihilate anything regardless of its natural potencies, provided only that it has an obediential potency to His command.[32] In explaining his solution and the arguments against it, the author mentions Aquinas along with Simplicius and Averroës as holding for a twofold alteration, one corruptive and the other perfective.[33] He cites also Aquinas's opinion that, on the day of judgment, the heavens will not be corrupted substantially but

29 St. Thomas does not state the conclusion in this way in any of the foregoing references nor would most Thomists say that it is his conclusion (see fn. 24). In *De aeternitate mundi* he does allude to the question of infinites in act, but this is merely to state that the question has not yet been solved (Marietti ed., n. 310, p. 108). The terminology used by the author is to be found, however, in later scholastics and particularly in Soto's *Questiones* on the *Physics* of Aristotle, Bk. 3, qq. 3-4, and Bk. 8, qq. 1-2.

30 56.19 and 27, citing 1a, q. 68, a. 1, where the author is critical of Aquinas's statement: "This was the opinion of Plato, who regarded heavenly matter as made of the element fire." He writes: "Plato videtur consensisse cum Aegyptiis: verum noluit caelum esse tantum igneum, ut male illi adscripsit D. Thomas ubi supra, sed maxime constare tamen ex caeteris elementis sive ex summitatibus illorum et, ut ait Proclus, ex delitiis, maxime vero ex terra et igne." (56.26-30).

31 60.27, citing Aquinas's commentary on the *De caelo*, Bk. 3 [lect. 8] and the *Metaphysics*, Bk. 7 [lect. 1]. The author here appears to be quoting Aquinas, whereas in actuality he is summarizing and interpreting his argument.

32 Ratio huius est, quia divinae potentiae non est necesse ut respondeat potentia naturalis, qua res ex sua natura sit corruptibilis, sed satis est potentia quaedam quam obedientialem appellant theologi, qua omnia creata subiciuntur Deo" — 65.22-26. The expression "potentia obedientialis" derives from Aquinas (*De virtutibus in communi*, q. un., a. 10 ad 13) and gained acceptance among theologians in later centuries; other medievals, such as Alexander of Hales and St. Bonaventure, used the related expression "potentia obedientiae."

33 69.13.

only with respect to certain of their accidents.[34] The fifth question is a
rather lengthy disquisition on whether or not the heavens are composed
of matter and form, and here Aquinas is given more attention than in
any other part of the *Juvenilia*. The author first identifies St. Thomas's
position as being that the heavens are composed of matter and form,[35]
but then notes that Aquinas differs from many other Aristotelians in
holding that the matter of the heavens is different in kind from the matter here below.[36] Later he cites approvingly an argument taken from
Aquinas to prove that the heavens are composed of matter and form
and replies to a whole series of objections that have been raised against
the Thomistic arguments.[37] Again, he quotes the proofs given by
Thomas in the commentary on the *Physics* to show that there can be a
potency in the heavens, and then gives further arguments to show that
this implies that matter is also there, while using the general dichotomy
between potency and act as a principle throughout.[38] The author is convinced that the heavens are not composed of a matter that is of the
same kind as that here below. Here his principal adversary seems to be
Giles of Rome, who in turn is arguing against Aquinas,[39] but whose
arguments the author is at pains to refute. The sixth and final question
of this tractate is concerned with the animation of the heavens, and
here the author cites Aquinas as interpreting Aristotle differently in
various works. In the *Summa contra gentiles,* as he reads it, Aquinas
seems to state that Aristotle held that the intelligences are actually
forms of the heavenly bodies,[40] whereas in the *Summa theologiae* and in
the question *De spiritualibus creaturis* Aquinas seems to hold that the
intelligences merely assist the heavens and are otherwise not their
souls.[41] The author's conclusion is that, although it might be true that
Aristotle regarded the intelligences as actually informing the heavenly
bodies, more probably his opinion is that they are merely forms that
assist such bodies in their motions, and for this he again invokes the
authority of St. Thomas and other scholastics.[42]

34   69.22, citing *In 4 sent.,* d. 48, [q. 2, aa. 2-5].

35   76.24 and 29, citing 1a, q. 66, a. 2; *In 8 phys.,* lect. 21; *In 1 de caelo,* lect. 6; *In 2 sent.,* d. 13,
q. 1, a. 1 [ad 3].

36   77.5. The best exposition and analysis of Aquinas's teaching on this subject is Thomas Litt,
Les Corps célestes dans l'univers de saint Thomas d'Aquin (Louvain 1963), 54-90.

37   82.21.

38   85.11, citing *In 8 phys.,* lect. 21; also 86.4.

39   93.22-24; "Aegidium...dum arguit contra D. Thomam..."

40   105.27, citing *Contra gentiles,* Bk. 2, c. 70.

41   107.20, citing 1a, q. 70, a. 3 (given erroneously as a. 6); *De spiritualibus creaturis* [q. un., a.
6]. This inconsistency is discussed at length by Ferrariensis in his commentary on the *Contra gentiles,* Bk. 2, c. 70, n. 3, where he offers reasons why St. Thomas may have wished to leave his interpretation of Averroës open on this point.

42   108.19, mentioning "Scotus, Durandus, et alii scholastici."

The second broad division of the *Juvenilia* is not so well organized as the first and contains a number of ellipses or omissions that make for difficulty in recognizing its intended structure. It is probable, however, that this was planned to embrace two tractates, the first on alteration in matter (*De alteratione in materia*) and the second on the elements (*De elementis*). The tractate on alteration is the shorter of the two and seemingly was made up of only three questions. The first question is missing except for the last few lines of the text, which state a conclusion suggesting that the question was concernéd with the nature of alteration, its subject, and its terminus. The second question treats of intension and remission as a species of alteration, and here St. Thomas is mentioned at the beginning as one of the authorities in this matter.[43] Otherwise he is not cited, although the members of his school are given close attention, as will become apparent below. The last question discusses the parts or degrees of qualities (*De partibus sive gradibus qualitatis*) and consists only of a series of six *praenotamina* relating to the latitudes and degrees of qualities. In the fifth of these the author notes that intensification does not come about through addition alone, but in some way requires a greater intensification in the subject, and this is how he thinks St. Thomas can be understood when he holds that intensification results from the eduction of a form in such a way that it becomes more radicated in the subject.[44]

The second tractate is devoted entirely to the elements, and apparently was to consist of four parts, of which only portions of the first two are extant. After a brief introduction on the nominal definition of an element, where Aquinas is cited,[45] the first part is devoted to the nature of the elements (*De quidditate et substantia elementorum*), and four questions are allotted to this. St. Thomas is not mentioned in the first two questions, treating respectively of the definitions of the elements and their material, efficient, and final causes. He *is* cited, however, in the third question, which inquires into the forms of the elements, for his opinion that these are substantial forms, with which the author himself agrees.[46] The fourth question is whether the forms of the elements undergo intension and remission, and here again St.

---

43 111.23; see p. 307, infra.

44 121.19. St. Thomas speaks of a greater participation of the form by the subject (1a2ae, q. 52, a. 2; 2a2ae, q. 24, a. 5), but within his school it became common to speak of the form being more "radicated" in the subject.

45 124.2, citing *In 1 phys.*, [lect. 1].

46 130.33, citing *In 2 de gen.*, [text] 16 [actually lect. 2, n. 1]; *In 3 meta.*, [text] 27 [actually lect. 8].

Thomas is cited as an authority along with various members of his school, as will be noted below.[47]

The second part of the tractate on the elements is seemingly concerned with their qualities and accidents in general, and is apparently made up of four questions. These discuss: (1) the number of primary qualities; (2) whether these are all positive or whether some are privative; (3) whether all four qualities are active; and (4) what the role of the primary qualities is in activity and resistance. St. Thomas is mentioned only in the third question, where his opinion on what constitutes the passivity of a quality is listed among the notes at the beginning of the question.[48] Finally, in a question which seems to be interpolated between the first two parts of this tractate and probably belongs to the first part, although it is not numbered in the proper sequence for this, St. Thomas and his school are given significant notice. The question discussed is whether elements and natural things have termini of largeness and smallness, and here, among the authorities, St. Thomas is cited for holding that the elements have an intrinsic terminus of smallness but that they have no terminus of largeness.[49] In the author's solution to this question he holds that in relation to God, no natural things have maxima and minima, and this despite the fact that some authorities have taught that a quality such as grace cannot be increased intensively to infinity. Other authorities, he says, including some interpreters of St. Thomas, are able to hold the contrary, by distinguishing what can be done by ordinary power and what by the absolute power of God.[50]

This completes the citations of St. Thomas in the *Juvenilia,* which is intended to provide the framework for our subsequent analysis. For reasons of completeness we will now mention more summarily the contexts in which Galileo mentions Aquinas in writings that proceeded not merely from his pen but leave no doubt about their being his own composition. The first of these is the group of manuscripts assembled by Favaro in Vol. I of the *Opere* under the general title *De motu,* parts of which have been translated into English and annotated by I. E. Drabkin.[51] In this material there are two direct citations of Aquinas and

47   133.30; see p. 312, infra.
48   167.29.
49   144.18, citing *In 1 phys.*, t. 36, 38 [lect. 9, nn. 10, 13]; *In* [1] *de gen.*, t. 41 [lect. 17, n. 6]; 1a, q. 7, a. 3; p. 313, infra. Note here and in fn. 46 supra that the author's method of citing Aquinas's commentary on Aristotle is not the usual one, and may indicate that he took the citations from a secondary source.
50   146.14; for a fuller discussion, see pp. 313-316, infra.
51   Galileo Galilei, *On Motion* and *On Mechanics.* Comprising *De Motu* (*c.* 1590), translated with Introduction and Notes by I. E. Drabkin, and *Le Meccaniche* (*c.* 1600), translated with Introduction and Notes by Stillman Drake (Madison 1960); see pp. 1-12.

one marginal notation, associating him with an opinion being discussed in the text. The two direct citations both relate to St. Thomas's distinctive teaching that motion through a vacuum would not take place instantaneously;[52] Galileo is in agreement with the conclusion, but apparently not with the reasoning Aquinas and others use to support it. The marginal note occurs in a chapter where Galileo is discussing the cause of the increased acceleration at the end of a body's fall, and refers the reader to St. Thomas's exposition of Aristotle's reason, namely, "because the weight of the body is more concentrated and strengthened as the body approaches its proper place."[53] Although these are the only explicit mentions of Aquinas, it should be noted that many of the matters discussed in these manuscripts relating to motion bear on distinctive views of St. Thomas and his school. Even a cursory examination, however, would enlarge this paper beyond reasonable limits, and thus the material relating to motion must be left for further exploration elsewhere.

Of the remaining citations of Aquinas a goodly number occur in Vol. III of the National Edition, where Galileo is discussing mainly astronomical matters. One citation is St. Thomas's elucidation of Aristotle's statement that there is no goodness in mathematics, because mathematicians "abstract from matter, motion, and final causality."[54] Two other references are to Aquinas's teaching on the movement of the heavens,[55] and two more to his views on the plurality of worlds as contained in his commentary on the first book of Aristotle's *De caelo*.[56] Yet another reference is to the *Summa contra gentiles,* where Aquinas's authority is invoked to show that it is "ex fide" that the heavens will stop moving at the end of the world.[57] These last three citations, it may be noted, refer to matters already discussed in the *Juvenilia* and show Galileo's continued preoccupation with topics about which he wrote in his early notebooks. Four other citations invoke St. Thomas's assistance in the interpretation of Sacred Scripture, two of these occurring in Galileo's letter to the Grand Duchess Christina already mentioned in connection with Cajetan.[58] Finally, in Vol. IV, Aquinas is mentioned twice, along with others, for his opinion that shape is not the cause of

---

52   284.8 and 410.21; see Galileo, *On Motion*, p. 49 and p. 50, fn. 24. This distinctive teaching of St. Thomas is discussed at length in another article in these Commemorative Studies by J. A. Weisheipl, "Motion in a Void: Aquinas and Averroës," Vol. I, pp. 469-490.
53   316, fn. 1; see Galileo, *On Motion*, p. 85, fn. 1.
54   III, 255, citing 1a, q. 5, a. 3 ad 4.
55   III, 284 and 346.
56   III, 353 and 354, citing *In 1 de caelo* [lect. 16, nn. 6-7].
57   III, 364, citing *Contra gentiles,* Bk. 1, c. 20.
58   III, 290; V, 333-334 (for the English of this, see Drake, *Discoveries,* 210); XIX, 359.

motion, but of its being slower or faster.[59] These particular references are worthy of detailed examination in the context of fuller discussions of the manuscripts *De motu,* as has already been observed.

B. *Citations of Thomists*

With this general overview established it is now possible to deal at greater depth with points in St. Thomas's teaching that were taken up and developed by his followers. Although there are fewer references in the *Juvenilia* to Thomists than there are to St. Thomas, the former occur where points of doctrine are being subjected to closer scrutiny and thus shed as much light on the author's knowledge of Thomism as do the more extensive references to Aquinas.

That the author was aware of the existence of a Thomistic school seems incontestable in the light of his reference to "Thomists" (*Thomistae*). In the first place where he uses this term he identifies four members of the school, all Dominicans and easily recognized for their professed loyalty to St. Thomas. The context is in a discussion whether the heavens are a composed body, understanding this in the sense of composed of matter and form. The author writes:

> All of the Arabs also, with the single exception of Averroës, assign a composition to the heavens; as Avicembron in the book *Fons Vitae,* from Albert and from St. Thomas in the first part [of the *Summa theologiae*], q. 66, a. 2; Avempace, from the first book of *De caelo,* tract. 1, c. 3; Avicenna, in the first [book] of *Sufficientia,* c. 3; and a large number of Latins also, as Albertus Magnus in the first [book] of the *Physics,* as above, the eighth [book] of the *Physics,* tract. 1, c. 13, and in the book *De quatuor coaequaevis,* q. 4, a. 3, where he says also that this was the opinion of Rabbi Moses; St. Thomas, in the first part as above, and in the eighth [book] of the *Physics,* lesson 21, [n. 3], and in the first [book] of *De caelo,* lesson 6, [n. 6], although in the second [book] of *Sentences,* d. 13, q. 1, a. 1 [ad 3], he does not differ from Averroës; similarly all Thomists, as Capreolus in the second [book] of *Sentences,* d. 12; Cajetan in the first part, as above; Soncinas in the twelfth [book] of the *Metaphysics,* q. 7 [given erroneously as q. 3]; Ferrariensis, in the second [given erroneously as the third book] *Contra gentes,* c. 30; ...[60]

---

59 IV, 424 and 738.

60 76.22-33. In this and other texts quoted in this section, unless otherwise indicated I have verified all citations of St. Thomas and Thomists and noted any errors of the author; I have not done this, however, for other authorities cited. For St. Thomas I have used the standard Leonine and Marietti editions, together with the Mandonnet-Moos edition of the commentary on the *Sentences,* while for the Thomists I have used the following: Capreolus, *Defensiones theologiae divi Thomae Aquinatis,* ed. C. Paban and T. Pègues, 7 vols., (Tours 1900-1907); Cajetanus, *Commentaria in Summam Theologiae Sancti Thomae* as printed in the Leonine edition of the *Summa,*

Before and after this text there is a fairly comprehensive citation of authors ranging from Plato and the Stoics to sixteenth century philosophers. Following a rather extensive discussion of the matter-form composition of the heavens and the kind of matter found in them, the author raises the question how the various matters might be said to differ. He writes: "You may ask here, what is it that differentiates these matters? Capreolus thinks that they differ by diverse forms, whereas Cajetan [that they differ] in themselves."[61] In his answer the author seems to side more with Cajetan than with Capreolus, although allowing that "the matters differ also in their order to the forms."[62] Then, following a disquisition on the implications of this for the corrup-tibility of the heavens, the author raises another question:

> You may ask here, what is to be said concerning the matter of the celestial spheres? Is it one or many, just as the spheres are many? It is to be said that if the heavenly spheres differ specifically among themselves, the matter of each sphere is different from the matter of the other, as Albert thinks in *De quatuor coaequaevis*, q. 2, a. 6, and Cajetan in the first part, q. 66, a. 2, [n. 7]. Yet the contrary is held by Capreolus in the second [book] of *Sentences*, d. 12, q. 1, a. 3, Soncinas in the twelfth [given erroneously as the tenth book] of the *Metaphysics*, q. 10, and others.[63]

Here again the author sides with Cajetan, as against Capreolus and Soncinas, that a different matter is to be found in each of the heavenly spheres. The reason he gives is that if there were a single matter in the heavenly bodies and their forms were to differ specifically, that matter would be in potency to several forms, and then, when it exists under one form it would be deprived of another and be in potency to it; therefore there would be an intrinsic principle of corruption in the heavens. Having stated this, he notes the reply of "Capreolus and others" that this would not happen, because heavenly matter is not an apt subject of privation and the form of the heavenly body so informs the matter that it exhausts the matter's potency entirely.[64] The author responds to this,

---

and *Commentaria in De anima Aristotelis*, ed. P. I. Coquelle (Rome 1938); Soncinas, *Acutissime questiones metaphysicales* (Venice 1505); and Ferrariensis, *Commentaria in Summam Contra Gentiles*, as printed in the Leonine edition of the *Contra Gentiles*.

61 96.30-32. The reference to Capreolus is *In 2 sent.*, d. 12, concl. 2a; Cajetan's argument is in *In Iam*, q. 66, a. 2, n. 7, and is directed against Giles of Rome and Scotus.

62 97.2-3.

63 100.34-101.4. The "others" possibly refers to Javelli, *In 10 meta.*, q. 22. For Javelli I have used *Totius rationalis, naturalis, divinae ac moralis philosophiae compendium... his adjecimus in libros physicorum, de anima, metaphysicorum ejusdem questiones...*, 2 vols. (Lyons 1568).

64 101.17-19. In the place cited (see fn. 61), Capreolus is arguing against Durandus, Aureoli, and Giles of Rome. The "others" probably refers to Soncinas, *In 12 meta.*, q. 7, and Javelli, *In 10 meta.*, q. 22.

in turn, that it is open to all the objections that he has made against the arguments of Giles [of Rome], which connect the sameness of the matter with the sameness of its potency. Here again he answers an objection of Capreolus that this argument cannot be applied to the matter of the heavenly bodies, because although sublunary matter can admit privation, celestial matter cannot.[65] "On the contrary," writes the author, "for if the matter of the heavens is in potency to several heavenly forms, it can be the subject of privation, and secondly, if this is not the reason why matter is the subject of privation, Giles could say that matter that is not of the same definition as an inferior [type] is not the subject of privation from its nature but from the fact that it receives a form with [its] contrary."[66] After further extended discussion, the author concludes that since the matters and the forms of the heavenly spheres are different, one planet is essentially different from any other, since the planets are to be identified with their spheres, whereas all of the stars of the firmament have the same species.

Of the various Thomists mentioned in the *Juvenilia,* Ferrariensis receives the least detailed consideration, being mentioned only for the three opinions: (1) that the world could have existed from eternity, where he is said to agree with John Canonicus and "many moderns";[67] (2) that the heavens are composed, as in the text cited above; and (3) that it is the teaching of Aristotle that the intelligences are forms actually informing the heavens, where he is listed for his commentary on the text of St. Thomas.[68]

From what has been said up to now, the author of the notes recorded in the *Juvenilia* can be regarded as being quite sympathetic to the teachings of St. Thomas and his school, while being cognizant in the cases mentioned of differences between Cajetan and Capreolus, and generally siding with Cajetan. When, however, we come to the next series of topics relating to the intension and remission of forms and special problems pertaining to the elements, we find that the attitude towards the Thomistic school becomes more critical, and that the Thomistic conclusions and the arguments in their support are generally contested.

---

65   101.29-232. Here the reference is to *In 2 sent.,* d. 12, a. 3, in reply to Giles's third and fifth arguments and *passim.*

66   101.32-102.2.

67   32.6, citing *In 8 phys.,* q. 15. I have perused Ferrariensis's *Quaestiones luculentissimae in octo libros physicorum Aristotelis* (Venice 1619) in the Dominican library at Salamanca, but do not have it at hand to verify this citation; there is also an earlier edition (Rome 1577) which I have not seen. John Canonicus, or Juan Marbres, was a Spanish Scotist of the first half of the fourteenth century. The "plerique recentiores" probably refers to nominalists such as Durandus, Gregory of Rimini, Gabriel Biel, and William Ockham as well as to contemporary Thomists.

68   105.27, citing *In 2 contra gentiles,* c. 70.

The author begins his treatment of intension and remission by stating generally that this is the process by which a quality is varied according to more or less, and by noting the importance of the topic, namely, that, since it is found in almost every alteration, one cannot understand how alteration comes about if he does not understand intension and remission; and, since every action comes about through intension and remission, this process must be understood if one is to understand how any body acts on another. Immediately following this he lists the authorities from which he will draw his arguments, as follows:

> Authors who have treated of this matter are: St. Thomas in the first [book] of *Sentences,* d. 17 [given erroneously as d. 16] q. 2, a. 2, and in the first part of the second part [of the *Summa theologiae*], q. 52, a. 2, and in the second part of the second part, q. 24, a. 5; Capreolus, in the first [book] of *Sentences,* d. 17, q. 2; Herveus in *Quodlibet* 6, q. 11; Gandavensis [Henry of Ghent] in *Quodlibet* 5, q. 19; Soncinas in the eighth [book] of the *Metaphysics,* [q. 21]; Giles [of Rome] in the first [book] of *De generatione,* q. 19, and *Quodlibet* 5, q. 13, and *Quodlibet* 2, q. 14; Burley in the tract *De intensione et remissione*; Durandus in the first [book] of *Sentences*, d. 17, q. 7; Gregory [of Rimini], same place, q. 4, a. 1; Scotus, same, q. 4; Ockham and Gabriel [Biel], same, q. 7.[69]

The author then begins with three *praenotamina,* in the second of which he observes that both alteration and intension are successive, although he notes that it is possible that some alterations take place instantaneously. His reasoning is as follows:

> Alteration is successive, not only from the fact that the subject is altered in one part and then in another, but also by reason of form, insofar as the remiss comes to be intense, and the other way around, in the same part of the subject. And that such a successive intension exists may be proved [as follows]: because, even when the whole subject has been altered, there will yet follow an alteration that comes to be successively. Moreover: certain alterations exist that do not happen successively on the part of the subject, since all of its parts are altered together, as is apparent from the first book of the *Physics,* [comm.] 23, an example of which, according to Aristotle, is freezing; and nevertheless it is certain that some of these take place successively; therefore by reason of form, as Alexander [of Aphrodisias] rightly notes from Simplicius, fourth book of the *Physics,* comm. 23 in t. 22. Nor can you object that Aristotle sometimes states that alteration is only continuous on the part of the subject; from which it seems to follow that there is no succession on the part of the form, and hence no intension either. For, from those things that have been said on the continuity of motion the reply should be obvious: for they cannot be

---

69   111.23-112.2. In verifying citations from Herveus I have used his *Quodlibeta undecim cum octo... tractatibus* (Venice 1513), which includes the treatise *De unitate formarum.*

intrinsically continuous on the part of the form, but they can be on the part of the subject and of time; beyond which, since Aristotle manifestly concedes that there is intension in quality, he necessarily also admits succession in alteration, beyond that which takes place on the part of the subject.[70]

The third of the *praenotamina* also includes some interesting material that pertains to our later analysis and should therefore be cited at this point. This is the author's classification of the various ways in which intension can take place in qualities:

> Indeed intension can be in quality in two ways: first, consecutively; in which way, for example, health is intensified and diminished with the intension and remission of the qualities in which temperament consists; and in this way also relation is said to undergo intension and remission by reason of its foundation; secondly, per se and properly. This again takes place in two ways: first, through mixture with a contrary, in which way, for example, the less hot always has some cold mixed with it; secondly, without the admixture of a contrary, as happens in light, in which there is a more or less either on the part of the agent, as it is more or less a light source, or on the part of the subject: for a subject that is less disposed receives less light and, if it is more disposed successively, it is also more illuminated. For intension properly speaking is that which is found in true alteration, and which is with the admixture of a contrary: concerning which there arises a difficulty as to how intension takes place in alteration. It should be noted that we can estimate an intension to have taken place in an alteration in two ways: first, extrinsically, when no change has taken place in the quality but only in something else: which can take place in two ways: for either the quality can be intensified from a greater disposition of the subject or from the expulsion of the contrary: secondly, intrinsically, when some change has been made in the quality that is intensified; which also can take place in two ways, either through a new production of the quality, or in some other way.[71]

Immediately following this preliminary material, the author states his own conclusions and proceeds to argue in their favor. The first of these conclusions reads as follows:

---

70   112.36-113.18. Most of the distinctions on which this discussion is based are to be found in Soncinas, *In 8 meta.*, q. 22, where he is inquiring whether the intensification of forms is a continuous motion. The discussion of freezing (*congelatio*) is quite similar to that in Toletus, or Francisco de Toledo (1533-1596), *Commentaria in libros de generatione et corruptione Aristotelis* (Venice 1575), Bk. 1, q. 6, 4ª concl. The reading of the Venice 1602 edition is as follows: "Nec in hoc est id universaliter verum: sunt enim alterationes quae secundum subiecti partes simul fiunt, ut patet de coagulatione et congelatione, de quibus multoties diximus." — fol. 17va.

71   113.21-114.6. This particular mode of classification is not found in any of the Thomistic authors cited, although it is consistent with Soncinas's discussion in *In 8 meta.* q. 22, and with Capreolus's sixth conclusion in *In 1 sent.*, d. 17, q. 2, a. 1, "quod aliquae formae intensibiles intenduntur non solum secundum majorem participationem subjecti, sed etiam per additionem alicujus."

I say that first, intension does not take place through an extrinsic change alone: that is, because, granted the extrinsic change, an intension would follow in the quality itself; for then the intension would take place not from the disposition of the subject nor from the expulsion of the contrary, but from an increase on its own part; or, secondly, [it takes place] through the expulsion of the contrary or the disposition of the subject, with the quality remaining the same indivisibly in itself.[72]

Five different arguments are given in support of this position, in the third of which the interesting statement is made that "motion is nothing more than a *forma fluens*."[73] Then space is left for a second conclusion, which, however, is missing from the manuscript. Following this the author states his third conclusion, which reads: "I say, third, that in intension the prior part of the quality does not perish."[74] Five major arguments are again given in support of this, the last of which has many supporting syllogisms and distinctions. At the conclusion of all these the author makes a summary statement that, as it turns out, is transitional to the next conclusion he wishes to draw. He writes:

It therefore must be concluded that intension comes about through the production of a new quality in such a way that, when the latter part comes, the prior remains. Indeed this also can take place in two ways: first, that those later degrees that are added be produced in single instants; and in this way the intension would be discrete, as the Thomists prefer: secondly, in such a way that it come about successively, by a certain continued action.[75]

---

72   114.7-12: "Dico, iam primo, intensionem non fieri per solam mutationem extrinsecam: idest, vel quia, facta mutatione extrinseca, sequatur intensio in ipsa qualitate; nam tunc intensio non fieret; vel ex dispositione subiecti, vel ex expulsione contrarii: sed ex sui ipsius augmento [sic]; vel, 2°, per expulsionem contrarii, aut subiecti dispositionem [MS: dispositione], manente eadem qualitate indivisibili secundum se." I have retained Favaro's punctuation, despite the difficulty it makes for translation. The two alternatives seemingly contained in this conclusion are consistent, nonetheless, with Capreolus's sixth conclusion as given in fn. 71.

73   114.25.26. This statement would seem to align the author with the nominalist view of motion, rather than with the realist view which identified motion as a "fluxus formae." For a discussion of the distinction between "forma fluens" and "fluxus formae," see E. J. Dijksterhuis, *The Mechanization of the World Picture*, tr. C. Dikshoorn (Oxford 1961), 174-175. It is noteworthy, however, that Herveus Natalis speaks of motion in the same manner: "... illud non potest esse aliud nisi forma fluens que communiter ponitur esse ipse motus..." *Quodlibet* 2, q. 13 (Venice 1513), fol. 59ra. Herveus's arguments in this locus are similar to those discussed in the *Juvenilia*.

74   115.32. The position that the prior part of the quality perishes in intensification is identified by Javelli (*In 8 meta.*, q. 6) as that of Walter Burley [in his *De intensione et remissione*] and of Gregory of Rimini, *In 1 sent.*, d. 17, q. 4, a. 2. Gregory, in this locus, attributes the position to Burley and to Godfrey of Fontaines.

75   117.26-31. The Thomists to whom the author refers seem to be Herveus, *Quodlibet* 2, q. 13, and Soncinas, *In 8 meta.*, q. 22. According to Soncinas, the intensification of forms can be continuous in three senses: (1) in the Heraclitean sense of continually going on; (2) in the sense of deriving continuity from the parts of the subject being altered, either without the corruption of a previous part as in heating or with corruption of a previous part as in illuminating; and (3) in the sense of being continuous on the part of the form being intensified. Soncinas holds that St. Thomas

Note here that "the Thomists" are referred to as a group and that the author merely lists their opinion without commenting on it in one way or another.

The fourth conclusion, however, addresses this point directly and sides against the Thomistic school. The author's conclusion and the arguments in its support read as follows:

> I say, fourthly, that intension comes about continuously. [This] is proved, first: because otherwise it would follow that alteration is not one motion, because instants are not continuous but time intervenes, nor would it be motion, because it would not be the act of a being in potency, as has been proved in the *Physics*. [It] is proved, secondly; because, if a form or quality is produced through instants, either the agent does nothing in the time intermediate between the instants, or it does something. If it does nothing, this is absurd: because the agent then has been applied and has a sufficient active power, and the patient is indeed disposed; therefore it acts maximally, since no reason can be assigned why it should have acted a little previously and no longer acts. If, on the other hand, it does not act maximally, [this is] because some time must elapse between the first and the second action lest there be continuity; but for discontinuity any time at all is sufficient and, however much be assigned, it is enough to have less, and less to infinity; therefore a determinate time should never have been assigned: [and] therefore there should never be action. And if the agent does act, either it produces something of that quality, and thus successively; or it merely disposes. But, leaving out that it cannot always be shown that the agent disposes or how it disposes, if it disposes it induces some quality in the thing: either therefore this disposition and quality is induced successively, and so a successive quality is given; or through instants, and then the same question returns.[76]

denies that the intension of forms is continuous in the third of these senses. He writes: "St. Thomas holds the contrary opinion, namely, that the intension of forms is not a motion that is strictly and completely continuous; in fact, an intermediate rest intervenes, since the altering body, if it is sufficiently close to the patient, begins to act on the patient causing in it as perfect a form as it can; and afterwards the body acted upon rests for some time under that form, and is uniformly disposed according to it until, either because of a greater disposition of the subject or because of more power in the agent or from some other cause, it can make that form more perfect" (fol. 109rb). The Latin reads as follows: "Sed sanctus Thomas tenet opinionem contrariam, scilicet quod intensio formarum non sit motus simpliciter et omnino continuus; immo incidit quies media, quoniam corpus alterans si sit sufficiens et non impeditum in primo instanti quo est sufficienter approximatum passo incipit agere in passum causando in ipsum tam perfectam formam quam potest; et postea mobile per aliquod tempus quiescit sub illa forma, et secundum eam uniformiter se habet; donec aut propter maiorem dispositionem subiecti, aut propter maiorem virtutem agentis, vel ex aliqua alia causa possit magis perficere illam formam..." This teaching, it should be noted, was not accepted by Spanish writers under the influence of Domingo de Soto, being rejected as not authentically Thomistic by Toletus and then, in more definite fashion, by Domingo Banez in his *Commentaria et Quaestiones in duos Aristotelis de generatione et corruptione libros* (Salamanca 1585), a work almost exactly contemporaneous with the writing of the *Juvenilia*. See fn. 98, infra.

76   117.32-118.15. These arguments are given by Javelli, *In 8 phys.*, q. 7, as objections to the Thomistic position, although he connects no names with the objections, speaking only of "via

Up to this point there has been no discussion of the Thomistic opinion, but now the author proceeds:

> Nor do you say with the Thomists that heat having been produced, at the same instant it is then extended to the other parts of the subject, for that first part in which heat is already produced is closer to the agent; therefore the agent, having left that, will not act on the more remote parts. Add [to this] that it would follow that the agent does not act any less in the closer part than in the most remote, nor does it first induce the first degree in the closest part [any more] than in the most remote. [The] argument] is confirmed: because a form is produced successively because it resists a contrary; therefore it cannot be produced through instants alone: because it would otherwise follow that each part would be produced in an instant, and, therefore, without resistance and all at once. Therefore it must be concluded with Simplicius on the eighth [book] of the *Physics*, 12 in t. 23, Giles in the first [book] of *De generatione* on t. 20, Jandun in the eighth [book] of the *Physics*, q. 8, and others, that intension and remission come about continuously. [77]

Here, then, is the first explicit rejection of a teaching of the Thomistic school, although it is noteworthy that the particular Thomists are not mentioned *nominatim*, nor is there any indication of differences of opinion that might exist within Thomism on this particular conclusion.

Having finished this exposition of the intension and remission of qualities, the author next turns his attention to special questions relating to the elements, among which are found the question "Whether the forms of elements undergo intension and remission?" Here he divides the authorities into two groups, the first including the Averroists and the Scotists, among others, and the second including Avicenna, St. Thomas and the Thomistic school, nominalists, and others. The two groupings are of interest for the diversity of the thinkers enumerated within them, and for this reason are translated here in their entirety:

nostra" and the "multi" who are opposed to it (ed. cit., pp. 602-604). Diego de Astudillo, O.P., in his *Questiones super libros de generatione et corruptione* (Valladolid 1532), Bk. 1, q. 10, traces the opposition back to Burley and "all the nominalists," who hold that the motion of intensification is "simpliciter continuus"; his own position he states as follows: "motus intensionis et remissionis non est continuus sed successivus ... multae mutationes instantanee sibi succedentes" (fol. 21ra). Toletus, while arguing in the same vein as the author of the *Juvenilia*, does not identify the source of his arguments, except to mention a special teaching of Giles of Rome, that alteration is discrete with respect to the parts of the subject but continuous with respect to intensification, and to note that John or Jandun seems to follow Giles. The position that alteration is continuous in both of Giles's respects is identified by Toletus as "fere communis" (ed. cit., fol. 16vb).

77 118.-27. The arguments here are drawn from Soncinas, *In 8 meta.*, q. 22, fol. 110rb; the author's mention of Giles and Jandun, together with the form of his arguments, suggests some dependence on Toletus, *In 1 de gen.*, q. 6, 1a concl., as mentioned in the previous note. Immediately following the text cited, in 118.27-119.4 the author goes on to answer an objection; this too is taken from Soncinas, loc. cit., fol. 109va.

The first opinion is that of Averroës, in the third [book] of *De caelo,* comm. 67; Nifo and Paul of Venice at the end of the first [book] of *De generatione*; Zimara, proposition 20; Taiapetra, second book, tract. 4; Jandun in the eighth [book] of the *Metaphysics,* q. 5; Achillini, book two of *De elementis,* a. 3; Contarenus, book three; Alexander, in the eighth [book] of the *Metaphysics,* t. 10; all of whom say that the substantial forms of the elements undergo intension and remission, to which can be added Scotus, in the eighth [book] of the *Metaphysics,* q. 3, whom Antonius Andreas follows, eleventh [book] of the *Metaphysics,* q. 1; Pavesius, in the book *De accretione;* John Canonicus, in the fifth [book] of the *Physics,* q. 1; who affirm the same thing of any substantial form that is educed from the potency of matter, so as to exclude the rational soul ...[78]

The second opinion is that of others who deny that forms undergo intension and remission. This is that of Avicenna in the first [book] of *Sufficientia,* chapters 10 and 11, and in the first part of the first [book] of doctrine, third [part], chapter 1; whom Averroës opposes. The same is the opinion of St. Thomas in the opusculum *De mixtione,* and in the second [book] of *Sentences,* d. 15, [q. 2, a. 1], and in the first [part of the *Summa theologiae*], q. 76, a. 4 [ad 4], and there also Cajetan; Capreolus, in the second [book] of *Sentences,* d. 15, a. 1, concl. 2, and in the solutions to arguments against that; Soncinas, in the eighth [book] of the *Metaphysics,* qq. 25 and 26, and in the tenth [book] of the *Metaphysics,* q. 27, and elsewhere; Gregory, in the second [book] of *Sentences,* d. 15, q. 1; Ockham, *Quodlibet* 3, q. 4; Marsilius, in the first [book] of *De generatione,* q. 22; Themistius, in the second [book] of *De anima,* t. 4; Philoponus, in the second [book] of *De generatione,* comm. 33: who, however, teach only this, that the forms of the elements do not remain actual in the compound; but from this the other follows. Moreover, the same opinion is defended by Durandus in the first [book] of *Sentences,* d. 17, q. 6; Henry, *Quodlibet* 3, q. 5; Nobilius, q. 3 in chap. 3; Buccaferrus in t. 18; many of the commentators in the first [book] of *Microtecni,* comm. 15; Herveus in the tract *De unitate formarum* [qq. 15-18]; Giles, in the first [book] of *De generatione,* q. 18; Albert, in the first [book] of *Techni,* chap. 25; and Javellus, in the eighth [book] of the *Metaphysics,* q. 6 [given erroneously as q. 5].[79]

---

78   133.8-16.
79   133.28-134.9. The *De mixtione* of St. Thomas has the fuller title, *De mixtione elementorum ad magistrum Philippum,* and is printed in the Marietti ed. of the *Opuscula philosophica* (Rome 1954), pp. 155-156; see especially n. 433, p. 155, and nn. 436-437, p. 156. The author's reference to Aquinas's *In 2 Sent.,* d. 15, may be based on conjecture, since Capreolus has a long discussion of the subject in this *locus;* St. Thomas has only a tangential reference to it in q. 2, a. 1. Cajetan's arguments are directed against Scotus, Henry of Ghent, and the Averroists; see Vol. 5 of the Leonine ed., n. 19, p. 227. Javelli discusses the intension and remission of substantial forms in both q. 4 and q. 6, but not in q. 5, although he does state in q. 6, "hanc opinionem pertractavimus in q[uaestione] praecedenti," whereas the treatment is actually to be found in q. 4; perhaps this is the source of the author's miscitation.

Note that in this listing of the second group the Thomists are put in different places; first there is St. Thomas, with whom is mentioned Cajetan, Capreolus, and Soncinas, and then, after an enumeration of eight other thinkers, Herveus, followed three names later by Javelli. From the one enumeration of *Thomistae* in the *Juvenilia,* it is obvious that the author recognized Cajetan, Capreolus, and Soncinas as Thomists, and from the authorities listed at the beginning of the section *De intensione et remissione,* Herveus is grouped with Capreolus and Soncinas; with regard to Javelli, this is the only explicit mention of him in the *Juvenilia,* but there is indirect evidence that the author used him for summaries of Thomistic teaching.

After this presentation of the various opinions, the author appears to side with those in the second grouping, for he states immediately after the text just cited: "This second opinion is proved true from these arguments."[80] He then goes on to list four different arguments in some detail, proving that the forms of the elements do not undergo intension and remission. Following this, however, he lists a number of arguments *sed contra* that have been held by proponents of the first opinion. Unfortunately the question is not complete, and does not proceed beyond the listing of four objections. These are not answered, but it is probable that had the question been completed the resolutions of their arguments would have been given in a way that would safeguard the proofs offered in favor of the second opinion.

The last question wherein the opinion of Thomists are referenced is that devoted to the problem, "Whether elements and other natural things have termini of largeness and smallness?" As in some previous questions, the preliminaries include the various definitions and distinctions that will be employed in the discussion, and these make up eight *praenotamina.* These are followed by a listing of four opinions, of which the first is of some interest:

> The first opinion is [that] of those saying that all natural things, elements excepted, have intrinsic termini of largeness and smallness; elements, on the other hand, have an intrinsic terminus of smallness, but none of largeness: so St. Thomas in the first [book] of the *Physics,* t. 36, 38, *De generatione,* t. 41, and the first part [of the *Summa theologiae*], q. 7, a. 3; Capreolus, in the second [book] of *Sentences,* d. 19, [q. un.]; Soto, in the first [book] of the *Physics,* q. 4; and all Thomists.[81]

---

80   134.9-10.
81   144.15-20. For the identification of the references to St. Thomas, see fn. 49 supra. To verify the reference to Soto I have used the 2d ed. of his *Quaestiones super octo libro physicorum Aristotelis* (Salamanca 1555) and have checked this against the Venice 1582 edition, which may have been available to the author. Among "all Thomists" one would have to include Cajetan,

Note the significant inclusion of Soto's name after that of Capreolus, with the implicit acknowledgement that he is to be enumerated in the Thomistic school. Soto is the only Spanish Dominican mentioned by the author, although he is aware of other Spanish writers such as Pererius[82] and Vallesius.[83] Spanish Dominicans differed from Italian Dominicans in their treatment of some questions discussed in the *Juvenilia,* and thus this supplies an interesting point of comparison for judging the author's knowledge of variations within the Thomism of his day.

Following the foregoing enumeration, five arguments are offered in support of the first opinion, and these will be discussed later. The remaining three opinions that are listed, immediately following these arguments, are those of Averroës and the Averroists, the opinion of Paul of Venice, and finally the opinion of Scotus, Ockham, and Pererius. Then the author lists ten assertions or conclusions which he wishes to establish, and in the first and seventh of these he makes mention of individual Thomists. The first conclusion and its proof read as follows:

> I say, first: it seems certain, whatever others may think, that no things have maxima and minima in relation to God: not indeed that they can go to infinity, for concerning this elsewhere; but only God can, by absolute power, increase and diminish any created thing forever and ever. And this indeed is proved of living things [as follows]: for they require quantity, as something extrinsic, for their operation and conservation; but God can supply the concursus of any extrinsic cause; therefore [etc.].
> Concerning qualities, however, Scotus and Durandus in the third [book of *Sentences*], d. 13; Richard and Giles in the first [book of *Sentences*], d. 17; Henry, *Quodlibet* 5, q. 22; Cajetan, in the third part [of the *Summa theologiae*], q. 7, a. 3 [given erroneously as a. 4], and q. 10, and in the

Ferrariensis, and Javelli; other Thomists who taught this doctrine but are not mentioned in the *Juvenilia* include Gratiadei (John of Ascoli), Peter Crokart of Brussels, and Diego de Astudillo; Toletus also followed the Thomistic teaching on this subject.

82 Benedictus Pererius, or Benito Pereyra (c. 1535-1610), Spanish Jesuit philosopher and Scriptural exegete who spent most of his teaching life in Rome. His *De communibus omnium rerum naturalium principiis et affectionibus* (Rome 1562) is cited five times in Vol. I of Galileo's *Opere,* approvingly for its treatment of questions relating to the eternity of the universe and critically for its discussion of falling bodies. Pererius is somewhat eclectic but in his preface accords St. Thomas a place of honor among the philosophers, while favoring at times Scotistic or nominalist teachings himself. The Thomists he cites include Herveus, Capreolus, Cajetan, Ferrariensis, and Soncinas (see pp. 173, 197, 223, 227, 265).

83 Francisco Vallés (1524-1592), Spanish philosopher and physician who composed an exposition and Commentary on Aristotle's *Physics* (Alcala 1562), to which he appended his *Controversiarum naturalium ad tyrones pars prima, continens eas quae spectant ad octo libros Aristotelis de physica doctrina* (Alcala 1563); the latter is cited in the *Juvenilia,* p. 170. Vallés taught at Alcala, where he was a friend of Gaspar Cardillo de Villalpando (1527-1581), a classical Aristotelian who also commented on the *Physics* (Alcala 1566), but whose texts were soon replaced at Alcala by Soto's more scholastic commentaries. Vallés mentions Soto in his *Controversiae* but is generally opposed to his teaching.

second [part] of the second [part], q. 24, a. 7, speaking of the quality of grace, deny that a quality can be increased to infinity intensively; because, since some qualities might have been created and limited by grace, the properties of the essence must have a certain limit, granted intrinsic, of intensification. But on the other hand Capreolus, in the third [book of *Sentences*], d. 13, q. 1, and in the first [book of *Sentences*], d. 17, q. 2, a. 2 [given erroneously as q. 4]; Almainus and Gregory, same place; Ockham, same place, and in the third [book of *Sentences*], d. 13, q. 7; Soto, in the first [book] of the *Physics,* q. 4, a. 2, where he shows that this is the opinion of St. Thomas in *De Veritate,* q. 29, a. 3; and that if, in the third [given in text as 13] part [of the *Summa theologiae*], q. 7, a. 12, he seems to say the contrary, this should be understood of ordinary law; they say: although quality of itself has a certain terminus in intensification, nevertheless by [God's] absolute power it can be increased. And this reason can be assigned: because qualities are not so intrinsically the instruments of forms that they essentially include the latitude owed to the form....

And so I say, first, that no quality of itself, abstracting from an order to the subject or the agent, has a certain terminus in intensification; but it does not tend to infinity simply, because perhaps this is repugnant to a created nature, but to infinity syncategorematically. For which reason I say, secondly, the same quality, of itself, abstracting from the subject, does not require for itself a certain terminus. Add [to this] also, that the opinion of Capreolus is very probable.[84]

The text goes on to enumerate various objections and the replies that may be given to them, and the exposition reveals the author's respectable knowledge of the discussions current among nominalists and late scholastics generally.

The seventh conclusion is obviously directed against the Thomistic opinion, for it reads: "I say, seventhly, that elements and homogeneous compounds of themselves have no termini either extrinsic or intrinsic of largeness or smallness."[85] The proof is divided into two parts, the first consisting of four arguments to show that the elements have no termini of smallness, or *minima*. After this, the author continues:

And these reasons prove that there is no minimum. It is much more easily proved that there is no maximum, especially since this is denied by

84   145.32-146.28. Cajetan is aware that he is disagreeing with the majority Thomistic opinion on this matter; mentioning the *Thomistae*, he adds "inter quos forte ego aliquando fui" [*In 2am 2ae*, q. 24, a. 7, n. 3 (Leonine ed., Vol. 8, p. 183)]. Capreolus's arguments are directed against Aureolus, Durandus, Ockham, and Scotus, among others. Soto is aware of Cajetan's arguments, cites two of the three *loci* given in the *Juvenilia,* and gives a fairly lengthy refutation of Cajetan's teaching.

85   152.11-12. This is the thesis of Vallesius, Villalpandus, and Pererius (see fns. 82 and 83); it is opposed to the teaching of Soto, Javelli, Astudillo, and Toletus, among others, including the Averroist John of Jandun.

no one, except by Cajetan, in the first part [of the *Summa theologiae*], q. 7, a. 3. For Aristotle says in the second [book] of *De anima*, [text] 41, that fire can be increased to infinity. And this is obvious: for, if straw be added to the maximum, it will certainly be increased; for to say that the straw is not going to be burned, or, if it is burned, that in that event fire would be turned into air, this seems plainly ridiculous.[86]

This refutation of Cajetan is the only argument against *maxima,* and the author then turns to his remaining conclusions.

As to the rest of the question, there is no indication by Favaro that the treatment is incomplete, but one may suspect that it is from the fact that the solutions of the arguments that relate to the conclusions are limited to a refutation of the five arguments that have been given in support of the first opinion, that, namely, of the Thomistic school. It may be, however, that the author felt that the variations introduced in the second, third, and fourth opinions had been sufficiently accounted for in his own conclusions and in the arguments given in their support. If such is the case, then it would seem that the point of the entire question is to refute this particular Thomistic teaching.

Since the author's understanding of the arguments given by Thomists in support of their conclusions, and also his arguments against them, are of critical importance in judging his knowledge of Thomism, these arguments and the author's reasons for rejecting them are presented here in their entirety.

PROPOSITION: All natural things, elements excepted, have intrinsic termini of largeness and smallness; elements, on the other hand, have an intrinsic terminus of smallness, but none of largeness.[87]

FIRST ARGUMENT:

[Proof]

[This] is proved, first, from the authority of Aristotle, in the first [book] of the *Physics,* 36, where he says this; and in t. 38 he offers an argument against the ancients that, if there is no maximum and minimum, is worthless. For so he concludes against Anaxagoras: if anything can be separated from anything else, there is no minimum; but all natural things have a minimum; therefore, etc. Nor can you say that Aristotle supposes this contrary to Anaxagoras: for here Simplicius notes, in his comment 34, that Anaxagoras denied a minimum; and this seems probable, since he thought that anything could be separated from anything else. Moreover,

86   153.8-14. Cajetan's arguments are directed against Scotus [Leonine ed., Vol. IV, pp. 76-79, esp. n. 8 (p. 77) and n. 12 (p. 77)]. These arguments are discussed at length by Soto, *In I phys.,* q. 4, a. 2.

87   144.15-17.

Aristotle, in the second [book] of *De anima,* 41, teaches that everything constituted by nature has a definite terminus of largeness and smallness.[88]

[Reply]

Therefore, to the first argument of the first opinion I reply that Aristotle says that similar things have a minimum [when he is arguing] *ad hominem* against Anaxagoras. For, although, as I said, it seems probable from Simplicius that Anaxagoras denied a minimum, nevertheless Anaxagoras was defending two repugnant assertions. In the first he said that the first principles of all things are certain similar parts, and because of this, minimal; and from their mixing each thing is thought to be, and is named from, that species of which it contains the greater number of parts: for Simplicius attributes this to him, in the first [book] of the *Physics,* comm. 34. In the second [assertion] he was saying that anything can be separated out of anything: nor did he advert to the fact that this second [assertion] is repugnant to the first; for, if anything can be separated out of anything, one will never arrive at a minimum. Therefore Aristotle, so that he might use the second assertion to argue against Anaxagoras, supposes the first *ad hominem.* For in the locus of the second [book] of *De anima* he speaks of living things, and indeed there he says that fire does not have a terminus of largeness.[89]

SECOND ARGUMENT:

[Proof]

Secondly, by reason of Aristotle in the first [book] of the *Physics,* 36, if the homogeneous parts of an animal have no terminus of largeness and smallness, the animal also will have none; but this is false; therefore, [etc.]. The minor [premise] is obvious. The inference is proved [as follows]: for, if there can be flesh of any size and bone of any size and nerves and arteries, there can also be a head of any size. [The argument] is confirmed: if there can be homogeneous parts of any size whatsoever, there is no reason why, if God put them all together, there cannot be a man of any quantity whatsoever.[90]

---

88   144.20-29. The argumentation seems to be drawn from Soto, *In 1 phys.,* q. 4, aa. 2 and 3.

89   156.12-25. I have not been able to locate the source of these arguments; they are somewhat similar to the exegesis of Aristotle offered by Vallesius in his *Controversiae,* nn. 4 and 5, and are possibly based on Pererius or Villalpandus, both of whose works I have studied in the university library at Salamanca but do not have at hand for a precise verification.

90   144.29-145.1. The argumentation is probably drawn from Soto, *In 1 phys.,* q. 4, a. 2, and from Javelli, *In 1 phys.,* q. 19, who gives essentially the same reasoning as Soto. Others who earlier argued in similar terms include Astudillo, *In 1 phys.,* q. 8, and Peter Crokart of Brussels, *In 1 phys.,* q. 2, a. 5. These last-named little known Dominicans were influential in the formation of Francisco Vittoria and Soto and thus indirectly influenced the rise of "second scholasticism." Astudillo's commentary and questions on the *Physics* was finished on July 4, 1530, at five o'clock in the morning, as he states in the colophon, and is bound with his questions on the *De generatione* (Valladolid 1532); Peter Crokart's arguments are to be found in *Argutissime, subtiles et fecunde questiones phisicales magistri Petri de Bruxellis, alias Crokart* (Paris 1521).

[Reply]

To the second, I deny the inference: for, although the parts can be as large as one likes, nevertheless the living thing cannot be as large as one likes. The reason for the disparity is that similar parts need no determinate quantity for their operation; but living things do require [this]. For this argument concludes demonstratively against the ancients who denied a substantial form, for which reason they could not formally distinguish a whole from its part; and, moreover, they could not say that the whole required anything except by reason of parts. If therefore the parts do not require a determinate quantity they could not say why the whole requires [it]. But those who posit a substantial form can assign a reason for the disparity. [91]

THIRD ARGUMENT:

[Proof]

Thirdly, those things that are from nature are determinate. [92]

[Reply]

To the third [argument] I reply: if this proposition has this meaning, that all accidents and all conditions in each natural thing are determinate from the nature of that thing, the proposition is completely false. For matter is a natural thing; and nonetheless it is indeterminate; and the same for the elements. And [this] is confirmed [as follows]: for, according to almost everyone homogeneous things, such as the elements, do not have a determinate maximum terminus of largeness. If on the other hand the sense is, that which naturally belongs to a thing always belongs to it in the same determinate manner; this is true. For, since nature does not change, whatever it does once it does always. Moreover, since the elements of their nature have an indeterminate quantity, they will always have [it] indeterminate. [93]

FOURTH ARGUMENT:

[Proof]

Fourthly, we see that things are corrupted by attrition, by breaking, and so forth; but this would not be so, unless there were a minimum; therefore [etc.]. [94]

---

91   156.26-35, reading *requirat* for *requirant* in line 34. The line of reasoning here seems to be Scotistic and is similar but not identical to that discussed and refuted by Javelli, *In 1 phys.*, q. 19. It is also stated and answered by Peter Crokart, *In 1 phys.*, q. 2, a. 5.

92   145.1-2. This brief argument is expanded at considerable length by Soto, Javelli and Crokart in the *loci* cited, and by Cajetan in his commentary on the *De anima*, chap. 4, q. 4, and *In 1am.*, q. 7, a. 3, nn. 5, 6, and 9.

93   157.1-11. I have not been able to locate this argument in precise form, although it is somewhat similar to that offered by Vallesius, *Controversiae*, n. 5 (fol. 7r) and may be based on Pererius or Villalpandus. An intimation of the argument is also to be found in Crokart, loc. cit.

94   145.2-3. This is based on Soto, *In 1 phys.*, q. 4, a. 3. The argument is also implicit in Javelli, *In 1 phys.*, q. 19, in his refutation of the Scotistic position.

[Reply]

To the fourth [argument] I reply that the thing cut is corrupted by the violence [or force] of the ambient [medium]; things that are crushed, however, [are corrupted] either because they rarefy or because they are cut: for we are speaking of elements within their proper nature, according as they can subsist and operate with any quantity no matter how small.[95]

FIFTH ARGUMENT:

[Proof]

Fifthly: if there were no minimum even in homogeneous things, it would follow that there is no minimum in sight; but this is absurd; therefore [etc.]. The major [premise] is apparent: if there is not a minimum fire, for example, when it conserves light, there would not be a minimum visible object; therefore, not sight either. The minor [premise] is Aristotle's, in the book *De sensu et sensibili,* chap. 6; and it is proved by reason: for, the smaller the visible [thing] is, the stronger must be the power that perceives it; therefore, if there would be no visible minimum, there would be no maximum seeing power; therefore, it would increase to infinity.[96]

[Reply]

To the fifth [argument] I reply by denying that it follows that if there be no minimum there would be no sensible minimum. For a greater power is required for perceiving a smaller thing: therefore, although, if we divide fire, it would remain lucid of its nature, nonetheless this cannot be perceived by any sense; because no sense is so intense that it can perceive such an object.[97]

This, then, completes the exposition of the teachings of St. Thomas and the various Thomists that are contained in the *Juvenilia.* The matter that they provide would seem to be sufficient to form some judgment of the knowledge of Thomism that is manifested in the *Juvenilia* and the sources from which it may be drawn, to which topics we now turn.

---

95   157.12-15. A Scotistic argument, similar to those refuted by Javelli, loc. cit.

96   145.3-10. This type of argument is to be found in Peter Crokart, *In 1 phys.,* q. 2, a. 5, but otherwise is not to be found in the Thomists mentioned in the *Juvenilia,* apart from a passing remark in Soto, *In 1 phys.,* q. 4, a. 3, which might be interpreted in this fashion.

97   157.16-20. This line of reasoning is found as early as the mid-fourteenth century in Albert of Saxony's questions on the *Physics* (Venice 1516), Bk. 1, q. 9, "Utrum cognitio totius dependeat ex cognitione suarum partium?" It is repeated by authors in the nominalist tradition and by those arguing against them, such as Crokart, *In 1 phys.,* q. 2, a. 5.

II. The Thomism and the Sources of the *Juvenilia*

As can be seen from the foregoing, the *Juvenilia* contain a wealth of information that sheds light on Galileo's intellectual formation at Pisa and his general sympathies regarding philosophical issues that were being debated at the time. Here we shall have to restrict ourselves to those few points where his notes bear directly on St. Thomas and the Thomistic school, leaving for later study his relationships to classical and other positions. From the texts that have been given, however, and the annotations of their likely sources contained in the footnotes up to this point, it is possible to draw some tentative conclusions regarding the general milieu of Galileo's instruction at Pisa and the sources from which either he or his professors drew their inspiration.

A. *The Thomism of the* Juvenilia

In general, it seems fairly safe to conclude that the author of the *Juvenilia* is correctly informed on the teachings of St. Thomas and the Thomists whom he cites, and is sympathetic to their conclusions and the main lines of argument in their support. He is somewhat eclectic, however, and is not always accurate in his citation of the *loci* he purports to use. In one instance, while disagreeing with those whom he identifies as "the Thomists," he actually defends a position that was to be urged by Domingo Banez, writing only a year later, as the authentic Thomistic position.[98] The argumentation on this particular point was current at the time of composition of the *Juvenilia* and shows an up-to-date knowledge of the literature that had recently appeared and debates going on in Spanish and Italian universities.

These general conclusions will now be substantiated, first from the viewpoint of the author's knowledge of, and agreement with, the teachings of St. Thomas and, second, with his comparable relationship to the Thomistic school.

Not unexpectedly, considering the atmosphere in sixteenth century Pisa, St. Thomas is held in great respect by the author as the foremost

---

98   See fn. 75, supra. Banez devotes seven questions in his commentary on Bk. 1 of *De generatione* to the subject of alteration (ed. cit., pp. 50-82); of these, q. 6 is entitled "Utrum alteratio sive intensio sit motus continuus?" (pp. 73-77). In the first article of this question Banez analyzes the teachings of Thomists, including Capreolus, Soncinas, Javelli, Ferrariensis, and Astudillo, and concludes that their view is erroneous and not consonant with St. Thomas's teaching. His second article is devoted to the question "Utrum detur minimum in accidentibus que intenduntur?", and here he analyzes the roots of his teaching in Soto's questions on the first book of the *Physics*, q. 4, a. 3, and refutes the interpretation of "quidam novus philosophus" whom I have been able to identify as Toletus.

among Catholic Doctors and is treated with deference; this extends even to points on which he disagrees with St. Thomas but utilizes his argumentation benignly in support of his own position. The opinion or argumentation of St. Thomas is cited in ten of the questions discussed in the *Juvenilia,* and in eight of these the author sides with Aquinas's conclusions; in the remaining two, while disagreeing with one teaching or another, he does not directly oppose any of Aquinas's statements but prefers rather to argue against the positions of his commentators. The following is a listing of these questions, with a comment on the extent of the author's agreement or disagreement with St. Thomas:

1. *The unity and perfection of the universe.* [99] The author agrees with St. Thomas that there is only one universe, and urges Aquinas's support for his teaching that God could have made the universe more perfect in an accidental way, but not essentially so.

2. *Whether the world could have existed from eternity?* [100] The author here presents three conclusions, all of which he attributes to St. Thomas, although the third is rejected by Thomists as not being the authentic teaching of Aquinas.

3. *Whether the heavens are a union of simple bodies, or composed from them?* [101] The author's conclusion is that the heavens are a body distinct from the four elements and not a compound formed from them; this he recognizes as also the teaching of St. Thomas.

4. *Whether the heavens are corruptible?* [102] The author proposes a twofold conclusion: that they are probably incorruptible by nature, but not incorruptible in such a strict sense as to limit God's power in corrupting them if He so wished, since He alone is *ens necessarium.* The author invokes St. Thomas and other theologians in support of this double conclusion.

5. *Whether the heavens are composed of matter and form?* [103] The author again proposes a twofold conclusion: that they are so composed, but that the matter of the heavens is not the same as the matter here below. He adduces St. Thomas's support for both elements of this teaching.

6. *Whether the heavens are animated?* [104] Here the author concludes that the heavens are not animated by a vegetative or by a sensitive soul,

99   27.21.
100   32.2.
101   55.2.
102   63.13.
103   70.4.
104   103.11.

and that the problem of their being animated by an intellective soul can best be solved by holding that the intelligences are merely the movers of the heavens; in thus functioning they assist the heavenly bodies rather than inform them the way in which a soul informs a body. This he again presents as the teaching of St. Thomas.

7. *On intension and remission.*[105] Here the author concludes that the intensification of a quality requires more than an extrinsic change in the quality, that in such intensification the prior part of the quality does not perish, and that such intensification takes place in continuous fashion. St. Thomas is mentioned only as an authority on this topic, and is not otherwise discussed, although the opinion of "the Thomists" that intensification is not continuous is rejected. (Thomists after Banez, as has been noted, could agree with all three of the author's conclusions).[106]

8. *What are the forms of the elements?*[107] Here the author offers a threefold conclusion: that the forms of the elements are not proper alterative qualities and that they are not motive qualities, but that each element has its proper substantial form distinct from all others. This he proposes as the teaching of St. Thomas.

9. *Whether the forms of the elements undergo intension and remission?*[108] Here the author answers in the negative, giving the arguments of St. Thomas and the Thomistic school in support of his conclusion.

10. *Whether elements and other natural things have termini of largeness and smallness?*[109] Here the author offers ten conclusions, most of which resolve arguments raised in the nominalist schools that flourished after St. Thomas's death. Of the three conclusions that relate to Aquinas's thought, the author is in agreement with two (one regarding God's power with respect to maxima and minima, and the other regarding the termini of living things and heterogeneous compounds) and rejects the third (regarding the termini of elements and homogeneous compounds).

Of the 24 sub-conclusions that go to make up the answers to these ten questions relating to Aquinas's teaching, therefore, only two or three conclusions, depending on how one views the continuity of in-

105   111.13.
106   See fns. 75 and 98, supra.
107   129.23.
108   133.2.

109   138.29-30. It may be noted here that the question of *minima naturalia* comes up again in Galileo's *Discourse on Floating Bodies* and *The Assayer*, but in these places Galileo betrays no influences of the Thomist position. See William R. Shea, "Galileo's Atomic Hypothesis," *Ambix* 17 (1970), 13-27.

tensification as Thomas's teaching, imply a rejection of the Angelic Doctor. These two or three are basically Scotistic conclusions; and all three, perhaps by coincidence but noteworthy nonetheless, were taught by Vallesius, whereas the two less arguable ones were taught also by Pererius.[110]

The situation with respect to the Thomists falls into the same general pattern as that with respect to St. Thomas, except that in the former case the author is less restrained in expressing his disagreement with one or other member of the school. As we have seen, he cites seven Thomists: Herveus, Capreolus, Soncinas, Cajetan, Ferrariensis, Javelli, and Soto. Among these, there is little evidence of any serious study of Herveus or Ferrariensis, whereas for the remaining five it appears that the author read one or another of their texts with some degree of care. On one question he prefers Cajetan's teaching to that of Capreolus, on another, Capreolus's over that of Cajetan; he is definitely opposed to Soncinas's teaching on intensification; he uses Soto extensively for Thomistic views on maxima and minima, while disagreeing with some of his conclusions; Javelli he seems to find useful as a compendium of Thomistic teachings, particularly as a guide to the thought of Capreolus and Soncinas.

A more detailed characterization of the author's agreements and disagreements with the Thomistic school will become apparent from the following listing of the topics in relation to which their teachings are discussed:

1. *The nature of celestial matter.*[111] The author agrees with the Thomistic teaching that the heavens are composed of matter and form and that their matter differs from the earthly matter of the sublunary region. He prefers Cajetan's explanation to Capreolus's as to the nature of this heavenly matter, and also sides with Cajetan (against Capreolus and Soncinas) in holding that there is a different type of matter in each of the heavenly spheres.

2. *The continuity of intensification.*[112] Here the author is directly at variance with the teaching of Herveus, Capreolus, Soncinas, and Javelli. Soto has nothing explicit on this thesis, although he does lay the groundwork for a different interpretation of intensification in his tract

---

110 See fns. 24, 70, 76, 77, 82, 85, 89, and 93. Valesius teaches that creatures could not have been produced from eternity in his commentary on the eighth book of the *Physics,* and that intensification is continuous and that elements have no natural intrinsic terminus of largeness or smallness in n. 5 of his *Controversiae.* Pererius holds that one cannot demonstrate, one way or another, that corruptible creatures could have existed from eternity in Bk. 15, c. 13 of his *De communibus,* and that elements have no natural minima in Bk. 10, c. 23, of the same.

111 76.7-103.9.

112 111.14-119.4.

on natural minima, from which Banez was to draw his inspiration for what was later to become the accepted Thomistic teaching.[113] The author was acquainted with this section of Soto's questionary on Aristotle's *Physics*, but apparently did not grasp its connection with the problem of the intensification of qualities.

3. *The intensification of elemental forms.*[114] Here the author's solution is identical with that of the Thomistic school, among whom he enumerates the teaching of Herveus, Capreolus, Soncinas, Cajetan, and Javelli on this point. His own arguments are directed against Averroës and his followers, and also against Scotus and his school.

4. *Problems associated with maxima and minima.*[115] Among the ten conclusions reached by the author in his attempt to resolve these problems, only two bear on the teachings of the Thomistic school. The first is that, in relation to God, things do not have maxima and minima in the sense that God can always make them larger and smaller, but not in the sense that they will become actually infinite in a categorematic sense.[116] In stating this conclusion, he opposes himself to Cajetan and aligns himself with Capreolus, while using Soto's citation of a text of Aquinas in support of Capreolus's interpretation. The second conclusion relates to the termini of largeness and smallness as found in elements and homogeneous compounds, and here the author rejects Cajetan's opinion that elements have an intrinsic terminus of largeness — an opinion that is rejected as unintelligible by Soto[117] and is not common to the school. The author rejects also the teaching of Thomists generally that elements have an intrinsic terminus of smallness, using mainly Soto's arguments in his rejection of this conclusion, and opting rather for the Scotistic solution.

To summarize, then, on two of the four topics (n. 1 and n. 3), the author is in complete agreement with the Thomistic school, and on one topic (n. 1) engages in an intra-mural dispute wherein he favors the more recent opinion (Cajetan's) over an earlier teaching (Capreolus's). On a third topic (n. 4), he agrees with the more theological conclusion

---

113 On Banez, see his *In 1 de gen.*, q. 6, a. 2 (ed. cit., pp. 74-77). For a brief sketch of the history of this thesis in Thomism, see A. M. Pirotta, O.P., *Summa philosophiae Aristotelico-Thomisticae* (Turin 1936), II, pp. 315-329, esp. n. 456, pp. 317-318.

114   133.1-136.22.

115   138.29-157.20.

116 Cf. 146.24, 148.25-28, where the author allows the possibility of an infinite in a syncategorematic sense. The terms categorematic and syncategorematic derive from the nominalist controversies over infinity in the fourteenth century.

117 Soto states: "Caietanus adducens illic auctoritatem Aristotelis contra S. Thomam effingit nescio quam distinctionem, certe, ut pace doctissimi authoris dixerim, parum physicam." *In 1 phys.*, q. 4, a. 2 (ed. cit., fol. 14rb).

of the Thomistic school (God's power), while disagreeing with its thesis bearing directly on natural philosophy (elemental minima); his intra-mural arguments here favor Capreolus over Cajetan. On a fourth topic (n. 2), while disagreeing with the accepted Thomistic teaching of his time, he himself argues for a position that was later to be recognized as the authentic teaching of Aquinas. When these results are taken together with the author's attitude towards St. Thomas himself, they support the conclusion that the author is well acquainted with Thomistic teaching, and, if not a Thomist in the strict sense, is generally sympathetic to this school.

As a final point relating to the author's knowledge of Thomism, a comment should be made on the accuracy of his citations. He refers to St. Thomas 29 times in the *Juvenilia,* ten times with no identification of *loci* and 19 times with a total identification of 31 *loci.* Of these 31, 25 are correctly given in the manuscript and 6 are incorrectly given (ac-cepting Favaro's reading of the MS), although they are verifiable on correction. Similarly, with respect to the various Thomists, these are mentioned 25 times in the *Juvenilia,* three without any identification of *loci* and the remaining 22 with an identification of 26 *loci.* Of these, 20 are identified correctly and six are given incorrectly, although verifiable upon correction. The close to 25% occurrence of errors, all of which have been identified in the citations of the texts or in their ac-companying footnotes, may turn out to be significant for further research on the sources of the *Juvenilia.* Should similar errors be located in any of the printed texts that were available to the author, they would provide a key to his use of secondary sources. The twelve errors, it should be mentioned, are all understandable in terms of the difficulty of locating and citing texts, and may be an indication that the *Juvenilia* are Galileo's own composition, when, as a university student, he was still learning the techniques of accurate scholarship while working with primary sources.

B. *The Sources of the* Juvenilia

This brings us to our final consideration, namely, that of the im-plications of this study for a better understanding of the sources of the *Juvenilia.* Here only a brief indication will be given with respect to four different hypotheses: (1) that the *Juvenilia* are original with Galileo, representing his own work with primary sources: (2) that they were copied by Galileo from one or more secondary sources; (3) that they were Galileo's class notes based on the lectures of one or more of his professors at the University of Pisa; and (4) that they were a summary

Galileo prepared for himself with an ulterior motive in mind by
borrowing or cribbing from the notes of others,[118] possibly students who
attended lectures he himself had missed.[119]

The first hypothesis, as has been pointed out by Favaro,[120] is quite
unlikely considering the neatness of the autograph and clues of its
having been transcribed from another manuscript. These include
several spaces left vacant in the original writing and then filled in later
either with cramped lettering or with sentences flowing over into the
margins. There are also expressions that are written down, then crossed
out as not making sense in the context, only to appear a line or two
below in their proper place. Yet the transcription, if such it is, was not
made slavishly, as there are also evidences of words being changed and
expressions being altered to convey a clearer and more consistent sense.
Moreover, it could be that Galileo was actually recopying his own
poorly written notes; in this connection, there is certainly no a priori
reason for excluding the possibility that such notes were the composition of a twenty-year old university student. The work on Thomistic
theses that we have analyzed is not appreciably superior to what a bright
twenty-year old Italian or Spanish seminarian might do even in our own
day. In the century before Galileo, Giovanni Pica della Mirandola had,
at the age of 23, challenged all comers to debate 900 selected theses in
philosophy, theology, and science, and it should be remembered that
Galileo was as much a genius as Pico in his own right. The question as
to what primary sources might have been available to Galileo for such a
composition poses no serious problem. Among the authors we have
discussed the most recent would be the works of Pererius (Rome 1562),
Vallesius (Alcala 1563), Javellus (Lyons 1568), and Ferrariensis's commentary on the *Physics* (Rome 1577). Although Soto's commentary and
questionary on the *Physics* was not published in Italy until the Venice
1582 edition, at least six Spanish editions had appeared before this date,
beginning *c.* 1545.[121] I have found copies of Spanish editions of Soto's

---

118   This possibility has been suggested to me by Prof. Stillman Drake, of the University of
Toronto, in a private communication dated July 22, 1971, after having read this paper. He also
suggested a number of clarifications and information that enabled me to eliminate an error of fact
in the original draft. I wish to take this opportunity to thank him publicly for his interest and
assistance.

119   Following a suggestion of Prof. William R. Shea, of the University of Ottawa, in a private
communication from Cambridge, England, dated July 28, 1971, who also read the paper and, independently of Prof. Drake, came up with a similar proposal; to him I also acknowledge my debt
with thanks.

120   *Opere*, I, 10-12.

121   See V. Beltran de Heredia, *Domingo de Soto, O.P., Estudio biografico documentado*,
(Salamanca 1960), 527-528.

works in Italian libraries, and suspect that Vallesius's work was similarly available in Italy shortly after its publication. Thus there is nothing to exclude the possibility that Galileo could have worked with these sources and made his own synthesis from them. The strongest argument against this hypothesis, of course, is that the notes contain too many references. Galileo was notorious for having read *very* little, and although a bright young man of those days could have controlled a hundred books of the kind cited, it is extremely unlikely that Galileo really did so.

The hypothesis that the *Juvenilia* were copied by Galileo from one or more secondary sources is still tenable in the light of our study. Here the sources either could have existed in manuscript form, or they could have been printed sources. Regarding the latter possibility, there is no evidence of direct copying from any of the Thomistic authors mentioned in this study. Should Galileo have copied from a manuscript source, the consistency of the treatment of topics relating to Thomism suggests that this was the work of one man, or at least work done under the direction of one teacher.

The third hypothesis, that the *Juvenilia* are Galileo's class notes based on lectures at the University of Pisa, is similar to the last possibility. Here, again, the consistency of the treatment suggests that the notes are based on the lectures of one professor. By way of general characteristics, this man would be an eclectic Aristotelian with scholastic leanings, quite well acquainted with and sympathetic to the teachings of the Thomistic school, but accepting nonetheless some Scotistic theses and a few interpretations deriving from Averroës. He would be knowledgeable with respect to the classical Greek commentaries, and would also know and appreciate the nominalist arguments that were common among the "Latins." He would be acquainted with developments at both Spanish and Italian universities, and would appear to be sympathetic to the writings of two members of the newly-formed Society of Jesus, Pererius and Toletus.[122]

Who this professor might be is a question that is not easily answered. To my knowledge only two candidates have been proposed to date,

---

122 The Society was officially confirmed in 1540. Toletus became the first Jesuit cardinal; shortly after being received into the Society, he was called to Rome from Spain in 1559 to teach philosophy and later theology at the Roman College. He himself had studied theology at Salamanca under Soto, who regarded him as a favored disciple. Pererius entered the Society as a youth in 1552 and likewise taught philosophy and theology, including Scripture, at the Roman College.

Francesco Buonamici and Flaminio Nobili.[123] With regard to Buonamici, the results of this study would be adverse to his identification as the professor who formed Galileo's youthful mind. A perusal of Buonamici's *De motu* shows a quite different citation of authors from that in the *Juvenilia,* with strong emphasis placed on Averroës and classical commentators such as Alexander of Aphrodisias and Simplicius.[124] Buonamici cites St. Thomas with about half the frequency of Averroës, and occasionally mentions "Thomistae," but he does not identify any Thomists nor does he discuss their teachings in any detail. He accepts the Averroist teaching on the forms of the elements, and has not progressed beyond Walter Burley and James of Forli in his discussion of the intension and remission of qualities.[125] Thus the general tenor of his thought is quite different from that contained in the *Juvenilia.* Certainly Buonamici would not be identified as a Thomist or as one sympathetic to the teachings of this school.

Because of the difficulty of tracing any correspondence between the thought patterns of Buonamici and the young Galileo, Eugenio Garin has recently called attention to Galileo's "quotations from the lectures of Flaminio Nobili."[126] From the viewpoint of this study, however, there are difficulties with this suggestion also. Whereas Buonamici is not cited in the *Juvenilia,* Nobili is cited three times, and in two of these the author is quite harsh in his rejection of Nobili's teaching. The first rejection is with regard to the question, "What are the forms of the elements?" Nobili's teaching is listed as the first opinion, "that the forms of the elements are something made up of primary qualities and some substantial form."[127] The author goes on: "But this is unintelligible, nor does he [Nobili] seem to sufficiently understand the nature of a substantial form."[128] The second rejection occurs in the context of a discussion as to how the primary qualities are related to resistance. After giving his own conclusions, the author writes: "And from this is apparent the error of Nobili, who, in the first [book] of *De*

---

123 For details concerning Buonamici's life and works, see my article on him in the *Dictionary of Scientific Biography* (New York 1970), II, 590-591. I have not been able to locate any biographical information on Nobili, but see fn. 126 infra.

124 I have used the Florence 1591 folio edition of Buonamici's *De motu* and have counted the number of citations of authors in Bks. 4, 5, and 8 of this work; these contain the chapters that most relate to the elements, local motion, and alteration.

125 On the forms of the elements, see ed. cit., pp. 745-753; on intension and remission, see pp. 759-763.

126 Eugenio Garin, *Science and Civic Life in the Italian Renaissance*, translated by Peter Munz (New York 1969), 140; see also 97-113.

127 129.27-29.

128 129.29-30.

generatione, doubt 11 on chap. 7, has distinguished a twofold resistance: one of animals, which would consist in a certain endeavor, itself a kind of action; another in other things, which he has reduced to an impotency for receiving; where, as you can see, he has accepted the extrinsic cause of resistance for resistance [taken] formally, when these should be distinguished."[129] The third citation is merely an enumeration of Nobili along with St. Thomas and others as holding that the forms of the elements do not undergo intension and remission.[130] All three citations of Nobili refer to his *De generatione,* which I have not seen. But from even these three indications of its contents, one may doubt seriously whether Nobili could be the professor hidden behind the *Juvenilia.*

This leaves the fourth hypothesis, which gains its plausibility mainly from the exclusion of the other three. As Professor Drake has pointed out in his private communication,[131] Galileo was a medical student at Pisa from 1581 to 1583; in the latter year he became fascinated with mathematics, and in 1585 he left the university to devote himself to that discipline. In the intermediate year, 1584, seeing that he was not going to pursue medicine, he may have started to compile lectures on natural philosophy with a view to obtaining a better paying job than a mathematician could then hope for. This could have led him to make his own synthesis of extant materials, depending largely on secondary sources. Such an explanation is rendered even more plausible by the suggestion of Professor Shea, in his private communication,[132] to the effect that Galileo might have gotten hold of the notes of students who went to lectures he himself had not attended, and made a summary for himself, perhaps as a primer to undergo an eventual examination. This would explain elements of Galileo's personal style that are recognizable in the *Juvenilia,* while it would also serve to account for the atypical, non-Galilean citation of so many sources.

From these largely negative results, and from the tentative nature of the reasoning leading to them, it would be premature to attempt to draw any conclusions as to the identity of the author of the *Juvenilia.* It should be stressed, of course, that this study has been based on only one aspect of the contents of this work, namely, its relation to St. Thomas and to Thomism generally. Viewed from this perspective, when attempting to identify anyone known to be at Pisa in 1584 as either the

129   172.1-6.
130   134.6.
131   See fn. 118, *supra.*
132   See fn. 119, *supra.*

author of, or the inspiration behind, the *Juvenilia,* one would almost find as much support for the candidacy of Galileo himself as for anyone who has thus far been proposed as his teacher.[133]

133   The first draft of this article was completed on May 20, 1971, and some revisions were made on December 11, 1971, at which time the manuscript was submitted for publication. Since the latter date, a considerable amount of work has been done on Galileo's early writings both by the author and by Professors A. C. Crombie and Adriano Carugo, who are publishing their findings under the auspices of the Domus Galileiana in Pisa in a book to be entitled *Galileo's Natural Philosophy.* In general all of this work confirms the thesis only tentatively advanced in this study, namely, that the *Juvenilia* were probably composed by Galileo himself, with little or no direct use of primary sources but with a recognizable dependence on the writings of Pererius and Toletus, and also with some borrowings from Christopher Clavius's commentary on the *Sphaera* of Sacrobosco. The author has also had the opportunity meanwhile to consult the Galileo manuscripts in Florence, and has found that some of the mis-citations of sources attributed to Galileo in this article are actually Favaro's mis-readings of Galileo's handwritten numerals. Again, a study of the thus far unedited logical writings of the young Galileo, entitled *De precognitionibus et precognitis in particulari* and *De demonstratione,* transcriptions of which have been generously loaned to the author by Carugo, show a similar interest in Thomism. Of the 24 authors cited in addition to Aristotle, Cajetan and Aquinas rank among the first five on the basis of frequency of citation; also, two or three references are made to another Dominican, Franciscus [N]eritonensis, who was a professor at Padua and was probably one of Cajetan's teachers. — Note added by the author in galley proof on November 20, 1972.

DOCUMENTS SUR LES ORIGINES ET LES PREMIÈRES ANNÉES DE LA COMMISSION LÉONINE

Pierre M. de Contenson O.P.

DONNÉES HISTORIQUES ET PROBLÈMES

La décision de Léon XIII et ses suites.

LE pape Léon XIII annonca sa décision que soit publiée une nouvelle édition des œuvres de S. Thomas dans la lettre *Iampridem considerando* adressée au cardinal Antonin de Luca, Préfet de la Congrégation des études, datée du 15 octobre 1879.[1] Le motu proprio *Placere nobis* du 18 janvier 1880 définit les caractéristiques de l'édition nouvelle et confie sa réalisation à trois cardinaux: Antonin de Luca, Jean Simeoni, Préfet de la Congrégation pour la Propagation de la Foi, et Thomas Zigliara, des Frères Prêcheurs.[2]

---

[1] Il ne peut être question de reproduire ici in-extenso les actes pontificaux que nous mentionnons. Dans l'Edition léonine, tome I, on trouvera reproduits: l'encyclique *Aeterni Patris*... du 4 août 1879, "De philosophia christiana ad mentem sancti Thomae Aquinatis Doctoris angelici in scholis catholicis instauranda", voir pp. iii-xvi; la lettre au cardinal A. de Luca, préfet de la Congrégation des études, *Iampridem considerando* du 15 octobre 1879, "De Academia S. Thomae Aquinatis Romae instituenda deque nova omnium operum eius editione curanda", pp. xix-xxi; le motu proprio *Placere nobis* du 18 janvier 1880, "De operibus S. Thomae Aquinatis ex integro edendis", pp. xxv-xxvi. Ces mêmes textes se trouvent aussi dans A. S. S. 12 (1879) 97-115, 225-228, 337-338. Ci-dessous nous citons partiellement certains actes de Léon XIII: ainsi *Iampridem*...n. 4; *Placere nobis*... n. 5, *Volumen tertium*... pp. 379-380, *Quum certa*... n. 140.

[2] Il sera souvent question ci-dessous du cardinal Zigliara. A son sujet nous ne pouvons que renvoyer aux notices de dictionnaires et autres recueils, voir par ex. ASOP 1 (1893) 258-253; également *Memorie Domenicane* 45 (1928) 265-275 et 78 (1961) 86-100. Né le 20 octobre 1832 à Bonifacio (Corse), Tommaso Maria Zigliara (Francesco) fut étudiant dominicain à Rome et Pérouse, il est prêtre en 1856. Ses liens avec l'évêque de Pérouse Vincenzo Gioacchino Pecci, futur Léon XIII, sont bien connus: le père Carbó, promoteur du thomisme, était l'ami de Mgr Pecci, qui partageait son élan thomiste; il devint le professeur du jeune Zigliara qui fut ordonné prêtre par Mgr Pecci, lequel proclamait son admiration pour la qualité de la pensée thomiste de Zigliara. Lecteur à Corbara puis à Viterbe, Zigliara fut pro-régent du collège St. Thomas de Rome de 1873 à 1879 (il eut pour successeur dans cette charge le père Frati dont il est question ci-dessous, pp. 370-382 et nn. 104, 115). Le nouveau pape, Léon XIII, s'empressa de créer cardinal, le 12 mai 1879, T. Zigliara, qui devint préfet de la Congrégation des études en 1888 et mourut le 10 mai 1893. Concernant le cardinal T. Zigliara, A. Baudrillart cite un mot de Mgr d'Hulst à l'abbé Pisani le 23 janvier 1887: "...toujours le plus bienveillant et le plus fermé des hommes...," *Vie de Mgr d'Hulst* (Paris 1912), t. I, p. 536.

Sur Paolo Carbó, de nationalité espagnole et qui vint en Italie en 1835 pour être Lecteur à Viterbe en 1844, à Pérouse en 1849, régent du Collège Saint-Thomas à Rome en 1852, voir par exemple I. P. Grossi, "Un'Accademia Tomistica alla Minerva. Note d'Archivio", *Memorie Domenicane* 75 (1958) 226-248; voir également A. Walz "Sguardo sul movimento tomista..." cité ci-dessous n. 14.

La préparation de l'édition commence immédiatement sous la direction effective du cardinal Zigliara qui s'entoure de collaborateurs dominicains. Le 11 décembre 1882, ce groupe de collaborateurs est organisé en collège doté d'un président. Par la lettre *Volumen tertium* du 2 octobre 1886, Léon XIII impose un bouleversement du plan de l'édition et des consignes concomitantes obligent à renoncer aux méthodes de travail suivies jusqu'alors pour se contenter de faire un travail sommaire. Enfin en 1892-1893, le statut de l'entreprise d'édition de S. Thomas est radicalement modifié: la direction et la responsabilité du travail sont confiés au Général des Dominicains. A chaque fois, ces décisions sont accompagnées des mesures administratives et financières correspondantes.

Ainsi l'édition de S. Thomas d'Aquin dite "Edition léonine" a été décidée il y a plus de quatre-vingt-dix ans et, après des avatars successifs, la responsabilité de mener à bien ce projet a été remise directement au Maître de l'Ordre dominicain il y a au moins quatre-vingts ans. Cette relative ancienneté place donc les débuts et les premières mutations de l'entreprise que l'on appelle maintenant "Commission léonine"[3] sous le regard de l'historien. Ce dernier ne peut manquer de s'y intéresser car cette Commission constitue à son origine un élément notable et original du mouvement thomiste dans la deuxième moitié du XIXe siècle.

Questions et problèmes.

Il se trouve que les Actes de l'autorité et les documents plus ou moins officiels déjà publiés concernant les débuts de la Commission léonine attirent l'attention de celui qui les lit même candidement par certaines particularités: on y relève parfois des formules un peu étranges, à qui il arrive même d'être apparemment contradictoires entre elles, soit quand on passe d'un document à l'autre, soit à l'intérieur d'un même document. En voici deux exemples parmi d'autres:

a) Dans *Iampridem considerando* du 15 octobre 1879[4] et *Placere*

---

3 Sur le titre officiel de l'édition décidée par Léon XIII, "Edition léonine", voir ci-dessous n. 66. Nous n'avons trouvé aucun texte qualifiant de "Commission..." le groupe des trois cardinaux. Il semble que pour désigner l'équipe des éditeurs le titre de "Commission léonine" ne devint courant que très tardivement; on le trouve dans un tract de propagande pour l'édition manuelle de *Summa contra Gentiles* édité en 1934, dans une circulaire officielle de M. S. Gillet, Maître de l'Ordre, du 15 juin 1935 à l'occasion du décès du père P. P. Mackey, enfin en 1946 dans les *Actes* du chapitre général O.P. de Rome, c. III, n. 76. Le premier nom officiel du groupe de Dominicains travaillant en équipe à l'Edition léonine est celui de "Collège des éditeurs de S. Thomas", voir ci-dessous n. 115.

4 "Iampridem considerando...Demum quo latius spargatur ac disseminetur Angelici Doctoris sapientia, constituimus omnia eius opera de integro in lucem edere, exemplo s. Pii V. Decessoris Nostri, rerum gestarum gloria et vitae sanctitate praeclari; cui quidem in ea re tam felix contigit exitus, ut Thomae exemplaria, iussu illius evulgata, permagni sint apud viros doctos, summoque

nobis du 18 janvier 1880,[5] le pape Léon XIII insiste sur le nécessaire recours aux manuscrits et sur la qualité scientifique qui doit caractériser l'édition projetée; alors que, dans *Volumen tertium* du 2 octobre 1886, l'accent est mis presque exclusivement par Léon XIII sur une publication la plus rapide possible[6] cependant que dans *Quum certa* du 4 octobre 1893 le même pontife rappelle qu'il faut suivre les normes précisées dans *Placere nobis*.[7]

b) Plus radicalement, comment expliquer l'intervention personnelle du pape par *Volumen tertium* du 2 octobre 1886 pour que la *Summa theologiae* soit mise en chantier immédiatement et les commentaires d'Aristote remis à plus tard, ainsi que les consignes draconiennes, ruineuses de toute velléité de travail vraiment critique? Quelle explication donner alors que, dans *Placere nobis* du 18 janvier 1880 et même dans *Volumen tertium*, le même Léon XIII insiste sur la pleine liberté donnée et maintenue aux cardinaux pour organiser la publication, particulièrement l'ordre et les délais de parution, comme ils le jugeront le meilleur pour satisfaire les exigences initiales du projet?

studio requirantur. Verum quanto plus editio illa est rara, tanto magis alia desiderari coepta, quae nobilitate ac praestantia cum Piana comparari possit. Ceterae enim cum veteres tum recentiores, partim quod non omnia s. Thomae scripta exhibeant, partim quod optimorum eius interpretum atque explanatorum careant commentariis, partim quod minus diligenter adornatae sint, non omne tulisse punctum videntur. Certa autem spes est, huiusmodi necessitati consultum iri per novam editionem quae cuncta omnino sancti Doctoris scripta complectatur, optimis quoad fieri poterit, formis litterarum expressa, accurateque emendata; iis etiam adhibitis codicum manuscriptorum subsidiis, quae aetate hac nostra in lucem et usum prolata sunt... Observantur quidem animo rei gerendae cum magnitudo, tum difficultas; nec tamen deterrent quominus ad eam magna cum alacritate quamprimum aggrediantur. Confidimus enim in re tam gravi, quae ad commune Ecclesiae bonum magnopere pertinet, adfore Nobis divinam opem et ..."

5 "Placere Nobis, omnia sancti Thomae Aquinatis Opera de integro publicari, superiore anno significavimus...

Primum itaque, ne almae Urbi Nostrae haec pereat laus, editionem, quam supra diximus, reservatam esse volumus Officinae librariae Sacri Consilii Christiano nomini propagando, clarae iam ob alia magnae molis et laudati operis edita volumina.

Editioni autem curandae destinamus ac praecipua auctoritate praeesse volumus tres sanctae Romanae Ecclesiae Cardinales; scilicet Antoninum de Luca..., Ioannem Simeoni..., Thomam Zigliara ex Familia Dominicana, ad disciplinam s. Thomae apprime institutum atque eruditum. His autem ius et potestas esto statuendi ac decernendi Nostro nomine quidquid ad rem pertinere intellexerint. Quare prospiciant ut omnia ac singula Angelici Doctoris Opera integra prodeant... Similiter curent et provideant ne literarum optima forma, ne accurata emendatio, ne intelligens in rerum singularum delectu iudicium desideretur; ac demum constituant quo ordine, quo tempore singula volumina in lucem oporteat proferri.

Quod vero ad expensas attinet, argenteorum italicorum CCC millia Nos ultro damus atque addicimus suppeditandis sumptibus in praesenti necessariis. Reliquo autem tempore necessarios suppeditari volumus ex eiusdem Sacri Consilio Fidei propagandae aerario: cui tamen quidquid erit vendendis exemplaribus redactum pecuniae, tamdiu in rem cedat, quoad par ratio fuerit acceptorum et expensorum. Si quidquam eidem accrevisse contingat, accrescentem pecuniam omnem insumi iubemus in lucubrationes eorum Scriptorum edendas, qui s. Thomae Aquinatis illustrandis operibus maxime excellant..."

6 Voir ci-dessous pp. 379-381.

7 Voir ci-dessous n. 140.

Le recours aux études et même aux polémiques déjà publiées, et elles sont nombreuses touchant aux premières années de la Commission léonine, ne permettent pas d'éclairer totalement les difficultés.[8] Bien au contraire, elles font souvent surgir dans l'esprit des gerbes nouvelles d'interrogations. Ces interrogations, nous semble-t-il, peuvent être regroupées en trois problèmes fondamentaux:

1. Pourquoi, comment et sous quelles influences, Léon XIII a-t-il mûri si rapidement après son élévation au pontificat suprême son projet d'une édition nouvelle des *Opera omnia* de S. Thomas, alors qu'il existait déjà ou que se publiaient alors des éditions très satisfaisantes et en tout cas bien suffisantes pour l'usage scolaire?[9]

2. Quels sont les principes de travail suivis par les premiers éditeurs et grâce auxquels ils ont pu sortir les trois premiers tomes de l'édition dans les six années qui ont suivi la fondation?

3. Comment expliquer la mutation du plan d'édition par voie d'autorité et l'imposition d'une méthode de travail qui semble bien avoir nui gravement à la qualité de l'œuvre produite, méthode dont les éditeurs n'ont pu pleinement se dégager que de longues années après?

Notre projet.

Il ne peut être question de présenter une histoire synthétique de la Commission léonine qui soit satisfaisante, même si on la limite à une période très déterminée des origines. En effet l'histoire générale du néo-thomisme est encore à élaborer, bien que diverses études et de multiples documents sur ce sujet aient été récemment publiés.[10] Or, comme nous l'avons déjà dit plus haut, la Commission léonine dans ses débuts est une des composantes du mouvement néo-thomiste.

Puisque, pour cette période, on en est encore aux monographies, nous avons cru pouvoir apporter une modeste contribution en ce domaine en signalant ou en exploitant certains documents inédits contenus dans les archives romaines des éditeurs de S. Thomas; pour ce faire, nous les rapprochons à l'occasion de faits bien connus par ailleurs, de documents officiels ou encore d'autres informations sur la même époque

---

8   On trouvera des renseignements sur la majeure partie de ces publications diverses dans les études de Cl. Suermondt, "Kort overzicht en lijst van S. Thomas' werken", ETL 2 (1925) 236-244, "De principiis recensionis operum S. Thomae Aquinatis in editione Leonina", *Angelicum* 3 (1926) 418-465, voir également *Bulletin thomiste* 2 (1927) [35]-[50], "Le texte léonin de la 1a Pars de S. Thomas. Sa révision future et la critique de Baeumker", *Mélanges Mandonnet*, Tome I (Paris 1930) 19-50, "Il contributo dell'edizione leonina per la conoscenza di S. Tommaso", *Scholastica ratione historico-instauranda* (Acta congressus scholastici internationalis, Roma 1951) 233-283; de G. F. Rossi, "L'Autografo di San Tommaso dal Commento al III° libro delle Sentenze", *Divus Thomas* (Piac.) 35 (1932) 532-585, "Il quarto pionere della commissione leonina P. Clemente Suermondt", *Divus Thomas* (Piac.) 57 (1954) 90-119.

9   Voir ci-dessous n. 14.

10   Voir ci-dessous n. 11.

qui ont été publiées en ordre dispersé. Telle ou telle publication ayant déjà jeté quelque lumière sur les faits et les problèmes mentionnés ci-dessus, nous serions pleinement satisfait si les compléments de documentation que nous tentons d'apporter ajoutaient encore un peu de clarté. Nous savons cependant que bien des aspects ou des faits isolés resteront encore dans l'ombre.

Les documents présentés ici se sont trouvés tout naturellement groupés en trois dossiers correspondant à autant d'étapes distinctes du processus qui a finalement abouti à la production de l'Edition léonine. Cette édition est encore en cours de réalisation, mais il se trouve que les plus récents tomes parus, qui sont publiés plus d'un siècle après les plus anciens des documents ici présentés, se trouvent directement inclus dans les perspectives déjà ouvertes par la première de ces étapes dont nous parlons.

On trouvera proposés ci-dessous à l'attention:

1. Un ensemble de lettres et documents concernant un projet d'édition scientifique des *Opera omnia* de S. Thomas antérieur de plus de dix ans au projet léonin.

2. Une série de lettres et d'autres pièces donnant des informations concrètes sur la recherche de manuscrits et leurs premiers collation-nements éxécutés dans divers pays d'Europe à la demande et sous la direction du cardinal Zigliara.

3. Divers documents et renseignements sur les dix premières années de travail de la Commission léonine et sur les avatars de son statut tant au plan scientifique, que juridique et financier.

LE PROJET UCCELLI-DALLET D'UNE ÉDITION SCIENTIFIQUE
DE S. THOMAS EN 1869

Les documents.

Pour expliquer la décision de Léon XIII de mettre en route, sous la direction du cardinal Tommaso Zigliara, une nouvelle édition de S. Thomas, on se réfère tout naturellement au mouvement néo-thomiste qui se développe dans la seconde moitié du XIXᵉ siècle.[11] L'édition

11 Le mouvement néo-thomiste au XIXᵉ s. et plus largement la renaissance thomiste au siècle dernier ont bénéficié dans les dernières années d'un nombre considérable d'études, engendrant d'ailleurs parfois des polémiques sources de nouvelles publications. On voit revenir assez souvent, par exemple dans la revue *Divus Thomas* de Plaisance ou dans *Aquinas*, des articles sur le néo-thomisme, particulièrement en Italie, ces études sont signées de noms tels que ceux de F. Duranti, C. Fabro, A. Fermi, R. Masi, I. Narciso, F. Olgiati, A. Pelzer, G. F. Rossi, G. Stella, C. Vasoli, A. Walz, A. C. Zangrandi, etc. Nous ne pouvons citer ici tous les auteurs et tous les travaux que nous avons personnellement consultés; renvoyons donc une fois pour toutes à ce qui est signalé ou recensé dans le *Bulletin thomiste*: X, nn. 2081-2133; XI, nn. 2109-2133; XII, nn. 2497-2552; XIII, nn.400, 409-412; XIV, nn. 688-699. Nous citerons plus explicitement ci-dessous l'une ou l'autre de

léonine constitue manifestement, en effet, une expression importante de ce mouvement néo-thomiste, et tout d'abord dans l'esprit du pape lui-même.[12] On évoque aussi l'émulation suscitée chez les dominicains, la jalousie même peut-être, par les solides travaux du père Fedele da Fanna préparant une nouvelle édition des œuvres de S. Bonaventure.[13] Enfin, outre les nombreuses autres entreprises d'éditions complètes ou partielles d'œuvres de S. Thomas élaborées avec plus ou moins de bonheur au cours du XIXe s.,[14] on mentionne tout particulièrement la stimulation résultant des travaux de l'abbé Paul Antoine Uccelli sur les autographes de S. Thomas et ses inédits ou supposés tels.[15] Ces travaux révélaient qu'il y avait peut-être encore bien des découvertes à faire en ce domaine et que toutes les éditions de S. Thomas déjà publiées risquaient d'être beaucoup plus imparfaites encore qu'on ne le supposait.

ces publications, mais nous renonçons à redire ici ce qui a déjà été dit ailleurs. Il reviendra à un historien de regrouper un jour toutes ces études et de les concilier en une synthèse. Remarquons simplement que, contrairement à ce qui est suggéré dans le *Bulletin thomiste*, X, p. 929, nous pensons conclure de tout ce que nous disent les études récentes sur Léon XIII et ses activités ou engagements intellectuels, que c'est bien le thomisme que le pape entend restaurer et non pas seulement une philosophie chrétienne éclectique; les allusions à S. Bonaventure ou à S. Anselme que l'on relève sous la plume pontificale ne peuvent être invoquées pour minimiser les fortes convictions spécifiquement thomistes du cardinal Pecci, même si dans sa première encyclique de souverain pontife il ne parle de S. Thomas d'Aquin que de façon allusive: lettre encyclique *Inscrutabili* du 21 avril 1878, voir *A.S.S.* 10 (1877-1878) 585-592, où S. Thomas est mentionné p. 590 à propos de la bonne philosophie propre à bien former la jeunesse "quemadmodum nos exemplo scriptisque suis Magnus Augustinus et Angelicus Doctor, caeterique christianae sapientiae Magistri docuerunt."

12   C'est bien ce qui ressort de tous les actes de Léon XIII qui traitent de l'Edition léonine, voir par exemple le passage de *Iampridem considerando* cité ci-dessus n. 4.

13   C'est en 1874 qu'avait paru l'ouvrage du père Fidelis a Fanna, *Ratio novae collectionis operum omnium sive editorum sive anecdotorum S. Bonaventurae proxime in lucem edendae manusriptorum bibliothecis totius Europae perlustratis* (Torino 1874). Sur l'auteur voir V. Meneghin O.F.M., *Il P. Fedele a Fanna dei Fratri Minori 1838-1881* (Vicenza 1940). En fait, l'énorme travail codicologique et paléographique de Fedele da Fanna n'a pas été exploité autant qu'il aurait pu l'être par les éditeurs franciscains de S. Bonaventure. Le père Fedele étant mort à 43 ans le 12 août 1881, le premier volume sortira quinze mois après ce décès alors que les franciscains avaient décidé en 1870 de mettre en chantier cette édition.

14   Sur les nombreuses éditions d'œuvres de S. Thomas entreprises depuis le projet avorté de Tommaso Soldati à la fin du XVIIIe s., voir par ex. J. J. Berthier, *Sanctus Thomas Aquinas "Doctor Communis" Ecclesiae* (Roma 1914); mais surtout M. Grabmann, *Die Werke des Hl. Thomas von Aquin* (BZGPTM, XXII (Münster i.W. 1949) passim; voir aussi A. Walz, "Sguardo sul movimento tomista in Europa nel secolo XIX fino all'enciclica Aeterni Patris", *Aquinas* 8 (1965) 351-379, concernant Migne voir p. 357, pour les éditions italiennes p. 367. On retrouve cette même étude p. 139-167 du volume collectif *Gaetano Sanseverino*, qui n'est qu'une reprise du fascicule 3 d'*Aquinas* 8 (1965) sous une nouvelle couverture et avec une pagination autonome.

A la même époque, il y eut des projets multiples d'éditions des œuvres de S. Bonaventure, voir Fedele da Fanna, *Ratio novae...*, pp. 21-23, et aussi *S. Bonaventurae Opera omnia*, I (Quaracchi 1882) pp. VII-VIII.

15   Sur P. A. Uccelli, voir S. Merkle, "Antonio Uccelli und Thomas Contra errores Graecorum", *Römische Quartalschrift* 35 (1927) 209-246, mais également la liste des œuvres dans M. Grabmann, op. cit. note précédente, pp. 38-39 n. 59, à condition d'y ajouter au moins l'édition, à tirage très limité et actuellement introuvable, de la partie autographe du *Super Isaiam* faite à Milan en 1847.

Toute une série de documents inédits conservés dans les archives de la Commission léonine manifeste l'existence et la consistance d'un projet d'édition antérieur de dix années à la décision de Léon XIII. Ces documents fourmillent de détails qui conduisent à penser que ce projet, qui d'ailleurs avorta très vite, a très probablement exercé une influence notable sur la genèse et la maturation de l'idée qui est à l'origine de l'Edition léonine.

Voici la liste des documents concernant le projet Uccelli-Dallet qui se trouvent dans les archives de la Commission léonine:[16]

[1]   P. A. Uccelli à A. V. Jandel, Naples 14 mars 1869.
[2]   A. V. Jandel à P. A. Uccelli, réponse à [1], main de R. Bianchi, 17 mars.
[3]   P. A. Uccelli à A. V. Jandel, réponse à [2*].
[4]   Conditions pour un traité avec un éditeur, main de V. Ligiez.
[5*] V. Ligiez à P. M. Rouard de Card, brouillon, 5 mai; voir ici n. 29.
[6]   P. A. Uccelli à A. V. Jandel, mai 1869.
[7*] A. V. Jandel à P. A. Uccelli, réponse à [6], brouillon main de V. Ligiez, Marino 20 mai; voir ici pp. 347-349.
[8*] J. Dallet à A. V. Jandel, Langres 21 mai; voir ici n. 56.
[9*] A. V. Jandel à J. Dallet, réponse à [8], brouillon main de A. V. Jandel, juin; voir ici p. 349.
[10] P. A. Uccelli à J. Dallet, brouillon main de V. Ligiez, Rome 15 juin.
[11*] J. Dallet à A. V. Jandel, Langres 24 juin; voir ici p. 349.
[12*] A. V. Jandel à J. Dallet, réponse à [11*], brouillon main de V. Ligiez, Rome 3 juillet; voir ici pp. 349-350.
[13] T. M. Thiriet à V. Ligiez, Flavigny.
[14] T. M. Thiriet à J. Dallet, projet de contrat Uccelli-Dallet, Flavigny 2 août.
[15] J. Dallet à V. Ligiez, Langres 4 août.
[16] V. Ligiez à J. Dallet, réponse à [15], brouillon, Paris 6 août.
[17] J. Dallet à V. Ligiez, Langres 7 août.
[18] V. Ligiez à J. Dallet, brouillon, Paris 8 août.
[19] P. A. Uccelli à V. Ligiez, Rome 8 août.
[20*] R. Bianchi à V. Ligiez, Rome 10 août; voir ici n. 57.

---

16 A chaque fois nous indiquons pour les lettres l'auteur et le destinataire puis le lieu de rédaction et la date, mais quand nous n'avons eu en mains qu'une copie ou un brouillon ou encore un simple schéma de réponse, nous le signalons car nous ne pouvons pas être certain que la lettre réellement envoyée a comporté un texte identique en tout point à celui que nous avons eu sous la main.

Pour pouvoir le désigner plus commodément par la suite, nous donnons à chaque document un numéro d'ordre entre crochets. La numérotation a suivi dans la mesure du possible l'ordre chronologique; parmi les pièces non datées, certaines n'ont pu être situées que de façon approximative, mais on n'a retenu que les documents appartenant manifestement à cette période et à cette affaire.

L'astérisque qui affecte certains numéros indique que le document correspondant est cité ici soit intégralement, soit pour la partie concernant notre objet, ou bien, dans le cas de la pièce [39], qu'elle est fidèlement résumée.

[21]   A. V. Jandel à V. Ligiez, télégramme, Jaroslav 12 août.

[22*] A. V. Jandel à V. Ligiez, Lemberg 14 août; voir ici p. 351.

[23]   J. Dallet à V. Ligiez, Langres 13 août.

[24]   V. Ligiez à J. Dallet, brouillon, Paris 16 août.

[25]   P. A. Uccelli à V. Ligiez, doublet de |19|, Rome 18 août.

[26]   J. Dallet à V. Ligiez, Langres 18 août.

[27]· Projet de contrat P. A. Uccelli-J. Dallet, main de V. Ligiez.

[28]   Projet de contrat P. A. Uccelli-J. Dallet, main de V. Ligiez.

[29]   Projet de contrat V. Ligiez-J. Dallet, main de V. Ligiez.

[30]   P. A. Uccelli à V. Ligiez, 20 août.

[31]   V. Ligiez à J. Dallet, réponse à [26], brouillon, Paris 23 août.

[32*] M. Chéry à V. Ligiez, Rome 27 août; voir ici n. 58.

[33]   P. A. Uccelli à V. Ligiez, Rome 27 août.

[34]   P. A. Uccelli à V. Ligiez, Rome 31 août.

[35]   J. Dallet à V. Ligiez, Langres 3 septembre.

[36*] P. Monvoisin à V. Ligiez, Paris 4 septembre; voir ici n. 52.

[37*] T. Bourard à V. Ligiez, voir |24|, Dijon 11 septembre; voir ici p. 343-344.

[38]   C. Bayonne à V. Ligiez (?).

[39*] P. A. Uccelli, présentation du projet d'édition; voir ici n. 34.

[40*] P. A. Uccelli, à V. Ligiez, Rome avant la fin de 1869; voir ici n. 60.

Les principaux protagonistes de l'entreprise sont J. Dallet, libraire-éditeur à Langres (France), l'abbé P. A. Uccelli[17] et les dominicains V. Ligiez[18] et T. M. Thiriet.[19] Les autres correspondants impliqués sont tous dominicains: A. V. Jandel, Maître de l'Ordre; R. Bianchi, procureur général; Marcolin Chéry, français à Rome;[20] P. Monvoisin, Th. Bourard et C. Bayonne, de couvents français; enfin le père Rouard de Card, provincial de Belgique.

17   Nous nous contentons ici de signaler à l'attention et d'exploiter sommairement des pièces des archives de la Commission léonine; mais il est bien évident que, pour achever de préciser les rôles respectifs de P. A. Uccelli et de ses correspondants, il faudrait chercher ailleurs des pièces complémentaires particulièrement à la Bibliothèque vaticane dans les dossiers Ms. lat. 10139 à 10150.

18   Sur le père V. Ligiez voir par exemple I. P. Grossi, "Un' accademia tomistica alla Minerva. Note d'archivio", *Memorie Domenicane* 75 (1958) 226-248, voir p. 229 n. 7. Sur sa collaboration avec P. A. Uccelli et son rôle comme éditeur du volume posthume d'Uccelli, voir S. Merkle, art. cité ci-dessus n. 15, p. 226. Ligiez fut socius du Maître de l'Ordre à partir de 1866 et jusqu'à la fin de 1879.

19   Le père Th. M. Mannès Thiriet, de la Province de France, a été lecteur à Flavigny de 1867 à 1875. Ses liens avec certains religieux romains promoteurs du thomisme apparaissent dans la lettre [13] où il mentionne les pères Gugliemotti et Carbó; on sait le rôle important joué par ce dernier et ses relations avec le futur Léon XIII et T. Zigliara, voir I. P. Grossi, art. cité ci-dessus n. 2, passim.

20   Sur le père Marcolin Chéry, qui vint à Rome en février 1868 avec le cardinal Bonaparte et fut nommé consulteur de la Congrégation de l'Index en janvier 1870, voir I. P. Grossi, art. cité ci-dessus, p. 231 n. 12, mais surtout les renseignements biographiques des pp. 218-222 de l'article de P. Vallin, "La collégialité épiscopale selon le P. Marcolin Chéry", *Rev. Sc. ph. th.* 51 (1967) 217-226.

Origines, grandes lignes et motifs du projet.

Nous n'avons aucun renseignement direct sur les premières origines du projet. Il est clair qu'au début il y a, d'une part, J. Dallet[21] et sans doute des dominicains français, et P. A. Uccelli,[22] d'autre part; la liaison entre les deux étant faite par les autorités dominicaines de Rome.[23] Les pères Ligiez et Thiriet deviennent alors les intermédiaires permanents et les plus actifs soutiens de l'entreprise.[24]

Au moment de son élaboration la plus achevée dans l'esprit de Dallet,[25] d'Uccelli[26] et des pères Ligiez[27] et Thiriet, c'est-à-dire vers mai-juin 1869, le projet se présente ainsi dans ses grandes lignes:

Faire une édition des œuvres complètes du Docteur angélique qui soit directement fondée sur les manuscrits les plus authentiques exploités de la manière la plus scientifique possible;[28] quand il y en aura, ce seront les autographes ou les originaux qui seront collationnés. On commencera d'ailleurs cette édition par deux volumes qui seront l'œuvre d'Uccelli lui-même et qui seront précisément consacrés aux œuvres de S. Thomas dont nous avons une partie autographe.[29] Pour les

---

21 Au moment où l'affaire commence à mal tourner, on saura rappeler à J. Dallet que c'est lui qui a pris l'initiative première de tout le projet [24], voir [2].

22 En mars 1869, P. A. Uccelli présente déjà des projets au Maître de l'Ordre [1] [2].

23 C'est le Père Général qui oriente Uccelli vers Dallet avec qui la curie généralice est déjà en correspondance à la suite de propositions faites par Dallet [2].

24 Il ressort des documents que V. Ligiez agit en France en tant que représentant autorisé d'Uccelli pour traiter avec Dallet [10][16][35], mais comme il est en même temps 'socius' du Maître de l'Ordre il engage en fait plus que ne l'avait prévu le père Jandel, d'où des échanges difficiles, par ex. [20*][21][22*][32*] etc. Par ailleurs le rôle actif du père Thiriet est éclatant dans ses propres lettres, Uccelli lui rend hommage plusieurs fois, par ex. [19][34].

25 Ainsi les lettres [8*][15][17].

26 Il faudrait citer toutes les lettres d'Uccelli qui insiste généralement sur les deux premiers volumes mais dans d'autres documents il envisage toute l'édition, voir [10] et surtout [39*] que nous résumons ci-dessous n. 34.

27 Voir par exemple [5*][29].

28 Dans les documents le titre de l'édition est "édition des Œuvres de St. Thomas d'après les mss orginaux ou contemporains" voir par ex. [10] mais aussi [33][34] et aussi [39*] résumé ci-dessous n. 34.

29 Cela est redit dans tous les projets de contrat et dans les présentations de l'œuvre, ainsi [14][27][28] etc. Il est à noter qu'Uccelli semble considérer comme étant de S. Thomas les textes qui se trouvent dans son autographe de Naples alors qu'il s'agit en réalité d'œuvres de S. Albert copiées par S. Thomas. Voir par exemple ce qu'écrit V. Ligiez au père Rouard de Card au moment où il lui demande d'obtenir l'envoi à Rome d'un ms. de Bruges [5].

"Peut-être connaissez-vous D. Uccelli, le paléographe qui semble nous être envoyé providentiellement pour dénicher de partout où ils gisent dans la poussière et l'oubli, et surtout pour déchiffrer les écrits autographes de St. Thomas d'Aquin. L'une de ses plus précieuses trouvailles en ce genre est l'autographe des commentaires que notre Docteur Angélique a écrit (sic) sur *tous les* ouvrages de St. Denys l'Aréopagite, et qui sont inédits en grande partie. Cet autographe qui est à Naples, a fourni la preuve que ce qui a été imprimé de ces commentaires parmi les œuvres du B. Albert le Grand, est bien réellement de son disciple; et qu'en outre des livres *De caelesti hierarchia*, *De ecclesiastica hierarchia* et *De mystica theologia*, notre grand Docteur a encore commenté

autres volumes, éventuellement pour contrôler le travail d'Uccelli dans les deux premiers,[30] le travail sera accompli par les soins "d'une commission romaine chargée de la collation des textes... ainsi que de la correction des épreuves",[31] mais "les pères dominicains de France et de Belgique devront aussi contribuer..."[32] et d'ailleurs on prendra des collaborateurs "partout où le besoin s'en fera sentir".[33]

Les raisons d'entreprendre une telle édition sont très explicitement exposées par les promoteurs:[34] P. A. Uccelli met en avant l'actualité de

le livre *De divinis nominibus* et les *lettres de St. Denys*. Seulement le précieux autographe a été lacéré et mutilé par une dévotion indiscrète, et pour suppléer aux lacunes qu'elle y a ouvertes, il faut nécessairement recourir aux rares copies qui en ont été faites. D. Uccelli en a trouvé une au Vatican, mais fort défectueuse. On sait qu'il en existe une autre au Séminaire de Bruges, et ce serait un grand service à nous rendre que de nous la prêter pour quelque temps. Il est grandement question d'imprimer cet ouvrage de St. Thomas. Le S. Père qui a eu connaissance de la découverte qui en a été faite, désirerait qu'il soit publié avant le Concile, et l'Ordre aurait lui-même à cette publication un grand intérêt, car ce serait le commencement de la réédition des œuvres complètes de notre Docteur Angélique revues et collationnées sur les textes originaux ou les copies les plus authentiques, réédition qu'il est grand temps que l'Ordre entreprenne pour arracher ces précieux écrits à la spéculation mercantile qui en compromet de plus en plus la doctrine et l'intégrité..."

30   Uccelli lui-même avait proposé le père Gatti [33]; sur cette question de censure par l'Ordre dominicain, question qui préoccupe beaucoup les autorités romaines de l'Ordre, voir [7*] et [32*], ici pp. 347-349 et n. 58.

31   Cette commission, dont il est question plusieurs fois par ex. [15][29], n'existe que dans l'imagination anticipatrice des promoteurs et en particulier de V. Ligiez qui propose un projet de contrat à Dallet, commençant ainsi [29]: "Le R. P. Ligiez de l'Ordre de St. Dominique agissant en son nom et au nom d'une commission de P. dominicains constituée à Rome par ses soins, et Mr Dallet...forment le présent traité..."

32   Voir par exemple [12*][13][16].

33   Ainsi dans [16], ce recrutement de collaborateurs est présenté comme la raison d'être de la venue du père Ligiez en France en juillet-août.

34   Il faudrait citer trop de documents [5*][8*][10][15][17][29], nous nous contentons de résumer ici une présentation de l'entreprise rédigée par Uccelli lui-même et qui est malheureusement trop longue pour être citée *ad litteram* [39]:

— Uccelli part de l'actualité du thomisme et de la nécessité de fonder le renouveau thomiste sur une édition de valeur. Il parle des mérites de la Piana mais souligne ses défectuosités et les critiques dont elle a été l'objet par des hommes compétents. Les éditions postérieures, étant des reprises, ne font que reproduire les mêmes imperfections. Le rôle précurseur de T. Soldati à la fin du XVIII s. est présenté surtout à cause de ses idées en matière de recherche des mss.; Uccelli a lui-même bénéficié du très important fichier de Soldati.

— Le véritable problème, c'est de faire un bon usage de l'information codicologique et paléographique rassemblée, à cause du très grand nombre de mss qu'il faudra considérer.

— L'édition devra débuter par des documents sur la vie de S. Thomas, les catalogues de ses œuvres, les approbations pontificales de sa doctrine, une dissertation expliquant la valeur de ces approbations au plan théologique, mais cette introduction doit permettre aussi de situer historiquement chaque œuvre de S. Thomas et cela donnera à l'édition une valeur sans pareille par comparaison aux autres éditions de S. Thomas.

— Il faut rechercher les autographes, aucune autre édition ne l'a fait, et pour ces textes autographes on fera une édition diplomatique avec quelques fac-similés.

— On devra à chaque fois indiquer les mss collationnés pour l'édition, ceux qui auront été consultés et enfin ceux que l'on aura éliminés, de telle façon que les explications de ces choix permettent aux spécialistes de contrôler et éventuellement corriger le travail.

— Là où il y a des autographes, on s'en tiendra strictement à eux; en leur absence, on aura recours aux meilleurs mss et pour juger de l'authenticité d'un ms. on tiendra compte de son lieu de conla pensée de S. Thomas et ce qu'elle peut apporter au monde moderne, la nécessité de fonder le renouveau thomiste sur une bonne édition du texte même de S. Thomas et, par suite des défauts des éditions disponibles, l'obligation de faire cette bonne édition en suivant les normes scientifiques les plus rigoureuses en matière d'édition de textes.[35] Il arrive que dans les motifs invoqués se mêlent assez maladroitement des soucis doctrinaux élevés et des considérations mercantiles, le mélange produisant un effet cocasse.[36] On insiste sur le fait que les raisons d'agir sans retard ne manquent pas: il y a d'une part la concurrence résultant de la publicité commençante pour un projet analogue et il ne s'agit pas de se faire prendre de vitesse;[37] mais d'autre part le concile est imminent et le pape désire que les inédits de S. Thomas soient publiés avant l'ouverture de ce grand rassemblement écclésiastique, qui pourrait offrir par ailleurs des possibilités exceptionnelles de diffusion de l'édition.[38]

servation, de ses détenteurs successifs, des dates qu'il peut porter et de l'écriture du texte, de telle façon qu'on retienne les mss les plus anciens mais en prenant garde qu'un ms. récent peut être une copie d'un ms. très proche de l'origine. Il faudra déterminer les filiations des mss et établir leurs familles généalogiques. Les variantes seront indiquées en bas de page, avec référence au texte, "col metodo Maurino". Mais on utilisera aussi les éditions valables en particulier les éditions princeps et celles qui furent plus soignées.
— Les textes bibliques et patristiques seront conservés tels qu'ils se trouvent et on ne les retouchera pas à la moderne. On pourra justifier les formulations citées par S. Thomas en recourant pour la Bible à l'édition Sabatier, etc.; en effet, précise Uccelli, S. Thomas ne lit pas avec la Vulgate moderne et de son temps les études textuelles sur la Bible se développent particulièrement à Saint-Jacques. U. souligne que les façons de procéder de Nicolai sont erronées.
— Chaque œuvre sera précédée de l'excellente dissertation que De Rubeis lui a consacrée mais avec des ajouts et les compléments nécessaires.
— Chaque ouvrage aura son index propre. A la fin de l'œuvre totale on publiera un index général et la *Tabula aurea* de Pierre de Bergame mais corrigée et augmentée.

35   [39*] résumé dans la note précédente est un document assez éloquent en lui-même pour qu'il n'y ait pas lieu de citer les nombreux autres allant dans le même sens.

36   [5*] cité ci-dessous n. 29, voir aussi [8*] cité n. 56.

37   Le problème de la concurrence que pourrait faire le projet Vivès au projet Uccelli-Dallet d'édition des *Opera omnia* de S. Thomas revient sans cesse dans les documents, voir [5*][8*][13][17][18][22*][23][24][34][37][38]. On notera en particulier que Vivès avait fait des offres à Uccelli mais repoussées par ce dernier [13]. La participation de l'ex-dominicain Fretté au projet Vivès aggrave les choses au plan psychologique: on le considère comme un transfuge qui aurait eu connaissance du projet Dallet quand il était dominicain et qui serait passé à l'ennemi avec l'idée de ce projet [23][24]. Enfin cette rivalité se complique d'une polémique dans l'*Univers* [17][18][24][37*]. Tout cela d'ailleurs ne fait que stimuler le projet Uccelli-Dallet et en particulier le désir des maîtres d'œuvre de publier dès que possible un manifeste publicitaire [6][8*][17][22*][23][25][26][34][37] et particulièrement un article qu'aurait préparé T. M. Thiriet [26] etc. Louis Veuillot ayant refusé de couvrir le développement de publicités concurrentes dans son journal, [24][37*] etc. On sait que l'édition Vivès (Paris) sera publiée dans les années 1871-1880.

38   [5*][6][19][25][30].

Atouts et handicaps du projet.

Ce projet Uccelli-Dallet était sans doute intéressant et par bien des aspects assez solide. Un des meilleurs atouts de l'entreprise venait de la part qu'Uccelli devait prendre au travail mais aussi aux principes même de l'édition. Quelles que soient les critiques que l'on a pu faire très justement à certains de ses travaux,[39] Uccelli apportait avec lui un souci scientifique et une expérience concrète de l'édition de textes tout à fait hors du commun.[40] En outre, il semble bien, à l'en croire, qu'il avait ses petites entrées au Vatican et qu'il avait déjà réussi à intéresser le pape Pie IX, ainsi que son entourage peut-être, à cette entreprise en projet.[41] Il est clair que, du côté des Dominicains français, l'idée trouvait des encouragements; elle correspondait d'ailleurs à certaines aspirations du temps pour un renouveau tout à la fois thomiste et scientifique. Quant à la concurrence, elle contribuait en fait à stimuler l'ardeur des promoteurs.[42]

La correspondance relative au projet montre que l'entreprise se développe assez rapidement et peu à peu se précise: on échange des textes de contrats commerciaux,[43] on cherche à recruter des collaborateurs,[44] on pense à la publicité à faire,[45] etc.

Pourtant, dès l'automne 1869 donc à peine plus de six ou sept mois après sa mise sur pied, l'affaire est liquidée, du moins sous sa forme d'entreprise d'édition des *Opera omnia S. Thomae*. Les raisons de cet échec sont évidemment complexes et l'essentiel ne se trouve sans doute pas dans les écrits qui nous restent, mais on peut essayer de cerner quelque peu le processus.

On est d'abord frappé de voir combien les discussions se développent sur des points secondaires et s'y enlisent.[46] En outre, toutes les

---

39 Voir par ex. S. Merkle, art. cité ici n. 15.

40 Sur le souci scientifique qui anime U. voir le document exemplaire [39*] résumé ci-dessus note 34. Quant à son expérience concrète, nous pensons bien évidemment à ses travaux en codicologie et en paléographie, mais aussi au fait qu'il avait déjà été publié et qu'il avait par exemple traité avec Migne (Paris) pour l'édition du *Contra Gentiles* (il revient très souvent sur ce contrat qui semble lui avoir laissé des souvenirs amers. Par comparaison à J. Dallet et aux dominicains français, Uccelli est très lucide sur le temps et le nombre d'hommes qu'il faudra pour élaborer l'édition complète [19][25]; il sait qu'on ne peut fixer exactement tout cela à l'avance, il faut commencer et on verra bien, en conséquence le contrat d'édition doit rester ouvert à des développements.

41 Voir en particulier [6][19][25][33] et [7] cité ci-dessous pp. 347-349.

42 Voir ci-dessus n. 37.

43 [4][14][27][28][29] etc., voir note ci-dessous n. 37.

44 Ainsi par ex. [11*][12][13][16].

45 Voir [8*][22*], ici n. 56 et p. 351.

46 Alors que des points très importants restent totalement dans le vague: ainsi le temps nécessaire et le nombre d'hommes indispensable pour faire le travail, la méthode heuristique à adopter dans la quête codicologique, etc., le dossier est encombré de projets multiples de contrats à peu près identiques, de discussion sur tel ou tel point de détail qui étaient alors encore loin de se poser concrètement. Il faudrait citer ici toutes les lettres d'Uccelli et bien d'autres encore, voir

correspondances témoignent des nombreux malentendus qui séparent les divers interlocuteurs.[47] J. Dallet voit les choses du point de vue d'un éditeur commercial, il entre difficilement dans certaines requêtes d'Uccelli tenant pour une part pourtant au caractère très particulier d'une édition diplomatique. De leur côté, les Dominicains français sont enthousiastes, mais eux-mêmes ne perçoivent pas toujours non plus les raisons techniques de toutes les exigences d'Uccelli. En outre, ils ne précisent guère jusqu'à quel point leurs propos engagent les autorités religieuses dont ils dépendent pourtant et qu'ils représentent même d'une certaine façon.[48]

Les difficultés qui surgissent tiennent aussi pour une part non négligeable à certains traits de caractère d'Uccelli: sa susceptibilité d'auteur[49] et d'inventeur, ses revendications au plan des redevances financières ou en nature,[50] son esprit quelque peu minutieux et compliqué, son impatience d'être publié,[51] peut-être aussi son intérêt trop exclusif pour le secteur qui lui revient en propre dans le projet: les autographes et inédits, ou supposés tels par lui, etc.

Du côté des dominicains français, des difficultés ont certainement surgi également. Il y avait un gros pas à franchir entre l'élaboration imaginative de projets enthousiastes et la mise sur pied concrète d'une entreprise dont les dimensions réelles n'avaient sans doute pas été perçues par des Dominicains trop néophytes dans le domaine de l'édition de textes. Le recrutement de collaborateurs, en particulier, n'a pas été aussi facile qu'on ne l'imaginait, et ceci pour des raisons diverses mais qui finalement se renforçaient mutuellement: voici par exemple cette lettre du père Bourard de Dijon, elle est du mois de septembre[37]:

> Nos affaires ne vont pas vite, vous avez pu voir, si vous suivez l'*Univers*, que ma lettre n'y brille que par son absence. J'ai vu Lafon, j'ai vu L. Veuillot, rien n'a servi. De dernier m'a dit, avec quelque apparence

---

par ex. [4][13][14][19][27][28][29][31][35]. Les démêlés financiers qu'Uccelli a déjà eus avec Migne encombrent l'horizon des discussions [3][19][33], on ergote sur le nombre des services de presse [19][25][30][33], les modalités des corrections d'épreuves [19][30][34], des détails typographiques [19][26], les droits d'auteur en cas de réédition [33], le choix d'un arbitre si un litige survient [34], etc.

47   Ainsi entre J. Dallet et V. Ligiez [15][16]. Uccelli est très lucide sur l'inévitable tension entre l'éditeur commercial et l'érudit [33].

48   Voir [16]: la double personnalité de V. Ligiez, représentant légal d'Uccelli en Fance d'une part et "socius" du Père Général d'autre part, ne clarifie pas les choses, voir ci-dessus n. 24 et le paragraphe suivant ici pp. 346-351.

49   Nous avons cité [7*], ici pp. 347-349, qui est assez éclairant à ce point de vue.

50   Voir ci-dessus n. 46 et par ex. [3][19][33] etc.

51   En août, Uccelli s'étonne de n'avoir pas encore reçu les premières épreuves alors qu'aucun contrat n'a encore été conclu [19][25]; voir aussi [12*] cité ici pp. 349-350.

de raison, que pour une entreprise encore en voie de conception, il ne se sentait pas le courage de travailler à la démolition d'une œuvre déjà née. Si bien que voilà notre protestation à plat.

Quant à notre édition, les éléments n'en sont pas encore assez sortis du chaos, je crois, pour que vous traitiez avec un éditeur quelconque. Je dois vous dire aussi que vous n'avez peut-être pas tous les droits pour compter sur les collaborateurs de votre choix. Le petit T., que vous avez fait aller de Flavigny à Paris, dit à qui veut l'entendre, et cela m'a déjà été répété deux fois, que tout son amour pour St Thomas et la doctrine ne saurait le déterminer à passer dix ans pour *collationner des points et des virgules*. Comprenez-vous que ce petit trouve la besogne au-dessous de lui? Notre Docteur Uccelli lui-même n'est pas à l'abri de tout reproche. On ne lui croit pas assez de théologie, assez de connaissance des principes, pour s'en rapporter à lui dans la correction des textes traditionnels.

Si bien que nous en sommes toujours à peu près au point de départ.

Ici, j'ai trouvé le vieux Père Bissey. Cet homme de cœur se mettait à ma disposition pour l'œuvre, et il me vient l'idée que si, nous trois, vous, lui et moi, nous nous attelions à Paris à cette œuvre, nous la pourrions faire mais comment nous mettre tous les trois à Paris. Voilà... Adieu, bien cher Père, je ne vous demande pas de prier Dieu pour cette œuvre qui est ma vie, je sais que vous y mettez votre cœur, mais priez pour moi qui suis toujours un misérable pécheur et votre dévoué ami en Notre Seigneur.

Cette lettre témoigne bien des difficultés rencontrées pour recruter des collaborateurs.[52] Elle manifeste aussi quelle ignorance du travail im-

---

52 Malgré sa longueur, nous pensons devoir citer ici la lettre du père P. Monvoisin: même si elle représente une opinion qui n'était peut-être pas majoritaire, elle nous paraît très intéressante pour l'époque [36]:
"Le jour de votre départ, vous vous le rappelez, je me présentais chez vous au moment où vous fermiez votre valise; ma pensée était de vous demander un quart d'heure d'entretien et de vous exposer les idées qu'avaient fait naître en moi deux jours de réflexion sur l'entreprise dont vous m'avez parlé. La proximité de votre départ et la crainte de vous déranger me fermèrent la bouche, et je n'entamais pas la question: vous me permettrez de le faire aujourd'hui. Ce sera avec d'autant plus de maturité que j'ai reçu les réponses de plusieurs Pères graves et sérieux à qui j'avais cru devoir m'en rapporter.
Mon avis, et c'est le leur aussi, est que je ne puis accepter le travail que vous m'offrez. Certainement c'est une œuvre très belle, digne des veilles d'un Frère Prêcheur; je ne puis qu'y applaudir, et tous mes vœux, s'il est permis à un jeune Père de parler ce langage, sont de voir cette entreprise, œuvre colossale, aboutir. Heureux encore et dignes d'admiration, sont ceux qui s'y dévouent. Mais je le répète, il m'est impossible d'apporter à cette œuvre ma part de travail laquelle d'ailleurs aurait été bien faible, et au-dessous de ce que vous êtes en droit d'exiger.
Si vous voulez connaître quelques-unes des raisons qui m'arrêtent, je n'en fais pas un secret. Avant tout, et ce n'est pas fausse modestie de ma part, je ne crois pas être l'homme qu'il vous faut. Sans doute le travail et l'étude me plaisent, et beaucoup, mais c'est une étude qui parle au cœur et à l'esprit, un travail où l'on profite, où l'on sème pas en vain. Mais quant à ces recherches laborieuses, pour ces collations longues et pénibles de manuscrits et de mots, je n'ai ni l'attrait qu'elles supposent pour les commencer, ni la patience qu'elles demandent pour les poursuivre, ni l'aptitude qui les mène à bonne fin.
Ensuite, je suis effrayé par la longueur du travail, et par le rôle auquel je serais réduit, ce temps écoulé. Vous savez que j'ai peu d'aptitude pour la prédication et que ce genre de travail exige de

pliquée par le projet et plus largement quelles illusions nourrissaient l'espérance des partisans de l'édition. Elle montre en tout cas combien, en septembre 1869, l'affaire était peu élaborée.

Ceci bien souligné, il nous semble pourtant qu'en l'occurrence c'est l'attitude des autorités dominicaines de Rome qui a été déterminante et qui a ruiné le projet.

moi une sérieuse préparation. Or dans huit ou dix ans — car l'édition de St. Thomas ne peut s'achever à moins — que ferai-je? à quoi serai-je bon, ayant consacré mon temps et mes forces à un travail aride, desséchant. Comment pouvoir aborder la chaire qui exige une imagination jeune, une intelligence vive? Impossible. Entrerai-je dans le lectorat? Vous savez que deux fois les portes m'en ont été fermées. On ne me les ouvrira pas alors car les raisons qui m'en ont fait exclure aujourd'hui dureront encore demain.

Je ne veux pas vous parler ici, et peut-être pourtant en aurai-je le droit, d'une raison d'amour-propre. Comment veut-on que je me consacre à pâlir, pour les éditer, sur les œuvres et les idées d'un auteur pour lequel on me repousse coup sur coup d'une carrière que je croyais être la mienne, celle de l'enseignement. Que ceux-là qui sont les défenseurs d'office de St. Thomas, qui ont charge de l'expliquer, prennent à cœur la charge de le mettre au jour, pur de toute faute. Je le comprends et je leur laisse ce soin.

J'ajouterai encore une réflexion qui à mes yeux a son poids.

Il est téméraire et ambitieux à un jeune homme de dire qu'il a ses idées, surtout lorsque ces idées sont opposées à celles d'un docteur comme St. Thomas. Cependant, pardonnez-moi ici cette témérité. Et quand je dis opposées à St. Thomas, c'est plutôt à la scolastique, ou à la philosophie, à la science subie et acceptée par St. Thomas, comme par tous les hommes de son temps. D'autres partagent complètement les mêmes vues. Souvent nous avons causé ensemble de travaux sur St. Thomas et toujours nous sommes tombés d'accord pour repousser toute édition complète et nouvelle. A quoi bon? Celles qui existent suffisent, disions-nous. Et d'ailleurs, ce n'est pas là notre fait. Il faut pour ces sortes d'œuvres une dépense d'hommes et de temps que nous trouvions devoir être mieux employés ailleurs, à supposer toutefois que nous ayons jamais trouvé les hommes et le temps nécessaires. Mais voici quel projet nous aimions à caresser. Choisir dans St. Thomas les œuvres principales, celles que vous appelez si élégamment genuina, écarter tous les commentaires, toutes les œuvres supposées. Ainsi au fond nous borner à ses deux sommes, à ses questions disputées et à quelques opuscules. Puis éditer ces ouvrages avec des notes donnant, chose indispensable de nos jours, la clef de la scolastique, mettant la science thomiste en regard des idées et des sciences plus nouvelles; portant notre jugement, et au besoin rejetant ce qui a vieilli, ce qui est hors de saison, pour ne conserver de la doctrine de St. Thomas que ce qu'elle a de solide, de beau, d'éternel, et la part est grande encore... Projet chimérique, disais-je à quelqu'un, contre lequel il n'y aura jamais assez d'obstacles ni d'anathèmes, mais projet que nous considérons comme le plus nécessaire et le plus fructueux dans l'état actuel des esprits. Avec de pareilles idées, abusé si vous le voulez par la préférence des conceptions modernes, devenu par la force des choses adversaire de St. Thomas dont je reste pourtant un admirateur enthousiasmé et que j'étudie tous les jours, comment voulez-vous que je me mette au service d'une œuvre que j'admire, que j'apprécie, que je voudrais voir heureusement terminée! mais qui sort du cadre de mes études et du champ dans lequel seul j'ai résolu de travailler.

Inutile de poursuivre plus loin cet exposé de mes sentiments. Il n'a rien d'intéressant pour vous. C'est, pour conclure, c'est avec regret que je me vois obligé de me retirer de vos côtés. En toute autre rencontre j'aurais aimé, jeune soldat dans les camps de la science et de la vérité, à faire mes premières armes sous les auspices d'un chef aussi expérimenté, d'un guide aussi savant. C'eut été pour moi tout bonheur et tout profit; mais puisque le ciel m'a refusé l'armure nécessaire, et que la providence m'a laissé me ranger sous un autre drapeau, agréez mes regrets. Permettez-moi de rester ce que je suis et croyez moi à jamais.

Votre très respectueux serviteur et votre frère."

L'attitude des autorités dominicaines de Rome.

Les documents paraissent bien montrer que la cause principale de l'échec du projet Uccelli-Dallet provient du comportement des autorités dominicaines centrales. Ce comportement est d'ailleurs complexe; il convient de ne pas le caricaturer, car il pouvait se réclamer de raisons que l'on ne peut toutes considérer comme négligeables. [53] On peut cependant résumer l'analyse en une phrase et dire que c'est surtout la prudence temporisatrice du père A. V. Jandel qui a fait échouer l'entreprise.

Dans le cadre général d'une répugnance pour toute hâte ou précipitation en matière de responsabilités à endosser ou de réalisations à promouvoir, une telle répugnance étant sans doute bien romaine dans son inspiration, la prudence de l'autorité dominicaine suprême a pour fondement en l'occurrence: [54]

— une certaine suspicion pour un travail d'édition de textes qui serait purement paléographique et critique, une réserve à l'égard de tout travail de ce genre qui ne serait pas vérifié et donc authentifié par des théologiens "spéculatifs";

— une très grande méfiance à l'égard des travaux d'Uccelli, dont on suspecte la valeur au plan de la critique textuelle en même temps que l'on doute fortement de la solidité doctrinale et de l'orthodoxie thomiste de la pensée personnelle de l'auteur;

— un pressentiment des exigences très poussées que devrait satisfaire une telle entreprise au plan scientifique et technique, pressentiment conjugué avec la conviction que l'Ordre ne dispose pas alors des hommes capables de mener le travail, c'est-à-dire tout à la fois de le diriger et de le contrôler;

— un refus de courir le risque de produire un travail inférieur à ce qu'il devrait être; ce refus est d'ailleurs inspiré plus par des motifs de prestige à ne pas compromettre que par un véritable souci de valeur scientifique a promouvoir.

Cette prudence du père A. V. Jandel s'exprime dès les premiers documents émanant de lui, mais on voit qu'elle n'est d'abord ni comprise, ni même entendue, par les interlocuteurs du Maître de l'Ordre. Il en résulte un malentendu qui va se développant et qui finalement conduit à la fermeture du dossier.

53   Nous ne savons pas si la situation politique en Italie en ce temps et son incidence possible même en matière de recherche de mss a pesé sur les décisions ou la psychologie du Maître de l'Ordre, mais l'œuvre déjà publiée d'Uccelli n'était pas sans défauts, voir S. Merkle, art. cité ci-dessus n. 15. Quant aux ressources de l'Ordre dominicain de cet époque en hommes capables de comprendre les exigences scientifiques d'une telle édition et disponible un temps suffisant pour l'accomplir, elles étaient plutôt faibles.

54   Voir par exemple [7*][12*][37*], documents cités ici respectivement pp. 342-350, 343.

Certes les tout premiers documents témoignent d'excellentes relations entre Uccelli et le Maître de l'Ordre, A. V. Jandel. [55] Uccelli travaille en quelque sorte pour le compte de l'Ordre à Naples, il est d'ailleurs reçu dans un couvent dominicain et, au moins pour une part, ses frais divers sont couverts par le Père Général; mais ce dernier n'engage pas pour autant sa responsabilité personnelle ni celle de son Ordre, il encourage seulement une recherche menée par un érudit.

Dès le 20 mai, il apparaît qu'un malentendu commence à poindre entre le père A. V. Jandel et l'abbé Uccelli, ce malentendu étant d'ailleurs amplifié par leur grande différence de conceptions et de mentalité. A Uccelli qui lui écrit, avec bien des lamentations d'auteur incompris, pour insister sur l'urgence de certaines décisions, le Maître de l'Ordre répond en des termes qui nous dispensent de citer la lettre d'Uccelli [6], il la reprend en effet point par point [7*]:

> Je regrette que la conversation que nous avons eue la semaine dernière vous ait causé quelque peine, et afin de prévenir de nouveaux malentendus, je me détermine à répondre par écrit à la note que vous m'avez remise avant mon départ pour Marino. Je ne dirai rien des plaintes que vous me faites au sujet du silence gardé vis-à-vis de vous par nos Pères sur vos précédentes publications: je puis en être peiné, mais je ne peux intervenir pour les obliger à lire vos ouvrages et à vous en faire l'éloge, si mérité qu'il soit, et je ne pense pas que vous ayez cette intention. Je ne vois donc dans cette plainte que le signe d'une susceptibilité plus ou moins motivée, que je respecte, tout en la regrettant.
>
> Ce qui m'a vraiment surpris, c'est que vous étendiez cette plainte au silence gardé sur votre dernier opuscule de puchro, et cela en répondant à la conversation dans laquelle précisément je vous avais prévenu que ce travail était soumis à un commission d'examen, je vous avais même nommé les 4 examinateurs, et vous aviez paru pleinement satisfait. Il me semble que dès lors vous auriez dû comprendre que le retard que vous accusez, loin de provenir d'indifférence ou de non curanza, était au contraire le résultat et la preuve de l'importance que nous attachions à votre publication et au grand travail dont elle n'était qu'un 1er morceau détaché.
>
> Il est probable qu'au moment où je vous écris, la commission aura assez avancé son travail pour avoir pu déjà vous communiquer ses observations, et que celles-ci vous auront démontré l'étude sérieuse dont votre opuscule avait été l'objet, et l'étude bien plus sérieuse encore que réclamera tout votre manuscrit, avant de pouvoir songer à mettre la main à l'impression comme vous le désireriez.
>
> Ici les rôles semblent intervertis puisque c'est moi qui suis obligé de vous mettre en garde contre la furia francese. Si votre travail peut atteindre le degré de correction et d'exactitude nécessaires pour arriver à la publicité dans des conditions satisfaisantes, ce sera sans contredit une

---

55 Ainsi [1][2][3].

grande gloire pour vous d'avoir ajouté un nouveau fleuron à la couronne du St. Docteur dont vous aurez reproduit une œuvre inédite et jusqu'alors inconnue. Mais il faut pour cela que l'œuvre soit vraiment et de touts points digne du nom et du génie de St Thomas: une publication incorrecte, parce qu'elle serait trop hâtive, vous ferait peu d'honneur, et exposerait à une juste et sévère critique ceux qui l'auraient patronnée.

Aussi, quand même votre empressement d'auteur vous porterait à passer par dessus les intérêts de votre propre réputation, je vous déclare sans hésiter que je ne consentirai jamais à accepter la solidarité de la publication d'un écrit attribué à St Thomas et dédié à Pie IX, tant qu'elle n'offrira pas toutes les garanties que l'ouvrage est vraiment digne du génie de St. Thomas, et de l'auguste personne du Souverain Pontife.

Si ces retards vous déterminaient (comme vous en avez déjà manifesté la pensée) à vous adresser aux PP.Jésuites pour commencer sans délai la publication de votre manuscrit, ce serait à vous de voir si vous n'auriez pas lieu de regretter plus tard, dans l'intérêt du manuscrit lui-même, qu'il n'eut pas été soumis à de nouvelles corrections, et à une révision plus sévère éxécutée par l'Ordre dépositaire des traditions thomistes: mais je vous laisserai faire, plutôt que de m'associer à une œuvre imparfaite; et si cela arrive, je suis sûr que les hommes impartiaux apprécieront ma réserve et comprendront qu'elle ne peut être trop scrupuleuse, puisqu'elle est inspirée par mon respect et ma vénération pour St Thomas et pour Pie IX. Vous pouvez donc dès à présent vous décider en pleine liberté et connaissance de cause, car rien ne me fera changer.

Je n'ai nullement la prétention d'être initié aux communications que vous avez reçues *ab altissimo*; mais je crois bon de vous faire part d'une observation qui m'est seulement venue *ab alto*. On s'étonnait de la légèreté avec laquelle vous parliez au dehors des éditions *actuelles* et de l'enseignement *actuel* de St Thomas, comme si le manuscrit que vous aviez découvert pût être de nature à opérer une révolution dans la doctrine Thomiste, et à rendre douteuse ou suspecte l'autorité de cette doctrine, telle que notre Ecole en a transmis au monde la tradition depuis 6 siècles. Une pareille imagination serait trop puérile pour que je puisse songer à vous l'attribuer. Je suppose bien plutôt que votre enthousiasme fort naturel pour la précieuse découverte que vous avez eu le mérite de faire, aura empreint vos paroles d'une teinte d'exagération *praeter intentionem*; mais il me semble utile de vous mettre en garde contre elle, puisqu'on me l'a signalée.

Enfin, quant aux conditions matérielles et financières sur lesquelles vous désirez que je prenne l'initiative, il me paraît trop juste que vous avez tout le bénéfice d'une publication dont vous aurez eu presque tout le travail, et si vous la faites avec notre collaboration, et que vous tombiez d'accord avec l'éditeur dont je vous ai communiqué les offres, c'est vous qui recevrez toute la somme, déduction faite seulement des avances que nous aurons faites pendant tout ce temps pour concourir à votre travail, et dont il sera tout naturel que l'Ordre rentre en possession. Je tiendrai du reste à ce que ce soit vous même qui traitiez avec l'éditeur et qui signiez le contrat; car ne prétendant aucune part aux bénéfices en faveur de l'Ordre, je ne veux pas non plus assumer une part de responsabilité.

Dans l'espoir que vous serez satisfait de la franchise et la loyauté de ces explications nettes et précises, je vous renouvelle, Mr l'abbé, la sincère expression de mes sentiments dévoués.

Presque au même moment, J. Dallet écrit au Maître de l'Ordre avant tout pour obtenir son autorisation de commencer la publicité, il fait valoir la concurrence qui résulte de la propagande pour l'édition Vivès.[56] Voici la décision du père Jandel [9]:

Répondre que n'acceptant plus la solidarité de l'édition projetée dans les conditions actuelles, on ne peut que l'engager à s'entendre avec les Pères de la Province pour le cas où ils veuillent s'en charger et assurent leur collaboration.

Mais J. Dallet écrit à nouveau au Père Général pour l'informer de l'accueil favorable reçu par lui à Flavigny en vue d'une collaboration des dominicains de cette maison d'études. Il lui pose alors la question suivante |11|:

Il me tarde, Révérendissime Père Général, de mettre la main à l'œuvre promptement et de connaître les bases principales sur lesquelles doit reposer cette grande entreprise, ainsi que la part de responsabilité que veut y prendre l'ordre de St Dominique, sous sa direction et patronage. Je serai heureux, Révérendissime Père Général, si dans une lettre prochaine vous voulez bien fixer et arrêter les conditions définitives et me donner l'autorisation de commencer immédiatement.

Voici la réponse du père Jandel [12]:

Votre lettre du 24 Juin me prouve que je ne me suis pas bien fait comprendre dans ma précédente réponse, et je m'empresse de bien préciser la situation afin de rendre pour l'avenir toute erreur impossible.

---

56   C'est le document [8]: "J'avais espéré commencer presque immédiatement la publication des œuvres complètes de Saint Thomas par le manuscrit inédit de D. Uccelli; mais ce travail n'étant pas encore arrivé à toute la perfection désirable, j'attendrai malgré mon impatience et me soumettant à votre décision, puisque de nouveaux délais vous paraissent indispensables pour assurer à cette grande œuvre une parfaite exécution.

Néanmoins, Révérendissime Père Général, permettez-moi d'insister sur l'urgence d'une annonce immédiate, sinon positive, au moins évidente, qui me donnera le titre de votre éditeur et qui portera à la connaissance du public théologique la grande publication qui se préparera sous votre direction et sous votre patronage.

Cette annonce, pour me servir des expressions contenues dans votre lettre du 15 avril dernier, indiquerait les avantages et le mérite de cette grande œuvre, de manière à faire taire toute concurrence; et il y a urgence à agir promptement pour arrêter les entreprises des concurrents *qui exploitent aujourd'hui* le nom du S. Docteur.

M. Vivès a déjà fait plusieurs annonces concernant cette publication *avec manuscrits inédits*; ces annonces souvent répétées depuis quelques mois ont déjà procuré des souscriptions à cet éditeur et chaque jour de retard lui en apporte de nouvelles.

Je ne crois pas exagérer en disant qu'il y a urgence et j'ose espérer que vous voudrez bien cette fois, dans l'intérêt de l'œuvre et du succès de la publication, et pour mon intérêt particulier qui y est engagé, partager mes craintes et m'autoriser à faire immédiatement toutes les annonces nécessaires et possibles.

J'ai le projet d'aller à Rome pour le prochain concile et de profiter de l'occasion unique qui me sera présentée d'assister à cette grande réunion de tous nos prélats et de leur faire connaître cette importante publication..."

D. Uccelli est persuadé que, pendant qu'on réimprimera les Commentaires déjà publiés sur S. Denys l'Aréopagite, il aura mis la partie inédite du manuscrit en état d'être livrée à l'impression. Je crois, au contraire, qu'il ne faudrait pas moins d'un an ou deux, d'un travail très sérieux pour préparer, *comme il faut*, cette publication (et je ne sais même pas encore si l'on y réussirait). Dans cet état de choses, je n'ai rien voulu entreprendre avant que le travail de correction préparatoire du manuscrit fut assez satisfaisant et assez avancé pour nous garantir le succès. D. Uccelli et d'autres avec lui ne goûtent pas cette lenteur Romaine, et veulent presser l'exécution; je n'ai ni le droit, ni l'envie, de m'y opposer ou de l'entraver; je fais même les vœux les plus sincères pour que l'entreprise soit couronnée d'un plein succès; mais je n'y prends aucune part, et je n'en accepte ni pour moi, ni pour notre Ordre, la responsabilité. Si nos Pères de France veulent individuellement aider D. Uccelli de leur concours, ils sont parfaitement libres de le faire, mais à leurs risques et périls, comme D. Uccelli lui-même. Je n'ai donc plus à m'occuper des conditions d'exécution d'un travail auquel je demeurerai étranger, et dont je décline formellement toute solidarité tant en mon nom qu'en celui de notre Ordre.

Veuillez prendre acte de cette déclaration, qui est pour moi tout à la fois un acte de loyauté et une garantie, et recevez de nouveau, Monsieur, l'expression de mes sentiments dévoués.

Fr. A. V. Jandel, M. Gén. des Fr. prêch.

P.S. — Je m'aperçois que je n'ai pas répondu *explicitement* à votre proposition relative à l'édition des œuvres complètes de S. Thomas: cependant cette réponse est, au fond, contenue dans ce qui précéde; car les commentaires sur S. Denys devant être comme le *prodrome* de cette nouvelle édition, je ne puis entreprendre celle-ci tant que je ne suis pas sûr du succès de ceux-là. Et puis, bien que je sois convaincu que l'on peut dès à présent, à l'aide des études faites et des matériaux déjà recueillis, entreprendre une édition de S. Thomas bien supérieure aux précédentes, je ne crois pas toutefois le travail suffisamment complet pour que notre Ordre en accepte la responsabilité; parce que quand un grand Ordre assume l'initiative d'une œuvre aussi importante, il ne lui suffit pas de faire mieux que les autres, on est en droit d'exiger qu'il fasse *très bien*; or, pour faire *très bien*, nous ne sommes pas prêts, et nous aimons mieux laisser à d'autres plus pressés que nous, et à l'égard desquels on n'a pas le droit d'être aussi exigeants, le mérite d'un progrès incontestable, bien qu'incomplet.

Confirmée par ailleurs,[57] cette position du Maître de l'Ordre s'exprime à nouveau dans un télégramme [21] suivi d'une lettre [22]

---

57 Voici ce qu'écrit le procureur général des Dominicains [20]: "Per la *réédition des œuvres de St. Thomas* voi conoscete le intenzioni del P. Generale a cui sono conformi le mie. — L'Ordine non può prendervi alcuna parte finchè non sono le cose al punto da riescire e con onore — Ora credo, che siamo troppo lontani da questo punto; e qualunque programma sarebbe un fuor d'Opera. Non divido con voi il timore, che altri ci rubino le mosse." Voir aussi [32*] cité note suivante.

adressés respectivement de Jaroslav et de Lemberg, Pologne. Voici l'essentiel de la lettre:

> Au reçu de votre lettre du 31/7, je vous ai télégraphié en toute hâte à Paris, pour prévenir les complications qu'aurait entraînées votre signature apposée au prospectus Dallet. Il est clair, en effet, que le motif qu'on avait de désirer votre signature était précisément celui qui devait vous empêcher de la donner; c'était me rendre et rendre l'Ordre évidemment solidaires d'un acte provenant de mon socius et par là m'engager et engager notre Ordre vis à vis du public. Or, cet engagement et *cette solidarité, je n'en veux à aucun prix*, pas même pour la réédition des œuvres complètes, et je crois avoir de bonnes raisons d'en agir ainsi. Si vous aviez signé le prospectus, je me serais trouvé dans une très pénible alternative, obligé ou de vous désavouer publiquement dans les journaux, ou de renoncer à vous conserver à Rome, afin de constater par le fait que votre prospectus n'était que l'œuvre d'un religieux individuel de la province de France.
>
> Per carità, défiez-vous de la furia francese, et ne me créez pas sans nécessité de nouveaux embarras et de nouveaux ennuis; j'en suis déjà bien assez abreuvé en ce moment!

Cette phobie de A. V. Jandel pour la *furia francese*, qui s'exprime dans la lettre |22*| mais également ailleurs |7*|, citées ci-dessus pp. 347-349, doit sans doute être référée à un horizon beaucoup plus vaste et plus ancien que cette affaire d'édition, mais elle caractérise bien une des composantes de l'attitude des autorités dominicaines de Rome en l'occurrence.[58] Il convient de le signaler puisque de juillet 1869 aux dif-

---

58 Une lettre du père Marcolin Chéry, voir ci-dessus n. 20, nous paraît très explicite sur de nombreux aspects de toute l'affaire et sur les conceptions des dominicains romains |32|: "Si le Père Mauffroy (sic) était de ce monde, il vous dirait: N'alleumes si vite! Vous voulez lancer un prospectus pour l'édition des œuvres de S. Thomas et vous ne savez par encore sur qui compter! Si vous faites fond sur D. Uccelli, vous comptez sans votre hâte. Il n'est pas capable d'avoir la direction théologique d'une œuvre: le pauvre cher homme est capable de palir sur un manuscrit, d'en déchiffrer plus ou moins heureusement les caractères, mais de l'entendre, c'est autre chose! Aussi le P. Procureur Général regarde comme une grande légèreté de vouloir à tout prix exalter le travail de cet homme, quand une commission composée d'éminents théologiens (Gatti, Nardini, Pierrotti, Bianchi) l'a trouvé défectueux en mille endroits. Il en sera ainsi de toute la publication, et l'on peut juger de l'œuvre entière par le fragment sur le beau. Du reste, tout ce qu'a fait Uccelli en est là. Son édition du Contra Gentes fourmille de bévues des plus grossières et ce qu'il appelle des variantes ne sont souvent que des erreurs de copiste. Nous ne pouvons accepter de travailler avec Uccelli, qu'autant qu'il sera un simple manœuvre, nous apportant un texte qui sera revu consciencieusement par nous. C'est toute la part qu'il peut avoir dans une publication théologique. Voici ce qu'hier nous avons décidé avec le Procureur Général: l'Académie se chargera de la publication des Œuvres de St. Thomas, elle employera D. Uccelli à la révision des manuscrits et prendra seule la direction théologique. Quand son travail sera avancé, elle enverra en France deux ou trois de ses membres qui surveilleront l'impression et qui n'auront pas autre chose à faire. Car, pour une œuvre capitale comme celle-là, on ne peut se contenter d'envoyer les épreuves à Rome, il faut que les correcteurs soient sur les lieux. De plus il faut des hommes versés dans l'étude de S. Thomas et n'ayant aucune charge qui les contraigne de s'adonner à un autre travail. La publication ne peut se faire que dans ces conditions et le Révérendissime Père Vicaire est disposé à désavouer publiquement tout prospectus lancé en dehors d'elles. Vous n'avez encore aucun élément, vous ne pouvez pas même soupçonner si votre œuvre est viable et vous voulez lancer un prospectus: encore

ficultés que connaîtra la Commission léonine en juin 1882 et avril-octobre 1886, il se sera écoulé bien peu d'années et pourtant on verra alors les autorités dominicaines les plus élevées, sous la pression du Saint-Siège il est vrai, faire tout pour accélérer le rythme de publication de l'édition léonine, sans hésiter à risquer de sacrifier la qualité scientifique en vue d'accélérer la productivité.[59]

Epilogue: Projet Uccelli-Dallet et Edition léonine.

Avant la fin de 1869, il y a rupture définitive entre P. A. Uccelli et J. Dallet.[60] Uccelli réalisera à Rome son projet de publication des autographes.[61] Quoi qu'il en soit du faisceau de causes qui provoquent

une fois: *n'alleumes si vite* L'édition préparée par ceux que vous nommez les transfuges n'est pas capable de nuire à celle que nous pourrons faire, mais au contraire, elle assurera le succès de la nôtre. Car ceux qui veulent s'en mêler n'ont aucune valeur théologique, excepté Fretté et encore je ne sais s'il est de taille à soutenir pareille besogne. Ne nous payons pas de mots: nous ne sommes pas en mesure de commencer cette publication: le moment n'est donc pas venu de parler, mais d'agir en silence. Laissons la grosse caisse et les chapeaux-chinois à qui en a le goût. C'est d'ailleurs la pensée du Père Général, et si vous ne voulez pas vous attirer une déconvenue et jeter l'éditeur dans une impasse, vous attendrez que les choses soient plus mûres. Vous ne paraissez pas vous douter de ce que serait une réimpression des œuvres de S. Thomas; vous en parlez, comme s'il s'agissait de l'*epitome historiae sacrae* ou du *De viris.* Il faut pour cela des hommes et du temps et vous n'avez guère plus de l'un que de l'autre." Cette lettre explique certains détails du document [7*] cité ci-dessus. Les membres de la Commission à laquelle il est fait allusion sont bien connus de ceux qui ont étudié le renouveau thomiste, voir par exemple I. P. Grossi, art. cité ci-dessus n. 30 à propos du P. Gatti, passim.

59   Voir ci-dessous pp. 369-386.

60   Cette lettre d'Uccelli à V. Ligiez, écrite de la Minerve, est la dernière du dossier [40]: "Caro e stimabile Padre e amico. Il mio dovere è di avvertirvi come io vedendo tante lungagini e difficoltà da parte dello stampatore avrei accettato l'offerta che mi fa la Propaganda di stampare le mie cose. Quindi la prima lettera che scriverò sarà probabilmente di licenziare il Signor Dallet. Tanto vi serva di regola. Il contratto non è ancora firmato ma la cosa è stabilita e spero tra poco si darà principio alla stampa. Intanto voi non fate sembianza o parola di nulla collo stampatore; a luogo e tempo poi lo diremo. Intanto è bene che voi lo sappiate e posciate prepararvi a riportare in Italia il mio manoscritto. La Propaganda potrà facilmente far venire da Bruges anche il ms. del Seminario. In ogni modo all'occasione del Concilio potremo parlare al Vescovo di quella città. Il Marietti stampatore e socio di Propaganda sarebbe molto favorevole anch' all'edizione di tutte le opere di S. Tomaso. Ora pensiamo a tirarci di questo laborinto come dite voi. Io sono mal contento di Dallet. A me non sembra il vedere in lui che un uomo avido di danaro, senza nessun impegno e idea per superare il difficoltà pronto ad invogermi in una lite se gli torna a conto; mi sembra brut-tissimo anche il capitolo di far io dei compensi se le correzioni superano l'ordinato. Parola elastica, ignobile, e indegna. Obbligare un povero studioso a misurare le correzioni! — Impaziente di rivedervi al vostro ritorno mi segno tutto vostro obbligatissimo devotissimo Pietro Antonio Uccelli."

61   En 1878, imprimé par la Polyglotte de la Propagande, paraît de P. A. Uccelli l'ouvrage suivant: *S. Thomae Aquinatis...: Summae de veritate catholicae fidei contra gentiles quae supersunt ex codice autographo qui in bibliotheca Vaticana adservatur.*
En 1880, édité grâce au père Ligiez, paraît *S. Thomae Aquinatis... In Isaïam prophetam, In tres Psalmos David, In Boetium de hebdomadibus et de Trinitate expositiones, accedit anonymi Liber de fide Sanctae Trinitatis a S. Thoma examinatus in opusculo contra errores Graecorum una cum ipso opusculo et altero contra Graecos, Armenos et Saracenos. Omnia quae supersunt ex autographis cetera vero ex optimis codicibus et editionibus,* cura et studio Petri Antonii Uccellii, imprimé par les mêmes presses. Sur le rôle du père V. Ligiez voir S. Merkle, art. cité ici n. 19.

cet épilogue, de l'ensemble des documents concernant l'affaire se dégage clairement un certain ensemble de faits. Dès 1869, avec des encouragements venant du pape et de son entourage, l'idée d'une édition de S. Thomas fondée sur une exploitation la plus scientifique possible des autographes et des manuscrits les meilleurs avait été étudiée assez sérieusement par les autorités domincaines. Il n'est aucunement question de faire pièce aux franciscains futurs éditeurs de S. Bonaventure,[62] mais sous l'influence des travaux d'Uccelli on veut publier un texte de haute valeur qui déclassera définitivement les éditions antérieures et les entreprises contemporaines d'exploitation commerciale de l'œuvre du Docteur angélique. Cette édition nouvelle donnera un fondement textuel solide à l'essor d'une philosophie et d'une théologie thomistes qui permettront au monde moderne de sortir de ses impasses idéologiques. L'idée d'une commission de dominicains rassemblés à Rome pour élaborer l'édition est explicitement au centre du projet, mais avec cette idée complémentaire que la commission romaine bénéficiera des informations recueillies ailleurs par d'autres collaborateurs eux aussi dominicains. Si l'on remarque en outre que l'échec du projet résulte pour une large part de la haute idée que l'on se fait de l'œuvre à entreprendre et des grandes dimensions de l'investissement en hommes, en années de travail et aussi en argent, que suppose un tel projet, mais que toute l'affaire aboutit en un certain sens à l'hypothèse de mener à bien un jour, mais à Rome même, une entreprise de cet ordre, comment ne pas penser que le projet du pape Léon XIII d'une édition Léonine, projet lancé dix ans plus tard, a pour une large part pris ses racines dans la tentative de 1869, restée pourtant sans grande suite immédiate?[63]

Dans ce volume ne se trouvent éditées que des œuvres authentiques de S. Thomas, à l'exception naturellement du *Libellus*. Parmi les facteurs qui ont incité Uccelli à limiter prudemment son programme par rapport aux projets qu'il formait dix années plus tôt, on doit sans doute compter le jugement émis par la commission de théologiens dominicains appelés à se prononcer sur l'authenticité du *De pulchro*, voir ci-dessus p. 347 document [7*]. Ce jugement a été certainement négatif car les membres de la commission n'étaient ni codicologues, ni paléographes, mais ils connaissaient assez la pensée et la langue de S. Thomas pour porter un jugement correct sur un texte extrait d'un Commentaire sur les Noms Divins par Albert le Grand.

62   Voir ci-dessus n. 13.

63   Certains passages du document [39*] d'Uccelli, résumé ci-dessus n. 34, préfigurent de très certains passages des Actes de Léon XIII, voir ci-dessus n. 4. Par ailleurs, il est bien évident que quelques dominicains romains ou français qui avaient été mêlés au projet de 1869 étaient encore en situation de dire leur mot en 1870-1880. On notera en particulier que le père V. Ligiez est encore socius du supérieur général des Dominicains en 1879 et qu'il restera à Rome auprès du Maitre Général comme archiviste de l'Ordre jusqu'à sa mort en 1898.

L'enquête Heuristique du Cardinal Tommaso Zigliara.

Les documents.

Dans une lettre circulaire du 9 novembre 1879 le père Joseph-Marie Sanvito, vicaire général de l'Ordre dominicain,[64] invite les religieux qui dépendent de lui à répondre à l'invitation du pape Léon XIII de prendre S. Thomas comme maître à penser. Il annonce, parmi d'autres, la décision du pape de faire procéder à une nouvelle édition des œuvres de S. Thomas[65] et il précise alors que des hommes compétents sont déjà au travail.[66] En février 1880, une chronique de la publication française l'*Année dominicaine* fournit d'ailleurs quelques précisions supplémentaires qui donnent une idée assez nette de l'enquête déjà commencée:[67]

> Le projet relatif à une nouvelle édition complète des Œuvres de saint Thomas d'Aquin continue à être l'objet de la sollicitude du Souverain Pontife. Des commissions nommées à cet effet à Rome et à l'étranger sont chargées de collationner les meilleures éditions parues jusqu'ici avec les manuscrits originaux renfermés dans les bibliothèques. La commission nommée à Rome est présidée par Son Eminence le cardinal Zigliara qui s'est mis en relation avec un certain nombre de religieux des différentes provinces de notre Ordre pour mener activement les recherches et le collationnement des manuscrits. Les RR. PP. Chapotin et Beaudouin s'en occupent particulièrement pour ce qui regarde notre province de France; ils ont devant eux tous les trésors de notre Bibliothèque nationale à explorer, sans parler de ce qui se trouve encore dans les bibliothèques de province. On espère qu'un premier volume pourra être publié dans le cours de cette année.

64 Après la mort du père Jandel le 11 décembre 1872 et à cause de l'impossibilité de réunir un chapitre général à Rome pour lui élire un successeur, l'Ordre dominicain fut gouverné par un vicaire général, le père J. M. Sanvito. Finalement en 1879, grâce à une élection par correspondance, un nouveau Maître de l'Ordre fut élu, le père J. M. Larroca; cette élection fut confirmée le 30 septembre par le pape; le nouveau Maître fut institué par la Congrégation des évêques et réguliers le 7 janvier 1880 et finalement installé comme Général de l'Ordre le 1ᵉʳ février à 18h30; il avait 66 ans et était dominicain depuis l'âge de 17 ans. Le lancement de l'Edition léonine coïncide donc avec un changement dans les dirigeants de l'Ordre dominicain. La circulaire du père Sanvito ne paraît pas avoir été publiée de façon accessible.

65 "...Cum laetitia annunciamus providissimum Leonem XIII ex eo quo flagrat studiorum amore excelso disposuisse consilio, ut omnia S. Thomae aurea Opera iterum typis subiiciantur, sicuti olim a S. Pio V, accitis ex Ordine doctissimis Viris, fuerunt edita, una cum Commentariis Card. de Vio et Franc. Silvestri Ferrariensis, quae editio omnium princeps XVIII grandioribus voluminibus continetur..."

66 "...Iam viri eruditi desudant, ut eiusmodi editio Piana quoque correctior, et auctior in lucem prodeat. Ita Leonis nomen in horum operum editione, sicut antea illud Pii, ad posteros cum gloria transibit..."

67 *Année dominicaine* 1880 (février), Chronique, p. 73.

Cette chronique de l'*Année dominicaine* se poursuit par la présentation du texte du motu proprio *Placere nobis* du 18 janvier 1880.[68] D'autres informations du même genre ont sans doute été publiées à la même époque, nous n'avons pas cherché à les collecter. Il y a dans les archives de la Commission léonine toute une collection de lettres qui éclairent et précisent les assertions du père J. M. Sanvito et de l'*Année dominicaine*. Il nous a paru intéressant de signaler ici ces lettres à l'attention des historiens; bien que certaines d'entre elles aient déjà été utilisées en diverses études,[69] la série en tant que telle est inédite, en tout cas nous nous efforçons ici de les exploiter sommairement en les rapprochant de quelques autres documents contemporains déjà publiés mais qui en reçoivent une lumière nouvelle en même temps qu'ils contribuent à donner consistance à l'interprétation de la série.[70]

Voici la liste des pièces auxquelles nous nous référons dans les présentes pages:[71]

[41] C. Reynen à C. Bianchi, v. [42], Huissen 4 novembre 1879.
[42] C. Bianchi à T. Zigliara, Amiens 14 novembre 1879.
[43] H. Guillermin à J. M. Larroca, Toulouse 1 décembre 1879.
[44] H. Guillermin à J. M. Larroca, fin 1879.
[45] M. D. Chapotin à T. Zigliara, Paris 18 décembre 1879.
[46] E. P. Balme à T. Zigliara, Lyon 19 décembre 1879.
[47] X. Fauchet à T. Zigliara, Poitiers 29 décembre 1879.
[48] C. Reynen à T. Zigliara, Huissen 11 janvier 1880.
[49] H. Denifle à T. Zigliara, Graz 11 janvier 1880.
[50] R. M. Biolley à T. Zigliara, Tirlemont 12 janvier 1880.
[51*] F. P. Balme à T. Zigliara, Lyon 27 janvier 1880; voir ici pp. 364-365.
[52] F. P. Balme, relevé de mss, 27 janvier 1880.
[53*] M. D. Chapotin à V. Ligiez, Paris 2 février 1880; ici n. 89.
[54] T. Bonora à T. Zigliara, Bologna 4 mars 1880.
[55] C. Reynen à T. Zigliara, Huissen 6 mars 1880.
[56] A. Hoogland, "Manuscriptum in Biblioteca Ultrajecti in Hollandia".
[57*] R. M. Biolley à T. Zigliara, Tirlemont 2 avril 1880; voir ici n. 86.

---

68 Voir ci-dessus n. 5.
69 Ainsi par exemple par A. Walz, voir article "Denifle" dans GHGE p. 222; mais également P. A. Redigonda, "Il P. Enrico Denifle O. P. 1844-1905. Cenni bibliografici e alcune lettere", *Memorie Domenicane* 69 (1952) 101-136 et 70 (1953) pp. 65-99.
70 Redigonda, op. cit. ci-dessus, ne cite aucun des documents de notre série mais il donne le texte d'autres lettres qui complètent notre ensemble. Nous nous réréferons ici à Redigonda XII (Denifle à Larroca, Lyon 13 novembre 1882; R. p. 95), et à Redigonda XIII (Denifle à Larroca, Barcelone 24 novembre 1882; R. p. 96). Nous citons ci-dessous in extenso un brouillon de lettre de Denifle à Larroca publié par D. M. Planzer dans *Divus Thomas* (Frib.) 8 (1930) 447-448, voir ici n. 99.
71 Comme ci-dessus pp. 337-338 les pièces sont classées et numérotées selon l'ordre chronologique certain ou supposé et on indique par l'astérisque accolé au numéro d'ordre que la pièce correspondante est citée *ad litteram*, voir ci-dessus n. 16.

[58]   P. Tovani à T. Zigliara, Foligno 19 mai 1880.

[59]   P. Tovani, relevé de mss de Pérouse d'après Vermiglioli.

[60]   F. Rivas à T. Zigliara, Ocana 15 juin 1880.

[61]   F. Rivas à J. M. Larroca, Ocana 22 juin 1880.

[62]   T. Bonora à T. Zigliara, Bologna 23 juin 1880.

[63]   L. Galea à T. Zigliara, Valetta (Malta) 2 août 1880.

[64]   M. D. Chapotin à V. Ligiez, 23 novembre 1880, résumé de la main de
       V. Ligiez.

[65*] M. D. Chapotin à T. Zigliara, Paris 22 décembre 1880; voir ici n. 88.

[66*] T. Esser à T. Zigliara, Vienna 4 mars 1881; voir ici p. 366.

[67]   E. Sicardi à T. Zigliara, Modena 30 novembre 1881.

[68]   M. P. Manovel à T. Zigliara, Salamanca 25 mars 1882.

[69]   P. Tovani à T. Zigliara, mss de Pérouse, juin 1882.

[70*] H. Denifle à T. Zigliara, Orihuela 8 décembre 1882; voir ici n. 92.

[71]   H. Denifle à J. M. Larroca, Valladolid 19 décembre 1882.

[72*] H. Denifle à C. Bianchi, Madrid 2 janvier 1883; voir ici n. 91.

[73]   H. Denifle à C. Bianchi, Madrid 5 janvier 1883.

[74]   H. Denifle à T. Zigliara, Madrid 9 janvier 1883.

[75*] H. Denifle à C. Bianchi, Madrid 19 janvier 1883, voir ici n. 91.

[76)   H. Denifle à T. Zigliara, Barcelona 3 mars 1883.

[77]   L. Di Maggio à A. Frühwirth (?), Palermo 2 mars 1895.

De ces documents,[72] nous avons essayé de dégager tous les renseignements qu'ils contiennent sur la méthode suivie par le cardinal Zigliara en vue de recueillir les informations codicologiques, et même paléographiques, destinées à être utilisées par lui-même et ses collaborateurs pour élaborer l'édition léonine. Nous précisons d'abord cette méthode telle que les documents exploités ici permettent de la connaître,[73] puis à partir de ces mêmes documents nous proposons quelques réflexions sur la portée et les limites d'une telle tentative, réflexions qui permettront peut-être de mieux comprendre certains problèmes ou évènements ultérieurs de la Commission léonine.

72   A part [52][56][59] qui sont purement et simplement des relevés ou descriptions de mss, les autres pièces sont les lettres adressées au cardinal Zigliara, au Maître de l'Ordre: J. M. Larroca puis A. Frühwirth, au procureur général des Dominicains: C. Bianchi, au "socius" français du père général: V. Ligiez. Outre un prêtre séculier: L. Galea [63], et le père Bianchi [42], les auteurs de ces documents sont les dominicains C. Reynén, prieur provincial des Pays-Bas [41][48][55], et A. Hoogland [56] de la même province; R. M. Biolley [50][57*] de Belgique; H. Guillermin [43][44], M. D. Chapotin [45][53*][64][65*], X. Faucher [47], de provinces françaises; les italiens T. Bonora [54][62], P. Tovani [58][59][69], E. Sicardi [67], L. Di Maggio [77]; deux espagnols: F. Rivas [60][61], M. P. Manovel [68]; enfin deux autrichiens: T. Esser [66*] et, le plus important de tous, H. Denifle [49][70*] à [76].

73   Ici encore, notre documentation est très incomplète. Nous n'avons pas essayé de rechercher d'autres documents complémentaires soit dans d'autres archives parallèles, soit même dans d'autres sections des archives de la Commission léonine elle-même. Nous nous contentons ici de présenter un dossier d'archives en le commentant.

La méthode heuristique du cardinal.

Les documents manifestent que le processus d'enquête mis en route par le cardinal Zigliara au début du dernier trimestre de 1879 est très simple dans son principe. Il comporte les phases suivantes:

a) recherche de collaborateurs, ou plutôt de correspondants, pour les divers pays susceptibles de posséder des manuscrits d'œuvres de S. Thomas dans leurs bibliothèques.

b) recherche, repérage et relevé descriptif de tous ces manuscrits par les correspondants recrutés à cet effet.

c) par ces mêmes correspondants, collationnement des manuscrits donnant le texte des commentaires de S. Thomas sur le *Perihermeneias* et les *Postérieurs Analytiques* d'Aristote.

Pour le recrutement des collaborateurs (phase a), le cardinal s'adresse à l'Ordre dominicain afin d'obtenir dans chaque pays des religieux compétents et disponibles pour le travail. Les autorités dominicaines de Rome se mettent à son service: en même temps que sa circulaire du 9 novembre 1879 ou un peu auparavant, le père Sanvito semble avoir envoyé à tous les prieurs provinciaux et conventuels une lettre demandant que l'on signale les noms de religieux experts en paléographie susceptibles de collaborer avec le cardinal ainsi que les manuscrits et œuvres inédites de S. Thomas dont ils pourraient avoir connaissance;[74] le procureur général de l'Ordre rencontre au nom du cardinal les prieurs provinciaux de Belgique, Paris, Lyon et Toulouse; il écrit également au prieur provincial des Pays-Bas[42]. De son côté le socius pour l'Italie, le père Frati, écrit pour procurer des collaborateurs [62].

C'est de cette façon que se trouveront recrutés les pères suivants: deux pères de la province des Pays-Bas, dont le père A. Hoogland [42][49][55]; de Belgique, le père R. M. Biolley [41][42][50][57]; de la province de France (Paris), les pères M.D.Chapotin [42][53][64][65] et probablement R. Beaudouin [53];[75] de la province de Lyon, les pères F. P. Balme [46][51*][52] et X. Faucher [47]; de la province de Toulouse, le père H. Guillermin [43][44]; de la province d'Autriche-Hongrie, les pères H. Denifle [49][76] et T. Esser [66*]; d'Espagne, le père

---

74 C'est ce qu'affirme Redigonda, op. cit. p. 122. Cette affirmation semble confirmée par [41][43][44] si du moins ces trois lettres sont adressées au vicaire général ou au procureur général en réponse à cette invitation du père Sanvito.

75 Plus tard le père Larroca essaiera d'obtenir le père Beaudouin comme socius et collaborateur de T. Zigliara, voir ci-dessous p. 370. Certains documents écrivent "Beaudoin" et non Beaudouin, mais le père lui-même dans tous les actes officiels écrit et signe Beaudouin (archives Prov. de France, III-F-2 p. 291 et p. 302), de même dans ses lettres personnelles.

76 Sur la façon dont H. Denifle a été recruté pour la Léonine, voir Redigonda, op. cit. pp. 122-123. L'auteur, p. 122, cite une lettre du père Anselmi, prieur de Graz, déclarant en 1879 que depuis plus de dix ans le père Denifle parlait de la nécessité de faire une édition des œuvres de S. Thomas

F. Rivas [60][61]; d'Italie enfin, les pères P. Tovani [58][61], E. Sicard [67] et L. Di Maggio [77]. Nous ne citons ici que les cas signalés par les lettres que nous exploitons.[77] Nous savons qu'il faudrait ajouter beaucoup d'autres noms pour avoir une liste complète,[78] mais les noms mentionnés ci-dessus ont valeur d'exemple. Au contraire, d'autres correspondants de notre dossier répondent peut-être tout simplement à la circulaire de Sanvito et ne paraissent pas recrutés comme correspondants attitrés.

Le repérage et le relevé descriptif des manuscrits contenus dans les bibliothèques des divers pays (phase b) a commencé aussitôt que les religieux correspondants ont été désignés et ont reçu les instructions du cardinal. Voici les seules enquêtes dont quelque témoignage ait été noté par nous:[79]

Les bibliothèques des Pays-Bas ont été prospectées par A. Hoogland et son compagnon, mais aussi par d'autres pères appelés en renfort [48], le prieur provincial paraissant avoir pris lui-même la direction effective des opération [42][55].

En Belgique, le travail a été entrepris par R. M. Biolley avec l'aide d'autres dominicains [57].

En France, les bibliothèques de Paris ont été prises en charge par M. D. Chapotin [45]. X. Faucher a dû prospecter l'Ouest du pays [47]. Pour Lyon, c'est F. P. Balme [46] qui a vu également Grenoble, Chambéry, Annecy et, en Suisse, Genève [51*][52]. Pour le Sud de la France, on peut noter les enquêtes successives: Avignon, Aix et Toulouse [43][44] par H. Guillermin; Avignon [46][51*], Carpentras, Nîmes, Tarascon et Montpellier [51*] par F. P. Balme; Avignon, Nîmes, Narbonne, Perpignan par H. Denifle.[80] Ce même H. Denifle a d'ailleurs dépouillé en outre tous les catalogues départementaux de France.[81]

à l'exemple du travail entrepris par les franciscains pour S. Bonaventure, mais ajoutait qu'il serait tout à fait insuffisant de se contenter d'une édition analogue à celle de la Somme par Uccelli. Voir ci-dessous, p. 369, les circonstances de la nomination de Denifle comme socius pour qu'il puisse travailler comme collaborateur de T. Zigliara à Rome. Sur H. Denifle, voir P. A. Redigonda, art. cité ci-dessus n. 69: Heinrich Seuse Denifle (Joseph) né le 16 janvier 1844 a fait ses études comme dominicain entre 1866 et 1870 successivement à Graz, Rome et Saint-Maximin; à Rome il fut élève de T. Zigliara. Il devint ensuite Lecteur à Graz avant de venir à Rome en 1880. Voir ci-dessous p. 369 et n. 94.

77 Se référant à une lettre du père Bianchi, proc. gén., du 14 novembre 1879 (Arch. gén. O. P. XIII 176), Redigonda, op. cit. p. 119 n. 62, mentionne le nom du père Chapotin, mais ajoute celui du père Bayonne.

78 Dans ses notes inédites qui fourmillent sur les débuts du travail léonin, le père Mackey, voir ci-dessous n. 107, mentionne les noms de pères qui ont pris part au travail soit par correspondance, soit autrement, dès 1880: Denifle, Chapotin; Gaudenzi, Puebla Beaudouin, Balme. Chatillon, Poli, Costello, Berthier, Ligiez, etc. Comme on peut le constater, il y a des rencontres entre la liste du père Mackey et la nôtre, mais chacune donne des noms qui ne figure pas sur l'autre.

79 Voir ci-dessous n. 85.

80 Redigonda XIII.

81 Voir ci-dessous n. 99.

Dans les pays de langue allemande, H. Denifle a vu plus de 24 bibliothèques[82] et T. Esser au moins celle de Klosterneubourg [66*].

En Italie, on peut relever: Bologna, T. Bonora [54][62]; Todi, H. Denifle;[83] Perugia, P. Tovani [58][69]; Modena, E. Sicardi [67]; sans doute Palermo, L. Di Maggio [67][77].

Enfin dans la péninsule ibérique, le travail entrepris en Espagne par F. Rivas [60][61] a été repris[84] et étendu par H. Denifle avec ses visites à Madrid, l'Escorial, Salamanque, Valladolid, Osma, Ségovie, Avila, Gérone, Barcelone, Vich, Lérida, Saragosse, Tarragone, Valence, Tolède, Cordoue et enfin Lisbonne et le Portugal [70*] à [76].[85]

Certaines informations, concernant l'Ile de Malte [63] et Salamanque [68], voir [72*] par exemple, ne semblent pas venir de correspondants réguliers.

Le collationnement des manuscrits donnant les Commentaires de S. Thomas sur le *Perihermeneias* et les *Postérieurs Analytiques* d'Aristote (phase c) est conçu par le cardinal de la façon suivante: on comparera le texte fourni par chaque manuscrit au texte de l'édition Piana, on notera toutes les variantes du manuscrit par rapport à la Piana, on enregistrera en outre toutes les notes marginales du manuscrit |45||53*||55||57*| |61||65*|. Il est manifeste que ce travail était présenté comme prioritaire et comme devant être accompli dans les délais les plus courts possibles.

Limites et défauts de la méthode d'enquête.

Considérée dans ses principes essentiels la méthode mise en œuvre par le cardinal Zigliara ne peut qu'être chaleureusement approuvé. Pour mener à bien une édition critique et particulièrement celle de S. Thomas, ne faut-il pas en effet chercher à recruter en nombre suffisant des collaborateurs capables et, avec leur aide, tout d'abord constituer un répertoire descriptif le plus exhaustif possible de tous les manuscrits d'œuvres de S. Thomas puis ensuite pour chaque œuvre collationner, par comparaison à un texte pris comme texte de référence, tous les manuscrits de cette œuvre, en notant soigneusement les particularités adjacentes qui pourraient éclairer le travail?

Ceci dit, on peut se demander si le cardinal avait par avance bien perçu l'étendue exceptionnelle et les exigences scientifiques de la tâche

---

82 Comptant au total au moins 560 mss de S. Thomas, voir ci-dessous n. 99.
83 Redigonda XII.
84 Sur le P. Rivas voir ci-dessous p. 362 et n. 92.
85 Nous savons par ailleurs que le père H. Denifle a profité de son poste de socius du Maître de l'Ordre, et des voyages qui en résultaient, pour compléter son étude déjà entreprise des catalogues de mss de Grande Bretagne et des pays adjacents par des visites sur place. Voir DHGE et LTK "Denifle", et Redigonda p. 131.

qu'il promettait d'accomplir avec son équipe. Les difficultés inhérentes à une telle entreprise étaient-elles en permanence suffisamment présentes à son esprit? On a un peu l'impression qu'il s'est lancé en ignorant presque tout des dimensions réelles et des problèmes concrets impliqués par le travail qu'il pensait pouvoir obtenir de ses correspondants, à tel point que la question se pose de savoir si c'est véritablement lui qui a imaginé la méthode ou bien si celle-ci n'aurait pas été conçue par quelqu'un d'autre, quelque spécialiste, et mise en œuvre avec maladresse, précipitation, et simplisme par le cardinal? Quoi qu'il en soit, les faits sont là pour montrer que les moyens et le temps prévus étaient tout à fait insuffisants eu égard au but poursuivi et aux données qu'il s'agissait d'exploiter.

A cette époque, il était en effet impossible de trouver dans chaque pays un nombre suffisant de Dominicains suffisamment confirmés en paléographie et disponibles pour le travail. Certains des collaborateurs du cardinal étaient sans aucun doute médiocres au plan technique, ou physiquement incapables, ou encore trop occupés par ailleurs.

C'est ainsi que, avec le père Réginald van der Venne missionnaire à Curaçao, le P. Hoogland de la Province de Hollande est proposé par son provincial, parce qu'il est archiviste de sa province et "bien versé à lire des manuscrits ou documents anciens"; il sera effectivement collaborateur du cardinal, mais en outre les pères Hyacinthe Derksen et Constant Suermondt sont également proposés à cause de leur "science philosophique et théologique" et parce qu'ils "ont bien de goût de ces choses et pourront bien se rendre habiles en ces arts" |41|, c'est dire nettement qu'ils n'ont alors aucune formation paléographique.

Quant au Père Biolley, présenté comme bon paléographe |41||42|, il se révèle totalement ignorant des principes mêmes qui devraient présider au collationnement de manuscrits en vue d'établir un texte critique.[86] A en juger par les autres lettres, il n'est d'ailleurs pas le seul

---

86 [57] "Eminence, Les prédications continuelles dont j'ai été chargé depuis le temps où le T.R.P. Provincial me communiqua votre lettre du 5 Janvier, m'ont empêché jusqu'ici de voir les manuscrits des œuvres de S. Thomas. Je n'ai pu que parcourir les catalogues des grandes bibliothèques, et dresser la liste ci-jointe de tout ce que contient la Belgique à ce sujet. Parcourir tous ces manuscrits d'un bout à l'autre me serait un travail impossible: il faudrait y consacrer des mois, sinon des années, et le petit nombre de religieux, les autres occupations fort multipliées, le bon ordre et l'intérêt de la communauté s'opposent à des absences prolongées, votre Eminence le comprend aisément. De plus, je viens de lire dans la revue *la Scienza e la fede* (fasc. 692) que M. Uccelli a déjà vu ces manuscrits: peut-être pourrait-on profiter de ses recherches, et ne pas recommencer un travail qu'il a déjà fait mieux, sans nul doute, que je ne pourrai le faire.

Une autre difficulté encore s'est présentée, Eminentissime Père. Je n'ai pu me procurer le texte sur lequel j'aurais voulu noter les variantes. Le couvent que j'habite ne possède qu'une faible partie des Œuvres de S. Thomas. Les deux couvents de notre province qui les possèdent, tiennent à les conserver et ne consentent nullement à les dépareiller. Que faire dès lors?

Il y aurait, je crois, un moyen facile de tout concilier et de ne pas perdre le temps à un travail

collaborateur du cardinal à tout ignorer des rudiments d'une méthode qui n'était guère familière à Zigliara lui-même, à en juger par les consignes beaucoup trop sommaires données par lui à ses correspondants précisément pour ce qui est des collations à faire, à en juger aussi par sa décision de faire imprimer dès septembre 1880 le premier tome de l'Edition léonine;[87] sur ces deux points voir [61]. Un autre collaborateur de l'entreprise et qui semble bien avoir intensément et sérieusement travaillé pour le cardinal, le père Chapotin, manifeste lui aussi une certaine méconnaissance des lois élémentaires du travail critique.[88] D'ailleurs, en dépit de l'intérêt des travaux qu'il a effectivement produit dans le domaine historique, le père Chapotin avait été présenté au père Bianchi par son prieur provincial comme très habitué aux bibliothèques et habile dans la lecture des textes anciens, ce qui était certainement vrai, mais aussi comme bon paléographe, ce qui est moins assuré. Le

---

inutile. Oserais-je le proposer à votre Eminence?... Ce serait de me faire envoyer au fur et à mesure qu'on avance dans le travail que'.ques pages d'un exemplaire type, en y soulignant les passages sur lesquels on désire connaître les variantes. Il va sans dire qu'il serait inutile d'envoyer les parties desquelles nous ne possédons en Belgique aucun manuscrit. Ainsi l'examen serait plus court, plus aisé, et aboutirait à des résultats beaucoup plus pratiques pour ceux qui sont chargés de rédiger le texte définitif.

Je prie instamment votre Eminence de vouloir bien me faire donner la solution de ces difficultés: je serais heureux de pouvoir au plus tôt, lui prouver par mon travail les sentiments de respect et de dévouement que lui porte son très humble et très obéissant serviteur Fr. Raymond M. Biolley."

87 Voir ci-dessous n. 109.

88 Voir par ex. [53*][65*], voici [65]

"La lettre que Votre Eminence m'a fait l'honneur de m'écrire en date du 13, m'est arrivée au milieu de prédications qui ne m'ont pas permis d'aller immédiatement à la Bibliothèque Nationale. Je me hâte de réparer ce retard, et de répondre successivement aux questions de Votre Eminence.

1° Des deux manuscrits 16101 et 16154 le second seulement provient de la Bibliothèque de l'ancienne Sorbonne. J'en ai transmis l'ancien N° à Votre Eminence par le P. Ligiez il y a quelques semaines, en réponse à l'unique question qui m'était posée. Quant au manuscrit 16101, il ne porte pas de N° ancien et j'en ignore la provenance.

2° Nous avions d'abord préféré le manuscrit 16101, parce que l'exécution en est plus soignée. Mais parvenus à peine au quart du travail, nous avons reconnu que le texte du 16154 était beaucoup plus parfait, et nous ne recourions plus guère au 16101 que dans les cas où le texte du 16154 nous paraissait imparfait ou la lecture trop difficile.

3° Il n'y a aucune note au texte; seulement quelques corrections dans le 16154, et nous en avons tenu compte. En général ces corrections consistent simplement en quelques mots ajoutés après coup et par une autre main pour réparer des omissions faites par le premier copiste.

Les deux manuscrits me paraissent être à peu près de la même époque, c'est à dire fin XIIIᵉ ou commencement du XIVᵉ siècle...

Quant au second volume, quand pourrai-je m'en occuper? Mes aides sont partis en Angleterre et au Tyrol, et Votre Eminence sait que je n'ai ni assez d'intelligence ni d'assez bons yeux pour travailler seul. J'en ai demandé d'autres au T.R.P. Provincial qui n'a encore désigné personne.

D'ailleurs, nous ne sommes pas encore fixés dans nos asiles même provisoires, et d'un autre côté, nous sommes trop heureux d'être demandés pour les prédications d'avent, de carême, de Mois de Marie, puisqu'aujourd'hui plus que jamais la question du pain quotidien se pose la première, et non sans de cruelles anxiétés pour les Supérieurs..."

père Chapotin lui-même proteste de son incompétence et de son besoin d'être aidé au plan paléographique [45][53*][65*]; il propose qu'un autre religieux lui soit adjoint pour la collation des mss. [89]

De son côté le père Rivas proteste de son ignorance absolue en paléographie: lui-même ne peut lire la cursive médiévale; d'ailleurs, selon lui, personne en Espagne ne peut la lire [60][61]. Il suggère donc de transférer les manuscrits espagnols à Rome où ils pourront être étudiés sérieusement [61].

Aux limites tenant au peu de compétence, viennent s'ajouter celles provenant d'états de santé déficients: Balme [51*], Chapotin [65], Denifle [49], ou encore de l'indisponibilité résultant par exemple de la prédication: Biolley [57*], Chapotin [53*][65*]; ce dernier précise bien qu'il s'agit là d'une nécessité pour que les couvents puissent financièrement survivre. [90]

Les conditions de l'époque aggravaient singulièrement les choses pour les plus fragiles: les pères Denifle et Balme semblent avoir particulièrement souffert des fatigues des voyages, des changements d'alimentation, du froid. [91] Quand il n'y avait pas des inondations empêchant tout déplacement [61].

---

89 [53] "J'ai l'honneur de vous adresser par une occasion, qui me semble plus sûre que la poste, notre travail sur le *Perihermenias*, en vous priant de vouloir bien le présenter à S. E. Mgre le Cardinal Zigliara. Vous voyez que nous avons eu beaucoup de choses à noter; au commencement, nous avons signalé des différences minimes, mais à mesure que nous avons vu se multiplier les variantes, nous nous sommes restreints à ce qui a paru au P. Beaudoin avoir une réelle utilité pour la correction du texte et pour l'intelligence de l'œuvre de notre Saint Docteur.

Nous avons comparé le texte de l'édition de S. Pie V à deux manuscrits de l'ancienne Sorbonne, aujourd'hui de la Bibliothèque Nationale, tous deux du XIIIe siècle, les seuls d'ailleurs que l'on possède ici du *Perihermenias*. L'un, exécuté avec grand soin, est souvent inexact; l'autre, extrêmement difficile, est plus exact. Quand un changement important nous a paru devoir être introduit et qu'il appartenait à la fois aux deux manuscrits, nous l'avons généralement signalé afin de donner plus de valeur à la correction proposée.

Avant d'aller plus loin, nous voudrions savoir si ce travail répond à la pensée et au désir de Son Eminence et, s'il y a lieu, recevoir ses observations.

Le R.P. Beaudoin va repartir jeudi, et il reste encore les deux *Postérieurs Analytiques*. Est-ce qu'on est pressé à Rome de les avoir? S'il était nécessaire de terminer ce travail promptement, peut-être y aurait-il lieu de me faire rester, par un échange, à Paris pendant le Carême: nous pourrions travailler avec le T. R. P. Villard, qui parait désireux de mettre le nez dans ces vénérables vieilleries, ou avec le R. P. Delorme, que l'on dit très versé dans ces matières; vous savez, mon Très Révérend Père, que je ferai ce que vous voudrez. Mais je désire bien vivement que mon voyage de Rome, déjà retardé du commencement de l'hiver jusqu'à Pâques à cause des grandes prédications de la saison, ne le soit pas encore et indéfiniment: les travaux qui m'y attirent, et qui me permettront enfin de voir Rome, ont aussi bien leur intérêt et leur importance..."

90 Voir en particulier [65][53] cités ci-dessus. Nous n'avons aucune information sur la façon dont étaient couvertes les dépenses effectuées pour la préparation de l'Edition léonine par les correspondants et spécialement les itinérants, à l'exception d'une allusion de Cl. Suermondt à propos des voyages de H. Denifle, dans "Le texte léonin de la prima Pars", p. 46 n. 1, mais cette allusion est trop vague et aussi trop passionnelle pour qu'on puisse faire fonds sur elle.

91 Ainsi [46][70][71], voir aussi Redigonda XII. Citons ici partiellement [72] où le père

D'autres difficultés ou obstacles ont retardé ou restreint le travail des collaborateurs, mais, plus directement liées à la technicité même de l'entreprise, elles auraient pu être soupçonnées à l'avance. Il y eut ainsi la difficulté ou l'impossibilité de pouvoir disposer d'exemplaires de la Piana comme texte de base pour les collations [57*][61]. Mais tout d'abord, les enquêteurs se sont heurtés aux horaires peu pratiques de certaines bibliothèques soi-disant publiques, à la multiplicité des démarches à faire pour accéder aux collections privées, et très souvent aux catalogues insuffisants, à l'absence de catalogue et même au manque de classement rationnel de certaines bibliothèques, particulièrement en Espagne.[92] Mais la difficulté principale est venue du

---

Denifle nous donne un témoignage direct, et combien savoureux, de certaines épreuves et difficultés que H. Denifle et F. P. Balme ont dû affronter:

"J'ai reçu hier votre lettre, et je remercie beaucoup. Excuser que je ne écrirait pas avant, comme j'ai promis. A Salamanque j'étais incapable pour faire quelque chose en cause de mon estomac. Les français ont une cuisine inexplicable, et pour cela tous sont malades, aussi le P. Vicaire général du Perpignan.

Je crois que l'Eminenz après quelques jours Platon doit recevoir. Pour S. Thomas je trouvais rien à Valladolid, Salamanque (dans la bibliothèque il y a rien d'autre que les disputes sur la grâce) et Segovie. Mais à Segovie le P. Gregoire Revilla m'a donné une belle relique du N. S. Père Dominique — je porterai au P. Général. Le P. Manuel à Salamanque m'a donné le manuscrit du Vitoria sur 1. part. du St. Thomas. Sur la predestination et reprobation il a les preuves tout à fait come Bauer. Ici j'aspette toujours encore une billet pour la bibliothèque privé du Roi, et pour Escorial. Les Espagnols modernes ne se pressent pas. Sono iomadoni! J'ai fini à Madrid et demain l'Eminence recevra la liste. Le P. Balme est encore avec moi. Avec Votre lettre est venue une autre de son P. Provincial, dans quelle il exprime votre intention. Le P. Balme *est content*. Il me quittera après 2 semaines — il est trop fatigué. Les rotis oiseaux ne volent pas aussi en Espagne dans la bouche. Mais pour la paléographie il est bien capable quoique tardif. A Avila j'ai trouvé une charmante communauté. C'est un vrai plaisir! J'étais seul là. Le couvent est immense comme à Salamanque, et les Espagnols le remplissent parfaitement. J'assistais à la fonction du 1ᵉʳ soir. Le P. Général ou le P. Pueblo doivent raconter les détails de cette fonction. Semel in anno ridet Apollo.

Une fois Vous, Revme Père, dever aller en Espagne. Ce un pays magnifique. Malheureusement ont les français et la révolution beaucoup des bibliothèques et des manuscrits détruits...

Le P. Balme écrira après quelques jours. La partie de 'La fé' est content pour encyclique du Pape. La partie du 'Siglo futuro' moins. Cette division est un malheur."

H. Denifle et F. P. Balme ne réagissaient d'ailleurs par toujours à l'unisson, les difficultés pouvaient s'en trouver aggravées. Voici, parmi d'autres que l'on pourrait citer en ce sens, le document [75]: "Bona festa et ad multos annos! Aujourd'hui, je pars pour Cordova. Pour Lisboa j'ai reçu d'Autriche une recommandation pour l'ambassadeur autrichien. Je suis content. Les manuscrits philosophiques sont rares, mais plus rares encore les commentaires sur la Bible. Les manuscrits théologiques sont abondantes et pour la plus grande partie plus anciens que dans les autres pays. Maintenant Andalousie et Portugal! Hélas, j'oublie toutes les fatigues. Le P. Balme a pris mal du pays. La persévérance n'est une plante, qui croît en France. Mi pare... Fr. Enrique Denifle O.P."

92 Voir par exemple les lettres du père Denifle, en particulier [61][70*][72*]; voici le texte de [70]:

"Je mande ici ce que j'ai trouvé jusque présent. Le P. Rivas n'a pas bien travaillé. Souvent il a pris seulement les notes des catalogues, qui sont très imparfaits. Quelques bibliothèques il n'a pas connue. Les fatigues du voyage sont très grandes. Une grande difficulté offre le chapitre de Barcelone. Ils ne veulent pas qu'on garde la riche bibliothèque. Peut-être que j'ai plus fortune retour-

très grand nombre de manuscrits d'œuvres de S. Thomas, le plus souvent dispersés à travers le monde entier et, comme nous venons de le dire, dans des locaux souvent inabordables et dans des ensembles sans inventaire ou classement acceptable. A une époque où les moyens techniques étaient sommaires et les possibilités humaines limitées, ce très grand nombre de manuscrits intéressant l'Edition léonine rendait impossible la réalisation rapide d'une édition scientifique véritablement sérieuse des œuvres de S. Thomas d'Aquin. Or le personnel a été recruté, les consignes données et les délais d'achèvement des volumes determinés à l'avance comme si aucune difficulté importante ne risquait d'intervenir.

Certes, bien que des travaux antérieurs de même nature, telles que les entreprises précédentes d'éditions d'*Opera omnia* de S. Thomas et surtout la préparation de l'édition de S. Bonaventure par le père Fidelis a Fanna, eussent pu éveiller leur attention, le cardinal Tommaso Zigliara ne doit peut-être pas être critiqué trop sévèrement non plus que Léon XIII pour n'avoir pas soupçonné à l'avance toutes les difficultés que nous avons évoquées ci-dessus, ou du moins leurs dimensions véritables qui étaient en l'occurrence colossales, le cas de S. Thomas débordant très largement par exemple celui de S. Bonaventure. Mais il se trouve que le cardinal a été très vite et très clairement prévenu par certains de ses collaborateurs plus perspicaces. Il est bien certain qu'il a eu un écho des sentiments développés par H. Denifle dans la lettre que ce dernier a sans doute envoyée au Maître de l'Ordre et qui a déjà été publiée.[93] Mais à cette lettre, il faut ajouter deux lettres inédites adressées au cardinal lui-même, par le père Balme d'une part, par le père Esser d'autre part. Dès janvier 1880, le père Balme écrit ceci au cardinal |51|:

> ...J'ose vous prier, Eminence Révérendissime, de vouloir bien me permettre de vous soumettre, pour le meilleur succès de l'entreprise, quelques réflexions qui me paraissent aussi urgentes que dignes d'être prises en considération. C'est autorisé parce ce que, depuis plusieurs années, j'ai vu pratiquer par le P. Fidèle de Fanna Récollet pour l'édition des œuvres de St. Bonaventure, et aussi par ma propre expérience en pareille matière, que je me crois suffisamment en mesure de vous soumettre ces réflexions.
> S'il ne s'agit, Eminence, que de publier une édition des œuvres de St.

nant à Barcelone. Demain je pars pour Madrid, où spécialement la bibliothèque nationale est très grande.

On ne trouve pas un manuscrit trop moderne ou sur carte; presque tous sont anciennes. Mais beaucoup des manuscrits furent brullés par les français et pendant la révolution."

Quand on compare de tels témoignages, qui datent d'un siècle, aux comptes rendus de voyage de ceux qui aujourd'hui font encore le même travail de recherche pour conduire jusqu'à son achèvement l'Edition léonine, on se prend à penser que les choses n'ont guère changé depuis l'enquête Zigliara.

93 Nous citons cette lettre plus loin, voir ci-dessous n. 99, afin de la mettre dans ce qui nous paraît être son véritable contexte.

Thomas plus correcte et plus complète que les précédentes en tenant compte des travaux antérieurs, ce sera chose facile et il n'est guère besoin de se livrer à de grandes et pénibles recherches; mais si on veut faire un travail exceptionnel, qui donne le dernier mot de la question, qui réponde aux intentions solennellement exprimées de Sa Sainteté Léon XIII et soit digne de la dévotion de l'Ordre et de votre Eminence à Notre Saint Docteur, il devient indispensable de faire pour cette édition ce que, pour les Œuvres de St. Bonaventure, fait l'Ordre des frères Mineurs par l'impulsion de son Général et sous la direction du P. Fidèle de Fanna! L'ouvrage que ce dernier a publié à Turin chez Marietti intitulé "Ratio novae collectionis operum omnium S. Bonaventurae" en donne une idée, et le petit travail que je viens de faire moi-même à Avignon m'a montré jusqu'à l'évidence que c'est une nécessité qui s'impose si on tient à réussir. Il faudrait donc en premier lieu faire vérifier par des hommes compétents dans toutes les bibliothèques, tous les manuscrits des œuvres de St. Thomas des 13°, 14°, 15° siècles jusqu'à la découverte de l'imprimerie; car souvent les manuscrits les plus précieux et les plus authentiques se découvrent là où on s'y attendrait le moins et où personne n'en soupçonnerait l'existence. De plus il y a souvent autant de variantes que de feuillets dans un manuscrit et comment faire un choix judicieux si l'on n'a pas toutes les pièces en main?

2° Ce premier travail fait en Italie, en France, en Espagne, en Allemagne, en Angleterre, etc. etc., et le compte rendu vous en étant fait et soumis, il faudra que l'on copie intégralement les textes les plus anciens, ceux que vous indiquerez en suivant l'ordre de publication qui sera adopté — plus on aura, sur un texte, de copies, plus la critique s'exercera avec profit. On assure que le P. Fidèle a sur un seul texte jusqu'à 20 et 30 copies: il est impossible de songer à ce que la même personne déchiffre un manuscrit et, séance tenante, compare et fasse le choix des variantes à adopter.

3° Quand donc toutes les copies que l'on aura pu obtenir d'un manuscrit seront réunies à Rome, il y aura lieu, ce me semble, pour une commission nommée par Votre Eminence, de les collationner entre elles et de faire aussi avec une critique mûrie et en connaissance de cause, choix du meilleur texte et des variantes les plus autorisées.

4° Ce sera alors le moment d'imprimer sûrement et avantageusement...

Il serait aussi très utile que les différentes pères qui collaborent à cette œuvre, au moins en France, se connaissent, puissent se voir, s'entendre, échanger leurs vues, afin d'adopter la même méthode d'investigation et le même plan et en même temps, afin de se faire réciproquement part des résultats de leur expérience dans ce travail tout nouveau pour la plupart.

Pardonnez-moi, Eminence, ma témérité! C'est votre bienveillance d'un côté et le désir de l'autre de voir mener à bonne fin une si belle entreprise qui m'ont déterminé à vous écrire cette lettre.

Qu'aurait écrit le père Balme si, comme nous le savons maintenant, il avait soupçonné que pour certaines œuvres de S. Thomas il n'est pas question de 20 ou 30 copies mais plutôt de 150 à 200? En mars de l'année suivante, c'est le père Esser qui, à son tour, met en garde le cardinal contre trop de précipitation en des termes eux-aussi très explicites [66]:

> Et qui non posso tacerle una mia osservazione, la quale propongo però con tutti i respetti alla mia ignoranza, al savio e prudentissimo parere di Vostra Eminenza: Se si commincia a lavorare prima di cognoscere *tutti* i manoscritti delle diverse opere di S. Tommaso, dispersi nelle diverse bibliotheche di tutto l'orbe cattolico, ben facile potrebbe capitare il caso che, dopo finito un volume, si troverebbe ancora uno o più codici migliori di questi, di cui si è adoperato per quel volume, di modo che tutto questo lavoro sarebbe inutile, o almeno dovrebbe comminciarci da capo. Percio secondo il mio parere — ma forse secundum insipientiam loquor — anzi tutto dovrebbe farsi un Catalogo o cosidetto *Clavis Codicum*, nel quale tutti i codici trovabili sarebbero registrati, numerati; distinti secondo il loro valore, etc. Allora si avrebbe un fondamento certo e firmissimo, si saprebbe, dove si trovano i migliori codici per le diverse opere, ed il lavorare del resto sarebbe ben facile e spedito. — Mi perdoni la Vostra Eminenza, questa mia libertà, e mi creda, che non ho detto, quanto dissi, per una certa criticandi cacoethes, ma si per il solo e puro interesse, che prendo di un lavoro tanto glorioso non solamente per la di lei persona Eminentissima, ma ancora, per mezzo di essa, per tutta quanta la nostra santa religione.

Ces deux lettres des pères Balme et Esser au cardinal, également celle du père Denifle, témoignent de la lucidité de leurs auteurs respectifs sur les véritables dimensions et les exigences scientifiques de l'entreprise. [94] Nous ne savons si le cardinal a reçu d'autres avertissements allant dans

---

[94] On notera que leur franchise à l'égard du cardinal n'a pas empêché les pères Balme et Denifle de continuer à travailler pour la préparation de l'édition léonine, voir [70*] à [76] et également Redigonda XII, XIII. En septembre 1882, le père Denifle avoue qu'il a plus de courage qu'auparavant, Redigonda XII.

Pour ce qui est tout particulièrement du père Denifle, les documents signalés ici, [49][70*] à [76] et Redigonda XII et XIII, permettent de situer à sa vraie place la lettre de Denifle que nous citons ci-dessous n. 99 à la suite de D. M. Planzer. Il semble que la publication de ce brouillon isolément de son contexte ait incité à majorer le prétendu découragement de certains des premiers collaborateurs du cardinal qui auraient abandonné parce que le travail n'était pas mené avec assez de rigueur scientifique. Le cas du père Denifle est alors toujours cité avec comme exemple la lettre révélée dans *Divus Thomas*, voir par ex. R. Aubert, "Aspects divers...", p. 197 n. 105 où R. A. renvoie d'ailleurs à "Denifle" du DHGE. Or le cas du père Denifle nous montre précisément qu'après sa lettre très négative pour le projet, sans doute de 1880, il fait sur ordre un voyage très long et fatigant, faisant des recherches dans le sud de la France et dans toute la péninsule ibérique, voir ci-dessus p. 359. C'est sa nomination comme sous-archiviste du Saint Siège, en décembre 1883, qui mit un terme à sa coopération à l'édition léonine et non son désaccord, sans doute très réel, sur la méthode ou plutôt l'absence de vraie méthode du cardinal Zigliara. Voir ci-dessous n. 99. Une lecture cursive des documents mentionnés ici et concernant Denifle permet de lire avec une certaine philosophie les appréciations si divergentes portées autrefois sur l'apport du père Denifle à l'édition critique des œuvres de S. Thomas: voir par ex. card. Ehrle, *Franziskanische Studien* 11 (1924) p. 32; Cl. Suermondt, "Le texte léonin..." n. 1 de p. 46; les notices "Denifle" de DHGE et de LTK. Comme collaborateur du cardinal Zigliara à l'étape heuristique du travail, H. Denifle a accompli un travail considérable, voir par ex. Redigonda pp. 126-132, et s'il n'a sans doute pas collaboré au collationnement proprement dit, ses idées méthodiques appuyées par une forte personnalité ont certainement eu elles-aussi une certaine influence sur le groupe romain.

le même sens, en tout cas on ne relève aucun indice permettant de faire croire que ces lettres ont eu un effet quelconque. Faut-il s'en étonner? En la personne du cardinal Zigliara et a travers lui, les trois érudits s'adressaient à un milieu ecclésiastique beaucoup trop replié sur lui-même et beaucoup trop ignorant du développement de la recherche historique et de ses développements techniques à cette époque pour pouvoir comprendre la portée d'avertissements donnés pourtant très clairement mais par des hommes qui eux étaient plutôt en avance sur leur temps par leur conception de ce que devrait être un véritable travail de critique textuelle.

Bilan sommaire.

Au terme de cette présentation et de ces réflexions sur la méthode heuristique du cardinal Zigliara et sa mise en œuvre concrète, on ne peut que souligner la justesse des intentions fondamentales[95] et en souligner les fruits.[96] Mais en même temps, on est amené à constater que dès les débuts de la Léonine se constitue un malentendu entre les autorités qui veulent une édition scientifiquement excellente mais réalisée dans les délais les plus brefs et les techniciens qui déclarent in-

---

95 Il faut rendre au cardinal cette justice que l'on ne peut relever dans les documents des allusions de sa part à des critères d'orthodoxie doctrinale, philosophique ou théologique, ou encore à des capacités spéculatives particulières qu'il faudrait exiger des éventuels collaborateurs, alors que certaines remarques auraient pu lui en donner l'idée [41][43] et que sa relative ignorance du travail critique et ses antécédents intellectuels personnels auraient bien pu le conduire à partager le souci typiquement romain de sécurité conceptuelle en tout domaine, comme si en l'occurrence elle pouvait avoir une incidence bénéfique sur la valeur scientifique du travail d'un éditeur critique. On a vu combien ce facteur a été influent dix années auparavant, ci-dessus p. 347. Il est tout à l'honneur du cardinal qu'il semble donc avoir admis, au moins implicitement, que pour mener à bien une telle tâche il fallait avant tout une équipe de bons codicologues et surtout de bons paléographes pour la premières étape du travail; la seconde étape étant conduite par de bons techniciens de la critique textuelle, ayant donc un esprit assez méthodique mais également formés par une longue expérience dans ce domaine, leur tâche consistant précisément à exploiter le plus objectivement possible le donné paléographique rassemblé au cours de la première étape. Il est vrai qu'il ne faut peut-être pas attribuer au cardinal Zigliara plus d'idées précises qu'il n'en avait en réalité: au fond le recrutement de collaborateurs ne dépendait pas tellement de lui, il prenait ceux qu'on voulait bien mettre à sa disposition; d'autre part, ceux qui précisément lui proposaient des sujets avaient peut-être eux quelques principes de sélection: ce qui dispensait précisément le cardinal d'en avoir. On a vu plus haut que ce sont collaborateurs directs du Maître de l'Ordre qui recrutaient pour le cardinal, voir ci-dessus p. 357. Il n'en reste pas moins que dans le cas d'œuvres comme celles de S. Thomas, à cause de l'état du donné manuscrit, la critique interne n'a pratiquement que très peu à intervenir: des préoccupations prématurées d'orthodoxie théorique et de rectitude doctrinale ne pourraient que risquer de compromettre la rigueur scientifique du travail d'établissement du texte.
96 L'équipe des "collaborateurs du cardinal Zigliara" qui deviendra ensuite le "collège des éditeurs" voir ci-dessous pp. 371-377, ne semble pas avoir toujours apprécié de façon assez objective le travail des "correspondants", témoin cette remarque du père Mackey pour les mois de janvier à juin 1880 "Le misure prese in questo tempo non hanno avuto felice esito, e non ne rimane nessuno risultato se non il conoscimento di gran' numero di codici". Le but même d'une enquête heuristique n'est-il pas précisément d'apporter d'abord une information codicologique?

conciliables ces deux exigences et s'orientent résolument vers la
réalisation d'une publication encore plus rigoureuse au plan scientifique
que ne l'imaginaient ceux qui l'ordonnaient, mais repoussent alors
dans le futur non défini le terme de l'œuvre. Certains fruits assez amers
de ce malentendu verront très rapidement le jour dans les années
immédiatement suivantes. Il est bien évident qu'un tel malentendu est
toujours sur le point de poindre à nouveau, si tant est qu'il ait jamais été
totalement dissipé.[97]

Les Editeurs de S. Thomas de 1879 à 1894

Il est bien certain que dans l'esprit même du cardinal Zigliara
l'établissement de répertoires descriptifs de manuscrits d'œuvres de S.
Thomas et la collation des manuscrits d'une œuvre en se référant à un
texte de base et en notant les éventuelles notes marginales ne pouvaient
représenter qu'un travail préparatoire à l'élaboration proprement dite
de l'édition. Une fois cette première étape accomplie, comme nous
l'avons vu grâce au travail de correspondants, une étape nouvelle devait
nécessairement suivre, consistant en une étude critique du donné
paléographique fourni par les collations pour aboutir à l'établissement
d'un texte proposé à l'impression typographique, avec les préfaces et les
apparats correspondants.

Pour mener à bien cette seconde étape, capitale, le cardinal avait
évidemment besoin de l'aide de collaborateurs résidant à Rome et
travaillant à ses côtés. L'histoire du groupe de ces collaborateurs, que
l'on appelle aujourd'hui Commission léonine, est jalonnée par des crises
et des transformations dont l'étude n'est peut-être pas sans intérêt pour
tous ceux qui s'intéressent à la technique de l'édition de textes. Ici encore, nous n'avons pas la prétention d'écrire une histoire complète de la
Commission léonine mais simplement de présenter certaines pièces,
pour une part inédites, que nous avons crues intéressantes et d'en
dégager quelques conclusions qui ont peut-être encore quelque intérêt
et même une certaine actualité.[98]

---

97 Comment expliquer autrement que, sans consulter les spécialistes, on ait encore récemment
pu faire dire que l'Edition léonine serait terminée d'ici quelques années, alors que les exigences
scientifiques en matière d'édition critique sont plus rigoureuses que jamais et que les moyens d'investigation et de consultation ont fait des pas de géant, accroissant par là même très lourdement
les délais incompressibles nécessaires pour mener à bien ce genre de travail.

98 Les documents exploités ci-dessous ne constituant pas comme précédemment un dossier,
nous n'en donnons pas ici une liste récapitulative. A chaque fois que nous nous référons à un
document, nous en donnons le texte d'après l'authentique ou la minute officielle, ou encore d'après
la copie qu'en a faite le père Mackey, v. ci-dessous n. 107.

Pour être comprises, ces pièces doivent être insérées dans la trame historique où elles s'insèrent naturellement et dont le découpage est imposé par les faits eux-mêmes, d'où les paragraphes successifs de cette dernière partie.

Les collaborateurs du cardinal Zigliara, éditeur de S. Thomas, 1880-1882.

C'est le cardinal lui-même qui avait reçu mission de mener à bien l'édition léonine. Pour ce faire il lui fallait nécessairement recruter à nouveau des collaborateurs, mais alors des collaborateurs qui travailleraient sur place à ses côtés. H. Denifle, en dépit de sa résistance,[99] est nommé "socius" du Maître de l'Ordre afin qu'il soit en situation d'aider le cardinal: il est déjà à Rome avant le 28 octobre 1880.[100] Le nouveau Général, le père J. M. Larroca, avait d'ailleurs essayé d'appliquer le même processus au père Beaudouin pour assurer au cardinal l'aide de ce religieux français considéré comme bon

---

99 N'est-ce pas pour préparer sa réponse au Maître de l'Ordre qui l'invitait à venir à Rome comme socius, que Denifle rédigea le brouillon publié par D. M. Planzer dans *Divus Thomas* (Frib.), 8 (1930) 447-448? Sa réticence s'expliquerait peut-être alors, pour une part par son peu d'inclination à devenir socius du Père Général, car il lui était plus facile d'essayer d'esquiver cette charge en arguant de difficultés pour lui à collaborer avec le cardinal. Si notre hypothèse est exacte, comme le suggère la première phrase de la lettre, il faudrait dater le document d'avant le 28 octobre 1880, date d'arrivée de Denifle à Rome, après une nouvelle instance du Père Général. Voici en tout cas le texte:

"Romae verosimiliter adiuvare deberem Em. Cardinal. <Zigliara> in editione operum S.Thomae; et hoc ex causis infra referendis intimo meo contradicit. Viginti quatuor bibliothecas in Germania perlustravi, in quibus 560 manuscripta librorum Thomae inveni; adhuc manent circa viginti bibliothecae perlustrandae. Em. Cardinali quantocius catalogum mittam saltem illorum manuscriptorum saec. 13 et 14. Perlustravi etiam catalogos impressos, in quantum sunt publicati bibliothecarum des départements, ut dicunt, Galliae, et inveni manuscripta "non" minoris numeri. In Italia, ut mihi Fid. a Fanna dixit, eodem numero inveniuntur. Quid faciendum? Si centum homines insimul laborarent, non perficerent opus tam brevi tempore, ut Summus Pontifex vult. Debent manuscripta comparari, eligi, in classes dividi. V. gr. ex commentariis super Metaphysicam inveni 12 manuscripta quae deberent adhiberi; et eodem numero sunt in Physicam, in Ethicam et in Animam. Et sic est in Gallia, in Italia, in Hispania forsan. Quis hoc praestabit? Duo anni solummodo teruntur, ut bibliothecae in Europa perlustrentur et quisque sciat, quot manuscripta sunt in illis. Sex annis non sufficiunt ad comparationem manuscriptorum. Peto, quisnam praestabit per dimidium vel unum annum? Est physica impossibilitas. Et ideo omnes docti in Germania et aliqui Galli, quibuscum conveni, mihi dixerunt, quod si Summus Pontifex consilium suum non mutabit, Em. Card. solummodo codices Vaticanos vel etiam Parisienses adhibeat et dicat in fronte editionis: "correcta iuxta codices Vaticanos et Parisienses"; aliter ordo noster et ipse Summus Pontifex in detrimentum veniret, quia critici, ut iam audivi, primo contra Card. et nostrum ordinem insurgent et deinde etiam contra Summum Pontificem. Altera difficultas est: multae bibliothecae in Germania post combustionem bibliothecae docti Mommsen non sunt tam faciles ad manuscripta transmittenda, sicut fuit prius. Quomodo nunc comparare? Bibliothecae iacent in regionibus protestantium, ubi deberent fratres morari per plures annos! Dicat hoc Em. Cardinali et credat experto et referat Summo Pontifici. Pulchritudo in editio <ne> est accidens: essentia est editio iuxta rectas regulas criticorum."

100 Voir Redigonda, p. 118. En fait, nous l'avons vu, H. Denifle continue à rechercher des mss dans toute l'Europe, mais il ne travaille pas aux côtés du cardinal.

théologien et professeur, mais le Maître de l'Ordre s'est trouvé contraint de renoncer à ce dernier projet.[101]

D'après les notes du père Mackey, on peut reconstituer ainsi les étapes successives de la constitution du groupe de ceux qui seront les vrais collaborateurs du cardinal: juin 1880, arrivée à Rome du père Constant Suermondt qui commence à travailler à peu près seul:[102] le 1er avril 1881, arrivée du père Hoogland et, le 25 juin, du père Lyttleton.[103] A la même époque, le père Frati est recruté mais pour travailler directement avec le cardinal et il n'est pas considéré comme "adetto al lavoro".[104] D'autres viennent s'adjoindre au groupe puisqu'en septembre 1881, sans compter le père Pierotti chargé des finances en tant que "sin-

101   Au début de septembre 1880, le père Larroca, Maître de l'Ordre, écrit au père Chocarne, provincial de France, qu'il choisit le père Beaudouin, lecteur et maître des étudiants à Flavigny, comme "socius". Le 15 du même mois, le père Chocarne écrit au Père Général qu'il ne peut lui donner le père Beaudouin, indispensable à Flavigny, etc. Le père général étant absent de Rome, c'est le père Bianchi qui reçoit cette lettre à Rome, il écrit au père Chocarne le 27 septembre qu'il transmet immédiatement la lettre du 15 septembre au père Larroca et intervient dans le même sens. Le 4 octobre, de Mazères (France), le père Larroca écrit au père Chocarne: "Je regrette moi aussi de priver votre Province du bien qu'y fait le Père Beaudoin (sic) et je le laisserez (sic) tranquille s'il ne s'agissait que d'un simple socius, mais je dois penser à aider notre cardinal dans l'édition des œuvres de St. Thomas. Veuillez donc lui communiquer ma détermination à ce qu'il se prépare à partir pour Rome dès qu'il le pourra...". En fait, dès le 7 octobre, le père Larroca, tenant compte encore d'autres interventions, écrit au père Chocarne qu'il lui laisse le père Beaudouin (Archives de la Prov. de France, III-C-6). Dans la notice nécrologique du père Beaudouin, signée par le père Ambroise Gardeil et publiée dans l'*Année dominicaine* de 1907, on lit que le père Beaudouin alla passer à Rome, en septembre 1877, l'examen "ad gradus" et que "à l'occasion de cet examen, le P. Zigliara le présenta au cardinal Pecci..." p. 198; on y lit également que le père Beaudouin "ami du cardinal Zigliara" p. 201, fut un des premiers membres de l'Académie S. Thomas d'Aquin, voir I. P. Grassi, op. cité ci-dessus.
102   On a vu plus haut que le père Suermondt avait été signalé au cardinal Zigliara quand celui-ci recherchait des correspondants, voir ci-dessus [41].
Le père Constant Suermondt, né en Hollande le 3 novembre 1850, profès dominicain le 23 octobre 1870, arrive à Rome pour la Léonine en 1880 à l'âge de trente ans; il sera frappé de paralysie définitive à 75 ans le 26 janvier 1925, alors qu'il corrigeait les épreuves du tome XIV de l'Edition; il meurt le 31 janvier 1925, après avoir travaillé 44 ans pour la Léonine. Notices dans Edition léonine, t. XIV, p. vi, dans *Memorie Domenicane* 70 (1953) 273-274.
103   Comme on le verra ci-dessous, p. 377, le père Hoogland ne restera pas longtemps à la Léonine. Quant au père James Lyttleton, né en Irlande le 14 novembre 1851, profès dominicain le 3 mai 1869, il arrive à la Léonine le 25 juin 1881 et meurt le 28 janvier 1909 après 27 ans de travail pour l'Edition. Notices dans Edition léonine, t. XVI, pp. v-vi, dans ASOP 11 (1913-1914) 150-151.
104   Cette formule est du père Mackey. Voici le texte de la lettre par laquelle Mgr. Boccali, secrétaire privé de Léon XIII, sollicite du Maître de l'Ordre l'affectation du père Frati:
"Rmo Padre Generale. Il S. Padre, per l'importanza grandissima che annette alla nuova edizione di tutte le Opere di S. Tommaso d'Aquino, desidera che l'Emo Cardinal Zigliara, il quale ne ha la cura, abbia l'aiuto di persone capaci sulle quali possa riporre intera fiducia. Una di queste è il Rmo P. Frati Reggente del Collegio di S. Tommaso alla Minerva; di cui peraltro l'Emo Card. Zigliara non potrebbe ulteriormente valersi, a motivo della Scuola di Teologia al medesimo affidata. Quindi ho l'onore di significare alla P. V. Rma essere desiderio del S. Padre che il lodato P. Frati sia messo a disposizione dell'Emo Card. Zigliara; e che l'insegnamento di S. Tommaso, finche non siasi potuto trovare un altro soggetto pienamente idoneo, sia provisoriamente affidato al P. Gaudenzi, chiamato recentemente a Roma e destinato ad assistere la P.V. Rma nell' Officio Generale.
Godo di poter confermare alla P.V. Rma i sensi della mia venerazione, con cui mi è grato professarmi della P.V. Rma. Vaticano, 3 nov. 1880, Devmo Servitore."

daco" de la Minerve,[105] l'équipe de travail se trouve constituée des religieux suivants: Suermondt, Lyttleton, Palmer,[106] Cuschieri et Carruana, enfin Mackey.[107] Sauf le père Lyttleton qui réside à San Clemente, ils vivent ensemble à la Minerve, maison généralice, et travaillent près des appartements du cardinal.

Cette équipe travaille "sur les variantes des manuscrits", le père Suermondt dirigeant la partie paléographique, alors que le cardinal avec l'aide du père Frati s'occupe personnellement de l'élaboration du tome I dont l'impression commence à la Propagande en juin 1881. Là, un prêtre assure jusqu'au 28 décembre 1881 le travail de correction typographique, après cette date ce travail retombera sur le groupe qui est malheureusement atteint au même moment par des départs notables. En effet, le 13 février 1881, le père Palmer retourne en Angleterre; le 27 février, ce sont les pères Cuschieri et Carruana qui rentrent à Malte. Il ne reste donc plus que les pères Constant Suermondt, Albert Hoogland, Jacques Lyttleton et Pierre-Paul Mackey comme "collaborateurs du cardinal Zigliara".[108] Un premier fruit du travail, le tome I de l'édition léonine, est terminée le 30 juillet 1881.[109]

La première crise et la mutation qui en résulte, 1882-1886.

Selon le père Mackey, la période qui s'étend de juin 1882 à décembre de la même année est marquée par de nombreuses difficultés tenant à la diversité des conceptions qui s'affrontent. Mais ces difficultés nous sem-

---

105 Il s'agit seulement des finances pour la vie quotidienne. En effet, l'administration de l'édition et les problèmes financiers y afférant relèvent des cardinaux et de la Propagande. A ce plan, on devance les développements du travail d'édition, puisque dès juin 1880 plus de 50.000,00 L sont dépensés en matériel typographique et que le premier contrat pour le papier est passé avec la Propagande le 5 mai 1880.

106 Dans une lettre du père Larroca au père Bianchi, de Gande (sic) et du 30 septembre 1881, on relève le passage suivant: "Sono contento assai che il P. Palmer sia utile e che il Cardinale ne sia contento. Se riesce a avere contento il P. Fratti (sic) puo andare avanti l'edizione."

107 Le père Peter Paul Mackey est né en Angleterre le 4 décembre 1851, profès dominicain le 10 octobre 1872, il arrive à Rome pour la Léonine le 22 septembre 1881, en 1929 devenu à peu près aveugle, il cesse de travailler à l'édition à laquelle il a donné 48 années de sa vie, il meurt le 23 avril 1935 à Rome. Notices dans Edition léonine, t. XVI, pp. v-vi, dans ASOP 22 (1935-1936) 140-142 et 449-456.

C'est aux notes inédites du père Mackey et au registre où il copiait toutes les pièces intéressant l'histoire de la Commission léonine que nous avons emprunté tous les détails et les textes qui figurent dans ces pages sans indication d'origine.

108 C'est ainsi qu'ils sont désignés dans la demande présentée à la Sacrée Congrégation pour l'interprétation du concile de Trente et satisfaite par elle le 28 mars 1882: désormais les pères A. Hogland (sic), J. Lyttleton, C. Suermondt et M. P. Mackey, "collaboratores Eminentissimi Domini Cardinalis Zigliara", pourront être autorisés par le Maître de l'Ordre à réciter Matines et Laudes du lendemain à partir de deux heures de l'après-midi, mais "durante munere, per modum tamen actus et non habitus, pro suo arbitrio et conscientia". Le père Raymond Bianchi accorde la permission demandée le 7 avril 1882.

109 L'impression d'une partie importante du volume avait commencé en juin 1881.

blent toutes dominées par l'espèce de crise que déclanche une lettre du cardinal Zigliara au Maître de l'Ordre en date du 12 juin 1882:

Reverendissimo Padre Maestro Generale:
Nell'udienza del 3 corrente Giugno ebbi l'onore di parlare col. S. Padre sulla sistemazione definitiva del personale necessario a proseguire la nuova Edizione delle Opere di S. Tommaso. Dopo l'udienza credetti mio dovere d'informare la Paternità vostra Reverendissima che Sua Santità metteva a disposizione de' religiosi collaboratori un quartiere dell'Accademia Ecclesiastica, assumendosi in pari tempo le spese di vitto, vestito, viaggi, ecc.Aggiungevo che sarebbe desiderabile di portare a 12 il numero de' religiosi per poterli distribuire a gruppi, e sollecitare cosi la stampa, affidando a ciascuno gruppo la preparazione di un' opera. Qualora un tal numero d'individui capaci non si poterre avere subito in pronto, si lasciava alla saviezza di V. P. Reverendissima di prendere tempo e di limitarsi per ora al personale necessario per preparare il secondo volume.
In passato la Paternità Vostra Reverendissima mi si mostrò molto soddisfatta di vedere questa nuova Edizione affidata dal S. Padre al nostro Ordine, il quale veniva cosi a continuare la gloriosa opera de' nostri maggiori, e mi aggiungeva che a cio occorendo parecchi religiosi, avrebbe preso le opportune disposizioni per chiamare in Roma questi religiosi medesimi. E ricordo pure ch'Ella mi manifesto l'intenzione di scegliere a suoi soci i padri Gaudenzi, Denifle e Beaudouin, acciocchè anch 'essi prestassero la loro opera. Riferii, come era dovere, il tutto a Sua Santità, la Quale accolse queste notizie con visibile compiacenza; e però rifiutò il concorso premurosamente e con insitenza offertole da persone estranee all' Ordine nostro. E nell' ultima udienza mi ripetè: Ai mezzi provvederò io; l'Ordine Domenicano, non ne dubito, si metterà con zelo, a curare une Edizione che ridonda a tanto suo onore. Dopo ciò fui non poco sorpreso e addolorato nel sentire le P.V. Reverendissima affaciare delle difficoltà intorno al personale necessario a preparare il secondo volume, quasi che non si possa disporre di un individuo senza compromettere, sono sue espressioni, l'avvenire di una provincia. Per conseguenza non che aumentare il numero, già scarso, de' collaboratori, c'è forse pericolo di perdere alcuno di quelli che hanno lavorato per il primo volume. Confesso che non so persuadarsi che l'Ordine nostro sià ridotto a questi estremi; ma comunque sia, è al tutto necessario che sieno manifeste al Santo Padre le precise intenzioni della Paternità Vostra Reverendissima. E siccome il medesimo S. Padre si è degnato servirsi di me per communicare le sue Sovrane intenzioni al Capo del nostro Ordine, mi sento in dovere di dare a Sua Santità discarico della missione affidatami.
A questo fine prego la Paternità Vostra Reverendissima a volermi dire Se Ella può e vuole accettare dal S. Padre il compito di far proseguire l'Edizione delle Opere di S. Tommaso da' nostri religiosi domenicani. Deporrò subito nelle mani del Sommo Pontifice la risposta che la P. V. Reverendissima vorrà darmi. La quale risposta mi pare debba essere sollecita, accioche, qualora ella creda esse di non poter secondare le sapienti mire di Sua Santità. Questa abbia tempo di trovare fuori dell' Or-

dine personne capaci di proseguire l'Edizione, della quale sta per pubblicarsi il primo Volume.

A scanso poi di malintesi mi preme di aggiungere che qualora la risposta al quesito proposto sia affermativa, sarà in piena facoltà della P.V. Reverendissima ordinare personale, lavoro e direzione in quel modo che ella crederà opportune. In tal caso, come appunti fu fatto per l'Edizione Piana, il Santo Padre fornisce i mezzi, l'Ordine fa l'Edizione. Che se il mio concorso sarà giudicato di qualche utilità, lo presterò volentieri in quel modo che posso migliore, ponendomi sin d'ora a disposizione della P.V. Reverendissima.

Con distintissima stima ho il bene di professarmi Della Paternità Vostra Revma Devotissimo Servo vero, fr. Tommaso Ma Card. Zigliara, de' Pred.

Comme on le voit, il ne s'agit pas d'un différent entre le cardinal et le Père Général,[110] mais c'est le pape qui s'adresse aux Dominicains par l'intermédiaire du cardinal: il met à la disposition du groupe d'éditeurs un quartier de l'Académie des nobles ecclésiastiques et s'engage à payer les frais de séjour et autres, mais il demande qu'il y ait douze religieux appliqués au travail. La lettre menace de chercher des éditeurs en dehors de l'Ordre des Prêcheurs si les Dominicains ne peuvent faire face à la tâche.[111]

Le 17 juin 1882, le conseil généralice des Dominicains décide que l'Ordre accepte la responsabilité d'assurer l'édition mais à condition que tous les problèmes financiers soient réglés aux dépens du pape.[112]

---

110 Si l'affaire éclate ouvertement en 1882, une certaine tension existait déjà entre le père Larroca et le cardinal l'année précédente comme paraît en témoigner une lettre du Maître de l'Ordre au père Bianchi datée de Galway (Irlande) 8 août 1881; cette lettre n'a certainement pas été antidatée par un par inadvertance puisque les archives de la Province de France contiennent une lettre du Père Général datée du 8 août 1882 montrant que la Maître de l'Ordre est à cette date à Rome et non à Galway. Voici un extrait de la lettre de Galway du 8 août 1881:
"Amo servare silenzio su quanto si riferisce al Cardinal piutosto che scrivere. Egli dirà quanto gli piace, sta bene. Vedo che anche in questa facenda si vuol fare ricadere tutta la colpa sopra di me. Sta bene. Tutto questo non mi disturba affato, perche il peggio che potrebbe succedermi, sarebbe il meglio per me. Che l'Ordine possa pensare da se all'edizione delle Opere di san Tommaso, potrebbe dirlo uno che non fosse Domenicano. Se il Cardinale si ritira ci penserà il S. Padre. Il male per noi si è che, come io temei fin dal principio, questa facenda fa nota a tutti la miseria nostra..."
111 La lettre du cardinal manifeste que des propositions pressantes et insistantes furent effectivement faites au pape en vue d'une reprise de l'Edition par d'autres éditeurs non dominicains.
112 "In Consilio habito coram iisdem (i.e. Rmo P. Mtro generale cui assidebant Rmus Proc. Generalis, Adm. Rdi PP. Fr. Thomas Gaudenzi Prov. Dacie, Fr. Josephus Carbery Prov. Scotiae et Fr. Henricus Chatillon Prov. Terrae Sanctae), perlectis litteris, quibus, nomine Summi Pontificis Leonis XIII fel. reg. Emus Cardinalis Zigliara Rmo Magistro Generali proponebat ut operum D. Thomae typis noviter edendorum curam et directionem, ipsius Summi Pontificis expensis, Ordo noster assumeret: Patres a Consiliis per quatuor suffragia, uno sese abstinente, propositum acceptandum esse decreverunt, ea tamen lege, ut certas conditiones ad rem pecuniariam spectantes atque per aliquot Patres ad hoc specialiter a Magistro Ordinis nominatos determinandae Smo. Dno. Ntro. suppliciter exponerentur, quibus videlicet operis incepti prosequtio certa tutaque in posterum fieret..."

Le 18 juin 1882, le Maître de l'Ordre rend compte de cette délibération au cardinal dans les termes suivants:

> Eminenza Reverendissima:
>
> Prima di dare una risposta definitiva alla pregiatissima lettera dell'
> Eminenza Vostra in data del 12 corrente mese, ho creduto conveniente
> convocare i PP. del mio consiglio, giacchè trattandosi di cosa assai grave,
> e che impegna per molti anni l'Ordine intero, non ho giudicato di
> potermi assumerne totalmente la responsabilità.
>
> I Padri sono stati unanimi nell' accettare in massimo l'offerta fatta con
> tanta degnazione e con tanta bontà dal S. Padre all' Ordine nostro, cui
> sarebbe disdoro grandissimo per noi il non accogliere con ossequiosa e
> riconoscente alacrità. Credono per altro di dover subordinare une tale ac-
> cettazione ad un progetto, che valga ad assicurare la Nobilità, e con-
> tinuazione dell' Opera importantissima, progetto affidato ad una speciale
> commissione, che sarà quanto prima sottoposto all' approvazione della
> Santità Sua.
>
> Prego pertanto la E.V. Revma di assicurare il S. Padre che l'Ordine, a
> cui indegnamente e non solo ma eziandio poco utilmente presiedo,
> fidando nell' aiuto di Dio, nella benedizione di S. Santità, e nella
> cooperazione efficacissima dell'E.V.R. che vorrà, come per l'addietro,
> continuare nella direzione dell'opera, è pronto a intraprendere il difficile
> compito, appena la Santità Sua si degnerà di accogliere benignamente il
> progetto, che Le verrà umiliato....

Après ces échanges de documents et la présentation au pape du tome I
le 18 août 1882,[113] présentation dont on peut penser qu'elle a quelque
peu détendu l'atmosphère, on commence l'année scolaire 1882-1883 en
travaillant à la préparation du tome II. Mais, en application des
décisions précédentes, les éditeurs sont transférés le 11 décembre dans
une partie des bâtiments de l'Académie pontificale des nobles ecclésiastiques.[114] Ce regroupement en une communauté spéciale visait

---

113 C'était la fête de S. Joachim, dimanche dans l'Octave de l'Assomption et par là la fête
patronymique du pape.
Ce premier volume porte le titre suivant: "Commentaria in Aristotelis libros Peri Hermeneias et
Posteriorum Analyticorum cum synopsibus et annotationibus Fr. Thomae Mariae Zigliara O.P.,
S.R.E. Cardinalis". Comme on le voit, la paternité du travail est reconnue au cardinal Zigliara et
on ne présente pas l'édition comme fondée sur une étude critique des manuscrits; il est intéressant
de comparer ce titre à ceux des tomes II et III d'une part, voir ici n. 123 et n. 129, et d'autre part à
celui du tome IV, voir ici n. 135.
En fait ce premier tome témoigne d'un certain souci d'utilisation des manuscrits accessibles, il
se réfère à la Piana mais garde sa liberté à l'égard de cette édition: pour le *Perihermeneias*, il est
renvoyé à 5 mss et à trois éditions outre la Piana; pour les *Postérieurs Analytiques*, toujours en plus
de la Piana, 3 éditions et 18 mss sont mentionnés. Actuellement nous connaissons 21 mss de l'*In
Perihermeneias* et 55 mss de l'*In Post. Analyt.*
114 Le pape savait ce qu'il offrait comme résidence puisqu'il avait lui-même séjourné pendant
un an à l'Académie en 1832. La partie des bâtiments qui devait servir de résidence au groupe de la
Léonine avait l'avantage d'être contigu à l'appartement du cardinal De Luca, l'un des membres de
la commission cardinalice. Mais en fait, le 12 juin 1883, l'équipe déménagera pour s'installer dans

sans aucun doute à éliminer les difficultés internes évoquées ci-dessus et qui provenaient peut-être d'une part de ce que tous les membres de l'équipe ne logeaient pas ensemble et d'autre part de l'insertion de l'équipe dans une communauté de religieux dominicains plus vaste et qui acceptait sans doute difficilement la présence d'un groupe voué à une activité très spéciale, menant donc un genre de vie singulier, et ayant en tout cas un régime financier qui lui était propre. Nous ne savons si ce dernier point a eu de fait une grande importance, mais nous croyons utile de le souligner, car les composantes financières de toutes ces crises et évolutions semblent avoir généralement pesé de façon notable sur les psychologies et c'est au fond bien normal.

Enfin, comme conséquence inéluctable du transfert mais aussi comme son complément au plan des hommes, le père Hyacinthe Frati est promu par le Maître de l'Ordre à la charge de "praeses" du *Collège des éditeurs*. Cette nomination du 11 décembre est acceptée par l'intéressé le 13 du même mois.[115] Une telle nomination n'implique pas une modification substantielle du statut des éditeurs; à un groupe isolé, il fallait de toute nécessité donner une tête.[116] En fait, si le cardinal garde nominalement la présidence scientifique jusqu'à sa mort, sa participation effective décroît par degrés et il en arrive assez vite à ne plus participer du tout au travail d'une équipe qui n'est d'ailleurs plus logée à proximité immédiate de ses propres appartements. Selon le père Mackey, dès que le transfert est accompli, le père Frati se comporte comme le vrai chef du travail scientifique, mais cette équipe de religieux dominicains est logée dans les bâtiments du Saint-Siège et voit toutes ses dépenses assurées directement par l'administration vaticane.

---

une autre partie de l'Académie "all ultimo piano dell'Accademia, coll'entrata S. Chiara 33" précise le père Mackey.

115 "...Collegio Fratrum Ordinis nostri operibus D. Thomae denuo edendis addictorum, ac in aedibus Pontificiae Academiae Ecclesiasticae, jussu et magnificentia SS. D.N. Leonis PP. XIII fel. regn. adunatorum, de idoneo praeside, qui eorumdem Fratrum bono et incremento incumbat, providere volentes, te Adm. Rdum Patrem Magistrum Fr. Hyacinthum Frati, de cuius doctrina, zelo, prudentia ac regendi dexteritate notitiam plenam habemus, matura consideratione delegimus, cui praefatum munus in dicti Collegii profectum et in tuae obedientiae meritum demandemus. Quapropter harum serie nostrique auctoritate Officii te memoratum Adm, R.P. Mag. Fr. Hyacinthum Frati; absolventes prius ab omni vinculo excommunicationis aut quovis alio Ecclesiastico impedimento, si quod forte innodatus existas, ad effectum dumtaxat Praesentium consequendum, instituimus et facimus, teque institutum et factum declaramus praedicti Collegii Praesidem, cum omnibus juribus, gratiis et privilegiis, quibus huiusmodi Praesides in Ordini nostro gaudere solent et debent: Mandantes tibi in virtute Spiritus Sancti et sanctae obedientiae, sub formali praecepto, ut hoc munus et onus incunctanter accipias. Porro omnibus Patribus et Fratribus quomodolibet ad praefatum Collegium pertinentibus sub eodem formali praecepto mandamus, ut te tanquam verum et legitimum Praesidem suscipiant, habeant et venerentur tibique in omnibus et per omnia religiose pareant et incunctanter obediant. In nomine Patris et Filii et Spiritus Sancti..."

116 Du point de vue de la structure religieuse dominicaine, le Collège et son "praeses" sont placés sous l'autorité du père Bianchi, procureur général, délégué par le Maître de l'Ordre pour régir la Léonine.

Sur les nouvelles bases posées ainsi en fin de 1882, la vie de la Léonine se continuera jusqu'en 1885 sans bouleversements révolutionnaires. L'intelligence des évènements subséquents suppose, nous semble-t-il, que soient rappelés brièvement et selon leur ordre chronologique les faits les plus importants qui jalonnent le travail des éditeurs de S. Thomas.[117]

Pendant l'année scolaire 1882-1883 on "collecte les variantes pour le second volume." Le pape reçoit en audience les pères Larroca et Bianchi puis tous les collaborateurs,[118] il témoigne aussi de sa bienveillance en accordant aux éditeurs de S. Thomas certains privilèges touchant à leur vie religieuse en communauté dominicaine, privilèges qui étaient à l'époque assez recherchés[119] mais surtout réservés aux professeurs; le 20 mars 1883, Léon XIII assigne aux collaborateurs une somme totale annuelle de 10.000,00 L[120] et le 19 mai 1883 ils reçoivent l'autorisation exceptionnelle de pouvoir sortir les manuscrits de la Bibliothèque Vaticane.[121]

En septembre 1883, arrivent les pères Van Dyck et Weiss mais ce dernier repart pour l'Allemagne le 17 juin[122]; alors que le 13 de ce

---

117 Ici encore nous exploitons les notes du père Mackey.

118 "Questa è l'unica volta che i collaboratori sono stato ricevuto dal Sto Padre" écrit le père Mackey.

119 "Die 27 Ianuarii 1883 Sanctissimus Dominus Noster Leo PP. XIII, preces benigne excipiens infrascripti Patris Magistri Generalis Ordinis Praedicatorum, concedere dignatus est, ut Patres eiusdem Ordinis, qui operam suam praestant pro nova Editione Operum Doctoris Angelici Sancti Thomae Aquinatis, tamquam Lectorem in actu habeantur, adeoque juribus ac privilegiis Lectoribus actu legentibus a Legibus Ordinis concessis, gaudere possint et valeant. Contrariis non obstantibus quibuscumque. Datum Romae in Conv. Nostro S. Mariae s. Minervam die et anno ut supra. Fr. Josephus Maria Larroca, Mag. Ordinis."

Il est clair que l'enjeu de telles faveurs était le recrutement de futurs éditeurs et la persévérance de ceux qui étaient déjà appliqués au travail. Il ne convenait pas que cette affectation spéciale les prive de privilèges dont ils auraient automatiquement bénéficié s'ils avaient suivis la carrière à laquelle les destinaient normalement leurs aptitudes.

120 Cette somme doit être versée par le procureur de la Propagande. En septembre 1883, pour la seule résidence à S. Chiara 33 sera conclu un contrat de 5.000,00 L par an mais dont seulement 4.000,00 seront à payer.

121 Note de Mgr Ciccolini, "Primo Custode della Bibl. Vaticana",du 19 mai 1883 au père Bianchi. Il transmet le texte d'une note qu'il a reçue de Mgr Boccali et dont voici la teneur: "Vaticano 17 maggio 1883. Nell'interesse dell'edizione che tanto Gli sta a cuore, il S. Padre permette che si estraggono dalla Biblioteca Vaticana i codici e libri di rara edizione che occorreranno ai Collaboratori Religiosi Dominicani per la ristampa delle Opere di S. Tommaso. Dispone però che si prendano tutte le necessarie cautele per la conservazione e restituzione dei codici e volumi estratti e principalmente quella che se ne renda garante il Rmo Proc. Generale P. Bianchi. — G. Boccali, Cam. Segr. Parta. di S.S."

122 D'après certaines lettres du père Albert Marie Weiss, de 1883 et 1884, il semble qu'il ait reçu l'ordre d'arriver à Rome avant l'été 1883, mais qu'à cause de publications en cours il ait reçu l'autorisation de n'arriver qu'au milieu d'octobre; en avril 1884, sa santé laisse à désirer. En tout cas, il paraît beaucoup plus préoccupé de ses publications personnelles que de tout autre travail. Notice du père A. M. Weiss, ASOP 17 (1925-1926) 603-614.

même mois, le tome II était terminé,[123] il sera présenté le 22 juin au pape par les cardinaux Simeoni, Zigliara, les pères Larroca et Bianchi, le cavaliere Melandri.[124] Le travail pour préparer le troisième volume commence immédiatement tandis que l'attention du pape ne faiblit pas: en août-septembre 1884, il forme le projet de transférer le collège des éditeurs à S.-Nicolas de Tolentino près du Collège arménien, mais ce projet n'aboutira pas; et le 13 septembre, Léon XIII témoigne à nouveau de sa faveur aux membres de la Léonine, toujours en leur reconnaissant au sein de leur Ordre des privilèges particuliers.[125] Enfin, le père Bianchi étant mort le 25 juin, il avait fallu lui nommer un remplaçant provisoire pour que soit assurée la continuité de la gestion financière[126] jusqu'à ce qu'il soit remplacé en septembre 1885 dans ses fonctions de délégué du Père Général sur la Léonine par le père Marcolin Cicognani, nouveau procureur général de l'Ordre dominicain.

Si la condition matérielle du collège des éditeurs semble alors satisfaisante, c'est leur petit nombre qui va, au moins pour une part, se trouver à l'origine de nouvelles et graves difficultés: en effet, si le père Huysman était venu rejoindre le groupe en septembre 1884, les pères Hoogland et Van Dyck étaient retournés en Hollande le 27 juillet 1885, et le groupe se trouve alors réduit, sous la présidence du père Frati, aux pères Suermondt, Lyttleton, Mackey et Huysman.

Le changement de programme et de méthode, 1886-1892.

La crise survenue en 1882 ne devait pas être la dernière qui affecterait la Commission léonine. Une nouvelle crise, extrêmement grave dans ses conséquences sur la qualité du travail, se déroula pendant une

---

123 "Commentaria in octo libros Physicorum Aristotelis ad codices manuscriptos exacta cura et studio Fratrum Ordinis Praedicatorum". L'édition utilise 23 mss, nous en connaissons maintenant 64, mais cette édition de 1883 a une réelle valeur critique.

124 Le cavaliere Melandri était chargé de la conduite de l'impression typographique des volumes à l'imprimerie de la Congrégation pour la Propagation de la Foi.

125 "In audientia diei 13 Sept. anni 1884 SS. D. N. Leo PP. XIII benigne annuens precibus infrascripti Magistri Ordinis PP. Praedicatorum, indulgere dignatus est ut anni quibus Religiosi sui Ordinis, qui tunc in praesenti tum in posterum adlaborabunt ad novam editionem Omnium Operum S. Doctoris Thomae Aquinatis ab Ipso SS. D. N. Leone PP. XIII injunctam Ejusdemque sumptibus munificentissime exaratam, iisdem computentur ac si in Ordine legissent, pro gradibus in eodem Ordine consequendis ad Magisterium inclusive dispensatis tum examine ad gradus, tum aliis conditionibus a Legibus Ordinis praescriptis. Contrariis non obstantibus quibuscumque. In quorum fidem etc. Romae die et anno ut supra. Fr. Josephus Maria Larroca, Mag. Ordinis."

126 Lettre du cardinal Zigliara au cardinal Simeoni du 28 juillet 1885: "Il Padre Pierotti, Parocco della Chiesa di S. Maria sopra Minerva, in Rome, continua a tenere, sotto la dipendenza del Padre Generale de' domenicani, l'amministrazione del danaro necessario ai collaboratori per la nuova edizione delle Opere di S. Tommaso, già affidatagli dall'ora defunto P. Bianchi. Quindi egli rimane autorizzato a riscuotere da Propaganda le solite quote semestrali. Bacio umilissimamente le mani all'E.V. Reverendissima, e con distintissima stima mi onoro di professarmi dell'Em. V. Revma Umilissimo Devotissimo Obbedientissimo Servo suo fr. Tommaso Maria Zigliara."

bonne partie de l'année 1886. Les raisons de cette nouvelle crise sont en somme de même nature que celles qui sont à l'origine de la précédente: il s'agit encore de l'impatience des autorités devant la lenteur du travail accompli eu égard au coût très lourd de l'entreprise.

Les documents concernant cette crise de 1886 sont tout à fait explicites sur l'enjeu qui est mis en cause. Nous avons d'abord deux lettres du cardinal dominicain A. Bausa, maître du Sacré Palais. Elles visent à obtenir une accélération de la fabrication du tome III:[127]

> Vaticano. 4 Aprile 86. Padre Reverendissimo. Come le dici a voce, le ripeto che il Santo Padre m'incaricò di parlare energicamente, e efficacemente per la pronta consegna del volume di San Tommaso. Inutilmente ho parlato, e non so quello che io debba dire Martedì prossimo. Chiedere danaro, e non dare il lavoro è l'eccesso della follia. Ecciti I frati al lavoro, o rinunzino all'opera. Mi creda suo Devoto servo.
> Fr. A. Bausa.
> Vaticano, 6 Apr. 86. Molto Rdo Padre Maestro. Il Santo Padre mi ha interrogato sull'esito della missione affidatami. L'ho assicurato che la pubblicazione del volume di San Tommaso sarà accelerata. Ho parlato delle difficoltà incontrate, e della importanza accezionale di questo lavoro. Ho chiesto il suo consiglio, e mi ha esternato essere anche sua opinione che debbasi pubblicare la parte apocrifa. Io l'ho lasciato pienamente calmo, e benevolo. Vegga ella, Padre Maestro, di accelerare il lavoro, e mi tenga informato perchè io posso riferire a suo tempe al santo Padre, e impedirne i lamenti. Stia bene e mi creda suo Devoto Servo.
> Fr. A. Bausa.

Le 9 mai de la même année, Monsignore G. Boccali, secrétaire privé de Léon XIII, écrit à son tour au Maître de l'Ordre afin d'obtenir une accélération de la publication:[128]

> Reverendissimo Padre Generale. E' per espresso incarico ricevuto da Sua Santità che debbo rivolgermi alla Paternità Vostra Reverendissima e rinuovarle le piu vive premure affinchè tutta l'edizione abbia da procedere d'ora in poi senza troppo lunghi ritardi. Il S. Padre è dispiacente che nei vari anni gia trascorsi siasi pubblicato solo il 1° e il 2° tomo. Anche dall' estero sono giunte a Sua Santità lettere di personaggi che s'interessano dell' edizione e che ne hanno cominciato l'acquisto; nelle quale lettere unitamente al dispiacere del ritardo si esprime il

---

127 Bien que le père Mackey les suppose adressées toutes deux au père Frati, les en-tête semblent suggérer que la première est adressée au Maître de l'Ordre, le père Larroca, ou au procureur général, le père Cicognani; alors que la seconde est directement destinée au père Frati.

128 En bas de cette lettre, on peut lire une note du père Frati ainsi libellée: "Io non ho encora parlato della sospensione nè coi frati nè colle stamperia. fr. G. Frati. Verrò dimatina." Le père Frati aurait donc eu connaissance avec sept mois d'avance de la décision notifiée officiellement le 3 octobre.

Une annotation nous apprend que cette lettre a été reçue le 17 mai par le père Larroca.

desiderio di vedere pubblicati più sollecitemente gli altri volumi. In vista de tutto ciò voglia le Paternità Vostra Reverendissima dare le più efficaci disposizioni affinchè l'edizione sia condotta con quella maggiore speditezza che è compatibile colle diligente preparazione richiesta da publicazione di tal natura.

Conpinto l'incarico, non mi resta che presentare alla Paternità Vostra i sensi di distintissimo ossequio con cui mi è grato da professarmi, Della Paternità Vostra Reverendissima, Devotissimo servo.

Vaticano, 9 Maggio 1886   G. Boccali.

Le tome III dont il est question dans ces trois lettres sera terminé le 18 juin 1886[129] et le 28 juin l'équipe commence le travail pour préparer l'édition du Commentaire de S. Thomas sur le *De anima* d'Aristote. Mais la crise, déjà bien révélée par les documents cités ci-dessus, éclate de façon fracassante: Une lettre de Léon XIII est adressée aux cardinaux I. Simeoni et T. Zigliara, les deux survivants de la triade originelle. Portant officiellement la date du 3 octobre 1886, elle ordonne de renoncer au plan d'édition établi dès l'origine[130] et de s'attaquer immédiatement à la publication du texte des deux Sommes:[131]

Dilectis Filiis Nostris Joanni Simeoni, Thomae Zigliara, S.R.E. Cardinalibus

Leo PP. XIII

Dilecti Filii Nostri, salutem et apostolicam benedictionem. — Volumen tertium ex operibus sancti Thomae Aquinatis, quod novissimo tempore prodiit curis vestris in lucem, perspeximus laboriosa adornatum industria et exquisito iudicio, prorsus ut non minoris esse pretii quam duo illa priora videatur. Qua de re meritas debitasque laudes libenti animo tribuimus tum vobis, tum iis ex Ordine Dominicano sodalibus, qui in eodem incepto constanter non minus quam scienter vobiscum elaborant: ac simul confidimus, non de futurum vobis illud vehementer optabile maximeque dignum doctis laboribus praemium, sapientum approbationem. Porro accurandae editionis rationem, quam instituistis, institutam intelligenter esse, res loquitur ipsa: conficiendoque operi, quod habetis in manibus, consentaneum est tantum vos sumere temporis, quantum necesse intellexeritis esse.

---

129 "Commentaria in libros Aristotelis De caelo et mundo, De generatione et corruptione et Meteorologicorum ad codices manuscriptos exacta cura et studio Fratrum Ordinis Praedicatorum." Le regret du pape que ne soient pas publiées les parties des commentaires qui ne sont pas de S. Thomas (voir la lettre du 6 avril 1886) explique sans doute que l'édition de ces parties apocryphes figure dans le tome III comme un ajout raccroché après coup et insérées après les index, voir tome III, pp. i-cxlviii. Pour le *In De Caelo*, 11 mss sont utilisés, nous en connaissons 38; pour le *In De generatione...*, 3 mss utilisés, 4 sont connus maintenant. Pour le *In Meteor.*, 2 mss seulement sont utilisés, nous en connaissons maintenant 11, dont 6 donnent 3 leçons inédites, voir A. Dondaine et L. J. Bataillon dans AFP 36 (1966) 81-152. Cependant ce troisième tome, comme le précédent, a lui aussi une bonne tenue critique.

130 Ce plan avait été exposé par le cardinal Zigliara dans le premier volume, voir Edition léonine, t. I, p. xxxviii.

131 Cette lettre "Volumen tertium" a été publiée en tête du tome IV, pp. vii-viii.

Verumtamen inter ceterorum voluminum apparatum, cui longior est
opera necessaria, valde cupimus ut utriusque Summae editio maturetur.
Quod fieri celerius videtur posse, quia sunt illa quidem ex operibus sancti
Thomae maxime cognita et saepenumero formis litterarum impressa, et
multis eruditorum virorum laboribus explanata. Ex altera parte
cogitatione permovemur assidui usus: nam quicumque in philosophia
theologiaque serio versantur et aliquid volunt dignum iis disciplinis attingere, nihil habere solent utraque Summa familiarius. Itaque quanto
citius illas nitide et emendate, quod est diligentiae facultatisque vestrae,
publicaveritis, tanto magis utilitatem properabitis iis omnibus qui
eiusmodi studiorum dediti sunt generi. Nobis autem tam gratum feceritis,
quam quod maxime: neque enim estis nescii quam vehementer et quibus
de causis optemus ut sapienter Angelici Doctoris late propagetur.
Quamobrem voluntati ingenioque vestro rem omnem commendamus: in-
terea que auspicem caelestium donorum et paternae benevolentiae
Nostrae testem vobis et adiutoribus vestris apostolicam benedictionem
peramanter in Domino impertimus.

Datum Romae apud S. Petrum die III Octobris An. MDCCCLXXXVI.

Pontificatus   Nostri   Nono

Leo P. P. XIII

On remarquera que, dans cette lettre, comme dans la lettre de Mgr
Boccali, la dernière phrase du premier paragraphe laisse les artisans de
l'édition juges des délais d'élaboration, mais leur interdit d'aller au-delà
du minimum indispensable.

La portée de la décision pontificale révèle ses véritables dimensions
avec une note du 3 septembre 1886 remise au père Frati par le père
Marcolin Cicognani, procureur général des Dominicains. Cette note
oblige les éditeurs à renoncer à tout souci proprement critique puisqu'ils
doivent reproduire le texte de la Piana, tout en tenant compte éventuellement de quatre éditions plus récentes, et se contenter d'indiquer
en note et sans explication critique les variantes contenues dans les
seuls manuscrits du Vatican. En outre, c'est le cardinal Zigliara et lui
seul qui pourra en cas d'absolue nécessité décider de s'écarter du texte
de la Piana. De telles directives contredisent radicalement les vues
initiales du pape Léon XIII. Elles ruinent avec tant d'évidence tout
espoir de faire une édition ayant quelque valeur au plan de la critique
textuelle qu'il n'y a pas lieu d'y insister.[132] Mais il nous fallait donner la

132 "Metodo da tenersi nello stampare la Somma teologica di S. Tommaso ed i commenti del
Gaetano.
    1°. Per la Somma di S. Tommaso servirà da testo la Piana, tenerdo conto dell'edizioni del
Donato, de' Teologi di Lovanio et dell'edizione di Padova, ossia dell'edizione del De Rubeis, che
riassume le tre predette.
    2°. Le varianti de' codici vaticani si metteranno tutte quante ut jacent, cioè senza osservazioni
alcune, in nota a piè dell'articolo di S. Tommaso prima de'commentarii del Gaetano. Quivi pure si
noterà la lezione Piana, quando questa sarà evidentemente erronea. Questi cambiamenti però della
Piana saranno fatti esclusivamente da S. E. il Cardinal Zigliara.

teneur exacte de cette note pour expliquer la facture des tomes qui
allaient être publiés après une telle crise. Ajoutons que la mutation im-
posée par l'autorité s'accompagne de nouvelles dispositions financières
mais leur détail ne nous est pas connu. [133]

Après l'intervention du pape que nous venons de rappeler et pour
plus de cinq années, aucun évènement capital ne vint bouleverser la
structure de la Commission léonine, ni le travail engagé par décision
supérieure sur un nouvel objet et en suivant de nouvelles méthodes, elles
aussi imposées d'en haut. On ne reviendra pas ici sur le dommage qui
en résulta pour l'édition au point de vue de la qualité scientifique des
volumes produits. On sait que le responsable technique avec la ténacité
qui caractérise les hommes de sa race, s'efforcera de faire peu à peu
éclater le carcan dans lequel l'autorité avait cru pouvoir contenir l'effort
de recherche et de réflexion critiques. [134]

Il faut bien reconnaître que l'intervention pontificale fut extrêmement efficace au plan qui intéressait par dessus tout le Souverain Pontife: la rapidité de la production. Dès décembre 1886, c'est-à-dire moins
de trois mois après la décision du pape, on commence à imprimer les
premières pages du tome IV, le premier de la *Somme de théologie*. [135]
Le 21 juillet 1887, le travail pour préparer l'édition des 43 premières

---

3°. Quanto a citazioni di autori si starà a quelle di S. Tommaso *ut jacent* nell'articolo; le
citazioni poi particolareggiate degli editori saranno quelle della Piana *ut jacent*; e così pure quanto
ai dubbii di Pietro da Bergamo. — Si numereranno gli' articoli progressivamente come nella prima
Parte della Piana.
4°. Riguardo al Commentario del Gaetano, se si potrà trovare un'edizione più antica e più
corretta della Piana, si stamperà quella; altrimenti si stamperà la Piana *ut iacet*, passando oltre in
ogni caso e non fermandosi punto sopra errori anche manifesti; e così anche per le divisioni de'
Paragrafi.
5°. L'indice della Somma si stamperà in fine di tutta la stessa Somma. L'indice del Gaetano si
stamperà come sta nella Piana, alla fine però di ciascuna parte."
On notera la multiplication de la formule "ut jacet" ou de ses équivalents. On pourrait penser
que le vrai problème est totalement absent de l'horizon intellectuel des autorités, puisque le titre
même de cette note indique que l'on envisage l'impression (typographique) de la Somme de
théologie et non l'édition au sens de travail pour établir le texte; mais il est à remarquer que
d'autres documents antérieurs parlent aussi d'impression des œuvres de S. Thomas au lieu de
parler d'édition au sens complet du mot, il ne faut donc pas trop serrer de près les significations.
133 Le père Mackey mentionne le fait sans l'expliquer, mais la première lettre du cardinal
Baussa, du 4 avril 1886, montre bien l'incidence des questions financières sur l'affaire.
134 Bien avant les commentaires donnés par son neveu, voir articles du père Clément Suermondt signalés ci-dessus n. 8, le père Constant Suermondt, avec une discrétion adaptée à chaque
fois aux circonstances du moment, s'est lui-même expliqué très clairement à plusieurs reprises:
tout d'abord dès le t. IV, Préface p. xiii; puis dans le t. VIII, p. xi; enfin dans le t. XI, p. xii b *in
situ* mais dont les phrases essentielles ont été récemment citées par A. Brounts, "Nouvelles
précisions sur 'pecia'. A propos de l'édition léonine du commentaire de Thomas d'Aquin sur
l'*Ethique* d'Aristote", *Scriptorium* 24 (1970) 343-359, voir les notes 7 et 10 des pp. 344-345 où il est
précisément question de la crise de 1886.
135 "Pars Prima Summae Theologiae a Quaestione I ad Quaestionem XLIX ad codices
manuscriptos vaticanos exacta cum commentariis Thomae de Vio Caietani Ord. Praed. S. R. E.
cura et studio fratrum eiusdem Ordinis."

questions de la Somme (*De Deo uno*) était achevé, c'est-à-dire presque tout le texte de ce tome IV dont la préparation fût pleinement terminée le 22 décembre 1887, l'impression finie et la présentation au pape faite en 1888. Commencé au début de 1888, le travail sur le tome V est achevé le 10 juillet 1889. On commence à travailleur sur le tome VI en septembre 1889, à l'imprimer en février 1890, il est achevé le 9 janvier 1891. Quant au tome VII, on commence à l'imprimer en mars 1889 et il sera achevé en 1892, c'est le quatrième de la *Somme de théologie*.

Pendant ce temps au plan des personnes, à part la promotion du père Lyttleton comme maître en théologie le 31 décembre 1888, il n'y a à signaler que la nomination du père Frati, le premier président du Collège des éditeurs, au poste de Secrétaire de l'Index en mai 1889.[136] Il restera nominalement président jusqu'à sa mort survenue le 6 juillet 1894 mais sa collaboration au travail cesse avant la fin de 1889 et d'ailleurs il partira définitivement du groupe en mai 1893. A partir de mai 1889, il n'y a donc plus que quatre religieux: Suermondt, Lyttleton, Mackey et Huysman, travaillant sous la responsabilité théorique du cardinal Zigliara.

Le transfert à l'Ordre, 1892-1894.

C'est en 1892-1893 que l'entreprise d'édition des œuvres de S. Thomas d'Aquin connut sa mutation administrative la plus importante depuis sa fondation par Léon XIII en 1879-1880. Cette mutation consista en un transfert de la responsabilité totale de l'entreprise: officiellement dirigée depuis 1880 par une commission cardinalice de trois membres mais pratiquement sous la responsabilité du seul cardinal Thomas Zigliara, qui en 1892 était d'ailleurs l'unique survivant de la triade initiale, l'édition léonine fut totalement prise en charge par l'Ordre dominicain et passa donc sous la responsabilité du Maître de l'Ordre. L'initiative de cette mutation administrative semble avoir été prise par le cardinal Zigliara. En effet, sous la présidence du père André Frühwirth, nouveau Maître de l'Ordre ayant pris possession de sa charge le 31 octobre 1891, le conseil géneralice des Dominicains délibère le 4 avril 1892 sur une proposition du cardinal Zigliara au Maître de l'Ordre. Voici le compte-rendu de cette délibération:

> Praeside Rmo Ordinis Magistro, adstantibus Rmo P. Fr. Marcolino Cicognani, Procuratore Generali, et A A. RR. PP. Magistris et Sociis, Alberto Lepidi, Josepho Dominico Martinez, Dominico Maria Scheer et Ceslao Ruby exposita et discussa sunt sequentia: En tribus Emis S. R.

---

136 On peut noter également le décès du Maître de l'Ordre, le père Larroca, le 8 juin 1891.

Ecclesiae Cardinalibus, quos SS. D. N. Leo Papa XIII, per motum proprium die 18. Januarii 1880 praefecerat curandae novae editioni operum D. Thomae Aquinatis, defunctis jam duobus, unus superstes est Emus Cardinalis Thomas Zigliara, qui pluribus ex causis in hoc consilium devenit, ut, cum venia et assensu Romani Pontificis, incepta editio curis Alumnorum Ordinis Praedicatorum, sub ductu Rmi Magistri Generalis, deinceps continuaretur, ac Deo dante, perficeretur. Hujus tamen consilii, priusquam ad SS. D. N. Leonem XIII. deferretur, Emus Cardinalis participem fecit Rmum Ordinis Magistrum, ab eo inquirens, utrum, quatenus Sanctitas Sua hanc propositionem ratam haberet, ipse Rmus Magister Generalis, nomine Ordinis, onus et officium illam exequendi vellet acceptare.

Censuit autem Rmus Ordinis Magister, in negotio tanti momenti, priusquam firmum responsum daret, exquirenda esse vota graviorum Patrum. Praemissa igitur matura deliberatione, unanimi voto, per secreta suffragia, statuerunt:

Licet res, de qua agitur, ardua nobis futura sit et laboribus plena, operam Ordinis non esse in casu denegandam, dummodo opportunis mediis et provisionibus postea determinandis, Ordo eximatur et immunis maneat ab expensis et sumptibus occasione susceptae editionis faciendis.

Ita est.

Dès le lendemain, le 5 avril 1892, le Maître de l'Ordre informe le cardinal Zigliara en lui communiquant copie du compte rendu de la décision prise par le conseil généralice "intorno alla continuazione della stampa delle opere di S. Tommaso". Comme on le voit par cette dernière formule et par le texte même du compte rendu reproduit plus haut, l'attention est encore surtout portée sur l'impression des volumes et les frais ou dépenses occasionnées par le travail typographique. Les questions de paléographie et de critique textuelle ne sont même pas envisagées, donc a fortiori sont passées sous silence les exigences scientifiques minimales pour que l'entreprise puisse se poursuivre dans des conditions acceptables. Or, à cette date, il n'y a plus que quatre religieux pour constituer l'équipe de travail. On peut s'étonner de ce silence sur ce que l'on juge peut-être essentiel, mais on trouvera normal que les incidences financières du projet de transfert administratif n'aient pas été négligées[137] et que les Dominicains n'aient pas voulu

---

137 A titre de compléments des renseignements donnés ici dans d'autres notes, voir ci-dessous n. 143, mais aussi afin de dissiper certains racontars sur un prétendu "trésor de la Léonine", il paraît bon de donner quelques indications sur les aspects financiers de l'entreprise léonine. Les documents manquent pour reconstruire une comptabilité détaillée qui serait d'ailleurs fastidieuse. Voici quelques exemples empruntés aux notes du père Mackey, ils révèlent des ordres de grandeur:

Considérons d'abord les dépenses. L'impression des sept premiers tomes de l'Edition a coûté 142.009,41 L (I: 32.732,89; II: 17.193,31; III: 23.088,81; IV: 18.840,90; V: 25.531,08; VI: 16.164,85; VII: 12.907,40). Pendant ce même laps de temps, il a fallu dépenser au moins 150.000,00 L en

s'engager sans recevoir à ce plan de sérieuses assurances. [138]

En fait, l'opération de transfert des responsabilités et l'opération corrélative de transmission des fonds destinés à assurer le fonctionnement de l'entreprise se sont effectuées par des étapes successives dont voici les stades essentiels: En juillet 1892, se déroule une première opération complexe de liquidation de comptabilités diverses et de transmission de fonds. [139]

dépenses techniques complémentaires des frais d'impression proprement dits, il est vrai qu'il faut inclure dans ce dernier chiffre les dépenses faites en 1880 pour l'achat d'une machine typo et de caractères d'imprimerie, soit 50.000,00 L dont on peut penser qu'il n'y aurait pas lieu de les renouveler de sitôt. A ces dépenses touchant de près ou de loin l'impression, se sont naturellement ajoutés les frais d'entretien des membres du collège des éditeurs, car leur travail à plein temps pour l'Edition ne leur permettait pas des activités apostoliques rapportant des honoraires, à l'exception naturellement des messes quotidiennes célébrées par chacun d'eux. Nous savons par exemple que les dépenses de pension et de vie courante pour les membres du collège des éditeurs se sont élevées à 72.258,78 L de février 1880 à juillet 1886 (pour cette période on compte 10.884,54 L de "vestiaire, blanchissage, poste, café, sucre et tabac", mais nous ne savons si cette somme est incluse ou non dans celle indiquée précédemment).

Comme le pape s'y était engagé, voir ci-dessus n. 5, toutes ces dépenses ont été pour l'essentiel couvertes par le Saint-Siège. Ainsi, pour l'entretien des religieux entre février 1880 et juillet 1886, le pape donne 19.000,00 L et la Congrégation pour la Propagation de la Foi 43.000,00 L, cette dernière somme représentant sans doute le total de versements successifs effectués en application de la décision pontificale du 20 mars 1883 assignant chaque année pour les collaborateurs de la Léonine un total de 10.000,00 L que devait verser le procureur de la dite Congrégation, voir ici n. 120. Dans la même période de février 1880 à juillet, il y a une rentrée totale de 11.227,04 L en intentions de messes, etc. De leur côté, les dépenses typographiques et annexes devaient être assurées par le revenu d'un capital de 300.000,00 L versé par le pape en 1880, voir ci-dessus n. 5, et géré par le cardinal Simeoni et Mgr Jacobini. Nous savons que ce capital était placé pour moitié à Banco di Roma, avec un revenu de 5%, et pour l'autre moitié à Banco Guerrini. En fait le revenu était certainement inférieur à la dépense typographique, en dépit du profit résultant de la vente des ouvrages de 1882 à 1893, puisqu'en 1884 le pape donne 10.000,00 L pour l'impression du deuxième volume.

138   Nous ne savons si ce sont les difficultés financières, ou certaines incidences du processus de transfert engagé de fait avant avril 1892 par le cardinal Zigliara, qui expliquent la note suivante du père Mackey pour le mois de mars 1892:

"Ora passano due anni interi senza che sia permesso di riprendere la stampa, cioè sino a Marzo 1894. Intanto si fa qualche preparazione." On constate en tout cas que le travail typographique pour le t. VIII ne commença en effet qu'en mars 1894; après une interruption à cause d'un désaccord sur le papier, il s'acheva le 14 mai 1895 sauf pour ce qui concerne la préface.

139   Le 15 juillet 1892, le cardinal Zigliara verse au père Frühwirth 8.000,00 L pour l'édiition Léonine. Le 25 juillet 1892, le compte géré par le cardinal Simeoni et Mgr Jacobini est fermé: 81.691,80 L de capital sont transmis à Mgr Mario Mocenni, secrétaire de la commission cardinalice pour l'administration des biens du Saint-Siège; 1.601,80 L représentant le revenu produit par le capital précédent sont remis au cardinal Zigliara qui les transmet le 27 juillet au père Frühwirth.

D'autre part, une décision du 2 septembre 1892 ordonne le transfert des fonds gérés par le cardinal Simeoni, fonds prévus pour l'impression et les dépenses adjacentes, au même Mgr Mocenni. C'est cette décision qui nous révèle ce qui reste du capital de 300.000,00 L constitué à l'origine par Léon XIII: il subsiste alors 21.736,80 L à Banco di Roma et 80.090 à Banco Guerrini, soit au total 101.826,00 L. Mais le document précise "Il fruttato di questo fondo che verrà aumentato da Sua Santità per far fronte alle spese per la continuazione della sudetta edizione dovrà passarsi d'ora innanzi, per ordine della stessa Santità Sua al padre Generale dell' Ordine de'

Le processus reprend un an après, alors que le cardinal Zigliara était mort le 10 mai 1893. Le procureur général des Dominicains fait le 11 novembre 1893 un rapport sur l'affaire du transfert. Le 4 octobre, le pape Léon XIII adresse une lettre apostolique au Père Général de l'Ordre par laquelle se trouve transférée au Maître Général des Dominicains la mission qui avait été confiée en 1879 aux trois cardinaux.[140] Cette décision ne va pas sans soulever de graves inquiétudes mais cette fois encore on ne considère que les incidences financières de l'affaire;[141] il ne semble pas que d'autres problèmes aient été soulevés. Quoi qu'il en soit, la décision du pape est mise en application: le secrétaire de la commission pour l'administration des biens du Saint Siège transfére au Maître de l'Ordre l'administration financière[142] et les

Predicatori. Si prega la S.V. (i. e. Mgr Mario Mocenni) ad accusare ricevuta di questa consegna al sottoscritto." Au même moment, juillet 1892, avait eu lieu la liquidation des comptes typographiques à la Propagande et de la gérance du cavalier Melandri qui en avait été chargé et qui reste débiteur de 5.000,00 L envers la Léonine, note le père Mackey. Enfin, le 2 septembre 1892, une lettre de Mgr Mocenni informe l'Ordre dominicain qu'il y a en banque 101.826,80 L et que les intérêts de ce fonds seront versés tous les six mois au Maître de l'Ordre "per far fronte alle spese per la continuazione della suddetta edizione."

140   Voici le texte, que l'on trouve dans l'Edition léonine, t. VIII, pp. vii-viii:
"Quum certa Nobis spes esset fructus uberrimi qui promanaret ad studia provehenda rerum divinarum solidaeque philosophiae, si nova accuraretur editio operum S. Thomae Aquinatis, partibus omnibus expleta, eo appulimus animum ab ipsis Nostri Pontificatus exordiis. Atque hoc cogitatum Nostrum litteris explicavimus quas idibus Octobris anno MDCCCLXXIX dedimus ad clarae memoriae Virum Cardinalem Antoninum de Luca Praefectum Sacro Consilio Studiis disciplinarum regundis. Ibi et illud adiecimus, placuisse Nobis ut ea ederentur opera cum probatissimis interpretum illorum commentariis. Tum pressius rem urgentes anno subinde insequto a.d. XV Kalendas Februarias, per alias litteras Nostras motu proprio datas huic editioni curandae praefecimus memoratum Cardinalem de Luca, aliosque duos ex eodem Sacro Collegio delectos Viros, Ioannem Simeoni et Thomam Zigliara, quibus ius potestatemque fecimus statuendi Nostro nomine quidquid ad eam rem pertinere intelligerent. Nec segniter illi manus rei gerendae admoverunt, et septem quae jam prodiere volumina dilucide studium demonstrant quo illi contenderint Nostris obtemperare mandatis. Quum vero mors eos praeripuerit, opere nondum absoluto, hujus incepti persequendi perficiendique munus Dominiciano Ordini, cui praes, mandare decrevimus. Tanta est enim in eius alumnis peritia doctrinarum quas summus ille Magister christianae sapientiae tradidit, tanta eorum studia in Illum, cuius nomine ordo universus honestatur mirifice, ut efficiatur. Viris itaque a Te, Dilecte Fili, ex religiosa Familia tua eligendis eam curam demandamus, eosque volumus iis uti praesidiis quae in praedictis Litteris nostris a.d. XV Kalendas Februarias datis anno MDCCCLXXX significavimus, operique sui perfunctionem ad eas normas exigere quas a tribus quos diximus S. R. E. Cardinalibus repererint constitutas. Laeta interim spe erecti operi progresso favorem non defore opemque Divinam quae benigne aggredientibus adfuit, Apostolicam Benedictionem paternae caritatis testem Tibi, Dilecte Fili, et Ordini universo cui praesides peramanter impertimus."

141   Recopiant une lettre du père Cicognani au Maître de l'Ordre, du 22 octobre 1893, le père Mackey note "Si trattava della questione finanziaria." Voici cette note:
"...L'affare dell'edizione delle Opere di San Tommaso, come giace al presente, sarebbe un onere insopportabile per l'Ordine. Al momento, Rmo Padre, non ho che adoperarmi per avere mezzi da mantenere i Padri, e battere, battere forte per ottenere un fondo o un assegno sicuro dal S. Padre..."

142   Le 26 octobre 1893, le directeur de la typographie de la Propagande informe le père Cicognani, procureur général des Dominicains, que de 1880 jusqu'au milieu de l'année 1893 la vente a produit 93.239,15 L.
Chaque tome était tiré en trois qualités différentes, à raison de 500 ex. pour la 1ʳ, 500 ex. la 2ᵉ et

fonds concernant l'édition léonine. [143] Enfin, toujours comme conséquence de la décision pontificale, le 8 janvier 1894, l'équipe de Dominicains travaillant à l'édition quitte l'Académie pour retourner s'installer à l'Ospizio de la Minerve. C'est d'ailleurs une équipe bien réduite qui rejoint cette maison dominicaine: il ne reste plus que trois Léonins, Le P. Huysman ayant regagné la Hollande le 20 juin 1892. [144]

En continuité avec la commission primitive mais sous un statut administratif tout différent, [145] une nouvelle commission pauvre en nombre d'hommes et également en ressources financières allait courageusement poursuivre l'entreprise.

Epilogue.

Le déménagement de l'équipe léonine quittant les locaux de l'Académie Pontificale des nobles ecclésiastiques, le 8 janvier 1894, pour aller s'installer dans des bâtiments réguliers au milieu d'une communauté dominicaine canonique est le dernier acte, mais que l'on peut considérer comme particulièrement symbolique, du long processus qui fit passer la Commission léonine du statut de groupe de trois cardinaux, ou plus réellement d'un cardinal directeur, dirigeant une équipe de travail, à celui d'un groupe structuré de religieux travaillant sous la responsabilité des autorités supérieures de leur Ordre. Ce processus était sans doute inéluctable: la responsabilité passe d'un homme responsable à une institution, par là est assurée la pérennité de l'entreprise mais au risque de la dévitaliser et de la fonctionnariser. En tout cas, il

---

1.000 la 3ᵉ. Voici quelques-uns des prix de vente à cette époque: t. II, 10,69-8,15-7.09; t. IV, 11,50-9,00-7,90; t. V, 12,88-10,08-8,81; t. VII, 7,95-6,15-5,35.

143 D'après le père Mackey, le père Cicognani aurait reçu nominalement, c'est-à-dire fictivement, une somme de 100.000,00 L. Cette dernière précision paraît très vraisemblable à qui fait l'effort de combiner ensemble les chiffres cités ci-dessus nn. 105, 120, 137, 139 et 142, afin de reconstruire approximativement le bilan financier de l'affaire pour les treize premières années de son administration. Il est possible que les 80.000,00 L dont on ne trouve pas trace de transmission représentent la valeur estimée alors du stock des volumes imprimés à l'Ordre. Ce stock devait être assez considérable puisque les volumes étaient tirés à 2.000 exemplaires et que les ventes avaient été les suivantes: t. I, imprimé en 1882, 610 ex. vendus en juin 1885 et 814 au total à la fin de 1888; t. II, imprimé en 1884, 493 ex. vendus en juin 1885 et 734 au total fin 1888; t. III, imprimé en 1884, 547 ex. vendus à la fin de 1888.

144 Le promotion du père Mackey à la maîtrise en théologie en juin 1892 ne pouvait malheureusement pas tenir lieu d'un renforcement de l'équipe en travailleurs.

145 Désormais c'est le Maître de l'Ordre qui passe contrat avec la Propagande pour l'impression: le nouveau contrat est conclu le 15 février 1894 et il sera modifié le 12 décembre 1894. Pour l'essentiel, le statut administratif de la Commission dominicaine pour l'édition des œuvres de S. Thomas n'a plus connu de nouvelles mutations jusqu'à maintenant, exceptées la mise à sa disposition de ressources nouvelles purement locales au Canada pour la section d'Ottawa créée après le chapitre général des Dominicains de 1949, et la création de la Saint Thomas Aquinas Foundation qui soutient financièrement toutes les autres sections depuis 1964.

semble bien qu'à toutes les étapes de ce processus le grand projet de Léon XIII se soit heurté aux mêmes difficultés: tension entre l'autorité qui désire une production rapide et les techniciens au travail qui veulent produire un travail de qualité, difficulté permanente pour avoir une équipe assez nombreuse et assez qualifiée, enfin problèmes financiers insolubles sinon par des expédients. L'histoire ultérieure de la Commission léonine devait bien montrer qu'aucune de ces difficultés ne se trouvait éliminée par l'établissement complet et définitif dans un nouveau statut administratif et un nouveau style de vie quotidienne.

Célébrant le septième centenaire de S. Thomas en commémorant à retardement les quatre-vingt-dix ans de l'Edition léonine et de son équipe d'éditeurs, nous espérons avoir choisi une voie qui ajoute quelques bribes à la documentation déjà mise à la disposition des historiens de métier, leur permettant par là de mieux situer dans leur contexte et dans leurs détails certains actes de Léon XIII et de son entourage. Nous formons en outre le voeu que cette publication de certains documents extraits des archives de la Commission léonine, à vrai dire d'intérêt historique limité, incite au moins les responsables d'autres archives ou dépôts de documents à révéler les trésors qui dorment peut-être dans leurs casiers, ou en tout cas à signaler leur existence. Telle pièce en apparence insignifiante prend en effet beaucoup plus d'intérêt une fois remise dans son contexte et rapprochée éventuellement d'autres pièces conservées ailleurs mais relevant du même ensemble historique.

Mais nous n'avons pas écrit seulement pour les historiens et archivistes, nous osons penser que notre travail permettra à tous de mieux mesurer le travail considérable et les mérites des premiers ouvriers et chefs d'équipe de l'entreprise d'édition critique des œuvres de S. Thomas. Il nous a paru que c'était pour le responsable actuel de cette édition un devoir de tirer les devanciers de l'oubli où les enfonce inexorablement le cours du temps et de leur rendre un hommage qui leur a parfois été mesuré bien chichement, sinon même refusé avec beaucoup d'injustice. Ceci tenant surtout, nous l'espérons, à une ignorance des véritables conditions dans lequelles les premiers léonins avaient dû travailler pendant de longues années, tout en étant contraints précisément, pour sauver l'avenir, de rester discrets sur ces conditions imposées par l'autorité.

Nous sommes en outre tout à fait convaincu que les difficultés et contradictions qui ont affecté, même avant sa naissance mais ensuite tout au long de son développement, l'entreprise léonine d'une nouvelle édition des *Opera omnia* de S. Thomas ne sont pas purement fortuites.

Bien au contraire, à la lumière des développements qui se sont produits ultérieurement, ces difficultés et contradictions paraissent bien substantiellement liées à la nature d'un tel projet; on doit donc toujours les considérer comme imminentes. Une étude consacrée à ces épisodes déjà anciens mériterait donc de retenir aussi l'attention de ceux qui se soucient peu du passé comme tel mais qui ont des responsabilités sur le présent et l'avenir de l'édition critique de S. Thomas. Peut-être même, par analogie, une telle étude pourrait-elle être instructive pour tous les directeurs d'entreprises de même type. Il est vrai qu'il est peut-être naïf d'espérer que les leçons d'un passé même à peine centenaire pourraient être mises à profit par ceux qui aujourd'hui construisent le futur, tant il est clair qu'il est difficile d'échapper au fatal déterminisme en vertu duquel les mêmes causes produisent les mêmes effets. Et c'est bien pourquoi, en ce domaine de l'édition critique comme en tant d'autres qui entrent pourtant dans le champ de la liberté humaine, on voit d'époque en époque se reproduire les mêmes erreurs et se propager les mêmes illusions. Mais, corrélativement, on voit aussi se déployer, dans ce même domaine, des efforts patients et une ténacité qui, envers et contre tout, assurent quand même la continuité du projet.[146]

146 Au terme de ces pages, il est juste que j'exprime ma gratitude au père A. Dondaine qui m'a signalé l'existence des dossiers des archives léonines exploités ici, aux membres de la section du Saulchoir de la Léonine qui ont bien voulu lire son manuscrit et me communiquer leurs remarques, à H. Shooner qui a mis toute son expérience de paléographe à mon service pour le déchiffrement de certains documents qui pour n'être pas médiévaux n'en étaient pas moins difficiles à lire, au père A. Duval, archiviste de la Province de France (Paris) de l'Ordre dominicain, pour ses renseignements et remarques, à Madame Yannick Joubert enfin pour les dactylographies de très nombreux textes cités ici.

VII

ST. THOMAS IN THE 20TH CENTURY

CRÉATION ET HISTOIRE

M. D. Chenu O.P.

CE n'est pas seulement dans la commune sensibilité du peuple
chrétien que la création est exprimée par des images et représen-
tations étrangères à l'histoire; les énoncés métaphysiques eux-mêmes ne
sont pas sans prêter à une interprétation de la création — soit l'acte
créateur, du côté de Dieu, soit la dépendance ontologique, du côté de la
créature — comme en dehors du temps. Même à qui a su coordonner
une vision évolutive du cosmos avec l'Absolu créateur, la création
comme telle, à l'état pur, comme relation de Créateur à créature, n'est
pas liée au temps. On sait avec quelle tenace assurance saint Thomas
d'Aquin a enseigné, au grand scandale des *murmurantes*, qu'un "commencement" du monde n'est pas inclus dans l'intelligibilité de la
création. L'histoire semble donc n'être qu'un élément adventice, si
urgent soi-il de fait, à la conception de l'acte créateur. Ainsi se présente
l'image de la transcendance, dans ce Dieu "éternel", en sa toute suffisance. N'est-ce pas déjà le faux dieu, immobile et muet, du déisme de
Voltaire et de Sartre?

Sans céder à un superficiel concordisme avec le problème contemporain de l'historicité du monde et de l'homme, il est permis de
repérer dans l'analyse des maîtres spéculatifs du moyen âge, en particulier de saint Thomas d'Aquin, les points d'appel à fonder dans la
Création même la réalité *historique* de l'univers, l'origine *théologique*
de l'histoire.[1]

FONDEMENT ANTHROPOLOGIQUE DE L'HISTOIRE

L'économie de la création ne peut être comprise sans l'homme, qui lui
donne avec son accomplissement sa signification, terrestre et "céleste".
Voici: l'homme, créé pour lui-même, mais aussi comme maître du
monde et de son histoire, participe ainsi à la création. Il est partenaire

---

1 D'un bout à l'autre, référence sera faite aux chapitres de l'ouvrage de M. Seckler, *Das Heil in
der Geschichte. Geschichtstheologisches Denken bei Thomas von Aquin* (München 1964), trad. fr.
Le salut dans l'histoire (Paris 1967), où il aborde ce problème. Ainsi répondrai-je, en communion
de pensée, à la référence qu'il fait généreusement à ma propre reflexion, en particulier dans mon
article "Situation humaine: corporalité et temporalité," 2ᵉ éd. dans *L'Evangile dans le temps* (Paris
1964), 411-436.

de Dieu dans la construction du monde. La réalisation de cette virtualité de l'homme implique corrélativement l'expérience de la réalité en tant qu'histoire. L'homme est impensable en dehors de l'histoire, en même temps qu'il confère à l'univers une dimension historique.

Ce n'est pas là caprice de Prakhriti. L'acte de créer implique dans sa "production" une "multiplication", une "distinction"[2]: c'est-à-dire que Dieu ne peut émaner "quelque chose" sans que ce soit, au sens originel du mot, un *univers*. En effet la raison de l'entreprise divine se trouve dans l'urgence d'un Amour qui éprouve le besoin — si l'on ose dire — de se communiquer à un autre, en lequel il mette sa complaisance, comme en une représentation à la fois autonome et immanente, puisque aucun être ne peut être hors de l'Etre ou en une quelconque addition. "Dieu créa l'homme à son image, à l'image de Dieu il le créa": telle est la densité rationnelle du texte religieux de la Genèse (1: 27).

Or qui dit représentation de Dieu se trouve devant l'inévitable multiplicité: Dieu ne peut être représenté suffisamment par une créature finie; la multiplication diversifiée des créatures est la suppléance de leur débilité. "Dieu a produit les choses dans l'être pour communiquer sa bonté aux créatures, et la représenter en elles. Et parce qu'elle ne peut être représentée efficacement par une seule créature, il a créé des choses multiples et diverses, de telle manière que ce qui manque à l'une pour représenter la divine bonté, soit suppléé par l'autre. Ainsi la bonté qui est en Dieu simple et unique, se trouve dans les créatures démultipliée et différenciée. En conséquence, c'est tout l'univers qui participe parfaitement la bonté de Dieu et la représente, plus qu'aucune créature".[3] Cette Unité, en puissance d'émanation, dans la conjonction de l'Un et du Bien, est la raison de la souveraineté du Créateur, pour laquelle Bonaventure crée le mot de *primitas*.[4]

Cette nécessité métaphysique est ressentie par certains mystiques, chrétiens ou non, comme une défaillance radicale, et par les néoplatoniciens comme l'origine d'une dispersion, d'une chute permanente, que l'incessante prolifération des êtres ne peut ressaisir.[5] La

---

2 "Productio" et "distinctio": c'est à partir de ces deux catégories que saint Thomas développe son traité de la création dans la *Somme*, I pars, qu. 47, et tous les chapitres 40 à 46 de la *Somme contre les Gentils*, livre II.

3 "Utrum rerum multitudo et distinctio sint a Deo", *Summa Theologiae* I, 47, 1. Cf. *Contra Gentiles* II, 45.

4 Cf. J. G. Bougerol, *Lexique de saint Bonaventure* (Paris 1969), s. v.

5 Analyse technique de cette admirable tentation, dans l'histoire de la pensée grecque et arabe, par saint Thomas, *De Potentia* 3, 16: "Utrum ab Uno primo possit procedere multitudo." Réponse: La perfection de chaque individu dans l'unité, n'est réalisable que dans un univers lui-même unifié: "Sicut Deus est unus, ita et unum produxit, non solum quia unumquodque in se est unum, sed etiam quia omnia quodammodo sunt unum perfectum, quae quidem unitas diversitatem partium requirit". Ibid. ad 1.

"dyade"—entendez la rupture première de l'Unité—est au principe de la détresse, de la malédiction originelle du monde.[6] Que l'homme soit ainsi livré au flux de l'histoire est le signe d'un irréparable échec à son unité. D'où la répugnance de certains théologiens à l'histoire, fût-ce l'histoire du salut.

Saint Thomas ne cède pas à cette interprétation pessimiste. L'entreprise est au contraire œuvre de "sagesse": réaliser l'émanation de son Etre dans une coordination de ces êtres finis, c'est "l'univers", qui est un *ordo*.

Au sommet de cet univers, de cette "hiérarchie", *ordo sacer* (Denys), l'homme en récapitule les "degrés", en être et en valeur, auxquels il imprime leur dynamisme ontologique, dans une articulation progressive de leurs niveaux. En lui, toutes les énergies, de la matière à l'esprit, accèdent à la conscience. L'homme humanise la nature. L'histoire est ainsi le lieu humain de la Création. Vision biblique du monde, sous son appareillage grec, et non vision antique.

HISTOIRE ET SOCIABILITÉ

De cette réalisation progressive de l'image de Dieu dans le monde, la constitution même de l'homme — ce "microcosme" — est effectivement le centre névralgique, là où la divinisation s'investit dans l'humanité, non seulement en ses individus éphémères, mais dans la continuité de l'*univers* — matière comprise — et de son histoire.

Car la multiplication, à ce haut niveau aussi, est dans la logique de l'entreprise créatrice. Certes les individus humains sont des "personnes", dignes d'amour comme telles, dans la communion de l'image de Dieu; elles sont voulues pour elles-mêmes, et la multiplication des personnes est une fin en soi. Cependant, chaque individu est radicalement insuffisant à réaliser sa nature en plénitude: l'homme n'est homme que dans la communauté de tous les hommes. C'est à ce point qu'il est, par nature, "social": articulation rigoureuse de l'individu et de l'espèce pour que soit réalisable, concrètement, la perfection. Ce n'est pas par une vague suppléance que la nature est assouvie par le génie de l'espèce, dans une prolifération permanente: l'intention de la nature rencontre le but de la Création, représentation durable du Créateur dans une réalité extra-divine. Le maintien biologique de l'espèce n'est

---

6 Entre tant d'expressions de ce grand thème néoplatonicien, banalisé au moyen âge, cf. le manuel du temps *Historia scolastica* de Pierre Comestor, Gen. c. 4; PL 198, 1059: "Binarius infamis numerus est in theologia, quia primus ab unitate recedit; Deus autem Unitas est, et sectionem et discordiam detestatur".

point la manifestation matérielle d'un éternel recommencement, dans des individus juxtaposés; il compose la trame d'une multiplication qui donne son sens à l'évolution temporelle. Le temps n'est plus seulement la succession ponctuelle d'instants physiques, nombre immanent du mouvement; il est la mesure intérieure d'une destinée, incluse en quelque manière dans le dessein éternel d'une providence transcendante, actualisée dans la conscience, personnelle et collective.

Or, pour saint Thomas, à l'encontre de ses contemporains qui le condamnèrent pour ce "matérialisme", cette genèse de l'histoire par l'articulation de l'espèce et de l'individu se fait par et dans la matière; la matière est le principe de l'individuation. L'homme ne devient une personne que dans un corps; son "incarnation" est à la fois le principe d'individualité, de sociabilité, d'historicité. L'ange n'a ni sociabilité ni histoire; il est stérile, dans sa suffisance. Parce qu'il n'est pas un pur esprit, mais un esprit qui s'anime dans la matière, l'homme n'est présent à lui-même qu'en sortant de soi. Il ne se voit dans sa réalité intérieure qu'en se tournant vers le monde des objets et des hommes. Il n'est personne que lorsqu'il est avec une autre personne; la conscience de soi est la conscience d'un soi-dans-le-monde, une conscience d'être avec les autres hommes. Ainsi la structure métaphysique de l'homme comporte une ouverture radicale à l'histoire et une dépendance de l'histoire. C'est donc dans le tissu social élémentaire que s'exerce historiquement l'acte créateur, si'il est vrai que l'homme est, par son corps, non seulement un être-dans-le-monde, mais un individu qui ne s'accomplit que par son ouverture à l'autre.[7]

Un certain personnalisme, tout centré sur l'intériorité, ne rend pas compte du devenir social, malgré l'exaltation des amours intersubjectifs. De fait, ce spiritualisme est insensible, en même temps qu'à la réalité de l'histoire et à son intérêt humain, à la dureté objective des rapports de justice sur lesquels la société structure ses droits. Le bien commun, dit au contraire saint Thomas, *divinius est* que la somme des libertés personnelles. "Bonum ordinis diversorum est melius quolibet illorum ordinatorum per se sumpto; est enim formale respectu singularium sicut perfectio totius respectu partium".[8]

La conception hylémorphique aristotélicienne, à laquelle recourt saint Thomas dans son anthropologie, radicalise à ce point, de manière imprévisible pour le Philosophe, l'historicité de l'homme. La densité du

---

7 Cf. K. Rahner, *Hörer des Wortes*, 2ᵉ ed. (München 1963), p. 147 ff. Ed. Schillebeckx, *Intelligence de la foi et interprétation de soi*, dans *Théologie d'aujourd'hui et de demain*. Congrès de Chicago, 1966 (Paris 1967), 122-125.
8 *Summa contra Gentiles* II, 45.

temps vécu se double de la densité des générations qui composent la société. L'histoire est, par définition, sociale. Histoire de l'homme, elle embraye sur l'histoire de la nature. Les instants du temps et les libertés des individus ne deviennent une histoire que par et dans une sociabilité des hommes qui vivent dans ce temps. L'histoire est le lieu humain de la Création.

*

* *

Ainsi mesurons-nous la double dimension de la Création, dans l'*ordo* qui manifeste son émanation, l'unité de son émanation. Les choses créées sont non seulement en relation avec l'Etre créateur (*ordo ad deum*), mais en relation entre elles (*ordo ad invicem*). Sans doute cette seconde articulation est-elle réductible à la première, puisqu'elle a pour raison d'être de conduire l'univers à sa fin, la représentation analogique de la perfection de l'Etre pur; mais elle a sa consistance propre. La perfection de l'univers est entièrement immanente au monde. "Post bonitatem divinam, quae est finis a rebus separatus, principale bonum *in ipsis rebus existens* est perfectio universi".[9] Cet *ordo rebus inditus* a un sens déchiffrable, sans détriment pour le sens transcendant, dans la réalité de Dieu dans l'au-delà, *bonum separatum*. Tel est précisément le "mystère" de la Création.

Tout ceci implique que, si la relation absolue et unique à Dieu forme l'horizon fondamental et co-conscient de nos multiples relations conscientes avec le monde et à l'intérieur de celles-ci, cette relation absolue entre dans la conscience qu'a l'homme de lui-même dans et par les relations relatives à nos semblables et au monde. Aussi ne pouvons-nous pas séparer cette relation absolue à Dieu de nos relations historiquement conditionnées et intramondaines, à ce monde et à ces semblables. Nous ne pouvons donc pas formaliser cette relation à Dieu et l'abstraire de la trame historique de notre existence.[10]

Un double courant anime ainsi la Création, l'un qui aimante directement chaque chose vers son Créateur ("Ad hoc unaquaeque res tendit ut participet ipsum, et assimiletur ei inquantum potest"[11]); l'autre qui

---

9 *Summa Theol.* I, 22, 3; et on ajoute: "...perfectio universi, quae quidem non esset si non omnes gradus essendi invenirentur in rebus". Une fois de plus, la Création implique démultiplication, dans l'unité hiérarchique de l'univers.
Cf. aussi *Summa Theol.* I, 103, 2, ad 3m: "Finis universi est aliquod bonum *in ipso existens*, scilicet *ordo* ipsius universi."
10 Cf. Ed. Schillebeeckx, op. cit., p. 125, qui continue: "Par rapport à moi, Dieu, le Transcendant, n'a d'autre fondement que la contingence et la gratuité de mon existence historique".
11 *Summa Theol.* I, 103, 2.

ordonne les choses à la perfection de l'ensemble créé, dont elles sont des parties. L'infidelité au corps social en tant que tel, dans la construction de l'univers, au delà du contrat des individus et de la liberté des amours, est un échec à la Création, dont l'humanité est le démiurge.[12] Telle est la loi du "retour" vers Dieu, selon la dynamique même de l'émanation.

FONDEMENT THÉOLOGIQUE DE L'HISTOIRE

Emanation-retour: c'est le grand thème néoplatonicien de l'*exitus*, qui vient donc ici sous-tendre l'intelligence de l'historicité de l'homme. A l'encontre d'une interprétation strictement aristotélicienne de la philosophie de saint Thomas, on a remis en place et en valeur, dans sa vision du monde, les éléments néoplatoniciens. Non seulement on a rendu leur fécondité aux sources vives que furent pour lui Denys et le *Liber de causis*, sans parler d'Avicenne, tous les deux commentés en pleine page, non seulement on a reconnu dans le plan de la *Somme théologique* l'architecture et le dynamisme de l'*exitus-reditus*, mais on a décelé dans le tissu même de la pensée de l'Aquinate des trames soutenues de métaphysique néoplatonicienne. Le traité de la création est le secteur le plus propice à ce discernement. L'opération est d'autant plus significative que ce recours au néoplatonisme pour fonder le dynamisme historique de la création, pour articuler temporalité et éternité, va à l'encontre de la logique idéaliste et essentialiste du système. Paradoxe d'autant plus vif que l'opération est menée en concurrence avec l'aristotélisme, étranger pour sa part à toute ouverture au créationnisme dans une divinité Acte pur. Ce paradoxe animait déjà la prétention de Boèce, dans son projet de faire concorder Platon et Aristote.

Il ne faudrait certes pas céder à une réaction inverse: la notion thomiste de création reste élaborée sur l'axe de l'être, et non sur une émanation à partir de l'Un, inaccessible au delà de la multiplicité des "idées", créatrices et créées à la fois, théophanies de cet Un qui, dans sa surexistentialité, ne peut être engagé dans une création des êtres, pas plus qu'il n'en peut être connu. *Superexaltata unitas* (Denys, *De divinis nominibus*, c. 5). Si plein de révérence soit-il pour Denys, saint Thomas se dégage de ce transcendantalisme absolu, et assure l'individualisation des relations des créatures à Dieu.

Denys cependant demeure présent, en sous-œuvre, pour écarter, comme incompatible avec la doctrine de l'Un, une représentation trop

---

12 Bonhoeffer dit aujourd'hui, dans son *Ethique*: "Il s'agit d'avoir part aujourd'hui à la réalité de Dieu et du monde, de telle manière que je n'éprouve jamais la réalité de Dieu sans celle du monde, et vice versa."

humaine de l'intelligence divine traitée comme le lieu des "idées", dans des déterminations et des multiplications produites par une activité idéologique. Il n'y a pas des "vérités éternelles", dont les réalités temporelles, dans l'univers et dans l'humanité, ne seraient qu'une projection sans consistance propre, tout étant déjà fait en Dieu. Les créatures préexistent en Dieu, mais leur idée n'est autre que l'essence créatrice. L'Un n'est aucunement une réserve d'essence. Il n'y a en Dieu aucune complexité, parce qu'il n'y a aucune référence réelle à ses créatures; leur connaissance, et avec elle, leur participabilité, est impliquée dans la connaissance que Dieu a de lui-même. Ainsi la relation de créature a ceci de déconcertant pour la logique humaine des relations, qu'elle est unilatérale, du seul côté de la créature. Dieu ne peut être relatif à un autre, car, si un autre est, il est en Dieu. La diversité et la multiplication, loi de l'émanation créatrice et de la perfection de l'univers, ne contredisent point l'Ab-solu du Créateur. La transcendance est dialectiquement la garantie de l'immanence. Ces deux dimensions de l'acte créateur composent, en même temps que la vérité de la nature, la densité de l'histoire. Parce que l'emprise créatrice est totale, *profundens totum esse*, elle n'entre pas en concurrence avec la créature: "impermixtio causae primae ad res alias".[13] La transcendance garantit, avec la pureté totale de l'acte créateur, l'auto-réalisation de l'être créé, qui dans l'homme accède à la conscience et à l'histoire.

On saisira mieux les ressources du néoplatonisme dionysien, sous les nécessaires rectifications que lui apporte saint Thomas, en le comparant au platonisme augustinien, alors excellemment exploité dans l'exemplarisme de saint Bonaventure. Autant Augustin, comme chrétien, est pénétré de l'immanence de Dieu dans la nature et dans l'histoire, personnelle et collective, autant il reste court, en instrumentation philosophique, dans son ontologie de l'immuable transcendance de l'Essence, pour rendre raison d'un devenir où le temps n'est que la décomposition inintelligible de l'éternité, seul lieu de l'être et de la vérité. Les activités et la croissance des êtres ne sont que le déploiement de ce que les formes éternelles précontiennent. L'existence de chaque chose et la durée qui la mesure ne sont que la réfraction visible des essences invisibles, qui, elles, dans leur vérité, ne naissent ni ne périssent. L'histoire n'est plus qu'une ombre. Le monde n'est pas la demeure de l'homme.[14]

---

13 *Expositio super Librum de causis*, prop. 20. Lire tout le chapitre. "Unde, cum essentia (causae primae) sit maxime una, quia primum principium est secundum se unum et bonum, consequens est quod causa prima uno modo, quantum est ex parte sua, agat in res et influat in eas. Sed ex ejus influxu res diversimode recipiunt, quaedam plus et quaedam minus, unaquaeque secundum suam proprietatem."

14 Cf. E. Gilson, *Le thomisme*, 4° éd. (Paris 1942), 190-191.

Saint Thomas n'a rien d'un historien; mais sa conception de l'homme-dans-le-monde fournit les bases d'une sociologie où l'efficacité et l'intelligibilité des causes secondes, loin de concurrencer l'éternelle Providence de Dieu, la réalisent dans le temps et dans la vérité terrestre de l'histoire, la sainte et la profane. Dans le thomisme, "l'emprise créatrice de Dieu donne consistance à la durée temporelle".[15]

*

*   *

Si Dieu n'a aucune relation réelle avec la créature comme avec un objet, on ne peut chercher dans la créature la cause de l'initiative créatrice: elle est toute entière en Dieu. Dieu ne peut vouloir que soi-même, lors même que, par surabondance, il se veut et s'aime dans les participations finies de sa propre perfection. Si motif il y a, il lui est coessentiel. Son vouloir, sa bonté en expansion, sont son être même et son essence.[16]

Mais précisément la bonté est par essence communicative; la suprême Bonté est suprêmement communicative. *Bonum est diffusivum sui.* De cet axiome dionysien, qui pourrait incliner à une "naturelle" émanation, saint Thomas tire admirablement parti, pour manifester la suprême gratuité de la création dans la liberté souveraine du Créateur. L'initiative procédant de l'amour va rompre l'apparente antinomie de la transcendance et de l'immanence, et donner un sens au monstre logique d'une relation unilatérale de la créature à son Créateur. Telle est en effet la toute puissance ce cette communication du Bien, que les créatures ne sont pas la projection d'un égoïsme, mais des êtres voulus, réalisés, aimés, pour eux-mêmes. L'univers, en cela encore, a consistance en ses natures, dont la "propriété" n'est point dissoute, ni instrumentalisée, ce qui serait une dérision de l'amour.[17] L'Amour, ici, porté selon sa loi à son incandescence, confère à "l'autre" totalement émané de lui, une consistance telle que cet autre est vraiment autre, comme si Dieu entrait dans la dépendance de celui qu'il aime. Le contraire d'une aliénation de

---

15 A. Hayen, "La connaissance humaine selon saint Thomas," *Rev. phil. de Louvain*, 1956, 589.

16 *Expositio super Librum de causis*, prop. 20: "Habet enim causa prima bonitatem bonificam, id est quae est principium bonitatis in omnibus. Bonitas autem cause primae est ipsum suum esse et sua essentia, quia causa prima est ipsa essentia bonitatis."

17 *De potentia* 5, 4: "Deus creaturarum universitatem vult *propter seipsam*, licet et *propter seipsum* eam vult esse; haec enim duo non repugnant. Vult enim Deus ut creaturae sint propter ejus bonitatem, ut eam scilicet suo modo imitentur et repraesentant; quod quidem faciunt in quantum ab ea esse habent et *in suis naturis subsistunt....* Sic enim Deus unamquamque naturam instituit, ut ei non auferat *suam proprietatem.*"

la créature. Par le mystère de l'acte créateur, nous nous élevons au mystère de l'amour gratuit et libre. Identité de l'Etre et de l'Amour: c'est le sens de la genèse créatrice. La dépendance ontologique est transmuée par la certitude d'un amour.

Si toute chose est saisie par un pareil amour, ainsi inviscéré en toute créature, "le mouvement universel de la nature se définit à la fois comme une auto-réalisation et comme un dépassement de soi. Tout être est habité par un sens de transcendance. Dans la terminologie que reprend saint Thomas, ce sens de transcendance s'appelle *amour*. Toute créature aime donc le tout plus que soi-même, et Dieu plus que le tout".[18] Ce comportement "extatique" fait partie de la condition vécue de la créature, c'est-à-dire d'un être fini, dépendant, qui trouve dans cette dépendance même le seul achèvement possible et adéquat à sa nature. Le "retour", par le dynamisme même des natures, selon leur "émanation".

Que si, dans cet univers des êtres et des natures, nous considérons et nous situons l'homme, qui en est le démiurge et la conscience (cf. notre première réflexion), nous franchissons le seuil de l'instinct de l'esprit, *voluntas ut natura*, de l'intelligence, de la liberté, de la responsabilité. Toutes choses, toutes formes, toutes valeurs, en lui récapitulées, revêtent une nouvelle existence, dans l'unité de l'univers, macrocosme et microcosme, où la Nature et l'Histoire embrayent l'une sur l'autre. "L'homme achève, à son niveau, le processus d'intériorisation et de réflexion qu'esquissait déjà la dialectique du mouvement. Il l'achève dans une immanence spirituelle dont les affinités avec le tout confèrent aux choses d'ici-bas une nouvelle unité et une nouvelle existence".[19] Quand le chrétien investit sa foi en l'Incarnation de Dieu dans "cette créature en attente de sa libération" (Rom. 8: 22), il l'appellera la Nouvelle Création.

En débouchant ainsi sur la foi chrétienne, nous sortons en quelque sorte de la ligne de notre méditation sur la Création. Nous ne pouvons faire autrement, si la Création implique Histoire, dès lors que Dieu est lui-même entré dans l'Histoire. Mais dès avant cela, la notion de Création a débordé la pure analyse philosophique de la causalité et de l'Acte pur: elle s'est ouverte à la "religion" — relation de la créature au Créateur — disons, hors toute ambiguïté, au "mystère". Sans doute est-ce le mot adéquat, s'il est vrai que l'Amour résout seul l'antinomie entre un Dieu qui, s'il est Dieu, est incommunicable et inaccessible dans sa suffisance, et un Dieu dont la Bonté est substantiellement communicable de soi. *Unum et Bonum*.

18 St. Breton, *Saint Thomas d'Aquin* (Paris 1965), 51-52.
19 St. Breton, op. cit., p. 59.

ST. THOMAS' DOCTRINE OF SUBJECT AND PREDICATE

A POSSIBLE STARTING POINT FOR LOGICAL REFORM AND RENEWAL

Henry Veatch

LOGIC was hardly St. Thomas' forte. Apart from his commentaries on Aristotle's *Perihermeneias* (which only goes through Ch. II of Book II) and the *Posterior Analytics,* the passages are comparatively[1] few and far between in which St. Thomas might be said to have given anything like an *ex professo* treatment of questions of logic. Nor, as far as we know, is there any place in his writings where he seems to have shown any special competence in, much less made any distinctive contribution to, what today would be called formal logic in the strict sense.

No doubt, the immediate effect of such an admission can only be to make St. Thomas lose caste with most, if not all, of today's formal logicians — supposing that he ever enjoyed caste with them in the first place. Still, discredit in such quarters need not necessarily mean that St. Thomas should simply be written off as a lost soul in matters of logic. For one thing, doctrinaire logicians to the contrary notwithstanding, there surely is more to logic than formal logic; and that more could even be well-nigh all-important. For another thing, so far as St. Thomas' own scattered and various comments of a non-formal nature on the subject of logic are concerned, these have not only borne a not inconsiderable fruit in the past, but they also — a fact which may not be so generally known — have begun to bear a kind of fruit among logicians even in the present day. Thus, witness the writings of Professor Geach. For we have his own word for it that he wishes to bear unmistakeable, even if rather solitary, testimony to the importance of St. Thomas as a non-formal logician. And although some may find the

---

1 This term we use quite advisedly, particularly in view of the remarkable array of citations having to do with logic that Father Robert Schmidt has assembled in his book *The Domain of Logic according to Saint Thomas Aquinas* (The Hague 1951). The author explains that the aim of his study is "to present the doctrine of St. Thomas on the domain of logic and on the nature of this science directly from the works of St. Thomas." Nor can it be denied that the aim is impressively borne out by the performance.

logical fruit that is thus produced by the graft of Geach upon Aquinas to be a rather strange fruit, it at least is not a forbidden fruit save only perhaps in respect of its comparative unintelligibility.

a. *St. Thomas' Principle of Predication: Wholes Must be Predicated of Wholes*

Be this as it may, in this present study we should like to single out a particular feature of St. Thomas' teaching in regard to the logical relation of subject-predicate,[2] which we believe merits a more careful consideration and perhaps even a long overdue exploitation. Unhappily, it would appear to be a feature that has been largely passed over in silence by most contemporary authorities whose judgment is especially deserving of respect. Thus Geach,[3] directly in his various and highly sophisticated attempts to rehabilitate St. Thomas' teaching in regard to subject and predicate, and to approximate that teaching to the more recent views of Frege, seems to have studiously avoided even mentioning this particular point in St. Thomas' treatment of the topic. No more does Father Schmidt — to mention a scholar of very different interests and background from Geach — consider that this point merits any special discussion or treatment in his monumental study of *The Domain of Logic according to Saint Thomas Aquinas.*[4]

Could it be, though, that the not inconsequential remark about "the stone which the builders rejected" etc. might have a figurative, and hopefully a not irreverent, application even in the history of logic! In any case this neglected point which we have chosen to single out is one which St. Thomas seems to enunciate most clearly in Chapter II of the *De Ente et Essentia.*[5] There the principle emerges — and certainly it does not sound like a very significant principle when it does first emerge — that in the matter of predication, it is never a part that is

---

2   In the ensuing discussion, we shall speak more or less indifferently of the relation of subject to predicate and of predicate to subject. Not that the two are the same; rather it is as Fr. Schmidt notes: One can speak of "the relation of attribution or predication, in which the predicate of the proposition is the subject of the relation. It would be possible to consider the relation in the other direction, making the subject of the proposition its subject. We should then have the relation of *subjicibility* or of *subjection*. Since subject and predicate are correlative, we always have the two relations at the same time." (Op. cit., p. 239, n. 169).

3   The only essays of Geach to which we shall have occasion to refer in this study are "Subject and Predicate" in *Reference and Generality* (Ithaca 1962) 22-46, and "Form and Existence" in *God and the Soul* (New York 1969) 42-64.

4   See the reference given in note 1 above.

5   Unless otherwise indicated, our references to this work will be to the second edition of Father Maurer's translation, *On Being and Essence* (Toronto 1968).

predicated of a whole, but always a whole of a whole.[6] And the illustration used is of the term "humanity" which, St. Thomas explains, "signifies" man's very nature or essence, or "that by which man is man."[7] At the same time, "humanity" may not be predicated of any individual man. One cannot say, for example, "Socrates is humanity"; rather one has to say "Socrates is human" or "is a man."

Moreover, the explanation which St. Thomas gives of this seemingly trivial fact of logic, or even of grammar, is that since "humanity" signifies the essence of man just as such — i.e. taken in precision both from designated matter as well as from such accidental features and characteristics as pertain to individual men like Socrates[8] — Socrates' human nature or essence, considered in this way, is but a part of the concrete whole which is the individual man, Socrates. Accordingly, our not being able to predicate "humanity" of "Socrates" may be taken to exemplify that first part of Aquinas' general logical principle in regard to predication, viz. that a part cannot be predicated of a whole.

But now contrast the term "man" or "human being." Although this term, no less than "humanity," does indeed signify the essence of man, it nevertheless "expresses it as a whole, because it does not prescind from the designation of matter, but contains it implicitly and indistinctly ... that is why the term 'man' can be predicated of individuals."[9] Here, then, we have an explanation of that other half of St. Thomas' principle, viz. that in the matter of predications only wholes may be predicated of wholes.

b. *Three Points of Commentary on the Principle*

What, though, is one to make of this rather odd-sounding principle that St. Thomas seems thus to have enunciated in the *De Ente et Essentia*? In answer, we propose to put forward and discuss three major considerations which we hope may serve more or less as commentaries on the principle.

---

6 Although it might be supposed that in matters of logic Aquinas did little more than follow the lead of Aristotle, the fact is that on any number of points St. Thomas went far beyond his master in an effort to clarify, expand, and interpret Aristotle's teaching. Certainly, unless we be very much mistaken, on this very point about the necessity of predicating wholes of wholes, St. Thomas is putting forward a logical principle which is nowhere explicit in Aristotle, if it is even so much as implicit with him.

7 Maurer translation (op. cit.), Ch. II, n. 11, p. 43.

8 For an alternative statement of the same point, cf. St. Thomas, *In Meta.*, Liber VII, lectio V, nn. 1378-1380.

9 Maurer, op. cit., n. 13, p. 44.

1. Clearly, the principle is one which St. Thomas appears to think is proper to logic and to logic alone. For not only does he advance it as a principle governing the distinctively logical relation of predicate to subject[10] in propositions; but in addition, he chooses to exhibit the distinctive character of this logical relation by contrasting it with what one might not improperly call "ontological" relations.[11]

Specifically, in the passage which we have cited from the *De Ente et Essentia,* the contrast is drawn between the relation of predication in "Socrates is a human being" and the relation of Socrates to his humanity. The latter relation, presumably, is one which holds between an individual man, Socrates, and his nature or essence, or that in virtue of which he is a man, viz. his humanity. Now surely, such a relation must be of the kind we have termed "ontological." That is to say, it is a real relation, or a relation that may be said to hold *in rerum natura.*[12] In fact, it is just such a relation as the scholastics later came to call that of essence to supposit, and which Aristotle seems to have worried himself sick over, to say nothing of his readers, in Book Z of the *Metaphysics.*

However, it is not merely the ontological relation of supposit to essence that could have been used to point the contrast with a properly logical relation like that of subject to predicate. No, for the ontological relation of substance to accident might have done just as well, or even that of matter to form or of potency to act. For example, just as one may say "Socrates is a man," but not "Socrates is humanity," so also one may perfectly well say "Socrates is bald," but not "Socrates is baldness." Baldness, indeed, is but an accident[13] of the substance, Socrates.

---

10 Cf. note 2 above.

11 This is clearly not a Thomistic term. Yet in view of the use of the word "ontology" by any number of contemporary American philosophers, we thought it not unilluminating to speak of "ontological relations," in contrast to "logical relations," as a way of pointing up much the same contrast as interpreters of St. Thomas are wont to draw between "real relations" and "relations of reason" or "rationate relations," as Father Schmidt would call them (op. cit. Part II, ch. VI).

12 Since it is definitely not within our competence, it is fortunate that it happens not to be within our responsibility in this paper on the logical relation of predication to discuss the nature and kinds of real or ontological relations. That so-called predicamental relations would be examples of the latter would certainly be beyond dispute. Yet in pointing up the contrast between a logical relation like that of subject-predicate and various real relations, St. Thomas does not tend to use examples of predicamental relations. Instead, he uses examples more like those of supposit-essence or substance-accident. Now formerly it was not unusual for interpreters of St. Thomas, following John of St. Thomas, to call relations of the latter type "transcendental relations." After Krempel's strictures, however (see his *La Doctrine de la relation chez Saint Thomas,* Paris 1952), both this term, as well as the notion which it expresses, seem to have fallen into rather bad odor. As a result, it has become somewhat difficult accurately to characterize the exact ontological status that St. Thomas would ascribe to such relations as were formerly called "transcendental." For our purposes, though, it is enough if we simply consider them as real relations in contrast to logical relations and let it go at that.

13 Of course, in strictness "baldness' is not an accident at all, being only a privation and not

Moreover, such an accident might be said to have been no less a part of the total complex of substance-plus-accidents that comprised the man, Socrates, than was Socrates' essence, considered just as such, a mere part of that total concrete whole that was the man Socrates. Accordingly, both of these ontological relationships would exemplify what in Aquinas' terminology would be relations of whole to part, whereas, as we have seen, what is requisite for a logical relationship such as that of subject-predicate is that it be a relation of whole to whole.

Besides, so long as we are drawing upon a somewhat rough and ready Aristotelian and Thomistic ontology for examples, we might well have used, as we have already remarked, examples of matter-form or potency-act, no less than those of supposit-essence or substance-accident. Here again, one might say, these are examples of real relations: matter is really related to form, as is potency to act. Presumably, also, just because they are real relations, they cannot and must not be taken to be relations of subjects to predicates. Thus matter cannot, strictly speaking, even be said to be its form, any more than a substance can ever be its accident. Indeed, if a substance were an accident — say, a quantity or a quality or what not, — then it would truly be an accident and not a substance at all. So also if the ontological distinction between matter and form is to be maintained, then matter can never as such be said to be a form.

So much, then, for our first point of commentary on St. Thomas' principle of predication that only wholes may be predicated of wholes.

2. As for our second consideration, it bears more directly on the somewhat awkward terminology involved in saying that one has to predicate wholes of wholes. For what can St. Thomas mean by this? It can hardly be said to be idiomatic English — though this, doubtless, could hardly be reckoned a disability, so far as St. Thomas is concerned. What is more disturbing, though, is that even as technical jargon it is none-too-illuminating. Happily on this score, though, St. Thomas seems not to have been content with mere jargon. Instead, he undertakes to clarify the notion of a relation of whole to whole in terms of what he holds is a certain identity between the two. What is being propounded or asserted, he says, in any affirmative subject-predicate proposition is a kind of identity as between subject and predicate:

> ... sciendum est quod in qualibet propositione affirmativa vera oportet quod praedicatum et subjectum significent idem secundum rem

properly subsumable under any of the ten categories. (Cf. *On Being and Essence*, Ch. I, nn. 2 and 3). However, there can be no objection to our treating baldness as if it were an accident, just for purposes of illustration.

> aliquo modo, et diversum secundum rationem ... Manifestum est
> enim quod *homo* et *albus* sunt idem subjecto et differunt ratione; alia
> enim est *ratio hominis* et *ratio albi*.[14]

Note that St. Thomas does not say here that the relation of subject to predicate simply is one of identity, in the sense that the subject may be said to be identical with the predicate.[15] Rather what he says is that such a relation signifies a kind of (*aliquo modo*) identity *secundum rem*. And even this is puzzling. Still, it is not hard to see in a general way what Aquinas is driving at here. For to say of a man, for example, that he is white is not to say that he is a white peacock or a white elephant or a white monkey or a white whale, or even a white anything else, but simply that he is a white man.[16] Not only that, but the white man that one might be said to be talking about or to be referring to in the predicate of the proposition, "the man is white," can only be the same identical man as the one referred to in the subject of the proposition. In other words, so far as one is concerned to know what the subject and predicate terms in the proposition refer to or are about,[17] they are about

14 St. Thomas, *Summa Theologiae*, I, 13, 12.

15 It is on just such a misunderstanding that Prof. Grossmann's criticisms of such a doctrine of predication are based. Despite, or perhaps because of the misunderstanding, however, the criticisms are exceedingly illuminating. Cf. *Reflections on Frege's Philosophy* (Evanston 1969), 98-104.

16 Geach is very scornful of this way of construing what might be called the identity-factor in affirmative predications. Thus in "Form and Existence" (op. cit. p. 43) he takes Lewis Carroll to task for having committed just such an error: "Lewis Carroll professes to find a difficulty over saying 'some pigs are pink'; as it stands, this suggests an impossible identity between certain things (pigs) and a certain attribute (signified by 'pink')! He seeks to remove this difficulty by expounding the proposition as meaning 'some pigs are pink pigs,' where 'are' signifies real identity. But 'pink pigs' means 'pigs that are pink', and there is as much or as little difficulty about this phrase as about the predication 'pigs are pink' at which he stumbles."
Surely if this criticism is meant to apply to Aquinas as well as to Lewis Carroll, then it does seem nothing if not gratuitous. Aquinas never even supposes "an impossible identity between certain things (pigs) and a certain attribute (signified by 'pink')"; rather he insists that the identity can never be between certain substances and their attributes, but only between substances. And once one is clear on this score, then what of it if "some pigs are pink" means "some pigs are pink pigs"? If Geach counters by saying that "pink pigs" means "pigs that are pink," of course it means this, and more: it means "pigs that are pink pigs." The supposed circularity in the explanation, in short, is only in Geach's imagination.

17 It is just here that Geach would doubtless take violent exception. For as he understands the relation between subject and predicate, it is only subject terms that can be said to name or refer to anything, whereas predicates never refer, but are only "true of" their subjects. Hence even to raise the question as to what a predicate term in a proposition may be supposed to be referring to is simply rediculous. Cf. "Subject and Predicate," op. cit., especially pp. 31-34.
However, the answer to this objection would seem fairly obvious. Making all due allowance for the possibility that Geach may be using "refer" in a somewhat Geachian, not to say Pickwickian, sense, it would nonetheless seem that for a predicate to be true of its subject, it would surely have to be about that subject; and how could it be about its subject without in some way or other making reference to it?
This is not to say, of course, that the predicate refers to the same thing the subject does in exac-

the very same thing, viz. in this instance a particular human being who happens to be white.

Very well, if we let this suffice as an explanation of how subject and predicate terms can signify the same thing *secundum rem,* just how are we to understand, directly in conjunction with it, the further suggestion that subject and predicate signify something different *secundum rationem?* Perhaps we might avail ourselves of a kind of metaphor here and say that this difference *secundum rationem* really means no more than that the same thing is being viewed or considered under a new or different guise or aspect. Thus in terms of our examples thus far, we might say that in speaking of a man as being white, we are really considering him under the guise of his being white; or to say that Socrates is bald is to consider him simply under this particular aspect.

Now the point of this somewhat metaphorical way of putting the matter is to bring out the peculiar significance of the expression *secundum rationem.* For Socrates is not really different from the bald Socrates; nor is the man referred to in the other example really different from the man who is white. Rather in each case it is one and the same thing in fact (*secundum rem*) that is nevertheless considered somewhat differently — i.e. it is considered under a different guise or aspect (*secundum rationem*).

To sharpen the point, we might contrast such a situation in which one and the same thing is considered under a different guise or aspect with a situation in which one and the same thing has in fact become different. As an example of the latter, Socrates, we might say, from not having been bald, became bald. Here the difference is surely a real difference, and not a mere logical difference or rationate difference: at one time Socrates was without the property or accident of baldness; at another time he had changed, so as actually to have this accident. In contrast, in the assertion "Socrates is bald" the difference between what is signified or understood by the subject term and what by the predicate is not a difference between one and the same thing that has become really and in fact different. Rather it is exactly the same whole (say, Socrates plus the accident of baldness) that is referred to by the predicate as well as by the subject: the only difference is that in the subject Socrates is not considered or recognized or understood as being bald, whereas in the predicate he is. In other words, the difference is

tly the same way as the subject does. For the one does so in the manner of a subject and the other in the manner of a predicate. Thus in an affirmative predication one is saying something about something else (*dicit intellectus aliquid de aliquo. In III De An.,* 11, n. 760); hence the predicate only refers to the same thing as the subject *via* the subject or through the subject, whereas the subject refers directly.

only a difference of consideration, or a difference in what might be called the guise or aspect under which the same identical thing is seen or viewed.

Moreover, this very capability according to which one and the same thing (*secundum rem*) can nevertheless be considered or understood or recognized under different guises (*secundum rationem*) is a distinctive capability of the human intellect, a capability which renders possible just such logical relations or relations of reason as that of subject-predicate.

3. Our points of commentary thus far have sufficed, we would hope, to make it clear both how the subject-predicate relation of whole to whole is a purely logical relation that needs to be sharply distinguished from all ontological or real relations, as well as how this logical relation must needs be construed as a rather special kind of relation of identity. What it now remains for us to do in this our third consideration is to try to make clear just how this subject-predicate relation functions as a tool or instrument of knowledge. For it is basic to St. Thomas' entire conception of logic that "logic as an instrumental science [should be] ordained to the knowledge of things" (*logica ordinatur ad cognitionem de rebus sumendam*). [18] Accordingly, the subject-predicate relation that is involved in propositions can hardly be an exception to this rule: it too must be ordained to a knowledge of things. Not only that, but sharply as this purely logical relation of subject-predicate has to be contrasted with ontological relations like that of matter-form, or essence-supposit, or substance-accident, etc., it must at the same time be recognized that it is precisely in and through such a relation, that relations of this latter type can come to be known. How, though, can this be? How is it that in order to know and to formulate our knowledge of so-called ontological relations, which, as we have seen, do not involve the identity factor [19] that is present in subject-predicate relations, we must needs employ precisely that logical relation of subject-predicate in which the identity factor is a most prominent feature? Or to put the question a little differently: supposing that subject-predicate relations in logic are thus ordained to a knowledge of real relations in things and in *rerum natura*,

---

18 Schmidt, op. cit., 83-84. The reference for the quotation from Aquinas that Fr. Schmidt cites is *In I Peri.,* 2, n. 3.
19 We are embarrassed to know how best to designate that factor of identity which is present in affirmative subject-predicate propositions and which we sought to explicate in section 2 above. Sometimes we shall speak simply of an "identity relation" between subject-predicate, and sometimes of an "identity factor" in the relation of subject-predicate. Such designations or labels can unfortunately be misleading; but some sort of designation has to be used and we would hope that what we have said in section 2 may be a sufficient guard against misunderstanding.

just what is the source and character of that instrumentality which these logical relations of predication would appear to have that thus enables them to mediate a knowledge of such real relations as substance-accident, matter-form, etc.?

c. *The Relevance of St. Thomas' Principle of Predication to Some Contemporary Theories of Meaning*

Apparently, to judge from what we have said thus far in the foregoing section, our point about predication is turning out to be not so much a point of commentary as of question. And so it is. What's more, to speak of this question we propose to make something of a detour through various theories of meaning that are closely associated with modern developments in logic, and which by way of contrast should enable us to appreciate rather better the distinctive instrumentality which the logical relation of predication, as St. Thomas conceives it, definitely affords. For if we are not mistaken there is no current theory of meaning which allows a place for a subject-predicate relation of the peculiar kind which St. Thomas had in mind; and unless we be even further mistaken, it is precisely because they lack a logical relation of just this kind that modern theories of meaning find themselves in the straits they do.

To be sure, in current discussions of either logic or semantics it may not be the habit immediately to juxtapose questions of logic to questions of meaning. Yet there is surely nothing amiss with approaching so-called theories of meaning precisely with a view to seeing just how, if at all, they would suppose various logical relations — such as that of subject-predicate, for example — to be "ordained to a knowledge of things." In other words, just how do logical relations mean, and what is there about them that enables them to mean or signify in the way they do?

Now the first such theory of meaning in the context of which we should like to consider such a question as to how subject-predicate propositions mean, or how they are ordained to a knowledge of things, is none other than the theory which has been called "the referential theory of meaning," or sometimes the "picture theory." And although this theory in its strict and proper sense should be associated solely with Wittgenstein in his earlier period, it might not be too far wrong to say that what is roughly characteristic of such a theory of meaning is simply that it holds that the meaning of a word or term in a language is just that thing or entity in fact or in reality which it names or to which it refers. Thus the meaning of the term "St. Thomas Aquinas" would simply be the real St. Thomas. Indeed, as is well known, Ryle later came to designate the theory rather derisively as the "'Fido'-Fido theory."

In any case what is interesting about this theory for our purposes is that under its aegis any number of modern logicians were influenced in the direction of supposing that the structure of logical propositions should ultimately be such as merely to picture or mirror the structure of the corresponding facts. Or put a little differently, one could say that on this view all of the various elements in a proposition had to be such that they could be set in one-to-one correspondence with elements in the corresponding fact. Thus consider such well-known pronouncements of the early Wittgenstein as:

> In a proposition there must be exactly as many distinguishable parts as in the situation it represents.[20] The configuration of objects in a situation corresponds to the configuration of simple signs in the propositional sign.[21]

Perhaps, though, a quotation from Russell might serve even better to bring out the import of this theory of meaning, so far as the structure of logical propositions is concerned:

> Take (say) the proposition, 'Socrates was before Aristotle'. Here it seems obvious that we have a relation between two terms, and that the constituents of the proposition (as well as of the corresponding fact) are simply the two terms and the relation, i.e. Socrates, Aristotle, and *before*... We may represent the general form of such propositions by 'x Ry', which may be read 'x has the relation R to y'.[22]

Quite patently, here is an account of propositions and of the relation of subjects and predicates in propositions that is very different from that of St. Thomas. An immediate and superficial difference is that on Russell's view — and the same would be true for Wittgenstein and Frege as well — a proposition may well have not just one subject but several. Thus in Russell's example of the proposition "Socrates was before Aristotle," "Socrates" and "Aristotle" are both of them subjects of the proposition, and the predicate which joins or relates them is the relation of the one being "before" the other. In fact, to borrow Wittgenstein's terminology, those elements of the proposition which he calls the "simple signs" and which may be taken to refer to what he calls the "objects" in the corresponding real "situation" — these might be considered to be the subjects of the proposition; and likewise, that element in the proposition which Wittgenstein calls "the configuration" of "simple signs" and which is held to refer to "the configuration of objects" in

20 L. Wittgenstein, *Tractatus Logico-Philosophicus*, trans. by Pears and McGuiness (London and New York 1961), 4.04.
21 Ibid., 3.21.
22 B. Russell, *Introduction to Mathematical Philosophy* (2nd edition, London 1920), 198.

the real situation — this element might be considered to be the predicate of the proposition.

No sooner, though, is the relation of subject, or of subjects, to the predicate in a proposition conceived in this way, than St. Thomas' view of the subject-predicate relation as being a kind of relation of identity is ruled out altogether. For quite patently it makes no sense to speak of any sort of identity *secundum rem* as between the subjects, "Socrates" and "Aristotle" on the one hand, and the predicate "before" on the other.[23] But further, as we saw, it was just such a purely logical relation of identity as between subject and predicate that in St. Thomas' eyes served to distinguish such logical subject-predicate relations from any and all ontological relations in the real world. Once, though, the relation between subject and predicate ceases to be thought of as a relation of identity in this sense, and immediately the bar is removed to conceiving of subject-predicate relations as being on all fours with relations in the real world. And this was just as Russell and Wittgenstein intended that it should be. For as they saw things, the logical structure of a logical proposition, so far from having to be different from, needed to be exactly the same as, or to be isomorphic with, the corresponding ontological structure of that fact or state of affairs in the real world which that proposition was supposed to represent or be about.

With this, though, we begin to see just how this particular view of subject-predicate relations in propositions turns out to be peculiarly congenial to a referential theory of meaning of the kind here being considered. For if it be asked just how it is that propositions so structured are able to mean or signify the things they are supposed to mean or signify, the answer is that they do so simply in virtue of that isomorphism or sameness of structure as between the subject-predicate structure of the proposition and the structure of the corresponding fact that the proposition is supposed to mean or represent. How diametrically opposed, then, is such a referential theory of meaning to the Thomistic theory. For St. Thomas, a logical proposition is ordained to a knowledge of things precisely because, the relation between subject and predicate being one of identity, it is therefore never to be confused with those relations in the real world which such a logical relation is designed to signify or intend.[24] With the advocates of the referential

---

23 This point of criticism we have developed at much greater length in our book *Two Logics* (Evanston 1969), ch. I.

24 Needless to say, we are using this term in what we take to be its Thomistic sense. Cf. *In II Sent.*, 38, 1, 2 sol.: *Intendere enim dictur quasi in aliud tendere.* See Father Schmidt's discussion, op. cit., chapter V.

theory, however, it is quite otherwise: only in so far as logical relations are isomorphic with real relations, are they able to serve as instruments for our knowing the things of the real world. In other words, on this theory of meaning the entire case for the instrumentality of logic, so far as meaning or knowledge is concerned, turns just on such an isomorphism.

d. The Inadequacy of a Mere Isomorphism as a Vehicle of Meaning

Given this opposition, then, between the referential theory of meaning and the Thomistic theory, which of the two is the better? Well, it should not be difficult to see how the referential theory simply breaks down as an adequate account of meaning. Moreover, the inadequacy would appear to be traceable simply to an excessive reliance upon that supposed isomorphism between logical structures and real structures, which on the referential theory is taken to be the sole ground for understanding just how and why logical relations and devices are able to function as vehicles or instruments of meaning.

For example, take just a crude illustration, say, the two uprights of a six-foot wooden ladder. To say that these two pieces of wood are quite alike could well be true: they might be of the same length, have the same breadth and thickness, could be made of exactly the same kind of wood, etc. Not only that, but it could also be the case, that the holes for the rungs in the one upright exactly corresponded to those in the other. In fact, though it is unlikely that we should ever speak of it this way, there could indeed be said to be a genuine isomorphism as between the one upright and the other. And yet surely it would be absurd to suppose that the one knows the other, or even represents the other, simply in virtue of the isomorphism between them. But so likewise, a mere isomorphism between the form of a proposition and the form of the corresponding fact would not of itself suffice for anyone to say that there was a knowledge of the one by the other.

Of course, one could respond to this by insisting that we have explicated the example of the sides of the ladder at once improperly and unfairly. For indeed it is ridiculous to say that no more is needed than that two things should be alike, or isomorphic, for the one thing to be said to know the other. Rather it is the case that when two things are alike, then the one can perhaps come to be known not so much by the other as *through* the other. Thus through a knowledge of a proposition I can come to know a fact that corresponds to it and is isomorphic with it. And even as regards the clumsy example of the two uprights of the ladder, it is surely the case that through a knowledge of the one I can indeed come to know something about the other that is just like it.

All well and good. And yet just how is it that through one thing we can come to know another like it? The mere fact of a likeness or similarity between the two does not suffice to explain a knowledge of the one by the other. This we have just seen. Nor can one suppose that for there to be such a knowledge, both the thing and its likeness must somehow first come to be known, and then compared the one with the other. Not only would this plunge one very quickly into the morass of the old copy theory of knowledge, but in addition as an explanation of knowledge it simply begs the question. If to come to know something I must do so by first coming to know its likeness, or something that is isomorphic with it, then how is this latter knowledge to be brought off? Must it be in terms of a still prior likeness or isomorphism? But this must seemingly lead to an infinite regress.

No, it is clearly necessary to give over entirely this kind of reliance upon isomorphism and proceed on a very different tack if we are ever to get clear just what sort of a logical instrumentality[25] is requisite in order that knowledge may be achieved. And is not the tack to be followed just that which St. Thomas proposes in his account of predication? For take anything that I, or that anyone else for that matter, might wish to know about, be it fish or fowl, be it substantival or adjectival, be it material or spiritual, be it universal or particular, be it absolute or relative, or whatever. Surely, the procedure toward knowledge in such cases cannot be one of first constructing a logical simulacrum of that which one seeks to know about, and then somehow coming to know the one through the other. Instead, the procedure would seem to have to be based on the very elementary consideration that whatever it is that I am seeking to know about, I can only come to know it in terms of what it is. That is to say, I must attempt to determine what that subject[26] is that I am thus subjecting[27] to my investigation. Suppose, for instance, that it is Socrates that I wish to know about. Presumably I will come to recognize

---

25 It should be noted perhaps that in this essay we are not attempting to address ourselves to more fundamental epistemological issues. Instead, we are considering only certain logical doctrines as being ancillary to various theories of meaning or knowledge.

26 The term "subject," of course, is ambiguous as between what might be called the logical subject and the real subject. For example, Geach simply lays down the rule that, as he uses the terms "subject" and "predicate," they will always be linguistic terms; I shall never call a man a logical subject, but only the name of a man — the name 'Peter,' not the Apostle, is the subject of 'Peter was an Apostle'..." ("Subject and Predicate," op. cit., p. 22). Although it is, of course, entirely proper for Geach thus to restrict his use of "subject," since the ordinary use of the term is ambiguous, we shall find it convenient in this essay not to limit the meaning to a single meaning, but rather to play on the ambiguity as far as possible. Of course, if it is not clear from the context which meaning is the relevant one, we shall then indicate as much. For example, in the present instance the subject meant is clearly the real subject.

27 On this use of "subjection," cf. the reference to Fr. Schmidt in note 2 above.

or to acknowledge him to be a human being and not a god or a torpedo fish, or to be bald and snub-nosed rather than aristocratic-looking or with an Afro-hair-do. But in any case, whether it be in terms of what he is essentially or accidentally, my learning and coming to know about Socrates has to be in terms of what he is.

e. *The Reaffirmation of the Subject-Predicate Relation and its Relevance to the Theory of Meaning as Use*

Must not this, though, bring us right around again to the subject-predicate relation in St. Thomas' sense, as being the only proper instrument of knowledge so conceived? That is to say, rather than that the proposition should have a structure that is isomorphic with that of which the proposition is supposed to be about, it is important instead that the proposition have a structure that will serve to relate by a kind of identity that which the proposition is about (the subject)[28] and that which that subject is understood as being (the predicate). Or put a bit differently, rather than a correspondence with the real, what is needed is that the proposition should set up a kind of identity between the real and that which it is being thought or understood or conceived to be. And what is this if not to understand that very thing which one is seeking to find out or know about, but to understand it (i.e. *idem secundum rem*) under a particular guise or aspect (i.e. according to a particular *ratio*)?

Perhaps we may go even further and suggest that by restoring again to its once central position in logic the subject-predicate relation as St. Thomas understood it, it might be possible to rescue the theory of meaning from the sort of impasse which it seems to have reached largely at the hands of the partisans of the old referential or picture theory. For while it is true that the picture theory has pretty much gone out of fashion largely as a result of Wittgenstein's own conversion from a referential theory to a theory of meaning-as-use, one wonders if the replacement of the former by the latter may not have involved throwing the baby out with the bath.

What seems to have happened is something like this. Isomorphism having been given up as the resource for explaining how logic could be ordained to a knowledge of things, it is as if the latter-day champions of

---

28   Here clearly the real subject is meant. As Geach remarks, just as "the name 'Peter,' not the Apostle is the subject of 'Peter was an Apostle,'" so also "what the predicate in 'Peter was an Apostle' is predicated of is Peter, not his name; for it is Peter, not his name, that is being said to have been an Apostle" ("Subject and Predicate," op. cit., pp. 22-23). Cf. note 26 above.

meaning-as-use[29] had decided that perhaps language or logic need not be ordained to a knowledge of things at all — at least not in any realistic sense.[30] Instead, the various logical and linguistic uses that we employ, not just in our efforts to know, but in living our lives generally, are but so many "language games" that we play. And these language games, by the very fact that they are games and that we play them, are considered to have their origin in us and in what Wittgenstein called our basic and rudimentary "forms of life." In other words, instead of trying to account for the character of our language games, and more generally of our language and logic as a whole, in terms of their suitability and appropriateness for disclosing the independently existing structures of nature and of the way things are, these thinkers tend rather to account for things being the way they are on the ground of their being so structured and ordered by our language forms and ultimately by our so-called form of life.

And so it is that the currently fashionable theory of meaning-as-use would seem to boil down to little more than a variant on Kant's theme of Copernican revolution in philosophy, with the result that the role of logic must cease to be understood in terms of its being ordained to a knowledge of things, and must instead be understood ultimately in terms of its capacity for being elevated to a transcendental logic.[31] That is why if logic is ever to return to its more traditional role of being ordained to a knowledge of things, the first step must be to revive St.

29   Although it is certainly true to say that the neo-Wittgensteinians have given up the isomorphism of the old picture theory, we would not wish to imply that they gave it up as a result of quite the same criticisms of isomorphism as we ourselves sought to detail in section d above.

30   Needless to say, "realism" as it is here being used does not signify realism as opposed to nominalism, but rather realism as opposed to various forms of idealism. It is what Prof. Bergmann would call realism2, as contrasted with realism1. Cf. *Logic and Reality,* passim (Madison 1964).

31   This interpretation of Wittgenstein's theory of meaning-as-use is confirmed by a most interesting discussion which W. D. Hudson gives in his *Modern Moral Philosophy* (New York 1970) 51-52: "Every language game goes down in the last analysis to certain concepts, or rules of inference, or both, which are tacitly presupposed and which logically constitute that universe of discourse. An example would be the concept of a physical object. The empirical evidence, on the basis of which we talk about physical objects, is discontinuous. Now we see the table; now we go into the next room and see it no longer; now we return and there it is. Though there has been a break between our observations of it, we nevertheless think of it as identical on the two occasions. Someone may raise the question: are we entitled to do so?... There is a logical gap here, then, between evidence which is *discontinuous* and what it is invoked to support which is continuous. Are we entitled to jump this gap as we do?... Professor P. F. Strawson, dealing with the skeptic who answers that question in the negative, points out that "a condition of our having this conceptual scheme is the unquestioning acceptance of particular-identity in at least some cases of non-continuous observation." The skeptic, says Strawson, "... pretends to accept a conceptual scheme (sc. that of common sense or natural science in which we speak of physical objects on the strength of empirical observation) but at the same time quietly rejects one of the conditions of its employment. Thus his doubts are unreal ... because they amount to the rejection of the whole conceptual scheme within which alone such doubts make sense."

Thomas' ancient principle of predication that only wholes may be predicated of wholes. For it is precisely the identity factor that is involved in predication as so conceived that enables the subject-predicate proposition to serve as the vehicle and instrument of our knowledge of things in terms of what they are. In short, it is just this subject-predicate relation no less that would seem to be the very gage and surety of a genuinely realistic theory of meaning.

f. *A Final Note on Professor Geach*

Now is this not a properly eloquent note on which to end this paper? How we wish that it might be! But unhappily it is certain to strike many as being a false note for no other reason than that our entire exposition and defense of St. Thomas' doctrine of subject-predicate would appear to be radically at variance with what the formidable Professor Geach has had to say on the same topic. Now it is neither possible nor appropriate to try to deal with Geach's views regarding the matter either of subject-predicate in general or of St. Thomas' views thereon in particular in any mere addendum to an otherwise completed discussion. But at least some indication and comment as to the major points at issue would seem called for.

And to bring the issue directly to a head, the following quotation from Geach should suffice:

> For Aquinas, the real distinction between a form and the self-subsistent individual (suppositum) whose form it is comes out in the logical distinction between subject and predicate (I a, q. 12, art. 12; q. 85, art. 5, ad 3um).[32]

Surely, such a flat pronouncement cannot fail to strike anyone as other than astonishing in view of the analyses and arguments which we have presented thus far. For does it not fly directly in the face of St. Thomas' careful differentiation of (1) the logical distinction between subject and predicate (e.g. "Socrates" and "human being") from (2) the real distinction between a form (e.g. humanity) and the self-subsistent individual (e.g. Socrates)? How, then, can Geach possibly equate the logical relation of subject-predicate with an ontological or real relation like that of supposit-essence (or form)? And must not such an equation have the unhappily retrograde effect of leading us right back into the toils of the referential theory of meaning, when as a matter of fact our only hope of progress out of these toils would seem to lie in following

32 "Form and Existence," op. cit., p. 47.

Aquinas along the lines of what we have called the identity theory of predication — a theory which Geach, it would seem, not only denies, but denies even to Aquinas?

But is this quite fair to Geach? After all, in the passage quoted he does not say that the real distinction of essence (*sc.* form) from supposit *is the same as* the logical distinction between subject and predicate; instead, he says only that the former distinction "comes out" in the latter. And certainly this somewhat metaphorical way of putting the matter is quite unobjectionable, provided it be rightly understood and interpreted. But does Geach anywhere or in any way make provision for such a "right" understanding and interpretation?

To this question we rather suspect that the answer can only be negative and this for two reasons. For one thing, Geach nowhere to our knowledge either mentions or explains what Aquinas is most careful not just to point out, but to lay stress upon, viz. that while one can quite properly speak of the relation of predicate to subject on the analogy[33] of the relation of form to matter, it is nevertheless equally important to recognize that the two relations are not the same. Quite the contrary, in one of the two passages that Geach refers to, Aquinas underlines this very difference — a fact which Geach passes over in silence. Thus in I, 85, 5, ad 3, St. Thomas remarks:

Unde compositioni et divisioni intellectus respondet quidem aliquid ex parte rei: *tamen non eodem modo se habet in re sicut in intellectu.*[34]

Now it is quite clear from the context that the respective compositions and divisions *in re* and *in intellectu* that St. Thomas is here referring to are compositions and divisions of matter and form. And what is the reason that Aquinas gives for insisting that these respective compositions and divisions of matter and form *in re* and *in intellectu* must be carefully distinguished from one another? The answer is stated clearly and unequivocally directly in the same passage:

Tamen differt compositio intellectus a compositione rei: nam ea quae componuntur in re sunt diversa; compositio autem intellectus est signum *identitatis*[35] eorum quae componuntur.

---

33 Father Schmidt uses this very notion in one place: "... by an analogical application of matter and form to intellectual composition, the predicate serves as the formal part of the proposition and the subject as the material: "Praedicatum est quasi pars formalis enuntiationis, subjectum autem est pars materialis ipsius."" Op. cit., p. 225. The quotation is from *In I Perih.*, 10, n. 23.

34 Our italics.

35 Our italics.

But this brings us to our second reason for thinking that Geach is not concerned to distinguish the matter-form relation *in re* from the matter-form relation in the case of subject-predicate, but rather is content to leave the impression that the two relations are structurally the same, or at least are isomorphic with one another. For not only does Geach pass over in silence all evidence to the effect that Aquinas considered the matter-form relation in the case of subject-predicate to be little more than metaphorical; but he also studiously avoids ever mentioning that identity factor in the relation of subject-predicate, which we have been at pains to show is the real ground for St. Thomas' insistence that a logical relation like that of predicate to subject must never be confused with a real or ontological relation like that of form to matter. Thus as we have seen in the one passage that Geach himself refers to (I, 85, 5, ad 3), St. Thomas explicitly declares that *compositio intellectus est signum identitatis eorum quae componuntur.* Not only that, but in that other passage to which Geach makes explicit reference, viz. I, 13, 12, we have already noted how Aquinas says that what is signified by the subject and the predicate in an affirmative proposition is *idem secundum rem,* although *diversum secundum rationem.*

Why, then, is it that Geach in his reference to both of these passages never gives his readers any intimation that they both contain unequivocal assertions as to the presence of an identity factor in affirmative predication? We believe that the answer is that Geach is doubtless radically suspicious of St. Thomas' way of understanding predication in terms of identity and would like to play down as much as possible this particular feature of his teaching. Nor is it to be denied that superficially at least Geach's suspicions on this score — supposing that he really does harbor them[36] — are perhaps not altogether gratuitous. For Geach is doubtless worried lest any attempt at understanding subject-predicate in terms of identity is likely to lead to what he calls "the old two-name or identity theory of predication, which flourished in the Middle Ages, and still keeps appearing in new guises:

36 This qualification has to be added, because Geach does say at one point that if a predicative expression can be treated as a name, then "it *is* possible to state the truth-condition of an affirmative predication as an identity of reference between two names ... Aquinas uses this way of stating truth-condition quite often, and has in consequence been wrongly regarded as holding the two-name theory" ("Form and Existence," op. cit., pp. 43-44). Unfortunately, Geach never explains how then Aquinas manages to avoid the two-name theory. Not only that, but since Geach seems to consider that a necessary condition of subscribing to such an identity of reference between two names is to treat the predicate as a name, this must mean that in his eyes St. Thomas does treat the predicate as a name. But this last, Geach seems to feel, is almost the beginning of all evil in logic. It is puzzling, therefore, to know just why and how Geach can consider his own views on subject and predicate to be so consonant with those of St. Thomas.

the theory that a true predication is effected by joining different names of the same thing or things, the copula being the sign of this real identity."[37]

Needless to say, in this present discussion we cannot go into Geach's many and varied strictures upon the two-name theory. Suffice it only to say that one could well accept many of his criticisms and still insist that the identity theory of predication, at least as Aquinas expounds it, just does not lead to such enormities. Indeed, Geach would seem even to admit as much himself.[38] Besides, if the commanding error of the two-name theory is simply that in effect it really denies that in predication we ever say anything of significance about the subject at all, the predicate being no more than a new name or a new word for the same thing, then clearly St. Thomas' theory of predication does not fall afoul of any such error. For although, according to him, subject and predicate do signify the same thing *secundum rem,* they also signify something different *secundum rationem.* Moreover, as we have construed such diversity *secundum rationem,* what it means is that the predicate term serves to point up features in the subject which the subject term did not specify, but which nevertheless are really there in the subject.

In other words, Geach's worry lest the identity-factor in predication lead inescapably to the two-name theory is surely a gratuitous worry, so far as St. Thomas' doctrine is concerned. But gratuitous or not, it is a real worry so far as Geach is concerned and would appear to have led him into a very dubious interpretation of St. Thomas. For in effect what Geach would seem to have done is to have retained only a part of St. Thomas' teaching in regard to subject and predicate, viz. that part in which St. Thomas insists that subject and predicate signify things that are different *secundum rationem.* But the other part of the same doctrine where Aquinas insists that subject and predicate signify the same thing *secundum rem* — this Geach plays down so conspicuously that one wonders if he does not mean to repudiate it altogether.

Besides, there is still another reason why Geach might have reason to be suspicious of the identity factor in predication. For his own doctrine of subject and predicate being no less profoundly influenced by Frege than it is by Aquinas, Geach is most anxious to maintain what he calls "an absolute distinction between names and predicables."[39] And the im-

---

37 Ibid., p. 43.
38 Cf. note 36 above.
39 "Subject and Predicate," op. cit., p. 34. The word "predicables" here Geach is using as roughly synonymous with "predicates" in the usual sense.
For Geach's explanation of his preference of "predicable" over "predicate," see ibid., pp. 23-24.

port of the distinction's being taken to be thus "absolute" is that "a name can occur in a proposition only as a logical subject";[40] and as for what Geach calls "predicables":

> A predicable applies to or is true of things; for example Peter struck _____'[41] applies to Malchus (whether it is actually predicated of Malchus or not). This relation must be sharply distinguished from the relation of name to bearer, which is confounded with it in the 'Aristotelian' tradition under the term 'denoting.' A predicable never names what it is true of, and 'Peter struck _____' does not even look like a name for Malchus.[42]

Now apparently what Geach is aiming at here is indeed the quite dubious view that there is a ready and easy interchangeability and perhaps mutual substitutivity of subject and predicate terms in propositions. As Geach himself puts it: "A term, as conceived in Aristotelian logic, is supposed capable of being a subject in one proposition and a predicate in another."[43] And that is bad!

Nor is there any doubt but that this is bad, if as a logical doctrine it leads to the consequence that one fails to recognize that a subject term has a very different function to perform in a proposition from a predicate, and a predicate from a subject. For the subject serves to point up what in the proposition one is concerned to know about or to find out about; and the predicate serves to indicate what one has come to recognize or see or understand that subject as being. Clearly, given this difference of function, a term in a proposition, in so far as it is functioning as a subject, could not possibly function as a predicate. And similarly, as we have already had occasion to note, a predicate term in a proposition, although it could hardly be denied that it must at least in some sense be taken to refer to that which it is being predicated of, still does not refer to that which the subject refers to in quite the same manner as the subject. It refers to it, as we suggested earlier,[44] *via* the subject, or perhaps through the medium of the subject.

Now if this is all that Geach means by his insistence that a predicate in a proposition can never be said to "name" what the subject names, but only to be "true of" what is thus named by the subject,[45] all well and

---

40   Ibid., p. 31.
41   The example here may seem a bit odd-sounding. However, Geach is careful to explain that a proposition must not be thought to admit of "only one subject-predicate analysis. 'Peter struck Malchus' is at once a predication about Peter and a (different) predication about Malchus; either 'Peter' or 'Malchus' may be taken as a logical subject..." Ibid., p. 28.
42   Ibid., p. 32.
43   Ibid., p. 34.
44   See note 17 above.
45   A remark that perhaps should be made not only with reference to the point which Geach is

good. Yet Geach does not stop here. For in wishing to make the difference between subject and predicate an "absolute" one, as he calls it, he would appear to be confusing a very proper difference in function between subject and predicate terms in propositions with an absolute ontological difference between the sorts of things *in re* that such subject and predicate terms can mean or signify. Put crudely, it is as if for Geach a subject term could never signify anything but a primary substance or a "self-subsistent individual (*suppositum*)"; whereas a predicate could never signify anything but a form.

Surely, though, this is simply preposterous. Indeed, it reminds one of the predicament that Frege got into with his absolute distinction between what he called "concepts" and "objects," and as a result of which he found himself compelled to admit that a concept could never be the subject (*sc.* object) of a proposition — that is to say it was not anything that an assertion could ever be made about. Even Geach acknowledges that Frege went too far here.[46] And yet he seems not to be aware of just how Frege went astray or how he, Geach, might be able to avoid getting into a like predicament.

Actually, though, neither the truth of the matter nor the way it is to be explained would seem so very difficult. For surely, when it comes to possible subjects of propositions, in the sense of possible things that propositions might be about, just anything and everything might be the subject of a proposition — individuals or universals, accidents or substances, "concepts" or "objects," possibles or actuals, real beings or beings of reason, you name it, and at once it can become the subject of a

here making, but with reference to any number of other such points as well is that St. Thomas' theory of subject-predicate is almost bound to give rise to misunderstandings in the present day, particularly since no adequate symbolism (at least not by modern standards) has ever been devised to represent all the facets that are involved in St. Thomas' view of subject-predicate propositions. Lacking this symbolism, it is impossible to formalize such propositions so as to be able to determine just what their so-called logical powers may be. Nevertheless, for an extremely interesting beginning at providing something like an adequate symbolism for subject-predicate propositions, we should like to refer to a brilliant, but as yet unpublished article entitled "Substance Logic" by Eddy M. Zemach and Eric Walther.

Of course, one can hardly devise an adequate means for symbolizing such propositions, unless one first has a right understanding of just what such subject-predicate propositions were conceived to be by St. Thomas. To such an understanding we would hope that this present paper may make some slight contribution.

46   For the relevant quotation from Frege, as well as Geach's discussion of it, see "Form and Existence," op. cit., p. 47. The trouble with Geach's discussion is that he seems never to face up to what we should imagine is the real issue here, viz. how the real subject of a proposition can ever be other than simply a self-subsistent individual or *suppositum*. Instead, in a commendable effort to avoid the extremes of both realism (Bergmann's realism!) and nominalism, Geach develops a most labored account of predicates as forms. The only trouble is that all of this would seem to have but little to do with the case, at least not with the case of how things other than self-subsistent individuals can ever be real subjects of propositions.

proposition! Nevertheless, even though in this respect there can be no restrictions of any kind on what can be the subject of a proposition, there are of course quite definite restrictions on the way in which terms in propositions can function as subjects (or as predicates for that matter). In other words, in trying to set up his absolute difference between subject and predicate, Geach would seem to be making the same mistake as Frege: he confuses the difference between the way subjects and predicates function in propositions with an absolute ontological difference between the kinds of things that subjects and predicates are able to signify. Moreover, this confusion would seem to spring ultimately from Geach's failure to appreciate the identity-factor in subject-predicate propositions. Not realizing that this identity-factor does not need to be, and certainly ought not to be, interpreted as eliminating all difference between subject and predicate, Geach would seem to want to disregard it altogether. But disregard this factor, and the structure of propositions begins to appear indistinguishable from the corresponding ontological structures which the former are supposed to signify or represent. Unfortunately, though, to interpret St. Thomas in this light is but to implicate Thomistic realism in the difficulties of the so-called referential theory of meaning. Is it any wonder, then, that Professor Geach's proffered guidance through the arcana, alike of St. Thomas' teaching and of the logical doctrine of subject and predicate, should perhaps be eyed with no little suspicion?

IL NUOVO PROBLEMA DELL'ESSERE
E LA FONDAZIONE DELLA METAFISICA

Cornelio Fabro C.S.S.

I tentativi di "conciliare" la posizione di Heidegger in generale con la concezione della verità del Cristianesimo ed in particolare con la concezione dell'essere di S. Tommaso non vanno aldilà della buona volontà alla quale lo stesso Heidegger non ha prestato alcuna attenzione.[1] Diverso è invece il giudizio se il problema è portato sul piano critico-teoretico del "significato" delle istanze di Heidegger, lasciando da parte ogni velleità di concordismo esteriore di semantiche superficiali. A nostro avviso, come per gli altri filosofi essenziali dell'epoca moderna, l'opposizione radicale che Heidegger, nella linea del pensiero moderno, ha creduto di opporre al realismo, sfociando nella critica radicale ad ogni dualismo metafisico ed in particolare al creazionismo cristiano, presenta dei pretesti e delle istanze positivi ma esattamente nel senso opposto a quello voluto dai concordisti. Cioè non si tratta tanto di accordo dottrinale fra Heidegger e S. Tommaso, che non ci può essere su nessun punto, quanto di convergenza d'istanze nella tematica e problematica di fondo e quindi nella rottura di una situazione com'è il pensiero contemporaneo che ha superato l'ultimo punto di resistenza ed è precipitato nel nichilismo. Si tratta, se la formula può andare, di una divergenza convergente o convergenza divergente che stimola a nostro avviso un confronto di estrema tensione per una dialettica positiva fra Heidegger e S. Tommaso: convergenza di istanze, divergenza di prospettive — ma più che le formule, sono i problemi stessi che devono guidare il confronto. E sui problemi la convergenza fra i due pensatori non può rivelarsi che a livello sempre più profondo, malgrado la distanza nel tempo e la differenza nella cultura.

Possiamo infatti dire che ambedue "pensano a ritroso" ossia seguono il metodo regressivo di "ritorno al fondamento" (*Rückgang in den*

---

[1] Questo tipo di "concordismo" estrinseco è stato diffuso ad opera della scuola maréchaliana, fedele alla metafisica di Suarez, il quale ha sostituito alla distinzione tomistica reale di *essentia* ed *esse* la distinzione modale estrinseca di *essentia* ed *existentia* a cui Heidegger attribuisce con ragione la perdita della verità dell'essere in Occidente.

Grund)[2] ch'è proprio dei pensatori essenziali. Ambedue vedono questo fondamento nella riduzione all'essere ossia mediante l'illuminazione dell'ente o essente nell'essere. In ambedue la (conoscenza della) verità dell'essere precede la (conoscenza della) dipendenza causale ossia non identificano realtà (esistenza) con effettualità e non fondano la realtà sulla causalità. Di conseguenza ambedue rifiutano la distinzione (modale) di *essentia* ed *existentia* e la considerano la principale responsabile sul piano teoretico dell'oblio dell'essere e del volontarismo assoluto del nichilismo occidentale. Infine ambedue, in quanto convengono nel riportare (fondare) la realtà-verità dell'essente e dell' essenza all'essere, distinguono nel modo più netto la natura dalla grazia e la ragione dalla rivelazione.[3] In questo senso, anche se può sembrare paradossale, nessun pensatore presenta una convergenza di istanze speculative così profonda e radicale con S. Tommaso come Heidegger: è impossibile oggi pensare ad una ripresa veramente operante del tomismo passando sopra alla lezione heideggeriana. E questo per una duplice ragione: anzitutto perché Heidegger ha scrutato a fondo l'istanza positivo-negativa del pensiero moderno — quella del *cogito* che si attua come *volo* — che ha portato alla sostituzione della verità con la "certezza" (*Gewissheit*) ed allo svuotamento della distinzione di *essentia-existentia* precipitando nel nichilismo della volontà di potenza; poi, perché ha rilevato nell'intrico e nell'opposizione dei sistemi la permanente unità di fondo dei problemi.

Il vigore speculativo dell'istanza di Heidegger viene dalla ripresa del plesso di ente-essere (ἐόν-εἶναι) di Parmenide, offuscato subito a vantaggio dell'essenza nel pensiero greco e portato al completo oblio nel pensiero moderno: orbene esso è stato riscoperto nella linea speculativa pura da S. Tommaso che ne ha garantito l'emergenza originale con la distinzione (reale) di *essentia* ed *esse* con la quale intendiamo riassumere sia il valore ad un tempo dell'istanza heideggeriana, sia l'impertinenza della sua critica nei confronti del tomismo ed infine la soddisfazione che ha la sua istanza nella concezione tomistica dell'*esse* come *actus essendi* partecipato di cui la dipendenza causale è una "proprietà" non la realtà, come invece accade nell'estrinsecismo di tipo agostinista-nominalista-suareziano. In questa ripresa del plesso ἐόν-εἶναι di Parmenide, l'ἔστιν non è l'"è" come copula della proposizione,[4]

---

2 Cf. M. Heidegger, *Was ist Metaphysik?*, Einleitung, V. Aufl. (Frankfurt a.M. 1949), p. 7 ss.

3 Ambedue perciò si oppongono alla caduta del pensiero nella "scienza" (*Wissenschaft*) come si fa oggi, o nella "fede" (*Glaube*) come nel nominalismo ed in larghi strati del pensiero moderno da Cartesio a Jaspers, oppure nella "speranza" (*Hoffnung*) come il neo-marxismo utopista di E. Bloch e la teologia neo-luterana della speranza (Moltmann, Pannenberg...).

4 Per questa protesta e rivendicazione, vedi: M. Heidegger, *Der Spruch des Anaximander*, in "Holzwege", (Frankfurt a.M. 1950), spec. p. 323 s.

come l'intende il pensiero moderno (e già prima il nominalismo) con la risoluzione della verità a certezza: esso nomina lo εἶναι dello ἐόν, l'essere presente del presente. L'ἔστιν corrisponde alla pura pretesa dell'essere e perciò vien prima della distinzione della οὐσία in prima e seconda, in *essentia* ed *existentia*...L'ἐόν di Parmenide pertanto è pensato a partire dalla nascosta e non rilevata pienezza del non-nascondimento, ch'era familiare alla prima Grecità, anche se non si poteva ancora, né si sentiva la necessità, di sperimentare sotto ogni aspetto questa pienezza essenziale: ma, per miserando destino, nel corso della storia del pensiero l'essere (dell'essente) fu ridotto al rango del concetto più vuoto e generico. Bene, è questo ricupero che tocca realizzare fino in fondo. Ora Heidegger osserva che le altre parole fondamentali del primo pensiero greco quali φύσις, λόγος, μοῖρα ed ἔρις, ἀλήθεια ed ἕν sono scaturite dall'esperienza dello ἐόν degli ἐόντα ch'è espresso senza ausilio di concetti: il λόγος (λέγειν : raccogliere, riunire) è sperimentato [a partire] dalla ἀλήθεια, ch'è il nascondere-disvelante e così all' ἐόν si appaia lo ἕν. Mettiamo allora in chiaro come punto di partenza il problema decisivo per l'eventuale salvezza della metafisica dal fallimento in cui si trova, mediante un ripensamento della "storia dell'essere" (*Geschichte des Seins*) che non è affatto un tornare al passato ma un riportarsi a ciò che si è mostrato come l'iniziale (*das Anfängliche*). Questo ritorno Heidegger lo chiama — con un termine preso da Hölderlin — "ricordo" (*Andenken*) e, sfruttando l'etimologia del termine tedesco, usa anche: *Erinnerung* (interiorizzazione intensificata = *Er-innerung*) che dà il senso del compito. Di qui il titolo ambivalente ma efficace: *Die Erinnerung in die Metaphysik* il quale esige la comprensione simultanea di "la memoria nella metafisica" e di "interiorizzazione nella metafisica" poiché il panorama storico (del primo compito) deve portare alla realizzazione del secondo per la salvezza della metafisica e dell'uomo in essa.

Heidegger perciò può scrivere che "... la memoria nella metafisica si dà a pensare come un'epoca necessaria nella storia dell'essere, che e come di volta in volta l'essere determina la verità dell'essente, che e come l'essere da tale determinazione apre un campo di progetti per la spiegazione dell'essente, che e come tale determinazione spinge dall'interno (*stimmt*) anzitutto alla pretesa dell'essere e da tale spinta interiore costringe un pensatore a parlare dell'essere."[5] Tale ricordo della storia dell'essere esige sempre dall'essenza dell'umanità storica che, prima della dipendenza dell'uomo da forze ed energie, l'essenza dell'uomo sia fatta entrare nella verità dell'essere. L'essente è, così conclude Heidegger come aveva cominciato. Il suo essere contiene la verità,

---

5 M. Heidegger, *Nietzsche* (Pfullingen 1961), Bd. II, p. 481s.

ch'esso "è". E qui egli tocca il punto critico della sua ricerca che abbiamo già individuato in apertura, sfuggito (mi sembra) all'esuberante letteratura heideggeriana, e che tocca tenere ben fermo per afferrare l'inserzione dell'istanza originale tomistica sul fondamento dell'ente sfuggita sempre ad Heidegger.

Il fatto, egli osserva d'accordo con Aristotele e S. Tommaso, che (*Dass*) l'essente è, questo dà all'essente il privilegio d'indubitabilità dal quale si eleva alla questione di "ciò" (*Was*) che l'essente è. L'essenza (*Was-sein*) è così l'essere ch'è attinto anzitutto a partire dall'essente. In questo si manifesta che l'essere stesso si dà soltanto alla determinazione nella forma dell'entità per portare mediante tale determinatezza stessa soltanto l'essente come tale nell'essenza. Perciò contro l'essenza (*Wassein* = idea) si distingue allora anzitutto espressamente l'esistenza (*Dass-sein*). E' la distinzione, che già conosciamo, di *essentia* ed *existentia* che porta secondo Heidegger tutta la metafisica e che ha il suo peso nel sigillo essenziale della *existentia*, ma mediante la quale — aggiunge Heidegger — non si può mai attingere la distinzione iniziale che porta e connette tutta la metafisica.

Nella denunzia dell'influsso nefasto che ha avuto nella civiltà e cultura dell'Occidente il predominio della distinzione di essenza ed esistenza sta il merito di Heidegger con l'invito a ripensare a ritroso il problema di Parmenide ed a recuperarne l'intima esigenza speculativa. Quand'egli poi afferma che "... la storia dell'essere non è né la storia dell'uomo e di un'umanità, né la storia del rapporto umano all'essente e all'essere"[6] per concludere che "la storia dell'essere è l'essere stesso e soltanto questo": l'essere per Heidegger — per l'ultimo Heidegger dopo la *Kehre* di *Zeit und Sein* come per il primo di *Sein und Zeit* — è l'accadère puro come essere puro, l'eventarsi dell'evento, nella medesimezza del darsi dell'essere dell'ente all'uomo e dell'apprendere dell'essere da parte dell'uomo, dove l'unica distinzione è quella dell'essente e dell'essere (*Seiende-Sein*).

Parlare di una "concordanza" fra S. Tommaso ed Heidegger non ha senso, non più che per Hegel, Kant, Spinoza e qualsiasi filosofo moderno: quelli che l'hanno tentato, hanno potuto farlo badando soltanto ai semantemi di essere-ente ma trascurando l'accusa fondamentale in cui Heidegger coinvolge, a torto come vedremo, lo stesso S. Tommaso con tutta la tradizione filosofica occidentale: l'oblio dell'essere a causa della distinzione di *essentia* ed *existentia*, come si è detto. Soltanto mostrando il distacco di S. Tommaso da quella tradizione e l'opposizione che quella tradizione ha fatto a S. Tommaso,

---

6 M. Heidegger, *Nietzsche*, ed. cit., Bd. II, p. 488s.

si può aprire il passaggio a quel confronto: un confronto, come si è detto, di convergenza-divergente, di convergenza nella radicalità delle istanze, di divergenza altrettanto radicale nella prospettiva speculativa. Questa divergenza ha il suo nodo nel rifiuto totale da parte di Heidegger della dipendenza causale. Procederemo, per questo confronto, secondo il metodo genetico nella scia di Heidegger.

LA PROSPETTIVA DI SVILUPPO

Dopo il lampo illuminante dell'essere di Parmenide è seguito, per Heidegger, il progressivo oblio (della verità) dell'essere fino alla sua totale scomparsa. Per S. Tommaso viceversa, assistiamo nell'avanzare del pensiero umano alla scoperta progressiva della verità dell'essere dell'ente[7] in una crescente consapevolezza della sua struttura e della sua prima origine: "Antiqui philosophi paulatim et quasi pedetentim intraverunt ad cognitionem veritatis." Nella descrizione delle tappe di questo cammino ascendente egli segue il modello aristotelico circa il *naturalismo* dei primi filosofi: "A principio enim quasi grossiores existentes non existimabant esse entia nisi corpora sensibilia. Quorum qui ponebant in eis motum, non considerabant motum nisi secundum aliqua accidentia, ut puta secundum raritatem et densitatem, congregationem et segregationem." Al fondo resta la materia increata, ciò che vale anche per Platone ed Aristotele: "Et supponentes ipsam substantiam corporum increatam, assignabant aliquas causas huiusmodi accidentalium transmutationum, ut puta amicitiam, litem, intellectum, aut aliquid huiusmodi."

(La scoperta del plesso materia-forma). La seconda tappa è la scoperta della forma sostanziale, principio dell'essere e della sua unità e perfezione: "Ulterius vero procedentes, distinxerunt per intellectum inter formam substantialem et materiam, quam ponebant increatam; et perceperunt transmutationem fieri in corporibus secundum formas essentiales. Quarum transmutationum quasdam causas universaliores ponebant, ut obliquum circulum, secundum Aristotelem, vel ideas, secundum Platonem." Nessun sospetto quindi, ancora in S. Tommaso, dell'importanza di Parmenide ed Eraclito, sepolti dalla storiografia aristotelica nella categoria semplicistica di naturalismo e riscoperti nel loro effettivo contributo speculativo dalla critica moderna. E' esplicita però anche in lui, non meno che in Heidegger e con riferimento

---

7 Cf. *S. Th.* I, 44, 2 ("Utrum materia prima sit creata a Deo"). Vedi anche: *De Pot.* III, 5 ove però S. Tommaso fa fermare lo sviluppo — come terza tappa — a Platone e ad Aristotele e divide la prima tappa della *S. Theol.* in due (forme accidentali, forme sostanziali individuali) attribuendo a Platone ed Aristotele la scoperta dello *ipsum esse* universale.

teoretico più pertinente, come diremo, l'avvertenza del "limite" della posizione platonico-aristotelica della scoperta della forma da parte di Platone ed Aristotele: "Sed considerandum est quod materia per formam contrahitur ad determinatam speciem; sicut substantia alicuius speciei per accidens ei adveniens contrahitur ad determinatum modum essendi, ut *homo* contrahitur per *album*. Utrique igitur consideraverunt ens particulari quadam consideratione, vel inquantum est *hoc ens*, vel inquantum est *tale ens*. Et sic rebus causas agentes particulares assignaverunt." La requisitoria di S. Tommaso che insiste sulla determinazione dei principi va molto più a fondo di quella di Heidegger che si limita alla denunzia del plesso estrinseco di *essentia-existentia* per cogliere l'oblio dell'essere. S. Tommaso coglie questo oblio da parte dei due massimi filosofi agli antipodi di Heidegger, nella mancata "origine" della materia prima la quale, rimanendo in sé senza principio, del tutto inintelligibile, finisce per rendere impossibile l'afferramento della verità dell'essere.

Perciò l'Angelico ammette una terza epoca filosofica nella fondazione dell'essere: (La scoperta del plesso *ens-esse* e la creazione della materia prima) "Et ulterius aliqui erexerunt se ad considerandum ens inquantum est ens: et consideraverunt causam rerum, non solum secundum quod sunt *haec* vel *talia*, sed secundum quod sunt *entia*. Hoc igitur quod est causa rerum inquantum sunt entia, oportet esse causam rerum, non solum secundum quod sunt *talia* per formas accidentales, nec secundum quod sunt *haec* per formas substantiales, sed etiam secundum omne illud quod pertinet ad esse illorum quocumque modo. Et sic oportet ponere etiam materiam primam creatam ab universali causa entium."[8] Certamente qui gli "aliqui" sono i neoplatonici greci, arabi e latini.

Ciò che anzitutto risulta da questo primo passo del confronto è la convergenza di S. Tommaso e Heidegger secondo un tipo di metodo

---

8   Questa terza tappa, attribuita nella S. *Th*. alla filosofia ch'è seguita a Platone ed Aristotele e mancante nel *De Potentia*, sembra contraddire con la tesi dell'art. 1 ("Utrum sit necessarium omne ens esse creatum a Deo") che attribuisce espressamente il principio della creazione totale (partecipazione dell'essere) a Platone e ad Aristotele. La cosa più sorprendente è che nel *De Substantiis separatis* (1270-73) lo schema storiografico è di nuovo rivoluzionato e diventato più complesso, ma è conservata la divisione triadica secondo la successione: Anassagora, Platone, Aristotele, ove i "Naturales", che sono i Presocratici della storiografia moderna, formano ora il "prologo" della *triplex via* (cc. 1-2). Il netto distacco posto ora fra Platone ed Aristotele ha portato ad un confronto di accordo di fondo (*convenientia*) e di disaccordo su punti particolari (*differentia*) fra i due filosofi (cc. 3-4). L'accordo, oltre alla creazione, qui comprende la composizione di essenza ed *esse* (anche nelle creature spirituali) e la provvidenza universale (ed. Leon., Roma 1969, p. 46 s.). Sul "metodo regressivo-intensivo", usato da S. Tommaso nel riferimento alle sue fonti, vedi: C. Fabro, *La nozione metafisica di partecipazione secondo S. Tommaso d'Aquino*, III ed. (Torino 1963), p. 43ss., 75ss.

regressivo intensivo in quanto l'uno e l'altro vedono nei predecessori, assieme alle lacune, la presenza ascendente del "proprio" principio speculativo (l'*esse* come atto primo fondante per S. Tommaso, il *Sein* come presenza del presente per Heidegger). Una convergenza che sottende la divergenza ovvero l'antitesi radicale. S. Tommaso si muove riportando l'ente ai suoi principi operando per tappe, cioè dall'apparire che l'ente presenta mediante gli accidenti alla sua costituzione essenziale *ut tale ens* (essenza come sinolo di materia e forma, di sostanza e accidenti) alla costituzione radicale di *ens ut ens* (di *essentia* ed *esse*). Heidegger, che ha portato il principio moderno dell'identità di essere e conoscere alla sua esigenza radicale di avvertimento di presenza e assenza non conosce che l'opposizione di essere e non-essere (nulla). Perciò, mentre S. Tommaso sprofonda l'*esse* ad atto fondamentale ed unico della stessa forma pura e di tutto ciò che è ed appare nel reale, il *Sein* heideggeriano s'identifica con l'apparire puro ed il non-essere con lo scomparire.

Il significato pertanto del plesso *ens-esse*, già al primo passo di orientamento storiografico, è interpretato da Heidegger e S. Tommaso in senso diametralmente opposto e non poteva essere diversamente data la divergenza radicale dell'orientamento iniziale, realista in S. Tommaso, immanentista in Heidegger. S. Tommaso distingue tre livelli: l'apparire rispetto alle mutazioni accidentali sul fondamento della sostanza che contiene gli accidenti, il divenire rispetto alle mutazioni sostanziali sul fondamento della composizione di materia e forma grazie all'immanenza-emergenza della forma sulla materia e sul sinolo, l'origine prima della creazione grazie all'immanenza-emergenza dello *esse* sulla forma e sull'ente. Heidegger non conosce che il plesso di *Sein-Seiendes* e l'unico tipo di attuarsi nell'evento temporale ossia come puro apparire, unico contenuto (se così si può dire) neutrale e inesauribile (*Sein und Zeit, Zeit und Sein*) della verità. Già in questo primo confronto la somiglianza-dissomiglianza, fra i due pensatori, sembra chiarirsi in una somiglianza puramente esteriore ed in una dissomiglianza reale: a nostro avviso il loro incontro-scontro ha un significato più profondo e i due momenti non vanno separati ma devono convivere. Si tratta infatti che il problema teoretico della fondazione della verità del reale sorge, sia in S. Tommaso come in Heidegger, da esigenze similari ma è orientato in prospettive opposte. La stessa situazione si ripete nello svolgimento del confronto.

Il Punto di Partenza o "Cominciamento"

In Heidegger, come si è visto, il cominciamento è fatto con il plesso "l'essente è" poiché "nell'essente appare l'essere" e così "l'essente è il reale." In realtà però Heidegger è d'accordo con Hegel poiché quell'essere dell'essente è identico al non-essere e sta quindi per il semplice (essere dell') "apparire." Quando infatti Heidegger procede spiegando che "... nell'essente appare l'essere,"[9] l'essenza dell'essere è questo puro apparire (*erscheinen*) dispiegantesi mediante la temporalità del *Dasein* ch'è l'uomo. Ma mentre Hegel considera l'essere e il nulla come momenti astratti (dell'indeterminatezza dell'immediatezza) da superare col ricorso (mediazione) all'Infinito come fondamento e principio che sta "dietro le spalle," per Heidegger l'essere coincide con l'apparire ed il non-essere con lo scomparire, esso è principio e fine ad un tempo *nel* tempo ch'è senza fine. Per questo "...l'essere stesso è nell' essenza finito e si manifesta soltanto nella trascendenza della realtà umana (*Dasein*) che si è mantenuta fuori nel nulla."[10] Per Hegel il cominciamento è l'essere vuoto (dell'apparire puro) dell'immediatezza e perciò in questa sua astrazione è identico al nulla: si tratta perciò qui di un cominciamento apparente, provvisorio e didattico, per così dire, perché il cominciamento reale è fatto con l'Assoluto ed in virtù dell'Assoluto che "sta alle spalle" del soggetto conoscente e dà perciò la "spinta"[11] alla riflessione speculativa per attingere l'ultimo fondamento. Per Heidegger invece l'essere è il tempo come attuarsi dell'uomo nel mondo: cosi non c'è che il divenire storico, orizzontale ch'è identità di compresenza di essere e non-essere[12] nel rispettivo mutuo condizionarsi secondo la struttura dell'evento (*Er-Eignis*), come si è visto. Trascendenza e "metafisica" sono allora sinonimi anche per Heidegger, ma con significato capovolto: essi indicano il portarsi della coscienza (ovvero del *Dasein* ch'è la realtà umana) alla natura ($\varphi\acute{\upsilon}\sigma\iota\varsigma$, mondo...), il suo

---

9 "Im Seienden erscheint das Sein" (M. Heidegger, *Nietzsche*, ed. cit., Bd. II, p. 339, 488).

10 "Sein und Nichts gehören zusammen, aber nicht weil sie beide — vom Hegelschen Begriff des Denkens aus gesehen — in ihrer Unbestimmtheit und Unmittelbarkeit übereinkommen, sondern weil das Sein selbst im Wesen endlicht ist und sich nur in der Transzendenz des in das Nichts hinausgehaltenen Daseins offenbart" (M. Heidegger, *Was ist Metaphysik?*, ed. cit., p. 36).

11 Ed Hegel infatti parla di "impulso" (*Trieb*) che corrisponde al *conatus* di Spinoza, alla *vis activa* o *nisus* della monade di Leibniz... come Hegel stesso ricorda (cf. *Wissenschaft der Logik*, II. Buch, 1. Abschn., 1. Kap.; Lasson II, 59). E' un punto dell'hegelismo che merita di essere approfondito.

12 Di fì a poco infatti Heidegger con chiarezza esemplare: "Das menschliche Dasein kann sich nur zu Seiendem verhalten, wenn es sich in das Nichts hineinhält. Das Hinausgehen über das Seiende geschieht im Wesen des Dasein s. Dieses Hinausgehen aber ist die Metaphysik selbst" (*Was ist Metaphysik?*, ed. cit., p. 37).

farsi mondo e farsi nel mondo.[13] Non c'è più per Heidegger, come per nessun filosofo dopo il capovolgimento che l'idealismo ha fatto di Kant, un problema della conoscenza distinto dal problema metafisico: *Sein und Zeit* infatti non è che un'analisi di fenomenologia trascendentale del comportamento,[14] nel senso di una completa estroflessione della soggettività ch'è dissolta nella neutralità dello "es gibt" dell'evento.

Assai più complessa è la semantica del plesso tomistico di *ens-esse*, che corrisponde alla lettera al *Seiende-Sein* di Heidegger, sulla quale non si è fatta ancora completa luce da parte dei tomisti: a noi interessa questa volta rilevare soltanto i momenti principali della sua progressione teoretica.

A differenza di Hegel e Heidegger (e forse dello stesso Parmenide), che scivolano sul plesso intensivo del *Seiende* e fanno il cominciamento con il *Sein* come presenza vuota, S. Tommaso comincia con lo *ens* come il nodo di presa della realtà da parte della mente. Nei primi scritti il suggerimento (o pretesto) sembra venire da Avicenna, ma nello sfondo domina la posizione di Aristotele che attribuisce alla metafisica come oggetto proprio d'indagare sullo ὄν ἦ ὄν.[15] La ragione di questa precedenza assoluta che lo *ens* ha su tutti i semantemi sembra proprio la proprietà che lo ὄν ha di stare al vertice dei concetti; ma qui soccorre, a salvare lo *ens* dalla riduzione ad un prodotto di pura astrazione logica, l'affermazione aristotelica, decisiva per la metafisica tomistica, che "... l'ente non è un genere."[16] Ma il modo di arrivare alla posizione dello *ens*, in questo primo periodo almeno, sembra decisamente di natura logica ossia "riduttivo" formale. Ecco il testo forse più completo:

Dicendum quod sicut in demonstrabilibus oportet fieri reductionem in aliqua principia per se intellectui nota, ita investigando quid est unumquodque; alias utrobique in infinitum iretur, et sic periret omnino scientia et cognitio rerum. Illud autem quod primo intellectus concipit quasi notissimum, et in quod omnes conceptiones resolvit, est ens, ut Avicenna dicit in principio *Metaphysicae* suae [lib. I, c. IX]. Unde oportet quod omnes aliae conceptiones intellectus accipiantur ex additione ad ens. Sed enti non potest addi aliquid quasi extranea natura, per modum

---

13 Questa nozione di "trascendenza" può anche considerarsi come la risposta — e la sconfessione drastica — al progetto kantiano di passare dalla Critica della ragion pura alla cosidetta "Metafisica della natura" (cf. *Kritik der reinen Vernunft*, Vorrede, A XXI).

14 Di qui il favore che *Sein und Zeit* ha trovato presso alcuni psichiatri (Binswanger, H. Müller-Suur, J. Meinertz...).

15 "Ens et essentia sunt quae primo intellectu concipiuntur, ut dicit Avicenna in principio suae Metaphysicae" (*De ente et essentia*, Prol.; Baur 11, 3-6). Il richiamo ad Avicenna sembra di obbligo in questo periodo: *In I Sent.* 25, I, 4; 38, I, 4, 4ᵐ; *De Ver.* I, 1. C'è ancora nel più tardo commento alla Metafisica: lib. I, 1. 2, nr. 40. Per la formula di Aristotele, vedi: *Metaph.* IV, 1, 1003a21.

16 *Metaph.* III, 8, 998b22.

quo differentia additur generi, vel accidens subiecto, quia quaelibet natura essentialiter est ens; unde etiam probat Philosophus in III *Metaphys.* [com. 10], quod ens non potest esse genus.[17]

Il testo è complesso perché ha tutta l'apparenza di una deduzione formalista e contenutistica soprattutto con l'inciso: "Sed enti non potest addi aliquid quasi extranea natura, per modum quo differentia additur generi, vel accidens subiecto, quia quaelibet natura essentialiter est ens." E'vero che qui l'analisi è presentata nell'ambito formale delle categorie: nel primo momento la divisione dell'ente è presa a partire dai modi di essere che sono la sostanza e gli accidenti, quella è presa dall'essere principale e questi indicano le essenze o forme secondarie. L'*esse*, come *actus essendi*, che qui sembra lasciato nell'ombra, emerge invece subito nella deduzione seguente dei trascendentali ove spicca l'apporto neoplatonico e S. Tommaso torna infatti a richiamarsi ad Avicenna. L'*ens* è espressamente distinto dalla *res* proprio per questo che "... ens sumitur ab actu essendi, sed nomen rei exprimit quiditatem vel essentiam entis."[18] La distinzione fra atto (*esse*) e contenuto (*essentia*) è qui ormai esplicita ed è posta a fondamento della struttura della metafisica.

Sembra, questo procedimento, una deduzione di tipo logico essenzialistico, come farebbe pensare il prologo del nostro testo: "Sicut in demonstrabilibus oportet fieri reductionem in aliqua principia per se intellectui nota, ita investigando *quid est* unumquodque, alias utrobique in infinitum iretur..." Il "quid est" infatti fa subito pensare al τί ἐστιν aristotelico, richiamato anche da Heidegger, e perciò all'essenza, così che la riduzione ultima debba terminare nel concetto del contenuto più indeterminato qual è appunto lo *ens generalissimum* della Scolastica giustamente deprecata da Heidegger. Questo però è già escluso dallo sviluppo e dal seguito del testo tomistico, come si è visto, che mette in evidenza l'*actus essendi* il quale conferisce al semantema *ens* la struttura paradossale di plesso il più concreto e comunissimo ad un tempo. Una formulazione stimolante in questa direzione è contemporanea al *De ente*: "Primum quod cadit in imaginatione intellectus est ens, sine quo nihil potest apprehendi ab intellectu, sicut id quod primum cadit in credulitate intellectus sunt dignitates et praecipue ista, contradictoria non esse simul vera; unde omnia alia includuntur quodammodo in ente unite et distincte, sicut in principio."[19] L'espressione "unite et distincte" è un lampo di genio del giovane baccelliere che contiene la problematica dell'intera metafisica. E si può chiarire allora il significato che può avere la *additio* per il semantema *ens*: altra è la con-

17 *De Ver.* I, 1; ed. leon. (Romae 1970), p. 4b-5a.
18 *De Ver.* I, 1; ed. cit., p. 5b.
19 *In I Sent.* 8, I, 3; Mandonnet I, p. 200.

dizione (del concetto) di Dio, spiega S. Tommaso, il quale è in sé per-
fetto e non può ricevere aggiunta; altra è la condizione (del concetto) di
ens commune che astrae da ogni aggiunta "...ita quod non sit de ratione
eius quod fiat additio, neque quod non fiat, et hoc modo ens commune
est sine additione." E spiega: "In intellectu enim entis non includitur
ista conditio, sine additione; alias numquam posset sibi fieri additio,
quia esset contra rationem eius; et ideo commune est, quia in sui ratione
non dicit aliquam additionem, sed potest sibi fieri ut determinetur ad
proprium."[20] E questo avviene p. es. come nel genere animale comune
che prescinde dalle determinazioni che sono le differenze di *rationale* e
irrationale. La spiegazione è esemplificativa, perché S. Tommaso tiene
sempre saldo fin da principio che l'ente non è un genere. Ed è sotto la
spinta di questo principio aristotelico, combinato ancora con un
riferimento ad Avicenna, che l'Angelico arriva alla sua formulazione
originale del semantema *ens*:

> Ista definitio, secundum Avicennam, non potest esse substantiae: sub-
> stantia est quae non est in subiecto. Ens enim non est genus. Haec autem
> negatio "non in subiecto" nihil ponit; unde hoc quod dico, ens non
> est in subiecto, non dicit aliquod genus: quia in quolibet genere oportet
> significare quidditatem aliquam, ut dictum est, de cuius intellectu non est
> esse. Ens autem non dicit quidditatem, sed solum actum essendi, cum sit
> principium ipsum; et ideo non sequitur: est non in subiecto, ergo est in
> genere substantiae; sed oportet addi: est habens quidditatem quam con-
> sequitur esse non in subiecto; ergo est in genere substantiae.[21]

E' chiaro quindi che l'impressione dell'origine essenzialistica del
nostro semantema va abbandonata, anche se si può forse ammettere che
in questo primo periodo gli influssi aristotelici e platonici non sembrano ancora giunti ad una completa fusione come si può osservare
negli scritti della maturità. Comunque fin da principio la prima *Diremtion* trascendentale di *ens* e *res* per S. Tommaso è chiara: quello
rimanda all'*esse* e questa all'*essentia* come preciserà il *De Veritate*.[22]

Qui allora si fa evidente la differenza radicale iniziale fra Heidegger
e S. Tommaso e con essa si chiarifica la mediazione funesta che la
distinzione scolastica di *essentia* ed *existentia* ha operato per l'oblio
dell'essere consumato dal pensiero moderno con la risoluzione
dell'essere nell'identità di pensiero-volontà. Per Heidegger si presenta
soltanto il plesso di essente-essere (*Seiende-Sein*), ove l'essere dice la
presenza dell'essente e pertanto la sua *illuminazione*: il concetto di
essentia — come "contenuto" dell'ente derivato dalla ἰδέα — è il sot-

---

20 *In I Sent.* 8, IV, 1 ad 1; Mandonnet I, p. 219.
21 *In I Sent.* 8, IV, 2 ad 2; Mandonnet I, p. 222s.
22 Cf. *De Ver.* I, 1.

toprodotto del separatismo platonico assunto poi dal Cristianesimo, la *existentia* in quanto fondata sulla causalità estrinseca deriva dal creazionismo cristiano. Per S. Tommaso però è altrettanto saldo, quanto per Heidegger, che l'*esse* è l'atto dell'*ens* nel senso forte di ἐνέργεια come si è detto e come l'Angelico ha mantenuto da principio alla fine: "Esse dicitur actus entis in quantum est ens."[23] L'emergenza dell'*esse* (*actus essendi*) vale quindi per S. Tommaso come l'affermazione della consistenza primaria della realtà nel suo immediato presentarsi come verità dell'ente. L'istanza e la semantica dell'inizio, che implica insieme quella del fondamento, coincidono quindi in Heidegger e S. Tommaso: il loro significato però sta agli antipodi. L'ente e l'*esse* di cui parla S. Tommaso precede e fonda il pensiero e l'attuarsi della coscienza in generale; per Heidegger invece, anche se sembra respingere il soggettivismo immanentistico, l'essere del soggetto umano è il suo ec-sistere come trascendersi nel mondo — perciò può dirsi immanentismo ontologico e quindi monismo metafisico, come si è visto sopra. Abbagliato dall'estrinsecismo del plesso di *essentia-existentia*, Heidegger si è fermato al *Sein* come apparire e presentarsi che si risolve nel rapporto (*Bezug*) scambievole di uomo e mondo.

Per S. Tommaso invece l'*ens* è fondato in profondità nel duplice riferimento alla "essentia" come contenuto e allo "esse" come atto di cui risulta la sintesi in atto di ente come plesso semantico originario del reale esistente. La *existentia* dice perciò soltanto la realtà di "fatto" dello *ens*, attestato dall'esperienza: ossia la *actualitas* ch'è l'oggetto del giudizio di effettualità esistenziale: p.es. l'esistenza del mondo, dell'anima, di Dio, dei pianeti e degli astri... ed anche degli accidenti come salute, scienza, ricchezza, bellezza... e perfino delle privazioni come malattie e morte, ignoranza e vizio — "esistono" anch'esse, e come! Ma sia degli accidenti e tanto più delle privazioni non si può dire che abbiano l'*esse* e quindi che siano propriamente *entia*. *Ens* secondo S. Tommaso ha significato forte e si dice in senso proprio soltanto la "sostanza" che sussiste nella sua essenza in virtù del suo *actus essendi*. Il principio della sostanza è perciò il pilastro del realismo metafisico, che sta perciò agli antipodi dello storicismo ontologico dell'evento (*Ereignis*) di Heidegger. La sostanza è infatti — come *ens* a titolo primario — il portatore proprio dello *esse*: "Nam cum ens dicat aliquid

---

23 *Quodl.* IX, II, 3. Alcuni testi: "Nomen entis ab esse imponitur" (*In I Sent.* 19, V, 1); "Nomen entis nullo modo sumitur ab aliqua relatione sed ab esse... sed nomen rei imponitur a quidditate vel forma" (Ibid. 25, I, 4 ad 1); "Ipsum esse est quo substantia denominatur ens" (*C. Gent.* II, 54); "Res et ens significant omnino idem sed sec. diversas rationes. Hoc nomen res imponitur a quidditate tantum; hoc vero nomen ens imponitur ab actu essendi" (*In IV Metaph.*, 1, 2, nr. 553. Cf. nr. 558); "Esse idem est quod actus entis" (*Quodl.* XII, I, 1 ad 1).

proprie esse in actu, actus autem proprie ordinem habeat ad potentiam, secundum hoc simpliciter aliquid dicitur ens secundum quod primo discernitur ab eo quod est in potentia tantum. Hoc autem est esse substantiale rei uniuscuiusque. Unde per suum esse substantiale dicitur unumquodque ens simpliciter: per actus superaddictos dicitur esse secundum quid."[24] Lo schema aristotelico delle categorie resta quindi dominante, ma lo *esse* vi compare come principio attuale fondante che attua la sostanza come un tutto mentre per Aristotele l'atto della sostanza era la forma sostanziale.[25] E questo ci riporta alla riflessione iniziale ossia che l'*ens* è il semantema ad un tempo il più comune ed insieme il più concreto: "Ens quamvis sit communissimum tamen concretive dicitur."[26] Per Heidegger invece il plesso *Seiende-Sein* è e si esaurisce in un rapporto di comportamento trascendentale (*Bezug*), non fa capo ad un atto e ad un contenuto di una realtà ma al manifestarsi del comportamento di un soggetto e per un oggetto ch'è l'uomo storico nella dinamica del tempo.

Il parallelismo antitetico di Heidegger-S. Tommaso prosegue e si approfondisce. Nel plesso *Seiende-Sein* di Heidegger, la verità del *Seiende* è il *Sein* ossia il presentarsi come accadere puro e così il *Seiende* "cade" nel *Sein*. Il plesso invece di *ens* si biforca in *essentia* ed *esse* e così diventa il plesso trascendentale per la conoscenza della verità. Questo principio tomistico è di un'estrema densità d'implicazioni il cui sviluppo costituisce la messa in opera delle strutture portanti, non solo della conoscenza immediata e della scienza in generale e delle scienze applicate sia della natura come dello spirito, ma anzitutto e soprattutto della metafisica.

L'*ens* come plesso trascendentale dell'intelligibilità del reale: "Primum quod cadit in imaginatione intellectus est ens, sine quo nihil potest apprehendi ab intellectu, sicut primum quod cadit in credulitate intellectus sunt dignitates et praecipue ista, contradictoria non esse simul vera: unde omnia alia includuntur quodammodo in ente unite et distincte, sicut in principio."[27] Rileviamo i momenti fondamentali di questa trascendentalità, che corrisponde per antitesi a quella del *cogito-volo* moderno.

L'*ens* — come si è visto nei testi già citati — è certamente il *primum*

---

24   *S. Th.* I, 5, 1 ad 1. Così p. es. anche nel commento alla Metafisica: "Ens simpliciter dicitur id quod in se habet esse, scilicet substantia" (*In lib. XI*, 1. 3, nr. 2197); "Nam ens dicitur quasi esse habens, hoc autem solum est substantia quae subsistit" (*In lib. XII*, 1. 1, nr. 2419).
25   Perciò in uno degli ultimi commenti, S. Tommaso scrive: "Ens nihil aliud est quam quod est... significat rem quae habet esse" (*In Periherm.* c. 1, lect. 5).
26   *In Boeth. De Hebd.*, lect. 2.
27   *In I Sent.* 8, I, 3; Mandonnet I, p. 200.

nella sfera ontico-fenomenologica cioè il fondamento: "...*primum* quod cadit in imaginatione"; "*primum* quod cadit in intellectu... quod intellectus intelligit"; "*primum* quod cadit in conceptione humana."[28] La ragione di questa priorità è che *ens* dice l'essere in atto e l'essere in atto è essere nella propria verità e perfezione e corrispondere perciò al proprio destino (*Geschick*) come direbbe Heidegger. Questo destino per le realtà naturali e per l'uomo, in quanto si trova e opera nel tempo, si attua certamente nel tempo, ma non è detto che abbia nel tempo il suo primo fondamento e che ottenga nel tempo il suo ultimo compimento, come pretende Heidegger e l'antropologia trascendentale post-hegeliana. Per S. Tommaso al *transcendentale fundans originarium*, nel senso intensivo di ciò ch'è insieme il primo dato alla (della) coscienza e ciò che fa pensare ossia che mette in movimento il pensiero per il conseguimento della verità del reale, è l'afferramento primordiale del plesso di "ens": "Id quod primo acquiritur ab intellectu est ens et id in quo non invenitur ratio entis non est capibile ab intellectu."[29] In questa genesi trascendentale del conoscere le conoscenze posteriori, si badi bene, restano immanenti al plesso originario di *ens*, non soltanto — come presto si dirà — come "punto di partenza" da lasciare alle spalle ma come il principio di fondazione a cui si deve restare sempre attaccati come la garanzia dell'attacco con la realtà. "Hoc verbum *Est* consignificat compositionem quia non eam principaliter significat, sed ex consequenti; significat enim illud quod cadit in intellectu per modum actualitatis absolute: nam Est simpliciter dictum significat in

---

28 *In Boeth. De Trin.*, q. I, a. 3 ad 3. Rileggiamo ancora: "Ens est prima intentio intellectus" (*In I Sent.* 19, V. 1 ad ult.); "Primum cadens in apprehensione est ens..." (*In I Sent.* 25, I, 4); "Illud quod primum intellectus concipit quasi notissimum est ens" (*De Ver.* I, 1); "Cum ens sit quod primo cadit in conceptione mentis" (*De Ver.* XXI, 1); "Illud quod primo cadit in apprehensione intellectus est ens..." (*De Ver.* XXI, 4 ad 4); "Primum in conceptione cadit ens" (*S. Th.* I, 5, 2); "Intellectus per prius apprehendit ipsum ens..." (*S. Th.* I, 16, 4 ad 2); "Primum quod in intellectum cadit est ens" (*De Pot.* IX, 7 ad 15); "Cum autem ens sit primum quod in intellectu concipitur" (ibid.: "Ad ea quae in oppositum").

29 *In lib. De causis*, lect. 6; Saffrey 47, Pera nr. 174. Qui, alla fine della sua carriera, S. Tommaso s'ispira espressamente al principio di Proclo: "Πᾶν τὸ θεῖον αὐτὸ μὲν διὰ τὴν ὑπερούσιον ἕνωσιν ἄρρητόν ἐστι καὶ ἄγνωστον πᾶσι τοῖς δευτέροις".(Proclus, *Elementatio Theologica*, Prop. 123; Dodds 108). E' la ripresa, ora approfondita col neoplatonismo greco, dell' intuizione giovanile sopra ricordata, mantenuta nella maturità: "Primum quod cadit in imaginatione est ens, *sine quod nihil potest apprehendi ab intellectu*" (*In I Sent.* 8, I, 3); "...et in quod omnes conceptiones resolvit" (*De Ver.* I, 1); "...unde unicuique apprehenso a nobis attribuimus quod sit ens" (*S. Th.* I-II, 55, 4 ad 1); "In his quae in apprehensione hominis cadunt, quidam ordo invenitur. Nam illud quod primo cadit in apprehensione est *ens, cuius intellectus includitur in omnibus quaecumque quis apprehendit*" (*S. Th.* I-II, 94, 2).

actu esse."[30] Così si può dire che la posizione del cosidetto problema critico del conoscere coincide, per S. Tommaso, come a loro modo anche in Hegel e Heidegger, con la stessa posizione radicale della verità dell'essere.

LA DEDUZIONE TRASCENDENTALE DELLO "ENS" TOMISTICO

Essa si presenta in tre momenti o fasi di fondazione del conoscere nel suo articolarsi interiore e costitutivo primario: per le forme o essenze, per i trascendentali, per i primi principi.

a) *Le forme o essenze.*

Infatti l'ente esprime un contenuto in atto ch'è precisamente l'essenza reale, come si è visto nella prima *Diremtion* dello *ens*. Perciò l'essenza appartiene all'*ens* e come ha la sua realtà grazie allo *esse* dello *ens*, così trae da esso la sua intelligibilità: "Illud quod primo cadit in apprehensione intellectus est ens; unde oportet quod cuicumque apprehenso per intellectum, intellectus attribuat hoc quod est ens. Et ideo cum apprehendit essentiam alicuius entis, dicit illam essentiam esse ens; et similiter unamquamque formam generalem vel specialem, ut bonitas est ens, albedo est ens, et sic de aliis."[31] L'osservazione prepara l'emergenza intensiva dello *esse*, come atto di tutti gli atti e perfezione di tutte le perfezioni, come si dirà più avanti. E' questo il momento metafisico della *res*, come primo trascendentale, accennato sopra. S. Tommaso presenta la *res* come il primo "modo" (*modus*) "... secundum quod consequitur omne ens in se" in forma affermativa: "Non autem invenitur aliquid affirmative dictum absolute quod possit accipi in omni ente nisi essentia eius secundum quam esse dicitur: et sic imponitur hoc nomen *res*; quod in hoc differt ab ente secundum Avicennam in principio *Metaphysicae* quod ens sumitur ab actu essendi, sed nomen rei exprimit quidditatem vel essentiam entis."[32]

Qui però sorge un problema di fondo, rimasto finora nell'ombra. E' noto che S. Tommaso, fedele all'antropologia di Aristotele, attribuisce come oggetto proprio dell'intelletto umano l'essenza delle cose materiali conosciuta per astrazione, la quale sembra costituire così il

---

30 *In lib. Periherm.* c. 1, lect. 5.
31 *De Ver.* XXI, 4 ad 4.
32 *De Ver.* I, 1. Per il testo di Avicenna, cf. *Metaph.* I, 6 (ed. Veneta 1508, fol. 72rb). Assieme allo ens, fra i *primum cognita*, Avicenna include la *res* e il *necesse esse*.

punto di partenza per la conoscenza del reale: invece si è visto che l'oggetto proprio dell'intelletto è il plesso di *ens*.

Ma il problema ci sembra soltanto apparente, qualora sia visto all'interno della struttura del pensiero tomistico. La conoscenza per astrazione riguarda il "contenuto" cioè l'essenza ed è perciò una conoscenza che esige appunto la riflessione astrattiva, mentre l'apprensione dello *ens* è immediata e costituisce il primo passo di apprensione del reale.[33] Là si tratta di una conoscenza riflessa specifica cioè esplicita dell'essenza (*res*) come tale, limitata perciò ai costitutivi propri del suo contenuto come sono presenti nell'astrazione (dalla singolarità in cui si trovano nella realtà); qui invece si ha la apprensione implicita *globale* che mette il soggetto nel primo contatto *diretto* con la realtà. Il rapporto fra questi due momenti del conoscere non è di esclusione ma d'integrazione e di fondazione: cioè è quella del tutto alla parte e di pensiero spontaneo al pensiero riflesso. Questa connessione sembra suggerita da S. Tommaso con esplicito riferimento ad Aristotele: "Ens autem dicitur id quod finite participat esse et hoc est proportionatum intellectui nostro, cuius obiectum est "quod quid est" ut dicitur in III De Anima.[34] Unde illud solum est capibile ab intellectu nostro quod habet quidditatem participantem esse."[35] L'apprensione dello *ens* porta sull'affermazione della realtà in quanto nella sua complessità è presente e data alla vita cosciente del conoscente; la conoscenza dell'essenza è di natura specializzata e suppone come sostegno e punto di partenza quella di *ens*. Questo vale soprattutto nella concezione tomistica che esige nell'attuarsi dell'astrazione la "conversio ad phantasmata" ossia il riferimento al singolare esistente che è appunto tale in quanto è *ens*. Il progresso di S. Tommaso, anche questa volta, avviene in modo mirabile all'interno dei principi aristotelici:

> Intellectus autem humani, qui est coniunctus corpori, proprium obiectum est quidditas sive natura in materia corporali existens; et per huiusmodi naturas visibilium rerum etiam in invisibilium rerum aliqualem cognitionem ascendit. De ratione autem huius naturae est quod in aliquo individuo existat, quod non est absque materia corporali: sicut de ratione naturae lapidis est quod sit in hoc lapide, et de ratione naturae equi quod sit in hoc equo, et sic de aliis. Unde natura lapidis, vel cuiuscumque materialis rei, cognosci non potest complete et vere, nisi secundum quod cognoscitur ut in particulari existens. Particulare autem apprehendimus per sensum et imaginationem. Et ideo necesse est ad hoc quod intellectus

---

33 "Simpliciter enim dicitur res quod habet esse ratum et firmum in natura... sec. quod habet quidditatem vel essentiam quamdam; ens vero sec. quod habet esse, ut dicit Avicenna" (*In II Sent.* 37, I, 1; Mandonnet II, p. 944).

34 *De an.* III, 4, 429b10ss.

35 *In lib. De causis*, lect. 6; Saffrey 47, Pera nr. 175.

actu intelligat suum obiectum proprium, quod convertat se ad phantasmata, ut speculetur naturam universalem in particulari existentem. [36]

L'apprensione originaria dello *ens* è solidale con l'intero dinamismo della coscienza ed è presente perciò a tutti i livelli dell'attività dello spirito teoretico e pratico.

b) *I trascendentali.*

La rappresentazione (e la rappresentabilità) appartiene alla *res*, all'essenza, grazie al contenuto ch'essa "presenta" mediante il quale si pone nella realtà e l'una cosa si distingue dall'altra. La cosa si presenta anzitutto mediante l'esperienza nella propria situazione spazio-temporale e con le caratteristiche sensibili immediate p. es. le qualità caratteristiche dell'albero, della casa, del cavallo... La rappresentazione sensibile (e la rappresentabilità) sta pertanto a fondamento dell'oggettività (e dell'oggettivazione) del conoscere: nel realismo aristotelico essa fa capo, come si è visto, alla *conversio ad phantasmata* ch'è la mutua necessaria implicanza di senso e intelletto nella conoscenza della realtà. Questa implicanza indica la dipendenza stretta, continua e indispensabile, dei concetti puri ad ogni livello (sia generico e specifico, sia fisico, morale, estetico, religioso...) dai contenuti di esperienza interna ed esterna. Tale dipendenza radicale e sostitutiva dell'attività intellettuale noetica formale dalla sfera sensibile caratterizza, nel suo momento dinamico, il realismo del conoscere, il quale come comincia dal contatto diretto con le cose riguarda le cose che il mondo presenta al soggetto e termina alle cose stesse. La *conversio ad phantasmata* costituisce pertanto il processo di oggettivazione in *actu exercito* nel suo momento fondamentale il quale rivela (ed attua) ad un tempo la struttura trascendentale del soggetto di senso e intelletto e la struttura dell'oggetto ai suoi vari livelli intenzionali: di essente ed essere, di essente ed essenza, di essenza ed *esse*, di sostanza ed accidenti, di materia e forma... secondo l'intero intreccio costitutivo della realtà. Ma qui trascendentale ha il senso opposto a quello kantiano: esso indica la dipendenza dell'intelligibile dal sensibile, della rappresentazione dalla presentazione, del soggetto dall'oggetto...Secondo Kant invece — al quale si richiama ovvero ritorna Heidegger —

spazio e tempo sono soltanto forme dell'intuizione sensibile, quindi soltanto condizioni dell'esistenza (*Existenz*) delle cose come ap-

---

36 *S. Th.* I, 84, 7. Sulla connessione di questa dottrina con la concezione tomistica (finora trascurata) della *cogitativa*, cf. C. Fabro, *Percezione e pensiero*, II ed. (Brescia 1962), p. 198ss., spec. pp. 208-234.

parizioni (*Erscheinungen*); inoltre noi non abbiamo nessun concetto dell'intelletto quindi anche nessun elemento (*Elemente*) per la conoscenza delle cose se non in quanto può essere data un'intuizione corrispondente a questi concetti; di conseguenza noi non possiamo avere conoscenza di alcun oggetto (*Gegenstand*) in quanto cosa in se stessa ma soltanto in quanto esso è oggetto (*Objekt*) dell'intuizione sensibile cioè in quanto apparizione.[37]

Il trascendentale moderno ripete quindi, ma con movimento inverso e con significato opposto, la funzione della *conversio ad phantasmata*: qui infatti il momento formale (detto a priori) è tutto da parte del soggetto ed il conoscere perciò non termina alla cosa in sé ed all'essere ma all'apparizione. Il trascendentale moderno, come ha precisato con acume Heidegger, non è identico all'a priori ma è l'a priori che determina l'oggetto *come* oggetto, l'oggettività. Di qui il capovolgimento del concetto di "trascendenza," come si è visto sopra, nel senso di oggettività ossia di riferirsi del soggetto al mondo e (di avvertire) di essere-nel-mondo come essere storico. Questo avviene, si badi bene, mediante la rappresentazione dell'oggetto che ha nel soggetto l'origine (la possibilità) della sua rappresentabilità: quindi la sua oggettività è fondata a partire da qualcosa (l'a priori = spazio e tempo, le categorie, l'io penso...) che "gli viene-prima" e precisamente nel rappresentare. La pensabilità è perciò la rappresentabilità di qualcosa come condizione del conoscere. Io penso qualcosa.[38] Kant, ed il pensiero moderno in genere, cominciano con la *res* e non conoscono l'*ens*: stretto in quest'essenzialismo, il pensiero è anzitutto e soltanto presenza di contenuto ch'è sostenuto dalla rappresentazione e condizionato nel suo fondamento dalla capacità rappresentativa del soggetto, la *Denkbarkeit* come *Vor-stellbarkeit*. Perciò da questo deriva anche il significato opposto, osserva Heidegger, che ha l'intuizione (*Anschauung*) in Kant in quanto essa rimane fondata nella posizione fondamentale dello "Io penso" che attua l'oggettivazione come rappresentare.[39] Perciò alla domanda: che significa lo "Ich denke" di Kant? — Heidegger risponde, questo: "Io rappresento qualcosa come qualcosa"[40] e questo comporta l'unificazione (dei dati sensibili e dell'a priori). L'essere è la loro unità. Pensare è quindi unificare nel senso di rappresentare l'unità dell'essente.

---

37 Kant, *Kritik der reinen Vernunft*, Vorrede zur zweiten Aufl., B XXVs.
38 M. Heidegger, *Nietzsche*, ed. cit., Bd. II, p. 466.
39 Il "rappresentare" italiano non rende l'efficacia del tedesco *Vorstellen* che è il "porre prima cioè in anticipo" (*vor-stellen*) o "darsi-in-anticipo" (*Vor-sich-brungen*) come insiste Heidegger (l.c.).
40 "Was heisst dann das Kantische 'Ich denke'? Soviel wie: Ich stelle etwas als etwas vor" (op. cit., Bd. II, p. 461).

Ma questo è sempre un muoversi nella scia e dentro il formalismo (essenzialismo) scolastico della distinzione di *essentia* ed *existentia* che dà la priorità noetica al contenuto e la qualifica di attualità al fatto di produzione (dell'oggetto): da parte di Dio nel formalismo scolastico, da parte del soggetto conoscente nel pensiero moderno. Di qui la preminenza che assume l'uno, l'unità e l'unificazione, in quanto è a partire dal soggetto che sorge l'unità dell'oggetto ed è perciò reso possibile il suo presentarsi. Pensare è essenzialmente afferrare l'uno dei (nei) molti (ἓν παρὰ τὰ πολλά), nella linea dell'essenzialismo classico (Platone), raccolto nella ἰδέα. Esattamente all'opposto di S. Tommaso, per il quale l'uno viene al terzo posto, dopo l'*ens* e la *res* ed è quindi doppiamente fondato, come contenuto nella costituzione della *res* e come atto nella presenza dello *ens* portatore dello *esse* ch'è l'atto fondante. Pertanto si può dire che come la *conversio ad phantasmata* è la via della fondazione trascendentale della verità del contenuto (*essentia*) dell'ente, così la corrispondenza delle proprietà o modi dell'ente ovvero dei trascendentali è la via della chiarificazione dell'esplicitazione e dell'accrescimento interno che il reale ottiene nel soggetto spirituale. La *Diremtion* dei trascendentali non è affatto uniforme, essa però comporta un distinguere (restando) *dentro* l'ente: ciò significa che l'ente resta il presupposto e il fondamento, indispensabile ed inesauribile, ed insieme quindi che l'ente è il punto di arrivo delle determinazioni come dell'arricchimento portato dai trascendentali.[41]

La deduzione tomistica dei trascendentali non avviene quindi per "anticipazione" delle condizioni dell'unità oggettiva, ma per lo sviluppo dell'implicito nell'esplicito in modo però che l'esplicito è immanente nell'implicito e sta sempre saldamente attinente ad esso, gli appartiene necessariamente. La prima *Diremtion* non a caso è quella della *res*, di cui si è detto: essa esprime, come si è visto, la determinazione all'interno dell'ente del momento statico del contenuto nella sua distinzione dall'atto ch'è l'*esse*. Solo nel secondo momento interviene l'unità (*unum*) come determinazione dell'indivisione e integrità dell'ente ed è perciò una proprietà dell'ente stesso, fondata quindi sulla realtà dell'ente in atto: unità ch'è certamente, ai vari livelli, unificazione di essenza ed *esse*, di sostanza ed accidenti, di materia e forma, di anima e facoltà... e in generale di atto e potenza, ma è un'unità di unificazione che è compresa dal soggetto a partire dall'*ens* in quanto presentantesi nel presentarsi dell'*ens* a partire dalla riflessione sullo *ens* stesso come plesso sintetico originario. Il plesso allora di *ens-res-unum* costituisce

41 Cf. C. Fabro, *L'esse tomistico e la ripresa della metafisica*, in "Tomismo e pensiero moderno", (Roma 1969), p. 381ss.

una triade in sé assoluta ossia che si fa presente al soggetto come il plesso di esplicitazione statica del "fondamento": la *res* dice la realtà dell'essenza che appartiene all'*ens* e l'*unum* (con l'*aliquid*) dice il carattere intrinseco cioè costitutivo necessario di tale appartenenza a tutti i livelli. S. Tommaso perciò parla di "additio" per indicare che tutte le altre concezioni della mente sono posteriori all'ente e quindi non fanno che "aggiungere" all'*ens* nel senso di precisare l'uno o l'altro "modo" di essere e quindi si tratta sempre di un'aggiunta — nozionale soltanto, com'è ovvio — che appartiene e perciò resta intrinseca all'ente stesso che detiene il primato indiscusso del fondamento. L'*unum* ch'è la *negatio divisionis in ente* lungi dal fondare l'ente, come nel pensiero moderno, si fonda sull'ente e dice anzitutto l'*ens* (ma) in quanto si presenta in sé indiviso.[42]

L'"addere" allora, in cui consiste la funzione dei trascendentali tomistici, è fondato nell'ente e non fondante, è scoperto nella realtà dell'ente e non prodotto: si potrebbe dire che essi pongono il nuovo modo dell'ente con l'evento-intervento (*Ereignis*) della propria *additio*, in quanto lo suppongono: "Unum quod convertitur cum ente, quod quidem ponit aliquid, *in quantum ponit ipsum ens* cui solam negationem superaddit,"[43] cioè la negazione della divisione ch'è un modo positivo e perciò una perfezione assoluta dell'ente stesso. Fin qui allora assolutamente nulla di soggettivo in questi due tipi di "aggiunte," poiché esse sono assolute e imposte dall'ente stesso. La *additio* soggettiva, se così si può dire, avviene nei due ultimi trascendentali, il *verum* ed il *bonum* ma qui la soggettività di cui si parla nasce all'interno della realtà primordiale, oggettiva e oggettivante dell'ente, la precisa e l'arricchisce: perciò S. Tommaso afferma che "... verum et bonum *positive* dicuntur."[44] Tale positività consiste nel rapporto allo spirito che il *verum* ed il *bonum* conferiscono (esprimono) all'*ens*, in quanto lo mettono in rapporto con l'intelletto e la volontà; si tratta evidentemente di un carattere nuovo e perfettivo che così si aggiunge allo *ens*. Ora perché ciò avvenga, occorre che il soggetto di tale relazione sia equicomprensivo come l'ente e questo è soltanto lo spirito, la *mens*, l'anima spirituale, secondo l'indicazione aristotelica che "l'anima è in qualche modo tutte le cose"[45] mediante l'intelletto e la volontà. La

---

42 "Unum vero quod convertitur cum ente non addit supra ens nisi negationem divisionis, non quod significat ipsam indivisionem tantum, sed substantiam eius cum ipsa [importante per il realismo questo "substantia"]: est enim unum idem quod ens indivisum" (*De Pot.* IX, 7). E perciò "...inter ista quattuor prima primum est ens: et ideo oportet quod positive praedicetur; negatio vero vel privatio non potest esse primum quod intellectu concipitur, cum semper quod negatur vel privatur sit de intellectu negationis vel privationis" (Ibid., ad 6).

43 *De Pot.* IX, 7 ad 8.

44 *De Ver.* XXI, 1.

45 *De an.* III, 8, 431b21.

deduzione tomistica può ben essere interpretata come un'antropologia trascendentale, come oggi si dice, purché la trascendentalità dell'anima (nelle funzioni dell'intelletto e della volontà) sia intesa e fondata a partire dallo *ens* come fondamento oggettivo del conoscere e del volere e quindi precontenente, come recettività pura e libertà, la realtà e perfezione della verità e la realtà della perfezione del bene. Un'esposizione fra le più complete di questo altissimo momento teoretico è certamente la seguente:

> Oportet igitur quod verum et bonum super intellectum entis addant respectum perfectivi. In quolibet autem ente est *duo* considerare: scilicet ipsam rationem speciei, et esse ipsum quo aliquid subsistit in specie illa; et sic aliquod ens potest esse perfectivum dupliciter. *Uno modo* secundum rationem speciei tantum. Et sic ab ente perficitur intellectus, qui perficitur per rationem entis. Nec tamen ens est in eo secundum esse naturale; et ideo hunc modum perficiendi addit verum super ens. Verum enim est in mente, ut Philosophus dicit in VI *Metaphys.*; et unumquodque ens in tantum dicitur verum, in quantum conformatum est vel conformabile intellectui; et ideo omnes recte definientes verum, ponunt in eius definitione intellectum. *Alio modo* ens est perfectivum alterius non solum secundum rationem speciei, sed etiam secundum esse quod habet in rerum natura. Et per hunc modum est perfectivum bonum. Bonum enim in rebus est, ut Philosophus dicit in VI *Metaphys.* [comm. 8]. In quantum autem unum ens est secundum esse suum perfectivum alterius et conservativum, habet rationem finis respectu illius quod ab eo perficitur; et inde est quod omnes recte definientes bonum ponunt in ratione eius aliquid quod pertineat ad habitudinem finis; unde Philosophus dicit in I *Ethic.*, quod bonum optime definiunt dicentes, quod bonum est quod omnia appetunt.[46]

Così nel tomismo si parla di trascendentali al plurale come prospettive di determinazione in sé della realtà e espansione intenzionale della realtà nel suo rapporto allo spirito.

Facendo pertanto un breve bilancio della dialettica tomistica dei trascendentali, possiamo senz'altro meravigliarci del fatto che Heidegger mostri d'ignorarla completamente: essa infatti smentisce in pieno, e lo vedremo tra poco in modo più preciso, la sua denunzia dell'oblio dell'essere. Nella posizione tomistica infatti:

1. *Il fondamento* e primo oggetto del conoscere è l'*ens* nel senso forte in quanto esprime il plesso di soggetto ch'è il contenuto (*essentia*) e di atto (*esse*): l'*ens* quindi in quanto porta e contiene l'*esse*. Così lo porta e

---

46 *De Ver.* XXI, 1. Più concise sono le deduzioni di: *In I Sent.* 8, I, 3; ibid. 19, V, 1 ad 2; *De Ver.* I, 1; *De Pot.* IX, 7; *S. Th.* I-II, 94, 2.

lo manifesta. L'*ens-esse* è perciò da riconoscere il plesso intenzionale dell'appartenenza originaria ossia il *transcendentale fundans*.

2. *Il momento statico* ossia analitico del trascendentale è indicato dalla *res* che esprime il contenuto e dall'*unum* che esprime l'appartenenza intrinseca dei costitutivi dell'*ens*. La derivazione di questi due primi trascendentali è interiore all'*ens* ed è sostenuta dall'*esse*:[47] è in vista dell'*esse*, cioè per poter essere, che l'*ens* deve avere un contenuto (l'essenza) e deve risultare di principi che si appartengono.

3. *Il momento dinamico* o espansivo dell'*ens* riguarda la sua appartenenza al soggetto spirituale che si attua nel conoscere e nel volere: qui si attua in varie guise la dialettica d'immanenza e trascendenza ai vari livelli della riflessione e dell'azione. Qui prende rilievo il momento della libertà nella formazione del soggetto spirituale ch'è la persona responsabile del proprio destino, che non è amorfo ed estrinseco come il *Geschick* di cui parla Heidegger.

La conclusione immediata e sorprendente è che l'*ens* ed i trascendentali tomistici stanno agli antipodi della concezione della scolastica suareziana, a cui si rifà il kantiano Heidegger. Essi infatti unificano in sé l'estrema universalità e la massima concretezza: "Cum autem ens sit primum quod in intellectu concipitur oportet quod quidquid in intellectum cadit, intelligatur ut ens, et per consequens ut unum, et bonum. Unde cum intellectus apprehendat essentiam, unitatem, veritatem et bonitatem in abstracto, oportet quod de quolibet eorum praedicetur ens, et alia tria concreta. Et inde est quod ista denominant seipsa, non autem alia quae non convertuntur cum ente."[48] Una metafisica tomistica che intenda rispondere alle istanze del pensiero moderno dovrà approfondire questa dialettica e dinamica che i trascendentali attuano all'interno dello *ens*. Il fatto poi che i trascendentali si distinguono dallo *ens* solo *secundum rationem,* e non realmente, questo garantisce la pienezza e necessità intrinseca dell'appartenenza, dentro la distinzione,[49] di ciascuno con l'*ens* e di ciascuno con gli altri ponendo

---

47 La priorità dell'*ens* non ostacola né diminuisce ma fonda la realtà e universalità, pari a quella di *ens*, degli altri trascendentali: "Inter ista quatuor prima [ens, unum, verum, bonum] maxime primum est ens: et ideo oportet quod positive praedicetur; negatio enim vel privatio non potest esse primum quod intellectu concipitur, cum semper quod negatur vel privatur sit de intellectu negationis vel privationis. Oportet autem quod alia tria super ens addant aliquid quod ens non contrahat; si enim contraherent ens, iam non essent prima. Hoc autem esse non potest nisi addant aliquid secundum rationem tantum; hoc autem est vel negatio, quam addit unum, vel relatio, vel aliquid quod natum sit referri universaliter ad ens; et hoc est vel intellectus, ad quem importat relationem verum, aut appetitus, ad quem importat relationem bonum; nam bonum est quod omnia appetunt, ut dicitur in *I Ethic.*" (*De Pot.* IX, 7 ad 6).

48 *De Pot.* IX, 7 ad ea quae in oppositum objiciuntur.

49 A questo proposito S. Tommaso scrive: "Dupliciter potest intelligi aliquid sine altero. Uno

ad un tempo l'appartenenza intrinseca, nella distinzione, di verità e libertà a tutti i livelli della vita dello spirito. L'elevarsi poi alla considerazione dei trascendentali significa non soltanto porre le basi della metafisica operando il "ricupero" (*Verwindung*) proposto da Heidegger, ma comporta il porsi sul piano della considerazione assoluta che permette il passaggio alla sfera della "trascendenza" autentica, come S. Tommaso osserva distinguendo l'uno numerico dall'uno trascendentale: "Unum secundum quod est principium numeri, non praedicatur de Deo; sed solum de his quae habent esse in materia. Unum enim quod est principium numeri, est de genere mathematicorum; quae habent esse in materia, sed sunt secundum rationem a materia abstracta. Unum vero quod convertitur cum ente, est quoddam metaphysicum, quod secundum esse non dependet a materia."[50] Qui allora l'immanenza perfettiva richiama la trascendenza e questa s'integra in quella e la fonda nella pienezza dell'appartenenza come nella forma autentica di "presenza," affermata da Heidegger, ma non al modo di Heidegger, come l'essenza della verità dell'essere.

c) *La conoscenza dei primi principi.*

Heidegger ha denunziato con ragione l'identificazione e lo scambio di certezza e verità come la radice del capovolgimento del conoscere nell'agire e dell'intelletto nella volontà operata nel pensiero moderno a partire dal *cogito-volo* di Cartesio fino al *Wille zur Macht* di Nietzsche. Kant lo dichiara espressamente: "*Certezza e chiarezza*, due elementi che riguardano la forma della medesima [ricerca critica], sono da considerare come esigenze essenziali che si possono con ragione richiedere all'autore che osa affrontare un'impresa così scivolosa."[51] Orbene la connessione fra certezza e chiarezza ha luogo nella sfera della conoscenza determinata e perciò è posteriore al primo passo (cominciamento) rispetto al costituirsi del fondamento del conoscere. Sembra infatti che certezza e chiarezza, come sono nel linguaggio ordinario, non si possano applicare all'*ens* e ai trascendentali perché sono comprensivi di tutta la realtà e a tutti i livelli. Eppure l'*ens*, come si è visto, fa il cominciamento oggettivo sintetico del conoscere e si presenta come il

---

modo per modum enuntiandi, dum scilicet intelligitur unum esse sine altero; et hoc modo quidquid intellectus potest intelligere sine altero Deus potest facere. Sic autem ens non potest intelligi sine bono, ut scilicet intellectus intelligat aliquid existens non esse bonum. Alio modo potest intelligi aliquid sine altero per modum definiendi, ut scilicet intelligatur unum, non tamen intellecto altero; sicut animal intelligitur sine homine, et omnibus aliis speciebus: et sic ens potest intelligi sine bono. Nec tamen sequitur quod Deus possit facere ens sine bono, quia hoc ipsum quod est facere, est procedere aliquid in esse" (*De Ver.* XXI, 1 ad 2 quod in contrario objicitur).

50 *S. Th.* I, 11, 3 ad 2.
51 Kant, *Kritik der reinen Vernunft*, Vorrede, I Aufl., A 15.

plesso oggettivante veritativo fondamentale e perciò come il plesso evidente assolutamente e come la fonte per la fondazione di ogni evidenza sia nella sfera teoretica come in quella pratica. Nella posizione tomistica il primo passo con l'*ens* precontiene in modo implicito e perciò confuso tanto il momento dell'oggettività (*verum*) quanto quello della soggettività (*bonum*), tanto la sfera dell'essere (intelletto) quanto quella della volontà (libertà); però essi sono resi espliciti soltanto nel momento dinamico mediante la riflessione sulla vita dello spirito la quale conserva a questo modo la sua originalità e la distinzione delle due sfere della conoscenza e della libertà. Non ogni conoscenza è quindi trascendentale ma solo quella che porta sul fondamento e sui fondamenti di tutto il sapere prima del dirimersi nelle sue varie forme. Sta perciò agli antipodi Kant quando scrive: "Io chiamo trascendentale ogni conoscenza che in generale non si occupa tanto di oggetti, ma del nostro modo di conoscere gli oggetti in generale, in quanto questi devono essere possibili a priori."[52] Invece l'*ens* e i trascendentali i quali sono ad un tempo sintetici e necessari, sintetici mediante il plesso di appartenenza di una duplicità ch'è anzitutto propria ad ognuno e che poi si reduplica in quanto ognuno di essi (*unum, verum, bonum...*) contiene l'*ens*, poiché ognuno è implicito nell'*ens*; necessari poi in quanto ciascuno si presenta come un modo (di essere) che procede dall'*ens* così che ogni trascendentale nella sua nozione ha per soggetto l'*ens* ossia esprime prima l'*ens* e poi la modificazione che lo costituisce in proprio e lo distingue. Nulla vieta, se è questione soltanto di termini, che questa apprensione dello *ens* si possa anche chiamare *appercezione trascendentale* ed anzi con molta più ragione che non lo *Ich denke überhaupt* di Kant ch'è bensì *forma formarum* del conoscere ma analitica e vuota come già lo era il *cogito* di Cartesio. Kant, com'è noto, ricorda nell'Analitica "... la proposizione così invocata presso gli scolastici: quodlibet ens est *unum, verum, bonum*" (unità, verità, perfezione), ma dalla sua esposizione come dalla sua critica risulta il carattere puramente essenzialistico della sua interpretazione[53] legata alla Scolastica

52 Kant, *Kritik der reinen Vernunft*, Einleitung VI, A 12, B 25.
53 Kant infatti ignora completamente il carattere di fondamento che spetta al plesso di *ens*, anzi lo salta a piè pari e interpreta i tre trascendentali seguenti (*unum, verum, bonum*) come esigenze e criteri logici di ogni conoscenza delle cose in generale ossia come categorie della qualità cioè "... dell'*unità, pluralità* e *totalità*" — ossia come unità del concetto, come pluralità dei caratteri del concetto ed infine come totalità ossia compiutezza del concetto stesso. La critica di Kant è che non si può partire da un principio omogeneo come la quantità "... con lo scopo di collegare in una sola coscienza elementi conoscitivi *eterogenei*" (*Kritik der reinen Vernunft*, Elementarlehre, II. Teil, 1. Abt., § 12, B. 113). Per un confronto fra il trascendentale tomistico e quello kantiano cf.: C. Fabro, "The Transcendentality of *ens-esse* and the Ground of Metaphysics," *International Philosophical Quarterly* VI (1966), 389-427 (rist. in "Tomismo e pensiero moderno," ed. cit., p. 319ss.).

formalista ch'era giunta fino alla filosofia wolffiana dei suoi maestri. Per questo Kant inventa il giudizio sintetico a priori che tale non è, poiché i due elementi — data la loro origine completamente eterogenea, la materia dall'intuizione sensibile e la forma dall'intelletto (Io penso puro) — continuano a restare estranei l'un l'altro: di qui l'inevitabilità della risoluzione idealistica del pensare nell' agire (Fichte, Schelling).

Per S. Tommaso invece l'*ens* "... dicit aliquid proprie esse in actu,"[54] e l'atto non solo fa esistere ma è con ciò principio d'intelligibilità; perciò l'*ens* è il plesso trascendentale di ogni intelligibilità non solo rispetto ai concetti dai più generali fino ai più determinati, ma anche come il plesso trascendentale di validità di tutti i principi a cominciare dal primo ch'è il principio di non contraddizione. Un testo sintetico:

In his quae in apprehensione omnium cadunt, quidam ordo invenitur. Nam illud quod primo cadit in apprehensione, est ens, cuius intellectus includitur in omnibus quaecumque quis apprehendit. Et ideo primum pincipium indemonstrabile est quod non est simul affirmare et negare, quod fundatur supra rationem entis et non entis: et super hoc principio omnia alia fundantur, ut dicitur in IV *Metaphys*. Sicut autem ens est primum quod cadit in apprehensione simpliciter, ita bonum est primum quod cadit in apprehensione practicae rationis, quae ordinatur ad opus: omne enim agens agit propter finem, qui habet rationem boni. Et ideo primum principium in ratione practica est quod fundatur supra rationem boni, quae est, Bonum est quod omnia appetunt.[55]

Ed ora un testo analitico non meno sorprendente e comprensivo:

Cum duplex sit operatio intellectus: una, qua cognoscit quod quid est, quae vocatur indivisibilium intelligentia: alia, qua componit et dividit: in utroque est aliquod primum: in prima quidem operatione est aliquod primum, quod cadit in conceptione intellectus, scilicet hoc quod dico ens; nec aliquid hac operatione potest mente concipi, nisi intelligatur ens. Et quia hoc principium, impossibile est esse et non esse simul, dependet ex intellectu entis, sicut hoc principium, omne totum est maius sua parte, ex intellectu totius et partis: ideo hoc etiam principium est naturaliter primum in secunda operatione intellectus, scilicet componentis et dividentis. Nec aliquis potest secundum hanc operationem intellectus aliquid intelligere, nisi hoc principio intellecto. Sicut enim totum et partes non intelliguntur nisi intellecto ente, ita nec hoc principium omne totum est maius sua parte, nisi intellecto praedicto principio firmissimo.[56]

I due testi suggeriscono, ci sembra, le seguenti considerazioni.

---

54 *S. Th.* I, 5, 1 ad 1.
55 *S. Th.* I-II, 94, 2.
56 *In IV Metaph.*, l. 6, nr. 605.

a) *Contro l'apriori di Kant ed il cogito moderno.*

Il primo passo dello spirito, l'*Anfang*, è *cogito ens* nel senso primario fondante ossia di *cogito* anzitutto *ens* e *cogito* in quanto *menti adest* (è e si fa presente) l'*ens*. L'*ens* si potrebbe dire il plesso noetico fondamentale illuminante nel senso più attuale. Un altro testo tomista, precedente ai due citati, fa il punto con assoluto rigore speculativo:

> Cum natura semper ordinetur ad unum, unius virtutis oportet esse naturaliter unum obiectum: sicut visus colorem, et auditus sonum. Intellectus igitur cum sit una vis, est eius unum naturale obiectum, cuius per se et naturaliter cognitionem habet. Hoc autem oportet esse id sub quo comprehenduntur omnia ab intellectu cognita: sicut sub colore comprehenduntur omnes colores, qui sunt per se visibiles. Quod non est aliud quam ens. Naturaliter igitur intellectus noster cognoscit ens, et ea quae sunt per se entis inquantum huiusmodi; in qua cognitione fundatur primorum principiorum notitia, ut non esse simul affirmare et negare, et alia huiusmodi. Haec igitur sola principia intellectus noster naturaliter cognoscit, conclusiones autem per ipsa: sicut per colorem cognoscit visus tam communia quam sensibilia per accidens. [57]

Così l'*ens* non è soltanto come il trascendentale fondamentale kantiano (lo *Ich denke*) che deve poter "accompagnare" (*begleiten*) tutte le rappresentazioni e conoscenze e perciò resta estrinseco al contenuto, ma costituisce la prima origine permanente della intelligibilità dei contenuti stessi secondo la gamma dell'analogia: non solo però delle rappresentazioni e conoscenze, ma anche degli stessi primi principi e di quanto ad essi fa capo nella fondazione e struttura del sapere. Lungi perciò dall'essere il relitto ed il concetto vuoto dell'ultima astrazione, com'è nella tradizione formalistica, bisogna riconoscere che l'*ens* è non semplicemente un contenuto astratto ma il "contenente" di tutti i concetti in quanto esprime il plesso di contenuto (*res*) e di atto (*esse*) nella concretezza della loro sintesi.

b) *Contro il sintetismo formale della neoscolastica kantiana.*

Il nucleo di questa posizione è che l'*esse* è colto soltanto e propriamente mediante la copula del giudizio. Così l'essere dello *ens* da una parte, nel primo momento come concetto, non è che l'astratto formale dell'essenza e perciò comune a potenza ed atto, sostanza e accidenti, materia e forma, finito e infinito, contingente e necessario... e perciò è l'astratto dell'essenza che astrae ovviamente dall'esistenza. Dall'altra parte, e di conseguenza, l'essere come atto di esistenza è manifestato anzitutto e propriamente dalla funzione copulante del

---

57 *C. Gent.* II, 83 (ed. Taur. nr. 1678).

giudizio la quale si risolve sempre in una affermazione (o negazione) di essere in forma diretta col verbo essere e indiretta con gli altri verbi, in modo esplicito con il tempo presente indicativo e implicito con gli altri tempi e modi.[58] Quest'interpretazione sembra abbia dalla sua parte alcuni testi tomistici espliciti soprattutto delle opere giovanili i quali sembrano seguire lo schema ora indicato, cioè di far corrispondere alla *simplex apprehensio* l'afferramento dell'essenza ed al giudizio l'*affirmatio (et negatio)* dell'essere. Ecco:

> Cum sit duplex operatio intellectus: una quarum dicitur a quibusdam imaginatio intellectus, quam Philosophus, III *De Anima*, text. 21, nominat intelligentiam indivisibilium, quae consistit in apprehensione quidditatis simplicis quae alio etiam nomine formatio dicitur; alia est quam dicunt fidem, quae consistit in compositione vel divisione propositionis: prima operatio respicit quidditatem rei; secunda respicit esse ipsius. Et quia ratio veritatis fundatur in esse, et non in quidditate, ut dictum est, ideo veritas et falsitas proprie invenitur in secunda operatione, et in signo eius quod est enuntiatio, et non in prima, vel signo eius quod est definitio, nisi secundum quid; sicut etiam quidditatis esse est quoddam esse rationis, et secundum istud esse dicitur veritas in prima operatione intellectus: per quem etiam modum dicitur definitio vera.[59]

Se non che è sufficiente tenere presente il contesto perché il significato di questo testo, così come degli altri che lo ricalcano, risulti nella sua effettiva collocazione. Osserviamo pertanto che il problema dell'apprensione dello *esse* (come *actus essendi*) è qui fuori causa.

1. Vi si parla infatti della conoscenza nella sua sfera ordinaria e non dell'apprensione dello *ens* ch'è del tutto privilegiata. Nella conoscenza ordinaria dell'astrazione formale la essenza o *quidditas* è appresa nel suo contenuto oggettivo, prescindendo dall'esistenza e dallo *esse* che l'attua in concreto: posso pensare p. es. il cavallo, astraendo dalla sua esistenza di fatto e quindi senza pensare il suo *esse*.

2. D'altra parte anche il giudizio è considerato nella sua funzione puramente formale di sintesi, mediante la copula *è*, di S e P. Ma S e P

---

58 La posizione più esplicita di questa deformazione radicale del tomismo, ridotto ad heideggerismo, si trova nelle opere di K. Rahner: *Geist in Welt* (Innsbruk 1939) e *Hörer des Wortes* (München 1940). Cf. C. Fabro, *K. Rahner e l'ermeneutica tomistica*, II ed. (Milano 1973).

59 *In I Sent.* 19, V, 1 ad 7; Mandonnet I, p. 489. Nella stessa opera questa esposizione ritorna ancora con le stesse espressioni: "Cum in re duo sint, quidditas rei, et esse eius, his duobus respondet duplex operatio intellectus. Una quae dicitur a philosophis formatio, qua apprehendit quidditates rerum, quae etiam a Philosopho, in III *De anima*, dicitur indivisibilium intelligentia. Alia autem comprehendit esse rei, componendo affirmationem, quia etiam rei ex materia et forma compositae, a qua cognitionem accipit, consistit in quadam compositione formae ad materiam, vel accidentis ad subjectum" (*In I Sent.* 38, I, 3; Mandonnet I, p. 903).

possono trovarsi a tutti livelli del conoscere — non solo reale, ma anche possibile, fantastico, puramente logico... — e la copula *è* compie sempre la sua funzione di unire S e P anche quando non c'è nulla di essere a cui corrisponda nella realtà.

3. Di conseguenza l'essere della predicazione nel giudizio è puramente formale funzionale e non reale, tanto che può predicare l'essere anche di ciò che non ha realtà o essere alcuno ma è pura negazione o privazione (*mors est, bos non est leo...*). La "qualità" di essere della copula dipende pertanto dalla qualità (cioè dalla realtà costitutiva) del S e P e quindi dalla realtà del rapporto di S e P e qui vale il principio aristotelico che l'essere (predicativo) come tale non significa nulla. Nella considerazione formale la sede della verità è il giudizio il quale si attua mediante la copula *è* e quindi il giudizio è l'operazione ch'è sede (funzione) della predicazione dell'essere. Ma la "qualità" o sfera di tale essere deve risultare prima e altrove. Perciò S. Tommaso nello stesso contesto un po' prima scrive: "Cum autem in re sit quidditas eius et suum esse, veritas fundatur in esse rei magis quam in quidditate, sicut et nomen entis ab esse imponitur; et in ipsa operatione intellectus accipientis esse rei sicut est per quamdam similationem ad ipsum, completur relatio adaequationis, in qua consistit ratio veritatis. Unde dico, quod ipsum esse rei est causa veritatis, secundum quod est in cognitione intellectus."[60] L'essere della copula come tale ha significato (esistenziale) formale, non reale: afferma cioè l'esistenza del rapporto di S e P, ma la copula è in funzione della realtà del soggetto e del rapporto col predicato:[61] se questo è reale, reale è l'essere; se fantastico o solo logico, tale sarà anche il significato e valore dell'essere della copula. I due significati di *esse*, reale e logico, vanno nettamente distinti: "Esse dupliciter dicitur: uno modo significat actum essendi; alio modo significat compositionem propositionis quam anima adinvenit coniungens praedicatum subjecto."[62]

Perciò al fondo di tutti questi vari significati che può assumere l'essere nella riflessione, sta il significato fondamentale reale di *esse* qual è contenuto nell'apprensione del plesso originario di *ens* che va

---

60 *In I Sent.* 19, I, 1; Mandonnet I, p. 486. Più avanti, S. Tommaso distingue un triplice *esse*: la *quidditas*, l'*actus essentiae* e, al terzo posto, la *veritas compositionis in propositionibus* cioè dello *est* della copula. Di quest'ultima si legge: "Et secundum hoc est in intellectu componente et dividente quantum ad sui complementum; sed fundatur in esse rei, quod est actus essentiae, sicut supra de veritate dictum est" (*In I Sent.* 33, I, 1 ad 1; Mandonnet I, p. 766).

61 Si può dire pertanto che la *veritas formalis* del giudizio è fondata sulla *veritas materialis* dell'apprensione: "Veritas quae in anima causatur a rebus, non sequitur aestimationem animae, sed existentiam rerum" (*De Ver.* I, 2 ad 3).

62 *S. Th.* I, 3, 4 ad 2.

detto perciò in questo senso, un'apprensione "prelogica":[63] tale infatti è il senso da dare all'espressione base della nostra ricerca che "... id quod primum intellectus intelligit est ens." L'apprensione dello *ens* costituisce infatti il primo avvertimento che la mente ha della realtà e l'aggancio primo e fondante del soggetto con la realtà a cui si deve riferire ogni seguente attività spirituale.

La Distinzione Reale di "Essentia" Esistente (*Quod est*) ed Atto di Essere (*Esse, Actus Essendi*)

Ma il primo e più nevralgico punto di confronto fra Heidegger e S. Tommaso è la "fondazione" del primo plesso speculativo che ha affogato l'essere nel fare rimandando l'essere, ch'è in sé presenza e presenzialità, al fare e causare ossia risolvendo la presenza ch'è la realtà propria dell'essere, nella relazione di dipendenza ch'è estrinsecità ed estraneità. La formula classica di siffatta perdita radicale dell'essere è, come si è notato, la distinzione di *essentia* ed *existentia* della Scolastica decadente che Heidegger con ragione trova — come si è visto — anche a fondamento del pensiero moderno da Cartesio a Kant e fino a Nietzsche.[64] Il momento è di estrema importanza perché risolutivo per la fondazione della metafisica che intende ancorarsi al plesso di *ens* ed alla dialettica dei trascendentali: senza la distinzione reale di *essentia* ed *esse* — come (di) due principi immanenti allo *ens* stesso — manca il fondamento per la distinzione di *ens-res*, cioè di concreto reale e astratto formale, e di *ens-unum-bonum* cioè di concreto indeterminato e di concreto specificato per il soggetto spirituale ossia per la conoscenza (intelletto) e di determinato per la libertà (volontà). Si badi bene: è in questo momento che si deve superare, come vuole Hegel contro Kant, il condizionamento della metafisica dalla critica della conoscenza (*Erkenntnistheorie*)[65] e che si deve affermare, come vuole Heidegger, la priorità dell'essere sulla coscienza.[66] Ma la posizione di Heidegger non è facile e non è stata senza oscillazioni.

---

63 "Prelogico" è espressamente da intendere il *Sein* a cui rimanda il *Dasein* heideggeriano secondo le ricerche dell'ontologia fenomenologica di *Sein und Zeit*, messa in evidenza supratutto da E. Fink (cf. *Zur ontologischen Frühgeschichte von Raum, Zeit, Bewegung*, Den Haag 1957; *Sein, Wahrheit, Welt*, ibid. 1958; *Alles und Nichts*, ibid. 1959).

64 "Die Einheit von Wille zur Macht und ewiger Wiederkehr des Gleichen beruht in Zusammengehörigkeit von essentia und existentia, deren Unter scheidung hinsichtlich ihrer Wesensherkunft im Dunkel bleibt" (M. Heidegger, *Nietzsche*, ed cit., Bd. I, p. 381s.).

65 Cf. Hegel, *Phänomenologie des Geistes*, Einleitung; ed. Hoffmeister, spec. p. 63ss. Heidegger ne ha dato un mirabile commento nel saggio: *Hegels Begriff der Erfahrung*, in "Holzwege," ed. cit., p. 105ss.

66 La priorità dell'essere sul pensiero è un punto saldo per Heidegger: "Aber das Sein ist kein Erzeugnis des Denkens. Wohl dagegen ist das wesentliche Denken ein Ereignis des Seins" (*Was ist*

Heidegger sta fermo al plesso *Sein-Seiende*, come si è detto, e si mantiene nella tensione dell'ambito ontico (*Seiende*) ontologico (*Sein*) del puro apparire-accadere: si tratta appunto di risolvere e fondare il *Seiende* nel *Sein*, il plesso empirico dell'immediatezza hegeliana (*Unmittelbarkeit*) nel puro accadere dell'evento. Perciò Heidegger vede sempre il plesso dell'essere-ente dall'interno dell'atteggiarsi della soggettività umana trascendentale, ma egli ha anche capovolto la posizione hegeliana: per Hegel il *Sein* del *Seiende* è il momento dell'immediatezza astratta che deve "passare" al (nel) *Begriff*, per Heidegger il *Begriff* sarebbe un ritorno al *Seiende* e non la seconda autentica immediatezza, questa è il *Sein* come farsi presente del presente e come l'adeguarsi analitico-sintetico della presenza con se stessa dell'identità (*Sein*) con la diversità (*Seiende*), del permanente col transeunte. Heidegger infatti scrive:

> Ciò che è, ciò che accade. Ciò che accade è già accaduto. Ciò non significa ch'esso sia passato. Ciò ch'è già accaduto è soltanto ciò che si è raccolto nella essenza dell'essere, l'essenza di ciò e come ciò[67] ch'è la venuta dell'essere stesso — e sia pure nella forma del sottrarsi cessante. La venuta mantiene l'essente come tale nel suo non-nascondimento e questo resta per lui come l'essere non pensato dell'essente. Ciò che accade è la storia dell'essere, è l'essere come la storia del cessare.[68]

E' sempre la dialettica dell'apparire e scomparire dell'essente (plesso ontico) che rimanda pertanto al plesso (ontologico) di *Sein-Seiende* a quello più originario (metafisico?) di *Sein-Nichts* che Heidegger prende da Hegel ma in senso capovolto come si è detto.

Ora per Heidegger la *Diremtion* originaria di *Sein-Nichts*, che sottende e fonda quella di *Sein-Seiende* è svelata non da processi propriamente né conoscitivi né affettivi, ma grazie ad una impressione fondamentale ch'egli con un termine preso da Kierkegaard ha chiamato "angoscia" (*Angst*). Qui si vede, alla sua radice, la coerenza di Heidegger col vuoto ch'è costitutivo del *cogito* moderno e la sua antitesi di fondo con la posizione tomistica. Per S. Tommaso, come si è visto, il *primum quod intelligitur* come positività in sé di presenza reale che si

---

Metaphysik?, Nachwort; ed. cit., p. 43). Però si deve sempre tener presente che l'essere si disvela a partire dal comportamento (*Angst, Sorge* = angoscia, sollecitudine) dell'esistente ch'è sempre e solo l'uomo, non gli altri enti e neppure Dio: "Das Seiende, das in der Weise der Existenz ist, ist der Mensch. Der Mensch allein existiert. Der Fels ist, aber er existiert nicht. Der Baum ist, aber er existiert nicht. Das Pferd ist, aber es existiert nicht. Der Engel ist, aber er existiert nicht. Gott ist, aber er existiert nicht" (*Op. cit.*, Einleitung; ed. cit., p. 14 s. Cf. anche più sotto: Nachwort, p. 42).

67 Heidegger fa un gioco di termini riportando (e spiegando) il *Wesen* con il *Ge-Wesen*: qui il *Wesen* è sostantivo e infinito insieme e così *Ge-wesen* è participio (passato) e sostantivo. L'accostamento c'è già in Hegel e c'era già nel τὸ τί ἦν εἶναι di Aristotele.

68 M. Heidegger, *Nietzsche*, ed. cit., Bd. I, p. 388.

dà all'intelletto è l'*ens* in quanto ha l'*esse* ch'è l'atto per essenza e l'antitesi assoluta del nulla. Per Heidegger invece il *Sein* rimanda al *Nichts* e il *Nichts* è rivelato e attestato dall'angoscia: essa così costituisce l'unico aggancio per il *Sein*. Nell'ordine quindi bisogna dire: *Seiende-Sein-Nichts-Angst*, secondo un legame inscindibile e secondo un'appartenenza intenzionale che va percorsa in ambedue i sensi da *Seiende* ad *Angst* e da *Angst* a *Seiende*: è "... l'angoscia che fornisce l'esperienza dell'essere come dell'altro di ogni essente,"[69] dove si vede chiara la simultanea appartenenza di essere-essente e di essere-nulla. Heidegger fa quindi con Hegel una operazione ovvero riduzione analoga a quella della sinistra hegeliana con la decapitazione dell'Assoluto, ma in un certo senso la sua è ancor più radicale perché esige la negazione di tutti i valori in quanto questi sono contenuti e qualità del *Seiende* che formano invece lo scopo esplicito della rivoluzione marxistica. Due negazioni comunque — quella heideggeriana all'interno del *Sein* (come *Nichts*) e quella marxista — che convergono nell'appartenenza scambievole di *Sein-Seiende* e che restano all' interno del *Seiende* come abbattimento dello *statu quo* così da identificare la verità dell'essere con l'esistenza e stanno perciò agli antipodi della posizione tomistica.

Tale appartenenza scambievole, e la conseguente dialettica circolare, è negata per principio dal plesso tomistico di *ens-esse* in virtù della priorità che ha l'atto sulla potenza e del conseguente compito di fondamento che ha il reale sulla coscienza, sull'attività del conoscere e del volere. E' il darsi allora dello *ens* perché è *id quod habet esse* che attua il conoscere e mette la libertà dell'esistente spirituale in condizione di fare le sue scelte.

Ecco allora la progressione metafisica:

1. L'*ens* è il plesso trascendentale (concreto) originario che rimanda all'atto di essere (*esse*) che è doppio, come si è visto, ossia come principio di determinazione di un contenuto ed è l'essenza e come principio

---

69 "Eine Erfahrung des Seins als des Anderen [= Nichts] zu allem Seienden verschenkt die Angst." Il "nulla" di cui Heidegger parla non è vuota negazione ma — se così possiamo dire — l'intenzionalità ultima totale che scaturisce dall'angoscia, ciò quindi grazie a cui appare l'essente: "... questo nulla si mostra come l'essere" (*Aber dieses Nichts west als das Sein*). Quest'appartenenza doppia unitaria di Essere-Essente ed Essere-Nulla è costitutiva del plesso stesso della verità dell'essere: "Ohne das Sein, dessen abgründiges, aber noch unentfaltetes Wesen uns das Nichts in der wesenhaften Angst zuschickt, bliebe alles Seiende in der Seinlosigkeit. Allein auch diese ist als die Seinsverlassenheit wiederum nicht ein nichtiges Nichts, wenn anders zur Wahrheit des Seins gehört, dass das Sein nie west ohne das Seiende, dass niemals ein Seiendes ist ohne das Sein" (*Was ist Metaphysik?*, Nachwort; ed. cit., p. 41). La terza tappa, che sanziona l'appartenenza scambievole del doppio plesso di *Sein* e *Zeit* della filosofia antica e di *Seiendes* e *Nichts* del pensiero moderno, si legge nell'intervista di Heidegger con R. Wisser: *Martin Heidegger im Gespräch* (München 1970), p. 74s.

di attuazione come tale. Ossia l'essenza è il principio come contenuto intrinseco realizzato e l'*actus essendi* è il principio come atto realizzato e l'*actus essendi* è il principio come atto realizzante intrinseco. L'*ens* e l'*esse* certamente si appartengono — come si appartengono l'*essentia* e l'*esse* — ma non secondo una corrispondenza scambievole inscindibile: in questo caso si fa del piano fenomenologico il riferimento fondamentale e l'essere si dissolve come l'attuarsi del puro presentarsi, così come l'essenza dell'essere è dall'angoscia fatta emergere come il Nulla. Il tentativo, sferrato dagli scolastici heideggeriani, di recuperare il *Sein* heideggeriano allo *esse* tomistico, è compromesso perciò al suo primo punto di partenza: *Sein = Anwesenheit* cioè "presenza di coscienza."

2. Il plesso primo tomistico di *ens-esse* è perciò provvisorio e non costitutivo, come è invece in Hegel e Heidegger, poiché esso si esplicita nella coppia reale di *essentia-esse*. Questo *esse* va davvero preso come principio realizzante in senso forte e dominante quindi l'essenza ch'è il principio (contenuto) realizzato nell'ente: a questo livello metafisico di riflessione che può essere detta riduttiva fondamentale, l'*esse* è l'atto e la *essentia* è la potenza. Atto e potenza hanno qui il senso aristotelico originario che comporta la *emergenza* dell'atto sulla potenza: la prima istanza di questa emergenza è la composizione-distinzione reale di *essentia* ed *esse* la quale esprime secondo S. Tommaso il senso ultimo e fondamentale della "differenza ontologica" fra l'*ens* e l'*esse* ed in ultima radice fra la creatura ed il Creatore. Erra quindi Heidegger quando accomuna S. Tommaso alla Scolastica la quale intende l'*esse* come *existentia* e lo riduce perciò alla dipendenza causale.[70] L'*esse* è immanente all'*ens* come *atto* reale intrinseco all'essenza concreta ch'è perciò la sua *potenza* reale: la loro scambievole presenza e appartenenza originaria è solidale con la creazione. Ma l'*esse* di cui si parla non è la semplice dipendenza causale bensì il suo effetto che resta intrinseco all'ente, così come la *essentia* che compone con l'*esse* non è il semplice possibile — che Heidegger con Hegel interpreta come il nulla — ma è il contenuto reale dell'ente. Questa è una posizione assolutamente originale combattuta e abbandonata dalla Scolastica e ignota ad Heidegger.

3. Lo *esse* dello *ens* tomistico che fa composizione reale con la *essentia*, non va perciò confuso con la *existentia*. La *existentia*, bisogna affermarlo con forza, è un termine estraneo alla semantica della

---

70 Ma più errano quegli Scolastici che pretendono accordare Heidegger e S. Tommaso muovendo dall'identità di *esse* ed *existere* che porta alla negazione della distinzione reale di essenza ed *esse* (cf. p.es. H. Meyer, *M. Heidegger und Thomas von Aquin*, München 1964, p. 22ss.). Sulla medesima linea formalista sembra muoversi anche B. Rioux: *L'être et la vérité chez Heidegger et Saint Thomas d'Aquin* (Paris-Montréal 1963), spec. p. 248s.

metafisica tomistica: il suo apparire con la controversia fra Enrico di Gand e Egidio Romano (*esse essentiae, esse existentiae*) ha segnato la perdita della novità rivoluzionaria dello *esse* tomistico e l'inizio della *Seinsvergessenheit*, giustamente rilevata e deplorata da Heidegger. *Existentia*, come già si è accennato, è un fatto, una condizione di fatto, il fatto della realtà e della realizzazione (causazione) dello *ens* ed esso è comune perciò tanto all'essenza quanto allo *esse*, tanto alla sostanza come agli accidenti. In questo senso, riassumendo il peccato originale della deviazione speculativa dell'Occidente, Kant aveva ragione di affermare il più grave paradosso e assurdo che "... l'essere non è un predicato reale."[71] Per S. Tommaso, all'opposto, ogni realtà di verità, vita, bellezza, bontà... fa capo all'*esse* dell'*ens* come atto primo e fondamentale ch'è insieme immanenza assoluta (*actus essendi* dell'*ens* = *esse per participationem, esse commune* della creatura) e trascendenza assoluta (*esse purum, per essentiam* = Dio).

Questa risoluzione speculativa della verità dello *ens* tomistico, si chiarifica all'interno di tre eventi decisivi che confluiscono nella formazione del tomismo ignorati e trascurati sia dalla Scolastica come dal pensiero moderno e da Heidegger.

1. *L'emergenza dell'Uno sui molti con Platone mediante la nozione platonica di partecipazione* (μίμησις, μέθεξις) che innalza al di sopra del mondo mutevole degli enti della δόξα la verità immutabile di essere degli εἴδη raccolti nell'Uno: mentre il *Sein* di Heidegger elimina la distinzione di ἀλήθεια e δόξα.[72]

2. *L'emergenza dell'atto* (ἐνέργεια) *sulla potenza*, affermata da Aristotele e giustamente ripresa da Heidegger, realizzatore ed insieme emergente sulla potenza che raccoglie in sé perciò l'esigenza simultanea d'immanenza e trascendenza, mentre il *Sein* di Heidegger non può essere senza il *Seiende*. S. Tommaso, che arriva allo *esse* come atto primo, fonde mirabilmente l'istanza della trascendenza platonica con l'immanenza aristotelica: il tentativo fu ripreso da Hegel, ma l'esito era

---

71 Kant, *Kritik der reinen Vernunft*, A 598, B 626.

72 Ha interpretato l'*esse* di S. Tommaso nella linea stretta del panenteismo di Proclo-Ps. Dionigi lo studio di K. Kremer, *Die neuplatonische Seinsphilosophie und ihre Wirkung auf Thomas von Aquin*, (Leiden 1966). L'A. suppone che l'*esse commune* di cui parla S. Tommaso è identico con Dio (*Ipsum esse subsistens*) con la conseguenza di rivalutare espressamente l'argomento ontologico e di negare altrettanto espressamente la distinzione di *essentia* ed *esse* (p. 384 ss., 447 s.). L'A. però, sia detto a suo onore, dichiara il suo imbarazzo di fronte ai testi espliciti di S. Tommaso contrari alla sua interpretazione (p. 430). Per un'analisi più approfondita su questo punto cf. C. Fabro, "Platonism, Neo-Platonism and Thomismus: Convergencies and Divergencies," *The New Scholasticism*, 44 (1970), I, pp. 69-100 (rist. in "Tomismo e pensiero moderno," ed. cit., p. 435ss.).

compromesso dall'inizio con il *Sein* vuoto ch'era il peso morto della perdita dell'essere già consumata.[73]

3. *La rivendicazione della emergenza dello spirito sulla materia*, in cui ancora "concordano" Platone et Aristotele contro il materialismo (preteso o reale) dei Presocratici. Non così però una direzione del neoplatonismo medievale iniziata dal filosofo arabo-giudeo Avicebron e seguita da gran parte della scuola agostinista tradizionale la quale, per distinguere la creatura dal creatore sul piano metafisico, introdusse la composizione di materia e forma anche negli angeli e nell'anima umana. La contropartita di questa tesi nel tomismo è precisamente la distinzione reale, non più *in ratione essentiae* — poiché lo spirito è semplice per definizione — ma *in ratione entis*, ch'è precisamente la composizione reale di *essentia* ed *esse*,[74] di cui S. Tommaso è stato il primo ed è rimasto l'unico assertore nel suo tempo: una posizione di cui ora, dopo l'avventura del pensiero moderno, cominciamo a comprendere il pieno valore speculativo di fondamento. Da una parte infatti questa tesi è strettamente connessa alla furibonda polemica sulla unità o molteplicità delle forme sostanziali che divise i teologi specialmente tra la fine del sec. XIII e la prima metà del sec. XIV[75]; dall'altra parte, con l'affermazione della consistenza metafisica della creatura spirituale, dotata di un proprio *esse* che aderisce necessariamente all'essenza o forma assolutamente spirituale, essa permette il confronto diretto col trascendentale moderno ed il suo deciso superamento: esso si attua con l'affermazione della libertà radicale come capacità originaria di decidere del proprio essere con la scelta dell'ultimo fine.

A questo modo la distinzione reale di *essentia* ed *esse* è la chiave dell'originalità speculativa del tomismo e l'unica risposta radicale, all'interno del tomismo speculativo, della richiesta heideggeriana della "differenza ontologica" per il disvelamento dell'essere dell'ente che Heidegger per coerenza al suo immanentismo ha dovuto confessare di tenere legato nel plesso temporale dell'evento; non si vede allora come, con la proclamazione dell'orizzonte finito dell'essere dell'ente,

---

73 Alla ricerca dell'originalità della posizione tomistica come sintesi-superamento, nel senso della *Aufhebung* hegeliana, abbiamo dedicato la maggior parte dei nostri studi (cf. *La nozione tomistica di partecipazione secondo S. Tommaso d'Aquino*, I ed. Milano 1939, III ed. Torino 1963; *Participation et causalité*, Paris-Louvain 1960, ed. it. Torino 1961).

74 I testi classici della maturità sono spec.: *Q. De Spir. creat.*, a. 1 ("Utrum substantia spiritualis sit composita ex materia et forma"); *Q. De Anima*, a. 6. L'esposizione critica più analitica e drastica della posizione di Avicebron e dell'itinerario platonico-aristotelico della sua nuova nozione di partecipazione, culminante nella tesi della distinzione reale di *essentia* ed *esse*, S. Tommaso l'ha data nell'opuscolo incompiuto *De substantiis separatis* (cf. C. Fabro, *La nozione metafisica di partecipazione*[3], ed. cit., p. 62ss.).

75 Cf. F. J. Roensch, *Early Thomistic School*, (Dubuque Iowa 1964), spec. p. 188s.

Heidegger possa superare il limite dell'Estetica trascendentale di Kant ed aprire un varco per la metafisica. La richiesta heideggeriana della differenza ontologica non poteva certamente essere soddisfatta dalla sola distinzione aristotelica (fatta valere dagli Averroisti contro la distinzione tomistica di *essentia* ed *esse*) di sostanza ed accidenti ch'è puramente predicamentale. Né era più soddisfacente il ricorso unilaterale alla dipendenza causale estrinseca in cui si rifugiarono l'agostinismo teologico e la Scolastica barocca con la distinzione di *essentia* ed *existentia*, a cui ritornano oggi con flessioni neoplatoniche i fautori del nuovo trascendentalismo cattolico filokantiano e heideggeriano che Heidegger stesso ha confutato in antecedenza.

In conclusione: il problema radicale sul piano sia storico come speculativo per la fondazione della metafisica è quello sollevato da Heidegger, il ricupero dello *esse* come atto fondamentale, ma non però al modo di Heidegger ossia come "presenza del presente" ch'è il presentarsi transitorio dentro e mediante il tempo e quindi semplice presenza di (e come) *existentia*. L'*esse* è presenza di atto metafisico profondo come prima partecipazione dell'attualità assoluta, immanente all'essenza (finita), grazie al quale lo stesso *Esse per essentiam* ch'è Dio diventa immanente al finito "per essenza, per potenza e per presenza."[76] E' all'interno di questa formula, ancora enigmatica e audace, che s'inserisce la concezione tomistica della dinamica dello spirito finito per l'attuazione radicale della sua libertà, come ha visto giustamente il pensiero moderno. Ma il pensiero moderno era partito male, con l'astrazione totale dell'essenza ch'è il vuoto di coscienza ed è finito perciò nella dialettica orizzontale di essere-nulla, dell'apparire e scomparire dell'effimero gioco degli eventi in un mondo diventato senza senso.

Liberata dalle polemiche e dalle incrostazioni di un tipo di cultura, ch'era insieme troppo legata alla fisica e troppo teologizzante, la concezione tomistica dello *esse*, come atto intensivo emergente, è in grado di evitare sia la Scilla di una creaturalità statica di predestinazionismo assoluto della teologia statica, sia il Cariddi di una libertà come trascendentale puro della filosofia moderna ch'è il presentarsi dell'atto come apparire e scomparire in uno scorrere infinito, senza principio e senza fine.

76 *S. Th.* I, 8, 1-4.

ANALEKTIK UND DIALEKTIK

Zur Methode des Thomistischen und Hegelschen Denkens

Bernhard Lakebrink

ES kann keinem Zweifel unterliegen, dass das Thomistische Denken, wie es sich in den grossen Systemen der *Summa Theologiae*, der *Summa contra gentiles,* in den Quästionen *De veritate* und *De potentia* darstellt, nach strenger Methode verläuft, deren Geist diese breit angelegten und diffizil ausgeführten Konstruktionen bis in die letzten Winkel hinein inspiriert. Thomas selbst hat ebenso wie sein grosses Vorbild Aristoteles diese Methode mit sicherem Griff gehandhabt, ohne sie jedoch, wie etwa Kant die seinige, ausdrücklich zu reflektieren. So fehlt im Werk des Aquinaten ein gesondertes Kapitel, in dem seine Methodenlehre in aller Form entwickelt würde. Mehr noch als Kant hat Hegel — vor allem zum Schluss seiner Grossen Logik — mit höchstem Anspruch an unser philosophisches Nachdenken nicht eine "transzendentale" (im Vorblick auf mögliche Erfahrung angelegte), also bloss endliche Methode entwickelt, sondern eine Form des Denkens konzipiert, die er als absolut-unendliche oder als spekulative Methode begriffen hat.

Aber wenn Thomas und Aristoteles die Methode ihres Denkens und Systematisierens nicht ausdrücklich auf den Begriff gebracht haben, so heisst das nicht, dass sie bei der Kompliziertheit ihrer summativen Begriffsgefüge keinerlei Methode angewandt und benutzt hätten. Sie haben in der Fülle ihres Schrifttums auch hier und da, wenn auch noch so sporadisch, methodologische Erwägungen angestellt, die uns einen gewissen Einblick in die Konstruktionsgesetze ihres Denkens und in den Stil ihrer Systematik verstatten. So können wir die innere, zweifellos vorhandene Systematisierung ihrer Systeme herausanalysieren, um sie näher zu bestimmen und gegen andere Methoden — in unserem Fall gegen die Hegelsche Dialektik — abzugrenzen.

Wir bezeichnen nun die Thomistische Methode als *"Analektik"* im Unterschied zur *Dialektik* Hegels, zumal der Begriff der Analektik in der Analogielehre des Aquinaten seine greifbarste und einsichtigste Verwirklichung erfährt. Daher erscheint es als durchaus legitim, den ontologisch-sachhaften Begriff der Analogie zu dem der Analektik zu formalisieren, wobei aber stets festzuhalten ist, dass die Analektik nicht nur auf die Analogielehre des Aquinaten, wie er sie in der *Summa Theologiae* I, 13 entwickelt, beschränkt bleiben darf. Die Gesamtheit der Thomistischen Philosophie und Theologie ist von dieser Analektik als Methode beseelt; sie ist gleichsam deren Stilform, die das Gesamt des summativen Vertikalgefüges ebenso wie alle seine Einzelheiten und Gliedformen bestimmt, so wie ja auch die gotische Kathedrale bis in all ihre Strebepfeiler, Fialen und Arabesken hinein von dem einen Geist der Gotik inspiriert erscheint.

Das neuzeitliche Denken ist ganz besonders am Problem der Methodologie interessiert. Der rationalistische Deduktionalismus, die transzendentale Methode Kants, die spekulative Dialektik Hegels, die marxistische Ideologie, das positivistische Denken, die phänomenologische Methode Husserls — sie alle fordern immer wieder das Nach-denken unserer Tage heraus. Alles, was seit Schleiermacher und Dilthey um das Problem der sogenannten Hermeneutik in Geschichte und theologischer Exegese kreist, das alles hat mit dem Phänomen des Methodologischen zu tun. Erst der Existentialismus der Nachkriegszeit suchte sich dem *wissenschaftlichen* Bemühen um das Methodologische überhaupt zu entziehen, indem er die Philosophie und ihr strenges Denken der Willkür quasi-dichterischer Einfälle auslieferte und so die Wissenschaftlichkeit der Methode und damit alle systematische Philosophie aufhob. "Das Denken ist [nach Heidegger] kein Mittel für das Erkennen," zumal das Denken mehr und mehr in die Nachbarschaft des Dichtens hereingerät: "Beide, Dichten und Denken, brauchen einander."[1]

Die Methode der philosophischen *Wissenschaft* wird unter Missbrauch des Hegelschen Begriffs vom "Vorstellen" und unter Benutzung Nietzsche'scher Motive einem auch von Heidegger abgewerteten bloss "wissenschaftlichen *Vorstellen*" zugesprochen, wie es sich vor allem in Metaphysik und Technik ereignen soll. Im existentialen Denken hingegen "gibt es weder die Methode noch das [gegenständliche] Thema, während in den Wissenschaften... das Thema nicht nur durch die Methode gestellt [wird], sondern es wird zugleich in die Methode hereingestellt und bleibt in ihr untergestellt".[2] Diese "Nach-

1 Heidegger, *Unterwegs zur Sprache* (Pfullingen, 1969), 173.
2 *Ibid.*, 178.

barschaft des Denkens und Dichtens"[3] zerstört natürlich den wissenschaftlichen Charakter allen Philosophierens von Grund auf. Allgemeingiltigkeit, Objektivität und Lehrbarkeit geprägter Aussagen (Dogmen) werden unmöglich. Daher das auch für die moderne Theologie verbindlich gewordene Wort Heideggers: "Alle Formeln sind gefährlich".[4]

Auch die existentiale Theologie, vor allem die der Rahner und seiner Anhänger, hat sich dem objektiv verpflichtenden Gesetz einer bestimmten einheitlichen Methode längst entzogen. Rahner wirbelt transzendentalistisches und existentiales, dialektisches und Thomistisches Denken unbekümmert durcheinander (vgl. *Geist in Welt* und *Hörer des Wortes*), nachdem Maréchal bereits auf unglückselige Weise den Kantischen Transzendentalismus mit Thomistischer Methode auszusöhnen versucht hatte. Die verderblichen Folgen dieser Vernachlässigung methodologischer Redlichkeit und exakter Innehaltung eines von der Sache selbst her geforderten "modus procedendi" erleben wir heute angesichts der Tragödie nicht nur des philosophischen, sondern vor allem auch des theologischen Denkens.

Um so mehr sollten wir uns nicht nur immer wieder auf die unerschütterlichen Fundamente der philosophia perennis, insonderheit der Thomistischen Philosophie zurückbesinnen, sondern ineins damit auch die Orientierungsmacht und die zeit- bzw. geschichtslose Leuchtkraft seiner Methode, die versöhnliche und wahrhaft vermittelnde Milde, den Geist der Gerechtigkeit, d. i. des "suum cuique", ebendieses Denkens zu bedenken versuchen. Vor dem feindseligen Extremismus gedachter Positionen, vor der Unerbittlichkeit jäher Umschwünge im Begrifflichen überhaupt, vor dem "wilden Wechsel"[5] in Ding und Denken, der "das wesentlich Feste wankend" macht,[6] vor dieser selbst von Hegel gefürchteten Gefahr aller Dialektik weiss uns die Analektik Thomistischer Methode sehr wohl zu bewahren. Nicht von ungefähr begreift Hegel im Zeichen der grossen Französischen Revolution "das Wahre... als den bacchantischen Taumel, an dem kein Glied nicht trunken ist".[7] Nun will sich allerdings "die durchsichtige und einfache Ruhe", ohne die selbst in dialektischem Betracht keine Wahrheit möglich ist, nur schlecht wiederherstellen lassen, zumal ja nicht nur die logischen, sondern auch die "sittlichen Bestimmungen" in das dialektische Entstehen und Vergehen hineingerissen werden. Hegel

---

3 *Ibid.,* 189.
4 *Ibid.,* 81.
5 Hegel, *Wissenschaft der Logik* (Leipzig, 1932), II, 112.
6 *Ibid.,* 493.
7 Hegel, *Phänomenologie des Geistes* (Leipzig, 1937), 39.

verlangt deshalb eine Art irrationalen Fiduzialglaubens an den dialektischen Logos, zumal er uns keinen besseren Trostgrund an die Hand zu geben vermag als den Zuspruch: "Insofern die Dialektik... sittliche Bestimmungen aufhebt, [so muss man] zur Vernunft das Vertrauen haben, dass sie dieselben, aber in ihrer Wahrheit und dem Bewusstsein ihres Rechts, aber auch ihrer *Schranke* [!], wiederherzustellen wissen werde". [8]

Es sollte nicht lange dauern, bis der Durchbruch des geschichtlichen Denkens im 19. Jahrhundert alle feste Wahrheit in einen relativistischen Historizismus aufzulösen versuchte, und das mit einer nicht unberechtigten Berufung auf die Hegelsche Dialektik. Hegel selbst hat über seine dialektische Methode nun nicht nur in der Vorrede zur "Phänomenologie des Geistes" reflektiert. Vollends auf den Begriff gebracht erscheint sie erst zum Schluss der Grossen Logik, und zwar in der Lehre von der "absoluten Idee". [9] Auf dem Wege ihrer logischen Selbstvollendung hat die Idee alle bestimmten, d.h. inhaltlich-objektiven und somit begrenzten Entfaltungsphasen ihrer selbst durchlaufen, ähnlich wie das Lebewesen die Stadien von Jugend, Reifezeit und Alter. Am Ende ihrer selbst hat sich die Idee völlig in sich selbst zurückgezogen, alle Reichtümer ihres gedanklichen Lebens in sich hineinerinnert. Sein, Wesen und Begriff sind gleichsam ihre logischen Reifestadien, wobei der Begriff in seiner höchst vollendeten Gestalt als reine Form oder "*absolute Methode*" aufscheint.

Nunmehr ist alles an Inhalt, Objektivität, alle äussere Reflexion, die bisher noch in *unser* Wissen fiel, auf- und untergegangen in ebendiesen Schluss der reinen Idee als des vollendeten Begriffs. [10] Jetzt ist aller bisherige logische Inhalt mit seinen vielfachen Bestimmungen aufgezehrt, aufgehoben, einverwandelt in die *Inhaltslosigkeit,* als welche die *absolute Form* oder die reine Idee selbst ist. Die ganze Logik mit der Fülle ihres Nacheinanders an Bestimmungen war nichts anderes als die deduktionale Selbstvollendung bzw. Selbstverwirklichung der absoluten Idee. "Das ursprüngliche *Wort*..., das eine Äusserung ist, [ist] eine solche, die als Äusseres unmittelbar wieder verschwunden ist, indem sie ist; die Idee ist also nur in dieser Selbstbestimmung, *sich zu vernehmen*; sie ist in dem *reinen Gedanken*, worin der Unterschied noch kein *Anderssein* [erlangt hat], sondern sich vollkommen durchsichtig ist und bleibt." [11]

Die *logische* Idee hat sich also noch nicht in das *wirkliche* Anderssein in der Gestalt von Natur und Geist (Geschichte) entäussert. Sie

   8 Hegel, *Logik* II, 493.
   9 *Ibid.*, 483.
   10 Vgl. *ibid.*, 505.
   11 *Ibid.*, 485.

ist zunächst noch mit all ihren andershaften Bestimmungen ganz und gar in das Element ihrer selbst, d. h. des reinen Denkens, beschlossen und so immer noch bei sich. Die absolute oder vollendete Idee ist als das reine Denken ihrer selbst in diesen ihren Denken- bzw. Selbstbestimmungen (Sein, Wesen, Begriff) nur als das reine "*Wort*",[12] worin sie sich selbst nur für sich selbst ausspricht, ohne sich schon in dieser im Denken einbehaltenen Andersheit in das ganz Andere von Natur und Geist entlassen zu haben. Nachdem sich die Idee *innerhalb* des Denkens also ausgesprochen und den so gedachten Ausspruch oder das "ewige Wort" wiederum vernommen, d. h. in sich zurückgenommen und aufgehoben hat, allen andershaften Inhalt verflüchtigt und seine Mannigfaltigkeit von Bestimmungen wieder eingefangen hat in die reine *Form* des Denkens als den *aufgehobenen Inhalt*, so bleibt als dieser aufgehobene Inhalt die nunmehr reine Form noch zu bedenken. Das reine Denken ist jetzt nur noch als aufgehobener, überwundener, durch und durch zerdachter Inhalt seiner selbst. Das Denken als diese absolute Form, als Nicht-mehr-Inhalt, ist aber nichts anderes als die absolute Methode selbst, die alles Inhaltlich-Gedachte überwunden hat und sich nur noch in dieser Negativität des aufgehobenen Inhalts, d. h. als reine Form, bedenkt.

Die logische Wissenschaft oder das reine Denken schliesst damit, in der Fülle der geäusserten und im "Worte" ausgesprochenen Sach- und Inhaltsbestimmungen seiner selbst (Sein, Wesen, Begriff), sich nunmehr abschliessend, d.h. im *vollendeten* Begriff als dem zuletzt Gedachten, zu entdecken. Im Gedachten (Begriff) entdeckt das Denken (Begreifen) sein Selbst als die alle voraufliegenden Bestimmungen und Denkinhalte durchdringende und aufhebende "Seele und Substanz", als die "absolute Negativität", als "absolute Form", als die "*allgemeine absolute Tätigkeit*",[13] als die "*absolute Methode*".[14] Der reine Begriff hatte sich im Verlauf der Logik selbst zum Gegenstand (Inhalt) und schliesst nunmehr damit, "dies Begreifen seiner selbst [das in dem Inhaltlich-Gedachten verschlüsselte Denken selbst] zu erfassen, somit seine Stellung als Inhalt und Gegenstand aufzuheben und den Begriff der Wissenschaft zu erkennen",[15] d. h. ihre "Seele", "Tätigkeit", "Form" als "Methode" zu erfahren; denn alles das sind die Weisen des Begriffs selbst, die er als sich selbst oder sein Leben in der Wirklichkeit der logischen Wissenschaft zu erkennen vermag. Die Methode oder ab-

12 *Ibid.*
13 *Ibid.,* 486.
14 *Ibid.,* 490 f.
15 *Ibid.,* 505.

solute Form ist mithin das Leben des Logos selbst, seine absolute *Negativität*, weil er am Ende der Logik alle Gedankenbestimmungen seiner selbst (Sein, Wesen, Begriff) in sich zurückgefürht und *aufgehoben* hat.

Die analektische Methode des hl. Thomas hält demgegenüber jeden Hauch von Negativität aus Gottes Leben fern, mithin auch alle Veränderlichkeit und alles, was geschichtlich ist. Die Wirklichkeit Gottes ist analektisch die *absolute Positivität* seiner alles umgreifenden und in sich bergenden Form selbst. Während alle endliche Form (umgrenzte Wesenheit) das relative Nichts des Andersseins an sich trägt und deshalb von dem ihr an- und zugemessenen Sein selbst ("actu esse") real unterschieden ist, fallen Gottes unendliche Form und somit seine unbegrenzte Wirklichkeit der Fülle ineins. Daher ist keinerlei Differenz, auch keine Grenze bzw. Negation und Andersheit in ihm zu finden. "Cum Deus sit ipsa forma, vel potius ipsum esse, nullo modo compositus esse potest. Et hanc rationem tangit Hilarius 7 de Trinitate dicens: "Deus, qui virtus est, ex infirmis non continetur; *neque qui lux est, ex obscuris coaptatur*"".[16]

Das analektische Denken lebt von der uneingeschränkten Priorität des Affirmativen bzw. Positiven. Das gilt sowohl für seine logische Formalität als auch für das Prinzip seiner Ontologie. "Semper enim in rebus negatio fundatur super aliqua affirmatione, quae est quodammodo causa eius".[17] Es fehlt der Negation bzw. Privation jedwede Art von affirmativem Ansichsein, so dass sie ohne eine ihr zugrundeliegende, apriorische Positivität von Wirklichkeit nicht zu sein vermag. "Nam negatio vel privatio non est ens naturae, sed rationis",[18] oder "privatio entis fundatur in ente".[19] Analektisch lebt alle Ontologie ebenso wie die ihr zugeordnete Logik von der Priorität des Positiven. "Denn durch die Bejahung [κατάφασις] wird die Verneinung [ἀπόφασις] erkannt, und die Bejahung ist *früher* [προτέρα], wie auch das Sein früher ist als das Nichtsein [ὥσπερ καὶ τὸ εἶναι τοῦ μὴ εἶναι] ".[20] Alles Negative als solches hat keinerlei Seiendheit oder Wahrheit aus sich selbst, sondern empfängt beides allemal vom Verstande. In der *Wirklichkeit* der Dinge gibt es keine Negativität als solche, ebensowenig wie ein Allgemeines-an-sich ausserhalb unseres Verstandes anzutreffen ist. Weil das absolute Nichts alles Sein ein für allemal aus sich ausschliesst, so kann ihm auch keine Wahrheit innewohnen. Beides wird hier allenfalls vom Verstande

---

16   *Summa theologiae* I, 3, 7, c.
17   *Summa theol.* I-II, 72, 6, c.
18   *In IV Meta.* lect. 2, nr. 560.
19   *Summa theol.* I, 11, 2, c.
20   Aristoteles, *Anal. post.* I, 25, 86 b 34-36.

gleichsam ausgeliehen, so dass er über das Nichts zu urteilen vermag, *als ob* es so etwas wie ein Seiendes bzw. Wahres wäre. "Quod [non-ens] intellectui cuicumque aequetur, non est ex seipso non ente, sed ex seipso intellectu, qui rationem non entis accipit in seipso".[21]

Alle Seiendheit und Aussagbarkeit verdankt das Nichts somit dem göttlichen oder menschlichen Verstande. "Ens enim aliquo modo acceptum dicitur de non ente, secundum quod non ens est apprehensum ab intellectu".[22] Damit ist das fundamentalste Grundgesetz analektischen Denkens ausgesprochen: das Sein als solches schliesst alles Nichts ein für allemal aus sich aus, und zwar in logischem wie ontologischem Betracht. Das Widerspruchsprinzip in seiner Negativität und Exklusivität bildet nicht von ungefähr den *Anfang* unserer Denkbewegung. Dialektisch aber sind Negativität (Nichts) und Sein selbst bis zur Identität ineinander verschränkt. "Sein und Nichts ist dasselbe", heisst es im § 88 der Hegelschen Enzyklopädie. Für das analektische Denken aber ist die Negativität im Widerspruchsprinzip (Das Sein ist nicht Nichts) nur der verschärfte Ausdruck der totalen unaufhebbaren, unvermittelbaren Entfremdung von Sein und Nichts. Was aber für den *Begriff* des Seins gilt, das trifft erst recht zu für die *Wirklichkeit* des Seins selbst, das "esse subsistens", als welches Gott selber ist. Wenn für das dialektische Denken die absolute Idee so etwas ist wie die "absolute Form",[23] die "absolute Methode,[24] so gilt auch analektisch: Gott ist "*forma...* per se subsistens",[25] aus der alle Negativität, Potentialität, Veränderlichkeit, Geschichtlichkeit ausgeschlossen sind, eben weil Gott das Sein selbst ist. "Deus est actus purus, non habens aliquid de potentialitate".[26]

Die analektische Logik vertreibt mittels des Widerspruchsprinzips aus dem Sein selbst radikal jedwede Art von Nichtigkeit, so dass nicht die leiseste Vermittlung zwischen Sein und Nichts statthaben kann. "Inter contradictoria non est medium". Alle Negativität gilt nur als der verschärfte Ausdruck für diese Unmöglichkeit jedweder Art von Vermittlung zwischen Sein und Nichts. Ähnlich dienen auch alle negativen Aussagen über Gott nur dem unendlichen Über-Hinaus seiner Positivität und Seinsvollkommenheit. "Deus non sic dicitur non existens, quasi nullo modo existens, sed quia est *supra omne existens*, inquantum est suum esse".[27] Wenn analektisch von der Un-endlichkeit

21 St. Thomas, *De veritate* I, 5, ad 2.
22 *De veritate* I, 1, ad 7; vgl. *Summa theol.* I, 16, 7, ad 4.
23 Hegel, *Logik* II, 486, 501.
24 *Ibid.,* 490.
25 *Summa theol.,* I, 3, 2, ad 3.
26 *Ibid.,* c.
27 *Summa theol.,* I, 12, 1, ad 3.

Gottes die Rede ist, so ist auch hier die gedoppelte Negativität des
"Un" und "endlich" (un-begrenzt, in-finit) nur ein bescheidenes
Ausdrucksmittel unseres menschlichen Sprechens, um das uneinholbare
Über-Hinaus von Gottes ursprünglicher und verströmender Fülle auf-
zuzeigen, als welche er analog zu unserem Seinsbegriff wahrhaft der un-
vermittelte Anfang selbst ist. "Deus, cum sit *infinitus,* comprehendens
in se omnem plenitudinem perfectionis totius esse, non potest aliquid
acquirere, nec extendere se in aliquid, ad quod prius non pertingebat.
Unde nullo modo sibi competit motus. Et inde est quod quidam an-
tiquorum, quasi ab ipsa veritate coacti, posuerunt, primum principium
esse immobile". [28]

Dialektisch hingegen leben die Negativität und damit der Widerspruch im Herzen Gottes selbst und auch zutiefst in allen Dingen dieser
Welt. "Das *Nichtsein* des Endlichen [das "Un" des Endlichen] ist das
Sein des Absoluten". [29] Und wenn man dialektisch zwischen Positivität
und Negativität wertend unterscheiden will, so wäre "der Widerspruch
für das Tiefere und Wesenhaftere zu nehmen. Denn die Identität ihm
gegenüber ist nur die Bestimmung des einfachen Unmittelbaren, des
toten Seins; er aber ist die Wurzel aller Bewegung und Lebendigkeit". [30]
Je negativer und zugeschärfter der Widerspruch im Inneren von Gott
und Dingen revoltiert, um so jäher ist sein Umschlag in die Identität
bzw. Positivität. Die Identität ist somit niemals Ursprung und
Voraussetzung (Causa) der Negation, sondern umgekehrt: Die Identität
ist dialektisch allemal nur als das "*Resultat*"[31] der Negation, als die
"Negation der Negation", als das "Andere des Anderen". [32] So und nur
so ist beispielsweise das *Fürsichsein* möglich, sei es in Gestalt des
mechanisch-numerischen Eins (des Atoms, der Monade), des "Ich", des
"Geistes" oder "Gottes". [33]

In allem ist die Negativität, besser die "absolute Negativität", "das
Negative des Negativen",[34] das konstitutive Prinzip. Alles ist somit der
"absoluten Methode" unterworfen. Die Methode ist also alles andere
als die des analektischen Denkens, das sich allemal im behutsamen
Nachgang der Wirklichkeit des Wirklichen anzugleichen sucht, ja—um
des Seins und der Wahrheit willen — sich ihr in Botmässigkeit und
Dienstschaft zugeordnet (proportioniert) und verpflichtet weiss. "Scibile

28 *Summa theol.* I, 9, 1, c.
29 Hegel, *Logik* II, 62.
30 *Ibid.,* 58.
31 *Ibid.,* 499.
32 Hegel, *Enzyklopädie*, § 95; *Logik* II, 496.
33 *Logik* I, 149.
34 *Logik* II, 496.

non dependet a scientia, sed e converso".[35] Nicht der Geist und die Methode sind das Mass der Dinge, sondern "res est mensura intellectus nostri".[36] Dialektisch ist die absolute Methode das endliche Denken des Menschen, aber so, dass es in seiner Widersprüchlichkeit und Negativität (Endlichkeit) über sich hinaus getrieben und aufgehoben wird in das Denken Gottes selber, so dass Letzteres nicht Ursprung, wohl aber *Resultat* des endlichen Denkens ist. Der Fortgang, die Entwicklung des Denkens oder Begriffs über alle Endlichkeit hinaus, vollzieht sich nicht als "*eine Art von Überfluss*".[37] Gott ist nicht der absolute, aktuose Anfang, "actus purus", "diffusivum sui",[38] Gott ist dialektisch vielmehr immer nur das *Ende*. "Nur in seiner *Vollendung* ist es [das Sein des Anfangs] das Absolute".[39]

Die absolute Methode ist jenes Leben, das seinen Ausgang nimmt von seiner Anfangsbestimmung, als welche das Sein ist, das soviel wie Nichts bedeutet. Von dieser leeren Unmittelbarkeit und "abstraktesten und dürftigsten"[40] Äusserlichkeit als ihrer armseligen Vorausbestimmung geht die absolute Methode aus, wobei ihr zunächst unser Denken als "äusserliche Reflexion" als bloss "verständiges endliches Erkennen"[41] zuschauend beiwohnt. Kraft des ihm immanenten Widerspruchs wird dieser Anfang (Sein als Nichts, Identität als Nicht-Identität) über sich hinaus getrieben in sein Anderes, in seine erste Negation, als welche sich das *Wesen* zeitgt. Das *Sein* wird dialektisch als Unmittelbarkeit, abstrakter Anfang, als "Nichts, welches das Sein ist"[42] begriffen, besser noch als die "*Einheit* des Seins und Nichtseins... oder der *Identität* der Identität und Nicht-Identität".[43] "Dieser Begriff könnte als die erste, reinste, d. i. abstrakteste Definition des Absoluten angesehen werden".[44]

Diese Abwertung des höchsten und vollkommensten Begriffs, den das analektische Denken kennt, macht jede Versöhnung zwischen Analektik und Dialektik von vornherein unmöglich. Die katholische Theologie des 19. Jahrhunderts hatte durchaus recht, wenn sie — von einigen Ausnahmen abgesehen — im Gegensatz zum Heute zu einer Rezeption Hegelscher Denkmotive nicht bereit war. Auch analektisch

---

35 St. Thomas, *In I Sent.* d. 8, q. 4, a. 1, ad 3.
36 *Summa theol.* I-II, 65, 3, c.
37 *Logik* II, 490.
38 *Summa theol.* I, 5, 4, ad 2.
39 *Logik* II, 490.
40 *Enzyklopädie*, § 86.
41 *Logik* II, 491.
42 *Enzyklopädie*, § 89.
43 *Logik* I, 59.
44 *Ibid.*

ist das Sein der uranfängliche, erste und gerade so alles einbehaltende Begriff, der allem, wenn auch auf die verschiedenste Weise, also analogisch zukommt, mag es sich um Gott oder um die Materie, ja sogar um das Nichts als ein "ens rationis" handeln. Wenn unserem Denken der Aufstieg in die unendliche Weite des Transzendentalen und des Transzendenten möglich ist, so nur, weil es über diesen ganz und gar undialektischen, eben analektischen Begriff des Seins verfügt. Das Sein ist durch und durch analektisch eingefärbt und zwar aus zweierlei Gründen:

1) Weil es durch und durch analogischer Natur ist und so alle kategorialen, artlichen und "Einzel"-Begriffe *aktuell*, d. h. unmittelbar in sich selber trägt, im Gegensatz zu Art und Gattung, die ihre Unterschiede nur *potentiell*, also nicht unmittelbar *in* sich selbst enthalten. Diesen analektischen Primat des Begrifflich-Analogen überhaupt drückt Thomas also aus: "In praedicationibus omnia univoca reducuntur ad unum primum non univocum, sed *analogicum*, quod est ens";[45]

2) Das Sein selbst ist ebenso wie die ihm kongruenten Transzendentalbestimmungen ganz und gar undialektischer Natur, d. h. sie sind analektisch strukturiert, sofern sie als solche keinerlei Negativität in sich tragen. "Quaedam nomina significant ipsas perfectiones absolute *absque hoc quod aliquis modus participandi* claudatur in eorum significatione, ut ens, bonum, vivens, et huiusmodi; et talia *proprie* dicuntur de Deo".[46]

Das Sein selbst, als welches Gott ist, steht in seiner Fülle und Vollendung immer schon am Anfang, nicht aber am Ende seiner eigenen oder gar einer menschlichen Denk- und Seinsbewegung. "Deus est ipsum esse per se subsistens".[47] Daher ist es die natürliche Folge, dass Gott und nur Gott als das Sein selbst auch in den Dingen dieser Welt als die allein ihm gemässe Wirkung das *Sein* selbst erwirkt. "Cum Deus sit ipsum *esse* per suam essentiam, oportet quod *esse* creatum sit proprius effectus eius, sicut ignire est proprius effectus ignis".[48] Gerade um des Seins willen wohnt Gott nicht ausserhalb, sondern in der Herzmitte der Dinge selbst. "Esse est illud quod est *magis intimum* cuilibet, et quod profundius omnibus inest, cum sit formale respectu omnium quae in re sunt... Unde oportet quod Deus sit in omnibus rebus — *et intime*".[49]

Obwohl Gott als Prinzip der Dinge dank seiner unendlichen Entität und einmaligen Aseität unendlich über sie hinaus ist, verlangt dieses

45 *Summa theol.* I, 13, 5, ad 1.
46 *Summa theol.* I, 13, 4, ad 1. Vgl. auch *De veritate* 2, 11, c; *De potentia* 7, 2, ad 9.
47 *Summa theol.* I, 4, 2, c.
48 *Summa theol.* I, 8, 1, c.
49 *Ibid.*

Über-Hinaus dennoch sein innerstes Insein in der Kreatur. Diese widerspruchsfreie, eben seinsgemässe Spannung des Über-In ("supra-in") gehört zum Wesen der "analogia entis".[50] "Deus est *supra* omnia per excellentiam suae naturae, et tamen est *in* omnibus rebus ut causans omnium esse".[51] Alle Art von dialektischer Identität, also einer Identität von Identität und Nicht-Identität, eine *Unendlichkeit als Resultat* von transzendenter (metaphysischer) "Verstandes"-Unendlichkeit und hinfälliger Endlichkeit ist analektisch absurd. Daher kann es auch kein Werden oder gar eine Geschichte in Gott selber geben, wie die modernen Theologen wollen. Gott ist niemals in pantheistischem Sinn das Wesen von Welt, wie sehr er ihr auch — als ihre Wirklichkeit wirkend — zuinnerst innewohnt. "Deus est in omnibus rebus, non quidem sicut *pars essentiae*".[52] Der dialektische Pantheismus Hegels verflicht Endliches und Unendliches in die Einheit eines einzigen, in sich gegenläufigen Prozesses bzw. ein- und derselben Methode. "Das Endliche wird nicht vom Unendlichen als einer ausser ihm vorhandenen Macht aufgehoben, sondern es ist seine [des Endlichen] Unendlichkeit, sich selbst aufzuheben".[53] "Es ist nur die *Negation* [des Endlichen selbst], die sich in der *Negation aufhebt*".[54]

Statt des analektischen *"Über-In"* strukturiert dialektisch das *"Heraus-Hinein"* das Gott-Welt-Verhältnis. Dadurch werden Gott und Welt zu einer einzigen Einheit verschlungen, in eine *Identität* von Nicht-Identischen hineingezwungen. Die Dialektik behauptet, "das Unendliche [Gott] gehe zur Endlichkeit [Welt] *heraus*, darum weil es keine Wahrheit, kein Bestehen an ihm, wie es als abstrakte Einheit [von der alten Metaphysik] gefasst ist, hat; so umgekehrt geht das Endliche aus demselben Grunde seiner Nichtigkeit in das Unendliche *hinein*. Oder vielmehr ist zu sagen, dass das Unendliche ewig zur Endlichkeit herausgegangen, dass es schlechthin nicht ist, so wenig als das reine Sein, allein für sich, ohne sein Anderes an ihm selbst zu haben".[55]

Es zeugt von einem unentschuldbaren Missverständnis der Hegelschen Dialektik, wenn man heutzutage versucht, eine derartige Ontologie des Widerspruchs zu so etwas wie den "Prolegomena zu einer künftigen Christologie" aufzuwerten, um zugleich den — angeblich neuen — christlichen Gottesbegriff von dem "der griechischen Meta-

---

50 Vgl. E. Przywara, *Analogia entis* (München 1932).
51 *Summa theol.* I, 8, 1, ad 1.
52 *Ibid.*, c.
53 *Logik* I, 135.
54 *Ibid.*
55 *Ibid.*, 144.

physik" wegzuführen, "da sich dieser [angeblich] als zu statisch und zu transzendent erwies".[56]

Die "absolute Methode" oder die "unendliche Form", welche alle Inhaltsbestimmungen, deren dialektisches Auseinander- Hervorgehen, also den gesamten Verlauf der Logik bestimmt, erfasst erst am Ende der Logik als deren krönenden Beschluss sich selbst, denn aller Inhalt hat sich zur reinen Form, d.i. ins absolute Denken, selbst verwandelt. Nachdem sich die absolute Methode aus der anfänglichen Gedankenbestimmung des Seins zum Wesen entfaltet hat, setzt sie ebendieses Wesen als die "Negation des Seins". Weil nun das Wesen "das Negative des Ersten" (des Seins) ist, so ist es zugleich, "indem wir auf den weiteren Verlauf zum voraus Bedacht nehmen", das *erste Negative*.[57] Dieses erste Negative ist mithin nicht mehr der Anfang oder das Unmittelbare (Sein), sondern *das* [vom Sein her] *Vermittelte*" und "*enthält* überhaupt die *Bestimmung des Ersten* in sich. Das Erste ist somit wesentlich auch im Andern *aufbewahrt* und *erhalten*".[58]

Wir haben hier als Beispiele für die Formalität der dialektischen Methode die Bestimmungen von Sein und Wesen gebraucht. Natürlich könnten wir ebensogut als Beleginhalte für den Anfang bzw. die Unmittelbarkeit etwa das "Einzelne" (Logik II, S. 495) oder den "Keim des Lebendigen", die "Ursache", ja sogar die "Sonne"[59] benutzen, denn die "ganze Logik" enthält zahllose *Beispiele*"[60] dieser Art. Aber wie unterschiedlich die inhaltlichen Bestimmungen für die Form der Unmittelbarkeit oder des Anfangs auch sein mögen, hier steht ausschliesslich die *allgemeine* Form, die absolute Methode selbst in Frage, die all' jene Inhalte durchherrscht und in gedanklicher Bewegung hält. Das Erste (Sein) ist im Zweiten, seiner Negation, oder in dem so *Vermittelten* (Wesen) nicht nur enthalten, aufgegangen, sondern auch untergegangen. Was nun die positive Seite des Enthaltenseins anlangt, so kann zunächst einmal diese "*Einheit* als ein Satz ausgedrückt werden, worin das [jeweilige] Unmittelbare [z. B. Sein, Endliches, Eins, Einzelnes] als Subjekt, das Vermittelte [als die Negation jener Unmittelbarkeiten] als dessen Prädikat gestellt ist, z.B. *das Endliche ist unendlich, Eins ist Vieles, das Einzelne ist das Allgemeine*",[61] oder auch: Das Sein ist das Wesen u.s.f., wobei jedesmal das Prädikat als die Negation des Subjekts erscheint.

---

56 H. Küng, *Menschwerdung Gottes* (Freiburg, 1970), 553.
57 *Logik* II, 494.
58 *Logik* II, 495.
59 *Ibid.*, 490.
60 *Ibid.*, 495.
61 *Ibid.*

Weil nun hier das Unmittelbar-Anfängliche in dem Vermittelten, d.h. in seiner Negation, enthalten und aufbewahrt wird, si sind jene *positiven* Urteile gerechtfertigt. Da aber das Negative jenes Erste (Subjekt) nicht nur positiv erhält und aufbewahrt, sondern auch nichtet und in negativem Sinne aufgehoben, also destruiert hat, so erweist sich jene *positive* Form des Urteils als höchst einseitig und "unfähig..., das Spekulative und die Wahrheit in sich zu fassen. Die nächste Ergänzung desselben, das *negative* Urteil, müsste wenigstens ebensosehr beigefügt werden. Im Urteil hat das Erste als Subjekt den Schein eines selbständigen Bestehens, da es vielmehr in seinem Prädikate als seinem Andern aufgehoben ist; diese Negation ist in dem Inhalte jener Sätze wohl enthalten, aber ihre positive Form widerspricht demselben; es wird somit das nicht gesetzt, was darin enthalten ist; was gerade die Absicht, einen Satz zu gebrauchen, wäre".[62]

Mit anderen Worten: Jedes *positive* Urteil fordert sein entsprechend *negatives*, das jenes erstere aufhebt. Denn schon in der Zweiheit und damit Andersheit von Subjekt und Prädikat, die durch die Kopula (das Einzelne *ist* das Allgemeine) identifiziert werden, ereignet sich dialektisch der Widerspruch oder die Negativität als Konstituens auch des positiven Urteils. Wenn dem so ist, bleibt an die modernistischen Theologen von heute die verfängliche Frage zu richten, wie sie unter solchen Umständen die Hegelsche Dialektik für eine katholische Dogmatik nutzbar machen wollen. Wir werden übrigens in der Folge sehen, wie das analektische Denken des hl. Thomas uns die Urteilsstruktur und die innere Verspannung von Subjekt und Prädikat ohne die Zuhilfenahme von dialektischer Negativität zu deuten weiss.

Aber kehren wir zu Hegel zurück. Wir sahen, wie das Unmittelbare (Sein) auf seine Negation (das Wesen) hinbezogen, in diesem auf- und unterging. Die zweite Bestimmung (Wesen) ist so die vom Ersten her *vermittelte,* zugleich aber auch die weiterhin *vermittelnde.* Sie umschliesst nämlich das Erste als das aufgehobene Andere in sich selbst. Sie ist so das "zweite Negative" als das "*Andere eines Andern*" und ist so "*die gesetzte Dialektik ihrer selbst*".[63] Hier erst, am Schluss der Logik, tritt die Methode selbst, von allem inhaltlichen Ballast nunmehr befreit, offen zutage und erscheint erstmals als solche im Wissen als reine Form, so dass es sich in ihr jetzt erst als Methode oder als verflüssigte Formalität entdeckt. In dieser Form begreift das Wissen sich selbst als Wissen, so dass nunmehr die Aristotelische "$\nu\acute{o}\eta\sigma\iota\varsigma$ $\tau\tilde{\eta}\varsigma$

---

62 *Ibid.*
63 *Ibid.,* 496.

νοήσεως "[64] oder das " ταῦτον νοῦς καὶ νοητόν "[65] auch dialektisch zum Ereignis wird. Das Denken ist mehr als Inhalt, Gegenstand, Objekt bezw. durch diese begrenztes Subjekt, es ist reine Form, absolute Methode, Geist und Leben in allen Dingen, "unendlicher Progress",[66] "*allgemeine absolute Tätigkeit*, die [sich] selbstbestimmende und selbst realisierende Bewegung", die "*Substantialität der Dinge*, — d.h. der Begriffe, insofern sie der *Vorstellung* und der *Reflexion* zunächst als *Andere* erscheinen".[67] Hier wird der idealistische Grundzug der Hegel-schen Dialektik besonders deutlich, und man fragt sich, wie dieser Idealismus mit dem Realismus des christlichen Schöpfungsbegriffes in Einklang gebracht werden soll.

Jenes zweite Negative erwies sich, nachdem es das Erste bzw. Un-mittelbare in sich hineingenommen hat, nunmehr als das "*Andere eines Andern*". Diese in sich revolvierende Negativität und Andersheit er-weist sich nun als der "*einfache Punkt der negativen Beziehung auf sich*",[68] die ins Einfach-Punktuelle gleichsam eingezwängte unendliche Energie einer absoluten Negativität, das "Negative des Negativen"[69] in absoluter Konzentration.

Damit aber setzt der "*Wendungspunkt* der Bewegung der Begriffes"[70] ein, sofern die "Negation der Negation" analog dem grammatischen Prinzip: Gedoppelte Negation ergibt verstärkte Affirmation, sich nun-mehr als das "Aufheben des Widerspruches"[71] zu vollbringen beginnt. Der Widerspruch als solcher ereignet sich zunächst als die Aktuosität des Gedoppelt-Negativen, als die Feindseligkeit des Anderen *gegen* das Andere, und ist gerade so als diese *intime* Revolution "der innerste Quell aller Tätigkeit, lebendiger und geistiger Selbstbewegung, die dialektische Seele, die alles Wahre an ihm selbst hat, durch die es allein Wahres ist".[72]

Sofern nun dieser Widerspruch (dieses "Negative des Negativen") zugleich gerade wegen seiner verschärften Intensität in das Aufheben seiner selbst umschlägt, so vollbringt er zugleich im Widersprechen die *Einheit* seines Grundes als "das *innerste, objektivste Moment* des Lebens und Geistes, wodurch ein *Subjekt, Person, Freies* ist".[73] "Das Ding, das Subjekt, der Begriff ist nun ebendiese negative *Einheit* selbst;

---

64 *Enzyklopädie*, § 552.
65 *Ibid.*, § 577.
66 *Logik* II, 500.
67 *Ibid.*, 486.
68 *Ibid.*, 496.
69 *Ibid.*
70 *Ibid.*
71 *Ibid.*, 497.
72 *Ibid.*, 496.
73 *Ibid.*, 497.

es ist ein sich selbst Widersprechendes, aber ebensosehr der *aufgelöste Widerspruch*: es ist der *Grund*, der seine Bestimmungen enthält und trägt".[74] Es ist diese absolute Negativität, welche zum Ende der Logik sich in die *Einheit* einer übergreifenden *Subjektivität* erinnert und beruhigt, welche damit aber auch die letzte Spur von Endlichkeit, d. i. von "Gegensatz zwischen Begriff [endlichem Subjekt] und Realität [Objekt]" liquidiert und "die Einheit [setzt], welche die Wahrheit ist",[75] "den adäquaten Begriff",[76] "die sich wissende Wahrheit"[77] oder das "*erfüllte* Sein"[78] selbst erwirkt.

Was wäre die absolute Idee somit anderes als die Selbstverwirklichung des Begriffes im Medium der Wissenschaft (Logik), die "Causa sui",[79] die "*Realisierung des Begriffs*"[80] durch sich selbst und für sich selbst. Die allem Inhaltlichen "immanente Form"[81] hat sich zum Schluss ihrer systematisierenden Tätigkeit und logischen Selbstvermittlung als "der *eine identische Begriff*" realisiert, in dem "Subjekt, Methode und Objekt"[82] eins wurden und jetzt nur noch die absolute Form als solche herrscht, als die "höchste zugeschärfteste Spitze", als die "*reine Persönlichkeit*, die allein durch die absolute Dialektik, die ihre Natur ist, ebensosehr *alles in sich befasst* and hält".[83]

Damit ist nunmehr das "*Dritte*"[84] erstanden, die jetzt endlich *perfekte* Aufhebung von Vermittlung und Widerspruch, "der Begriff, der sich durch das Anderssein [Sein, Nichts, Werden, Dasein, Etwas, Anderes, Fürsichsein, Quantität, Mass, Wesen, Grund, Existenz, Inneres, Äusseres, Möglichkeit, Wirklichkeit, Substanz, Ursache, subjektiver Begriff, objektive Welt, Leben, Erkennen, Tun] realisiert hat und durch Aufheben dieser [inhaltichen] Realität [Andersheit] mit sich zusammengegangen ist und seine *absolute* Realität, seine *einfache* Beziehung auf sich, hergestellt hat. Dies *Resultat* ist daher die *Wahrheit*".[85] Dieses realisierte "Dritte" ist nun die absolute Persönlichkeit, das geeinzelte Allgemeine, das reine Wissen; zugleich aber ist es um seiner wiedergewonnenen Unmittelbarkeit willen erneut der Anfang, von dem die logische Methode ihren Ausgang nahm. Daher ist das göttliche

74 *Ibid.*, 62.
75 *Ibid.*, 496.
76 *Ibid.*, 407.
77 *Ibid.*, 484.
78 *Ibid.*, 504.
79 *Enzyklopädie*, § 153.
80 *Logik* II, 489.
81 *Ibid.*
82 *Ibid.*, 487.
83 *Ibid.*, 502.
84 *Ibid.*, 498.
85 *Ibid.*, 498 f.

Leben (absolute Methode) so etwas wie der "in sich geschlungene
Kreis",[86] der in sich zirkelt ohne Ende, zu welchem auch die zwei realen
Kreise von Natur- und Geistgeschehen immerzu zurückkehren. Natur
und Geist (Geschichte) sind nämlich im Gegensatz zu "Sein" und
"Wesen" nicht immanent-logische, sondern *transient-reale Anders-
heiten* der Idee, in welchen sie sich mehr noch als im Medium der
Logik, diesem "Reich der Schatten",[87] selbst realisiert.

Die Logik vollbringt sich innerhalb ihrer selbst als die "Triplizität"[88]
von Anfang (Sein), Vermittlung (Wesen) und aufgehobener Vermittlung
(Begriff), d. h. als Anfang, Mitte und Ende. Die Triplizität erscheint
aber auch als das Gesamt der Logik, das sich in die zwei anderen Kreise
von Natur und Geist entäussert hat, um aus ihnen in sich selbst zurück-
zukehren. Eine einzige absolute Methode durchherrscht also diese
ideal-logische und real-geistige Triplizität, macht alles und jedes zu immer schon aufgehobenen Momenten, zum Vermittelten in dieser einen
grossen Strömung, die *"als Kreis von Kreisen"*[89] in sich selber zirkelt.

Das Denken des Endlichen ist um dieser Endlichkeit seines Gegen-
standes willen selber endlich[90] und verbleibt so, bis sich zum Schluss der
Logik die Endlichkeit des Inhaltlich-Objektiven überhaupt in die absolute Methode formalisiert hat. Nunmehr ist unser endliches Denken
oder unsere "äusserliche... subjektive Reflexion"[91] in die Unendlichkeit
der methodischen Formalität hineinverwandelt, weil es in dem
aufgehobenen Inhalt als der reinen Form ein Begrenzend- Äusserlich-
Anderes nicht mehr gibt, sondern das Denken sich im *aufgehobenen*
Inhalt selbst gewahrt. Im Begriffenen begreift sich der Begriff, und der
Begriff begreift das Begriffene als sein Selbst und innerstes Wesen.
Dieses Sich- Begreifen ohne trennende Grenze zwischen Begriff und
Begriffenem hat sich aufgeklärt zur reinen Form. Es handelt sich somit
um "das Wissen des Menschen *von* Gott, das fortgeht zum Sichwissen
des Menschen *in* Gott",[92] oder auch um das Sichwissen des Menschen
als Gott, sofern der Mensch sich selbst durch die Negation seines endlichen Denkens, also von sich aus, als die freie Unendlichkeit Gottes
selbst erwirkt hat.

Mit dieser unendlichen Form des sich selbst denkenden Denkens ist
das Reich der Wahrheit angebrochen, *"wie sie ohne Hülle an und für*

---

86   *Ibid.,* 504.
87   *Logik* I, 41.
88   *Logik* II, 498.
89   *Ibid.,* 504.
90   Vgl. *ibid.,* 437.
91   *Ibid.,* 505.
92   *Enzyklopädie,* § 564.

sich selbst ist. Man kann sich deswegen ausdrücken, dass dieser Inhalt die *Darstellung Gottes* ist, *wie er in seinem ewigen Wesen vor der Erschaffung der Natur und eines enlichen Geistes ist*".[93] Wir müssen aber hinzufügen, dass dieses ewige Wesen, d. h. der Logos, als unendliche Form oder Methode nicht nur *vor* Erschaffung von Welt und Mensch, sondern ebensosehr *nach* ihnen als ihrer beider *Resultat* ist.[94]

Was hat nun angesichts dieser mystisch-pantheistischen Spekulation der Dialektik die Thomistische Analektik auszusagen? Nach Thomas ist der Zentral- bzw. Wendepunkt aller dialektischen Methode in der Gestalt der "Negation der Negation" eine an sich selbst unmögliche Sache. Eine "privatio privationis" oder "negatio negationis" kann sich nicht in den Dingen, auch nicht im gedachten Inhalt als solchem, sondern allenfalls in der abstrakten Formalität unseres Denkens selbst als "ens rationis" ereignen. "Unde relatio qua refertur ens ad non ens, non est nisi tantum in ratione: et similiter privatio, qua de ente negatur non ens, est in ratione tantum, ut privatio privationis, vel negatio negationis".[95] Wenn schon die einfache privatio bzw. negatio ihr Sein dem setzenden Verstande zu verdanken hat, um wieviel mehr also die gedoppelte Negation als "negatio negationis"!? Die Folge ist, dass diese Seinsanleihe des Negativen beim Verstande und die Aufwertung des Negativen zum ens rationis eine solch' in sich verbissene wechselseitige Intensität zweier Negationen gar nicht zulässt, wie sie die Dialektik verstattet. Denn durch die Einbildung des Seins ins Negative mildern sich zum Beispiel die *Kontradiktorien* von Sein und Nichts, soweit sie vom Verstande als zugleich bedachte seinem Einen Wissen innewohnen, zur Kontrarietät.

So bleibt nach Thomas für die jähe Härte des kontradiktorischen Gegensatzes nur der Raum des Sachhaft-Objektiven. Hier mögen sich Sein und Nichts unversöhnlich verfeinden oder besser, einander meiden und sich soweit als möglich aus dem Wege gehen ("elongatio"): das Denken umgreift dennoch beide und macht sie eben dadurch zu *Gedachten.* Was in Wirklichkeit einander *widerspricht,* im Denken wird es — weil Gedachtes — zur Kontrarietät herabgesetzt. "Quamvis enim *esse* et *non esse* non sint contraria, sed contradictorie opposita, si considerentur ipsa significata, prout sunt in rebus, quia alterum est ens et alterum est pure non ens, tamen si referantur ad actum animae, utrumque ponit aliquid esse. Unde *esse* et *non esse* sunt contradictoria".[96]

---

93 *Logik* I, 31.
94 Vgl. *Enzyklopädie*, § 574.
95 *In I Sent.* d. 24, q. 1, a. 3, ad 1.
96 *Summa theol.* I-II, 64, 3, ad 3; vgl. auch I-II, 35, 5, ad 2.

Das will besagen, dass die Realität der "contradictio" im Verstande zur "contrarietas affirmationis et negationis" entschärft wird. Es entspricht dem "sanften Gesetz" (media via) analektischen Denkens, dass das Wesen des kontradiktorischen Gegensatzes nicht so sehr im verbissenen Kampf des Gedoppelt-Negativen besteht, als vielmehr im stillen Ausweichen und in der maximalen Entfernung des Negativen vom Positiven oder des Möglichen vom Wirklichen. "Et isto modo in oppositione contradictoria *elongatur* potentia ab actu, quia in non ente simpliciter nihil potentiae est ad esse".[97]

Schon Platon — von der existentialen Theologie des Heute nicht mehr geschätzt — begreift das Verhältnis des Gegensätzlichen keineswegs als den *"einfachen Punkt* der negativen Beziehung auf sich",[98] als das Ineins zweier Negationen, sondern gerade umgekehrt als *Auseinanderstreben* der Kontradiktorien, als "elongatio" im Thomistischen Sinn, als die Nicht-Annahme des einen Gegensatzes durch den andern: " τὸ ἐναντίον τὸ ἐναντίον μὴ δέχεσθαι".[99] Niemals wird das eine Gegenteil zu dem anderen, sondern es flieht vor ihm oder löst sich beim Zusammentreffen beider restlos auf: " ἀπέρχεται ἢ ἀπολλύται".[100] Ganz im Sinne des Aristotelischen Widerspruchsprinzips kann und wird niemals eine Versöhnung bzw. Vermittlung des Gegensätzlichen als solchen durch Umschlag in ein Drittes erzwungen: " μηδέποτε ἐναντίον ἑαυτῷ τὸ ἐναντίον ἔσεσθαι".[101]

Eine aller Dialektik überlegene Besinnung stellt Thomas an, wenn er die Kontradiktorien von Sein und Nichts in das Gedachte an sich verlegt, das Denken selbst aber von ihnen vollends freihält. Ergibt sich aber dann nicht das folgende Problem, d. h. werden beide Kontradiktorien (Sein und Nichts) in dem objektiven Bereich des Dinglichen nicht selbst zu Seiendheiten, wird nicht trotz allem das Nichts wiederum aus einem blossen "ens rationis" zu einem "ens reale" angehoben? Thomas findet eine überraschende Lösung, die zudem ob ihrer präzisen Formulierung auch innerhalb der Dialektik kaum ihresgleichen hat. Die Thomistische Antwort lautet bündig: "In contradictoriis vero absolute *non* sunt *extrema realiter diversa*, quia non ens non est aliqua res. Sunt tamen extrema contradictionis semper *realiter non eadem*".[102] Sein und Nichts sind keine gleichgewichtigen gegensätzlichen Realitäten, weil das Nichts an sich selbst eben

---

97 *De IV oppositis*, cap. 1, nr. 622/Marietti.
98 *Logik* II, 496.
99 *Phaidon* 105 a, 2; ferner 104 b, 7-8.
100 *Ibid.*, 103 a, 1.
101 *Ibid.*, 103 b, 7-8.
102 *De IV oppositis*, cap. 3, nr. 594.

ausschliesslich nur Nichts ist. Zwischen beiden besteht nicht nur ein Seins-, sondern auch ein bestürzendes Wertgefälle, sofern das Sein als "nobilius extremum" vom Nichts als dem "extremum vilius"[103] allzeits geschieden bleibt, zumal nicht einmal der leiseste Ansatz ("potentia") von Seiendheit im Nichts erscheinen will. Aber das Sein in seiner Unvermittelbarkeit, Ausschliesslichkeit und Alleinheit genügt ja vollends, um seine *reale Nicht-Identität* ("realiter non eadem") mit allem Nichts uns in unüberbietbarer Evidenz schlicht und einfach in den Blick zu bringen. Das Widerspruchsprinzip bestimmt machtvoll die Objektivität des Dinglichen, ist dessen schlechthin prinzipiierendes Gesetz, die metaphysisch-transzendentale Bedingung aller Möglichkeit und Wirklichkeit, alles Endlichen und Unendlichen, sofern es zu seiner objektiven Giltigkeit nicht der *gegensätzlichen Realitäten*, wohl aber der *realen Gegensätzlichkeit* (Nicht-Identität) bedarf, die durch die Ausschliesslichkeit und Alleinigkeit des Seienden selbst unaufhebbar verbürgt und ein für allemal garantiert ist.

Die Dialektiker aller Zeiten, die der Antike wie die der Neuzeit, sind nach Thomas allemal "Sophisten", da sie Sein und Nichts im Grunde als gegensätzliche Sachheiten begreifen, die letzten Endes *generisch* ein und dasselbe sind. "Inde est quod sophistae decepti sunt putantes alterum extremum contradictionis, non esse scilicet, *in genere contineri*".[104] Das analektische Denken weiss sich selbst und seine ihm proportionierte Sache des Seins überhaupt auf unerschütterlichen Grund gestellt. Es gilt der Satz: Alles philosophische wie auch theologische Denken, das vom Widerspruche lebt, stirbt auch daran. Jedes Seiende ist seiner Natur nach sehr viel mehr auf die Proportionalität seiner immanenten Prinzipien, auf die Tranzendentalität von Frieden und Einheit im Inneren ("unitas sive pax")[105] seiner selbst so wie auf den Einklang mit dem Insgesamt von Welt gegründet. Das Endlich-Seiende ist analektisch alles andere als in tödlicher Ruhe erstarrt. Es wird in Atem gehalten durch die ihm einwohnende "virtus essendi",[106] weil Wesenheit und Sein, Potenz und Akt einander immer schon angemessen sind. "Potentia, cum sit receptiva actus, oportet quod actui *proportionetur*".[107] Aber die Proportion von Akt und Potenz verhindert nicht, dass sie *an sich* einander auch entgegengesetzt sind. "Id autem quod est in potentia tantum, non potest esse pars actus; cum potentia *repugnet* actui, utpote contra actum divisa".[108]

---

103 *Ibid.,* cap. 2, nr. 590.
104 *Ibid.,* nr. 592.
105 *Summa theol.* I, 103, 3, c.
106 *Summa contra gentiles* I, 20.
107 *Summa theol.* I, 75, 5, ad 1.
108 *Ibid.,* c.

Ebendiese in aller Zuordnung nicht aufgehobene Gegensätzlichkeit von Akt und Potenz, von Wesenheit und Sein, von Materie und Form stiftet jenes lebendige Zusammenspiel im Inneren der Dinge, damit ihre Wirklichkeit Ereignis werde. "Nulla res, in qua est aliud essentia et aliud esse, potest esse nisi *concurrentibus pluribus*, scilicet essentia et esse".[109] Längst bevor das existentiale Denken seine "ontologische Differenz" entdeckt zu haben glaubte, war sie als "distinctio realis" eine der Grundvoraussetzungen der analektischen Philosophie. Es ist nicht die Dialektik des zwangsgeeinten Widerspruchs, der inmitten der Dinge pulsiert als vielmehr der Einklang im Zusammenspiel ihrer physischen (Materie-Form) und metaphysischen (Wesenheit-Sein) Prinzipien, die — ohne die Spannung in ihrer Andersheit und Gegensätzlichkeit zu verlieren — die notwendige Voraussetzung hergeben, damit das harmonische Zusammenspiel oder die Konvenienz im Sein des Seienden und der immanenten Vielfalt seiner Momente sich vollbringen kann, denn: "Ens inquantum ens non habet rationem repugnantis, sed magis convenientis".[110]

Aber gilt nicht auch analektisch der — angeblich dialektische — Satz des Spinoza: "Omnis determinatio est negatio"?[111] Wir antworten: Längst vor Spinoza hat Thomas festgestellt: "In ratione distinctionis est negatio",[112] in aller Vielheit steckt auch analektisch Negativität und Andersheit. Thomas spricht in diesem Zusammenhang sogar von einer "negatio realis": "In multitudine est negatio vel privatio realis, secundum quod una res non dicitur esse alia, et huiusmodi distinctionem per negationem negat negatio importata in ratione unitatis. Unde dico, quod negatio ista in qua perficitur ratio unitatis, non est nisi *negatio rationis tantum*. Omnis enim respectus qui est entis ad negationem vel ad non ens, non est nisi rationis".[113] Im übrigen: was dialektisch von konstitutiver Bedeutung ist für Ding und Denken, die Wechselseitigkeit des Negativen nämlich, ist analektisch eine Absurdität. Denn jede Art von Negation, erst recht die gedoppelte Negation, die "negatio negationis", ist analektisch nur ein "ens rationis". Ebenso erweist sich das grammatische Prinzip, wonach gedoppelte Negation verstärkte Affirmation ergibt, allenfalls als ein "modus significandi", keinesfalls aber als ein "modus essendi".

Die Dialektik der "absoluten Negativität" erwies sich uns im Verlaufe der Methode als das "Zweite"[114] nach dem Sein als der "*ersten Un-*

109 *Summa contra gentiles* I, 22.
110 *Summa theol.* I-II, 29, 1, ad 1.
111 *Logik* I, 100.
112 *Summa contra gentiles* I, 71.
113 *In I Sent.* d. 24, q. 1, a. 3, ad 1.
114 *Logik* II, 494.

mittelbarkeit",[115] oder als das "*Negative* des Ersten"[116] und damit als das "Negative des Negativen" oder als das "*Andre eines Andern*".[117] Nirgendwo im methodischen Verlauf der logischen Bestimmungen gibt es ein markanteres Beispiel für ebendieses "Negative des Negativen" als das *Wesen selbst*.[118] Als die Negation des Seins und damit seines Negativen, kurz als das aufgehobene Sein (Schein) ist das dialektische Wesen aller Wesenheiten in seiner Reinform diese gedoppelte Negation oder besser noch "*diese Bewegung von Nichts zu Nichts und dadurch zu sich selbst zurück*".[119] In Gestalt dieser Rückkehr vollbringt sich die Identität dieser absoluten Negativität mit sich als das zum "Schein" gewordene oder aufgehobene Sein.

Analektisch ist allenfalls *im Denken* des reflektierenden Verstandes eine solche "negatio negationis" möglich, aber keinesfalls vermag sich im Bereich des Sachhaft-Objektiven oder gar des Physikalischen diese Art von negativer Reflexionsbewegung zu ereignen. Statt der dialektischen "Bewegung von Nichts zu Nichts" gilt analektisch: "Ex negatione in negationem non est *mutatio per se*".[120] Es dürfte auch heute im Zeitalter der Relativitätstheorie, wonach Masse-Energie angesetzt wird, keinen Physiker geben, der diese dialektische "Bewegung von Nichts zu Nichts" als physikalisches oder gar metaphysisches Prinzip zu akzeptieren vermöchte. Es bleibt dabei: Alle Verneinung als solche und erst recht das Kreiselspiel des Nichts zu Nichts hat immer nur als "ens rationis" im Verstande statt.

Mag sich auch die Vielzahl der Dinge als *Mangel* an Einheit oder die Blindheit als ein schmerzlicher Augen*fehler* erweisen, jedes dieser Defizientien hat seinen tragenden *Grund* in der Positivität des Einzel-Seienden oder in dem, was von der Wirklichkeit des Auges selbst noch übrig ist. Die Integrität der Wirklichkeit ist zwar jeweils angegriffen, sie hat je ihren echten Mangel, es fehlt an Sein, so dass der Verstand dieses fehlende Sein als seiendes Fehlen vor sich hinstellen und begreifen kann. Die Wirklichkeit leidet Mangel, ohne dass dieser Mangel selbst mit jener Wirklichkeit *gleichwirklich* wäre, an der er als dunkler Schatten haftet. Analektisch sind Sein und Bejahung allemal *früher* als Nichts und Verneinung, die allemal in jenen ihren positiven Grund haben müssen. Ohne dieses Fundierungs-Verhältnis wären sie (Vielheit-Blindheit) Nichts, absolutes Nichts. So gilt denn analektisch

---

115 *Ibid.*, 490.
116 *Ibid.*, 494.
117 *Ibid.*, 496.
118 *Ibid.*, 7 ff.
119 *Ibid.*, 13.
120 *In V Phys.* lect. 2, nr. 652.

unumstösslich: "Privatio entis *fundatur* in ente... et exinde contingit quod multitudo est quoddam unum, et malum est quoddam bonum, et non ens est quoddam ens".[121]

Das alles aber besagt nicht, dass das jeweils Positive mit dem Negativen dialektisch, d.h. als "negatio negationis", jemals *identisch* würde, nicht einmal, dass sie einander gegensätzlich gegenüberstünden, sondern nur, dass das Negative das Positive zu seinem Grund und Boden hat, der es begründet, und zwar dergestalt, dass unser Verstand dank dieses positiven Grundes auch das Negativ-Begründete als solches *sein* lässt. Die dialektische Methode verschärft die zweite Bestimmung, das Negative des Ersten, zum Negativen des Negativen, zum "Andern eines Andern," das ins *Dritte*, d.i. zu neuer Unmittelbarkeit, umschlägt, in der jenes "*Andere an sich selbst*"[122] aufgehoben und doch zuinnerst weiter pocht. In Wahrheit ist das "Andre des Andern" nicht in den wahren Frieden einer ausgewogenen Einheit überführt. Endlich und (abstrakt oder transzendent-) Unendlich, Mensch und Gott, werden dialektisch in die Gewaltsamkeit eines angeblich Wahrhaft-Unendlichen und damit in eine *Identität der Unruhe* hineingezwungen, die nur als absolute *Negativität* ihr Leben hat. Vermag dieses "Wahrhaft-Unendliche", die "absolute Idee", in dieser Not ihrer selbst zu existieren? Natürlich nicht! Die Not der Negativität zwingt die absolute Idee zu dem "*Entschluss*", sich in die Freiheit von Natur und Geist zu "entlassen,"[123] um alsdann aus beiden "Schlüssen"[124] in den der Logik zurückzuschwingen, die selbst nur als diese Rückkehr, als ihr eigenes *Resultat*, d.i. als absoluter Geist, zu sein vermag.[125]

Diese "Not Gottes" ist analektisch eine Absurdität, ja mehr noch: eine Blasphemie. Das "Andre *des* Andern" ist analektisch allemal zum "ἄλλο πρὸς ἄλλο,"[126] zum "aliud *ad* aliud"[127] und somit zum *Verhältnis* gegenseitigen Andersseins *auseinander*genommen und aufgrund dieser Distanzierung so verständigt, dass beide Andere eben nicht zur *Identität* umschlagen können. Identität und Nicht-Identität, (abstrakt-) Unendliches und Endliches, Positives und Negatives, das Andere hier und das ganz Andere dort koinzidieren analektisch niemals zu einer übergreifenden Identität absoluter Negativität, sondern erscheinen als wahrhaft vermittelt in einer *Mitte*, die auf höchst seinsgerechte Weise

---

121 *Summa theol.* I, 11, 2, ad 1.
122 *Logik* II, 496.
123 *Enzykopädie*, § 244.
124 *Ibid.*, § 571, 574 ff.
125 *Ibid.*, § 577.
126 Aristoteles, *Met.* 5, 1016 b 35.
127 St. Thomas, *In V Meta.* lect. 8, nr. 879.

dem Unendlichen gibt, was des Unendlichen ist, und dem Endlichen, was ihm gebührt. Erneut erweist sich: nicht der *Wider*-spruch, sondern der *Ent*-spruch als Konvenienz und Proportion beherrscht als allversöhnendes Prinzip das Seiende im Ganzen. In dieser Mitte werden nicht zwangshaft die Extreme von Identität und Nicht-Identität, von Unendlich und Endlich zusammengepresst zur Identität als absoluter Negativität, in jener Mitte sind sie zum voraus immer schon versöhnt. Jedes der Extreme bleibt, was es ist, so dass Unendliches dem Unendlichen und Endliches dem Endlichen höchst angemessen zugesprochen werden kann. "Medium enim inquantum habet convenientiam cum utroque extremorum, est quoddammodo [!] utrumque eorum; et ideo potest dici hoc ad illud, et illud ad hoc".[128]

Was ist diese Mitte als Konvenienz, als Proportion und Angemessenheit ihrer Extreme anderes als die Ähnlichkeit oder die Analogie, welche als wahrhafte Vermittlung zwischen Unendlich und Endlich, zwischen Gott und Mensch oder logisch-formell zwischen Identität und Nicht-Identität hin- und widerspielt? Gott bleibt Gott, Mensch bleibt Mensch, und dennoch hat ein analektisches Ineinanderscheinen statt, dem alle dialektische Identität zuwider ist. Nicht die Identität von Nicht-Identischen, sondern das begütigende Verhältnis der Ähnlichkeit garantiert die unberührbare Identität Gottes mit sich selbst, sichert aber auch der Kreatur ihr "proprium esse",[129] die Eigentlichkeit des "per se esse", des geschenkten Selbstseins, das nicht in der deduktionalen Strömung einer absoluten Methode untergeht und sich verliert. Das analektische Denken liebt die Dinge, zumal alles Sein mit dem Guten, d.h. seiner Appetibilität konvertibel ist. Die von der Dialektik abgewiesene "Zärtlichkeit für die Dinge"[130] umwirbt geradezu alle Kreatur, respektiert den Reichtum ihrer Eigenheit. Die Analektik entfernt alles dialektische Zugleich von Identität und Nicht- Identität, von Endlich und Unendlich, kurzum den Widerspruch selbst aus dem Herzen der Dinge. Das "proprium esse" der Welt lichtet sich zum "esse similitudinarium",[131] zum Ähnlichsein mit Gott. Selbst die Materie leuchtet noch im Lichte des unendlichen Seins, als welches Gott selber ist. "Materia... similitudinem quandam retinet divini esse".[132] Das analektische Denken ist nicht hairetisch, es zerreisst nicht die Proportion von Dingen und Denken in einen transzendentalen Verstand hie und ein unerkennbares Ding-an-sich dort, wie Kant und Maréchal,

---

128 *In V Phys.* lect. 1, nr. 648.
129 *Summa theol.* I, 6, 4, sed contra; *Summa contra gentiles* III, 107; *De veritate* 22, 10, c.
130 *Logik* II, 40.
131 *Summa theol.* I-II, 5, 6, ad 2.
132 *Summa theol.* I, 14, 11, ad 3.

Rahner und andere das möchten, sofern sie alle dem verfallen sind, was selbst Hegel als "subjektiven Idealismus"[133] brandmarkt. Die transzendentale Ähnlichkeit mit Gott verdankt alle Kreatur ihrer Teilhabe an seinem ewigen Sein. Daher gilt: Je vollkommener ihre kreatürliche Seinsverfassung, um so grösser ihre Ähnlichkeit mit Gott. "Quanto enim est aliquid perfectius, tanto est Deo similius".[134] Ähnlichkeit und Unähnlichkeit gehören als "per se entis accidentia",[135] als Modifikationen des Seins als solchen, in den allumfassenden Bereich der Transzendentalien. Im Lichte der Gottähnlichkeit leuchtet die Welt, und ein jedes Einzel-Seiende ist dem Insgesamt dessen, was ist, harmonisch eingefügt und zugeordnet. "Deus unamquamque creaturam fecit proportionatam universo".[136] Nicht in der *Identität* mit dem unendlichen Gott, der so als die Negation des Endlichen begriffen wird, besteht das Sinnziel des Geschaffenen, sondern das Höchstmass an Verähnlichung mit ihm beherrscht alles Sollen und Sich-regen dessen, was ist. "Id quod praecipue in rebus creatis Deus intendit, est bonum quod consistit in *assimilatione* ad Deum".[137]

Die Ähnlichkeit ist das Seins- und Wirkgesetz der Welt. Sie sichert den geschaffenen Dingen ihr Je-Einzelsein, ja macht die unsterbliche Geistperson des Menschen zum Herrn der Schöpfung. "Ipsa individua sunt de principali intentione naturae".[138] Überhaupt gilt analektisch der Primat des Einzelnen vor allem Allgemeinen, zumal das Endlich-Einzelne ein Mehr an Wirklichkeit besitzt denn alles Allgemeine. "Singularia sunt entia, et magis quam universalia, quia universalia non subsistunt per se, sed sunt solum in singularibus".[139] Und was die Sozialnatur des Menschen selbst und alle menschliche Gesellschaft überhaupt anlangt, so stehen sie analektisch im Dienste der geeinzelten Persönlichkeit. Wie beglückend, in Zeiten eines übersteigerten Sozialismus und einer sich verabsolutierenden Soziologie von Thomas zu hören: "Cum homo sit naturaliter animal sociale, indiget ab aliis hominibus adiuvari ad consequendum *proprium finem*".[140] Dieser analektische Sozialismus ist um des Einzelnen, der dialektische um der *Allgemeinheit* willen, mag sie in der Gestalt der Identität von Gott und Welt oder in der des dialektischen Kommunismus marxistischer Prägung begriffen werden. Ob der Unterdrückung und Aufhebung des

---

133   *Logik* I, 146.
134   *Summa theol.* III, 93, 1, ad 1, suppl.
135   *In IV Meta.* lect. 4, nr. 587.
136   *Summa theol.* I, 56, 2, ad 4.
137   *Summa theol.* I, 50, 1, c.
138   *Summa theol.* I, 98, 1, c.
139   *Summa contra gentiles* III, 75.
140   *Ibid.,* III, 112.

Einzel-Seienden ist Gott dialektisch so etwas wie mit und durch die Endlichkeit *"erfülltes Sein"*,[141] analektisch aber ist es aufgrund der uneinholbaren Transzendenz Gottes gerade umgekehrt: "Non est Deus ipsum *esse commune omnium"*,[142] denn dann wäre er die *Eine Allgemeinheit* der absoluten Methode oder der unendlichen Form selbst, die alles Endlich-Seiende im Sog ihrer Negativität zugrunderichtet. "Si igitur esse divinum esset formale esse omnium, oportet omnia simpliciter esse unum".[143]

Wenn nun das Einzelne dem Allgemeinen gegenüber ein Mehr an Wirklichkeit bedeutet, wie ist dann überhaupt ein *Urteil* möglich, das ja gerade vom Einzelnen das Allgemeine aussagt, weil beide *sachlich* identisch sind. "Oportet quod praedicatum et subiectum significent idem secundum rem *aliquo modo*, et diversum secundum rationem".[144] Diese Urteilsform, mit Inhalt aufgefüllt, ergibt etwa folgendes Beispiel: "Homo est animal; illud enim ipsum quod est homo, vere animal est".[145] Thomas setzt die Verschiedenheit von Subjekt und Prädikat auf das Konto unseres ur-teilenden Verstandes, aber so, dass er zugleich in deren Verbindung (*compositio*) durch die Copula die Identität der geurteilten Sache mit sich selbst zum Ausdruck bringt. "Identitas vero rei significat intellectus per ipsam compositionem".[146] Hegel hat uns bereits gesagt, dass diese Identifizierung von Verschiedenheit ("identitas diversitatis") oder der Satz: "Das Einzelne ist das Allgemeine"[147] der Widerspruch selbst sei.

Weil Denken und Sein dialektisch dasselbe sind, können sich Identität und Verschiedenheit nicht in den zwei verschiedenen Ebenen von "ratio" und "res", sondern nur in *ein- und derselben*, d. h. in "der absoluten *Einheit* der reinen Begriffs und seiner Realität"[148] ereignen. Diese "absolute Einheit" ("absolute Methode") durchherrscht ja dialektisch alles Geschehen, wenn jene Einheit auch in *unserem* abstrakten Verstandes-Urteil noch nicht in ihrer Vollendung sichtbar wird. Nach Hegel ist jedes affirmative Urteil ein Widerspruch und verlangt, wie bereits erwähnt, zu seiner Ergänzung sein negatives Gegenstück. Das analektische Denken hingegen bietet uns eine sehr viel sachgemässere Lösung, zumal es auch das logische Urteilen im Zusammenhange mit dem Seingeschehen überhaupt bedenkt. Das ἀνάλογον

---

141 *Logik* II, 504.
142 *Summa contra gentiles* I, 26.
143 *Ibid.*
144 *Summa theol.* I, 13, 12 c.
145 *Ibid.* Vgl. auch *Summa theol.* I, 83, 5, c.
146 *Summa theol.* I, 13, 12, c.
147 *Logik* II, 495.
148 *Ibid.*, 505.

συνορᾶν" ("proportionale conspicere"),[149] die Totalität des Seienden im Lichte der allwaltenden Ähnlichkeit zu betrachten, ist ein analektisches Grundgesetz. Danach hat unsere Ur-teilung von Subjekt und Prädikat in der *konkreten Identität* der Sache mit sich selbst ihren existentiellen Grund. Die geurteilte Sache selbst birgt eine ganze Fülle von Seinsbestimmungen in sich, die unser menschlich-diskursives, keineswegs intuitives Denken nicht auf einmal, sondern nur im Nacheinander logisch aufzugliedern vermag. Vor allem das organische Geschehen reflektiert sich in der Artikulation unseres ur-teilenden Verstandestuns. Im organischen Bereich verbirgt sich unter der Gestalt des *unentfalteten* Keimes ebendieselbe *ganze* Pflanze, die zur Hoch-zeit ihres Blühens den differenzierten Reichtum ihrer selbst in voller Pracht *entfaltet*.

"Id quod est genus prout praedicabatur de specie *implicabat* in sua significatione, quamvis *indistincte*, totum quod *determinate* est in specie, ita etiam et illud quod est species, secundum id quod praedicatur de individuo, oportet quod significet totum illud quod essentialiter est in individuo, licet *indistincte*; et hoc modo essentia Socratis significatur nomine hominis: unde homo de Socrate praedicatur."[150] In der Zweiheit der Begriffsgestalten von Subjekt und Prädikat (Einzelheit und Allgemeinheit) präsentiert uns der ur-teilende Verstand *ein- und dieselbe* Sache, aber in der *Unterschiedenheit* der Seinsweisen von Explizit und Implizit, von Differenz und Indifferenz, von Akt und Potenz. Die sich in der Zweiheit von Subjekt und Prädikat durchhaltende Identität der Sache selbst blitzt in der Copula des Urteils auf. Wie nun alles Urteilen und Begreifen, mit dem Seinsgeschehen überhaupt ineins gesehen, aus der Ähnlichkeit und Konvenienz der Dinge insgesamt gedeutet wird, das bezeugt das Wort des hl. Thomas: "Et ex hoc patet ratio quare genus et species et differentia se habeant *proportionaliter* ad materiam et formam et compositum in natura, quamvis non sint idem quod illa".[151] Keine dialektische Identität zwingt hier Denken und Sein, Begriff und Realität ineins, sondern die analektische Proportionalität belässt jeder dieser Ordnungen ihr volles Recht und ihre Eigenart und vermag sie gerade so zu Affinität und Wahlverwandtschaft mitsammen zu vermitteln.

Seinen höchsten Triumph feiert das analektische Denken bzw. sein Gesetz der Ähnlichkeit im Verhältnis von Gott und Welt, Endlich und Unendlich. Auch hier erweist sich alle dialektische Identität, wonach das *Sein* des Absoluten nur so etwas sein soll wie das *Nichtsein* des

---

149 Aristoteles, *Met.* IX, 6, 1048 a 39.
150 *De ente et essentia*, cap. II, 11.
151 *Ibid.*, II, 10.

Endlichen,[152] als unannehmbar. Gott ist analektisch so unendlich über alle Welt hinaus, bedarf in seiner Vollkommenheit nicht im mindesten irgendwelcher Andersheit, kennt in seinem ewigen Jetzt ("nunc stans") keinerlei Vergangenheit und Zukunft, ist somit in seiner absoluten Ungeschichtlichkeit allem Weltgeschehen immer schon vorweg. "Deus, cum sit infinitus, comprehendens in se omnem plenitudinem perfectionis totius esse, non potest aliquid acquirere, nec extendere se in aliquid ad quod prius non pertingebat".[153] Es gibt analektisch keinen Gott der Zukunft. Gott bedarf nicht der Natur und der Geschichte, um sich als das Nichtsein dieser Nichtigkeiten zu verwirklichen. Gott ist der absolute Anfang und *nur* der Anfang, niemals aber Resultat. "Deus est prima omnium causa, *excedens* omnia causata".[154] Alle Kreatur ist deswegen von ihm ganz und gar unterschieden, weil er selbst keine seiner Wirkungen essentiell zu sein vermag. Das besagt aber keineswegs eine Negativität von Ermangelung und Defizienz an ihm selbst, sondern die Positivität seines unendlichen Exzesses ("superexcedit")[155] über alles Geschaffene weit hinaus.

Aber wie sollen wir ob der Endlichkeit unseres Denkens dieses "excellens principium a cuius forma effectus deficiunt",[156] wie können wir dieses "pelagus substantiae infinitum"[157] überhaupt erkennen? Etwa so, dass wir jene unsere Defizienz und Endlichkeit auf Gott selber übertragen? Wir vermögen Gott nicht in seiner Absolutheit zu erfassen oder gar sein absolutes Selbst zu werden, wie die Dialektik will. Wir verbleiben im Umkreis dieser Welt, auch in unserem Gotterkennen. Aber weil die Welt von ihm verursacht und geschaffen, also seine *Wirkung* ist, vermögen wir im reflexen Schein ("similitudo refulgens")[158] dieser Wirkung doch irgendwie, d.h. analogisch, ihre "Causa prima" zu erkennen. Analektisch brauchen wir, um Gott zu erkennen, die Welt, weil sie seine gewirkte Schöpfung ist, nicht einmal zu verlassen, geschweige denn sie dialektisch zu nichten. Der "sursum ductrix analogia"[159] vertrauen wir uns denkend an, wobei sich uns ein dreifacher Weg eröffnet: die "via affirmationis, negationis et supereminentiae". "Deus est sapiens, non sapiens et supersapiens".[160]

Wir sprechen Gottes Wesenheit affirmativ jene transzendentalen

---

152 Vgl. *Logik* II, 62.
153 *Summa theol.* I, 9, 1, c.
154 *Summa theol.* I, 12, 12, c.
155 *Ibid.*
156 *Summa theol.* I, 13, 2, c.
157 *Summa theol.* I, 14, 11, c.
158 *Summa theol.* I, 12, 4, ad 1.
159 *Summa theol.* I, 106, 1, c.
160 Vgl. *De potentia*, 7, 5, ad 2.

Vollkommenheiten zu, die wir in seiner Schöpfung antreffen. "Cognoscimus eam [essentiam Dei], secundum quod repraesentatur in perfectionibus creaturarum".[161] Nachdem wir aber alle Endlichkeit und Geschöpflichkeit ebendieser innerweltlichen Seinsvollkommenheiten negiert haben, übersteigern wir die mittels jener Negation von aller Endlichkeit geläuterten Seinsbestimmungen noch dazu ins Ungemessene. Hegel hat dieser analektischen Methode entgegengehalten, dass solcherlei Verunendlichung des Endlichen durch unseren abstrakten Verstand nichts anderes als einen sinnlosen *Verstandeswiderspruch* ergeben müsse. "Dieser Widerspruch lässt auf diesem [analektischen] Standpunkte nur die nebulose Auflösung durch quantitative Steigerung zu, sie [die Seinsvollkommenheiten] ins Bestimmungslose, in den sensum eminentiorem zu treiben. Hierdurch aber wird die Eigenschaft in der Tat zu nichte gemacht und ihr bloss ein Name gelassen".[162] Hegel entwertet somit die Analogie zu einer blossen Aquivokation. In Wahrheit hat sein dialektischer Einwand die Transzendentalität der Ähnlichkeit, insonderheit die "analogia proportionalitatis" nicht erfasst. Danach ist die Welt Gott ähnlich und unähnlich zugleich. Aber diese "similis dissimilitudo" ist keineswegs ein Widerspruch, denn er wird gerade durch die Behutsamkeit und Subtilität analektischen Beziehungsdenkens, d.h. durch die von aller Dialektik nicht umsonst misskreditierten "*Insoferns, Seiten und Rücksichten*"[163] vollends ausgeräumt.

"Cum sacra scriptura dicit aliquid non esse simile Deo, non est contrarium assimilationi ad ipsum. *Eadem enim sunt similia Deo, et dissimilia; similia quidem secundum quod imitantur ipsum, prout contingit eum imitari, qui non perfecte imitabilis est; dissimilia vero, secundum quod deficiunt a sua causa*".[164] Trotz aller unendlichen Distanz und der je grösseren Unähnlichkeit zwischen Gott und Mensch reisst dennoch die kausative Beziehung des "Von-Gott-her" niemals ab. In aller Unähnlichkeit, sofern auch sie noch ein Verhältnis von Andersheit (Kreatur) zu Andersheit (Gott) besagt, bleibt ein Stück Ähnlichkeit erhalten, zumal die Formalität eines Verhältnisses von Verhältnissen (proportio proportionum) das an sich Un-endliche nicht ins Endlos-Unbestimmte entschweben lässt. Verhältnis hie und Verhältnis da bewahren *wesenhaft* die Formalität ihrer Verhältnismässigkeit zueinander, wie immer auch ihr Inhalt sich in dieser Formalität des "aliud ad

---

161 *Summa theol.* I, 13, 2, ad 3.
162 *Enzyklopädie*, § 36.
163 *Logik* II, 36, 40.
164 *Summa theol.*, I, 4, 3, ad 1.

aliud" bewähren mag. Verhältnisse als solche garantieren essentiell ein unmittelbares Verhältnis zueinander, sei ihr Abstand als Unverhältnismässigkeit auch noch so gross. Wenn schon *unsere* Weisheit nicht *Gottes* Weisheit ist, so verhält sich doch unser *Verhältnis* zu unserer Weisheit unmittelbar zu dem *Verhältnis*, das Gott zu seiner supereminenten Weisheit hat. So scheint ja auch die Unendlichkeit des Abstandes die Parallelität zweier Parallelen nicht zufzuheben. Daher gilt in all' unserer Endlichkeit von Sein und Denken dennoch das überaus beglückende analektische Prinzip: "*Sicut* infinitum est aequale infinito, *ita* finitum finito".[165] Eine Steigerung ins *Bestimmungslose* kann sich analektisch nie ereignen, weil die Steigerung ins Superlativisch-Eminente den Positiv des Ausgangs nie vollends negiert und auslöscht, sondern in der Verhältnismässigkeit der Verhältnisse von Endlich zu Endlich und Unendlich zu Unendlich allezeit salviert.

Die Analogie hält allemal die *Mitte* zwischen Univokation und Äquivokation, zwischen Identität und Nicht-Identität. Diese ùngebrochene Mitte ergab sich uns als das bestimmende Gesetz analektischen Denkens, mag es sich nun in Gestalt von Philosophie oder von Theologie ereignen. Daher gilt auch für die Philosophie und ihre Methode das Thomistische Prinzip: "Fides autem catholica *media via* incedit".[166]

165 *De veritate* 23, 7, ad 9; *Summa theol.* III, 92, 1, ad 6, suppl.
166 *De veritate* 24, 12, c.

GUIDE-LINES FROM ST. THOMAS
FOR THEOLOGY TODAY

E. L. Mascall

Should auld Aquinas be forgot
And never brought to mind?

IN view of the extent to which Roman Catholic theology and philosophy had for several centuries, and more especially since the encyclical *Aeterni Patris* of Pope Leo XIII in 1879, been dominated by something which at any rate believed itself to be authentic Thomism, it is perhaps not surprising that, in the ampler climate of Post-Vatican-II, it is widely assumed, within as well as without the Roman communion, that there is very little that we can learn from the Angelic Doctor at the present time and very little help that we can derive from him for the solution of our contemporary problems. To the question at the head of this paper many would reply with a confident and resounding "Yes!" This reaction I believe to be mistaken and, without either claiming that St. Thomas was infallible or forgetting that the middle of the thirteenth century is not the end of the twentieth, I believe that he can give us a great deal of assistance in the terribly confused intellectual situation in which we find ourselves today. With M. Gilson I would say that I value my intellectual freedom as much as anyone and that I claim the right to agree with a man when he says what seems to me to be true.

And first of all, in my opinion, St. Thomas provides us with an admirable example of the way in which a Christian thinker should make use of a philosophical system which has not itself emerged from the womb of the Christian revelation. Up to St. Thomas's time Christian theologians, in so far as they had made use of philosophy at all, had been much more attracted to Platonism than to Aristotelianism; St. Augustine and St. Anselm are, of course, the outstanding examples of this. In the mid-thirteenth century, however, the fashionable newcomer to the West was Aristotelianism; and it is understandable that, to old-fashioned people, it was highly suspect, not only because of its pagan origin (after all, Plato was pagan too) but also because of the Muslim medium through which it had been transmitted. In adopting it as a vehicle for Christian thought and communication, therefore, St. Thomas was manifesting that astounding intellectual audacity which, to quote M. Gilson again, was as marked an aspect of his character as was his equally astounding intellectual modesty. Partly, no doubt, this was due to his desire to argue with unbelievers in a language which they could understand; one of his two greatest works was explicitly written *contra Gentiles*. He was of all men the least likely to imitate the Bellman in *The Hunting of the Snark*, who addressed his hearers in four languages with which he himself was acquainted but entirely forget to address them in their own. Nevertheless, it is also clear that he believed the Aristotelian philosophy to provide, if not a perfect, at least a fairly adequate instrument for Christian purposes. What, however, I find most instructive is the way in which he handled his Aristotelian material; so far from bringing Christian doctrine in line with the modern thought of his day, he almost brutally brought the modern thought in line with Christian doctrine. I will give several examples of this.

The first is in the realm of cosmology. Modern writers, in their celebration of the victory of Copernicus and Galileo over Aristotle and Ptolemy, often overlook the fact that throughout the Middle Ages there was a spirited contest between the two geocentric systems of Aristotle and Ptolemy themselves. Briefly, the trouble was that Aristotle's system, while theoretically simple and attractive, was very unsuccessful in predicting the actual movements and positions of the planets, whereas the Ptolemaic system, while almost entirely successful (with one glaring exception) from the standpoint of prediction, was highly untidy and intricate. St. Thomas appears to have accepted Aristotle's arguments as providing the ultimate *physical* truth about the celestial bodies and their operations, but he was perfectly ready to accept the Ptolemaic system as a calculus for practical purposes, or indeed any other system which would perform with equal or superior efficiency the function of "saving the appearances".[1] What is of most importance, however, is the way in which the Angelic Doctor changes the whole metaphysical basis of the Aristotelian cosmogony. For Aristotle, the celestial orbs continue their uniform gyrations because uniform circular motion is theoretically the most perfect and therefore needs no further explanation or justification; it will therefore go on for ever. For St. Thomas, on the other hand, while he accepts the reality of secondary causality in the created realm, the orbs continue their motions just as long as God intends that they shall do so, and when his purposes for the

---

1   Cf. my *Christian Theology and Natural Science* (London, New York 1956) 51ff.

world have been achieved, their motions will come to an end.[2] Beneath a superficial identity it would be difficult to conceive a greater difference than this which is found between the cosmology of Aristotle and Aquinas. And beyond this there is a radical opposition between the two thinkers about the relation between God and the universe.

For Aristotle the first unmoved mover has no conscious concern with the world and is occupied solely with the contemplation of his own perfection, *noesis noeseos*. He is in no way responsible for the existence of the prime matter out of which the world is composed; it is as eternal and uncreated as he is himself. He is in a certain way responsible for the changes which the prime matter undergoes, for it constantly strives to imitate his perfection, but he is entirely unconscious of this and all the effort, so to speak, is on the world's side and not on his. He is the formal or exemplary cause of the world's development; he is in no way its efficient cause. Now the interesting point in this is that, when arguing for the existence of God in the *Contra Gentiles*, St. Thomas reproduces in great detail the arguments which Aristotle himself gives for the existence of a first unmoved mover,[3] but the unmoved mover at which he arrives is very different from that of Aristotle. I am not concerned here to argue whether St. Thomas or Aristotle or either of them is right in the conclusion which he reaches, but only to stress the way in which St. Thomas, even while he pays Aristotle the compliment of lifting his argument bodily, firmly and respectfully puts him right. It is as if he were saying "You mistakenly suppose that your argument leads to a first unmoved mover entirely concerned with admiring his own perfection; but I will show that it leads in fact to the God of Judaism and Christianity, without whose knowledge not even a sparrow falls to the ground."

An even more striking example of St. Thomas's obstinate loyalty to Christian belief is provided by his doctrine of the human soul. He quite complacently takes over Aristotle's teaching that the soul is the form of a man and the body is his matter. This immediately raises problems for the Christian which do not exist for the pagan. To begin with, this view seems to deny to the individual man that unique personal status which is involved both in the Christian emphasis on personal responsibility and in the Christian doctrine of salvation. If the different human beings that exist are merely so many numerically diverse particular instances of the universal "manhood", in the same kind of way as a number of

---

2 Cf. *De Potentia* 5, 5.
3 *Contra Gentiles* I, 13. Aristotle, *Physics* V-VIII, *Metaphysics* XI, XII. Cf. my *He Who Is* (London, New York 1943) ch. v.

lumps of cooking-salt are so many particular instances of the universal "sodium chloride", I can hardly be considered to have any ultimate significance. In the second place, what happens to the individual when the body dies? When the salt has decomposed, where is its saltness? And thirdly, all those personal characteristics and idiosyncrasies which make human beings at once so different and so interesting seem to be reduced to a purely trivial and accidental status. Are the things in which we differ from one another really of as little importance as this?

Now St. Thomas has an answer to all these objections, but it is one which does considerable violence to Aristotle. There is first the doctrine of the unity of the substantial form in man, for which the Angelic Doctor contended so stubbornly. Although the soul is united to the body as form to matter, its penetration of the individual does not stop there. As form, the soul subsumes into itself all those lower formalities which the body as an organised entity, animate, vegetative and corporeal, already possesses, so that the matter which it ultimately embraces is not merely the body of an animal but the fundamental *materia prima* itself. The soul, as human, penetrates to the deepest metaphysical root of the man; it does not just confer rationality on an ape or galvanise a corpse. Again, we are told that the soul does not merely *acquire* a temporary substantiality from its union with a particular particle of signate matter; it is a form existing *in se*, which *confers* substantiality upon the composite being. And finally, against the Averroists with their denial of personal immortality, we are told that the soul possesses individuality in itself and not through the matter which it informs, though it possesses it in virtue of its aptness to inform matter.

Now the objections which can be urged from the strictly Aristotelian standpoint to St. Thomas's modification of the Aristotelian doctrine are obvious. This, it will be said, is a philosophy in which only particulars exist and in which, at any rate as regards corporeal beings, forms are particularised only in union with matter; surely, therefore, the notion that the form can exist when the matter has departed is ridiculous. If, as is asserted, the soul is the form of the man, survival is impossible; we die like cows or cabbages. And even if this objection can be somehow rebutted, the difficulties are by no means over. For, if the form goes on existing after it is separated from the body, it must then exist either individualised or not. If it exists in separation individualised, then humanity as a universal has vanished; each soul is a different form and hence a different species, men are angels in disguise, and Descartes will be right after all. But if the form exists in separation unindividualised, then personal identity has gone; we merge at death into a universal soul and the Averroists are vindicated against St. Thomas. Has St. Thomas for once committed the dreadful crime of allowing his faith not to perfect his reason but to destroy it?

In chapter four of my book *Existence and Analogy* I have tried to answer these objections and I shall here only remark that it seems to me that when one has been forced to take account of them one arrives at a metaphysic of form and matter that is both more coherent and more profound than before. That, however, is not my present concern, which is with St. Thomas's deliberate refusal to alter Christian doctrine in order to bring it into superficial agreement with a fashionable philosophy of secularist type. It may be argued, not implausibly, that it is impossible to bring the Aristotelian doctrine of form and matter into line with the Christian belief about man, and that all that St. Thomas achieved was to make the Aristotelian doctrine incoherent. What cannot be denied is that St. Thomas was determined that the Christian belief must be preserved and that if the Aristotelian doctrine cannot be brought into line with it (though St. Thomas thought that it could) it is the Aristotelian doctrine that must give way. And here he has, I would hold, a lesson for us today, who are faced with the impact of other philosophical systems of secularist provenance than that of thirteenth-century Aristotelianism.

St. Thomas has often been criticised for having, as is alleged, compromised, or even identified, Christian theology with one particular philosophical system of his day. Both the drastic modifications to which he subjected Aristotelianism and the skilfull adoptions which he made of many of the features of Platonism sufficiently answer this charge. We may, however, note in passing the strange fact that this criticism has often proceeded from persons who are only too anxious to implicate Christian belief with some one particular philosophical system of their own time, as for example, Charles Gore with Kantianism, Paul van Buren with linguistic empiricism and Rudolf Bultmann with Heideggerian existentialism. Now it seems plain that, as they stand, some philosophical systems are flatly incompatible with Christian belief, such as the dialectical materialism of Marxism or the metaphysical nihilism of Buddhism. I would, however, emphasise the words "as they stand" in the previous sentence. It may conceivably be found, on careful and sympathetic investigation, that the features which appear to be inconsistent with Christianity are capable of modification or are merely superficial and accidental, and that their correction or removal makes the system not less but more adequate and coherent. On the other hand, a system may turn out to be incorrigible and quite incapable of reconciliation with Christian belief. The only way to settle the matter is to consider each case on its merits. We have certainly no reason to assume that only one philosophical system is consistent with Christianity or that only one can be a profitable partner for it. Some would certainly appear to be incompatible with Christianity, though this ought not to be hastily assumed. Some may have to be rejected, not because they are clearly incompatible with Christian belief but because they can be shown to be false on purely rational grounds. And even those mutually competing systems which are acceptable from the stand-point of Christian theology are likely to be mutually compatible in their most profound depths; for truths can never ultimately contradict one another. Furthermore we must not forget that both philosophical systems and Christian understanding are always in a state of develop-ment if they are healthy at all.

That there is a kind of philosophical pluralism that is theologically acceptable may be illustrated from the fact that St. Thomas in-corporated into his theological structure many features of Platonism; perhaps the most striking instance is his doctrine of the ideas in the mind of God. A much more comprehensive example is provided by a comparison between the "Aristotelian" theology of St. Thomas in the thirteenth century and the "Platonic" theology of St. Gregory Palamas in the fourteenth. At first sight — and indeed at second and third sight as well — they would seem to be not only philosophically but also theologically incompatible; nevertheless it is, I think, clear that, beneath extremely different linguistic and conceptual structures, these two great figures of West and East respectively were dealing with the same fundamental problems and giving ultimately the same Christian and Biblical answers.[4] Both Aquinas and Palamas give us luminous examples of the way in which a Christian theologian should handle a philosophical system which is not itself of Christian provenance. And I shall now give two modern instances which seem to me to be thoroughly in line with St. Thomas's attitude.

The first is provided by the massive and now little-known work *The Incarnate Lord* by Lionel Thornton, which appeared in 1928. Thornton had been much impressed by the "philosophy of organism" of Alfred North Whitehead, which was based on a first-hand acquaintance with the method and outlook of contemporary science and which was to receive monumental and definitive statement in Whitehead's Gifford Lectures *Process and Reality*. It seemed to Thornton that Whitehead's metaphysical system might provide the medium for a presentation of the Christian doctrine of the Incarnation that would be intelligible and attractive to thinking persons in a scientific and technological age.

4 Cf. my *The Openness of Being* (London 1971) 221 ff.

(That Thornton's laudable intention was largely frustrated by his un-
manageable literary style does not affect my present point). The
weakness of Whitehead's system lay in his thoroughly immanentist doctrine of God, an obstacle as formidable to Thornton's exploit as
Aristotle's doctrine had been to St. Thomas's. Thornton was, however,
convinced that this obstacle could be removed and that Whitehead's
system would be more adequate as a metaphysic and more amenable as
a medium of Christian doctrine after its removal. Thus, while Whitehead wrote "It is as true to say that God creates the World, as that the
World creates God",[5] Thornton insisted that "the essence of religion
consists in the concrete dependence of incomplete created individuality
upon absolute individuality as it exists in God."[6] Thornton was able, by
making this drastic revision of Whitehead's system, to produce a formulation of Christology which, while expressed in a contemporary
idiom, was thoroughly orthodox. It is, in my opinion, an almost perfect
example of expressing Christian truth in a modern idiom, as contrasted
with distorting Christian truth in order to bring it into line with modern
thought. It is perhaps revealing that Dr. W. N. Pittenger, who is a
whole-hearted supporter of "process-theology", has taken Thornton to
task for thinking it necessary, as a Christian thinker, to make
modifications in Whitehead's doctrine.[7]

My second instance will be that of Fr. Karl Rahner, who has been
described by Dr. John Macquarrie as the most outstanding of living
theologians.[8] The school to which he belongs draws its origin from the
work in the 1920s of Joseph Maréchal, who in an immense work entitled
Le Point de Départ de la Métaphysique attempted to reconstruct
Thomism by a quasi-Kantian critique in a way which he hoped would
lead to a more definitely theistic position than that of the Sage of
Königsberg. This "transcendental Thomism", as it has come to be
called, is alleged by strict Thomists such as M. Gilson to have no right
to the label "Thomist" at all. Nevertheless, Fr. Rahner's largest work
Spirit in the World is professedly a development of one of the basic
epistemological doctrines of St.Thomas, that the human mind in its perception of the world abstracts from, and returns to, the phenomena of
the senses. Whether or not it is genuinely Thomist in inspiration,
Rahner's system is certainly not Thomist in its idiom, for the latter is
derived from the German existentialist Martin Heidegger. What Rahner is doing in all this is seeking to find or construct a philosophical

5 *Process and Reality* (Cambridge 1929) 492.
6 *The Incarnate Lord* (London 1942) 362.
7 *The Word Incarnate* (London 1959) 107ff; *Christology Reconsidered* (London 1970) 19f, 101f.
8 *Principles of Christian Theology* (New York 1966) ix.

system which will be loyal to Christian truth and at the same time more congenial and intelligible to contemporary men and women than the traditional Catholic formulations. It thus presupposes the pluralist axiom, that Christian truth is capable of expression in more than one philosophical idiom. In practice one is sometimes inclined to doubt whether those who clamour for a healthy plurality in Christian theology really wish to do more than substitute one singularity for another. Certainly there is nothing particularly pluralistic about the impressive theological encyclopaedia *Sacramentum Mundi*, the most voluminous product of the Rahnerian school, which is almost entirely written in the idiom of transcendental Thomism. This is not, however, relevant to my present point, which is that Fr. Rahner and those associated with him, such as Coreth, Metz and Lotz, are quite deliberately and conscientiously attempting to make the existentialist idiom an adequate vehicle for the expression of Christian truth and are not trying to force the Christian faith into the predetermined mould of a secularist philosophy. Whether this particular attempt is altogether happy I am occasionally disposed to doubt. Whether or not the existentialist idiom comes with an immediate note of relevance and intelligibility to the average educated German I do not know, but it certainly fails to ring a bell with the average educated Englishman or American. Furthermore, so far as the English-speaking philosophical world is concerned, the idiom of existentialism is, if anything, rather less attractive than is that of traditional scholasticism. In the time of St. Thomas there were a number of philosophical schools, but they did at least talk the same language and they were able to argue with one another; whereas today if you put a British linguistic empiricist and a Continental existentialist or phenomenologist together in the same room each of them will have the greatest difficulty in recognising that the other is a philosopher at all. If we are to have pluralism in the theological and philosophical world, let us try at least to see that it is a genuine pluralism and not the substitution of one singularism for another. But, having said all this, I repeat that it is clear that, with whatever degree of success, Rahner and most of his school are trying to bring one contemporary philosophical system into the service of the Christian faith and are not, like some of the more radical of the *Avant-garde*, trying to force the Christian faith into the narrow and rigid mould of a quite intransigent secularism.

Thus, to summarise, the first lesson which St. Thomas has to teach us today is simply how we should go about the task of speaking Christian truth in a secular climate, while recognising that, whereas for St. Thomas the secular climate was that of a newly fashionable philosophical system, for us it is the climate of the whole culture in which we live. Behind this there lies, of course, St. Thomas's basic conception of the relation of the natural to the supernatural, with its view of the two orders as distinct yet organically related. It must be admitted that the theological manuals have frequently spoken as if grace and nature were comparable to two apartments on successive floors of a building, separated by a soundproof floor and ceiling and possessing no means of mutual communication, so that nature's sole function with respect to grace is to provide a support for the latter. Such a view inevitably leads to a dichotomy in which grace is concerned only with "religious" matters, in the narrowest sense of the term, and nature—the realm of the "secular"—first of all claims to be entirely autonomous and then claims to be the whole of reality. This view, however, can claim no support from St. Thomas. He did not, of course, work out the matter in detail with applications to our twentieth-century situation, but the basic principles for the discussion are quite explicit. "Grace does not destroy nature but perfects it",[9] and this not in the sense of making an extrinsic addition to it, for "grace presupposes nature"[10] and "grace is related to nature as the act of perfecting to that which is to be perfected";[11] this is the sense in which "nature is a preamble to grace".[12] Paradoxically, it is, I think, because of his firm conviction of the organic relationship of nature and grace that St. Thomas was unable to reach a satisfactory solution to the question of man's orientation to the beatific vision. Just because nature needed grace to perfect it, it must have some tendency, however inchoative and unthematic, towards grace and supernature; yet, precisely because grace is *gratuitous*, nature can neither expect, deserve nor demand it. Fr. Henri de Lubac's historical studies have done a good deal to elucidate the problem;[13] so have Fr. Rahner's exploration of the notion of a "supernatural existential"[14] and Fr. Robert W. Gleason's exposition of sanctifying grace as participation in the life of God himself.[15] Much still remains to be done, but without St. Thomas's principles as our guide-lines I do not see how we can avoid either sentimental religiosity and escapism on the one hand or downright secularism leading to atheism on the other.

Closely related to this is St. Thomas's doctrine about truth and our perception of reality. In insisting that truth consists in the conformity of

---

9 *Summa theol.* I, 1, 8, ad 2; *De Veritate* 27, 6, ad 1.
10 *Summa theol.* I, 2, 2, ad 1.
11 *De Veritate* 27, 5, obj. 17.
12 *In Boethium de Trinitate*, 2, 3.
13 E. g. *The Mystery of the Supernatural* (New York 1967) passim.
14 *Theological Investigations* (Baltimore 1961) I, chh. ix, x.
15 *Grace in Freedom* (New York 1969) passim.

the mind to reality — *adaequatio rei et intellectus*[16] — he might seem
to be uttering a platitude, but, if so, it is a platitude that has been
vigorously denied quite recently. Dr. Leslie Dewart's books *The Future
of Belief* and *The Foundations of Belief* expound at great length the
view that truth is purely subjective and relative. He repudiates both "the
epistemological position that truth is the adequation of mind to things
and... the metaphysical position that being is intelligible as such."[17]
"Truth and falsity", he tells us, "thus pertain neither to subject as such
nor to object as such. They pertain to the relation in which we render
ourselves present to ourselves and to the world."[18] The upshot of this is
that God himself has no reality outside our consciousness; he does not
exist, but he can be *present* in our consciousness and he cannot be
present anywhere else.[19] I have devoted a complete chapter of my book
The Openness of Being to an examination of Dewart's argument; here I
shall only point out that his doctrine is inherently self-destructive, for,
if truth does not consist in the conformity of the mind to reality,
Dewart's own mind, when he states his own peculiar view of what he
calls "truth", presumably does not conform to reality either. And so
there is no reason why we should believe what he says. He does apply
the word "reality" to God, but, as he uses the term, a *reality* is not a
being that *exists* but merely something that is *present* in, and only in,
our consciousness. Perhaps the chief value of Dewart's books lies in the
dreadful warning which they give of what happens when one abandons
the traditional view of the nature of truth.

To say that truth consists in the conformity of mind to reality — of
intellectus to *res* — carries with it the implication that the mind can
know reality and is not simply shut up in the enjoyment of its own
feelings. It is significant that the phase of the empiricist movement
which began with Locke and culminated with Hume discovered that, in
spite of its claim to be in line with the achievements and endeavours of
experimental science, it had eliminated from the realm of human
knowledge not only God but the physical world as well. Physical objects
became for Hume simply concatenations of impressions in the mind,
though Hume never managed to give a satisfactory account of the mind
in which they were concatenated. Nor have his successors been more
successful. Even Kant's attempt to preserve a *Ding an sich* or *nou-
menon* which is wholly real and non-subjective suffers defeat at the
hands of his doctrine that all we can know is the *phenomenon* which the

16   *Summa theol.* I, 16, 2, c.
17   *The Foundations of Belief* (New York 1969) 246.
18   Ibid. 270.
19   Ibid. 443.

mind has constructed in the act of perceiving. Dr. Errol Harris has recently drawn attention to the remarkable fact that the movement in philosophy which, above all else, prides itself on being in tune with empirical science has totally failed to give a plausible account of the inductive method which it has alleged to be the chief tool used by empirical science.[20] (He has also condemned the empiricist philosophers for misunderstanding the role played in science by the inductive method, but that is another story.) Dr. A. Boyce Gibson, in his recent work *Theism and Empiricism* has significantly listed at the head of his catalogue of "the Misadventures of Empiricism" the "empirical misadventure" which consisted in equating empiricism with sensation. He adds that "it is the linking of empiricism with sensationalism which, more than anything else, has made it implausible to talk about the empirical approach to God."[21] It would be an exaggeration to describe Boyce Gibson as a Thomist, but I find his remark all the more penetrating for this. For it is, I think, very remarkable that the one doctrine of perception which modern philosophers hardly ever discuss, and of which indeed most of them seem to be totally ignorant, is the one doctrine which provides just that kind of objectivity in perception which empirical science both needs and, more or less unconsciously, assumes. And this is, in its central features, the doctrine of St. Thomas. It holds that perception is an activity in which sense and intellect are both involved. This does not mean that in an act of perception there are really two acts performed by two different subjects, a sense which senses and an intellect which understands. There is one subject, the human being, who in one act of perception senses by his senses and apprehends by his intellect, the sensible impression being the *objectum quo* and the intelligible extra-mental thing the *objectum quod*. Provided this basic formulation is accepted, its elaboration and ornamentation, as we find them in St. Thomas and in such modern Thomists as M. Gilson and M. Maritain, seem to me to be secondary and optional; this does not mean that they are uninteresting or trivial, but it does mean that the central doctrine can stand without them. That the basic Thomist doctrine can hold up its head in the world of today and is capable of new and exciting development is demonstrated by Fr. Bernard Lonergan's monumental work in which he sets out to answer the two questions "What is happening when we are knowing?" and "What is known when that is happening?" Its title *Insight* is nothing but a translation of the

20 *Hypothesis and Perception* (London 1970) esp. ch. ii.
21 *Theism and Empiricism* (London 1970) 20. I have discussed this work at length in Appendix I to my book *The Openness of Being*.

Latin *intellectus*, stressing the power of the human mind to penetrate beneath the sensible surface of things to reach their intelligible essence.

Correlative with the Thomist doctrine of the understanding mind is the Thomist doctrine of the object understood. The proper object of the understanding, St. Thomas says, is being, and the correlative object of our human minds in their corporeal condition is the being of corporeal things. And to know beings other than oneself is a highly mysterious activity. As I have written elsewhere:

> To know a being is not to achieve some kind of external contact with it analogous to the impact of one material object on another. It is to achieve a real union with the being, to get it "into one's mental skin" or, from another aspect, to become identified, however imperfectly, with it. This is what is implied by the scholastic assertion that in knowledge the knower *becomes* the thing known, not entitatively but "intentionally". This is...highly mysterious, but it is a fact. It pertains inchoatively, on the level of pure sensation, even to sub-human animals, but it is on the level of spirit that this capacity to penetrate other beings, not physically but none the less really, reaches its full manifestation, and it comes to its climax in the mutual communication of spirits with one another. In us humans, compounded as we are of spirit and matter, it is not only mysterious but extremely complex. There is nothing in the intellect that was not first in the senses; the mind spontaneously turns to sensory representations, but, simply as mind, as intellect, as spirit, it can (intentionally) "become" all things. *Nihil in intellectu quod non prius in sensu; mens convertit se ad phantasmata; mens quodammodo fit omnia:* these well-worn tags are not statements of a theory about knowledge, they are a description of what human knowledge is.[22]

It is, I suggest, extremely important to stress that the correlative object of our minds in their embodied condition is extra-mental corporeal being. One hesitates to generalise about so protean a movement as existentialism, but it is, I think, a serious weakness of most forms of existentialism, Christian as well as atheistic, that they treat the human mind as if it was altogether detached from the rest of the universe. The universe appears as a mere environment, hostile or at best indifferent, into which the human subject finds himself "flung" (*geworfen*). This view of man and his situation is equally contrary to Christian dogma and (what may disquiet most of our contemporaries more) to modern science. For, in the physical aspect of his being, man is not *surrounded* by the material world, he is actually *part* of it. It is a most astonishing fact that, whereas the Middle Ages, for all their limited knowledge of the details of the physical realm, held firmly together the physical and

---

22 *The Openness of Being*, 190. I have added the word "human" to the last sentence.

the mental constituents of human nature, the last four centuries have seen an ever increasing divergence between the scientific and the philosophical realm, the former discovering more and more truths about the world of matter while philosophy has retreated more and more into the human subjectivity. It has often been remarked that Kant's so-called "Copernican revolution" was in fact about as un-Copernican as anything could be; for Copernicus removed man from the centre of the physical universe, while Kant began by placing him at the centre of the mental universe and never managed to get him away from it. St. Thomas's insistence that what we know in the first instance is not ourselves but extra-mental material beings is not only true in itself but, I would maintain, highly important for Christian apologetic today. It is, of course, fully compatible with that concern of God for man's welfare which is manifested in the Incarnation and in redemption. But without it we are in danger of that isolation of the doctrine of redemption from any doctrine of creation which almost inevitably leads to an introverted and escapist type of religion.

It would not be difficult to list a great number of individual points concerning which St. Thomas may have much to teach the world of the late twentieth century and to defend him against criticism and misunderstandings. For example, in reply to the common accusation that the category of substance ought to be abandoned as static and outmoded, it could plausibly be affirmed that, substance in its philosophical sense being equivalent to the Greek *ousia* or "being", it is difficult to see how one can do without it, and that if (which is doubtful) St. Thomas's doctrine of substance was too static, what is needed is not no doctrine of substance but a more dynamic one. I have, however, felt it better to concentrate on a few broad and basic issues and indeed space would not permit of anything more. Many of St. Thomas's views were, of course, not peculiar to him and some of them were not even peculiar to Thomists. But there is about him a serene urbanity and a patient sureness of touch which has much to teach us in these days of journalistic theology, when one slogan succeeds another with breathless rapidity and when it is apparently assumed that it is more important that one's views should be startling than that they should be true. In the last resort, I do not think it matters a jot whether our theology is Thomist; what matters is that it should be true. And this was in fact the precise position of St. Thomas. The most famous of the Augustinians may have shouted "Tell them Dr. Martin Luther will have it so!" But, whatever may have been the attitude of some of his disciples, I do not think that the most famous of the Dominicans ever settled an argument by saying "As the Angelic Doctor reminds us...."

NOTES ON CONTRIBUTORS

Marie-Thérèse d'Alverny was born in 1903 in Boën, France. She is director of research at the Centre national de la Recherche scientifique in Paris and *chargée de cours* at the Centre d'Etudes supérieures de civilisation médiévale in Poitiers. She was formerly keeper of the latin manuscripts in the Bibliothèque nationale in Paris. She is also chairman of the Bibliographical Commission of the International Union of the History of Science, and co-editor of the *Archives d'histoire doctrinale et littéraire du moyen âge*. She has published catalogues of latin manuscripts, studies and editions of texts concerning mediaeval philosophy and the history of science; she has also written on the relations of Islam and the West and on mediaeval translations from Arabic into Latin.

Georges C. Anawati, OP, was born in Alexandria, Egypt, in 1905. After studying engineering and chemistry at Lyons, France, he entered the Dominican Order. He studied philosophy and theology at the Saulchoir, and obtained the Ph. D. in Montreal. He is the director of the Dominican Institute of Oriental Studies in Cairo and the editor-in-chief of *Mideo*. He has taught at the Universities of Montreal, Alexandria (since 1955), Louvain, the Institute of Higher Arabian Studies in Cairo, the Angelicum, and the University of California.

Louis-Jacques Bataillon, OP, was born in Paris in 1914. He studied at the University of Paris, obtaining the Licence in 1936 and the Doctorate in Law in 1942. He entered the Dominican Order in 1945 and was ordained priest in 1950. In 1952 he was named Lector in Theology. Since 1952 he has been a member of the Leonine Commission.

Vernon J. Bourke was born in 1907 in North Bay, Ontario, Canada. He studied at St. Michael's College and the Institute of Mediaeval Studies in Toronto, obtaining the Ph. D. from the University of Toronto in 1937. He is *associé de la Société Philosophique de Louvain* (1953). He has been a member of the Faculty of philosophy at St. Louis University since 1931, and the director of the Thomistic Institute (1948). He is a former president of the American Catholic Philosophical Association, and was Aquinas Medalist in 1963.

Leonard E. Boyle, OP, was born in Donegal, Ireland, in 1923. He studied at Dublin and Oxford, where he took a doctorate in mediaeval history. He has taught at the University of St. Thomas (Angelicum) in Rome, and is professor of Latin Palaeography and Diplomatics at the Pontifical Institute of Mediaeval Studies in Toronto. He has written on the popularization of theology and canon law in the Middle Ages and has published a survey of the Vatican Archives and its mediaeval holdings.

Ignatius C. Brady, OFM, was born in Detroit, Michigan, in 1911. He entered the Franciscan Order in 1929 and was ordained priest in 1937. He studied at Duns Scotus College, Detroit, and the Pontifical Institute of Mediaeval Studies in Toronto, taking the Ph. D. from the University of Toronto in 1948. He has taught at Duns Scotus College, the Franciscan Institute in St. Bonaventure, New York, and the Catholic University of America. He was a member of the *Collegio Internazionale S. Bonaventura di Quaracchi* (1956-1959) and prefect of the theological commission from 1961 to the present. His specialites are Peter Lombard and mid-12th century Paris, and the Franciscan School at Paris.

Jean Châtillon was born in 1912 in Epinal, France. He was ordained priest at Metz in 1935. He studied at the Institut Catholique in Toulouse, where he obtained the doctorate in theology, then at the Angelicum in Rome, the University of Nancy and the Sorbonne. He holds the degree of Doctor of Letters from the latter university. He was professor of philosophy at the Grand Seminary of Metz from 1945 to 1950, and since then he has taught the history of mediaeval philosophy in the Institut Catholique in Paris. From 1961 to 1967 he was dean at this Institute. He has specialized in research in the philosophy and theology of the 12th and 13th centuries.

Marie-Dominique Chenu, OP, was born in 1895 at Soisy-sur-Seine, France. He entered the Dominican Order in 1913 and took his lectorship and doctorate at the Angelicum in Rome. He taught theology at the Saulchoir from 1920 to 1942, where he was rector from 1932 to 1942. He was the founder, and for many years the director, of the *Bulletin thomiste*. He is at present living at the Couvent de Saint Jacques in Paris.

Edmund Colledge, OSA, was born in 1910 at Tynemouth, Northumberland. He is a member of the English Vice Province of the Augustinian Friars, for whom he was ordained in 1967. He taught at the University of Liverpool, and is now professor at the Pontifical Institute of Mediaeval Studies, Toronto. He has written on the mediaeval mystics, and is a member of the editorial board of the *Archivio italiano per la storia della pietà*.

Yves Congar, OP, was born in 1904 in Sedan, France, and was ordained priest in the Dominican Order in 1930. He was professor of fundamental theology and ecclesiology at the Saulchoir from 1931 to 1954. From 1939 to 1943 he was interned at Colditz and Lübeck. He founded the collection *Unam Sanctam* (Editions du Cerf), and has written extensively on eccelesiology and ecumenism.

Pierre M. de Contenson, OP, was born in Paris in 1918. He entered the Dominican Order in 1945 and was ordained priest in 1950. He studied philosophy and theology at the Saulchoir and taught there as lecturer from 1952 to 1960, and as ordinary professor from 1960 to 1967. He was dean of theology from 1962 to 1964. He obtained the doctorate in theology from the Saulchoir in 1958. He was managing editor of the *Revue des sciences philosophiques et théologiques*, director of the *Bulletin thomiste*, and is now general director of the Leonine Commission for the critical edition of the works of St. Thomas. Since 1973 he has been on the staff of the Vatican secretariate for promoting Christian unity.

Michael Bertram Crowe was born in Cork, Ireland, in 1923. He received his higher education at University College, Dublin, the Dublin diocesan seminary, Holy Cross College in Clonliffe, the Lateran University in Rome, and the University of Louvain, where he obtained the doctorate in 1955. He was ordained priest in Rome in 1949. Since 1950 he has been on the staff of University College, Dublin, and since 1956 in the Department of Ethics and Politics. He was appointed by the National University of Ireland statutory lecturer in Ethics and Politics, University College, Dublin, in 1972.

Antoine Dondaine, OP, was born in Sennevoy-le-Bas (Yonne), France, in 1898. He was ordained priest in the Dominican Order in 1931. He attended the Ecole Saint Jacques, Joigny (Yonne), and studied philosophy and theology at the Saulchoir, becoming Master of Theology. From 1936 to 1952 he was a member of the Institut Historique Dominicain in Rome. Since 1952 he has been a member of the Leonine Commission, serving as its general director from 1952 to 1964. Since then he has been director of the section of Santa Sabina.

William B. Dunphy was born in New York City in 1926. He studied at the Pontifical Institute of Mediaeval Studies, Toronto, and the University of Toronto, obtaining the Ph. D. in 1953. He has taught at Fordham University, Manhattanville College, and Queens College, and is now professor of philosophy in St. Michael's College in the University of Toronto. He specializes in research in the philosophy of the 13th century.

Cornelio Fabro, CSS, was born in 1911 in Talmasson (Uldine), Italy. He is a member of the Congregation of Stigmatines and professor at the University Institute of Education and director of the Institute of the History of Atheism in Rome. He has written extensively on the metaphysics of St. Thomas and on modern atheism.

Louis Gardet was born in France in 1904. He made his university studies in philosophy. From 1930 to 1946 he lived in the Algerian Sahara, and for many years in the countries of the Maghreb and the Near East. He has lectured in the universities of Rabat, Algiers, Cairo, and the Lebanese University. From 1946 to 1972 he has taught comparative philosophy, and particularly Islamology, at the Collège Philosophique et Théologique in Toulouse. A specialist in Islamic thought, he is co-director with Etienne Gilson of the collection *Etudes Musulmanes*, and collaborator of the *Encyclopédie de l'Islam*.

Jean, Louis-Bertrand Geiger, OP, was born in Strasbourg, France, in 1906, and was ordained priest in the Dominican Order in 1931. He made his higher studies at the Saulchoir and at the Institut Catholique, Sorbonne, and Ecole des Hautes Etudes in Paris. He holds the degrees of Licence ès Lettres, Doctor of Philosophy, and Master of Theology. He has been professor of philosophy at the Saulchoir, visiting professor at the University of Montreal and St. John's University in New York. From 1966 he has been ordinary professor of philosophy at the University of Fribourg in Switzerland.

Etienne Henri Gilson was born in Paris in 1884. After studying at the University of Paris he obtained the agrégation de philosophie in 1907 and the Doctorat ès Lettres in 1913. He taught the history of mediaeval philosophy in various French universities and at the Collège de France. In 1929 he founded the Pontifical Institute of Mediaeval Studies in Toronto and was its director of studies until his retirement. He is a member of the French Academy. His immense bibliography contains studies on Descartes, St. Thomas, St. Bonaventure, St. Augustine, Dante, St. Bernard, and Duns Scotus, and in general on the philosophy and theology of the Middle Ages.

Bernhard Lakebrink was born in 1904 at Asseln near Paderborn. After attending high school at Paderborn he studied law, philology, and philosophy at the universities of Freiburg, Munich, and Bonn. After receiving his doctorate under A. Dyroff in Bonn he taught at a number of high schools in the Rhineland. In 1954, in Cologne, he acquired the right to teach in universities, and he was called to Freiburg as Ordinarius for philosophy. As early as 1934 he had turned against National Socialism in his "Studies on the Myth of the 20th Century." His scholarly work chiefly concerns High Scholasticism and German Idealism.

Francis J. Lescoe was born in Middletown, Connecticut, in 1916. He pursued higher studies at St. Mary's University, Baltimore, and was ordained priest in 1942. He did graduate work in philosophy at the Pontifical Institute of Mediaeval Studies and the University of Toronto and obtained the Ph. D. He is currently professor of philosophy and chairman of The McAuley Institute of Religious Studies, Graduate Division of St. Joseph College, West Hartford. He is the editor of The McAuley Lecture Series and has written on both mediaeval philosophy and existentialism.

Eric Lionel Mascall was born in 1905. He studied mathematics at Cambridge University from 1924 to 1928 and was ordained in the Church of England in 1932. From 1945 to 1962 he taught theology at Christ Church, Oxford, and from 1962 to 1973 was professor of Historical Theology at King's College in the University of London. He retired from this position in the summer of 1973. He has been Bampton Lecturer at Oxford and Columbia Universities and Gifford Lecturer at Edinburgh. He holds doctorates from Oxford, Cambridge and (honorary) St. Andrews.

Armand A. Maurer, CSB, was born in Rochester, New York, in 1915. He was ordained priest in the Congregation of St. Basil in 1945. He did his graduate work at the Pontifical Institute of Mediaeval Studies and the University of Toronto, from which he holds the Ph. D. degree. He is professor of philosophy at the Pontifical Institute and Graduate Department of Philosophy of the University of Toronto. He specializes in research in the philosophy of the 13th and 14th centuries.

Joseph Owens, CSSR, was born in 1908 in Saint John, New Brunswick, Canada. A member of the Redemptorist Order, he was ordained in 1933. His higher education was at the Pontifical Institute of Mediaeval Studies, Toronto, from which he holds the doctorate. He has taught at the Accademia Alfonsiana in Rome, Assumption University of Windsor, Purdue University, the Catholic University of America; for many years he has been professor of philosophy at the Pontifical Institute of Mediaeval Studies. He has written extensively on both Greek and mediaeval philosophy.

Anton Charles Pegis was born in 1905 in Milwaukee. He was professor of philosophy at Marquette and Fordham Universities before coming to the Pontifical Institute of Mediaeval Studies in Toronto. He was president of this Institute from 1946 to 1954. He is a Fellow of the Royal Society of Canada and past president of the American Catholic Philosophical Association. He has written extensively on ancient and mediaeval philosophy, particularly on the thought of St. Thomas.

Jaroslav Pelikan was born in 1923 in Akron, Ohio. He was educated in Concordia Seminary and the University of Chicago, where he took the Ph. D. in history in 1946. An ordained Lutheran minister as well as historian, he has taught successively at Valparaiso University, Concordia Theological Seminary, the University of Chicago, and Yale University, where he is Sterling Professor of Religious Studies. He is the editor of *Luther's Works* and the author of many volumes on the history of theology.

Walter H. Principe, CSB, was born in Rochester, New York, in 1922. He was ordained priest in the Congregation of St. Basil in 1949. Educated at the University of Toronto, the Pontifical Institute of Mediaeval Studies, and the Ecole Pratique des Hautes Etudes in Paris, he received the doctorate in mediaeval studies from the Pontifical Institute in 1963. He is a past president of the Canadian Theological Society. He is professor of the history of theology at the Pontifical Institute, professor of systematic theology and historical theology at the University of St. Michael's College, Toronto, and professor of the history of ideas at the Graduate Centre for Medieval Studies in the University of Toronto.

John Francis Quinn, CSB, was born in Dublin, Ireland, in 1925 and settled in Canada in 1948. He was ordained a priest in the Congregation of St. Basil and did his graduate studies in both the University of Toronto and the Pontifical Institute of Mediaeval Studies. He has taught philosophy and the history of mediaeval philosophy for eight years, primarily in the Pontifical Institute but also in the Graduate School of Toronto University. His special field of teaching and research is the doctrine of St. Bonaventure. He is now secretary of the Pontifical Institute. He has served on the editorial board of *St. Bonaventure 1274-1974*, a five volume series commemorating the seventh centenary of St. Bonaventure's death.

Beryl Smalley was born in Cheadle, Cheshire, England, in 1905, and was educated at St. Hilda's College, Oxford, and Manchester University. She holds the M. A. from Oxford and D. Phil. from Manchester University. She was lecturer in history at the Royal Holloway College, London University; research fellow, Girton College Cambridge; assistant in the Department of Western Mss. Bodleian Library; history tutor, fellow and later vice-principal, St. Hilda's College, Oxford. She is at present emeritus fellow of St. Hilda's.

Edward A. Synan was born in Fall River, Massachusetts, in 1918, and ordained priest for the archdiocese of Newark, New Jersey, in 1942. He was educated at Seton Hall, New Jersey, the Catholic University of America, the University of Louvain, the Pontifical Institute of Mediaeval Studies, and the University of Toronto. During World War II he served as chaplain, U.S.A.A.F. He holds the doctorate in philosophy from the University of Toronto. He is professor of philosophy and president of the Pontifical Institute of Mediaeval Studies.

Joris, Clemens-Maria Vansteenkiste, OP, was born in Torhout, Belgium, in 1910. He studied philosophy at Ghent and theology at Louvain and Rome, and was ordained priest in the Dominican Order in 1934. He was a member of the Leonine Commission in Rome and Ottawa from 1947 to 1953, and from 1954 he has taught the history of mediaeval philosophy and the introduction to the study of St. Thomas at the Angelicum in Rome. He is the editor of *Rassegna di Letteratura Tomistica* (New Series of *Bulletin thomiste*).

Henry Babcock Veatch was born in Evansville, Indiana, in 1911. He received his higher education at Harvard, receiving the Ph. D. in 1936. He has done special studies at Heidelberg University, the Pontifical Institute of Mediaeval Studies, and the Harvard Divinity School. He has taught at Harvard, Indiana University, Northwestern University, and he is at present professor of philosophy and chairman of the Department of Philosophy at Georgetown University. He has been president of the Metaphysical Society of America and Aquinas Medalist of the American Catholic Philosophical Association.

Gérard Verbeke was born in Waregem, Belgium, in 1910 and educated at the University of Louvain, from which he holds the degrees of Master and Doctor of Philosophy. Since 1942 he has taught at that University metaphysics, the history of ancient and mediaeval philosophy, and the relations between Greek philosophy and Christianity. He became a member of the Royal Flemish Academy of Belgium, president of the Institute of Mediaeval Studies at Louvain, vice-president of the International Academic Union, and visiting member of the Institute for Advanced Study, Princeton. He was elected president of the International Academic Union for the period 1971-74. He is the director of the *Aristoteles Latinus* and the *Corpus latinum Commentariorum in Aristotelem graecorum*, and member of the editorial board of the *Aristoteles Semitico-latinus* and the *Catalogus Translationum et Commentariorum* (New York).

William A. Wallace, OP, was born in New York City in 1918, and was ordained priest in the Dominican Order in 1953. He did graduate studies in the

Dominican House of Studies and the Catholic University of America, both in Washington, D. C., and at the University of Fribourg, Switzerland; he also did post-graduate work at Harvard University. He taught philosophy and theology in Dominican *studia* for over fifteen years, including a term as regent of studies of the *studium generale* in Washington. One of the principal editors of the *New Catholic Encylopedia*, he is currently professor of the history and philosophy of science at The Catholic University of America.

Angelus Walz, OP, was born in Basel, Switzerland, in 1893. He attended the University of Basel and entered the Dominican Order in 1912. He studied at Düsseldorf and the Angelicum, becoming doctor of theology in 1921. The same year he obtained the diploma from the Scuola Pontificia Paleografia e Diplomatica. He was professor at the Angelicum from 1921 to 1969, archivist of the Generalate 1923-1930, editor of the *Analecta OP* 1923-1926, and of the *Angelicum* 1934-1944. He is now chaplain in Strahlfeld, in the diocese of Regensburg.

James A. Weisheipl, OP, was born in Oshkosh, Wisconsin, in 1923, and was professed in the Dominican Order and ordained priest in 1949. He obtained his first doctorate in philosophy from the University of St. Thomas in Rome, 1953, and his second from Oxford University in 1957. He taught in the Dominican Studium in River Forest, Illinois, for eight years and at the Pontifical Institute of Mediaeval Studies, Toronto, for ten. He is Visiting Fellow at Corpus Christi College, Oxford, for 1973-1974.

INDEX

Numbers preceded by II refer to Vol. II. Thus: 345, 368 refer to these pages in Vol. I; II, 345, 368 refer to these pages in Vol. II.

Thomas Aquinas, St.: *passim*

Life

—legend of St. Thomas 13-28
—infancy narratives 19-20
—entry into Dominican Order 21
—miracles 22
—visions 25-26
—death 16-17
—canonization 17, 29-37

Writings

—dating of the *De Substantiis Separatis* 51-56
—title of *De Substantiis Separatis* 52
—authenticity of *De Substantiis Separatis* 57
—inauthentic sermons 67n, 75
—characteristic features of sermons 68
—sermons and *Catena Aurea* 67-75
—St. Thomas and classical and mnemonic verses 77-85
—his letter to the Abbot of Monte Cassino 87-108
—*Summa contra Gentiles* as theological 131
—dating of the *Summa contra Gentiles* 149
—time and place of his commentary on the *Nich. Ethics* 247-255
—nature and purpose of his commentaries on Aristotle 213-237
—purpose of his commentaries on the *Nich. Ethics* and *Metaphysics* 253, 255
—appraisal of his commentary on the *Nich. Ethics* 256-259